YE8687

THE PAPERS OF
BENJAMIN FRANKLIN

SPONSORED BY

The American Philosophical Society
and Yale University

ERIPUIT COELO FULMEN SCEPTRUMQUE TIRANNIS

Au GÉNIE D. FRANKLIN

Au Génie de Franklin

THE PAPERS OF

Benjamin Franklin

VOLUME 27   *July 1 through October 31, 1778*

CLAUDE A. LOPEZ, *Editor*

DOUGLAS M. ARNOLD, DOROTHY W. BRIDGWATER,

ELLEN R. COHN, JONATHAN R. DULL,

AND CATHERINE M. PRELINGER, *Associate Editors*

New Haven and London YALE UNIVERSITY PRESS, 1988

Funds for editing this volume of The Papers of Benjamin Franklin *have been provided by the Andrew W. Mellon Foundation, the J. Howard Pew Freedom Trust, the American Philosophical Society, and the National Historical Publications and Records Commission under the chairmanship of the Archivist of the United States. For all these sources of support the editors are most grateful.*

Library of Congress catalog card number: 59–12697
International standard book number: 0–300–04177–2

The paper in this book meets the guidelines for permanence and durability of the Committee on Production Guidelines for Book Longevity of the Council on Library Resources.

Printed in the U. S. A.

Contents

French surnames and titles of nobility often run to great length. Our practice with an untitled person is to provide all the Christian names at the first appearance and then drop them; a chevalier or noble is given the title used at the time, and details are provided in a footnote.

*Denotes a document referred to in annotation.

CONTENTS

x

CONTENTS

CONTENTS

CONTENTS

CONTENTS

List of Illustrations

Au Génie de Franklin   *Frontispiece*

Etching by Marguerite Gérard, after a design by Jean-Honoré Fragonard. The etching illustrates Turgot's famous epigram, which appears as a caption: *Eripuit coelo fulmen, septrumque tirannis,* "He snatched the lightning from the heavens and the sceptre from the tyrants." Minerva, behind Franklin, wards off lightning with her shield; Mars, at his feet, is about to slay Avarice and Tyranny while America, leaning on the Doctor's lap, surveys the scene calmly, a sheaf of arrows (symbol of the Thirteen United Provinces) in her hand. When it was announced on November 15, 1778, that this print was for sale at Fragonard's atelier at the Louvre, the *Journal de Paris* explained that the engraving had been executed by the artist's sister-in-law under his guidance. Reproduced by courtesy of the Yale University Library.

Réception de Franklin au Palais Royal par le Duc d'Orléans (Louis-Philippe), 1778   *facing page* 37

A lithograph of a painting by Charles-Auguste-Guillaume, baron de Steuben, made by Weber. Those represented are, from left to right: Stéphanie-Félicité Ducrest de Saint-Aubin, comtesse de Genlis, the "gouverneur" of the Chartres children; the five-year-old duc de Valois, future king Louis-Philippe, holding a drum; Louis-Marie-Adélaïde de Bourbon-Penthièvre, duchesse de Chartres; Louis-Philippe, duc d'Orléans; Louis-Philippe-Joseph d'Orléans, duc de Chartres; the comte de Pons-Saint-Maurice. Reproduced by courtesy of the Yale University Library.

La Vigne des treize cantons   *facing page* 123

A warmly pro-American drawing included by M. Richelet in his letter of July 18, 1778. Reproduced by courtesy of the American Philosophical Society.

xl

Marianne Camasse, comtess de Forbach and duchesse douairière de Deux-Ponts, and her sons Christian and Wilhelm von Zweibrücken (Deux-Ponts) *facing page* 273

This family portrait—the late duke appears in the painting that is being held up—comes from Adalbert Prinz von Bayern, *Der Herzog und die Tänzerin* (Neustadt/Weinstrasse, 1966), p. 81. The original is in a private collection in Paris.

Benjamin Franklin: engraving by François-Denis Née after Carmontelle *facing page* 288

Holding a copy of Pennsylvania's Constitution, the Doctor sits in the armchair that Louis Carrogis de Carmontelle used for so many of his portraits in profile; Franklin sat for this portrait in August, 1778. Engraving by François-Denis Née, *c.* 1781. Reproduced by courtesy of the Philadelphia Museum of Art, Mrs. John D. Rockefeller Collection.

Charles-Henri-Théodat, comte d'Estaing *facing page* 337

An engraving by Goldar after a painting by d'Haigue, published in John Andrews, *History of the War with America, France, Spain and Holland* (4 vols., London, 1785–1786), III, facing p. 302. Reproduced by courtesy of the Yale University Library.

Observing the Ephemera by Night *facing page* 433

A vignette published in René-Antoine Ferchault de Réaumur, *Mémoires pour servir à l'histoire des insectes* (6 vols., Paris, 1734–1742), VI, p. 1. A contemporary description called the insects "as dense as snowflakes in winter"; Réamur observed that those who happen to be born after sunset do not live to see the sunrise. See Gilbert Chinard, "Random Notes on Two Bagatelles," APS *Proc.,* CIII, 1959, p. 754. Reproduced by courtesy of the Yale University Library.

Anne-Catherine de Ligniville Helvétius *facing page* 670

An engraving by Huyot after an unidentified pastel, published in Mathurin François Adolphe de Lescure, *Les Grandes épouses* (Paris, 1884), p. 368. It depicts the widow as Franklin knew her: aging but still vigorous and vibrant.

Contributors to Volume 27

The ownership of each manuscript, or the location of the particular copy used by the editors of each rare contemporary pamphlet or similar printed work, is indicated where the document appears in the text. The sponsors and editors are deeply grateful to the following institutions and individuals for permission to print or otherwise use in the present volume manuscripts and other materials which they own.

INSTITUTIONS

Algemeen Rijksarchief, The Hague
American Philosophical Society
Archives du Ministère des affaires étrangères, Paris
Bibliothèque de la Société Eduenne, Autun
Bibliothèque Nationale, Paris
Connecticut Historical Society
Connecticut State Library
Cornell University Library
Dartmouth College Library
Detroit Public Library
Duke University Library
Franklin Library, Franklin, Massachusetts
Harvard University Library

Historical Society of Pennsylvania
Henry E. Huntington Library
Library of Congress
Massachusetts Archives
Massachusetts Historical Society
National Archives
National Maritime Museum
New York Public Library
Public Record Office
South Carolina Historical Society
United States Naval Academy Museum
University of Pennsylvania Library
University of Virginia Library
Yale University Library

INDIVIDUALS

William N. Dearborn, Nashville, Tennessee
M.D.A.F.H.H. Hartley Russell, on deposit in the Berkshire County Record Office, Reading, England

xlii

Method of Textual Reproduction

An extended statement of the principles of selection, arrangement, form of presentation, and method of textual reproduction observed in this edition appears in the Introduction to the first volume, pp. xxiv–xlvii. What follows is a condensation and revision of part of it.

Printed Material:

Those of Franklin's writings that were printed under his direction presumably appeared as he wanted them to, and should therefore be reproduced with no changes except what modern typography requires. In some cases, however, printers carelessly or willfully altered his text without his consent; or the journeymen who set it had different notions from his—and from each other's—of capitalization, spelling, and punctuation. Such of his letters as survive only in nineteenth-century printings, furthermore, have often been vigorously edited by William Temple Franklin, Duane, or Sparks. In all these cases the original has suffered some degree of distortion, which the modern editor may guess at but, in the absence of the manuscript, can not remedy. We therefore follow the printed texts as we find them, and note only obvious misreadings.

We observe the following rules in reproducing printed materials:

1. The place and date of composition of letters are set at the top, regardless of their location in the original printing; the complimentary close is set continuously with the text.

2. Proper nouns, including personal names, which were often printed in italics, are set in roman except when the original was italicized for emphasis.

3. Prefaces and other long passages, though italicized in the original, are set in roman. Long italicized quotations are set in roman within quotation marks.

4. Words in full capitals are set in small capitals, with

initial letters in full capitals if required by Franklin's normal usage.

5. All signatures are set in capitals and small capitals.

6. We silently correct obvious typographical errors, such as the omission of a single parenthesis or quotation mark.

7. We close a sentence by supplying, when needed, a period or question mark.

Manuscript Material:

a. *Letters* are presented in the following form:

1. The place and date of composition are set at the top, regardless of their location in the original; the complimentary close is set continuously with the text.

2. Addresses, endorsements, and notations are so labelled and printed at the end of the letter. An endorsement on a letter is to the best of our belief by the recipient, a notation by someone else.

b. *Spelling* of the original we retain when in English, and correct it in brackets or a footnote if it is abnormal enough to obscure the meaning: "they where [were]." The most common such abnormalities in French are omitting apostrophes where they belong or inserting them where they do not belong, and running two words together or separating a single word. These vagaries cannot be handled in the same way without disfiguring the text or overburdening the annotation, and we silently correct them: "d'ans les qu'els jai resté 8 ans edemy" becomes "dans lesquels j'ai resté 8 ans et demy."

c. *Capitalization* we retain as written, except that every sentence is made to begin with a capital. When we cannot decide whether a letter is a capital, we follow modern usage.

d. Words underlined once in the manuscript are printed in italics; words underlined twice or written in large letters or full capitals are printed in small capitals.

xliv

e. *Punctuation* has been retained as in the original, except:

1. We close a sentence by supplying, when needed, a period or question mark. When it is unclear where the sentence ends, we retain the original punctuation or lack of it.

2. Dashes used in place of commas, semicolons, colons, or periods are replaced by the appropriate marks; when a sentence ends with both a dash and a period, the dash is omitted.

3. Commas scattered meaninglessly through a manuscript are eliminated.

4. When a mark of punctuation is not clear or can be read as one of two marks, we follow modern usage.[1]

5. Some documents, especially legal ones, have no punctuation; others have so little as to obscure the meaning. In such cases we silently supply the minimum needed for clarity.

f. *Contractions and abbreviations* in general are retained. The ampersand is rendered as "and," except in the names of business firms, in the form "&c.," and in a few other cases. Letters represented by the thorn or tilde are printed. The tailed "p" is spelled out as per, pre, or pro. Symbols of weights, measures, and monetary values follow modern usage, as: £34. Superscript letters are lowered.

g. *Omitted or illegible words or letters* are treated as follows:

1. If not more than four letters are missing, we supply them silently when we have no doubt what they should be, and otherwise with a bracketed question mark.

2. If more than four letters are missing, we supply them in brackets, with or without a question mark depending on our confidence in the insertion.

3. Other omissions are shown as follows: [*illegible*], [*torn*], [*remainder missing*], or the like.

1. The typescripts from which these papers are printed have been made from photocopies of the manuscripts; marks of punctuation are sometimes blurred or lost in photography, and it has often been impossible to consult the original.

4. Missing or illegible digits are indicated by suspension points in brackets, the number of points corresponding to the estimated number of missing figures.

5. When the writer has omitted a word required for clarity, we insert it in brackets and italics.

h. *Author's additions and corrections:*

1. Interlineations and brief marginal notes are normally incorporated in the text without comment, and longer notes with the notation [*in the margin*] unless they were clearly intended as footnotes, in which case they are printed with our notes and with a bracketed indication of the source.

2. Canceled words and phrases are in general omitted without notice; if significant, they are printed in footnotes.

3. When alternative words and phrases have been inserted in a manuscript but the original remains uncanceled, the alternatives are given in brackets, preceded by explanatory words in italics, as: "it is [*written above:* may be] true."

4. Variant readings of several versions are noted if important.

Recent Changes in Editorial Policy:

Most of these are minor, such as omitting the notation "not found" after a document referred to in the text; but with the beginning of the mountainous material in the French period the criteria of selection have become much less inclusive. The various developments in policy are explained above, xv, xxiv; XXI, xxxiv; XXIII, xlvi–xlviii.

Abbreviations and Short Titles

AAE	Archives du Ministère des affaires étrangères.
AD	Autograph document.
ADB	*Allgemeine Deutsche Biographie* (56 vols., Berlin, 1967–71).
ADS	Autograph document signed.
AL	Autograph letter.
Allen, *Mass. Privateers*	Gardner Weld Allen, ed., *Massachusetts Privateers of the Revolution* ([Cambridge, Mass.], 1927) (Massachusetts Historical Society *Collections*, LXXVII)
Almanach des marchands	*Almanach général des marchands, négocians, armateurs, et fabricans de France et de l'Europe et autres parties du monde . . .* (Paris, 1779).
Almanach royal	*Almanach royal* (91 vols., Paris, 1700–92). Cited by year.
Alphabetical List of Escaped Prisoners	Alphabetical List of the Americans who having escap'd from the Prisons of England, were furnish'd with Money by the Commissrs. of the U.S. at the Court of France, to return to America. A manuscript in the APS, dated 1784, and covering the period January, 1777, to November, 1784.
ALS	Autograph letter signed.
Amer.	American.
APS	American Philosophical Society.
Archaeol.	Archaeological.
Assn.	Association.

Autobiog.	Leonard W. Labaree, Ralph L. Ketcham, Helen C. Boatfield, and Helene H. Fineman, eds., *The Autobiography of Benjamin Franklin* (New Haven, 1964).
Bachaumont, *Mémoires secrets*	[Louis Petit de Bachaumont *et al.*], *Mémoires secrets pour servir à l'histoire de la république des lettres en France, depuis MDCCLXII jusqu'à nos jours; ou, Journal d'un observateur* . . . (36 vols. in 12, London, 1784–89). Bachaumont died in 1771. The first six vols. (1762–71) are his; Mathieu-François Pridansat de Mairobert edited them and wrote the next nine (1771–79); the remainder (1779–87) are by Moufle d'Angerville.
Balch, *French in America*	Thomas Balch, *The French in America during the War of Independence of the United States, 1777–1783* (trans. by Thomas Willing Balch *et al.;* 2 vols., Philadelphia, 1891–95).
BF	Benjamin Franklin.
BF's accounts as commissioner	Those described above, XXIII, 20.
BFB	Benjamin Franklin Bache.
Bigelow, *Works*	John Bigelow, ed., *The Works of Benjamin Franklin* (12 vols., New York and London, 1904).
Biographie universelle	*Biographie universelle, ancienne et moderne, ou histoire, par ordre alphabétique, de la vie publique et privée de tous les hommes qui se sont fait remarquer* . . . (85 vols., Paris, 1811–62).

xlviii

Bodinier — From information kindly furnished us by Cdt. Gilbert Bodinier, Section études, Service historique de l'Armée de Terre, Vincennes.

Bodinier, *Dictionnaire* — Gilbert Bodinier, *Dictionnaire des officiers de l'armée royale qui ont combattu aux Etats-Unis pendant la guerre d'Indépendance* (Château de Vincennes, 1982).

Boyd, *Jefferson Papers* — Julian P. Boyd *et al.*, eds., *The Papers of Thomas Jefferson* (22 vols. to date, Princeton, 1950–).

Burke's Peerage — Sir Bernard Burke, *Burke's Genealogical and Heraldic History of the Peerage Baronetage and Knightage with War Gazette and Corrigenda* (98th ed.; London, 1940). References in exceptional cases to other editions are so indicated.

Burnett, *Continental Congress* — Edmund C. Burnett, *The Continental Congress* (New York, 1941).

Burnett, *Letters* — Edmund C. Burnett, ed., *Letters of Members of the Continental Congress* (8 vols., Washington, 1921–36).

Butterfield, *Adams Correspondence* — Lyman H. Butterfield *et al.*, eds., *Adams Family Correspondence* (4 vols. to date, Cambridge, Mass., 1963–).

Butterfield, *John Adams Diary* — Lyman H. Butterfield, *et al.*, eds., *Diary and Autobiography of John Adams* (4 vols., Cambridge, Mass., 1961).

Case of Silas Deane — [Edward Ingraham, ed.,] *Papers in Relation to the Case of Silas Deane* (Philadelphia, 1855).

Chron. — *Chronicle.*

Clark, *Wickes* — William Bell Clark, *Lambert Wickes,*

	Sea Raider and Diplomat: the Story of a Naval Captain of the Revolution (New Haven and London, 1932).
Clowes, *Royal Navy*	William Laird Clowes, *The Royal Navy: a History from the Earliest Times to the Present* (7 vols., Boston and London, 1897–1903).
Cobbett, *Parliamentary History*	William Cobbett and Thomas C. Hansard, eds., *The Parliamentary History of England from the Earliest Period to 1803* (36 vols., London, 1806–20).
Col.	Column.
Coll.	*Collections.*
Commons Jours.	*Journals of the House of Commons* (233 vols. to date, [London,] 1803–); vols. I–LI are reprints.
Crout, "Diplomacy of Trade"	Robert R. Crout, "The Diplomacy of Trade: the Influence of Commercial Considerations on French Involvement in the Angloamerican War of Independence, 1775–78" (Ph.D. dissertation, University of Georgia, 1977).
Croÿ, *Journal*	Emmanuel, prince de Moeurs et de Solre et duc de Croÿ, *Journal inédit du duc de Croÿ, 1718–1784* (4 vols., Paris, 1906–07).
Cushing, *Writings of Samuel Adams*	Harry Alonzo Cushing, ed., *The Writings of Samuel Adams* ... (4 vols., New York, 1904–08).
d.	*denier.*
D	Document unsigned.
DAB	*Dictionary of American Biography.*
DBF	*Dictionnaire de biographie française* (17 vols. to date, Paris, 1933–).

l

Deane Correspondence	*The Deane Papers; Correspondence between Silas Deane, His Brothers and Their Business and Political Associates, 1771–1795* (Connecticut Historical Society *Collections,* XXIII; Hartford, Conn., 1930).
Deane Papers	*The Deane Papers, 1774–90* (5 vols.; New-York Historical Society *Collections,* XIX–XXIII; New York, 1887–91).
DF	Deborah Franklin.
Dictionnaire de la noblesse	François-Alexandre Aubert de La Chesnaye-Dubois and M. Badier, *Dictionnaire de la noblesse contenant les généalogies, l'histoire & la chronologie des familles nobles de la France . . .* (3rd ed.; 19 vols., Paris, 1863–76).
Dictionnaire historique	*Dictionnaire historique, critique et bibliographique, contenant les vies des hommes illustres, célèbres ou fameux de tous les pays et de tous les siècles . . .* (30 vols., Paris, 1821–23).
Dictionnaire historique de la Suisse	*Dictionnaire historique & biographique de la Suisse* (7 vols. and supplement, Neuchatel, 1921–34).
Directory of Congress	*Directory of Congress: Biographical Directory of the American Congress, 1774–1961 . . .* (Washington, D.C., 1961).
DNB	*Dictionary of National Biography.*
Doniol, *Histoire*	Henri Doniol, *Histoire de la participation de la France à l'établissement des Etats-Unis d'Amérique. Correspondance*

	diplomatique et documents (5 vols., Paris, 1886–99).
DS	Document signed.
Duane, *Works*	William Duane, ed., *The Works of Dr. Benjamin Franklin* . . . (6 vols., Philadelphia, 1808–18). Title varies in the several volumes.
Dubourg, *Œuvres*	Jacques Barbeu-Dubourg, ed., *Œuvres de M. Franklin* . . . (2 vols., Paris, 1773).
Dull, *French Navy*	Jonathan R. Dull, *The French Navy and American Independence: a Study of Arms and Diplomacy, 1774–1787* (Princeton, 1975).
Ed.	Edition or editor.
Etat militaire	*Etat militaire de France, pour l'année* . . . (36 vols., Paris, 1758–93). Cited by year.
Exper. and Obser.	*Experiments and Observations on Electricity, made at Philadelphia in America, by Mr. Benjamin Franklin* . . . (London, 1751). Revised and enlarged editions were published in 1754, 1760, 1769, and 1774 with slightly varying titles. In each case the edition cited will be indicated, e.g., *Exper. and Obser.* (1751).
Ferguson, *Morris Papers*	E. James Ferguson, John Catanzariti, et al., eds., *The Papers of Robert Morris, 1781–1784* (6 vols. to date, Pittsburgh, Pa., [1973–]).
Ferguson, *Power of the Purse*	Elmer James Ferguson, *The Power of the Purse: a History of American Public Finance* . . . (Chapel Hill, N.C., [1961]).

Fitzpatrick, *Writings of Washington* — John C. Fitzpatrick, ed., *The Writings of George Washington* . . . (39 vols., Washington, D.C., [1931–44]).

Force, *Amer. Arch.* — Peter Force, ed., *American Archives: Consisting of a Collection of Authentic Records, State Papers, Debates, and Letters and Other Notices of Publick Affairs* . . . , fourth series, March 7, 1774 to July 4, 1776 (6 vols., [Washington, 1837–46]); fifth series, July 4, 1776 to September 3, 1783 (3 vols., [Washington, 1848–53]).

Ford, *Letters of William Lee* — Worthington Chauncey Ford, ed., *Letters of William Lee, 1766–1783* (3 vols., Brooklyn, N.Y., 1891).

Fortescue, *Correspondence of George Third* — Sir John William Fortescue, ed., *The Correspondence of King George the Third from 1760 to December 1783* . . . (6 vols., London, 1927–28).

France ecclésiastique — *La France ecclésiastique pour l'année* . . . (15 vols., Paris, 1774–90). Cited by year.

Freeman, *Washington* — Douglas S. Freeman (completed by John A. Carroll and Mary W. Ashworth), *George Washington: a Biography* (7 vols., New York, [1948–57]).

Gaz. — *Gazette.*

Gaz. de Leyde — *Nouvelles extraordinaires de divers endroits,* commonly known as *Gazette de Leyde.* Each issue is in two parts; we indicate the second as "sup."

Geneal. — *Genealogical.*

Gent. Mag.	*The Gentleman's Magazine, and Historical Chronicle.*
Gruber, *Howe Brothers*	Ira D. Gruber, *The Howe Brothers and the American Revolution* (New York, 1972).
Heitman, *Register of Officers*	Francis B. Heitman, *Historical Register of Officers in the War of the Revolution* . . . (Washington, D.C., 1893).
Hillairet, *Rues de Paris*	Jacques Hillairet, pseud. of Auguste A. Coussillan, *Dictionnaire historique des rues de Paris* (2nd ed.; 2 vols., [Paris, 1964]).
Hist.	*Historic* or *Historical.*
Hutchinson, *Diary*	Peter O. Hutchinson, ed., *The Diary and Letters of His Excellency Thomas Hutchinson, Esq* . . . (2 vols., London, 1883–86).
Idzerda, *Lafayette Papers*	Stanley J. Idzerda *et al.*, eds., *Lafayette in the Age of the American Revolution: Selected Letters and Papers, 1776–1790* (5 vols. to date, Ithaca, N.Y., and London, [1977–]).
JA	John Adams.
JCC	Worthington C. Ford *et al.*, eds., *Journals of the Continental Congress, 1744–1789* (34 vols., Washington, 1904–37).
Jour.	*Journal.*
JW	Jonathan Williams, Jr.
Kaminkow, *Mariners*	Marion and Jack Kaminkow, *Mariners of the American Revolution* (Baltimore, 1967).
L	Letter unsigned.
Larousse	Pierre Larousse, *Grand dictionnaire universel du XIXe siècle* . . . (17 vols., Paris, [n.d.]).

Lasseray, *Les Français*	André Lasseray, *Les Français sous les treize étoiles, 1775–1783* (2 vols., Paris, 1935).
Laurens Papers	Philip M. Hamer, George C. Rogers, Jr., David R. Chestnutt *et al.,* eds., *The Papers of Henry Laurens* (10 vols. to date, Columbia, S.C., [1968–]).
Le Bihan, *Francs-maçons parisiens*	Alain Le Bihan, *Francs-maçons parisiens du Grand Orient de France* ... (Commission d'histoire économique et sociale de la révolution française, *Mémoires et documents,* XIX; Paris, 1966).
Lee, *Life of Arthur Lee*	Richard Henry Lee, *Life of Arthur Lee, L.L.D., Joint Commissioner of the United States to the Court of France, and Sole Commissioner to the Courts of Spain and Prussia, during the Revolutionary War* ... (2 vols., Boston, 1829).
Lee Family Papers	Paul P. Hoffman, ed., *The Lee Family Papers, 1742–1795* (University of Virginia *Microfilm Publication* No. 1; 8 reels, Charlottesville, Va., 1966).
Lee Jour.	Journal of Arthur Lee, December 22, 1776, to September 26, 1777 (transcript, Library of Congress): see above, XXIV, lii n.
Lee Papers	*The Lee Papers, 1754–1811* (4 vols.; New-York Historical Society *Collections,* IV–VII; New York, 1872–75).
Lewis, *Walpole Correspondence*	Wilmarth S. Lewis *et al.,* eds., *The Yale Edition of Horace Walpole's*

	Correspondence (48 vols., New Haven, 1939–83).
Lopez, *Mon Cher Papa*	Claude-Anne Lopez, *Mon Cher Papa: Franklin and the Ladies of Paris* (New Haven and London,[1966]).
Lopez and Herbert, *The Private Franklin*	Claude-Anne Lopez and Eugenia W. Herbert, *The Private Franklin: the Man and His Family* (New York, [1975]).
LS	Letter signed.
l.t.	*livres tournois.*
Lüthy, *Banque protestante*	Herbert Lüthy, *La Banque protestante en France de la Révocation de l'Edit de Nantes à la Révolution* (2 vols., Paris, 1959–61).
Mackesy, *War for America*	Piers Mackesy, *The War for America, 1775–1783* (Cambridge, Mass., 1965).
Mag.	*Magazine.*
Mass. Arch.	Massachusetts Archives, State House, Boston.
Mazas, *Ordre de Saint-Louis*	Alexandre Mazas and Théodore Anne, *Histoire de l'ordre royal et militaire de Saint-Louis depuis son institution en 1693 jusqu'en 1830* (2nd ed.; 3 vols., Paris, 1860–61).
Meng, *Despatches of Gérard*	John J. Meng, *Despatches and Instructions of Conrad Alexandre Gérard, 1778–1780* . . . (Baltimore, 1939).
Meyer, *Armement nantais*	Jean Meyer, *L'Armement nantais dans la deuxième moitié du XVIIIe siècle* (Paris, 1969).
Meyer, *Noblesse bretonne*	Jean Meyer, *La Noblesse bretonne au XVIIIe siècle* (2 vols., Paris, 1966).
Morison, *Jones*	Samuel E. Morison, *John Paul Jones: a*

Sailor's Biography (Boston and Toronto, [1959]).

Morton, *Beaumarchais Correspondance* Brian N. Morton and Donald C. Spinelli, eds., *Beaumarchais Correspondance* (4 vols. to date, Paris, 1969–).

MS, MSS Manuscript, manuscripts.

Namier and Brooke, *House of Commons* Sir Lewis Namier and John Brooke, *The History of Parliament. The House of Commons 1754–1790* (3 vols., London and New York, 1964).

Naval Docs. William B. Clark, William J. Morgan *et al.*, eds., *Naval Documents of the American Revolution* (9 vols. to date, Washington, D.C., 1964–).

Neeser, *Conyngham* Robert Walden Neeser, ed., *Letters and Papers Relating to the Cruises of Gustavus Conyngham, Captain of the Continental Navy 1777–1779* (New York, 1915).

Nordholt, *Dutch Republic* J.W. Schulte Nordholt, *The Dutch Republic and American Independence* (trans. Herbert M. Rowen; Chapel Hill, N.C., 1982).

Nouvelle biographie *Nouvelle biographie générale depuis les temps les plus reculés jusqu'à nos jours* ... (46 vols., Paris, 1855–66).

Pa. Arch. Samuel Hazard *et al.*, eds., *Pennsylvania Archives* (9 series, Philadelphia and Harrisburg, 1852–1935).

Pa. Col. Recs. *Minutes of the Provincial Council of Pennsylvania* ... (16 vols., Harrisburg, 1851–53). Volumes I–III are reprints published in Philadelphia, 1852. Title changes

	with Volume XI to *Supreme Executive Council.*
Palmer, *Loyalists*	Gregory Palmer, ed., *Biographical Sketches of Loyalists of the American Revolution* (Westport, Ct., [1984])
Phil. Trans.	The Royal Society, *Philosophical Transactions.*
PMHB	*Pennsylvania Magazine of History and Biography.*
Price, *France and the Chesapeake*	Jacob M. Price, *France and the Chesapeake: a History of the French Tobacco Monopoly, 1674–1791, and of Its Relationship to the British and American Tobacco Trade* (2 vols., Ann Arbor, Mich., [1973]).
Proc.	*Proceedings.*
Pub.	*Publications.*
Quérard, *France littéraire*	Joseph Marie Quérard, *La France littéraire ou Dictionnaire bibliographique des savants, historiens, et gens de lettres de la France, ainsi que des littérateurs étrangers qui ont écrit en français, plus particulièrement pendant les XVIIIe et XIXe siècles . . .* (Paris, 1827–64).
Rakove, *Beginnings of National Politics*	Jack N. Rakove, *The Beginnings of National Politics: an Interpretive History of the Continental Congress* (New York, 1979).
RB	Richard Bache.
Repertorium der diplomatischen Vertreter	Ludwig Bittner *et al.,* eds., *Repertorium der diplomatischen Vertreter aller Länder seit dem Westfälischen Frieden (1648)* (3 vols., Oldenburg, etc., [1936–65]).

lviii

Rev.	*Review.*
s.	*sou.*
Sabine, *Loyalists*	Lorenzo Sabine, *Biographical Sketches of Loyalists of the American Revolution* . . . (2 vols., Boston, 1864).
Schelle, *Œuvres de Turgot*	Gustave Schelle, ed., *Œuvres de Turgot et documents le concernant* (5 vols., Paris, 1913–23).
Sibley's Harvard Graduates	John L. Sibley, *Biographical Sketches of Graduates of Harvard University* (17 vols. to date, Cambridge, Mass., 1873–). Continued from Volume IV by Clifford K. Shipton.
Six, *Dictionnaire biographique*	Georges Six, *Dictionnaire biographique des généraux et amiraux français de la Révolution et de l'Empire (1792–1814)* (2 vols., Paris, 1934).
Smith, *Letters*	Paul H. Smith *et al.*, eds., *Letters of Delegates to Congress* (13 vols. to date, Washington, D.C., 1976–).
Smyth, *Writings*	Albert H. Smyth, ed., *The Writings of Benjamin Franklin* . . . (10 vols., New York, 1905–07).
Soc.	Society.
Sparks, *Works*	Jared Sparks, ed., *The Works of Benjamin Franklin* . . . (10 vols., Boston, 1836–40).
Stevens, *Facsimiles*	Benjamin F. Stevens, ed., *Facsimiles of Manuscripts in European Archives Relating to America, 1773–1783* (25 vols., London, 1889–98).
Taylor, *Adams Papers*	Robert J. Taylor *et al.*, eds., *Papers of John Adams* (6 vols. to date, Cambridge, Mass., 1977–).
Taylor, *J. Q. Adams Diary*	Robert J. Taylor *et al.*, eds., *Diary of*

lix

	John Quincy Adams (2 vols. to date, Cambridge, Mass. and London, 1981–).
Trans.	Translator or translated.
Trans.	*Transactions.*
Van Doren, *Franklin*	Carl Van Doren, *Benjamin Franklin* (New York, 1938).
Van Doren, *Franklin-Mecom*	Carl Van Doren, ed., *The Letters of Benjamin Franklin & Jane Mecom* (American Philosophical Society *Memoirs,* XXVII; Princeton, 1950).
Villiers, *Commerce colonial*	Patrick Villiers, *Le Commerce colonial atlantique et la guerre d'indépendance des Etats-Unis d'Amérique, 1778–1783* (New York, 1977).
W&MQ	*William and Mary Quarterly,* first or third series as indicated.
Ward, *War of the Revolution*	Christopher Ward, *The War of the Revolution* (John R. Alden, ed.; 2 vols., New York, 1952).
Waste Book	BF's accounts described above, XXIII, 19.
WF	William Franklin.
Wharton, *Diplomatic Correspondence*	Francis Wharton, ed., *The Revolutionary Diplomatic Correspondence of the United States* (6 vols., Washington, D.C., 1889).
Willcox, *Portrait of a General*	William B. Willcox, *Portrait of a General: Sir Henry Clinton in the War of Independence* (New York, 1964).
WTF	William Temple Franklin.
WTF, *Memoirs*	William Temple Franklin, ed., *Memoirs of the Life and Writings of Benjamin Franklin, L.L.D., F.R.S., &c* ... (3 vols., 4to, London, 1817–18).
WTF's accounts	Those described above, XXIII, 19.

Note by the Editors and the Administrative Board

The amount of material within our rubric has forced us once again to limit the time span of this volume to four months, and to reduce drastically the percentage of relevant documents printed in full. The bulk of the commissioners' outgoing and incoming correspondence is already in print, meticulously annotated, in the *Adams Papers*. Except in a few special cases, therefore, we summarize all such correspondence regardless of its importance, refer the reader to the printed text and annotation, and supplement the latter only on the rarest occasions. As this volume was about to go to press, we learned that the publication of Volume VII of the *Adams Papers*, which had been kindly communicated to us in typescript, is delayed. Consequently we are unable to furnish page references for the texts and annotation of the documents addressed to or written by the commissioners during September and October, 1778.

Our other methods of reducing bulk are an extension of those in use since the beginning of the French period, for which see above, xxiii, xlvi–xlvii. We have chosen a number of categories in which we give one example and discuss other similar letters in a summarizing headnote. Those collective descriptions appear in the index under the following headings: commission seekers; emigrants; favor seekers; and intelligence reports. As a result, a bare sixty percent of the almost eight hundred documents in this volume are printed in full.

Douglas M. Arnold left the project during the preparation of this volume. His contributions to our work during his ten years on the staff have been noteworthy. We wish him well.

Barbara Oberg joined *The Papers of Benjamin Franklin* in September, 1986, and took part in the final revisions of this volume. She will be the editor of the series as of Vol. xxviii.

Introduction

As this volume opens, the American cause is gaining momentum. On the diplomatic front, Congress has decided to ignore the blandishments of the Carlisle peace commission; on the military front, a few days later, the long-awaited war between France and England finally breaks out in the Channel when Admiral d'Orvilliers' French fleet clashes with the forces of Admiral Keppel. The battle of Ushant (Ouessant) was indecisive; both sides, of course, claimed victory.

Yet, reading the commissioners' mail in Paris, one hardly gets the sense that major events were taking place. Rather than the sounds of war, they heard mostly the shrill voices of disgruntled individuals with complaints to air: French and American crewmen squabbling, John Paul Jones still determined to see his second-in-command courtmartialed, Jonathan Williams forever embroiled in dispute with his former friend Schweighauser who had supplanted him as official agent in Nantes.

The lack of news about Admiral d'Estaing's expedition added to this sense of remoteness. Where was he? What was happening? Nobody knew. Franklin had calculated that he should reach America by June 22[1] but it was not until July 8 that he dropped anchor off the Delaware Capes—just too late to strike at a huge British convoy carrying Loyalists and supplies to New York. Prevented from entering New York harbor, d'Estaing joined the American army and the Rhode Island militia in the siege of Newport, but had to give up after suffering damage in a storm; by the end of this volume Franklin and Vergennes were reassuring each other as to their faith in the admiral's drive and ability even though he had, by latest accounts, sailed off to Boston.

Now that it had sent Conrad-Alexandre Gérard as its minister plenipotentiary to Congress, the French government was working mostly through him, and the commissioners found

1. Schelle, *Œuvres de Turgot*, v, 558.

themselves without much to do. Their role consisted mainly in trying to raise funds in order to meet the bills piled up by Congress. They turned to the Netherlands to that effect and, working through Horneca, Fizeaux & Cie., the Amsterdam bank associated with Georges Grand, they floated the loan that had been discussed through the spring—a loan that started in high hopes but which would eventually prove unsuccessful. William Lee, meanwhile, frustrated by inactivity since he had not been recognized as American commissioner to the courts of Berlin and Vienna to which Congress destined him, complicated their task by negotiating on his own a separate loan for Virginia and signing the draft of a separate treaty of commerce with the Dutch merchant Jean de Neufville.

The only two noteworthy diplomatic events were, in July, the exchange of ratifications of the treaties signed the previous February and, three months later, the deletion from those treaties of articles 11 and 12 concerning export duties on molasses and other goods. Otherwise, the commissioners spent their time on such trivial concerns as arguing for the release of Izard's luggage and the free transit of the irascible Dr. Smith's worldly goods. Not a great diplomatic agenda.

Franklin personally poured energy into trying, with the help of his friend David Hartley, to set up an exchange of prisoners—an undertaking that proved difficult and elusive. Also, as was his wont, he turned his hand to propaganda, spreading good news about the credit of American paper money, the morale of Washington's army, and informing the French that their allies had been instructed by Congress to pray for Louis XVI while forbidden to do so for George III.[2] He saw to it that France be exposed to the most eloquent voice in Boston: as soon as they arrived the letters of the Reverend Samuel Cooper were communicated to the *Affaires de l'Angleterre et de l'Amérique*. Franklin himself may well have contributed at least one article, which we publish, to that semi-official periodical whose columns were always open to him. As always he kept a public posture of optimism and equanimity— even when informed that the retreating British had plundered

2. *Courier de l'Europe*, July 10, p. 18.

his house in Philadelphia. "Il n'en est pas moins gai" noted Turgot.[3]

The day-by-day business of the commission was handled most efficiently if none too happily by John Adams who felt that his efforts went unrecognized and unsupported. Twenty-eight years later, still smarting, he inserted in his *Autobiography* a devastating picture of his senior colleague's working habits: late for breakfast, indulging his vanity through the morning with fawning visitors, off to dinner every day. "Mr. Franklin kept a horn book always in his Pockett in which he minuted all his invitations to dinner, and Mr. Lee said it was the only thing in which he was punctual." Out for tea, after that, with those many ladies who vied to please him (they are listed by Adams as "Madame Hellvetius, Madam Brillon, Madam Le Roy etc. and others whom I never knew and never enquired for"). Franklin's evenings were spent in a variety of amusements, his life "a continual Scene of discipation." It took days to obtain his signature on the letters laboriously prepared by Adams and Lee.[4] Not even the Doctor's death could assuage the hatred that Adams eventually bore him.

The commission was truly disintegrating and agreed on one point only: it should disband. Franklin painted a bleak picture of the situation to the President of Congress,[5] and within the same week, in a rare expression of personal feeling, confided to Carmichael that he could not understand why Arthur Lee and Ralph Izard detested him so much. His only explanation: he was "too much respected, complimented and caress'd by the people in general, and a Deference a little too particular paid . . . by some in Power."[6]

The continuing paradox of Franklin's life during that period is the contrast between his popularity with the French and the low opinion of him entertained by his colleagues, a state of affairs that would last until his death and beyond, when the French National Assembly, acting at Mirabeau's suggestion,

3. Schelle, *op. cit.*, v, 561.
4. Butterfield, *John Adams Diary*, IV, 118–19.
5. To James Lovell, July 22, below.
6. To William Carmichael, July 29, below.

voted to honor his memory with official mourning whereas the American Senate refused to do so.

Adams had noticed that the Parisians looked upon the old Doctor as a sort of magician: "When they spoke of him, they seemed to think that he was to restore the golden age."[7] Facetiously, during the drought of the extremely hot summer of 1778, gardeners put the blame on him because he had supposedly promised Marie-Antoinette there would be no electrical storm all through her pregnancy![8] Instances of French eagerness to please him abound during these four months, from the light-hearted announcement by Chaumont's daughter and son-in-law that they were taking chess lessons in order to be worthier opponents,[9] to the King's heart-warming decision to free a certain convict because Franklin had asked it.[1]

The fascination of this volume lies in the insights it affords into Franklin's private life and his talent for escaping loneliness by slipping right into a cocoon of affection and warmth. Just as Mrs. Stevenson and Polly had given him a home in London while the Strahans provided a pseudo-family, so the Chaumonts in Passy catered to his every need. Mme. Brillon entertained him twice a week with chess and music. Their relationship changed profoundly during the summer, going on his part from the flaring of passion to the acceptance of more domestic terms, on hers from coquettishness to filial devotion. In the fall, we see him gradually switching his attention a mile or so down the road, to Auteuil, to where Mme. Helvétius, a much more suitable partner, closer to his age, widowed like him, and generally thought to be delightful in her down-to-earth way, entertained him frequently. She loved her dogs, her cats, the many birds in her aviary, her friends, her flowers, all with zest and joy. While the rather neurotic Mme. Brillon was surrounded by artists, the uncomplicated Mme. Helvétius

---

7. C.F. Adams, ed., *The Works of John Adams* (Boston, 1856), I, 660.

8. J. Ruwet *et al.*, eds., *Lettres de Turgot à la duchesse d'Enville* (Louvain and Leiden, 1976), p. 131.

9. Michel de Foucault to WTF, Aug. 22. APS.

1. From Marc-François Gauthier, July 5; from Vergennes, Aug. 22, both below.

could offer the intellectual stimulation of the *philosophes*, her late husband's colleagues, who still flocked to her house.[2]

For a man who had disliked and fought France a good part of his adult life, Franklin was charmed by the country's lifestyle. Even though he believed that he would soon be recalled home, now that the treaties had been signed, he dug deeper roots into French culture, with an abandon and a glee that no ambassador would ever dream of exhibiting today. The Foreign Service had not set any rules as yet, he made up policy as he went, and the policy he followed was to please and be pleased, to be grateful for the ally's help and not fret over the ally's lapses from Puritan behavior.

He entered the life of his Masonic Lodge.[3] He accepted invitations to take part in the scientific establishment, be it the Académie des Sciences, the Société Royale de Médecine, or the homes of individual scientists who begged him to witness their experiments. He started what would become a memorable collaboration with Parmentier, propagandist of the beneficent potato: along with the minister of war, the minister of the interior, the Paris police chief, several academicians, economists and other enlightened minds, Franklin attended, probably in late October, a banquet at which potato bread was served and highly praised.[4] He allowed a few more artists to depict him in various degrees of toga, laurel crowns, and allegory, our frontispiece being a case in point. To the French he was now both the witty Voltaire and the backwoods Rousseau that they had just lost.

Volume 27 also contains, of course, the news being sent from America. Franklin's son William, the former governor of New Jersey, had regained his freedom through an exchange and settled in New York. William already cast a dark shadow

---

2. For a ferocious portrait of Mme. Helvétius see the letter written by Abigail Adams in 1784: C.F. Adams, ed., *Letters of Mrs. Adams* (Boston, 1840), II, 55–6.

3. Although he generally could do no wrong in the eyes of the French, he was rebuked in print after a Masonic feast; did he really have nothing better to do than waste a whole day surrounded by poetasters and adoring young men? Bachaumont, *Mémoires secrets*, XII, 43.

4. Bachaumont, *Mémoires secrets*, XII, 15

across the future of his own son, Franklin's beloved Temple: Congress was warned that the young man might not be a suitable choice for secretary of the American mission. Silas Deane, the Doctor's close friend and partner in the early days in France, was in deepening trouble back home, in the initial phase of a crisis that would eventually affect the reputation of the commissioners and raise disturbing questions about the conduct of American foreign policy and the use of public money in Europe.

Finally, although the commissioners did not know it, their big problem was about to be solved. Congress, in order to meet the dictates of etiquette among nations, decided that the envoy to France should be of a rank equal to Gérard's: minister plenipotentiary. With the exception of Pennsylvania, the states voted for Franklin. The official announcement of this choice, made on September 14, would not reach Paris until February 12 of the following year. The commissioners' bickering, somewhat subdued by lassitude, was to last until then.

Two remarkable pieces of writing illuminate this volume. As tautly argued as a lawyer's brief and suffused with cold rage, Franklin's lengthy answer to the mysterious "Charles de Weissenstein," whom he believed to be the mouthpiece of King George, rejects the man's peace proposals with scorn: too little, too late, too English. Later in the summer "The Ephemera," brooding over the brevity and vanity of life, evokes with poetic shimmer a moment of personal discouragement. Be it to get rid of anger or overcome sadness, Franklin never forgot that his pen was his best friend and the best possible tool to recover his equilibrium and don once again his mask of serenity.

Chronology

July 1 through October 31, 1778

July 5: Opening of hostilities between Prussia and Austria.
July 8: D'Estaing's squadron reaches the Delaware Capes.
July 10: Louis XVI issues letters of marque against British shipping.
July 11–22: D'Estaing at Sandy Hook menaces New York.
July 12: Gérard is warmly welcomed at Philadelphia.
July 17: American commissioners and Vergennes exchange ratification of treaties.
July 18: Congress resolves to ignore letter from Carlisle commission.
July 19: British order reprisals against French shipping.
July 27: Battle of Ushant.
July 29–August 21: D'Estaing participates in siege of Newport.
August 2: British make public their orders against French shipping.
August 6: Gérard formally received by Congress.
August 11: Storm damages d'Estaing's squadron.
August 21/22: D'Estaing abandons Newport siege, sails for Boston.
September 4: W. Lee and Jean de Neufville sign draft of a commercial treaty at Aix-la-Chapelle.
September 6–7: BF visits Mme. Brillon at Anet.
September 11: Congress votes to appoint a minister plenipotentiary to French court.
September 14: BF elected minister plenipotentiary.
c. September 20: BF composes "The Ephemera."
September 26–28: BF visits Anet again.
September 28–October 5: Carmichael testifies against Silas Deane.

October 3: Final appeal by Carlisle commission.

October 22–26: BF's instructions as minister approved by Congress.

October 31: Vergennes sets date for exchange of declarations deleting two articles from Treaty of Amity and Commerce.

THE PAPERS OF
BENJAMIN FRANKLIN

VOLUME 27

July 1 through October 31, 1778

Editorial Note on Franklin's Accounts

Of the accounts discussed throughout the French period, the following still apply: I, III, V–VII, XI–XIII, XVII. We offer here a summary of entries which have not found a place elsewhere in our annotation, but which provide insights into Franklin's private and public life during the course of this volume.

Account I (XXIII, 19), Franklin's Wastebook, gives some of his expenditures: the purchase of printing types, for instance, which amounted to 333 *l.t.* paid on August 1 to Joannis. Other entries during these months include 18 *l.t.* for some small tools, 42 *l.t.* paid a joiner for cases, and 68 *l.t.*, 18 *s.* for a subscription to the *Affaires de l'Angleterre et de l'Amérique*.

Account III (XXIII, 19), whose entries are duplicated in many other accounts, is the most informative about the lifestyle of the Franklin household. The maître d'hôtel, M. Montaigne, was in charge of feeding the family and paying for postage, an expense borne in those days by the recipient. For doing this he was reimbursed 2473 *l.t.*, 19 *s.* for July, 1508.10.6 for August, 1626.1.3 for September and 1963.11.2 for October. Another servant, Dumont, who quit his service on August 10, was paid 154.19 for his last four months' wages. A man named Calais received 48 *l.t.* on July 22 for the price of his own meals when he waited on his master at someone else's party, as was the custom. Earlier in July Franklin had paid some 60 *l.t.* for seven weeks worth of washing. The earnings of the lowest helper on the domestic totem pole, Dennis (the *frotteur*), were about 30 *l.t.* a month, including his dinners at Paris and allowance for wine. The upholsterer received 78 *l.t.* on July 10 "for 6 Months Hire of 2 Beds & other Charges." For five months' use of Chaumont's carriage and horses and for postage, Franklin was charged 1732 *l.t.*

As to the household purchases, the expenses listed include such items as a payment of 1160 *l.t.* for 29 cords of wood, plus a gratuity of 1 *l.t.*, 4 *s.* for the man who delivered them.

Account V (XXIII, 20) also provides details about Franklin's life such as the 48 *l.t.* he contributed after having listened to a "Parish Charity Sermon," the 120 *l.t.* he charged the public for the five volumes of the *Atlas maritime* bought from M. Brillon and the 600 *l.t.*, 7 *s.* spent on the Fourth of July celebration. This account also reveals the date at which Franklin considered his mission to have begun and the amount of his salary. In an entry obviously written later he noted, under October 4, 1778: "To my Salary as one of the Com-

3

missioners of the United States at the Court of France from Oct. 4, 1776 is 2 years at 11428 Livres per annum as per Resolve of Congress 6. Augt. 1779 . . . 22,856.0.0."

Account XII (xxv, 3) shows that the third quarterly installment of the French government loan to Congress was paid on August 3 and amounted, like the other three, to 750,000 *l.t.*

To ["Charles de Weissenstein"][1]

ALS: Archives du Ministère des affaires étrangères

Sir,   Passy, July 1. 1778

I received your Letter dated at Brussels the 16th past.

My Vanity might possibly be flatter'd by your Expressions of Compliment to my Understanding, if your *Proposals* did not more clearly manifest a mean Opinion of it.

You conjure me in the Name of the omniscient and just God, before whom I must appear, and by my Hopes of future Fame, to consider if some Expedient cannot be found to put a Stop to the Desolation of America, and prevent the Miseries of a General War. As I am conscious of having taken every Step in my Power to prevent the Breach, and no one to widen it, I can chearfully appear before that God, fearing nothing from his Justice in this particular, tho' I have much Occasion for his Mercy in many others. As to my future Fame, I am content to rest it on my past and present Conduct, without seeking an Addition to it in the crooked dark Paths you propose to me, where I should most certainly lose it. This your solemn Address would therefore have been more properly made to your Sovereign and his venal Parliament. He and they who wickedly began and madly continue a War for the Deso-

1. In answer to his above, xxvi, 630–9, and probably not sent. JA said at the time that it had been, but later corrected himself: he and BF forwarded it to Vergennes, along with the letter and enclosures that provoked it, and asked advice about sending the reply; when no answer came, the decision was not to send it. Butterfield, *John Adams Diary*, IV, 149–53. There was no real reason to do so. BF had vented his feelings by writing the letter, and had made them known by forwarding it to Versailles.

lation of America, are alone accountable for the Consequences.

You endeavour to impress me with a bad Opinion of French Faith: But the Instances of their fruitless Endeavours to serve a Race of weak Princes, who by their own Imprudence defeated every Attempt to promote their Interest, weigh but little with me, when I consider the steady Friendship of France to the *Thirteen United States* of Switzerland, which has now continued inviolate Two hundred Years. You tell me that she will certainly cheat us, and that she despises us already. I do not believe that she will cheat us, and I am not certain she despises us; but I see clearly that you are endeavouring to cheat us by your conciliatory Bills; that you actually despis'd our Understandings when you flatter'd yourselves those Artifices would succeed; and that not only France, but all Europe, yourselves included, would most certainly and forever despise us, if we were weak enough to accept your insidious Propositions.

Our Expectations of the future Grandeur of America are not so magnificent, and therefore not so vain and visionary as you represent them to be. The Body of our People are not Merchants but humble Husbandmen, who delight in the Cultivation of their Lands, which from their Fertility and the Variety of our Climates, are capable of furnishing all the Necessaries and Conveniencies of Life, without external Commerce: And we have too much Land to have the least Temptation to extend our Territories by Conquest from peaceable Neighbours, as well as too much Justice to think of it. Our Militias, you find by Experience, are sufficient to defend our Lands from Invasion; and the Commerce with us will be defended by all the Nations who find an Advantage in it: We therefore have not the Occasion you imagine of Fleets or Standing Armies, but may well leave those expensive Machines to be maintain'd for the Pomp of Princes and by the Wealth of ancient States. We purpose, if possible, to live in Peace with all Mankind; And after *you* have been convinc'd, to your Cost, that there is nothing to be got by attacking us, we have reason to hope that no other Power will judge it prudent to quarrel with us, lest they divert us from our own quiet Industry, and turn us into Corsairs preying upon theirs. The Weight therefore of an independent Empire, which you seem so certain of our Inability to bear, will not be so great as you imagine: The Expence of our civil Government we have always borne, and can easily bear, because it is small. A virtuous and laborious People may be cheaply govern'd. Determining as we do, to have no Offices of Profit, nor any Sinecures or useless Appointments, so common in ancient and corrupted States, we can govern ourselves a Year for the Sums you pay in a single Department, or for what one Jobbing Contractor, by the favour of a Minister, can cheat you out of in a single Article.

You think we flatter ourselves and are deceiv'd into an Opinion that England *must* acknowledge our Independency. We, on the other hand, think you flatter yourselves in imagining such an Acknowledgement a vast Boon, which we strongly desire, and which you may gain some great Advantage by Granting or Withholding. We have never ask'd it of you. We only tell you, that you can have no Treaty with us but as an independent State: And you may please yourselves and your Children with the Rattle of your Right to govern us, as long as you have done with that of your King's being King of France, without giving us the least Concern if you do not attempt to exercise it. That this pretended Right is indisputable, as you say, we utterly deny. Your Parliament never had a Right to govern us: And your King has forfeited it by his bloody Tyranny. But I thank you for letting me know a little of your Mind, that even if the Parliament should acknowledge our Independency, the Act would not be binding to Posterity, and that your Nation would resume, and prosecute the Claim as soon as they found it convenient. We suspected before, that from the Influence of your Passions, and your present Malice against us, you would not be actually bound by your conciliatory Acts longer than till they had serv'd their purpose of inducing us to disband our Forces: but we were not certain that you were Knaves by Principle, and that we ought not to have the least Confidence in your Offers, Promises or Treaties, tho' confirm'd by Parliament. I now indeed recollect my being inform'd long since when in England, that a certain very great

6

Personnage, then young, studied much a certain Book, intituled *Arcana imperii*.[2] I had the Curiosity to procure the Book and read it. There are sensible and good Things in it; but some bad ones: For, if I remember right, a particular King is applauded for his politically exciting a Rebellion among his Subjects at a time when they had not Strength to support it, that he might in subduing them take away their Privileges which were troublesome to him: and a Question is formally stated and discuss'd, *Whether a Prince who, to appease a Revolt, makes Promises of Indemnity to the Revolters, is obliged to fulfil those Promises?* Honest and good Men would say, *Ay*. But this Politician says, as you say, *No*. And he gives this pretty Reason, that tho' it was right to make the Promises, because otherwise the Revolt could not be suppress'd; yet it would be wrong to keep them, because Revolters ought to be punish'd to deter future Revolts. If these are the Principles of your Nation, no Confidence can be plac'd in you, it is in vain to treat with you, and Wars can only end in being reduc'd to an utter Inability of continuing them.

One main Drift of your Letter seems to be, to impress me with an Idea of your own Impartiality, by just Censures of your Ministers and their Measures; and to draw from me Propositions of Peace, or Approbations of those you have inclos'd to me, which you intimate may by your means be convey'd to the King directly without the Intervention of those Ministers. You would have me give them to, or drop them for a Stranger I may find next Monday in the Church of Notre Dame, to be known by a Rose in his Hat. You, yourself, Sir, are quite unknown to me; you have not trusted me with your true Name. Our taking the least Step towards a Treaty with England thro' you, might if you are an Enemy, be made use of to ruin us with our new and good Friends. I may be indiscreet enough in many things: But certainly if I were dispos'd to make Propositions (which I cannot do, having none commit-

2. The personage was doubtless George as Prince of Wales; the book was [Marcus Zuerius Boxhorn], *Arcana Imperii Detecta: or, Divers Select Cases in Government* . . . (London, 1701).

ted to me to make) I should never think of delivering them to the Lord knows who, to be carried to Lord knows where, to serve no-one knows what Purpose. Being at this time one of the most remarkable Figures in Paris, even my Appearance in the Church of Notre Dame where I cannot have any conceivable Business; and especially being seen to leave, or drop, or deliver any Letter to any Person there, would be a matter of some Speculation, and might from the Suspicions it must naturally give, have very mischievous Consequences to our Credit here. The very Proposing a Correspondence so to be managed, in a Manner not necessary where Fair-dealing is intended, gives just reason to suppose you intend *the contrary*. Besides, as your Court has sent Commissioners to treat with the Congress, with all the Powers that could be given them by the Crown under the Act of Parliament, what *good Purpose* can be serv'd by privately obtaining Propositions from us? Before those Commissioners went, we might have treated, in virtue of our general Powers (with the Knowledge, Advice and Approbation of our Friends) upon any Propositions made to us. But under the present Circumstances, for us to make Propositions, while a Treaty is suppos'd to be actually on foot with the Congress, would be extreamly improper, highly presumptuous with regard to our Constituents, and answer no good End whatever.

I write this Letter to you notwithstanding (which I think I can convey in a less mysterious manner, and guess it may come to your hands), and I write it because I would let you know our Sense of your Procedure, which appears as insidious as that of your conciliatory Bills. Your true Way to obtain a Peace, if your Ministers desire it, is to propose openly to the Congress fair and equal Terms: And you may possibly come sooner to such a Resolution, when you find that personal Flatteries, general Cajolings, and Panegyrics on our *Virtue* and *Wisdom*, are not likely to have the Effect you seem to expect, the Persuading us to act *basely* and *foolishly* in betraying our Country and Posterity into the hands of our most bitter Enemies, giving up or selling off our Arms and Warlike Stores, dismissing our Ships of War and Troops, and putting those

Enemies in Possession of our Forts and Ports.[3] This Proposition of delivering ourselves bound and gagg'd, ready for hanging without even a right to complain, and without a Friend to be found afterwards among all Mankind, you would have us embrace upon the Faith of an Act of Parliament. Good God!—an Act of your Parliament! This demonstrates that you do not yet know us, and that you fancy we do not know you. But it is not merely this flimsy *Faith* that we are to act upon; you offer us *Hope*, the Hope of PLACES, PENSIONS and PEERAGES. These (judging from yourselves) you think are Motives irresistable. This Offer, Sir, to corrupt us is with me your Credential; it convinces me that you are not a private Volunteer in this Negociation. It bears the Stamp of British-Court-Character. It is even the Signature of your King.[4] But think for a Moment in what Light it must be view'd in America. By PLACES you mean Places among us; for you take care by a special Article to secure your own to yourselves.[5] We must then pay the Salaries in order to bribe ourselves with these Places. But you will give us PENSIONS! probably to be paid too out of your expected American Revenue, and which none of us can accept without deserving and perhaps obtaining a Su*spension*.—PEERAGES![6]—Alas, Sir, our long Observation of the vast and servile Majority of your Peers, voting constantly

3. This is not strictly accurate. Art. 7 of Weissenstein's proposed settlement stipulated that each party should keep what it had at the close of hostilities; Art. 16 provided that royal ships, military stores, etc. be returned to the crown and the rest sold for the benefit of the states. The texts of Weissenstein's two proposals are published in Stevens, *Facsimiles*, VIII, nos. 836–7.
4. "There were in the Letter infallible Marks," BF told JA, "by which he knew that it came from the King, and that it could not have come from any other without the Kings Knowledge. What these Marks were he never explained to me." Butterfield, *op. cit.*, p. 150.
5. Art. 1 of Weissenstein's proposed government of North America provided that no American might hold a British office of trust or profit without a Parliamentary dispensation.
6. Art. 6 of the proposed settlement secured offices or pensions or peerages to American leaders, among them JA, BF, Hancock, and Washington. JA's description of this proposal, in the passage cited in footnote 1, is highly inaccurate.

for every Measure propos'd by a Minister, however weak or wicked, leave us small Respect for that Title. We consider it as a sort of *Tar-and-feather* Honour, a Mixture of Foulness and Folly, which every Man among us who should accept from you, would be oblig'd to renounce, or exchange for that conferr'd by the Mobs in his own Country, or wear it with everlasting Infamy. I am, Sir, Your humble Servant   B FRANKLIN

Weissenstein

Notation: 1778. Juillet 1er. Docteur Franklin La Traduction est ci-jointe.

From Michael Comyn[7]   ALS: American Philosophical Society

Sir   Marseille 1. July 1778.

The Treaty of Friendship and Commerce happily concluded between the United States of America and France, rendering indispensable the Establishment of Consuls in the different Ports of this Kingdom for the Security and Advantage of the American Traders, I humbly take the liberty to offer my Services in this Capacity for the City of Marseille, and to request the favour of your Protection and recommendation to the Congress.

---

7. All we know about his background is the little revealed here, but his campaign for the consulship at Marseilles is abundantly documented. It began, as far as we know, a month earlier in Vienna, where a relative of his with the same name (which he spelled Comÿn) was first secretary of the French embassy. Comÿn was acquainted with Ferdinand Grand, the commissioners' Parisian banker, and wrote him on June 3 to recommend his kinsman in Marseilles, who had been instrumental in getting Count Pulaski and the chevalier de la Baume to the U.S. (Pulaski, occasionally confused with Count Potocki under various spellings, appears throughout their correspondence.) Comÿn added that he had given a memorandum on the matter to William Lee, who had promised to send it to Congress with his own recommendation. With that letter Grand received another of the same date and to the same effect, written by Comÿn but signed by his ambassador, the baron de Breteuil. Next, Michael Comyn, writing from Marseilles, sent the present letter enclosed in one of July 1 to Grand, which said much the same thing. Grand's reply of the 8th, now missing, was acknowledged by

Altho' I am a Native of Ireland, having constantly resided in France since the Age of Sixteen Years, and most of my Family being Established in this Country, I am perfectly Naturalized to it, and by twenty Years employment in Trade, have Acquired every Necessary Experience with respect to Commercial Matters; these Circumstances added to a competent knowledge of the English and French Tongues, and the Protection of his Ex[cellency] Le Baron de breteuil, the French Ambassador at Vienna with which I am honoured, induce me to hope for a preference; however I rely much less on these Motives, than on the Constant Zeal and Attachment which I have Manifested to America since the Commencement of the War in which it is at present Engaged. I reflect with pleasure on my having been instrumental in procuring for the Continental Army some Officers of distinguished Merit, particularly Count Pataski, who being totally ignorant where to Apply, I inclosed his Letters to Mr. Dean at Paris; these Letters, also those Written to Mr. Dean by Mr. Le Chevalier De la Baume and others, with the offers I then made him,[8] are evident prooffs of my Zeal for the Service of America at a time when the fate of that Country appeared very Uncertain. I could mention many Occasions wherein I have displayed my Attachment to the Americans, but shall pass them over to Avoid incroaching too much on your time. If I be so fortunate as to succeed in my request, my constant attention shall be to prove that I am not Unworthy of it, by fulfilling the Duty of Consul

---

Comyn on the 17th, when he thanked the banker for his support and furnished him a memorandum to Congress that he wanted the commissioners to sign. On the 22nd Comÿn sent Grand his acknowledgment from Vienna, and mentioned that Arthur Lee supported his brother in the application. At some point a M. Dunois, apparently a Marseillais friend of the applicant, wrote BF to add his own good word and to enclose his appeal to Count "Potocki" to make representations to Congress. On August 14 Michael Comyn warned Grand that competition was developing and urged him to work against it. The last extant communication in the series is another from Comyn, undated but addressed to BF as U.S. minister and hence probably in or after 1779, to solicit him once more. All these letters are in the APS.

8. For the two officers see xxiii, 419; xxiv, 445. We know nothing about Comyn's role.

with the Utmost integrity and the most Zealous attention to
the Interests of the American Traders. I should certainly feel
infinite satisfaction in being employed in the service of a brave
and free People, but how greatly would this satisfaction be
Augmented, could I Add the pleasing reflection of having Acquired it thro' the favour and Protection of a Person, as Universally as justly Admired, in the double Capacity of the Philosopher and statesman! I have the honour to be with great
truth and respect Sir Your most humble and Devoted servant,

MICHL. COMYN

Endorsed: Michael Comyn Application for Consul at Marseilles

From Samuel Cooper[9]   ALS: American Philosophical Society

My dear Sir,   Boston 1st. July 1778.

I have wrote you four or five Times not long since, but from
all our Arrivals from France of late have not the Pleasure of a
single Line, but I know your Crowd of important Business.
Accidentally hearing of a Vessel that sails for France this day, I
enclose you a Philadelphia Paper bro't by a swift Post last
Evening, and containing the Proceedings of the British Commissaries, and the Congress hitherto,[1] which you must be desirous to know as early as possible. The present Firmness of
Congress, is but half their Glory. Their Resolves, which I
transmitted you some Time ago, pass'd before they knew of
the Alliance with His most Christian Majesty, are noble indeed. They will persevere in spite of British Arms, Arts, or
Gold. Mr. S. Adams, in a Letter of 21. June, by this Post, writes
me, "I have never seen Congress more determind to support
the Independence of these States; nor more united in Measures for that Purpose." It is not unfavorable either to France
or these States that the British Commissioners, as you will

9. BF's old friend, the Boston clergyman.
1. The vessel was the *General Arnold*, which also carried the navy board's
letter of July 2: Taylor, *Adams Papers*, VI, 249–50, where the ship is called
the *Arnold Packet*. The paper was probably the *Pennsylvania Gazette* of June
20, mentioned by the committee for foreign affairs: XXVI, 666.

observe, stumbled at the Threshold, and in their first Communication to Congress, in order to slur the Measures of His most Christian Majesty in our Favor, advanc'd a Palpable Falsehood.[2] This will do them no great Credit in Europe, and will have a good Effect here. If they have nothing further to offer than they have already exhibited, they have come upon a Fool's Errand indeed: But it is like the British Ministry, who live upon Expedients for a Day. The first Essay of the Commissioners has not had half the Effect, in amusing or dividing the People that might have been expected; and the Cry ev'ry where now is: "Independence; and Fidelity to our Treaties." Our last Accounts from the Army, I give you, as I had them verbally, from the abovemention'd Express. Genl. Lee, and Maxwell, with about 2000 each, had been sent forward to watch and retard the Motions of the Enemy upon their leaving the City. Clinton's Army left it with Precipitation, and tho much was plunder'd and carried away, yet Nothing was destroy'd but war like Stores; and many Supplies left in the City. They encamp'd between Haddingfield and Billinsport, about 7 Miles from Philadelphia. Here they tarried two or three Days, which amus'd Congress as to their Design. They then remov'd to Mount Holly, where our Advice leaves them: Their Delay occasion'd by obstructing the Roads &c., gave Genl. Washington an opportunity to get before them, who by the last Accounts was not far from Princetown. His Army has been much reinforc'd by Continental Troops, and the Militia, especially in the Jerseys, have turn'd out briskly. He is said to have upwards of 20000 men; and Clinton from 12 to 15 thousand. In short, if our Reports may be depended on, the Situation of the latter is not unlike that of Burgoyne. But as Washington is not comparatively so much in Force as Gates was, I rather hope, than depend, that the Issue may be the same. Be that as it may, the Enemy by leaving Philadelphia are unravelling all they did last Year; our Prospects are brighten'd ev'ry day; and our Country, I think, will soon be compleatly deliv-

2. Cooper must have been referring to the Carlisle commission's following insinuation against France: "The insidious Interposition of a Power, which has from the first Settlement of these Colonies been actuated with Enmity to us both." Stevens, *Facsimiles*, XI, no. 1104, pp. 3–4.

er'd. We have just receiv'd Letters from France directed to the
Count d'Estaing, but have no Account to be depended on, of
his Arrival on the American Coasts. A short Notification, with
your and Mr. J. Adams' Signature, of a British Fleet of eleven
Sail of the Line, bound from St. Helen's to these Parts, Was
yesterday receiv'd by the Council,[3] and will be properly im-
press'd. I forgot to mention, that just before Clinton left the
City, about 3000 of his light Troops had embarqu'd and left it.
We have heard of the glorious Action of Capt. Jones. Our
Harbor looks alive with French Vessels, and a Number of late
Prizes. The Hopes of the Tories, and British Partizans, are now
as the Giving up of the Ghost. With much Esteem, and ev'ry
Attachment, I am my dear Sir Your's   SAML. COOPER.

Honorable Benjn. Franklin Esqr.

Endorsed: Dr. Cooper

Notation: 1st. July 1778.

From Georges-Adam Junker[4] and Other Applicants for Emigration

ALS: University of Pennsylvania Library

In the course of the four months covered by this volume, a number
of people turn to Franklin to secure his help in their plans to emigrate to America, to obtain the information necessary to make up
their minds, or to recommend other would-be emigrants. Such requests come from France, Switzerland, Germany, even England.[5]
They reveal two widespread misconceptions: that land in America
is free for the asking and that Franklin is as omnipotent as the King
of France, hence a source of unlimited patronage. Franklin must
have had some of these letters in mind when he wrote his *Advice to
those who would remove to America,* one of the *Bagatelles* he eventually
published on his own Passy press, in which he emphasized that the

3. The commissioners' warning of May 18: xxvi, 499.
4. A German emigrant (1720–1805) who had been in Paris since 1762
and made his mark there. He taught German at the Ecole militaire and had
become a royal censor: Larousse.
5. With the exception of Henry's letter, which is at the University of Pa.
Library, all the documents discussed below are at the APS. All the letters
are in French except Medel's.

14

first question asked of an emigrant to the New World was not *Who are you?* but *What can you do?*

Some people think of emigrating because they resent the iniquities of the old regime. On July 14, Geraud, writing from Bordeaux, explains that he has spent his youth traveling and acquiring knowledge in mathematics, physics, mineralogy and chemistry, especially metalworks and saltpetre. He wishes the Doctor himself would test him on scientific matters but travels have exhausted his small patrimony and he cannot afford the trip to Paris. He had hopes of a good position in the *régie des poudres*, only to be forgotten, which is not suprising in a country where "la protection inflüe pour beaucoup à la distribution des emplois." At thirty-five, he would have little trouble acquiring English, since he is already fluent in Italian and Spanish, and now his dream is to live among free people guided by honor and patriotism. Writing from Dijon on August 1st to both Franklin and Adams,[6] Pezerat ainé, Ecuyer, is also disgruntled by the French social system: "L'Espece d'Etre qui chés nous a le malheur d'etre a la fois Indigent et Gentilhomme est pour ainsi dire malheureux sans Ressource." Feeling compelled by the code of his class to leave his children at least as well off as their ancestors, he embarked on a lawsuit to recover their rightful share of the family fortune. He won his case but half his gains evaporated in bribes to judges, ushers and other legal sharks. He wants a new life among the virtuous Americans but before taking his wife, two small children and the family assets of about 15,000 *l.t.*, he needs a few answers. Supposing he were to clear some land, would he get it for free? If so, how much—converted, of course, into French measurements? Does the Government extend support before the land starts producing? How much does hired help cost? Would it be a better idea to use his small capital to start a foundry, and in that case how much should he pay his workmen? Would the commissioners hold his funds in Paris and furnish him an equivalent amount in America so as to avoid the perils of the sea? Is a practicing Roman Catholic deprived of any civil rights?

Still more questions are asked on August 3 by Tessier, a merchant from Cadillac, near Bordeaux. He too wants to clear some land with the help of ten farmers whom he would bring along under contract for a given time. Before getting ready to sail at the first rumor of peace, he wants to know whether the United States will provide emigrants with free passage, give them land upon arrival, support

6. Published in Taylor, *Adams Papers*, VI, 338–42.

them for a while, furnish them with housing and tools, exempt them temporarily from taxation, and allow them to bring their own bedding and linen. Heitz, a young lawyer currently employed at the archives of Strasbourg, sends, on September 8, a list of twenty-one questions having to do with agriculture, the price of various commodities, the safest time and the safest way to cross. Is liberty of conscience practiced in America? Is a man allowed to remain a bachelor? Should Franklin give him favorable answers, he is prepared to emigrate along with two friends.

Dusaray,[7] who writes on October 27, also plans to bring a number of people: his wife, six children, six farmers and their families, about twenty in all. He needs an adequate piece of land, not far from Philadelphia. He is, as he makes clear, an important man: *receveur des fermes* in Burgundy, at Mont Saint-Vincent; a relative, through his wife, of de L'Averdy,[8] he is well known to several of the farmers general. Had America still been under English rule he never would have thought of emigrating, but now, if Congress guarantees him good land, with woods, pasture and water, and advances him the necessary food, seeds, cattle and tools, he would gladly settle in the New World, trusting he would be treated there with the consideration due to a subject of the King of France.

Ship captain Guiot, writing from Nantes on September 20, "dans le moment le plus triste de ma vie," strikes a much humbler note. He too is willing to till the land, but on a small scale and by himself. The English, those pirates, seized his ship in July, 1776, off the coast of Guinea.[9] Now that the situation is deteriorating between France and England, he will never recover it and only wishes to bring his family and small holdings to any American province that will allow him to buy a plot of land. On August 21, a man called Charrière,[1] who describes himself as the lord of Cossonay near Versoix in

7. Or perhaps Busaray.

8. Clément-Charles-François de L'Averdy (1724–1793) had been comptroller of finances from 1763 to 1768. Michel Antoine, *Le Gouvernement et l'Administration sous Louis XV* (Paris, 1978), p. 149.

9. His ship was taken, he says, by the *Lord Dartmouth* acting on orders from the Governor of Senegal.

1. Ferdinand de Charrière was *châtelain de Cossonay*, near Lausanne, from 1736 to 1783, a position that the authorities in Bern had granted several times to members of that family. He eventually lost his fortune, and his son Henri-César, the last *châtelain*, had to sell the ancestral home. *Recueil de généalogies vaudoises* (Lausanne, 1923), I, 455–8. From information kindly provided by Prof. Pierre Deguise.

Switzerland, wonders in which capacity the Swiss might better be employed in the New World: in the army or in agriculture? Now that peace with England is at hand, some Swiss emigrants might take up domestic service or teach French. Whatever his reply, Franklin should keep it confidential since the writer's government would not take kindly to his project of collective expatriation. Charrière also wishes to warn Franklin that the people charged with the purchase of Swiss cheeses for export to America are not competent and that he would make a far better selection if entrusted with that mission.

Some intellectuals want to start a new life. Jean-Daniel Simon, a "ministre de la parole" who gives his address as Simon de Dieu, in Vieux Linange near Deux-Ponts, informs Franklin on August 22 that a small group of German scholars, five to eight people whose specialties comprise philosophy, law, theology and mathematics, wish to found a college in whichever American province Congress decides. Once provided with the necessary financial help and travel costs, they will open their school to young men of all religions. The curriculum, to be taught in German until the faculty learns English, will cover Latin, Hebrew, Greek, French, philosophy in all its branches, and the various sciences including medicine and surgery. Instruction in riding, fencing and dancing will also be offered. Some capital city would be the best location. On August 23, a man who refers to himself as Henry writes from Madrid. He is a French mathematician and something of a chemist now working as an engineer in Spain "par un hazard qui ne lui a pas été favorable." He has taught mathematics at the École Royale des Ponts et Chaussées for four years, has presented a much appreciated paper at the Academy of Sciences, worked in the mines of Guadalcanal and written, in Spanish, a treatise on pure mathematics.[2] Having heard that his brother, a former civil engineer, has just gone to America as captain of engineers, he desperately wants to go there too and will accept any kind of useful work.[3]

From Rouen, on August 25, comes a request signed by three rest-

2. His references in Paris are of the highest caliber: Jean-Rodolphe Perronet, first engineer of the ponts et chaussées (see his letter of Aug. 13), de Chesy his deputy, J.-B. Le Roy and Alexis Vandermonde, of the Academy of Sciences. He may well be the Dom Pedro Henry who published pieces on mathematics, hydraulic engineering and mineralogy in Seville in 1789 and 1790. From information kindly furnished by Charles Hendricks, of the Historical Division of the U.S. Army Corps of Engineers.

3. The brother was Jean-François Henry (1746–1801) ingénieur des ponts et chaussées, employed in Montignac (Dordogne) in 1777 and again

less young lawyers: Mollien, Poincheval and Brulley. They have received a fine education and are burning to put it to good use: what better place than Boston whose very name makes their blood run faster? They want to contribute to America's glory and sail as early as possible, no matter what the danger. Luckily they are all endowed with siblings who will be a source of solace to their parents.[4]

Another young man, Nithard, working as a clerk in Strasbourg, explains somewhat bitterly on September 18 that he is the oldest son of the captain of an infantry regiment in Alsace who, after thirty years of faithful service, left his widow and six children with nothing more than his Cross of Saint-Louis. The writer has just turned twenty-four, he knows German, French and Latin, has been clerking for eight years and possesses excellent testimonials to his thoroughness and zeal. Could Franklin help him obtain some work anywhere in America? Another applicant from Strasbourg, Carl Medel, presents his case on September 24, in German:[5] he is a schoolmaster in Neunkirchen, near Deux-Ponts, and would like to cross to America with his six little children. How expensive will the voyage be? Is there a danger of being captured? If Congress would pay their traveling expenses, several thousand German families would establish themselves in America.

Finally there is the case of the three young men who write from Paris on September 24. Jean Deversine, who lives in the Marais, is a candy maker; Honoré-Laurent Ferté makes lemonade; Louis Froment brews beer. They wish to practice their crafts in America because they don't see any future for themselves in France, as they are poor and their métiers are crowded. They hope that Franklin, who is America's father, will be their father too. They beg to be allowed on the first passenger ship leaving from Nantes and promise to apply themselves to any task requested on board. They hold certificates from the high magistrates of Paris attesting to their good con-

---

in 1794. Archives Nationales, f[14] 2243[2]. His biographical sketch there makes no mention of a stay in the United States. See also A. Brunot et R. Coquand, *Le Corps des ponts et chaussées* (Paris, 1982), p. 822.

4. Nicolas-François Mollien (1758–1850), the man who penned the letter, did well to remain in France. He had a brilliant career in the administration of finances and eventually served Napoleon who made him a count and Minister of the Treasury. Larousse. We have not been able to trace the other two young lawyers.

5. A brief résumé in French, in an unidentified hand, accompanies the letter.

duct and would be happy to serve some eminent person to whom Franklin would recommend them. Their plea ends with the consecrated formula: "Ils ne cesseront de prier pour la conservation des Jours precieux de son Excellence et une longue continuation de l'alliance."

Monsieur   à Paris, le 1er Juillet 1778.

Ayant à Vous communiquer une affaire relative au Service des Treize Etat-unis, j'ose Vous prier de vouloir bien me faire savoir l'heure et le jour où il Vous seroit commode de m'accorder un moment d'audience.[6] J'ai l'honneur d'être avec les sentiments les plus respectueux Monsieur, Votre très-humble et très-obéissant serviteur   JUNKER

Censeur Royal rue Rousselet, fauxb, St. Germain.

Notation: Junker 1er Juillet 1778.

To ――――[7]   ALS: American Philosophical Society

Sir,   Passy, July 2. 1778

I am exceedingly oblig'd by the exact Plan and Profile you have been so kind as to send me, of the hydraulic Machine at Chatou.[8] Be pleased to accept my thankful Acknowledgments of the Favour, and be assured that I am, with great Esteem, Sir, Your most obedient humble Servant   B FRANKLIN

6. His purpose is explained in a memorandum of his, dated July 4, that BF endorsed. It recommends a Sieur Gross, who had been an army surgeon and burgomaster of Hanau, Junker's birthplace; Gross wants to emigrate in order to join his sister in Philadelphia, and offers to take with him several young surgeons who are ready to serve. APS. Junker may have sent the memorandum either after an interview with BF or to further his request for one.

7. A virtually indecipherable notation on the verso, which may have no relation to the letter, can be read as "franclin et Ridly."

8. The machine was in fact nearby, at Marly, to provide water for that château and Versailles. The commissioners dined at Marly on June 2, when JA commented on the magnificence of the waterworks, and they visited them again on Aug. 17: Butterfield, *John Adams Diary*, II, 316, 318.

The Eastern Navy Board to the American Commissioners

LS: American Philosophical Society; copy:[9] Library of Congress

Navy Board Eastern Department Boston

Gentlemen   July 2d. 1778

We have the Honour to hand you by Capt. Ayres in the Arnold Packett, four Packetts Intrusted to our care for Conveyance by the Honble. Committee for Foreign Affairs.[1] We also Inclose the Gazettes of this Town Since our last. We wish them Safe to your hands as we presume they will give you all the Important Intelligence of this Country. We shall trouble you no further than to Inform you, that Capt. Ayres has the honour to hold a Captains Commission in the American Navy, and to recommend him to your Notice as an officer upon all Occasions ready to render his best Services to his Country. He has Orders to receive his directions from you for his future Conduct.[2] You will please to order him such Supplies as he may have occasion for. We have the Honour to be with the Greatest respect Your honours Most Obedient and most humble Servants   J WARREN[3]

Honble. Commissrs. of the United States of America

Addressed: The Honble: / The Commissioners from the United / States of America / Paris

Notation: James Warren Boston July 2d 78. Navy Board

9. In the hand of WTF.
1. For speculation on material in the packets see Taylor, *Adams Papers*, VI, 250 n, 347, 349 n.
2. John Ayres did not live long enough; see XXVI, 681 n.
3. The prominent Massachusetts politician had served on the navy board since its creation in 1777: XXV, 572 n.

Mr. and Mrs. Richard Bennett Lloyd[4] to Franklin and John Adams

AL:[5] American Philosophical Society

Thursday evening Chaillot Rue des Batailles
[July 2?, 1778[6]]

Mr. and Mrs. Lloyd present Compliments to Messrs. Franklin and Adams, and will do themselves the honour to dine with Them on Saturday next.

Addressed: Messrs. Franklin & Adams

Abraham Whipple to the American Commissioners[7]

ALS: American Philosophical Society; copy: Yale University Library

⟨Nantes, July 2, 1778: I received your letter of June 23[8] on the 30th; my orders are all that I could have wished. Officers and men are working with a will to get the ship ready, which she should be by the end of this month. I have space for more than the fourteen bales of blankets that Mr. Schweighauser has for me, and should gladly take the arms and stores that Mr. Williams, I understand, has on hand.[9] Please let me know soon so as not to delay stowing. I enclose, as instructed, a list of prisoners on board. Dispatches you send me will have my full attention. The mainmast I expect to be in tomorrow.⟩

4. For the two see XXVI, 343 n.
5. In the husband's hand.
6. We assume that they were accepting for the celebration on Saturday, July 4, to which the commissioners invited all the American ladies and gentlemen in Paris: Butterfield, *John Adams Diary,* II, 317; IV, 143–4. The year must be 1778, the last Lloyd spent in France. According to WTF's accounts, the cost of the dinner amounted to 600 *l.t.,* 7 *s.:* Account III, XXIII, 19.
7. Published in Taylor, *Adams Papers,* VI, 250–1.
8. See XXVI, 673–4. The letter contained sailing orders for Whipple's ship, the frigate *Providence.*
9. Until William Lee made Schweighauser the official agent at Nantes, JW had been in charge of repairing the old fusils that the commissioners had purchased and of assembling supplies to send to America.

From Charles Epp

ALS: American Philosophical Society

⟨Altorff,[1] July 2, 1778: The English are making a huge mistake in trying to fight a war overseas, especially against people as civilized as they are. Your leaders show wisdom in waiting for the enemy to overextend their supply lines. The danger for your country will begin after victory, when national consensus breaks down. My advice is not to give too much play to popular will, so easily manipulated by the ambitious. My own experience in the Swiss cantons[2] has shown me that, for all their defects, the aristocratic ones are better governed than the democratic, since brotherly love is an unrealistic notion. Please consider my remarks as coming from a wellwisher.[3]⟩

From Edme-Jacques Genet[4]

ALS: American Philosophical Society

Monsieur   A Versailles ce 2 juillet 1778

J'apprens avec le plus grand plaisir par la lettre dont vous m'avés honoré,[5] que vous approuvés l'usage que j'ai fait des lettres que vous aviés bien voulu me confier. J'ai actuellement deux n° des *affaires de l'angleterre* prêts à paroitre:[6] je n'attens que des nouvelles directes d'amerique, que j'espere recevoir par votre canal, suivant la promesse que vous avés daigné me faire de m'envoyer aussitôt, ce que vous jugeriés *fit for publication*. Vous serés sûr que dans les vingt-quatre heures les nouvelles ou lettres que vous aurés reçues seront répandues dans tout Paris.

Je voudrois bien pouvoir vous promettre de vous faire venir

1. A small town in the canton of Uri.
2. He signs himself "procureur au canton d'Uri."
3. BF's endorsement reads: "Charles Epp Swiss; his Remarks on republican Govermts Alsorff 2 juillet 1778."
4. Writing as usual in his capacity as editor of the *Affaires de l'Angleterre et de l'Amérique*. He had begun to draw information for it from JA as well as BF: Taylor, *Adams Papers*, VI, 190–3 *et seq.*
5. Of June 29: see XXVI, 696.
6. The issues, we assume, of June 25 and July 10: X, cahier XLVII and XI, part 2, cahier XLVIII.

régulierement de Londres, le *Lond. Ev. post* et le *Lond. Chronicle*. Mais dans l'Etat actuel de la correspondance entre Calais et Douvres, je ne puis pas répondre de la *régularité*. Cependant je ferai mon possible pour vous satisfaire au moins en partie.

Je vais expédier à mon ami M. Bridgen la lettre dont vous me chargés pour lui.[7] Je verrai auparavant s'il n'y auroit point d'occasion *safe* par les affaires etrangeres. Je suis avec respect Monsieur Votre trés humble et trés obeissant serviteur

GENET

P.S. J'ai fait traduire pour nos ministres la piece ci-jointe dont vous serés peut être bien aise d'avoir communication.

Addressed: Mr. Benjamin Franklin / député du Congres americain / a Passy

Notation: M. Genet 2 Juillet 78

From Henricus Godet[8]   ALS: American Philosophical Society

Sir   Amsterdam July 2d. 1778

Upon my arrival in town I was applyed to by one David Welch,[9] Who Says he was Second Lieutenant on board the Lexington Capt. Henry Johnson, and which was taken by a Kings Cutter the Lurt [*Alert*] Capt. Bazely and Carryed to Plymouth and putt into Mill prison, and Fortunately made his Escape out of Goal; and is now as you may reasonably Suppose, be in Want of Necessarys for Support. I pray you would take Such Steps as you may Judge Necessary; Should you think Necessary and prudent, I will Supply him and procure him a passage to any part of france that you may think most Convenient or will please to order; I am in Short Loath to Act in any Such Cases Without your agreeable orders; if Necessary I pray you would adress to Messrs. Reinhold Lappenberg & Schmieman, Merchants in Amsterdam Who are Wellwish-

7. The letter, now missing, was doubtless in reply to Bridgen's inquiry the previous April: XXVI, 376–7.
8. The St. Eustatius merchant who was now living in Amsterdam: XXV, 137.
9. Welsh's letter below of the same date was enclosed with this one.

ers to your Cause; and in my Absence will do the Needfull. In Expectation of your Speedy answer, I have the Honour to be Sir Your most Obedient Humble Servant   HENRS. GODET

Addressed: A Monsieur / Monsr. B. Franklin / a / Passi

Endorsed: Henry Godet abt Lieut Welsh

Notations in different hands: Amsterdam 2. juillet 1778. / A Mr. LeNeutre Ngt [Négociant] rue du petit Lyön

From Claude Mammès Pahin Champlain de La Blancherie[1]

ALS: University of Pennsylvania Library

A l'ancien college de Bayeux rue de la Harpe
Monsieur le Docteur,   le 2 juillet 1778

Je me serois mal expliqué, si vous aviez compris que je vous eusse prié de me servir de caution pour une somme quelconque empruntée pour me procurer un logement. J'avois seulement imaginé que, par l'interêt qu'on doit prendre à votre recommandation, M. de Chaumont auroit pu donner les mains à aider un établissement qui a mérité votre approbation, en m'avançant quelque argent.[2] Je pouvois l'espérer d'autant mieux qu'il est aisé de voir, que les dépenses seront toujours bien au dessous de la recette, que cela n'est pas dans ce moment, parcequ'il faut un commencement à tout. Quelque confiance que je doive avoir en l'honneur de votre protection, je sais trop ce qui vous est dû pour manquer de discrétion envers vous. Je vous prie de m'excuser, si j'ai laissé sur cela quelque équivoque. Je n'ai mis aucune borne à ma confiance en vous. J'ai déposé mes peines dans votre sein et je vous ai la plus grande obligation de la franchise avec laquelle vous avez

---

1. For this enterprising young Frenchman, see XXVI, 379–80.

2. The quarters in the Collège de Bayeux that he used for his weekly gathering were extremely cramped: *ibid.*, p. 536 n. Moving to the new ones would be expensive, and he had clearly asked BF, orally or in a missing letter, to intercede with Chaumont for a loan. Whether it was forthcoming we do not know, but a month later Elie de Beaumont made the move possible: see La Blancherie's letter of Aug. 5. The move to the rue de Tournon was announced in the Oct. 16 issue of the *Jour. de Paris.*

bien voulu me répondre, et je me félicite également d'avoir
reçu des témoignages de votre protection et de votre estime.
Il est vrai que si quelque chose eût pu me flatter c'eût été de
pouvoir annoncer dans toute l'Europe, que le Législateur des
Américains, étoit encore en france le bienfaiteur des Etrangers, des gens de lettres et des Artistes et c'étoit là véritablement la gloire que j'allois solliciter de vous. Je suis avec un
tres profond respect, Monsieur le Docteur, Votre tres humble
et tres obéissant serviteur   LA BLANCHERIE

Notation: La Blancherie 2. Juillet 1778.

From —— Richard and Other Favor Seekers

ALS: University of Pennsylvania Library

This note, like the one in the previous volume, summarizes letters
from a diverse group of people asking for favors;[3] as was the case
previously, we do not know whether they produced any result.

Three correspondents ask Franklin to forward letters. On July 24,
M. Lutterloh, Court Councilor of the Duke of Brunswick and Lune-
burg, hopes the Doctor will send the enclosed to his brother in the
American service and forward his brother's answer.[4] On the same
day, writing from Potsdam, Martin Paschke, who has just heard from
his son Frederic, assistant quartermaster general in the American
army, entreats Franklin to send the young man what may be his last
paternal blessing. He hopes that, with the Doctor's protection, his
son will be allowed to pursue in America a military career usually
reserved for men of high birth.[5] On September 17, Croiset, "juge du
point d'honneur"[6] at La Rochelle and a member of the Royal Academy of that town, pleads the cause of an honorable merchant from

3. See XXVI, 142–9. All documents summarized in the headnote, with the
exception of Martin (University of Pa. Library), are in the APS. Katz's letter
is in German, de La Blancherie's and Appreece's are in English, and the
remainder are in French.
4. For Col. Henry E. Lutterloh, see XXIII, 110–11 n.
5. Frederick Paschke was currently a lieutenant in the 4th continental
artillery; he later served in Pulaski's legion and as deputy quartermaster
general in the Southern department. Francis B. Heitman, *Historical Register
of Officers of the Continental Army* (rev. ed., Baltimore, 1982), p. 428.
6. A function usually fulfilled by the *maréchaux de France*, who decided
on the finer points of conduct of gentlemen and officers.

the nearby Ile de Ré, whose relatives, named Mazick, have established themselves in Charleston, South Carolina. Unable to meet Franklin while in Paris, Croiset sends him by post the package that is meant for Charleston. Its contents are meant only to establish commercial relations between France and America, a desirable goal.

Four people seek financial help. On August 28, a Mme. de Choisinet, living in Paris, begs Franklin to tide her over while she is waiting for some money she is certain to obtain. He owes such an act of charity to his reputation for philanthropy; her fate is now in his hands. No less desperate, Dom Bernard, a Benedictine monk of the Congregation of St. Maur in Châlon-sur-Saône, tells his story on September 14: during Lent he succumbed to the temptation of gambling and lost 3,840 *l.t.* He borrowed from various people to pay this debt and now does not have a penny to reimburse them. Should Franklin help him out and keep his shameful secret, he will pray incessantly for the noble cause of the Americans, "opprimés par des tyrans et des tigres."[7] The following day John Apreece, a former ensign in the 8th British infantry, wrote from St. Germain en Laye to tell Franklin he was bedridden and despondent. He had resigned his commission rather than draw his sword against the Americans. Although as nobly born as any in England (he was a cousin to Lord Harborough, Lord Mexborough and the late Sir Francis Delaval and his brother possessed an income of £5,000 a year) he had been subsequently ignored by his family and now was as truly miserable as anyone.[8] Ten days later Apreece repeated his appeal, adding that he had been in France for the past three years and that his old friend Lord Effingham[9] could testify to his good conduct and misfortune. The saga of Arnaud Matges, a dental surgeon who has fallen on hard times, is hard to follow: the *placet* he sent from Paris on October 9 is partly incoherent. He has been a master of his art, urged by

7. BF endorsed it: "Dom Bernard Benedictine wants me to pay his Gaming Debts—and he will pray for Success to our Cause 14. 7bre 1778."

8. Apreece (d. 1821) was the younger brother of Thomas Hussey Apreece (d. 1833), a prominent Huntingdonshire landowner and future baronet: Worthington Chauncey Ford, ed., *British Officers Serving in America, 1754–1774* ... (Boston, 1894), p. 10; *Victoria History of the County of Huntingdon* ... (3 vols., London, 1926–36), III, 226–9; *Gent. Mag.,* LII (1782), 312. For his cousins see Namier and Brooke, *House of Commons,* II, 309–10 and George E. Cokayne, ed., *The Complete Peerage* ... (13 vols., London, 1910–40), VI, 296; VIII, 684–5.

9. Thomas Howard, earl of Effingham (1747–91), an opponent in the House of Lords of the North government, for whom see *ibid.,* V, 13–14.

his patron, the late comte de Clermont, to give public demonstrations—with the result that envious colleagues plotted his ruin. Back with his family in Bordeaux in 1765, he was again opposed by the local surgeons and was eventually forced by poverty to wear such miserable rags that his patients felt under no compunction to pay him a decent fee. He walked all the way back to Paris in 1777, did not fare any better, and now sends Franklin a copy of his diploma along with an appeal for help. He has a destitute daughter and a sister-in-law to support in Bordeaux.[1]

One man seeks employment. Writing on August 24 from Bordeaux where, for lack of funds, he had to interrupt his proposed journey to Paris, Anne-Joseph de Panebeuf, *cadet de Gascogne*, introduces himself "en deux Mots": 34 years old, of noble birth, healthy, poor. Can Franklin suggest any way he could make a living while being of use to America? A similar request is made on September 14 by de la Blancherie,[2] a young nobleman who gives the château de Compiègne as his address. He has received a gentleman's education: a little music, both vocal and instrumental, a little mathematics, a little drawing. After some time with a rich uncle in Hispaniola, West Indies, which he left because he could not stand living among Negroes, he moved to Philadelphia where Samuel Mifflin[3] was his guardian, traveled extensively through the American colonies and learned English during his two-year stay. Back in France, restless, useless, untrained for any profession, he hopes Franklin will find him some work that would benefit the Americans whose kindness he appreciated.

Four individuals seek news of friends or relatives. N. Leleu, merchant and secretary of the Picardy chamber of commerce, inquires on July 19 about the fate of Pierre Ricot, captain of the *Benjamin*. The cutter, which left South Carolina on April 20, has undoubtedly been captured and taken back to America; the captain's family are desolate. Would Franklin use his influence to see that Ricot is treated well and exchanged promptly? Philipp Conrad Katz, registrar of the treasury for Budingen near Hanau, in Hesse, wonders on August 9 whether Franklin knows anything about his brother, Georg Theobald, who emigrated to Philadelphia with his family in

1. BF endorsed this letter: "Petition from a poor Dentiste."
2. Not to be confused with Claude Mammès Pahin Champlain de La Blancherie.
3. Samuel Mifflin (1724–81) has appeared briefly in vols. V–VIII. He was a colonel of the First Company of Artillery of Philadelphia: 6 *Pa. Archives*, I, 515.

1774. Are they still alive? A baronne de Lindau enquires from Eisenach in Hesse on September 25 about the fate of her son, an officer in the regiment of Hesse-Hanau, now a prisoner in Boston. Franklin's generous nature, so well known in her country, will certainly be moved by her plea; would he promise to forward the unsealed letter she plans to write to her son? On October 4, Mme. Robert Herault in Calais wonders whether Franklin has any news of the *Benjamin*, on which her husband is second in command. It sailed from Le Havre a full year ago, she has heard nothing and is in the throes of anguish.[4]

One more name is added to the list of those who believed Franklin had discovered a cure for dropsy in the form of tobacco ashes.[5] Cathallet Cotiere, in St. Sulpice de la Pointe (Languedoc), asks for additional information on October 3. A friend of his is about to die: please help.

Three people make an appeal for Franklin's intellectual patronage. A professor of mathematics in Rochefort, named Laureau, sends him, on July 16, a manuscript (now missing) on military matters. He had planned to add much detail but has been so busy during his current visit to Paris that further work was impossible. He trusts the Doctor to keep the utmost confidentiality about his memoir which shall be delivered by a friend, a sea captain who is dying to enter the American service along with another Frenchman. Laureau can vouch for their seamanship either at war or in trade. Would Franklin also forward "un mot" he has written to General Washington?

The abbé de Pellizer announces on October 21, from Paris, that the Spanish-French-Latin dictionary he has been working on is almost ready for the press; it has occurred to him that if he added the English language to it, the American's collaboration and protection would be of enormous value. He, the abbé, would become rich and American commerce would be promoted. On second thought, Franklin's protection alone would suffice.[6] On October 28, De

---

4. A notation by Chaumont says that the *Benjamin* was captured and taken to an English port.

5. See xxv, 178–9.

6. A protégé of the Spanish ambassador, Abbé Joseph-Emmanuel de Pellizer-Garcia occasionally read papers to the Académie des Sciences and may well have met BF there: *procès-verbaux*, C, fols. 221, 223. He does not seem to have carried out the grand plan mentioned here, but published a Spanish grammar in 1786 and several works on hydraulics and astronomy in the following years. *Catalogue de la Bibliothèque nationale.*

Belair[7] writes from Paris to ask Franklin to peruse an enclosed manuscript, the work of a friend. Any sign of approbation on his part will render the author extremely happy. Having heard nothing, he writes again on November 19 in a slightly irritated tone, and asks that Franklin respond directly to the author, Bardinet, whose name and address he now provides.[8] The manuscript Franklin has in his hands is the only complete version in existence. One month later, on December 28, De Belair repeats a message he had sent five days earlier (now lost): someone will pick up the manuscript on any day Franklin appoints.

Finally, there are the people who want to be appointed consuls in various French ports. President Pigault de Lepinoy, former mayor of Calais, sends word from that town on July 16: many foreign nations already have agents in Calais, it is high time for the United States to follow suit. His son, juge du point d'honneur, would help him fill the position which would be greatly enhanced by the title of infantry captain in the service of the United States: "Le Culte des François ne fut jamais dirigé vers l'interet; Il ne connoit que la Gloire et l'honneur."

Monsieur   De paris ce 2 juilliet 1778

Apres vous avoir assurer de mes respects La presente est pour vous prier de vouloir me fair Le plaisir s'il est a votre Connaissance de me donner des nouvelles de Monsieur Lebon, qui doit vous Etre attache En qualité d'un bureau de Correspondance pour L'amérique. Ce Monsieur Est de la Connaissance de monsieur penett Consul a nantes ainsy que de monsieur Coulo, et Mr. dagosta.[9] Des affaires interessantes M'oblige a vous importuner pour savoir de ses nouvelles; j'ose me flaté que vous voudrez me honnorer d'une reponse. Vous obligerez Celuy qui est avec Estime, Monsieur, Votre tres humble et obeissant serviteur   RICHARD

---

7. Possibly Alexandre-Pierre Julienne de Belair (1747–1819) who wrote several treatises on fortification and engineering. He became a general in 1793, a baron in 1813. *DBF*.

8. Bardinet is the author of a comedy entitled *Les Evénements nocturnes*, 1777. We have not found any trace of the dramatic poem mentioned here.

9. Pierre Penet was a former business partner of Couleaux and now of the d'Acosta brothers: see above, XXII, 469 n and Penet, D'Acosta frères et Cie. to BF below, Sept. 3. We know nothing of Lebon.

Mon adresse est place maubert chez Mr. ardoille[?] horloger pour me[?] remetre

Addressed: A Monsieur / Monsieur franquelin / Consul de Lamerique / A Chaiot

From David Welsh   ALS: Historical Society of Pennsylvania

Sir   Amsterdam July 2d. 1778

I seppose you have recd. my Letter of the 18th of last Month[1] which gives me A great deal of Un Easiness that I have not sence recd. aney Assistance from You as I am Distitude of Cash or aney friends to furnish me with aney untill they hear from you as they are gubious who I be. Mr. Hancock Wants to know if You should think it Propper for him to gow aney further or not as he was Purswaded by Some of the foar men of Plymouth Dock Yard to go and see you and if their was Aney encouriagement from You that they would three or four Hundred of them be verey glad to get off as soon it would permit them.[2] This Sir You will receive along with Mr. H. Godet letter and I hope You will Write as soon as Possiable to him so as he Would relieve me from my Distress and like wise Write me A few lines So as I may know how to Proceed after words. Sir In Complying with this request I am your most obedient and Humble Servant

DAVID WELSH
Formerley Secd. Lieutt. of the Brig Lexington

1. Above, xxvi, 658–9.
2. Philip Hancock lived at Plymouth Dock. He ultimately made his way to Paris where he offered to help formulate a plan for prisoner relief: see his letter below [after Sept. 2].

Charles-Guillaume-Frédéric Dumas to the American Commissioners[3]

ALS: American Philosophical Society; AL (draft):[4] Algemeen Rijksarchief

⟨The Hague, July 3, 1778, in French: What I said in my last about Amsterdam's borrowing[5] was much exaggerated; my informant was mistaken, and our friend van Berckel set me straight. Yesterday I communicated the treaty to him and to the Burgomaster of Amsterdam, and they were pleased with it;[6] now we have only to let the peat slowly catch fire. You will see, by the enclosed gazette and others, that I am using the material you sent me; it is having a positive effect. Ever since Saratoga I have given our friends here control of the battlefield. We learned this morning from the British papers that Keppel's fleet did nothing but take two frigates, begin hostili-

---

3. This letter from the Congressional agent in the Netherlands is published in Taylor, *Adams Papers*, VI, 251–3.

Dumas' cast of characters is so varied, and in his quest for secrecy and mystery he uses such various names and abbreviations that we believe it useful to introduce the figures who will appear with frequency in his correspondence. They are: Pieter van Bleiswijk, Grand Pensionary of Holland, functionally Dutch foreign minister, abbreviated as G—— P——; Engelbert François van Berckel, Pensionary of Amsterdam, proponent of trade between Amsterdam and America, called "notre ami," our friend; William V, Prince of Orange and Stadholder of the Netherlands, referred to as the Stadholder, the Prince, the Grand Personnage; the duc de la Vauguyon, French Ambassador to the Dutch Republic codenamed by Dumas the Grand Facteur or G—— F——; Laurent Bérenger, French chargé d'affaires in La Vauguyon's absence, called "le substitut"; Jean de Neufville, an Amsterdam financier who negotiates an agreement with William Lee, occasionally called only "le Marchand"; the States General, Their High Mightinesses, Leurs Hautes Puissances or only LL.HH.PP.; William Lee, often mentioned as Mr. L.

4. With significant differences from the ALS: Taylor, *Adams Papers*, VI, 253 n.

5. See XXVI, 692.

6. The treaty of amity and commerce between France and the United States, whose communication to the Dutch government was the subject of much discussion in our vol. XXVI.

ties, and then retire before the French coming out of Brest.⁷ It was good to hear of the arrival of the *Deane* because I knew that my friend Carmichael was on board.⁸⟩

John Paul Jones: Memorandum for the American Commissioners⁹
Copy: Harvard University Library

⟨[July 3, 1778:¹] I came to Paris when I learned on good authority that the minister wanted to speak with me on a matter of great utility to the United States.² Permission to sell the prizes, or an exchange of prisoners, was not in immediate prospect; and something had to be done to assuage the *Ranger*'s crew. The minister pledged me to reveal his plan to no one, so that I may not do so even to you, unless you get me released from my promise and allowed to inform him that you insisted. But I can assure you that the plan is consistent with my duty as an officer, and with American interests and the friendship of France; it will contribute to the success of our arms and cost nothing. Success, the minister emphasized, depends on complete secrecy. The affair was not of my seeking, and the trip to Paris accorded with my instructions and my duty. I acted on principle, and know that my past conduct has been amply approved.⟩

7. Keppel's battle with the frigate *Belle-Poule* and capture of her sister ships *Licorne* and *Pallas* marked the beginning of Anglo-French hostilities. Keppel's fleet returned to Portsmouth after the incidents; actually the French fleet at Brest did not put to sea until July 8: xxvi, 680; Dull, *French Navy*, 118–20.

8. The American frigate *Deane*, carrying William Carmichael and other passengers, reached New England at the beginning of May: xxv, 494 n.

9. Published in Taylor, *Adams Papers*, vi, 254.

1. Dated from the heading of the copy.

2. BF had written Jones confidentially three weeks earlier that he was about to receive the command of the "Frigate from Holland," the *Indien*: xxvi, 606–8. The minister was Sartine.

James Moylan to the American Commissioners

ALS: American Philosophical Society

Honorable Gentlemen   L'Orient 3d July 1778

The Frigate Boston Cap. S. Tucker is return'd to this port yesterday. On her Cruise she had taken four prizes, one of which loaded with Currants and Medecines the Cap. order'd to Boston, and the other three to this port, which are not yet arrived.

Mr. Livingston who set out this afternoon for Paris, will inform you the disagreeable cause of this vessel's return, and as Mr. Schwighawser (who I understand you have appointed Agent for this Province) has not yet had time to give his orders for supplying this vessels wants, I told Cap. Tucker that I wou'd furnish him with the necessarys, untill the receipt of them, or of your instructions,[3] in consequence of which I have pass'd with him through the diffirent ceremonys of his entrance &c. I have the honor to be respectfully Honorable Gentlemen Your assurd humble Servant   JAMES MOYLAN

Addressed: The Honorable Plenepotentiary / Ministers of the United States / of America / at / Passy

Endorsed by John Adams: Mr Moylan's Letter, 3d. July 78

Thomas Simpson to the American Commissioners[4]

ALS: American Philosophical Society

⟨Brest, July 3, 1778: Thank you for your interposition on my behalf. Captain Jones has released me from prison to sail for America, but holds me suspended until a court martial sum-

---

3. For Samuel Tucker and Musco Livingston, respectively, see XXVI, 216–17 n, 256 n. Moylan sounds as if he were sure that Schweighauser's authority had replaced his own in the agency at Lorient. In fact it had not, though he had good reason to suspect it; see our annotation of his letter of July 8.

4. Published in Taylor, *Adams Papers,* VI, 255–6. John Paul Jones's former first lieutenant had been imprisoned for supposedly disobeying orders while commanding one of the *Ranger's* prizes.

mons us to meet face to face. I enclose a copy of my parole. Immediately upon my release I inquired of Mr. Williams at Nantes about vessels bound to America; several are bound to the southern states, which are too far from my native New Hampshire for me to afford the journey, especially since I've received no wages as yet. Mr. Cutler[5] writes that Captain Whipple has offered me passage in the *Providence*, providing that she is bound for the northern states. I await his word, and can always sail with Captain Niles, who arrived this morning.[6]⟩

Samuel Tucker to the American Commissioners[7]

ALS: American Philosophical Society

⟨The *Boston*, Lorient, July 3, 1778: I arrived here after a cruise of twenty-four days, during which I took four prizes; one I sent to Boston and the others here. I returned so soon because I encountered Capt. Alexander Murray in the brig *Saratoga* with dispatches for you and the court and other important letters, which my officers saw. I started to convoy him, but went off on a number of chases and did not see him again until yesterday, bound for Nantes. Mr. Livingston, my second lieutenant, will present this and give you details.

Tell me whether I must take my prisoners to America. If so I shall build a prison for them aboard, and for some of my crew who are disaffected and whom I shall try, if I meet Capt. Whipple or Jones, and otherwise carry home. I am sorry to lose Mr. Livingston whose health will not endure another cruise. I should be glad to accompany Capt. Whipple. On

5. Samuel Cutler, an escaped prisoner who had reached Paris the previous November, was employed in JW's counting house in Nantes. See XXV, 171 n; JW to Congress, Sept. 10, 1778, APS.

6. Robert Niles, commander of the *Spy*. The ship brought the ratified treaties; they reached the commissioners on July 8 and on the 9th JA wrote that the news gave "universal Joy to this Court and Nation." See XXVI, 539; Butterfield, *John Adams Diary*, IV, 148. Simpson asked Niles on July 4 to represent his case to the commissioners in Paris. APS.

7. Published in Taylor, *Adams Papers*, VI, 256–7.

June 16 I encountered and evaded seven two- and three-deckers that I took to be the English fleet.⟩

Jonathan Williams, Jr., to the American Commissioners[8]

ALS: American Philosophical Society

⟨Passy, July 3, 1778: On your verbal instructions I have ordered the repair of arms at Nantes to be stopped and the workmen paid off according to the agreement.[9] Please let me know whether this is satisfactory.[1]⟩

From Fairholme & Luther[2]

ALS: American Philosophical Society

Sir   Isle de Rhè 3d. July 1778

We took the liberty of writing you twice, the last dated the 5th. Ultimo[3] advising the arrival here of an english prize and the necessity there is of having some person substituted here to act for the congress and at the same time making bold to offer our Services for that purpose and also to give a Security if necessary and that you thought proper to empower us with that trust, since which we are depriv'd of an answer.

The prize is still here and we are really puzled how to behave or act. The Admiralty informs us they have orders to sequester all prizes brought into these ports and to detain them 'till further orders from Paris. Our Custom house also say they can't let the wine ashore till they hear from the Farmers General, in what manner to receive the entry which 'till

---

8. Published in Taylor, *Adams Papers*, VI, 258.

9. With Mercier more than a year before: XXIV, 100–1. Only a fifth of the old fusils had been repaired: JW to Congress, Sept. 10, 1778, APS.

1. On the verso is a draft reply in JA's hand: "Passi July 10 1778. Mr. Williams. The within directions as given by you, being according to our verbal orders to you, are approved." This is followed by JA's notation, "ansd. July 10 1778 approved. see the Letterbk."

2. A local commercial firm: XXV, 206 n.

3. XXVI, 590–2.

they get proper orders they look upon as being foreign wine in a brittish bottom. In vain have we applied to both those officers, ever since the first arrival of the Prize which is now a Month past but can get no satisfactory answer which is the more necessary as the friggat the Providence, at present at Pain Boeuf, is in want of her Men who are here with the prize. We therefore most earnestly request you'll be pleas'd to have that matter clear'd up, in such a manner as to be a standing rule for any prizes that may come here hereafter. In expectation of the honour of your answer we remain most respectfully Sir Your most obedient and very humble Servant

FAIRHOLME & LUTHER

Addressed: A Monsieur / Monsieur Le Docteur Franklin / à Passey prés de / Paris

Notation: Ferholme & Luther 3 July 1778.

From Harriott Heathcote[4]

ALS: American Philosophical Society

St. Omer in Artois, July the 3d. 1778 Chez Monsr.
Symon rue St. Bertin

Amidst the multiplicty of bussines in which your Excellency is involv'd, many apoligies would be nessesary for troubleing you with this letter. But the man who could so nobely enter into the cause of Liberty and his Country must have a heart that will ever plead for involuntary errors. Upon that goodness alone it is that I must rely for takeing this liberty, for though unfortunately a stranger to Doctor Franklin's person, I was Long before I left my native soil well acquainted with his merrit.

4. Clearly the daughter of the Mrs. Heathcote who played whist and cribbage three times a week with Emma Thompson in St. Omer: above, XXIII, 292. As far as we know, the name meant nothing to BF; in 1777 he had sent his regards to Mrs. Heathcote because she was pro-American, but did not know her: *ibid.,* p. 298. He must have been unaware that she and her daughter, presumably during his stay in England, had been received by his family in Philadelphia. We have failed to find any trace of that visit.

Réception de Franklin au Palais Royal par le Duc d'Orléans
(Louis-Philippe), 1778

The very great civility my mother receive'd when at Phili-delphia from your Late Lady has Lain us under obligations never to be forgot while memory Lasts, and the politeness of Miss Franklin at the same time merrits acknowledgements of the warmest gratitude. And though some years have elaps'd since, yet do wee much wissh to hear of her wellfare, and the onely method I had was this I have now taken which if it proves successful will realy be an addition to my happiness.

My mother with me begg Leave to present most respectful Compliments to you and your Amiable Daughter. I have the honor to be with great respect your Excellencys most obedent and very humble Servant   HARRIOTT HEATHCOTE

P.S. That peace and tranquility may once more be restor'd to my native Country are my sincere prayers.

Addressed: His Excellency the Ambassador / of the United States of America / Doctor Franklin / Panchauds Banquier[5] / a Paris

Endorsed: Harriot Heathcote Thankful Enquiries

Notation: St. Anne en Artois. 3. juillet 1778.

From ——— Perrot and ——— Boyer

ALS: American Philosophical Society

Monsieur   Paris le 3. juillet 1778
On s'empressoit au Palais royal[6] à vous voir et à vous té-moigner la joie que Votre présence excitoit, vous vous êtes dérobé aux acclamations publiques et vous avez bien Voulu

---

5. Isaac and Jean-François Panchaud, prominent bankers and traders: Lüthy, *Banque protestante*, II, 426–7. Their father had been a London mer-chant, which may account for Harriott's using them.

6. A bustling enclave devoted to business and pleasure, the Palais-Royal comprised a vast array of restaurants, cafés, shops, amusement booths, gambling dens and meeting rooms of all kinds. See Howard Rice, *Thomas Jefferson's Paris* (Princeton, 1976), pp. 13–18. Even though we have found no written trace of the event, our guess is that BF had paid a courtesy call on Louis-Philippe, duc d'Orléans, as attested by the illustration on the facing page.

vous reposer un instant à la maison. Pouvons nous nous flatter que vous voudrez bien aussi accepter douze bouteilles de vins de Bourgogne: c'est une faible maniere de vous présenter son hommage, mais chacun cherche à vous présenter le Sien et nous sommes jaloux de vous faire agréer le nôtre; nous vous offrons, Monsieur, avec d'autant plus de Confiance ces Vins que, les récoltant nous mêmes, nous sommes surs de leur bonté: puissent-ils par l'usage que nous vous prions d'en faire, Contribuer à la prolongation de vos jours qui font l'honneur de Votre Patrie et de l'humanité. Nous vous suplions, Monsieur, de nous permettre d'avoir l'honneur d'aller vous faire notre cour et vous assurer du profond respect avec lequel nous Sommes Monsieur Vos tres humbles et tres obeissants serviteurs.

PERROT LE JEUNE
BOYER

Rue neuve des petits Champs Vis-a-vis celle Vivienne

> Graces à tes Projets, à tes Travaux hardis
> Ton Peuple a secoué le joug de l'Esclavage
> et respire à présent à l'Ombre de nos Lys:
> puisque de ta Vertu son bonheur est l'ouvrage,
> ne te derobes pas aux Voeux de Tout Paris
> francklin de l'univers a mérité l'hommage.

Notation: 3. Juillet 1778.

Endorsed: Perrot et Boyer Civility

From Claude-Carloman de Rulhiere[7]

AL: University of Pennsylvania Library

Ce vendredi, 3 juilliet [1778]

Rulhiere est venu pour avoir l'honneur de voir Monsieur franklin. D'après de nouveaux memoires très surs qu'il a recus de turquie, il est forcé de réformer en grande partie ce qu'il a dit de cet empire dans son histoire de l'anarchie de Pologne.[8]

7. For the poet, historian and diplomat see XXIII, 419, and XXVI, 290.
8. *L'Histoire de l'anarchie de Pologne et du démembrement de cette république* appeared posthumously in 1807. Quérard, *France littéraire*.

Comme il part demain pour la campagne où il passera deux mois dans la solitude, il compte y travailler à corriger cet ouvrage et à le finir s'il le peut. Il supplie Monsieur franklin de vouloir bien lui remettre ce qu'il en a entre les mains. Il lui adressera demain matin un homme sur,[9] auquel il le prie de remettre ce manuscrit. Rulhiere veut se presser d'achever ces tristes recits d'anarchie d'oppression et de ruine afin de s'occuper bientôt d'objets plus consolants. Puisse l'historien devenir digne de ce nouveau sujet, il presente à Monsieur franklin les plus respectueux hommages.

Notation: Rulhiere

From [Benjamin Vaughan][1]

AL: American Philosophical Society

My dearest sir,   July 3, 1778.

You will be a *little* out of humor with a set of your friends here, though *secretly* but little so, as you *must* understand the history of their pompous language. For my *own* part, I think it right to keep up the characters of the men into whose hands the country is likely to fall; for the sake of the people here and in America, and of our enemies; for their conduct has in general seemed unintelligble, and to have no bottom but courtiership and pride. I am sure there is a shape in which we shall *in fact* grow together again with America; and the characters on *each* side ought therefore to be mutually kept up. The more the distress of this country, the more it seems feasible; for nothing but distress could soften *us*, and *when* distressed, your people will quickly feel that it is not the business of America to let England go to the wall, and France and Spain have no check to balance their insolence and power. The difference of treaty before war and after war, is in my eyes nothing; for you

9. He sent a messenger on July 4 to pick up the manuscript and in a note expressed his regret at not having seen BF the previous evening. University of Pa. Library.

1. The last extant letter from BF's young friend and editor was in May: XXVI, 542–6.

will help France but coldly after your business is done, and I dare say carry on a large trade with us in the interim. We are certainly shockingly weak at this moment, and I believe it probable that the French may land and stay here for a season or so, though not permanently. The calamity will be dreadful for the moment, and leave us probably poor bankrupts, but not less firm as a people, for if this—does not change his administration and even system of government, he will lose his seat either to the enemy or his people. You may smile that the French don't terrify me; but it is happy when men upon the edge of calamity can spy a comfortable consequence or two.

The papers have got something concerning a treaty set on foot by Lord Bute for inviting in Lord Chatham. The following circumstances are *genuine*. Sir James Wright (whom some call a marplot) was the go-between; and Lord Bute expressed a wish to come into power with Lord Chatham, and in particular to take Lord Weymouth's post. Lord Chatham answered, that much as the country seemed lost to dignity and virtue, he was very sure they could distinguish between the man who had ruined it, and the man who had saved it, and who stood by in a cottage ready to save it again. The negotiation failed of course. Lord Chatham mean'd to have gone into a direct attack of Lord Bute on the day of his fit and some following days; in order as he said to pluck that viper from behind the throne. You may remember he began this topic.[2]

2. Reports of this negotiation were appearing in the London newspapers; see, for example, the *Public Advertiser*, July 1 and 3, 1778. Discussions between Sir James Wright, the former governor of Georgia (xv, 94 n) and Dr. Anthony Addington, Chatham's personal physician, had taken place earlier in the year. Chatham learned that Lord Bute, Wright's patron, desired Weymouth's position as secretary of state for the southern department. Chatham rejected the proposed coalition, instructing Addington to let Wright "know that his great patron and your village friend differ in this: one has brought the King and kingdom to ruin; the other would sincerely endeavor to save it." Francis Thackeray, *A History of the Right Honourable William Pitt* ... (2 vols., London, 1827), II, 365–7. For an account of the episode, some of the details of which were disputed by the principals, see *ibid.*, pp. 362–9, [633]–57. During his final speech in the House of Lords Chatham spoke of "something lurking near the throne" and misleading the

I hear that you have used the following expression; *"this great man doted before he died."* I am sure some very inaccurate man has been about you to misrepresent his words, if this phrase fell from you. I *know* who might have been that man; and he is notoriously inaccurate.[3]

The inclosed papers concern a certain minority-person's family. Perhaps Mr. A. Lee who was at school with him will undertake to enquire—in whose hands the property is at present? who receives the profits? whether the bulk of the land is in any, and in what cultivation? whether well managed? and what measures ought to be taken on the subject?[4]

I hear from my friend at Rotterdam, that nothing has been heard from you about the Legacy of 7 or 800 to the Maylander, which was mentioned to you at the Duke of Chaulnes last summer; and which you said should make the subject of an advertisement in the Mayland papers.[5]

By the by the name of the D. of C. puts me in mind, that they have not done with your points yet at the Society.[6]

My love to J. Williams, whom I deceived by two articles of news, one got from an admiralty lord, and the other from a Commissioner of the Customs; either directly or through good hands; but there is such changing of measures backwards and forwards, and such lying, that little intelligence can be had that is good.

---

government; this was doubtless the "topic" that Vaughan remembered. Cobbett, *Parliamentary History*, XIX (1777–78), 1025 n; see also above, XXVI, 366–8.

3. We have not located the source of this supposed quotation or identified the "very inaccurate man."

4. Lee's schoolmate, perhaps at Eton, eludes us.

5. The friend in Rotterdam might have been Benjamin Sowden, who had offered to transmit letters to England (XXIII, 601), but we have no evidence that he knew Vaughan or was concerned with a Maryland legacy. For Chaulnes, the naturalist, and his relationship with BF and Vaughan, see XXIII, 408 n; XXIV, 539 n.

6. For the recent debates in the Royal Society over the Purfleet episode, see XXVI, 625 and the references there. At issue were the pointed lightning rods that BF had recommended in 1772, for which see vol. XIX.

I dare tell you no news at the present moment; except that a West India packet has arrived after 10 weeks.[7] Yours with most[?]

Notations in different hands: B Vaughan / July 3. 78

Lewis (or Louis) Fevre (or Favre)[8] to William Temple Franklin

ALS: American Philosophical Society

Sir,   London, July 3d. 1778

The eagerness of gratitude to match at every means of shewing itself, will I hope plead my excuse for not missing so fair an opportunity of presenting to you this humble remembrance of my most attachful respects. My dutiful sense of Dr. Franklin's beneficence to me has never been one moment out of my mind. How much and how impatiently do I long to hear of his and your health. My best wishes ever attend you, and nothing could make me happier than their completion. My station in life may not obtain for them much weight with you, but if the heart could give them rank I could offer them you with a better grace, combined with the assurance of my remaining ever with the profoundest respect and the warmest gratitude, Sir, Your ever faithful and most obedient humble Servant   L. FEVRE

---

7. The *Grenville*, whose arrival was mentioned in the *Public Advertiser* on July 4.

8. A voice out of the past. The writer, after being BF's clerk for some years in England, entered Lord Shelburne's service; there he remained, highly esteemed, for the rest of his life: XIX, 438 n; XXII, 350. His name appears as both Fevre and Favre, and his signature here may be read either way. The first name, for which he used only the initial, is commonly given as Lewis; but because he was of French extraction we suspect that it was Louis. WTF replied on July 30, and docketed his draft "Le Fevre." He apologized for having been too busy to answer by the bearer, and assured him that he and his grandfather were keenly aware "of your friendship and the goodness of your heart." APS.

Mrs. Stevenson & Mrs. Hewson are well & retired in Surry. Mr. & Mrs. Faulkner are both dead.[9]

Addressed: To / William Temple Franklin Esqr. / Paris

Notation: Louis Le fevre 3 July 1778

John Bondfield to the American Commissioners[1]

ALS: American Philosophical Society

⟨Bordeaux, July 4, 1778: The *Union* left Edenton on June 6 and arrived here on the 2nd but unfortunately, after so short a passage, brought no news. Accounts come in of losses on the Carolina coast caused by pilots' misconduct; the inhabitants mislead our ships or refuse help, and the state government should take notice. Mr. Sartine has invited local merchants to unite in fitting out privateers, and offered to lend cannon for the duration at the King's expense.

Mr. James Willing led the party that cut off the English settlements on the Mississippi;[2] a vessel recently arrived here from New Orleans with a cargo estimated at a million livres. Many ships have come from the French islands; one learned from an English frigate that the British were only waiting to attack until they learn how Count d'Estaing behaves on reaching America. A rumor, probably fabricated here, tells of a battle between Washington and Clinton in which the latter prevailed.

The compliments of the day, which we plan to celebrate in the usual style.⟩

9. Mrs. Stevenson and Mrs. Hewson need no introduction. For the death of Mr. and Mrs. Magnus Falconar, relatives of Mary Hewson, see XXII, 301 n; XXVI, 41 n.

1. Published in Taylor, *Adams Papers*, VI, 260–1. Bondfield was the American agent and the commissioners' prolific correspondent in Bordeaux.

2. See XXVI, 377–8.

John Paul Jones to the American Commissioners

ALS: University of Virginia Library; AL (draft): National Archives; copy: United States Naval Academy Museum

Gentlemen   Passy July 4th. 1778

When Congress thought proper to order me to France it was proposed that the Ranger should remain under my direction and be Commanded by a Lieutenant, and as the French Ministry have now in contemplation Plans which promise Honor to the American Flag, the Ranger might be very Useful to Assist in carrying them into execution.

Lieutenant Simpson has certainly behaved amiss; Yet I can forgive as well as resent, And upon his making a proper Concession, I will with your Approbation not only pardon the past but leave him the Command of the Ranger. By this means, and by some little promotions and Attentions that may be consistent, I hope to be able to satisfy the Rangers Crew so that they will postpone their return as long as the service may require. I have the Honor to be with sentiments of due Esteem and Respect Gentlemen Your very Obliged, very Obedient very humble Servant   JNO P JONES

Their Excellencies the American Plenipotentiaries &ca.

Addressed: Their Excellencies / The American Plenipotentiaries / at the Court of / France.

Notations: Capn. Jones about Lt. Simpson / J.P. Jones to Amen. Plenips. 4 July 1778.

44

John Paul Jones: Memorandum[3]

Copy: Library of Congress

⟨Passy, June 5 [*i.e.* July 4–5],[4] 1778: "Plan for expeditions submitted to the American Plenipotentiaries and to the french minister of Marine by Com. Jones."

Three fast frigates with tenders might burn Whitehaven and its fleet, rendering it nearly impossible to supply Ireland with coal next winter.

The same force could take the bank of Ayr, in Scotland, destroy the town and perhaps the shipping at Clyde, along with Greenock and Port-Glasgow. The fishery at Campbeltown and some Irish ports are also worthy targets.

It might be equally expedient to alarm Britain's east side by destroying the coal shipping of Newcastle. Many important towns on the east and north coasts of England and Scotland could be burnt or captured.

The success of these enterprises will depend on surprise and dispatch; it is therefore necessary that the ships sail fast, and carry sufficient force to repel the enemy. If successful, any one of these projects would occasion almost inconceivable panic in England. It would convince the world of her vulnerability, and hurt her public credit.

Other projects might be to intercept Britain's West India or Baltic fleets, her Hudson Bay ships, or destroy her Greenland fishery.⟩

---

3. Published in Taylor, *Adams Papers*, VI, 261–3, where the problems of dating and of Jones's expeditions are fully annotated.

4. The error in the month, we are convinced, was a slip of the pen. On June 5 Jones was in Brest; see also his letter to the commissioners of Aug. 2, which refers to what we believe is this memorandum, of "July 4."

From —————— Carroll, Marquise d'Auzoüer[5]

ALS: University of Pennsylvania Library

Madame dauzouer hotel de flandre rue dophine
pres le pont neuf ce 4 julliet 1778[6]
Quoi que je vous sois, Monsieur, tres inconue permettez-moy
d'envoyer savoir l'heure ou je pourai avoir l'honneur de vous
voir demain, ou tout autre jour de votre comodité. J'ésperere
que vous voudrai bien m'accorder cette grace. Je suis une
proche parante de messieurs carrolls qui habitent anapolie
dans le meriland. Je vous assure, monsieur, que je prand beaucoup de part a tous les succés de votre patrie et que personne
ne sauroit être plus que moy, penetrée des sentimens de veneration qui vous sont dus. Avec lesquels j'ai l'honneur d'etre
Monsieur Votre tres humble et tres obeissante servante

CARROLL DAUZOÜER

Notation: Carroll 4 juillet 1777.

5. A close French relative, as she says, of the Carrolls of Carrollton. She
had been in touch with Charles Carroll, BF's companion on the mission to
Canada, as early as 1771, when she had written to ask him why he had not
paid her the visit he had promised during his school days in France years
before, and to inquire about the American branch of the family. His reply
ascribed his not keeping the promise "to a certain giddiness incident to
youth," and gave her a detailed genealogy. J.G.D. Paul, "A Lost Letter-
Book of Charles Carroll of Carrollton," *Md. Hist. Mag.*, XXXII (1937), 203–
8. She had either kept up the correspondence since then or was renewing it
with some vigor. On July 12 she wrote BF again from Paris, to regret that
the enclosed letters were probably too late to go with the dispatches of
which he had spoken; but she had recently written Mr. Carroll by Mr.
"Mayland" (James Moylan, the commissioners' agent at Lorient), "ce qui
multiplira mes lettres." She expressed her pleasure at meeting BF and her
enthusiasm for his cause, and added regards from her husband, "un gentilhomme qui vit dans sa terre dont il est le seigneur et de sa paroisse." They
were leaving in a fortnight for their country estate; if letters came for her
from Mr. Carroll, would he please forward them? University of Pa. Library.
6. The final digit could be read as a 7. But her husband referred in a
letter of Jan. 21, 1780, to a meeting that he and his wife had had with BF in
July, 1778, and she reminded BF of her visit in that year when she wrote
him on Oct. 12, 1784. APS.

From Arthur Middleton[7]

ALS: American Philosophical Society

Sir   Charles Town S. Carolina July 4th. 1778

Hoping that my Name is not entirely unknown to you, I take the Liberty of introducing Alexander Gillon Esquire to your Notice; a Gentleman, who, to oblige the State of So. Carolina has accepted the Commission of Commodore.[8] I promise myself no other recommendation of him is required, than the bare mention of his having chearfully given up his own Independance to assist in establishing that of America. He has thoughts of spending a short time in Paris, and any favours shewn him will confer an Obligation upon me. I am Sir with esteem and respect Your most obedient Servant

ARTHUR MIDDLETON

The Honble Benjamin Franklin Esquire.

Addressed: The Honble / Benjamin Franklin / Commissioner of the United States / of America / at the Court of Versailles.

Endorsed: South Carolina

Notation: Arthur Middleton Charlestown 4e juillet 1778.

---

7. A prominent South Carolina politician and the son of one of the largest landowners in the state: *DAB*. He and BF had served together in Congress.

8. Gillon (1741–94), born in Rotterdam, had become a South Carolina merchant and sea captain and attained prominence at the beginning of the Revolution. In February, 1778, he was appointed commodore in the state navy, and was commissioned to go to Europe to obtain three warships, if need be by raising a loan: *DAB*; Lowndes to the commissioners below, July 18. Middleton's and Lowndes's letters were only two of the recommendations that he carried with him; others are below, from Rutledge of July 9 and Gadsden of the 15th. BF answered all these on June 12, 1779. Library of Congress.

47

Théodore Jauge to William Temple Franklin[9]

ALS: American Philosophical Society

⟨Bordeaux, July 4, 1778, in French: I have sent no news since my return, but what I have now will win your and your grandfather's attention. For the past year and more we have been sending ships to North America. Many of them have been captured through the fault of your pilots, and we have now learned of a shocking example.[1] A vessel of ours anchored in Albemarle Sound and sent for a pilot; he refused to come at any price. The next day, when a frigate appeared, the crew cut their cables, ran aground, and escaped; their ship was looted and burned. Thus the pilot lost us a three-hundred-ton vessel with a rich cargo. Another of ours was taken in the Chesapeake and sent to New York. It is important that pilots who refuse to serve should be disciplined; they are said to be in league with the Loyalists, and I believe it.

How are you faring with the pretty demoiselles you met at M. Grand's?[2]⟩

Antoine-Raymond-Gualbert-Gabriel de Sartine to the American Commissioners[3]

ALS: Harvard University Library

⟨Versailles, July 5, 1778, in French: As I need Captain Jones for a certain expedition, I would like him to remain here. If this does not prove inconvenient, please leave him at my disposal, and give the command of his vessel to his second.⟩

9. The letter was clearly intended for BF. Jauge was, like his father Simon, in the shipping business in Bordeaux, and later in the year went into partnership with Jean-Louis Cottin: Lüthy, *Banque protestante*, II, 309. BF had extensive later dealings with the firm, but this letter makes clear that Jauge was already on good terms with the Passy ménage.
1. The activities of Carolina pilots must have been the subject of much discussion in Bordeaux; John Bondfield also complained in his letter to the commissioners above of the same date.
2. One of them surely was Ferdinand Grand's niece, Marie La Barre, for whom see XXIV, 400 n.
3. Published in Taylor, *Adams Papers*, VI, 265.

From Jacques-Donatien Le Ray de Chaumont

ALS and copy: Harvard University Library; copy: Archives du Ministère des affaires étrangères; two copies[4] and transcript: National Archives

This letter, enclosing an anonymous attack on Schweighauser, was not the only accusation against the agent. At about the same time, we assume, another was forwarded by Chaumont's neighbor Le Veillard: a Guernsey merchant has four privateers at sea, according to Le Veillard's informant, and his son "Aubray" (Dobrée) is Schweighauser's son-in-law and in charge of his office.[5] "Vous pensez que cecy a l'air d'une fable, cependant rien n'est plus vray." Guernsey is informed about American ships leaving Nantes, and they are regularly taken. The knowing laugh, and the Nantais commercial community is contemptuous of Congress.[6]

The enclosure in Chaumont's letter is undated and signed only "J." It points out that William Lee, when he appointed the American agent, was unaware that an English merchant from Guernsey by the name of Dobrée was the son-in-law of "M. Suegasse."[7] The agent, an elderly Swiss or German with no knowledge of English, uses this son-in-law to read and translate secret information about the coming and going of American ships; Dobrée, there is good reason to fear, passes on these secrets to two of his brothers who are in the shipping business on Guernsey. This warning, if well founded, deserves attention.[8]

It reached Arthur Lee on July 11, and the next day he asked Chaumont to furnish the writer's name. Not if the charge was true, Chaumont answered on the 13th, and its truth depended on whether Dobrée really had relatives on Jersey or Guernsey. Lee demolished this

4. The three copies in American archives are in the hand of Hezekiah Ford, serving as Arthur Lee's secretary; see XXVI, 685 n.
5. Pierre-Frédéric Dobrée had married Schweighauser's daughter the previous year: XXVI, 330 n. For the danger presented by the privateers from Jersey and Guernsey, see Kendall's letter of July 19.
6. The undated letter (APS) is in Le Veillard's hand, but we suspect that he was copying a note delivered to him. BF endorsed it "Remark about Guernsey Privateers."
7. Schweighauser, who also appears as "Suégasse" in a letter from the Cornic firm, July 16.
8. The original is with the ALS. The Harvard copy, dated Sept. 24, and made by Hezekiah Ford, adds that the body of the letter is in a different hand from the address to BF, which is now missing.

line of reasoning in his reply on the 22nd. Five days later Chaumont washed his hands of the matter: the anonymous writer may have been deceived; in any case since Arthur Lee seemed to regard the charge with indifference, he would do the same.[9] The commissioners, before long, seem to have decided to do likewise.[1]

Monsieur,   Passi ce 5 Juillet 1778.
   J'ay l'honneur de remettre a vostre Excellence un Billet a vostre adresse qui m'a été envoyé par unne personne habitante près des isles de Gersay et de grenezay, et qui est chargée de faire des recherches sur l'espionnage des anglais dans nos ports. Cette Personne n'a aucun interest particulier qui puisse la determiner a donner cet avis, pas d'autres motifs que Ceux qui interessent essentiellement Le Commerce de l'amerique Septentrionale. Je suis avec le plus respecteux attachement de votre Excellence, Monsieur, votre très humble et tres obeïssant serviteur   LERAY DE CHAUMONT
M. Benjamin Franklin

From Marc-François Gauthier[2]

ALS: University of Pennsylvania Library

Monsieur   Du 5 Juillet 1778.
   Les Grandes ames comme La vôtre Destinée par le ciel au Soutient des malheureux, doivent Toujours etre Touchée des

---

9. Copies and transcripts, National Archives.
1. After they had received, we assume, Dobrée's cogent defense of himself in his letter of Aug. 11.
2. He sent his letter with another, now in the same repository, undated and to an unnamed recipient, to forward to BF. This go-between was an American, for Gauthier refers to BF as "votre ambassadeur." He was a naval officer, to whom the convict stresses his knowledge of French coastal navigation and offers his services for three years at whatever wage may be given him. The officer, lastly, was in good standing with an unnamed duke, who in all likelihood was the duc de Chartres, commanding a division of the fleet at Brest. These clues indicate, almost beyond question, that Gauthier was writing to John Paul Jones, who in that case forwarded the appeal to BF and persuaded him to act upon it. The result was Vergennes' note of Aug. 22, informing BF that Gauthier had been released from confinement to enter the American service.

faiblesses humaine; c'est l'Espoir de Votre genereuse sensibi-
lité qui Engage le nommé Marc François Gauthier, de Vous
Supplier des larmes aux yeux, de Jetter sur sa situation déplo-
rable un de vos tendre regards de compation, en Daignant Le
retirer de L'abime, ou La Nation Britannique L'a plongé par
son intrigue ordinaire; intrigue que vous meme Eprouveriez
aujourd'huy si vous eussiez eté moins prudents. L'Infortuné
suppliant s'est Trouvé cinq Fois leur Prisonnier de guerre, il
n'y a point de Tourments qu'il n'ait Essuié de leur Part, mais il
n'en a point eté de même les trois fois qu'il a eté au pouvoir
des Americains qui l'ont traitté suivant son Etat de Prisonnier
du a un maître canonier; toute cette humanité ne peut être que
de mieux en mieux vous ayant pour Model, et fixant avec raison L'attention de tout L'univers tant a cause de vôtre sagacité,
qu'a cause de vôtre humanité. Le commerce de Londres vous
est connû, Monsieur. Le Suppliant s'y trouvant vers la fin de
L'année 1763, y recut du Nommé jean haristh [?] neg[ocian]t
La Somme de 111 *l.t.* 10 *s* qui [qu'il] lui paya en piece de deux
Sols monoye de france, pour solde de marchandises que Le
Suppliant, qui etoit pour lors Etablie a Dunkerque lui avoit
fournie. La ditte piece qu'on a dit avoir trouvé a bord d'une
fregatte francoise dont ils avoit fait la prise, se trouvant fausse,
il eu le malheur de se voir condamne par la cour des monoye
à Lille en flandre au mois d'avril 1764 a perpétuité de Galere
Etant soupçonné d'en avoir connû la fausseté, quoiqu'il eut
donné des preuves authentique et qu'il est encore den [dans]
le cas de faire, qu'il les avoient recues à londres.

Tel est le crime pour lequel le malheureux suppliant se
trouve pour toujours privé d'une Epouse et de quatre Enfants
qu'il a Laissés, et reduit aux fers au departement de Brest sous
le No. 1779, sans Espoir de les revoir Jamais, Si vous Détour-
nez de dessus son désastre, vos tendres regards de compas-
sion. Il en est digne, Monsieur, et il ne désire Sa Délivrance
que pour faire connoitre a son Roi ainsi qu'a vous qu'il n'a
rien de plus précieux que de repandre Jusqu'a la derniere
Goutte de son sang a son service ainsi qu'a celui de ses alliez.
Il vous seroit aisé très bienfaisant Seigneur d'obtenir du ministre Monseigneur de sartine La Remise de mes peines aux
offres que Je fais de m'embarquer sur un de vos premiers

Batimens qui peuvent être en relache dans les Ports de ce Royaume. Son Etat de canonier, qu'il a Exercé Jointe a la facilité avec laquelle il parle la langue anglaise, sont des objets qu'il croit être utile a sa demande; que ne vous devrait-il point Monsieur si touché de son Etat, vous lui obteniez Son pardon.

Ses Voeux et ses prieres sont et seront Eternelles à L'Etre des Etres pour Vôtre heureuse conservation et La prosperité de vos armes et de celles de sa majesté nôtre bienfaisant monarque, Monsieur.   MARC F[RANÇ]OIS GAUTHIER
forçat a Brest sous Le no. 1779.

Addressed: A Monsieur / Monsieur Francklin / ambassadeur Plenipotentiaire des Republiques Colonies / de l'Amérique, près Sa majesté Très Chrétienne, en Cour / de France; &a. &a. &a.

Notation: Gauthier forçat 5. Juillet 1778.

From Jean-Jacques de Lafreté[3]

ALS: American Philosophical Society

Magnanville le 5. Juillet 1778.

Nous ne retournerons à Surennes,[4] Monsieur, que dans 5. ou 6. jours; mon premier soin sera de vous aller rendre mes devoirs; Permettéz en attendant, que je vous recommande une affaire dont Messrs. Bouffé et d'Angirard,[5] auront, ou auront eûx l'honneur de vous parler, de la part de Messrs. Veuve Lalanne et fils, négocians à Bayonne, relativement au Navire l'Espérance, Capitaine Besrade, arrêté dit on Illégalement, et conduit à Newÿorck. Comme j'ai un intérêt dans ce navire, je

3. For the former postal official see XXVI, 289–90. See also C. Favre-Lejeune, *Les Secrétaires du Roi de la grande chancellerie de France* (2 vols., Paris, 1986), II, 761–2.
4. Magnanville was a small town near Mantes, Suresnes near Passy.
5. For Pierre-Gabriel Bouffé and Gabriel Bouffé see XXVI, 437 n. Dangirard is probably Jean-Baptiste-François, the Parisian banker, for whom see Lüthy, *Banque protestante*, II, 447.

me joins à ces Messieurs pour vous demander conseil et protection.[6]

Mad. De Lafreté[7] qui jouit d'une assés bonne santé me charge de mille complimens pour monsieur votre fils, et pour vous; J'ai l'honneur de le saluer et de vous assurer, Monsieur, du profond Respect avec lequel je suis, votre très humble et très obéissant serviteur LAFRETÉ

M.franklin à Passy

Endorsed: M. de la Freté and De Lalanne about a Ship Magnanville 5. juillet 1778.

To All Captains of Armed Vessels in the United States Service[8]

ALS (draft) and copy: Yale University Library

Gentlemen   Passy, near Paris, Jul 6. 1778.

Being well informed that William Gray, Esqr., formerly Provost-Marshal General of the Island of Jamaica, and Member of the Assembly there, has on several Occasions in his public Capacity and otherwise, manifested his Good Will to the American Cause and towards our Countrymen in general: I beg Leave to recommend him to your particular personal Civilities, in case the Fortune of War should put him into your Hands.[9] I have the honour to be, Gentlemen, Your most obedient humble Servant B FRANKLIN

One of the Commissioners from the United States to the Court of France

6. See XXVI, 675 n.

7. Daughter of the farmer general Isaac Jogues de Martinville.

8. Derived from a deleted notation on the ALS; another, in the same hand, identifies it as "Dr. Franklin's Rough Draft."

9. He held the former post in 1768 and served in the Jamaica assembly during the 1770's and 1780's; he died in 1788: *Caribbeana*, II (1911), 128. BF would not have issued such a pass lightly, but we have found no indication of the way in which Gray "manifested his Good Will to the American Cause."

To Daniel Roberdeau[1]   AL (draft): Library of Congress

Dear Sir,   Passy, near Paris, July 6, 1778

There is no Dissuading the young Gentlemen of this Country from going to seek Service in the Armies of America, when once they have taken that Fancy. I represent to them all, the Expence and Hazards of the Voyage, and the Uncertainty of their being employed when they arrive; but nothing avails; they will go, if it be only to serve as Volunteers. This is the Case of M. le Chevalier Dabzac, who purposes to have the Honour of delivering you this Line. He is recommended to me as a Gentleman of Character and good Accomplishments, and as his Zeal for our Cause gives him additional Merit, I beg Leave to recommend him to your Countenance, Protection and Counsels.[2] With the greatest Esteem I have the honour to be, &c.

Mr. Roberdeau

Recommendation D'Abzac

1. BF's old acquaintance, the Pa. militia officer and member of Congress: XXIV, 11 n.

2. BF indeed had been the object of a well-orchestrated campaign in favor of this tenth child of a prominent but impoverished branch of a Périgord family, the Abzac de la Douze. Describing the eighteen-year-old as tall and strong, the Abbé d'Aydie, his relative, wrote to the Chevalier de Beauteville who in turn asked an unnamed correspondent to obtain from BF a passport and "des lettres de recommandation un peu fortes." There is no indication that the youth ever reached America. Pierre de Buisson, chevalier de Beauteville to ———, May 24, 1778 (University of Pa. Library); Abbé d'Aydie to chevalier de Beauteville [May, 1778] (APS). For the Abzac de la Douze see *Dictionnaire de la noblesse*, I, 55–6.

54

From Julien-Pierre de La Faye[3] with a Postscript by
—— de Boisroger

ALS: American Philosophical Society

Monsieur   A Rocquencourt le 6 Juillet 1778.

Un Neveu de Mr. L'abbé Tailhié, si connu dans la Republique des Lettres par d'excellents ouvrages[4] desire ardament de faire un voyage en Amerique. Il s'embarqua l'année derniere pour s'y rendre mais ayant eté pris en Route par les Anglois, Il espere cette année qu'il sera plus heureux. Il desireroit Monsieur avoir de vous un mot de Lettre de recommandation pour ne point arriver en Amerique comme un homme inconnu. S'il n'y a point d'indiscretion a vous faire cette demande Je vous seray infiniment obligé si vous voulés bien luy donner cette satisfaction. J'ay l'honneur d'etre avec l'attachement le plus respectueux, Monsieur, votre très humble et très obeissant serviteur   DELAFAYE

Permettés que je fasse icy mille complimens a Monsieur votre fils.

[*In another hand*:] M. De Boisroger se joint a Mr. De la faye et Prie Monsieur franklin de recevoir de sa part les choses les Plus honnestes bien des compliments a Mr. son fils. Mr. De Boisroger et Mr. De la faye Prient Monsieur franklin de vouloir bien se ressouvenir de Mde. De Pontenet et des objets qui

---

3. The government official who was also a specialist in Roman mortar: XXIV, 65 n.
4. Abbé Jacques Tailhié, who died the same year, was an ancient, medieval, and Church historian: Larousse. Of his nephew we have found no trace.

l'interresse.[5] Ils esperent qu'a Rocquencourt[6] ils auront cet été
le Plaisir de le Posseder.

Endorsed: M Delafaye Tailhie Ponteney

Notation: 6. Juillet 1778

From Jean-Baptiste Le Roy

ALS: American Philosophical Society

Mon cher Docteur   Ce Lundy 6 Juillet 1778
    On m'a instamment prie de vous demander si vous pourriez
donner des lettres pour des personnes de connoissance à la
Caroline à l'honnête Négociant dont j'ai l'honneur de vous
envoyer la lettre.[7] De graces ne m'oubliez pas et par vous ou
par Monsieur Williams faites moi savoir la reponse que je dois
rendre à ce négociant   LE ROY

P.S. Il demande en même temps si vous pourriez lui faciliter
des retours sur France mais j'ai déja repondu à cet article que
le Commerce étant libre vous ne vous mêliez en aucune façon
de cette partie là.

5. Boisroger must have been a close friend or relative, for he was living
with La Faye. Mme. de Ponteney and her husband, friends of both, were
trying to sell merchandise in America: XXV, 47–8; XXVI, 581–2. Almost eight
weeks after this reminder they had heard nothing; perhaps BF had never
sent the answer that he had drafted to Mme. de Ponteney's letter of June 3.
In any case the husband stirred La Faye to write again, on Aug. 30, begging
BF for definite information: University of Pa. Library.
    6. The sumptuous estate located between Versailles and St. Germain that
La Faye would sell the following year to Monsieur, the King's brother.
Archives Nationales, Minutier central, LXXIX, 218.
    7. The merchant was Lalande Robinot, who had written Le Roy from
St. Brieuc on June 6 to ask his intercession with BF. The matter dragged on
for months. On July 18 or thereabouts Le Roy repeated his request. A few
days later, probably on the 22nd, he enclosed a letter of the 18th from
Baudouin de Guémadeuc, a master of requests, strongly recommending the
merchant and mentioning that his ship was the *Moissonneur.* All these letters
are in the APS. Le Roy soon returned to the charge, in an undated appeal
that spoke of the many times he had already importuned BF for the letter:

From Charles Gravier, comte de Vergennes

Two copies: Library of Congress

A Versailles le 6. Juillet 1778

Le Comte de Vergennes fait ses Remerciments à M. Franklin pour la Communication qu'il a bien voulu lui faire de son projet de Réponse;[8] il le lui renverra incessamment avec les Observations dont il le croit susceptible.

Nous venons d'être informés par une Voye prompte, que le 3. de ce mois il est arrivé à Brest un aviso de Boston; il y a aparence qu'il aura apporté des depêches pour M. Franklin, et nous sommes impatients d'être informés de leur Contenu.[9]

From David Welsh

ALS: Historical Society of Pennsylvania

Honourable Sir   Amsterdam July 6th 1778

I have had the luck of getting A Quainted with Monsieur Le Grand[1] last Sattyday whear as I maid my Cais knowen to him but he enformed me that he could not Suppley me with a Suffiecensey to Pay off my board and Carrey me to France with out Acquainting of you and receiving your Approbation of the same. He was kind Enouf to give me 2 Ducketts to pay for my washing and other Small Expences. Mr. Hope[2] has Enformed me that his friend in Paris had Delivired you the letter himself which gives me A great deal of Uneaseness that I have

---

University of Pa. Library. By late August it had been promised but not yet furnished; the moment it arrived the ship would sail: Le Roy to BF below, under Aug. 26.

8. BF's answer to Weissenstein on July 1.

9. The *Spy* had arrived at Brest on the 3rd but the commissioners had not yet received its news: see Simpson's letter above of that date. They had, however, a variety of reports carried earlier by the *Nymphe* (XXVI, 654–5) which they must have promptly made public. Under the dateline of July 6 the *Courier de l'Europe* published news from America provided by BF: IV (1778), 18 and see XXVI, 453 n.

1. Georges Grand.

2. The Dutch banker who refused aid: XXVI, 659.

not had aney Assistiance from you as I am in A Strange place
and neither Cash or friends. My last I have enclosed to you in
Mr. Godeats letter[3] by which I hope to receive your assistance
before you receive this. I hope Sir that will not loose now time
after receiving this as I am in Much distress onley haveing
what Cloas I got on My back. Sir I hope you doant reflect on
me on the Account of my Misfortune In regard of the Prias I
lost comeing to Bördix or in letting Allert Cutter take us.[4] Sir
I Can vendicate my Honour and Conduct Whilst I served on
board the Lexington as Soon As Called on. If I doant recive
aney assistance from you before the meddle of nixt week I
shall be badley off as my Landladey Expectes by that time if
you entend do aney thing for me you will doe it. Sir I hope
your Humanietey will not fail in assisting me as soon as
Posseable in my Distress. If you would be pleased to Send me
A few lines so as I may know whear to proceed two. I lodge
at Ann Magrath at the last Bible Warmer Street.[5] Sir with
Granting this request I remain Your Most obedient and
Humble Servant   DAVID WELSH
                        Formerly Second Leoutt. of the Lexington

Addressed in another hand: To / His Excellency Doctr Francklin /
Minister Plenipotentiary of / the United States of America. /
Passy

Notation: David Welsh July 6. 1778.

3. Henricus Godet's of July 2, enclosing Welsh's of the same date.
4. These were two separate incidents. Welsh, as second lieutenant of the
Lexington, had been made prize master of the *Hanover,* on March 21, 1777.
While he and two of his men were off the prize, replenishing from a French
ship, the *Hanover* was retaken and brought into Bordeaux: *Naval Docs.,* VIII,
238, 767–8. Welsh ultimately rejoined his ship. The cutter *Alert* captured
the *Lexington* on Sept. 19, 1777, after she left Morlaix: XXV, 525 n.
5. Where ship captains from America normally lodged: XXVI, 659 n.

58

Titus Ogden to the American Commissioners[6]

ALS: American Philosophical Society

⟨Lorient, [after] July [6],[7] 1778: On arrival at the beginning of April I consigned my ship and cargo to Mr. Moylan, who showed me his authorization as your agent, and I conceived the highest opinion of his abilities. When the *Boston* and her prizes appeared, I was astonished to have a foreigner, Mr. Puchelberg, who speaks no English and is little known here, claim to be agent by Mr. Schweighauser's appointment. He offered to make purchases for me; I enclose his bill to show that he knows how to charge. I should be glad for my country's sake if trust were put in a man of Mr. Moylan's character; we Americans are better served by a compatriot than by one who understands neither our language nor our ways.[8]⟩

John Bondfield to the American Commissioners[9]

ALS: American Philosophical Society

⟨Bordeaux, July 7, 1778: The *Sally*, which arrived here yesterday from Edenton, reports that the fourth regiment of Col. Maitland's expedition has been captured and that several ships, among them the *Roderigue* with a cargo of great value,[1] have arrived in the Chesapeake.

6. Published in Taylor, *Adams Papers*, VI, 336–7. Ogden identifies himself as a New Bern, N.C., merchant and master of the *Harmony Hall*, which brought a cargo of tobacco.
7. When the *Boston*'s prizes, which he mentions, arrived in Lorient. He went to Paris and was back by Aug. 1; see Moylan to the commissioners of that date. He must therefore have been writing not long after the 6th.
8. See the note on Moylan's letter to the commissioners, July 8.
9. Published in Taylor, *Adams Papers*, VI, 265–6.
1. John Maitland commanded a detachment of Royal Marines sent against American vessels in the Delaware: Namier and Brooke, *House of Commons*, III, 98–9. The *Fier Roderigue*, belonging to Hortalez & Cie. (XXII, 454), was then loading in the York River, and Beaumarchais' agent expected her to convoy to France ships loaded with goods for redeeming the American debt to the company; Virginia officials, however, seem to have had no such intention: Morton, *Beaumarchais Correspondance*, IV, 142–4 n.

Consorting here with agents and consuls of European states shows me the advantages that their countries derive from them; a similar arrangement might be useful for you. American trade is a new field, and you know nothing of its value in various regions; I and other agents elsewhere, especially if they had an order from Mr. de Sartine to local officials, might easily send you monthly reports of exports to and imports from America. This is a suggestion that might in time, if put into practice, be of great use.⟩

Francis Coffyn to the American Commissioners[2]

ALS: American Philosophical Society

⟨Dunkirk, July 7, 1778: I refer you to my letter of the 5th. Mr. Amiel has given the people here time to carry out the plan they put before you, but they failed; he then gave me your letter of June 26.[3] I might explain the conduct of those who tried to impose on you and wrong me, but the outcome vindicates me; I leave the explanation to Capt. Amiel. If any doubt remains I can show that those who tried to hurt me in the dark are afraid to justify themselves in the light.[4]

I enclose the commission, instructions, and bond, which to my regret are now useless, and will do my best to settle with the surgeon. As you seem to approve the intelligence I send you, I shall transmit it to America; should it go to your correspondents in the ports or directly to Congress?

A Dutch merchant captain who arrived yesterday from Portsmouth says that he saw the crews of the *Licorne* and *Pallas*[5] and two other vessels being taken to prison there on

2. Published in Taylor, *Adams Papers*, VI, 267–8.

3. The plan for outfitting a privateer for Amiel, in which Coffyn was involved as the commissioners' local agent, is discussed in our annotation to their letter to Amiel of June 23: XXVI, 672 n. Coffyn's of the 5th is missing.

4. See Poreau, Mackenzie & Cie. to BF, *ibid.*, pp. 693–4, and the letter following this one.

5. The two French frigates captured in the first engagement of the war: see Dumas to commissioners, July 3.

the 3rd, and that Admiral Keppel's squadron had been reinforced and was ready for sea. I shall send the American seamen who are here, according to your instructions, by the first
vessel for Nantes. But, as the English are expected to start
taking French ships, I am afraid those poor people, who have
already seen enough of English jails, will soon be captured
again. Privateers will probably be fitting out as soon as hostilities start; might it not be better to keep the men here until the
situation clarifies?

If Poreau's perfidious insinuations have prejudiced you
against me, for God's sake allow me to convince you of their
falsehood.⟩

Poreau, Mackenzie & Cie. to the American
Commissioners[6]   LS or ALS: American Philosophical Society

⟨Dunkirk, July 7, 1778, in French: When some Americans and
others appealed to us for support, we asked you for a privateer's commission. The Captain you chose seemed deserving
and trustworthy, but found the vessel too small for his large
ideas of glory. A more powerful one would have cost more
than twice the thirty to forty thousand livres we were willing
to risk. He refused us the commission that you meant for us,
and divulged to Coffyn, whom we knew to be trusted by the
British, information that we had confided in you. We were
unaware that Coffyn was an agent of Congress, and do not
believe that you could have given him our letter.[7] We are not
bound by a plan that we did not initiate and that costs more
than we can venture. Please send us the commission, to be
used as described by the one of us who spoke with you. Or
transmit it through the Prince de Robecq.[8] Or give it directly
into the hands of our representative, or of one of the Americans recommended to us.⟩

6. Published in Taylor, *Adams Papers*, VI, 269–71.
7. To BF, XXVI, 693–4.
8. The governor of French Flanders: *ibid.*, p. 693 n.

Musco Livingston to the American Commissioners

ALS: Pennsylvania Historical Society

Gentlemen   Paris 8 July 1778.

Inclos'd is A List of the prisoners on board the Boston, including those which he knows Capt. Tucker would wish to Exchange.[9] I have the Honour to be Gentlemen Your Most Obedient Humble Servant   M. LIVINGSTON

Addressed: The Honble. the Commissioners / to the United States of amer / ica; at / passy

Notation: Livingston 8. July 1778.

James Moylan to the American Commissioners[1]

ALS: American Philosophical Society

⟨Lorient, July 8, 1778: Two of Capt. Tucker's prizes arrived here on the 6th. I passed them through customs as from Portsmouth, New England. I have not had time to hear from Mr. Schweighauser, but have written to ask whether his authority extends to this port. If so I shall deliver them to his order unless you meanwhile instruct me differently.[2]

Friction between Capt. Tucker and the Frenchmen in his

---

9. The list, dated July 4 and signed by Livingston, gives no names: "four Captains of Ships, four mates: ditto, & Thirty Seven Seamen, or fore mast men."

1. Published in Taylor, *Adams Papers*, VI, 271–2.

2. As soon as the *Boston* arrived, a local merchant by the name of Puchelberg announced that he had been put in charge of her business; hence Moylan's inquiry of Schweighauser. Just after writing this letter the agent had his answer: Puchelberg was indeed authorized to act. Moylan immediately wrote his friend Jacques-Alexandre Gourlade (XXIII, 184 n), who was then in Paris, to say that he was perforce yielding his own claim but that something should be done; please tell Chaumont what would happen to American interests if such a man were in charge, and ask him to tell the commissioners: July 8, 1778, APS. Ogden gave them much the same warning; see his letter above, after July 6. A *modus vivendi* seems to have been arranged, Puchelberg handling prizes, Moylan dealing with prisoners; see the former's letter of Aug. 26, the latter's of Oct. 12, 21, and the commissioners to Moylan, Oct. 27.

crew has come before the admiralty court, but I hope will soon be settled.[3])

The American Commissioners to Schweighauser[4]

AL (draft):[5] Massachusetts Historical Society; two copies: National Archives

⟨Passy, July 9–10, 1778: We enclose an order on Desegray, Beaugeard fils & Cie. of Lorient for saltpetre, to be shipped to America as soon as possible. July 10: We also forward Mr. Williams' order on Mr. Cossoul for articles to be shipped in the same way.[6]⟩

Peter Amiel to the American Commissioners

ALS: American Philosophical Society

Honorable Gentlemen   Dunkirk the 9th July 1778
  Messrs. Poreau & Mackinzy of this place haveing wrote a Letter to Doctor Franklin; in which they have atempted to injure Mr. Coffyns character,[7] as I hope to be at Passy on Sunday next, beg it as a favor you'd suspend your Judgement till then, when I will lay before you every Particular that came to my Knowledge. I am with the greatest Respect Honorable Gentlemen Your Obliged Humble Servant   PETER AMIEL

Addressed: A Messieurs / Messieurs Franklin, Lee & / Adams,

---

3. On the contrary, it became worse; see ――― to commissioners, July 11, and Tucker to commissioners, July 12.
  4. Published in Butterfield, *John Adams Diary*, IV, 147.
  5. In Arthur Lee's hand; the postscript is in JA's.
  6. The order to Desegray was for 1,520 bags of India saltpetre. JW's order of the 10th on Cossoul was for arms, cloth, and medicines from Holland, sabers, uniforms from Montieu, copper, flints, and "All the Arms and Furniture repaired and unrepaired in the magazine." National Archives. So ended the contract with Mercier: XXIV, 100–1. Cossoul, a merchant from Nantes, eventually went into partnership with Elkanah Watson.
  7. See XXVI, 693–4; see also their letter to the commissioners of July 7.

Ministres plenipotentiaires / des Etats unis de l'Amerique, à la Cour / de France, / à Passÿ

Notation: Mr Peter Amiel Dunkirk 9 July 78

Francis Coffyn to the American Commissioners[8]

ALS: American Philosophical Society

⟨Dunkirk, July 9, 1778: I refer you to my letter of yesterday. This is to enclose a certificate from the admiralty court, to counter to some degree Poreau's insinuations against me. Tomorrow I send three other certificates and if they are insufficient will furnish whatever further proof you require; meanwhile Mr. Amiel will give you particulars.⟩

Richard Grinnell to the American Commissioners[9]

ALS: American Philosophical Society

⟨Dunkirk, July 9, 1778: I arrived here last August after serving on the *Belle Isle,* 74, as a midshipman impressed at sea; a London merchant got me my discharge. I went to Nieuwpoort, and told Mr. Nesbitt[1] that I wanted to be commissioned in Paris and then sail for Brazil to destroy the London fleet there. He put me in touch with Mr. Coffyn, who took my papers and advised me to write you. This I did, but after hearing nothing for two months accepted his offer of a vessel to go whaling off Brazil. I wrote to London, got ten Americans, and took four on the voyage with me; Mr. Coffyn sent the rest to Nantes. He wants me to go again, but I will not until I hear from the bearer, Capt. Amiel, whether I can serve my country. Mr. Nesbitt asks me to get as many Americans as possible from Lon-

---

8. Published in Taylor, *Adams Papers,* VI, 274–5, where the enclosure is summarized.

9. Published in Taylor, *Adams Papers,* VI, 275–7.

1. Jonathan Nesbitt, a Lorient merchant: XXVI, 12–13 n. Nieuwpoort is near Ostend.

don; I think a number will be able to escape and come by way of Holland.

True or not, I heard today that my brother, William Grinnell, first lieutenant on the *Columbus* when she engaged the *Glasgow*, is now at Brest in command of a frigate.

Please let me know how to proceed. I have promised Capt. Amiel to do nothing until I hear from him.⟩

From Jean Bochard de Champigny[2]

ALS: American Philosophical Society

Monsieur   Le 9 juillet 1778.

Je ne comprends pas ce qui peut empêcher votre Excellence de m'honnorer d'une réponse au sujet de mes foibles ouvrages dont en vain j'attends d'Elle depuis quelques mois les vingt et un Ducats qui manquent pour compléter sa souscription. Cela ne m'empeche cependant pas à m'acquitter de mon devoir, et je lui joins ici le troisieme volume de ma Traduction de l'histoire de Dannemarck qui vient de sortir de la presse ce qui ne fait que redoubler mes embaras, vu qu'il faut solder les comptes de mon imprimeur.

Aujourd'huy que votre Excellence est à paris pour y soutenir une rèpublique naissante, voudroit-elle tandis qu'Elle allegue qu'on a manqué aux Engagemens pris avec ses Constituens, rompre ceux qu'elle a pris avec moi? Elle scait mieux que personne que ceux de particulier à particulier sont plus sacrés que ceux des Souverains, et elle scait de plus que ma situation rend nécessaire la demande que je lui ai fait de l'argent qui me revient. Je me flatte donc qu'elle ne tardera pas à me le faire remettre, je l'en supplie ainsi que d'agréer les assurances du respect avec lequel je suis, Monsieur, de votre Excellence le très humble et très obéissant serviteur

LE COLONEL CHEVR. DE CHAMPIGNY

Amsterdam chez Mr. Cuthbertson dans le Kalverstraat

2. This impecunious and persistent author had been trying to get money out of BF since August, 1777, and his most recent appeal had been in May:

From ———— Deplaine[3]   ALS: American Philosophical Society

a verdun sur meuse le 9 juillet 1778.

J'ay lu avec plaisir mon cher frere dans l'année 2270 de laura-
guais page 387 article de philadelphie, l'etonante revolution
que L'amerique septentrionale doit a l'interet que tu prends au
bonheur de l'humanité. Une douzaine d'années ont amené un
evenement que l'auteur ne voyoit que dans un temps fort re-
culé. J'admire le prophête et encore plus le genie imm[ortel]
qui a plus de douze cent lieues de philadelphie dirige toutes
les manoeuvres de ses chers americains. J'ay mis ces vers au
bas de ton portrait de notre prelat (?) je te prie de les ecrire
sur le pieddestal de ton buste que j'ay vu l'an passé au Salon

> orbis hic auctoi sociavit foedere gentes
>   Fecit et encusso libera colla jugo.
> Ingens consilio coepit victoria fratrum,
>   cessabunt forti bella peracta manu.
> Anglia nequicquam ad pugnas tria regna cöegit:
>   contra Tarquinios Brutus hic alter adest.

Cet eloge est trop justement merité pour t'offenser, ce n'est
pas l'adulation qui te le donne. Poursuis ton grand projet et
vis assés longtemps pour y mettre la derniere main. Adieu.
Ton frere et ton ami   DEPLAINE

très zelé catholique et un peu quaker

Je t'envoye une plaisanterie de Pere jesuite de vigny de
nancy paroisse st. pierre. Il y a de la mauvaise humeur contre
toute espece de puissance il faut la pardonner a l'auteur qui
pleure encore sur les ruines de jerusalem.

J'ay fait pendant l'hyver en cinq mille vers latins les eloges

---

XXIV, 398–400; XXVI, 501. The details of what he wanted are explained in
BF's answer of July 24.

3. This document has us stumped. We have not been able to discover the
identity of this "slightly Quaker ardent Catholic," nor do we understand
his Latin or the joke the Jesuit de Vigny is supposed to have made.

de tous les illustres francois dans tous les [genres?] et de quelques villes qui mont envoyé des temoignages tres flateurs, et ont place avec honneur mes petits poemes dans leurs sales d'assemblée, tous ces eloges sont des morceaux detachés.

Addressed: Monsieur / Monsieur franklin / chancelier de la republique americaine / dans son hotel / a Passi près paris

From John Rutledge[4]   Transcript: Harvard University Library

Sir,   Charleston South Carolina July 9th 1778

Mr. Gillon, intending to pay his respects to you, requests a line of introduction which I take the liberty of giving him.[5]

This State having resolved to equip three Frigates, appointed him to the command of them with the Title of Commodore. He is about setting off for France to procure them, and I hope will meet with no difficulty in the business. You will find him a sensible, intelligent man, and as he has lately made a Tour through our different States and is well acquainted with occurrences, he will be able to give you information in some matters which you may wish to know. I will therefore trespass no longer on your time, than to tell you that the Grand alliance which you have obtained for us has diffused universal joy, and to request your acceptance of my best wishes, that you may long live in health to see and partake the fruits of the zeal and abilities which you have exerted for the service of your Country. I have the honor to be with great esteem and respect, Sir, Your obedient humble servant

J. Rutledge

J. Rutledge to B. Franklin

4. He had recently resigned as president of South Carolina to protest changes in the state constitution, but was elected governor under it the following January: *DAB*; Richard Barry, *Mr. Rutledge of South Carolina* (New York, [1942]), pp. 229–33.

5. For Gillon see Middleton's letter of July 4.

Franklin and John Adams to Rodolphe-Ferdinand Grand[6]

Copy and transcript: National Archives

⟨[July 10, 1778:[7]] We are agreed that Mr. Williams' bills on you, as listed herewith, be charged to the public account; he will be responsible to Congress or its agent, and to the commissioners, when called upon to render account of his expenditures. Our consent is not to be taken as approbation of his account or to influence the settlement of it.[8]⟩

The American Commissioners to Jonathan Williams, Jr.: Two Notes

ALS (draft): Massachusetts Historical Society; incomplete draft: American Philosophical Society; two copies: National Archives[9]

I.

Mr. Williams   Passy July 10. 1778.

We approve of the Directions given by you to stop the Reparation of the Arms at Nantes paying the Workmen their Wages, Gratifications and Conduct money according to agreement of which you inform us in your Letter July 3 1778.

ARTHUR LEE
JOHN ADAMS

6. Published in Taylor, *Adams Papers*, VI, 277–9, where the background is tentatively sketched. The letter, as explained there, was not from the commissioners, but from two of them who were at loggerheads with the third. We can add only one point. Lee had ordered Grand to disallow many of the bills in question, according to JW, and deduct them from the public account. The banker showed this letter to JW, who "presented him with Dr. Franklins and Mr. Adams's Approbation of these Bills to the amount of 191,000 Livres": JW to Congress, Sept. 10, 1778, APS. The present note, which mentions no sum, could scarcely be that approbation but could well be a reformulation of it.

7. For the dating see Taylor, *op. cit.*, p. 278.

8. See our annotation of JW to the commissioners, July 17.

9. The ALS draft is in Arthur Lee's hand. The incomplete draft of (I), written on the verso of JW's letter of July 3 (see the annotation of that letter), is in the hand of JA, as is one of the copies. BF's signature does not

68

II.

Passy July 10. 1778.
Mr. Williams is desired to send the Commissioners an order
for the Goods remaining on hand, including the sixty three
Barrels of Beef, to be delivered to Mr. J.D. Schweighauser of
Nantes or to his order.[1]   ARTHUR LEE
                                               JOHN ADAMS

Francis Coffyn to the American Commissioners

ALS: American Philosophical Society

Honored Gentlemen.   Dunkirk 10th July 1778
    In the letter I had the honor of writing to you yesterday by
Capn. Amiel, I inclosed a Certifficate from the officers of the
Admiralty.
    This serves to cover the three other Certificates I promised
in the Said letter, Vizt. one from the Bourgmaster and Magistrates, one from the President and Counsellors of the board of
Commerce, and an other from the Judge and Consuls in this
town.[2] All which I hope will Sufficiently convince you that
your confidence in me has not been illplaced, that in consequence of these proofs, you'll be pleased to favour me with
the continuation thereof, and in answer to this grant me a few
lines in approbation to my conduct, which has most wrong-
fully been censured; it is the sole satisfaction I require for the
injury my Ennemys have endeavour'd to do me, for on a
cooler reflection then that which Struck me at first, I think
they must find themelves (if they are Susceptible of any feeling) Sufficiently humiliated by the paralel I have drawn between their Character and mine, without inflinging on them

---

appear on these documents, but we have no reason to suspect that he refused to sign.
    1. Presumably in response to Whipple's offer, in his letter of July 2, to
take arms and stores that jw had on hand.
    2. The first is in the University of Pa. Library, the second and third in
the APS.

any other punishment however deserving. I shall drop this subject to take up one more agreable, which is to congratulate you and every frenchman and american on the arrival at Brest of the vessell which has brought over the ratiffication by Congress of the Treaties you had so gloriously concluded with the Court of France, in consequence of which I hope the Interest of both nations will be so well clogg'd and cimented together as to insure an everlasting duration. This is the Sincere and ardent wish of him, who has the honor to remain respectfully Honored Gentlemen Your most obedient and most devoted Humble Servant   FRANS. COFFYN

Hble. Dr. Bn. Franklin, Arthur Lee and John Adams Esqrs. at Passy

Notations: Coffyn Frans. 10 July 1778 / Coffyn

William Hodge[3] to the American Commissioners

ALS: University of Virginia Library, South Carolina Historical Society;[4] copy and transcript: National Archives

⟨Cadiz, July 10, 1778: I received only yesterday your letter of April 19. You tell me I am charged with almost 100,000 livres of public money. I gave Mr. Deane a detailed account of my receipts and disbursements and the charges of the Dunkirk merchants; my only charge was the trifling 2½ percent commission, which did not even cover my expenses. You will find that a balance is due me, as I was only responsible for a quarter of the cutter and Mr. Deane for the other quarter;[5] he doubtless took with him the papers relating to her and the lugger.

---

3. Deane's and the commissioners' agent, who had helped outfit the *Revenge* at Dunkirk and been imprisoned in the Bastille: XXIV, 243, 468–70. This letter is published in Taylor, *Adams Papers*, VI, 280–4.

4. In each the signature is preceded by "(signed)," but both are in Hodge's hand.

5. The remaining half formerly was owned by Congress: *Deane Papers*, II, 263.

Mr. Lee has informed Congress that he does not know how I used the large sum of public money I received. Ignoring expenses and what is due to the crew, he has told all his Spanish correspondents that Congress and I were jointly concerned with a privateer, and that they should pay me only half the prize money and send him the other half.

I shall now account for myself since I arrived in Spain. Mr. John Ross and I claimed the cutter as our property in consequence of an order from Mr. Deane, who had as much authority in public business as yourselves. I am surprised that Dr. Franklin signed your letter, for I heard him advising Mr. Deane to do as he did. Mr. Deane ordered Captain Conyngham to deliver us the cutter and put himself under our direction, which he did. He and Dr. Franklin avoided expense and trouble by giving us this vessel. Before my arrival she spent almost two-thirds of her time in port. Captain Conyngham did not give me enough to pay the crew's wages and prize money, some of the proceeds of the prizes having been stopped as a result of his taking a French brig and sending her in to San Sebastian.[6] I paid the officers and men from other funds, but not enough to satisfy them. I have not received a dollar more than what covered my expenses and will prove it. I distributed that money according to Congressional rules: I have taken receipts from all the men and do not care about their complaints. I found the ship with only a few officers; the men were in prison in San Sebastian, Bilbao, and elsewhere because of the capture of the French brig, and Captain Conyngham was offering to turn her over to the captain of a New England privateer in Bilbao.

As to your giving Captain Conyngham his future orders, you cannot do it without my consent as half-owner. I shall leave the whole matter to Congress, some of whose members understand business. We have had a report, I hope unfounded, that Captain Conyngham has been taken. I had intended to sail for home in a few days, but shall come to France instead to justify my conduct to you.

6. For this episode see XXVI, 498–9.

N.B. The prizes Captain Conyngham sent to Spain are stopped by order of the court, as a result of his taking the French brig.⟩

From David Hartley

ALS: American Philosophical Society; transcript: Library of Congress

Prisoner exchange was the focus of correspondence between Hartley and Franklin during the summer of 1778, and a major goal of Franklin's activity. He systematically collected names of British captives from American sea captains to meet the terms of the Admiralty, and negotiated with the French for an appropriate port and safe passage for the cartel ship. At the same time he tried to introduce a measure of flexibility into the Admiralty's proposal—this, without success. Hartley, repelled by the Franco-American alliance, pictured his own role as part of a larger plan for reconciliation between the Americans and British, while Franklin sought to channel the hopes of his friend into the specifics of an exchange.

Dear Sir   Golden Square July 10 1778

I only write you one line just to tell you that I have received no answer yet from the Admiralty relative to yours of the 16th of June.[7] I have applied several times, but I suppose they are employed about other matters. You may be assured that no assiduity shall be wanting on my side but I cannot command an answer. The affair which happened off Brest[8] has I presume in its consequences occupied the attention of the Ministry and of the Admiralty. I shall do my best to obtain all the objects mentioned in yours of June 16th. I wish it may be with Success. I shall write again to you soon. Believe me allways to be

---

7. Regarding the proposed exchange of British and American prisoners: XXVI, 626. Hartley was the British negotiator in the discussions that finally led to the first exchanges in 1779: Catherine M. Prelinger, "Benjamin Franklin and the American Prisoners of War in England during the American Revolution," *W&MQ*, 3rd ser., XXXII (1975), 272–6.

8. The outbreak of naval hostilities between France and England on June 17.

a friend to peace and to the rights of mankind and most affectionately yours   DH

To Dr. Franklin.

Endorsed: D.H. July 10. 1778.

The American Commissioners to Sartine[9]

Copies: Massachusetts Historical Society; National Archives (two)

⟨Passy, July 11, 1778: We received your Excellency's letter of the fifth regarding Captain Jones, and we readily consent to place him at your disposal.⟩

—————— to the American Commissioners[1]

AL: American Philosophical Society

⟨On board the *Boston*, Port Louis, July 11, 1778: Jerome Cazneau, sergeant of marines,[2] obtained shore leave and persuaded the other Frenchmen aboard to quit the ship. He did everything in his power to alienate them from returning to duty. The General,[3] though under orders to assist us, gave them the choice of staying or quitting, even though he was reminded that anyone who overstayed his leave for forty-eight hours without excuse forfeited all prize money. The trouble came from the complaints of a few Frenchmen about the strictness of Mr. Reed, our first lieutenant, and Mr. Bates, our third. We certify that the French have been indulged beyond what our regulations allow, and that those officers have the

9. Published in Butterfield, *John Adams Diary*, IV, 158.
1. Published in Taylor, *Adams Papers*, VI, 284–5, where it is printed as a letter from Reed and Bates. The document is more probably, we believe, a petition in their favor, which for some reason lacks signatures.
2. See XXVI, 584 n for another conspiracy on the *Boston* to which Cazeneuve was privy.
3. Gen. La Touche de Tréville is identified in our note on Tucker to the commissioners, July 12.

good will of every one else on board; thereto we append our names.[4] The General was too partial to his countrymen to allow those officers to vindicate or even speak for themselves, and reminded Capt. Tucker that we were within range of his cannon.⟩

From Emmanuel-Pierre de La Plaigne[5]

ALS: American Philosophical Society

Monseigneur,   Plimouth Le 11e Juillet 1778

Il m'est ordonné ce jour de me Rendre a oakhampton devon prisonier sur ma parole d'honneur avec ma famille et autres personnes qui étoient passagers avec moy dans le d'argentré; j'ay eû l'honneur d'écrire à votre exçellençe que j'étais de-poüillé de tout et sans argent quelconque.[6] Je la priais de vou-loir bien me secourir ne fussent que mes appointements qui me sont dus depuis le 26. May 1777. Je n'ay trouvé icy de Recours que dans le viçe consul des états genereaux qui a bien voulû m'obliger en ce moment de six guinees pour deux mois et qui veut bien se charger de faire passer à votre exçellençe la presente par la voye de hollande. Il est pret à obliger icy qui votre exçellençe jugera a propos d'avouer, et il merite Réelle-ment la confiançe. Aussi est-il le seul qui aye celle de mon état tout le monde me croyant un Negotiant. Je suis obligé de par-tire sur le champ et n'ay plus que le tems de vous demander votre protection et d'assurer votre exçellençe du profond Re-spect avec Lequel j'ay l'honneur d'etre, Monseigneur, Votre très humble tres obëissant et tres Respectueux serviteur

E.P. DELAPLAIGNE
Capt d'inf.

Les lettres et ordres dont votre exçellençe voudrait bien m'ho-norer me parviendraint surement par la voye de hollande à

---

4. Only the names of the two officers were appended, and they are not signatures but in the same hand as the rest of the text.

5. Georgia's agent in Europe who had recently been captured and im-prisoned. See xxiv, 83 n; xxvi, 185–6.

6. See xxvi, 688–9.

l'adresse de l'honnéte homme en question dont voicy M. gerrif [?] Tyasink viçe commissary to the states general at plymouth.[7]

Addressed: To his Excellency / Benjamin Franklin / Ambassador of the United / States at the Court of / Versailles / at / Paris

Endorsed: Delaplaigne

Notation: Plymouth 11. juillet 1778.

From Jacques-Nicolas Lallemant[8]

ALS: American Philosophical Society

A l'Orient de Paris
Très Respectable Frere,   Le 11 Juillet 1778.

Si la Jalousie pouvait entrer dans L'âme des Maçons, Touttes les Loges de Paris pourraient dans ce jour, être en proie à ce sentiment, pour disputer à celle Des Neuf Soeurs, l'avantage dont elle joüit maintenant en vous possédant pour un de ses Membres: mais ce qui peut seul dédommager ces Loges, est l'acte que vous venez de consommer, lequel vous réünissant au Corps de la Maçonnerie française, vous ouvre tous les Temples Erigés dans cette Capitale pour le bien de l'humanité.

La R[especta]ble∴ L∴ de la Paix qui a fixé une fête d'adoption à samedy prochain 18 du Courant à 3 heures après midi, au Ranelagh du Bois de Boulogne,[9] désire avec le plus grand empressement que vous lui fassiez la faveur de venir éclairer

---

7. Tasink, as he spelled himself, kept this letter for more than a month and then forwarded it with a covering note of Aug. 21. He was doing what he could for French and American citizens, he pointed out, and had provided La Plaigne with six guineas before the latter's departure for Okehampton on parole. Would BF, Tasink added, please recommend him to the French court to look after its interests in Plymouth? APS.

8. He had just moved from the Loge des Frères Amis to the Loge de la Paix: Le Bihan, *Francs-Maçons parisiens*, p. 278.

9. See XXVI, 697–8.

ses Travaux et y recevoir les hommages dûs à un frere aussi célèbre que vous par son savoir et ses vertus.

Cette L∴ me charge donc de vous faire agréer sa prière et se flatte que votre présence couronnera son attente.

J'ay la faveur d'être avec les sentimens de la plus profonde vénération et de la fraternité la plus parfaitte, par T∴ L∴ N∴ q∴ v∴ S∴ connus, et avec T∴ L∴ h∴ q∴ v∴ s∴ d∴[1] Très Respectable Frère, Votre très humble et très obéissant serviteur et f∴   LALLEMANT
                              Sécretaire de la L. de la Paix

On n'entrera qu'avec Les Billets cy joints Prix du Banquet p[ou]r un f. et une Soeur 12 lt. Il y aura Réceptions de femmes, Banquet Soupatoire à six heures du soir et Bal.

Endorsed: Lallemant Free Masons

To the Comtesse de Lameth[2]

ALS (draft): Library of Congress

[before July 12, 1778[3]]

It is with Pleasure I inform you, Madame, that a Cartel being settled in America for the Exchange of Prisoners, there is reason to hope the Chevalier de Bazantin, who has the Honour of being esteemed by you, is before this time at Liberty. I have upon your Recommendation which has great Weight with me written particularly to America concerning that Gentleman,

1. "Par tous les noms qui vous sont connus, et avec tous les honneurs qui vous sont dus."
2. In answer to hers of May 10: above, XXVI, 430–1.
3. When De Bout, the banker who was the countess's intermediary with BF, wrote him that he had received the letter and would forward it; he also thanked BF for returning a letter that he had asked on July 4 to have back: XXVI, 430–1 n. We assume that that letter was enclosed with this one, which was therefore written, in all likelihood, between the 4th and the 12th.

and shall be happy if it may be of Service to him.[4] I am, with
great Respect, Madam, Your most &c.   BF

Madame la Comtesse de la Methe.

To Madame la Contsse De la Methe 1778

Samuel Tucker to the American Commissioners[5]

ALS: American Philosophical Society

⟨On board the *Boston*, Port Louis, July 12, 1778: The Frenchmen I took on at Bordeaux have given me much trouble.
When we arrived here eight of them got shore leave; their
sergeant complained so much of their treatment that the
King's officers, including General La Touche of Lorient, came
aboard yesterday evening to ask them whether they would
stay or go ashore. They said they would go, since they were
volunteers. But I had enlisted them for Boston; I was not permitted to take volunteers, as I told the General.[6] Better to
leave them, he said, and let them forfeit their wages and prize
money; they had in fact drawn more than that from me and
the purser. The General told me that he was in command
while aboard. I produced my authority and the Congressional
regulations, under which the Frenchmen were guilty of sedition or mutiny. I commanded at sea, I told him. He would
complain to the court and the commissioners, he said, about
my two officers[7] who had mistreated the King's subjects; but

4. BF here made two attempts at a more courtly tone and then deleted
them both: "I am very sensible of the Honour done me by your very amiable and elegant Letter / Your very sensible and elegant Letter gave me
such an Impression of your."

5. Published in Taylor, *Adams Papers*, VI, 287–8.

6. La Touche de Tréville was *chef d'escadre* of a contingent that had put
into Lorient in the course of manoeuvers; in 1781 he became commandant
at Rochefort. See Sartine's first letter below, of July 18; see also Georges
Lacour-Gayet, *La Marine militaire de France sous le règne de Louis XV* (2nd ed.;
Paris, 1910), p. 533 n, and *Etat sommaire des archives de la Marine antérieures à
la Révolution* (Paris, 1898), p. 140 n.

7. Benjamin Reed and Benjamin Bates.

77

the two had done nothing contrary to my orders except box the ears of a Frenchman flogging a small boy. I do not blame them for what they did, only for not informing me. On the recommendation of a Mr. Frazier, late major in the continental army,[8] I took on this penniless sergeant in Bordeaux; he is going to join a French warship commanded by the General's son,[9] I understand, and so am not surprised that he was cleared. All the men wanted to return aboard, but I would not have them. My complement is a hundred and forty-six, with whom I shall put to sea and hope to join Capt. Whipple.⟩

From the Comtesse Conway[1]

ALS: American Philosophical Society

My dear papa   Auxerre twelve july 1778
   I Sand you a Concequence letter for my dear huusband, which I hope pleasure to forward to him, in which I am, and I will be highly oblige. Your truly tenderly daugheter

CONWAY

Thousand Compliments to messrs franklin, Williams and mr adams, my Sister joyn with me.

Notation: Madame Conway 12. Juillet 1778.

8. Probably John G. Frazer, who had crossed the Atlantic with John Paul Jones: Taylor, *Adams Papers*, VI, 77 n.
9. Actually his nephew, Louis-René-Madeleine Le Vassor de La Touche, later comte de Latouche-Tréville and a famous naval officer during the Revolutionary period; at this time he was commanding a corvette at Rochefort: Six, *Dictionnaire biographique.*
1. The wife of Gen. Thomas Conway; for her relationship with BF see above, especially XXIV, 486–7. On April 18 her father-in-law, Count de Conway, called upon JA in the hope of some word about his son (Butterfield, *John Adams Diary*, II, 302–3). Perhaps she was with him, for her later letters send regards to Adams. As the summer wore on she became more and more desperate for news of her husband. Several appeals to BF, such as one via her father-in-law (below, July 23), brought no reply; and in September she turned to WTF. Rumor, she told him on the 8th, had it that the General was ill and that BF knew it; was that true? By the 16th she had heard nothing, and wrote again: had she still any ground for hope? WTF

From ———— Herbaut de Marcenay[2]

ALS: University of Pennsylvania Library

Epinay ce 12 juillet [1778]

J'ai fait part monsieur à madame de breget des marques de votre souvenir et de l'invitation dont vous m'aviez charge, pour l'engager à aller diner un jour à passy. Elle serait bien flattée d'avoir l'honneur de vous aller chercher mais, étant à sa campagne, il serait peut être difficile de choisir d'ici à long-tems, un jour qui vous seroit commode, pour le voyage de passy. C'est pourquoi monsieur pour ne point differer le desir qu'elle a de passer des momens avec vous, elle vous prie de lui faire l'honneur de venir diner a épinay. Je me suis chargée avec d'autant plus de plaisir de cette négociation, que ce sera une occasion pour moi de vous renouveller l'assurance de mes sentimens, et vous savez monsieur combien je desire cultiver une société aussi aimable que la vôtre, et dont je scais appré-cier tout le prix. Choisissez donc le jour que vous voudrez, de la semaine prochaine, soit le lundi mardi mercredi, ou meme le jeudi. L'un de ces quatre jours sont égaux à ma soeur, mais ce qui ne lui sera point indifferent ainsi qu'a mr. de breget, ce sera d'avoir l'honneur de vous voir. Je vous promets aussi de leur part d'etre en petit comité et vous avez vû que je suis femme de parole. Amenez monsieur votre fils et monsieur le roy a qui je vais écrire pour lui proposer. Epinay est tres près de paris ainsi ce ne sera point un voyage ni long ni difficile. Ayez la bonté de me mander monsieur si nous pouvons nous

---

answered, but whatever he said did not calm her. By the 25th she had heard of Conway's duel (xxv, 555 n) but was not sure of the outcome, "ou Le bonheur et Le malheur de ma vie sont attaché." These three letters are in the APS. For further inquiries see de Gruffy to BF, Sept. 29.

2. Mme. de Marcenay and her sister, Mme. de Bréget, were the daugh-ters of a well known economist, Claude-Jacques Herbert, for whom see Quérard, *France littéraire.* Their husbands were both military men: Marcenay served with distinction in the artillery, and Joseph-Philippe de Bréget, a former captain of dragoons, was a lieutenant in Monsieur's *gardes du corps:* F. A. Gruyer, *Chantilly: les Portraits de Carmontelle* (Paris, 1902), p. 127; Bo-dinier. Mme. de Marcenay continued to seek BF's company; see Le Roy's letter under July 15 and hers of Aug. 22.

flatter de vous posséder? Vous comblerez de joie les deux soeurs; et moi je serai enchantée de vous assurer des sentimens avec lesquels j'ai l'honneur d'etre monsieur votre tres humble et tres obeissante servante   HERBAUT DE MARCENAY

Addressed: A Monsieur / Monsieur franklin / a passy

Notation: Marcenay 12. Juillet

From ———— de Reine[3]   ALS: American Philosophical Society

Monsieur Le docteur   a versailles le 12. juillet 1778.

Par ma lettre du premier mai dernier qui vous a été remise par M. brisson,[4] j'ai eu l'honneur de vous envoyer pour semence du Riz nababe, ce [c'est] la meilleur de dix especes que j'ai cultivé aux indes oriental, avec des harricots du cap de bonne esperance, si vous le desiré je suis en état de vous donner du riz du tibet, qui a la balle noire qui ne laisse point d'avoir son merite.

Vous avez vû, Monsieur, mes idées pour rafraichir nos êquipages a bord de nos vaisseaux pour evitter les inconvenient qui en resulte en donnant dans les combats des boissons enivrante; l'experiance m'a apris ainsi que vous en avez vû le detail dans ma premiere lettre, combien l'usage du caffé est salutaire, meme a tous egards.

J'ai eu aussi l'honneur de vous offrire la recette pour faire le vin d'orange.

Je vous prie, Monsieur, de recevoir ces vers avec bontés, ils ont étés acceuilly de meme par tous nos ministres.[5]

Il faut, Monsieur, pour animer la vertu dans tous les Etats, et singulierement la bravoure cette entousiasme qui allume ce feu divin!.. qui a fait dans tous les âges éclore les seuls grands

3. For the retired captain who sent BF exotic recipes see XXVI, 386.
4. The botanist Mathurin-Jacques Brisson: XIX, 126–7 n.
5. Both the recipe and the verses are missing.

hommes!.. J'ai l'honneur d'être avec respect Monsieur le docteur Votre tres humble et tres obeissant serviteur

De Reine

ancien capt. rue Sataury aux 4. bornes maison du chapelier
a M. Le docteur franklin a passy.

To [de Reine[6]] Draft:[7] American Philosophical Society

Passy ce [after July 12, 1778]
Les suffrages que vos vers ont obtenus, Monsieur, vous asseu-
rent de leur bonté, je voudrois savoir assez le françois pour
sentir tout leur mérite et je vous remercie de l'honeur que
vous m'avez fait de me les envoyer; j'ay reçu ce que vous aviez
chargé Mr. Brisson de me remettre et j'accepte le ris du thibet
a balles noires que vous m'offrez; je ne veux point que vous
preniez la peine de m'addresser la recette du vin d'orange, la
pensilvanie n'est pas assez propre a cette production pour que
nous puissions en faire usage. Je suis avéc reconnoissance
Monsieur Vostre tres humble et tres obeissant serviteur[8]

Notation: Written by [*deleted:* Le Roy] Le Veillard for Dr. Franklin

The American Commissioners to Francis Coffyn[9]

AL (draft):[1] Massachusetts Historical Society; two copies: National Archives

⟨Passy, July 13, 1778: Capt. Amiel brought us this morning
two letters from you[2] enclosing testimonials to your good

6. In answer to the preceding.
7. In Le Veillard's hand.
8. Someone here added the initials "B.F."
9. Published in Butterfield, *John Adams Diary,* IV, 159–60.
1. In JA's hand. All drafts in this repository, unless otherwise indicated,
are his.
2. Of July 9 and 10, above.

character. We had no doubt of it, and your trouble was unnecessary. A letter, it is true, did say that you were "somewhat too busy, in some particular matters,"[3] but this did not prejudice us against you. If you send news to America, write the Hon. James Warren at Boston or the Congressional committee of foreign affairs; English newspapers are always acceptable. But write nothing that is unconfirmed; misrepresentations that are floating about mislead the people. Give the American seamen you mention some employment, whether at Dunkirk, or at Brest or Nantes, that will save expense to their country.⟩

The American Commissioners to Schweighauser[4]

AL (draft): Massachusetts Historical Society; two copies: National Archives

⟨Passy, July 13, 1778: Load the *Boston* with whatever Capt. Tucker will take, and particularly with as much lead as he can carry and you can supply.⟩

The American Commissioners to Samuel Tucker[5]

AL (draft): Massachusetts Historical Society; two copies: National Archives

⟨Passy, July 13, 1778: On her last cruise the *Boston*, we understand, did not sail so well as before, doubtless due to some change in her ballast. Remove her present ballast if necessary, load whatever Mr. Schweighauser has for America, and take on lead to be delivered to the continental agent in America; so inform Congress or the navy board.

You are to join Capt. Whipple under his orders. If Lieut. Simpson applies for passage, accommodate him according to his rank.⟩

3. A paraphrase of a cryptic remark in Poreau, Mackenzie & Cie.'s letter above, XXVI, 693. The commissioners chose to ignore the comment that Coffyn was "the most unproper person for such a Trust."
4. Published in Butterfield, *John Adams Diary*, IV, 160.
5. Published in Butterfield, *John Adams Diary*, IV, 160.

The American Commissioners to Abraham Whipple[6]

AL (draft): Massachusetts Historical Society; copies: National Archives (two), Yale University Library

⟨Passy, July 13, 1778: We have ordered Capt. Tucker to join you for your cruises and homeward voyage; leave as soon as possible.⟩

To David Hartley

Two copies and transcript: Library of Congress

Dear Sir   Passy, July 13 1778

Inclosed is the List of our Prisoners, which by an accident was long in coming to us.[7] There are supposed to be about 15 more remaining in the Hospital, whose names we have not yet obtained, and about as many who being recovered of their wounds have been suffered to go home to England. If you continue in the Opinion of making the exchange at Calais,[8] you will send us the Papers necessary to secure the Vessel that shall transport the Men from the Ports where they are to that Place against Capture; as the marching them thither would be attended with great Inconveniencies, and many of them might desert on the way from an apprehension of being put on Board Men of war on their Arrival in England. I am ever Your affectionate humble Servant   BF

B. Franklin to M. Hartley

6. Published in Butterfield, *John Adams Diary*, IV, 160–1.
7. The commissioners had requested a list from Jones on June 10. Shortly thereafter they informed Hartley that the list, which they had not yet received, contained about two hundred names: XXVI, 605–6, 607, 626. Jones, who was en route to Passy, did not receive the letter until June 20 and presumably either had not prepared a list or did not have it with him. The list eventually furnished Hartley contained more than 250 names: see Hartley's notation of BF's letter to him, Oct. 20.
8. Hartley had transmitted the proposal in his letter of June 5: XXVI, 593.

From Frédéric-Charles de Baër[9]

ALS: American Philosophical Society

Monsieur   A Paris le 13 Juillet 1778.

Permettés moi d'implorer vos bons offices en faveur du Sieur Meyer porteur de la presente.[1] J'ai deja eu L'honneur la semaine passée de vous presenter cet Officier qui a servi avec distinction à bord du Ranger, Capne. Jones, et vous avés eu la bonté de lui promettre que vous voudrés bien veiller à ce que la part qui lui revient des prises que le Ranger a faites lui parvienne exactement. Oserois-je vous demander une nouvelle grace pour cet Officier? Je dois vous faire confidence qu'il est dans le dernier besoin. Sans Monsieur L'Ambassadeur, il n'auroit pas eu de quoi subsister à Paris. Maintenant il doit s'en retourner à Brest, et il n'a pas le premier sol pour faire ce voyage. Je n'ose plus importuner Monsieur L'Ambassadeur pour lui demander de nouveaux secours. Mais j'ai cru que si vous vouliés engager Mr. Jones à lui faire une avance d'une dixaine de Louis d'or à compte de ce qui doit lui revenir des prises, ce Capitaine non seulement ne risqueroit rien mais il rendroit encore le plus grand service à un honnette homme à qui il a réellement les plus grandes obligations. Ayés donc la bonté, Monsieur, d'interposer votre autorité et vos bons offices pour determiner le Cne. Jones à cette avance; vous ferés une bonne oeuvre digne de votre grande ame; je vous aurai en

9. A professor of theology at the University of Strasbourg and chaplain, as mentioned below, to the Swedish Ambassador to France, Gustaf Philip, count Creutz (Butterfield, *John Adams Diary*, III, 63 n). A man who joined vast erudition with great modesty, he was a corresponding member of the Académie royale des sciences and the author of works on a bewildering variety of subjects: *Nouvelle biographie;* Eugène and Emile Haag, *La France protestante* . . . (9 vols., Paris and Geneva, 1846–59), I, 214–15.

1. Jean Meyer, or Meijer, was a lieutenant in the Swedish army; he had offered his services to Silas Deane around September, 1777, and the following February enlisted as a volunteer on the *Ranger*. He had been Jones's second in command during the raid on Whitehaven and, Jones certified in 1780, behaved well in the engagement with the *Drake: Deane Papers*, II, 119–20; Charles Henry Lincoln, comp., *A Calendar of John Paul Jones Manuscripts in the Library of Congress* (Washington, D.C., 1903), p. 140; Morison, *Jones*, p. 140. A letter from Meyer to BF of Oct. 9, 1779 (APS) indicates that de Baër's introduction procured him a gracious welcome.

mon particulier une obligation bien sensible, et vous augmen-
terés, s'il est possible, les sentimens de veneration et de reconnoissance, avec lesquels j'ai L'honneur d'etre Monsieur Votre
très humble et très Obeissant serviteur

> De Baër
> Aumonier du Roi de Suede
> et Secretaire de l'Ambassade de S.M.

I beg you pardon, Sir to write to you in french, I would have
done it in English; but I am but a scholar in this Language.

Endorsed: De Baer Aumonier d'Ambassadeur de Suede

Notation: 13 Juillet 1778.

From Richard Bennett Lloyd

ALS: American Philosophical Society

Dear Sir,   Chaillot. Monday July 13th. 78.
   Mrs. Gibbes and Miss Stevens have just got a copy of the
Act passed in Sth. Carolina relative to *Absentees.*[2] They and
Mrs. Lloyd propose waiting on you and Mr. Adams this Eve-
ning should you be disengaged. I am, Dear Sir, with much
respect your obedient and very humble Servant

> Richard Btt. Lloyd

Addressed: Doctor Franklin / &c. &c. &c.

Notation: R.B Lloyd. July 13. 1778.

Franklin's Memorandum about the Walpole Company

ADS: New York Public Library

This memorandum is a key document in the story of Franklin's involvement with the Walpole Company. In 1774 he had ostensibly
resigned from it, because his presence among the promoters was a
political liability in their campaign for a land grant.[3] After his return

---

2. The two women and the act are identified in xxvi, 684–5.
3. xxi, 31–4.

to America, however, he continued to be active in the Company's affairs: he signed a power of attorney for its agent, endorsed a legal opinion in favor of its title, and participated in the reorganization of one of its components that was emerging again as a separate entity.[4] In 1777 he negotiated the return of the balance that remained of his initial payments to Walpole for his and his son William's shares of the purchase money and attendant expenses.[5] But as he indicates here, Franklin believed he retained his right to the land whenever the grant was made. He had dismissed the possibility of the crown as grantor, we believe, and now looked solely to Congress; the formal way in which he here records his claim indicates that he considered it a significant part of his legacy to his descendants.

[July 14, 1778]

Extract of a Letter from the honble. Mr. Thos. Walpole Tuesday July 7, 1778 to Dr. Bancroft.

"Pray make my best Compliments to Mr. Moses (i.e. BF). I am always flattered when he thinks of me and my Family. The Letter you mention he wishes to have returned, totally escaped my Memory. Perhaps I may not be able to lay my hand upon it immediately, but I will most certainly send it back soon."

Afterwards in the same Letter: "I have found Mr. Moses's Letter and will send it this Evening under Cover to G.H. & Co. not chusing to inclose it in this on Acct. of the Signature."[6]

The Letter mention'd above is the same that I now attach with a Wafer to this Paper. It was written on Request of Mr. Walpole, to obviate an Objection made by the Atty. General Thurloe to the Signing our Patent, viz. my being unworthy the Favours of the Crown. But I was still to be consider'd as an Associate, and was call'd upon for my Payments as before.

4. XXII, 19–21, 102–3, 325–6.
5. XXIII, 156–9, 264, 302–3, 431.
6. Walpole's letter is missing. He was returning the one in which BF withdrew from the Company (XXI, 33–4); "Mr. Moses" is an alias that we never before encountered. "G. H. & Co." is Girardot, Haller & Cie., the Parisian bankers.

My Right to two Shares, or two Parts of 72, in that Purchase, still continues, having paid all the Expence belonging to those Shares.[7] And I hope, that when the Troubles of America are over, my Posterity may reap the Benefit of them. I write this Memorandum at Passy in France, where I now am in the Service of the United States. July 14. 1778.   B FRANKLIN

Sartine to the American Commissioners[8]

Copies: Library of Congress (two), Massachusetts Historical Society (two), National Archives (three); transcript: National Archives

⟨Versailles, July 14, 1778, in French: The inhabitants of the islands of St. Pierre and Miquelon may receive few or no supplies, and be in great distress, if some of the victualers I have sent are intercepted; and by the time we hear of it there will be no remedy.[9] I have told the local authorities that they may depend on assistance from the United States, and the King would be glad if you would recommend, especially to the government of Boston, sending them supplies.⟩

Samuel Tucker to the American Commissioners[1]

ALS: American Philosophical Society

⟨On board the *Boston*, Port Louis, July 14, 1778: A letter of the 8th from Mr. Livingston tells me that a prisoner exchange is possible. I enclose a list of those on board, and a list of men recaptured, I suppose, in one of my prizes; the other two have already arrived. I am waiting on orders to join Capt. Whipple.

7. BF refers here to the legal expenses paid by Walpole for him before the unused balance was returned.

8. JA's own translation is printed in Butterfield, *John Adams Diary*, IV, 161. See also Taylor, *Adams Papers*, VI, 290.

9. These small islands off Newfoundland surrendered without resistance to a British force sent against them in September: G.R. Barnes and J.H. Owen, eds., *The Private Papers of John, Earl of Sandwich* . . . (4 vols., [London], 1932–38), II, 290.

1. Published in Taylor, *Adams Papers*, VI, 290–1.

He tells me he will be ready by the 20th and expects me to wait at the river's mouth.

The enclosed statement written by one of the marines and signed by five others will show the treatment they received from me and my officers.[2] Gen. Latuch [La Touche] will wait on you with an account of Sergeant Cazneau [Cazeneuve]; it is false, in that the sergeant is indebted to the ship. Every one begged me to take the marines back because they were destitute, but I refused all but those mentioned in the statement; them I took to show that their report was untrue.

Please, if possible, exchange Captain John Lee, taken in the brig *Fanney* [*Fancy*] and a brother of mine his master, Andrew Slyfield, who are in Mill Prison, and my nephew John Diamond. I should be glad to have a number of my captives exchanged for those in that prison. O that I were manned with Americans or others I could depend on! But I must do my best. P.S. The *Britannia* has just arrived,[3] and I am happy that my men are not prisoners.⟩

From Richard Bache

ALS: American Philosophical Society

Dear and Honored Sir   Philadelphia July 14. 1778

Once more I have the happiness of addressing you from this dearly beloved City, after having been kept out of it more than nine months. I have had the pleasure of hearing frequently from you of late, the last is dated the 25th. April, wherein you tell me that you have had no Letter from me since June 1777. I hope, my dear Sir, you don't suspect that Sally and I have been so remiss, as not to have wrote you in all this time, she has wrote you two or three Letters, I have wrote at least a dozen, which, considering that our situation

2. The "Declaration by French Crew Members of Frigate Boston" asserts that they have no complaint against Reed and Bates, that they have been even better treated than their American counterparts and that they are willing to follow Congressional regulations and to sail to Boston. Hist. Soc. of Pa.

3. For these men, see Kaminkow, *Mariners*. The *Britannia* was one of the *Boston*'s prizes: Taylor, *op. cit.*, 291 n.

has not been very stationary, is pretty well; but our Letters have been unfortunate. I was ignorant of Mr. John Adam's departure, or should have wrote by him. Sally is yet in the Country, and does not intend coming to Town 'till the hot weather be over, on account of her little Girl. I heard from them yesterday and they were well. I found your house and furniture upon my return to Town, in much better order than I had any reason to expect from the hands of such a rapacious crew; they stole and carried off with them some of your musical Instruments, viz: a welch harp, bell harp, the set of tuned bells which were in a box, Viol de Gambo, all the spare Armonica Glasses and one or two of the spare cases. Your armonica is safe. They took likewise the few books that were left behind, the chief of which were Temple's school books, and the history of the Arts and Sciences in french, which is a great loss to the public.[4] Some of your electric Aparatus is missing also. A Captain Andre also took with him the picture of you, which hung in the dining room,[5] the rest of the pictures are safe, and met with no damage except the frame of Alfred, which is broken to pieces. In short considering the hurry in which we were obliged to leave the Town, Sally's then situation, and the number of things we consequently left behind, we are much better off than I had any reason to expect. I have mentioned in four or five different Letters the Types you brought over with you from England being sold to the State of Virginia, and that the price of them was left for you to fix, as I knew not the cost or the value of them.[6] I should be glad to hear from you on this subject, that I might receive the Money and place it in the funds. Congress have not yet began to draw for the interest of money borrowed, as

4. Presumably BF's Amsterdam edition of the *Mémoires* of the Académie royale des sciences: XVIII, 70.

5. Capt. John André, whom the Americans later hanged for his part in the Arnold conspiracy, was aide-de-camp to Maj. Gen. Charles Grey, later first Earl Grey, to whom he presented the portrait by Benjamin Wilson. It remained in the Grey family until 1906, when the fourth Earl, then Governor General of Canada, gave it to the United States. APS *Proc.*, C, 371.

6. RB had disposed of BF's printing office, he reported in his letter above, XXV, 552.

soon as they do, I will remit you your bills. Your chest of papers left with Mr. Galloway I am told was broke open at Trevoes and the papers scattered about.[7] I shall go up thither today or tomorrow to look after them, if I can pick any of them up, shall take care of them. Governor Franklin is upon the point of being exchanged.[8] I have had two or three Letters from him, informing me that he enjoys better health than he had done in the begining of his confinement. Two days ago the french Ambassador arrived. I waited upon him yesterday, and was introduced as your son in Law, he received me very politely, told me he held dear every connection of yours.[9] This made me not a little vain. [*He*] told me he had a Letter for me, which he would wait upon me with, as soon as he had got his baggage on shore; I shall pay every proper respect and attention to your introductions, as soon as I am in a situation for it. I cannot help mentioning Mr. Holker, as a Gentleman that has made very sensible impressions on me.[1] It would have been a most fortunate event, had the fleet arrived three weeks earlier. They would have effectually crushed the British power in this part of the world; I am still in hopes this may be done,[2] but it would have been effected with greater facility had they met the enemy in our Bay or River. I am obliged to you for the

7. Trevose, Galloway's estate in Bucks County. For this pillage, the greatest single loss that BF's papers underwent, see I, xxi.
8. WF was finally released in late October. William H. Mariboe, *The Life of William Franklin, 1730(1)-1813, "Pro Rege et Patria,"* (Ph.D. dissertation, University of Pa., 1962), pp. 483-4.
9. Conrad-Alexandre Gérard had crossed with d'Estaing, who detached a frigate that landed him at Chester on the 12th. Meng, *Despatches of Gérard,* p. 147. On the 13th RB described his meeting with the minister in a letter to Sally: "The company that was with me said, I out did him in politeness, notwithstanding he is so polite a man." Yale University Library.
1. For Holker's mission see XXV, 238-9 n.
2. If the French had arrived two weeks earlier, a British observer agreed, "it is highly probable that our cause would have been totally ruined in America. Our fleet was at that time dispersed all over the American coast, New York was entirely defenseless, and the baggage and provisions for the whole army was then leaving the Delaware protected by a few frigates that would have been incapable of making the least resistance." Quoted in Willcox, *Portrait of a General,* p. 237.

extracts of Letters and other papers sent with yours of the 25th. April. I lament much that I do not understand french; I must endeavor to learn it. I have seen Mr. Lutterloh, and spoke to him relative to Count Wittgenstein's demand, he assures me that three months ago he remitted £400 Sterling to Mrs. Lutterloh in England with directions for her to remit this amount to the Count, which he says is all he owes him. From the paper you sent me the Count's demand is more. The Count had better send over a certified account and power of Attorney. It may then be in my power to recover the money due him, as Mr. Lutterloh has made a good deal of Money in our Service, and purchased an Estate at Potsgrove. I have wrote to the Adjutant General of our Army, requesting him to make every Inquiry to satisfy the friends of Frederick de Wernecke, and expect soon to receive his answer, whether or not such a person is in our Service. A Gentleman from Germany that lives here, and is acquainted with all the German Officers that come over, is of opinion that Captain Wernecke never came to this Country, but that he was lost with Mr. Zeller, whom he knew very well. I shall pay proper attention to the Duchesse de Melfort's Memoire, and endeavor to procure the satisfaction she wants relative to the Lands in New Jersey, but this will take up some time.[3] With most cordial Love and Duty I remain Dear and honored Sir Your most affectionate son

RICH: BACHE

3. BF's letter of April 25 has disappeared. Lutterloh's debt to Wittgenstein had resulted from recruiting the Count's subjects for the British in 1776; see Wittgenstein to BF, Jan. 25, 1780, APS. As for Frederick Warnecke, he was indeed alive and holding a commission in Williamsburg: see RB's letter below, Oct. 22. According to his brother-in-law, Warnecke had left Idstein in October, 1776 to enter American service: Langsdorf to JA, July 22, 1783, National Archives. He had been hired as state engineer of Va. in Oct., 1777, and was captured in January, 1781 at Richmond, where he was too drunk to flee the attack of Benedict Arnold: E.M. Sanchez-Saavedra, ed., *A Guide to Virginia Military Organizations in the American Revolution, 1774–1787* ([Richmond], 1978), p. 114. His relatives were still inquiring as to his whereabouts well after the Revolution; see National Archives, Papers of the Continental Congress, under Wernecke. For the duchesse de Melfort's questions about her land claims see xxv, 718–19.

I wish I could have sent to me from France 2 dozen of padlocks & Keys fit for Mails, and a dozen post horns, they are not to be had here.

Dr. Franklin

From Simon-Pierre Fournier le Jeune[4]

ALS: American Philosophical Society

Monsieur   Paris le 14 juillet 1778
J'ay l'honneur de vous réiterer votre demande de la fonte de Petit Romain par laquelle vous attendiés des modelles: Pour regler la hauteur en Papier, étant Prêt a la faire commencer, comme vous m'en avés Parû Pressé. Si votre courier d'anglettere est arrivé, et que vous daigné m'en faire Part vous obligérés celui qui a l'honneur d'être avec Respect, Monsieur, Votre très humble et très obeissant serviteur

FOURNIER LE JEUNE

Addressed: A Monsieur / Monsieur franklin / A Passy

Notation: Fournier le jeune 14. Juillet 1778.

From John Harris[5]

ALS: Historical Society of Pennsylvania

May it please you Excellency   Fortone July the 14th. 1778
The multiplicity of business you must be Engaged in, The flattering assurance of our being Exchang'd in a short time,

4. The member of the famous family of printers with whom BF was currently dealing: XXV, 577. An entry dated merely July in BF's Cash Book (above, XXVI, 3) records an outlay of 336 *l.t.* for 14 lots of type. For a discussion of the fonts BF ordered from the Fourniers, see Luther S. Livingston, *Franklin and his Press at Passy* (New York, 1914), 111–18.

5. The former commander of the *Mosquito*, a brig in Va. service, who had given John Thornton an account of his imprisonment in December; he was exchanged in 1779. See XXV, 415–16 n; Walter D. McCaw, "Captain John Harris of the Virginia Navy. A Prisoner of War in England, 1777–1779," *Va. Mag. of Hist. and Biog.*, XXII (1914), 160–72; BF to Harris, Aug. 12, 1779 (Library of Congress).

And my not being in imediete want was the motive of my not troubling you before, also supposing Mr. Thorton to have Inform'd you of the Station of every person here. Permit me now to Inform your Excellency that I had the Command of (a Cruizer) the Brigantine Moschetto bellonging to the State of Virginia and was taken by the King ship Ariadne Capt. Pringle on the 4th. June 1777 and brought here from Antigua in the Wind Augt. last. I have understood that an Exchange is now on foot for 200 of us. Your Excellency knows if there is truth in this report and would beg leave to Remind you that if such an Exchange should take place you would please to think on me and three of my Officers, Vizt. Capt. of Marines, Midshipman, and Boatswain which are all the Men I have here. I am in doubt that there are not Officers sufficient in France to Exchange for the number we have here. However I hope your Wisdom may cause that difficulty to be surmounted. I hope you would please to comunicate your sentiment to me through the same Channel you receve this which will be conveyd to the Revd. Mr. Wren and that good man will take a pleasure in Informing me of it.[6] When Mr. Thornton was here he was so harrased by the People that I had no oppertunity of knowing if there was a possibility of Drawing on the State of Virginia Thorough you Excellency's meen's for some small matter to purchase Necessaries shoul I be so fortunate to be among the number of those that was Exchanged or to supply me while here should it not be my fortune.

Your Excellency Character is such that I need not Apologize for this trouble I have given you. Believe me that I am among many thousands one who thinks it the greatest Honour to

6. For Capt. Thomas Pringle, who eventually rose to Vice-Admiral, see Alexander Pringle, *The Records of the Pringles or Hoppringills of the Scottish Border* (Edinburgh, 1933), pp. 325–7. Harris' three officers were Alexander Dick, Alexander Moore, and John Smith, respectively: William R. Cutter, "American Prisoners at Forton Prison, England, 1777–1779," *New-England Hist. and Geneal. Reg.*, XXXIII (1879), 36, 39. For Thomas Wren, the dissenting clergyman who was aiding American prisoners at Forton, see XXV, 416–17 n.

subscribe him Self Your Excellencys Most Humble and Obedient Servant   JOHN HARRIS

The Revd. Mr Wren desires his most respectful compliments to your Exell.

Addressed: Doctr: Benjn: Franklin / Paris

Endorsed: John Harris Prisoner

From David Hartley

ALS and incomplete copy: American Philosophical Society; transcript: Library of Congress

Dear Sir   Golden Square July 14 1778
   I have the following answers to make to you from the board of Admiralty, in relation to yours of the 16th of June. The prisoners to be exchanged from hence will be taken From Forton and Plymouth in proportion to their numbers in each place, and to consist of those who have been the longest in confinement. As to the distinction of the Seamen taken in the Merchants service, or in the service of the States of America, there is no such distinction in the prisons of Forton and Plymouth; they are all detained there under committments from some magistrate as for high treason; therefore no other distinction can be followed in their exchange but seniority as to their confinement. As to the passport for the ship which is to convey the prisoners from Brest to Calais, I am authorized to say that it will be granted by our Admiralty, if you will give me assurance that our ship going to Calais, shall have free entrance without molestation, and free egress with the prisoners in Exchange. There is but one point more in yours which I have not yet proposed to the board of Admiralty, viz. the general clearing of our prisons at once, upon your engagement to deliver an equal number in America to the Commander in Chief of the Navy or his order. I shall recommend this step very strongly to the board, and for that reason I chose to make it a seperate proposition and not to embarrass it with other details. I have several times proposed such a step to different members of the Administration long before you

94

made it as a request to me, I shall now make a written proposition of it in form.[7] I wish every thing to be done that may
tend to soften the minds of the parties to each other, to procure peace. You know the terms that I would recommend. I
am convinced that the people of the two Countries are not yet
alienated from each other, and in my opinion nothing could be
a compensation to either of them that they should ever become so. I will never remitt the utmost of my poor endeavours
to restore peace. Believe me ever Yours most affectionately

DH

To Dr Franklin

Notation: D.H. July 14. 1778

From ——— Martin   ALS: University of Pennsylvania Library

Monseigneur,   Dunkerque ce 14. juillet 1778.
Permetez que je m'adresse a Votre Grandeur, pour La suplier de me tirer d'inquietude sur le sort de mon fils ainé qui a
l'honneur d'etre connu de Votre Excellence sous le nom de
L'estarjette qu'il a pris d'un fief; il est parti de Nantes le 12. du
mois de Mars dernier a bord du navire nommé La Duchesse
de Choiseul appartenant a M. de Montieu;[8] depuis son depart
ayant fait rencontre le 20. avril d'un batiment venant de St.
Domingue a la Latitude et Longitude ci après noté, il m'a ecrit
le dit jour qu'il se portoit bien ainsi que tout l'equipage, plein
de bonne volonté et en etat de preter le côté a l'enemi s'il le
trouvoit a l'atterage. Comme il n'etoit pour lors qu'a 200 et
quelques lieux [lieues] de charles-town, ou il pouvoit arriver
vers la fin d'avril, et que plusieurs nouvelles sont venues de
vos colonies du premier au 20. may sans en avoir eu de lui, je
crains fort qu'il n'aye eté pris par les anglois roïalistes a L'at-

7. For the Admiralty's response, see Hartley's letter below, Oct. 9.
8. Louis Lestarjette (for whom see XXIII, 37–8) was by this time carrying
letters between Beaumarchais and his American agent de Francy. The *Duc
de Choiseul* was indeed captured by the British, but Lestarjette had arrived in
South Carolina by mid-July. Morton, *Beaumarchais Correspondance*, IV, 124,
140; for the ship's capture see XXV, 494 n.

terage. Je vous suplie, Monseigneur, au cas que vous ayez connoissance soit de son arrivée soit de sa prise, de vouloir bien me le faire mander, j'espere cette grace pour un pere tendrement attaché à son fils et aimé de toutte sa famille. Je suis avec un profond Respect, Monseigneur, de Votre Excellence Le très humble et très obeissant serviteur

> MARTIN
> tresorier extraordinaire des guerres,
> Ancien Maire et bourgmaitre de Dunkerque.

a la mer le 20 avril 1778
Latitude   28 degres.......10
Longitude   70................20

Notation: Martin 14 Juillet 1778.

From William Strahan   ALS: American Philosophical Society

Dear Sir   London July 14. 1778.

I wrote you by Post of the 13th. of last March; to which tho' you have not favoured me with an Answer, I cannot let our Friend Mr. Strange leave this Place to go where you are, without again paying my Respects to you; for to the Subject-matter of my last Letter, and not to any Abatement in your Friendship to me and mine I attribute your late Silence.[9] I shall therefore give you no farther Trouble of that Kind. Suffer me only to lament, as I dare say you do, the wide Difference between the present Times, and those in which (in your Letter to me of March 28. 1763. now lying before me) you wrote as follows:

"I congratulate you on the glorious Peace your Ministry have made: the most advantageous to Britain, in my Opinion, of any your Annals have recorded. As to the Places left or restored to France, I conceive our Strength will now soon increase to so great a Degree in North America, that in any future War we may with Ease reduce them all; and therefore I

9. The March letter (XXVI, 108–10) dealt with possible peace negotiations. Robert Strange, the engraver, had carried Strahan's letters before: XXIII, 226.

look on them as so many Hostages or Pledges of Good Behaviour from that perfidious Nation."

This Letter was in answer to one I wrote you by your Son, "who was then received," you tell me, "with the utmost Respect and even Affection by all Ranks of People." What a Reverse of Fortune! I was told last Winter by one Dr. Chandler, that he had been just informed that he was imprisoned in a Common Jail, and that his Wife had died last July at New York of a broken Heart. This Information I immediately laid before the People in Power, in case it might eventually lie in their Way to administer him some Relief. I know not what may have brought upon him this severe Treatment; but I think, whatever his Demerits may be in the Opinion of the reigning Powers in America, the Son of Dr. Franklin ought not to receive such Usage from them.[1]

You write me in a late Letter that Mr. Hall's Family were all well, and that Trade was as brisk with them as ever. Since that is the Case, I very much wonder I have not heard from young Mr. Hall these three Years past; nor has he remitted any part of the Balance then due to me, which is £363.10.11. tho' I have written to him again and again to remind him of it. You well know, that his honest Father would not have acted thus, and that no Situation of public Affairs would have prevented him from faithfully discharging his just Debts.[2] If you can, with any Propriety interpose in this Matter, I should be much obliged to you to mention this is in your next Letters, or to put me in the proper way to recover that Debt.

My Family, I thank God, continue all well and my Affairs

1. The 1763 letter is printed in x, 235–7. Thomas Bradbury Chandler had been an Anglican rector in New Jersey (above, IV, 72 n) until as a Loyalist he moved to England in 1775: *DAB*. For Elizabeth Franklin's death in July, 1777, and WF's unsuccessful request for leave from the Litchfield prison, see XXIV, 447 n.

2. David Hall, the father, had been BF's partner in the printing business. Strahan had complained early in 1777 that he had not heard from William, the son, in almost two years: XXIII, 227. In a later letter to David's widow he quoted a sentence of BF's reply (*ibid.*, p. 275) and mentioned in another paragraph writing William about the debt: April 7, 1778, Huntington Library.

prosperous. My Son George, the Parson, was lately married to a very agreeable and virtuous Girl, Daughter to a Mr. Robertson, Surgeon at Richmond, with whom [he] is likely to be extremely happy. My other two Sons, and your Wife are still single.[3] In Matrimonial Affairs I cannot, as in others, interfere, or accelerate their Motions. When Connexions of this Kind are quite voluntary, you well know they have the best Chance to be happy ones; and their Happiness is in this, as in all other Cases, my sole Object. They all remember you with great Esteem and Affection, and do not yet despair of seeing you here again—nor do I. But however that may be, or in whatever way Providence may see fit to dispose of us, be assured I shall ever remain Dear Sir Your affectionate and obedient Servant   WILL. STRAHAN

Mr Strange will inform you, that your old Friend Sir John Pringle is in perfect Health, and remembers you with wonted Esteem and Affection.

Endorsed: Strahan

Notation: July 14. 1778.[4]

Christopher Gadsden[5] to the American Commissioners

ALS: American Philosophical Society

Gentlemen.   Charles Town So. Carolina 15 July 1778

I cannot deny myself the Pleasure of endeavouring to introduce the Bearer Commodore Gillon to your Notice.[6] He hath been always very active in promoting the American Cause and been of great Service to it in several respects as well generally, as particularly to this State and our Assembly during its last Sitting appointed him Commodore of our Navy and in

3. William, Andrew, and BF's "wife" Peggy: XVII, 167 n.
4. Followed by a small sketch that looks like a half-inflated balloon.
5. The Charleston merchant who had served with BF in Congress: XXVI, 454 n.
6. See Middleton's letter above, July 4.

98

that Character he is sent to Europe to build or purchase three Frigates for this State. We have the highest Confidence in him as we are convinced he cannot have engaged in this Service, but from the purest Motives to serve the State and the Cause in general. Your Notice of him I am sure will be taken kindly by our State and particularly by Gentlemen Your most obedient humble servant CHRIST GADSDEN

P.S. For News I refer you to the Commodre. Few Men in this State are better inform'd, with regard to what is Stirring in the Continent in General, as to what particularly relates to this State.

Notation: Christ Gadsden Charlestown 15 juillet 1778.

Sartine to the American Commissioners[7]

Copies: Library of Congress (two), Massachusetts Historical Society

⟨Versailles, July 15, 1778, in French: Among the English prisoners on Belle Isle, taken from ships in French ports, are two who say they are Americans, James Niggins of Charleston, and John Selby of Baltimore. They want to be freed and sent home. They were on the *Hancock*, they say, en route to Charleston from Nantes when an English privateer took her and carried them to Falmouth; there, to avoid the press, they agreed to stay aboard their captor. Please tell me whether you know them, whether they have approached you, and whether you think them entitled to obtain their request.⟩

7. A translation is published in Butterfield, *John Adams Diary*, IV, 161–2.

From Jean-Baptiste Le Roy

AL: American Philosophical Society

Aux Galeries du Louvre ce mercredy matin
[July 15, 1778.[8]]

Mess. Kossakowsky et Strestsky gentilshommes Polonnois[9] qui vous remettront ce billet mon Illustre Docteur nous donnent à diner à Mde. Le Roy et à moi Jeudy prochain avec plusieurs académiciens. M. Strestsky nous fera voir ses curieuses experiences sur l'air inflammable dont j'ai eu l'honneur de vous parler.[1] Vous devriez être de la partie et ces Mess. le desirent vivement. C'est en conséquence même que je leur ai donné ce billet pour vous. Rendezvous donc mon cher Docteur à leurs Instances et aux miennes. Vous savez combien toutes les occasions où je puis passer quelques momens avec vous me sont précieuses.

Tourner s'il vous plait

Je viens de recevoir un billet de Mde. De Marcenay qui bien fâchée de ne vous pas voir vous propose d'aller diner chez sa

---

8. We are assuming that his postscript, mentioning a dinner with Mme. de Marcenay on Monday or Tuesday, refers to the same party about which she wrote BF on July 12, even though she gave the additional options of Wednesday or Thursday.

9. The abbé Remigian Corvini Kossakowski (1730–80) had been a Polish Jesuit before the suppression of the order in 1773. He then traveled abroad until he settled in Paris in the fall of 1776, where he stayed until his death and had the title of correspondent of the Polish educational commission (*Jour. de Paris*, Sept. 7, 1778, p. 999). His chief accomplishment there was to help the abbé Andrzej Strzecki, astronomer to the King of Poland, who had been sent to France to buy instruments for the observatory at Vilno. Strzecki completed his mission and returned home in early September. *Polski Słownik Biograficzny* . . . (29 vols. to date, Kraków, 1935–86) XIV, 284–6. Corvini Kossakowski wrote an undated letter (APS) accepting for them both a dinner invitation from BF for a Tuesday. Since he emphasized that Strzecki was on the verge of departure, an occurrence announced as imminent on Sept. 4 (*Jour. de Paris, loc. cit.*), our guess is that the dinner took place on Tuesday, Sept. 8.

1. On Aug. 29 Strzecki demonstrated to the Académie royale des sciences a British machine for experimenting with inflammable air: *procès-verbaux*, XCVII, fol. 292.

soeur à Epinay lundy ou mardy selon celui de ces jours qui vous conviendra. Faites moi un mot de reponse mon cher Docteur afin que je lui fasse savoir vos intentions et si vous acceptez.

Addressed: M. Franklin deputé du Congrès a Passy

From "Pierre Libertati" and Other Commission Seekers
ALS: American Philosophical Society

Once France entered the war, its eager young men had an obvious outlet for their martial energies. Many of the commission-seekers, henceforth, come from abroad—even from England—but there remains a trickle of French applicants, special cases who turn to Franklin for help.[2]

A seasoned officer addresses Franklin on July 24. Captain C.F. de Wiebel, once in the service of the Circle of Franconia, has fought in the Austrian army in the war against Prussia, served as an engineer in the Russian forces against Turkey, and in the army of Prince Dolgorouki marching on the Crimea.[3] He is enclosing the original, in Russian, of a letter written five years earlier by that prince, praising his engineering skills. A conspiracy brought him down as he was about to become the head of the engineers-geographers. Back at his home base, Erbac, he pursued his military studies and is now ready to spill his blood for America. Just let him have a commission equivalent to the one he held in Russia. Another officer writes from Geneva on October 12: De Stettenhoven hopes that, with the Doctor's recommendation, he will be able to enter the American army. He has served in Poland, first as a captain, ultimately as a major, and has the credentials to prove it. Antoine Deville explains on September 22 that he has already gone to Nantes on the advice of Franklin's friend, Baron de Benyowski,[4] whom he served as *intendant* and who gave him letters of recommendation before leaving for Austria. His

---

2. All letters summarized here are in the APS, with the exception of that from Duplacy, which is in the University of Pa. Library. All are in French except those of Ferrier, which are in English.

3. Prince Vasily Dolgorouki conquered the Crimea in 1771 after a two-week campaign. Larousse.

4. For whom see XXIV, 563–4 n.

background includes twenty-six years as a lieutenant in Malta, fighting the Turks, and four years as an auxiliary officer in the King's Navy. Having met Le Maire in Nantes,[5] he asked him for employ but was told that he should first procure a letter from Franklin.

In contrast with the training in foreign armies of the three previous officers, de St. Martin, who writes from Versailles on August 8, has no experience at all, only the depth of his "misérable infortune," the worst part of which is that he has been supported for five months by an infirm, destitute mother. His late father and grandfather were both captains in the Spanish service. He would enjoy the military life, yearns to travel, and would consider a sublieutenancy in America "un coup de fortune inespéré." Forgive his audacity in asking.

James Ferrier, a British candidate, writes from London on July 24. He is a cousin of Samuel Johnston, who will verify what he is about to say. After some years in the British service, he entered that of Portugal in 1762 and by 1774 had risen to the rank of brigadier general. During that time he served under that great master of artillery, Count La Lippe Buckebourg.[6] Now he feels he can be of great use to the United States by "regulating their artillery and putting it upon a footing at least equal to that of any at present in Europe." He is setting out the following day for Lisbon where he shall expect Franklin's answer. On August 30 he writes again, from Lisbon, to expand on his admiration for America and his fervent wish for an answer directed to him care of Thomas Mayne, in Lisbon. A duplicate of his previous letter is enclosed.

Joseph Ruault Duplacy, twenty-four, who writes on September 21 from Saint Brieuc in Brittany, is also connected with England. His problem is that, while French by birth, he grew up across the

5. Jacques Le Maire has been identified in XXVI, 34–5 n.

6. Ferrier (b. 1734), a Scotsman, was commissioned a lieutenant of the "Fireworkers" in 1758 and appeared in the British *Army Lists* from 1759 to 1761. He served in Portugal until 1780 and is said to have written *Sketches of Society and Manners in Portugal* ... (London, 1787) under the pseudonym of Arthur William Costigan. Friedrich Wilhelm Ernst, Graf von Lippe-Bückeburg (1724–77) had commanded the British troops in Portugal during the Seven Years' War. Lewis, *Walpole Correspondence*, XXII, 43 n, 48 n; Julian S. Corbett, *England in the Seven Years' War* ... (2 vols., London, etc., 1907), II, 322; Curd Ochwadt, ed., *Wilhelm Graf zu Schaumburg-Lippe Schriften und Briefen* ... (3 vols., Frankfurt am Main, 1976–83), II, 404, III, 549; *Grande enciclopedia portuguesa e brasileira* ... (40 vols., Lisbon and Rio de Janeiro, 1935–60), XI, 210, XII, 913.

Channel and spent eleven years in the British navy. In the course of nine voyages, he has acquired a vast experience of the sea and the rank of "second on a corvette." If Franklin who, he has heard, is in charge of naval affairs at Nantes, will grant him an equivalent rank, he will serve America faithfully. He knows English perfectly and has all the necessary certificates. The same request—to keep his current rank—is made on October 2 by Richaud, Chevalier de Servoulles,[7] presently serving the King of Sardinia as a first lieutenant garrisoned in Turin. Born in Provence to a well known but impoverished family, he had to seek service abroad. He would have joined the American cause long ago were it not for a few little debts that his parents seem unable to pay. If Franklin will take care of them, as well as of the expenses to bring him to the port of embarkation—furnishing him, of course, with letters of recommendation—he will resign on the spot and go wherever he is ordered. A postscript specifies that those debts amount to 600 Piedmontese pounds and that Franklin's letter containing the money should bear the right postage. If provided with the wherewithal, the young man will pay him a visit in Paris.

On August 22, writing from Metz, the Chevalier Delahaulsse offers his services. He has heard that BF is empowered to raise a new regiment of dragoons for Virginia; he feels confident that he could fight in it without losing his rank of lieutenant-colonel in the hussards of Conflans, a post he has held since the Foreign Legion of Conflans has been suppressed. He is a well-connected gentleman from Lorraine and can provide the best recommendations.[8] The former commander of that same Legion, the Chevalier de Prades, with thirty years' experience in the military, writes from Souillac in Quercy on October 10 that he is much appreciated by such important figures as the duc de Choiseul, the maréchal de Mouchy and M. de St. Paul, head of the War Office. His proposal is to raise a troop of deserters—not the first time that he would carry out such an assignment—bring them to any seaport Franklin wishes and from there to the French West Indies where he will lead them into battle. The only thing he asks in exchange is a pension of 1,200 *l.t.* for his family. Should the Doctor agree, he could be joined in this adven-

7. Louis Richaud de Servoulles (b. 1752) eventually left Sardinia and by 1793 was commanding a battalion in Gap. Bodinier.
8. A later letter, undated, from his relative Mme. or Mlle. de Jamogne, explains that Delahaulsse was responding to proposals made by de Loyauté (see XXVI, 35 n). She compares the Chevalier's bravery to that of the ancient Romans and wonders why he has had no answer from BF.

ture by his brother who fought in the last war as a captain in the legion of Lorraine.[9]

As usual, a number of friends and relatives send Franklin their recommendations on behalf of commission-seekers. Writing from Calais on July 15, Madame Brouttin Mollien des Sombres hopes Franklin will find military employment for her brother, twenty-one, "de vie et moeurs irréprochables," coming from a highly respectable family mostly connected with the army. Nature showered gifts upon him. "Moeurs irréprochables" are also credited to Baron de Ried, currently a tutor in the house of Comte de Stralenheim, who writes on his behalf from Ditschweiler [Dudweiler?] near Sarrelouis on October 25. The unfortunate young man had formerly been in the service of the Duke of Würtemberg, whose notoriously grandiose schemes precipitated the ruin of many honest people.[1] De Ried could build a new life for himself in America; he has already been to Canada, is well versed in engineering, in foundries and steelworks, and would be perfect at the head of a military school. He will come to Paris if Franklin so wishes. The writer, a "maréchal de camp au service du Roy," will be gratified to have contributed such a valuable person to "un Etat qui vous doit tout."

On an unspecified day in October, Comte de la Morliere, *intendant général des armées du Roy*, writes from Luciennes [Louveciennes] near St. Germain to introduce his twenty-one-year-old son who has been serving the king for three years but is burning to cross over to America.[2] Will Franklin grant them an appointment five or six days

9. Raymond de la Prade (b. 1726) was commissioned lieutenant in the régiment de Mailly in 1746 and held a variety of military appointments. He was still in France in 1779 and still alive in 1794. His brother Jean-Baptiste (b. 1730) was commissioned lieutenant in 1756 and took his pension in December, 1776. Bodinier. Choiseul and Lafayette's relative Mouchy need no introduction; St. Paul was a *premier commis* at the ministry of war.

1. Baron de Ried was clearly caught up in Karl Eugen (1737–93), duke of Württemberg's extravagant build-up of military forces, meant mostly for display. In 1762, at about the time of de Ried's service, Württemberg supported an army of more than 14,000 men, many of them not paid, for a population of less than 600,000 people. *ADB*.

2. Alexis-Charles Magallon de la Morliere du Tillet (1707–99) became lieutenant general in 1762. The son, Louis-Antoine, had recently fled from Martinique to St.-Domingue as the result of a quarrel. He later became captain of grenadiers, took part in the siege of Savannah, and was captured at Charleston in 1780. He subsequently entered the priesthood, his military career blocked by the Martinique affair. Bodinier, *Dictionnaire*, under Magallon.

hence? On August 4, another father, Person de Grandchamp, applies for his son.[3] He has long hesitated to do so, out of awe and respect, but Franklin has endeared himself so much to French hearts that he now takes the step. This son of his is gifted for the military life; he has studied fortification under his father's tutelage and has even written about it. He has been a *cadet-gentilhomme* for two years but without much prospect of advancement because the family is poor. He has left the service and has been eager to join the Americans ever since he read about the treaty of alliance. The father is happy to see those feelings in him and wishes he himself could have a second career to devote to the new country. Two days later he writes again: he had forgotten to give his address which is at Senoncourt near Verdun. Blame old age for such a lapse!

Monsieur,   Genève le 15 Juillet 1778.

Vous aurez s'il vous plait la bonté d'excuser la hardiesse, que prend un ami de la liberté de vous addresser la présente lettre, pour vous prier de lui faire la grace de lui marquer le plus promptement que votre commodité vous le permettra, qu'elles sont les conditions que vous feriez à un jeune homme, qui auroit envie d'aller au service du Congrès en Amérique. Il est agé d'environ 19 à 20 ans, Citoyen de Genève, ce qui vis à vis d'autres personnes ne seroit rien, paroit cependant devoir être de quelque poid vis à vis de vous, parce que qui dit Genevois, dit un grand ami de la Liberté; en effet comme vous ne l'ignorez surement pas, nos Ancêtres eurent aussi pendant fort longtemps, des guerres très opiniatres pour se mettre en liberté et pour l'affermir. Mais ce n'est pas le moment de vous entretenir de choses aussi peu essentielles pour vous que celles là, c'est celui de vous prier de reçevoir avec votre bonté ordinaire, les sentiments de respect, de vénération et d'admiration, que j'ai pour vous, Monsieur; auxquels vous me permettré de joindre les voeux les plus ardents, pour la gloire, la prosperité et la liberté des Etats unis de l'Amérique. Puisse le grand Administrateur des Etats continuer à les soutenir contre l'horrible tirannie que l'on veut établir sur eux, et a près que les membres

3. Claude-Nicolas Person de Grandchamp (1730–92) was captain of the royal grenadiers in 1774. The son was probably Charles, who attended the école militaire in Paris; he must not have had a distinguished career since there is no file on him at the War Office. Bodinier.

du sage Congrès, illustrés du mérite d'avoir procuré la liberté
à leur chère Patrie, auront été rassasiés de jours, il les couronne d'une immortalité bienheureuse. C'est là, Monsieur, les
voeux les plus ardents que fait celui qui a l'honneur de se dire
avec un très profond respect Monsieur Votre très humble et
très obeissant serviteur   PIERRE LIBERTATI

Pardonné si je ne me signe pas de mon veritable nom, mais
après que vous m'aurez fait l'honneur de m'écrire ici *poste res-
tante*, j'aurai celui de vous répondre sous mon nom véritable;
en vous remerciant si les propositions que vous me ferez
me conviennent, comme je n'en doute pas un moment; connoissant, Monsieur, autant que je sçais, votre intégrité, votre
équité, votre vertu et vos lumieres. Le dit   PL

Notation: Pierre Libertati Offr.

The American Commissioners to the Massachusetts Council[4]

AL (draft): Massachusetts Historical Society; two copies: National Archives

⟨Passy, July 16, 1778: We enclose a request from M. de Sartine,
which we promised to send you.[5] Americans will doubtless be
inclined to supply the islanders, and the northern states be
able to do so in the absence of, or perhaps even despite, British warships. We hope the attempt will be made; it will fetch a
good price and be a friendly and humane act. Please lay this
letter and the enclosure before the General Court.⟩

4. Published in Butterfield, *John Adams Diary*, IV, 163–4.
5. About St. Pierre and Miquelon: see above, July 14.

The American Commissioners to the President of Congress

AL (draft): Massachusetts Historical Society

⟨Passy, July 16, 1778: We enclose a letter from M. de Sartine[6] that we promised to communicate to Congress. We have no doubt—[7]⟩

The American Commissioners to Sartine[8]

AL (draft):[9] Massachusetts Historical Society; two copies: National Archives

⟨Passy, July 16, 1778: We shall take the first opportunity to send to Congress and the government of Massachusetts your letter of the 14th; it will, we are confident, lead to exertions for the relief of the islanders. Success is undoubted if British warships are withdrawn from the area; if not the difficulty will be great.

The enclosed letter from Mr. Schweighauser will show the troubles with prizes that still plague our frigates;[1] please give orders for their relief. We also ask that British prisoners already or subsequently captured by our ships be confined in your jails at our expense, until we either exchange them or send them to America.⟩

6. See the preceding document and Sartine's letter of July 14.
7. The draft, without the incomplete second sentence, is published in Butterfield, *John Adams Diary*, IV, 164. This letter, as explained there, was never sent; the commissioners decided to forward Sartine's request along with their letter of July 20.
8. Published in Butterfield, *John Adams Diary*, IV, 164–5.
9. In Arthur Lee's hand.
1. The letter, of the 9th, is missing; Schweighauser reminded the commissioners of its contents in his letter of July 16.

The American Commissioners to Schweighauser[2]

AL (draft): Massachusetts Historical Society; two copies: National Archives

⟨Passy, July 16, 1778: We have ordered Lieut. Simpson, commanding the *Ranger*, to sea as soon as possible; please furnish him promptly with what he needs. The British prisoners on these ships are to be left behind, in such custody as you advise; we shall try tomorrow to get the ministry's orders for their lodging.⟩

The American Commissioners to Thomas Simpson[3]

AL (draft): Massachusetts Historical Society; copies: National Archives (two)

⟨Passy, July 16, 1778: We have wanted to settle disputes among the *Ranger*'s officers for some time, and at last have the pleasure of sending you a letter from Captain Jones which allows us to reinstate you on board the *Ranger*. Upon receipt of this, you will take command of the *Ranger* as first lieutenant, join Captain Whipple of the *Providence*, and obey his orders respecting your future cruises and voyage to America. Leave the British prisoners in the custody of whomever Schweighauser advises.⟩

The American Commissioners to Abraham Whipple[4]

AL (draft): Massachusetts Historical Society; copies: National Archives (two), Yale University Library

⟨Passy, July 16, 1778: We have instructed Lieut. Simpson, on whom command of the *Ranger* devolves now that Capt. Jones

---

2. Published in Butterfield, *John Adams Diary*, IV, 163.
3. Published in Butterfield, *John Adams Diary*, IV, 162–3. The notation reads, "Deliver'd Capt Jones a Copy of the above Letter the 5 August 1778."
4. Published in Butterfield, *John Adams Diary*, IV, 162–3.

is on another service, to join you under your orders. The *Boston*, *Providence*, and *Ranger* should put to sea with all dispatch. Do your best to take or destroy British privateers within your reach. Leave your prisoners as Mr. Schweighauser directs.)

John Bondfield to the American Commissioners

ALS: American Philosophical Society

Honorable Sirs   Bordeau 16 July 1778

Permit me to lay before your honors the foregoing State which by your interpossion we flatter ourselves may be relieved.[5] I am most respectfully Honorable Sirs your most Obedient Humble Servant   JOHN BONDFIELD

The Honble. Benj Franklin Arthur Lee John Adams Esqrs.

Notation: Mr. [Bondfield] Bordeaux 1778

5. Bondfield's letter was written at the bottom of a request in French in another hand on behalf of Captain William Jones. Jones had had to pay much higher duty on the salt he loaded at Bordeaux than he would have had to pay at the Île de Ré or at Croisic, near Nantes. The request asks on Jones's behalf that Necker, director general of finances, order the farmers general to grant Americans the lower rate. For William Jones, captain of the brigantine *Nancy*, see Charles H. Lincoln, comp., *Naval Records of the American Revolution 1775–1778* (Washington, 1906), p. 398.

John Paul Jones to the American Commissioners

Copies: American Philosophical Society,[6] United States Naval Academy Museum, National Archives (two), Massachusetts Historical Society[7]

Gentlemen   [July 16, 1778]
    When I took Lieutenant Simpsons Parole I did not expect
to have been long absent from America: but as circumstances
have now rendred the time of my return less certain, I am
willing to let the dispute between us drop for ever by giving
up that parole which will entitle him to command the Ranger.
I bear no Malice; and if I have done him an Injury this will be
making him all the present Satisfaction in my power. If on the
Contrary he hath Injured me I will trust to himself for an
Acknowledgement. I have the honor to be with sentiments of
due Esteem and Respect Gentlemen Your very Obliged very
Obedient very humble Servant   (signed)   JNO. P. JONES

Notation: Simpsons Parole enclosed in a Letter from Capt.
Jones 16 July 78.

Jean-Baptiste Le Roy to the American Commissioners

ALS: American Philosophical Society

                                              16 Juillet 1778
Messieurs Les Députés du Congrès sont instamment pries de
tirer d'inquiétude un Pere et une Mere qui sont dans les plus
vives allarmes sur leur fils, dont ils n'ont, depuis très longtems,
aucunes nouvelles. Ce jeune homme qui est fils unique est
capitaine d'artillerie au service des Etats unis. Il s'appelle *Ga-*

---

6. In Jones's hand, along with his copy of Simpson's parole of June 10,
and preceded by the following note: "Copy of a letter from Captain Jones
of the American Navy to the Commissioners at the Court of France dated
at Passy the 16th day of July in the moment when they were about to give
Mr. Livingston a Commission and appointment to Command the Ranger."
This copy differs insignificantly from the others.
    7. In Arthur Lee's hand. JA copied this version in his *Autobiography*, IV, p.
165.

not.[8] Son Père est Lieutenant Colonel d'artillerie au service de France. On desire beaucoup que Messieurs les députés fassent passer cette note dans l'armée en amérique pour que les Parens ayent des nouvelles de ce jeune homme.   LE ROY

M. Ganot capitaine d'artillerie au service des Etats unis de l'Amérique Septentrionale.

Schweighauser to the American Commissioners[9]

ALS: Harvard University Library

Honorable Gentlemen!   July 16 [1778]
   Beging leave to refer you to mine of the 9 inst.[1] I have now to inform you that Capt. Whipple at his return to his Ship, having wrote to me that he wanted the goods you had pointed out to be sent by him in order to stow his hold properly, I made yesterday application to Mr. Williams' Clerk for the Continental stores in his Posession, when he told me that he had no objection to deliver them provided I wou'd give him an order upon you Gentlemen, for their amount. Which I could not comply with, having no directions from you to that purpose, which I hope you will approve. Mr. Ross being by some means apprised of this, has proposed some Powder belonging to the Public, which the Captain has accepted and is now occupied in taking into his Powder Room.
   Yesterday I sent the last boat with the Provisions and Slops on board and have now nothing else but what the Captain can

8. Louis de Recicourt de Ganot had crossed with Du Coudray and not been commissioned in the U.S. army. He quit the service, announced that he was returning to France for urgent family reasons, and asked for passage money; Congress paid him off. See two letters from Ganot to Congress, one undated and the other of Aug. 27, 1777: National Archives; *JCC*, VIII, 606; IX, 877, 903; Lasseray, *Les Français*, II, 388.
   9. This is the first extant letter from Schweighauser in English. It may have been composed by his son-in-law Dobrée. Schweighauser had been designated by the commissioners to provide goods for the *Providence*'s return voyage: XXVI, 673–4, and Whipple's letter above of July 2.
   1. Missing.

take when he receives his last dispatches. I am actually gathering the accounts, I hope to be able to make the general one shortly, in order to transmit you. I have the honor to be respectfully Honorable Gentlemen Your most Obedient and most humble Servant   J. DL. SCHWEIGHAUSER

Permit me to remind you of what I hinted to you in my last of 9 inst: of the necessity of taking the proper arrangements with the Farmers respecting the Prises, as it really appears clear to me that they shou'd not be consider'd, altho English, as the Produce of that Country. Leaving this to your better judgement beg leave to Subscribe myself as on the other side Honorable Gentlemen, Your most obedient and most humble Servant   J. DL. SCHWEIGHAUSER

To the Honorable Comissioners of the United States of America, at the Court of France, actually resident at Passy.

Jonathan Williams, Jr., to the American Commissioners   ALS: American Philosophical Society

Honourable Gentlemen   Passy 16 July 1778.
    In consequence of the Remittance made to me by Mr. Delap of Bordeaux[2] I have written the inclosed Letter[3] to the officers and people of the Ranger, which if you approve please to return to be copied and forwarded. I have the honour to be with great Respect Your most obedient Servant   JONA WILLIAMS J

The Honble The Ministers Plenipotentiary of the United States.

Notation: J. Williams 16 July 1778. to Commrs

    2. At the request of the commissioners, for the *Ranger*'s prizes: see their letter of June 24 to the Delaps, XXVI, 678.
    3. Missing.

From Cornic, Veuve Mathurin & fils[4]

LS: American Philosophical Society

Monsieur   A Morlaix le 16. Juillet 1778

Nous avons l'honneur de vous informer que nous venons d'apprendre avec peine que M. Suégasse [Schweighauser] de Nantes avoit nommé un particullier de cette ville pour correspondant du Congrès en ce Port. Cette Information nous mortifient d'autant plus que vous nous avez fait l'honneur de nous en charger depuis longtems par plusieurs de vos Lettres et par celles de M. Silas Dean. S'il en étoit autrement ce Désagrément oûtre qu'il nous priveroit de vous être utile nous seroit encore désagreable vis avis de tout Morlaix. Vous n'ignorez pas, Monsieur, tout le zèle et tout l'attachement que nous avons montrés de la maniere la plus distinguée dans touttes les occasions qui se sont presentée. S'il arrivoit donc dans ce moment dans cette Rade, des Dépeches, des Pacquebots, ou quelqu'autre vaisseau appartenans aux Etats unis, nôtre premier soin seroit de les accuillir, et de leur donner tous les secours et assistence dont nous sommes capables; mais aujourd'huy que ce Particullier qui n'est instruit d'aucune marche relative à ces sortes d'affaires (que vous sentez mieux que nous doivent Rester cachés à tous les yeux) se presenteroit ausi en vertu de sa Lettre qui ne peut que traverser nos opérations et dévoiler au Public ce qu'il faut qu'il ignore.

Nous esperons d'après ce que nous avons L'honneur de vous marquer que vous voudrez bien prévenir M. Lée (que nous n'avons pas encore celuï de connoitre) que depuis longtems vous nous avez honnoré de La Correspondance en cette ville pour qu'il écrive a son Correspondant M. Suegasse de Nantes de retirer les ordres qu'il à pû donner a ce particullier d'icy. Nous penserions que plustot seroit le mieux parcequ'il peut arriver de moment à aûtre des affaires importantes qui demandent autant de discretion que de celeritté vis avis des-

---

4. This is the name under which the firm has appeared above: XXIV, 4 n. The present letter makes clear that it consisted of Mathurin Cornic's widow and son.

quelles nous nous comporterons toujours avec le zele et L'Intelligeance que méritent les affaires des Etats unis. C'est dans ces sentimens que nous avons l'honneur d'etre avec tout le Respect possible, Monsieur, Vos très humbles et très obeissans Serviteurs VEUVE MIN CORNIC ET MIN FILS

Addressed: A Monsieur / Monsieur Le Docteur Franklin / ambassadeur des Etats unis de la / merique septentrionale / A Passis.

Endorsed: M Cornick & Fils Morlaix

From —— Levent

ALS: American Philosophical Society

Monseigneur   Paris ce 16. juillet 1778

Mr. le Comte de Canowe qui me veut du bien a eû l'honneur de présenter à Vôtre Excellence l'Almanach général des Marchands, dont le plan est généralement gouté,[5] mais cet ouvrage est éloigné de la perfection dont il est susceptible, et je ne pourrois espérer de l'y porter si le zèle patriotique n'y concouroit avec moy. Persuadé qu'il n'y a que les citoïens honnêtes qui soient animés de ce sentiment respectable je me suis adressé à différentes places de commerce du Royaume et de l'Etranger pour m'envoyer des mémoires détaillés sur les productions de leurs contrées et sur leur industrie avec les noms des meilleurs négocians, fabriquants, des Entrepreneurs des Manufactures, Banquiers, l'epoque des foires. J'ai la Satisfaction de voir qu'ils veulent bien seconder mes vues par les

---

5. We cannot identify the bearer, who must have been bringing BF the *Almanach* for 1778; its successor contains material dated after July. We have been unable to locate a copy of this 1778 volume, but that for 1779, the year in which Levent seems to have acquired a controlling interest, indicates the general plan. Towns and regions, largely French, appear alphabetically with brief mention of the products and manufactures of each, and in most cases a list of the principal merchants. The only American city we have found is Boston; it is given little space, and no merchants are named. Neither this nor the 1781 edition provides further details on America; hence BF could scarcely have provided the information that Levent is requesting.

renseignemens qu'ils me donnent pour l'Edition prochaine. Je prens la respectueuse liberté de reclamer les bontés de Vôtre Excellence à ce qu'il lui plaise m'en faire donner sur les principales places de l'Amerique, où je désirerois pouvoir en envoyer un nombre de cette année qui serviroient au moins de canevas, pour rediger les instructions que chaque principal négociant voudroit me faire parvenir. L'inclination naturelle de Vôtre Excellence à obliger et la Protection qu'elle daigne accorder à ceux qui tachent de se rendre utiles au bien général de la Societé me font espérer qu'elle voudra bien m'honorer de ses hautes Lumieres, et observations, sur cet ouvrage naissant. Je suis avec un profond respect Monseigneur de vôtre Excellence Le très humble et très obéissant serviteur

> LEVENT
> Directeur du Bureau d'Indication de L'Almanach général des Marchands rue Gaillon vis à vis l'hôtel de Richelieu

Endorsed: Levent Alma. of Merchts.

Notation: 16 July 1778

The American Commissioners to Vergennes[6]

LS: Archives du Ministère des affaires étrangères; copy: National Archives

⟨Passy, July 17, 1778: We enclose a resolution of Congress about the treaties, and request that it be laid before the King.[7] It will show him how he has won the hearts of that body and of the American people by a beneficence that time will never efface.⟩

6. Published in Taylor, *Adams Papers*, VI, 298. See also the commissioners to the president of Congress, July 20.

7. The substance of the enclosure (now missing), thanking the King for his "truly magnanimous conduct," is known only through the Congressional resolution of May 4: *JCC*, II, 457–8.

Dumas to the American Commissioners[8]

ALS: American Philosophical Society; AL (draft): Algemeen Rijksarchief

⟨The Hague, July 17, 1778, in French: I have seen the Grand Facteur and our friend[9] every day, but have waited to write until the States General adjourned. Increasing the army was the principal subject of debate; Amsterdam rejected the proposal, and it will not be adopted. Our friend differed on it with the Grand Pensionary, who has his strengths and weaknesses. He is rich, could be independent and wise, and if he had courage could make the republic play a role worthy of it; the Grand Facteur believes he is on our side, and says that our friend dislikes him for his courtier's flexibility. The Grand Pensionary fears Amsterdam, I believe, and my warning that it knew about the overtures to him accounted for his receiving me warmly.

Our friend assured me that the steps I have taken have publicized beyond contradiction the favorable American attitude toward the republic, and have strengthened Amsterdam and weakened the British party. I told him that failure on the Grand Pensionary's part to answer your letter would be offensive. As long as the court opposes formal consideration of the matter, he replied, the Grand Pensionary would not compromise himself by acting alone; but Amsterdam appreciates the communicating of the treaty and wants the most friendly relations with the United States.

War has been declared in Germany. The Dutch envoy to Berlin has reported the King's declaration of his position and of his spurned efforts at compromise; Prussian troops have reached Dresden, and the King has broken camp in Silesia.[1]

8. Published in Taylor, *Adams Papers*, VI, 298–304.
9. For an identification of the Grand Facteur, "our friend," and the Grand Pensionary see the note to Dumas' earlier letter, July 3.
1. The Prussian invasion of Austrian territory on July 5 opened the War of the Bavarian Succession, which produced weeks of languid hostilities before negotiations were resumed; see Paul P. Bernard, *Joseph II and Bavaria: Two Eighteenth-Century Attempts at German Unification* (The Hague, 1965), pp. 106–23.

116

The States General will reconvene tomorrow, to consider instructions to their envoy in London about the British seizure of two Dutch ships returning from St. Eustatius. You promised me, if I may remind you, a hundred louis semiannually for living expenses until Congress decided about me. I received the first instalment at the beginning of the year, but to survive until the end I need the second; should I apply to M. Grand in Paris?

Please send me a letter of recommendation, with names blank, in favor of a merchantman leaving Amsterdam for an American port. This would help good people who, on my advice, are taking this first venture in great secrecy.[2] Haste is required, for the vessel is almost loaded.⟩

Jonathan Williams, Jr., to the American Commissioners[3]

ALS: University of Virginia Library

⟨Passy, July 17, 1778: I appreciate your confidence in approving my drafts on Mr. Grand,[4] and am ready to account for them up to May 30; the expenses since I left Nantes will go on a new account. Might you not appoint some one to compare the bills and receipts with the charges, subject to your later approval?[5]⟩

2. Doubtless his business associates, de la Lande and Fynje (Finye): xxv, 700–1 n.

3. Published in Taylor, *Adams Papers*, VI, 304.

4. The commissioners as a whole had not approved them; only BF and JA had, conditionally, in their note to Grand of July 10.

5. The commissioners' request for JW's accounts (xxvi, 525–6) had plunged him into further difficulties. A severe illness had delayed his completing the accounts until the end of May when he took them with him to Passy; there he spent ten weeks in trying to get them accepted. Lee fought him every inch of the way—questioning his authority, demanding vouchers for everything, accusing him of private speculation with public funds. Hence JW's suggestion here of an independent audit. The commissioners did not answer him, and on Aug. 6 he informed them, below, that he would return to Nantes unless they ordered otherwise. Again he had no answer, and left on Aug. 10 with the whole matter unsettled. JW to Congress, Sept. 10, 1778, APS.

S. and J.-H. Delap to the American Commissioners

ALS or LS:[6] American Philosophical Society

Gentlemen   Bordeaux 18 July 1778.

We take the liberty of forwarding you Inclosed a Letter from Captn. William Hill Sargeant.[7] He informs us it is Requesting you to give him a letter of Marque Commission and that he has offered you our House as Guarantee that no improper use will be made of same. If this formality requisite and that you think us sufficient Security for any improprieties he may commit we beg leave to offer ourselves as such. We have the Honor to be very Respectfully Gentlemen Your obedient Humble Servants   S & JH Delap

To The Honble. B. Franklin Arth. Lee & Jno Adams Esqrs. Paris

Addressed: To / The Honble Benjamin Franklin / Arthur Lee, & / John Adams Esqrs. / Plenipotentiaries from the United States / of America at the Court of / Versailles

Notations in different hands: J & S H Delap Bordeaux 18 July 78 / reponder repondu

Rawlins Lowndes[8] to the American Commissioners

ALS: American Philosophical Society

Sirs,   Chas. Town So. Carolina. July 18th. 1778.

The State of South Carolina having Resolved to procure three Ships of War in foreign parts for the Protection of their

---

6. The text is in a different hand from the previous letter (XXVI, 425), either of which could have been written by the firm's surviving partner.

7. To the commissioners below, of this date.

8. A South Carolina lawyer, judge, and politician, who though conservative by temperament was loyal to and active in the state; at this time he was its president, succeeding John Rutledge. For his career see the *DAB* and Carl J. Vipperman, *The Rise of Rawlins Lowndes, 1721–1800* (Columbia, S.C., [1978]).

Coast and Trade, Have intrusted that Service to their Commodore, Alexander Gillon Esqr. a Zealous and approved Friend to the American States, who embarkes for France with some other Officers to manage that Business.[9]

The Legislature have appropriated to this Use the Sum of £500,000. Currency; And Goods and Effects purchased here to that Amount have been partly exported, and the remainder will soon be exported to France. But it is feared that the danger of Capture, the heavy Charge on Shiping, and the loss on the Sale of our produce, will reduce the Net proceeds in France considerably below the sum wanted. To Guard against the disappointment that would be Occasioned by these Contingencies, Mr. Gillon is furnished with the proper Credentials to enable him on the Faith and Credit of the Country to Negociate a Loan in Europe sufficient to make up any deficiency that may happen in the Sum granted that he may as soon as possible carry into Effect the intention of the State in procuring the said Armament.

I am therefore in behalf of the State of South Carolina, to request the favour of your Assistance and Countenance to Mr. Gillon, to give weight and success to his Application in a measure so interesting, and of such publick Utility to the United States in general, and to this in particular, for which purpose I take the Liberty of Introducing him to your Patronage and protection; And am with the greatest Respect and Regard Sirs Your Excellencies Most Obedient and Most humble Servants

RAW. LOWNDES

Their Excys, The Commissioners, representing the United American States, at Foreign Courts.

Notation: Raw Lowndes Charlestown 10. [*sic*] juillet 1778.

9. See Middleton's letter above, July 4. Gillon's other officers were three captains commissioned at the same time that he was, John Joyner, John McQueen, and William Robertson: Charles O. Paullin, *The Navy of the American Revolution* ... (Cleveland, Ohio, 1906), p. 435.

William Hill Sargeant to the American Commissioners[1]

ALS: American Philosophical Society

⟨Bordeaux, July 18, 1778: I lately arrived in a fast-sailing vessel from Virginia. The owners could not arm her there and gave me power to do so here; I therefore ask a commission for that purpose. During most of the war I served the state in a small trading ship. When she was condemned I took command of the *Dispatch*, a brigantine with eight four-pounders and a crew of twenty-five owned by St. George Tucker of Williamsburg.[2] Mr. Delap will stand security for me.[3] I should have visited you by now, to pay my respects and learn whether you had stores for the ship, if I had not had such trouble in keeping order among an American crew in this port. I shall be ready to sail in a week or so, and will await your orders.⟩

Sartine to the American Commissioners: Two Letters[4]

Copies: Library of Congress (two of each), Massachusetts Historical Society

I.

⟨Versailles, July 18, 1778, in French: Letters from Lorient tell of the trouble between the commander of the *Boston* and the French volunteers and sailors in his crew, of whom twenty-eight—twenty-five volunteers and three apprentices—have

1. Published in Taylor, *Adams Papers*, VI, 305–6. Sargeant was a privateer captain, later listed as a Philadelphian, who remained in the business for years before returning to the command of merchant ships: Charles H. Lincoln, ed., *Naval Records of the American Revolution* . . . (Washington, D.C., 1906), pp. 254, 400; Boyd, *Jefferson Papers*, IX, 645; X, 101–2.
2. The young lawyer who had gone home to Bermuda in 1775, and was now back in Virginia: XXII, 164–5; see also the *DAB*.
3. See the Delap firm to the commissioners of this date above, in which Sargeant's letter was enclosed.
4. A translation is published in Butterfield, *John Adams Diary*, IV, 166–7. One phrase, omitted in the translation of the first letter, we have supplied in our summary.

been sent ashore. Their grievance was against the first lieutenant and two other officers, who apparently mistreated them.
The facts came to the notice of the commissary and of M. de
La Touche de Tréville, *chef d'escadre*, who put in at Lorient in
the course of operations. The latter had also personal complaints, which he put before the Captain on boarding the frigate. When the men were landed the Captain did what he could
to restore their possessions, which had been pillaged by the
crew; they had difficulties, however, over their treatment.
They claim shares in two prizes sent to Lorient, but not in two
others sent to America. They were specifically enlisted in Bordeaux for a cruise, which the Captain insists extended to Boston; that was not, they say, in the articles. You should give
orders in the matter to avoid the expense of taking it to the
admiralty court. Let me know what you want done, so that I
may tell the commissary. He writes that he has offered the
Captain all possible facilities for enlisting new volunteers.

P.S. Mr. Schweighauser informs me that his agent in Brest[5] is
having trouble with the admiralty in selling the *Ranger*'s
prizes. I am writing to have the trouble stopped, and am so
informing Mr. Schweighauser.⟩

II.

⟨Versailles, July 18, 1778, in French: Several American vessels,
inactive in French ports, might be put to use in the common
cause. Our mutual interest will doubtless lead you to give the
necessary orders.⟩

Thomas Simpson to the American Commissioners

ALS: American Philosophical Society

May it please your Honours   Nantes 18th. July 1778.
    I wrote you by Captain Niles, that on receiving an answer
from Captain Whipple, I shou'd immediately follow his in-

5. Berubé de Costentin: see the commissioners' letter of Aug. 15.

structions, his letter came to hand the 12th, I embarked at Brest the 15th. and arrived here the 17th Instant, and am now to proceed for America in the Providence, where I hope to have the pleasure of being immediately bro't to trial.[6] I tho't my indispensible duty to inform you in what manner I have proceeded, And am Your Honours Most Obedient, Very humble Servant   THOM SIMPSON

Honourable the American Commissioners At Passi

Addressed: The Honourable Commissioners / for the United States of America / At / Passi

Notation: Lieut Simpson Nantes 18 July 78

From Ferdinand-François-Théodore-Joseph Pollart d'Hérimez[7]

ALS: American Philosophical Society

Monsieur   Ath, en hainaut autrichien, ce 18 juillet 1778

Des ordres de ma Cour en precipitant mon depart, m'ont privé du précieux avantage de prendre les votres. Je viens m'en dedommager, s'il est possible, par vous reiterer tous les sentimens qu'a tant de titres vous savez inspirer, et vous offrir mes services, si j'etois assez heureux de vous etre bon en quelque chose en ces quartiers. Le jour ou je pourrai vous obliger, Monsieur, sera bien assurement un des plus beaux de ma vie. J'apprends que l'escadre du m[arqui]s Destain est arrivee a Boston, et que philadelphie est evacuée, confirmez moi, je vous prie, cette important nouvelle, et ne me laissez pas ignorer aucun evenement qui concourt a assurer la liberté de vos freres; vous sçavez s'il me tarde de voir votre ouvrage couronnê: j'attends cette faveur de votre amitie, a laquelle j'ai quelque droit de pretendre, par l'attachement sincere et res-

6. Simpson did not hear of his appointment to command the *Ranger* until several days later; see his letter below, July 27.

7. The last châtelain (1754–94) of Ath, in the Austrian Netherlands. Some details about his life are to be found in a book about his daughter: A. Louant, *Une épistolière en Hainaut* . . . (Société des Bibliophiles belges, no. 46, Mons, 1970). From information kindly provided by C. Wyffels, Archivist-General of Belgium.

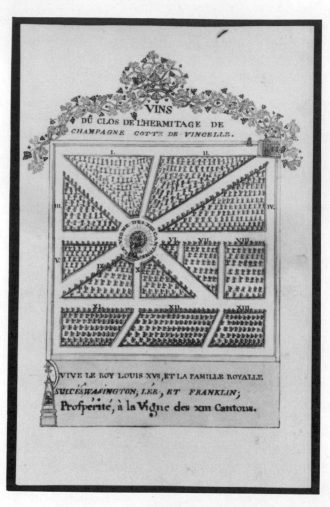

La Vigne des treize cantons

pectueux que je vous ai vouë. Ma femme me charge de vous
dire mille choses; je ne puis mieux vous les rendre qu'en vous
assurant qu'elle partage mes sentimens. Voici l'extrait d'une
Lettre que je viens de recevoir de notre armee, qui m'annonce
que la bombe est crevée.[8] Helas, en formant les voeux les plus
ardents, pour le succes des armes de l'auguste Souverain, que
nous idolatrons a si juste titre, nous gemissons avec vous,
Monsieur, sur les suites de cette guerre fatale. Le depart du
Courier m'empeche de m'etendre plus au long.[9] J'ai l'honneur
d'etre Monsieur Votre tres humble et tres obeissant serviteur

D'HERIMEZ
chatelain des villes et chatellenies d'ath

Endorsed: D'herimez

Notation: July 18. 79

From ——— Richelet   ALS: American Philosophical Society

L'hermitage de Chasseigne les Dormans
Monsieur   en champagne le 18 juillet 1778
   Je suis retirez du monde, et je n'en connois pas les usages:
je ne sais de nouvelles, que par une gazette de tous les mois.
   Ne soïez donc pas surpris Monsieur, si je ne vous donne pas
la qualité, que vous avez peutêtre a la Cour.
   Les gazettes annonçent L'Union de 13 provinces de
l'Amerique: par l'Effet du hazard, le petit manoir que j'habitte
se trouve aussi distribué sur 13 cantons.
   Cette Singularité, Monsieur, m'a determinez à acceptér
l'offre d'un maitre d'ecolle, pour en lever le plan, et j'ose vous
l'offrir.
   Il n'i à q'une petite journée de poste, de Paris icy: sur la
belle routte de Strasbourg.
   Vous trouvant a portée de la Champagne, dont les vins sont
renommez: si vous voulez voir les cottes qui le produisent,

8. The enclosure, dated Nîmes, July 6, 1778, tells of the outbreak of
hostilities between Prussia and Austria.
9. D'Hérimez sent BF another letter on Nov. 26, 1781, to congratulate
him on the victory of Yorktown. APS.

j'ose vous offrir l'hermitage, pour i faire le sejour qu'il vous plairoit.

Si l'offre que je fais Monsieur, vous paraissoit temeraire, permettez-moi de vous dire que ce seroit la fautte des papiers publics: ils annonçent une noble Simplicite dans votre façon de vivre; une entiere abnégation de faste. Et interieurement j'ai pensez, que pouvant vous fournir de quoi logér un sécrétaire, un Valet de Chambre, deux laquais; vous offrir un bon pottage, et par extraordinaire pour vous, deux entrées, vous pouriez vous contenter.

Si j'erre Monsieur, pardonnez-le moy en faveur de la veneration que vos vertus m'ont inspirées.

Si le hazard, qui occasionne cette lettre Monsieur, faisoit aussi, que Vous connussiez quelq'habitan de l'amérique qui voulut revenir en france, et acheptér une terre: j'en connois plusieurs, et de differents prix, qu'on m'a confiez êtres a vendre, sans etres aux affiches: et j'indiquerois volontier a qui il faudroit s'adresser pour negocier, et même les propriétaires. Je suis avec respect Monsieur Votre tres humble et tres obeissant serviteur   RICHELET

Ne soiez point surpris Monsieur, si cette lettre n'est pas timbrée de Dormans. Je la fais mettre à une autre poste: parceque si par hazard encore, mon desir s'acomplissoit, et que vous vinssiez comme atendu, ou qu'on le soupconnat, vous pouriez être interompu par la foulle d'habitans qui vouderoïent vous voir.

Si vous voulez savoir quel je suis? Vous pouvez Monsieur, faire informer près de Monsieur l'abbé de Breteüil, chancelier de Monseigneur Le Duc D'Orleans:[1] Je crois qu'il voudera bien dire si on peut m'en croire.

Endorsed: Richelet Invitation

Notation: Dormans 18. juillet 1778.

1. Elizabeth-Théodose Le Tonnelier, abbé de Breteuil, was the uncle of the baron de Breteuil, the French Ambassador to Vienna, and had chosen the chancellorship in preference to the embassy in Rome and the bishopric of Rennes. He was reportedly a libertine and certainly a wit. When Louis XV offered him the Abbeys of Foix and then La Charité, he remarked that the King had not deprived him of hope. Jean Grassion and Frans Durif,

From Joseph Kendall

ALS: American Philosophical Society

Respected Sir, Nantes July 19th 1778

Since I had the Honor of seeing you I have influenced a Relation (while in England) to discharge all my pecuniary obligations there, and am now at liberty to offer myself to you to serve in any capacity you may think me capable of.[2] My profession is that of a Surgeon, but will exert myself with pleasure in any other line, to the utmost of my abilities. I have been here about a Week. I came by the way of Guernsey and Jersey, the latter of which I left the begining of this Month, in company with 5 Prissoners on board a Dutch Ship bound for the Isle of Brehae.[3] I am sorry to inform you of the number of Privateers fitted out of those Islands, and their success in distressing our trade; from the former there are 21, the latter 16 beside 3 upon the Stocks. The adventures from Guernsey have taken 24 Vessels, those of Jersey 16, their force is from 16 6 po[unders] and 80 Men to half that Number of both. But they have already engaged many more in case of a War with this Country which they are in daily expectation of and they seem'd so confident of commissions to take French property that they delay putting out to Sea till their Commissions are sign'd. The Fox[4] and another Frigate with a small cutter is now upon that station, they were orderd in consequence of a French Ship of force cruising off those Islands. They have no Milatary but the new rais'd Regment of Highlanders commanded by Lord McCloud.[5] They are divided between the 2

---

eds., *Marquis de Bombelles: Journal* ... (2 vols., Geneva, 1977–82), I, 69 n, 73; see also pp. 123, 127.

2. Kendall had applied to BF for assistance in January, before offering his services to the British (see xxv, 466 n). We have no evidence that this letter elicited a response, but in a memorandum to Congress on May 12, 1784, he testified that he had been continuously employed as surgeon in the U.S. service since 1778. National Archives.

3. Bréhat, a tiny island in the Channel.

4. The British frigate which had been captured and retaken the previous year. Nathan Miller, *Sea of Glory*, (New York, [1974]), pp. 228–30, 254.

5. Lord John MacLeod (1727–1789) raised two battalions of Highlanders which became the 73rd Foot. See Sir James Balfour Paul, ed., *The Scots Peerage* ... (9 vols., Edinburgh, 1904–14), III, 82.

Islands, they are as yet but little acquainted with dicipline and near ⅓ are Sick. The Militia are much worse tho' exercis'd daily, evry 12th. Man is upon Guard at Night, notwithstanding which I shou'd think it no difficult matter to land in the Night with 25 or 30 Men and destroy the Shipping. The Principal Pier is that of St. Hillaire, distant near half a Mile from the Town, containing 38 Vessels and guarded only by 2 Men. When the tide is ebb, the Water does not come within half a Mile of the Pier, on which I build the probability of success in the attempt.

There is now an American Prissioner there ready to cooperate in any Plan you may think eligible or if you will procure him the means of escaping from the Island, he will attempt what is here intimated. This Person is Captn. McKirdy of Maryland, he disired me to mention him in this Manner to you.[6] I have such an opinion of the practicability of the Plan, that I have no objection to make one of 30 who may be depended upon to attempt it. I shoud have wrote to you sooner to have offer'd myself, but I thought I might have been able to get out with the Fleet under the care of the Providence and the Boston, which I cannot accomplish for the want of Money to purchase necessaries. I have a Passage offerd me in the former of these Vessels, but I am in such want of Clothes, that I must wait till an opportunity offers to go as Surgeon, if I cannot get any other assistance. Might I presume to intrude once more upon you, I shou'd be happy to recieve the means of getting either immediatly to America or into the Continental employ on board one of their Ships in France. The Ship will I beleive not sail till the begining of the next Week and if you will be so kind as to serve me by that time I shall ever acknowlege it as the greatest obligation, confer'd on Sir Your most obedient Humble Servant   JOSEPH KENDALL

Before I left London I informd Mr. Wharton of my wishes,

6. John McKirdy, who later commanded the Maryland schooner *Dove*. Charles Henry Lincoln, ed., *Naval Records of the American Revolution 1775–1788* . . . (Washington, 1906), p. 276.

and of my inability to get here, this however I have accomplis'd, but with many difficulties—for the rest I must wait the event.

Addressed: To His Excellency / Benjamin Franklin Esqr. / Ambassador from the United States / of N. America to the Court of/ Versailles

Endorsed: B. Kendal

From John Spencer   ALS: American Philosophical Society

Sir,   Nantz 19 July 1778

The Inclosed is a letter deliverd me when at Plymouth by a Capt. of the 1st Battalion of Georgia Continental Troops.[7] He has no doubt Painted his Sittuation to your Excellency, I need not theirfore take any notice on that head but Could Wish to have Every Relief Aforded him that Your Excellency Shall think Most Proper. I Remain With Respect Your Excellencys most Humble Servant &c.   JOHN SPENCER

Addressed: To His Excellency Benjamin Franklin Esqr. / Ambassador from the United States / of America[8] / a passÿ pres paris

Endorsed: Spencer

Notation: De B. De versailles

7. La Plaigne (above, July 11): for the letter Spencer is carrying see XXVI, 688–9.

8. Here is crossed out "to the Court of Versailles"; what follows is in a different hand.

The American Commissioners to the President of Congress[9]

AL (draft):[1] Massachusetts Historical Society; three copies and one transcript: National Archives

⟨Passy, July 20, 1778: The *Spy* brought us the ratified treaties with France. On the 17th we exchanged ratifications with the count de Vergennes; copies are enclosed.[2] War is not yet declared but hostilities have already commenced, the British and French fleets are at sea, and we hourly expect news of an encounter.[3] The Spanish treasure fleet has arrived but we still do not know Spain's real intentions. It seems highly probable she will join in a French war against Britain.[4] A war in Germany between the King of Prussia and the Emperor seems inevitable. We are doing all we can to obtain a loan and have a prospect of obtaining in Amsterdam some but not all of what is needed.[5] We ask Congress to be as sparing as possible in drawing on us. We enclose a copy of a letter from Mr. de Sartine.[6] Vergennes has agreed to drop articles eleven and twelve from the Treaty of Commerce as we understand you wish. Please send as soon as possible instructions and authorization for this. We recommend that Dumas be given at least £200 st. per year for his services. Although we have received congressional authorization to appoint commercial agents, Congress may wish instead to use the authority given it by

9. Published in Butterfield, *John Adams Diary*, IV, 168–70, with additional annotation in Taylor, *Adams Papers*, VI, 306–7.
1. In the hands of JA and Lee.
2. A copy of the French ratification of the Treaty of Commerce is at Harvard University Library; for the American ratification see *JCC*, XI, 462–3.
3. The French fleet with 32 ships of the line had sailed on July 10, the British with a slightly smaller number the following day: Dull, *French Navy*, 120–2; W.M. James, *The British Navy in Adversity: a Study of the War of American Independence* (London, 1926), pp. 125–7.
4. The commissioners were too optimistic. The Spaniards used their neutrality in an unsuccessful attempt to coax concessions from Britain: Dull, *French Navy*, 126–31. For the arrival of the treasure ships see *ibid.*, p. 127 n.
5. See XXVI, 338–9 n.
6. Above, July 14.

the commercial treaty to appoint consuls. At present the only commercial agents are John Bondfield at Bordeaux and J.D. Schweighauser at Nantes, both appointed by William Lee.[7]⟩

To Dumas

Abstract: Parke-Bernet catalogue (1963)[8]

⟨Passy, July 20, 1778: Franklin notifies Dumas of the ratification at Versailles of the Treaty of Alliance and the Treaty of Amity and Commerce[9] and authorizes him to "communicate the Treaty of Commerce to M. le Grand Pensionnaire."[1]⟩

Dumas to the American Commissioners[2]

ALS: American Philosophical Society; AL (draft): Algemeen Rijksarchief

⟨The Hague, July 21, 1778, in French: I have just received, translated and delivered a German letter to the Grand Facteur. The States General have adjourned and the Prince[3] is leaving for Los in Overyssel. No new instructions were given Count Welderen[4] concerning the British capture of two Dutch ships carrying tobacco for Messrs. Hope who are on good terms

7. The commissioners also recommended Americans be appointed as consuls and enclosed a memoir on their functions (Wharton, *Diplomatic Correspondence*, II, 652–3). The authorization to name commercial agents is given in XXV, 639–40; Bondfield's and Schweighauser's appointments are discussed at length in vol. XXVI. A third agent, Andrew Limozin, was chosen at Le Havre at the same time, but appears not to have exercised his powers: Ford, *Letters of William Lee*, II, 408.
8. Session of December 3: p. 19 of catalogue 2235.
9. See the preceding document.
1. Three weeks earlier Dumas had shown the Grand Pensionary van Bleiswijk the treaty but had not permitted him to retain a copy: XXVI, 691–2.
2. Published in Taylor, *Adams Papers*, VI, 307–8.
3. For the Grand Facteur, the Prince, and the States General see our annotation of Dumas to the commissioners, July 3.
4. Jan Walraad, graaf van Welderen, Dutch minister plenipotentiary at the court of St. James: *Repertorium der diplomatischen Vertreter*, II, 245.

with the British ministry. I am sending an article on the subject to the *Courier du Bas-Rhin*. The Grand Facteur has confirmed the capture of a British frigate by the French fleet.)

Hezekiah Ford[5] to the American Commissioners

ALS: American Philosophical Society

Honoured Sirs   Jersey. July. 21st. 1778
  In my Passage to Virginia, on Board a small Cutter, I had the Misfortune to be taken, and carried into Jersey. And as you are perfectly acquainted with my Sentiments (which I am still immoveably determined to retain, let the Consequences be what they will) I hope you will excuse the Freedom I have taken in solliciting your further Favours.
  Among the Passengers taken and brought in here, are, Mr. Channing and Lady, Mr. Blake, Mr. Harris, and Mr. Gilbank, of, and bound to, South Carolina. And Mr. Maury of, and bound to, Virginia.[6] We are under the disagreeable Necessity of going to England: from whence we shall take the earliest Opportunity to return. I have the Honour to be, Gentlemen Your Most Obedient Most Obliged, and very Humble Servant
                                                        H: FORD

Their Excellencies, Franklin, Lee, & Adams.

Notation: H Ford Jersey 21 July. 1778.

  5. The clergyman (XXVI, 615 n) had recently announced his intention of returning to America aboard the frigate *Providence* (*ibid.*, 701), but must have had an ill-considered change of mind.
  6. John Channing, Esq. had lived in England with his wife since 1769: *South Carolina Hist. and Geneal. Mag.*, XXI (1920), 14. For Mrs. Channing, the widow of John Izard, a relative of Ralph, see *ibid.*, LXX (1969), 96 n. William Blake is identified above, XXVI, 40 n. For Lieutenant John Gilbank of the 4th South Carolina Artillery (d. 1780), see Francis B. Heitman, *Historical Register of the Officers of the Continental Army* . . . (rev. ed.; Baltimore, 1932), p. 247, and his letter of Nov. 4, below. Maury is mentioned above, XXV, 454 n; in October Ford drew on him for 144 *l.t.*: Taylor, *Adams Papers*, VI, 361. Harris eludes us.

Musco Livingston to the American Commissioners[7]

ALS: American Philosophical Society

⟨Nantes, July 21, 1778: I arrived here last night, delivered my letters to Captain Whipple[8] and shall leave immediately for Lorient with his instructions for Captain Tucker.

I would be exceedingly obliged for a certificate or brief letter to the president of Congress mentioning what Captain Tucker said of my conduct aboard the *Boston*. I will return to Nantes in five or six days from whence I expect to obtain passage for America. If you send a letter here under cover to John Lloyd[9] I will be sure to receive it.⟩

From Heathcote Muirson[1]

ALS: Historical Society of Pennsylvania

Sir   Forton Prison July 21st 1778

The unfortunate situation I am in, I beg leave to make as an apology for my troubling you to peruse the following, unhappy, anecdote of my life.

I am the youngest son of Doctr. George Muirson of Suffolk County Long Island; and connected in the family of Doctr. Joshua Babcock of Westerly, whose son Mr. Adam Babcock married a sister of mine.[2] I early engaged in the service of my

---

7. Published in Taylor, *Adams Papers*, VI, 308.

8. Certainly the commissioners' letter of July 16 to Whipple and possibly those of that date to Simpson and/or Schweighauser.

9. A merchant identified in XXIII, 320 n.

1. A 1776 graduate of Yale College, Muirson had been committed to Forton Prison on July 4. He escaped and was paid 240 *l.t.* by the commissioners in February, 1779; by 1780 he had returned to America, where he was killed the next year while taking part in an expedition against a British fort on Lloyd's Neck, Long Island. Franklin B. Dexter, *Biographical Sketches of the Graduates of Yale College . . .* (6 vols., New York and New Haven, 1885–1912), III, 624–5; William R. Cutter, "American Prisoners at Forton Prison, England, 1777–1779," *New-England Hist. and Geneal. Register*, XXXIII (1879), p. 38; Alphabetical List of Escaped Prisoners.

2. George Muirson was a physician well known as a practitioner of inoculation by mercury; see XI, 356 n. Joshua Babcock, BF's old acquaintance,

Country, (contrary to the express orders of my Father and family, who, have positively refus'd me evry kind of support, so long as I continue in the Rebel service, as they please to term it.) In Octr. 1776, I was made a prisoner by Genl. Carlton on Lake Champlain, then acting as Capt. of Marines on board the fleet commanded by Genl. Arnold, and was permitted to return home upon my *Parole*, where I remaind a prisoner untill April 1778. I have been repeatedly solicited by my father and friends to return to them, making me evry offer they thought probable would tempt me, and even went so far as to procure me a pardon from Govr. Tryon,[3] (on the supposition that I was to deny the service of my country,) which I receiv'd, and destroy'd. Immediately after my exchange, I engaged in my former capacity on board the Brigantine Angelica of 16 Guns and ninety eight men, William Dennis Esqr. commander.[4]

We sailed from Boston 25th. of May, and had been at sea only five days, when we fell in with and were captured by the Andromeda frigate from Philadelphia, Genl. Howe being on board bound for England.[5]

We were brought to Spit Head, and after undergoing a ceremonious tryal, were committed as Pirates to this dismal Prison.

I have no desire Sir to boast of my Pedigree or connections, I only wish modestly to inform you who I am, thinking most probably you may have been acquainted with the persons or Characters of those I have mentioned, and by this means introduce myself to your Honor as a person destitute of friends and in want of almost evry necessary of life. It will be needless to enter into a long detail of my treatment. It is too much to

---

had last written in May; Adam was the third of his four sons: xxvi, 548–52; ix, 397 n.

3. William Tryon, last royal governor of New York, for whom see the *DAB*.

4. Capt. Dennis, a Rhode Islander, soon escaped from prison: Kaminkow, *Mariners*, p. 53 (where his name is given as William Davis).

5. Howe returned to England aboard the *Andromeda* after turning over his command to Sir Henry Clinton.

say that I was rob'd of evry thing except the clothes I had upon me; which obliges me to make my complaint in this channel and humbly ask your assistance.

If it is in your power Sir to give me any releif, either in effecting my exchange, or by any means conveying me a sum of money, I will obligate myself to remit the value of the same agreable to your Order.

At present I have very little fortune except what is in the Enemies possession on Long Island; Yet happily for me my brother in Law grants me evry thing I want which will enable me to answer evry obligation your Honor may please to lay me under. I am Sir with the greatest Respect Your Honors most Obedient Humble Servant   HEATHCOTE MUIRSON

His Excellency Benjamin Franklin

Addressed: His Excellency / Benja. Franklin Esqr Paris

Endorsed: Heathcot Muirson Prisoner

The American Commissioners to Sartine

AL (draft):[6] Massachusetts Historical Society; copy: National Archives

⟨Passy, July 22, 1778: We have received your letters of July 15 and 18. Niggins and Selby are unknown to us, but unless something appears to invalidate their story please grant their request. We are sorry for the dispute between two officers of the *Boston* and some French crewmen. Captain Tucker has sent us his account of the incident.[7] We believe that if the sailors enlisted to go to Boston they should return to the ship; if not, they have the right to leave and are entitled to their wages. We will write this to Captain Tucker.[8] We have ordered all our frigates to sail immediately.⟩

6. In the hand of JA with interlineations by Arthur Lee. The letter is published in Taylor, *Adams Papers,* VI, 309–10.

7. Which the commissioners summarize. They also enclosed a copy of the statement by satisfied French crewmen of the *Boston* mentioned in Tucker's letter to the commissioners, July 14.

8. See the commissioners' letter of the same day to Tucker.

The American Commissioners to Schweighauser

AL (draft): Massachusetts Historical Society; three copies: National Archives

Sir, Passi July 22 1778

Captain Robert Niles of the Spy at Brest,[9] has occasion for fourteen or fifteen Tons of Lead, which you will be so good as to order on board his Vessell, and if he should request any other Articles to make up a Cargo for the united States you will please to order them on board, out of those Merchandises or Arms &c. which you have on hand. We are

Please to send Us a List of the Articles you receive from Mr. Williams.

Mr. Schweighauser

P.S. Capt. Niles's Vessell has incured some Expence at Brest, which We desire you will discharge.

The American Commissioners to Jonathan Trumbull

AL (draft):[1] Library of Congress; copies: Massachusetts Historical Society, National Archives (two)

Sir, Passy, July 22. 1778

We received your Excellency's Letter of May 29. by Capt. Niles[2] with the Dispatches from Congress which you had intrusted him with, in good Order. He had a short Passage of 22 Days, and brought us the agreable News of the Ratification of the Treaties and of their being universally pleasing to our Country. We shall order some Lead to be shipt on board his Vessel, and have furnished him with the Money you mention, in ready Compliance with your Request. We are with great

---

9. For the arrival of the *Spy* see Simpson to the commissioners, July 3. Robert Niles is identified in xxvi, 539 n; the same letter explains this request for lead.

1. In BF's hand. The Mass. Hist. Soc. copy is published in Taylor, *Adams Papers*, vi, 310–11.

2. Above, xxvi, 539.

Esteem and Respect, Sir, Your Excellency's most obedient humble Servants.

His Excelly. Jonath Trumbull Esqr Governor of Connecticut.

Notation: To Jon. Trumbull by Capt. Niles. of the Spy. July 22. 1778.

The American Commissioners to Samuel Tucker[3]

LS:[4] Harvard University Library; AL (draft): Massachusetts Historical Society; two copies: National Archives

⟨Passy, July 22, 1778: If the French sailors enlisted in your books are to go to Boston, they should return to the ship and receive their due in wages and prize money. Otherwise, the cruise being complete, they are entitled to collect what is owed them, deducting advances, and to depart. We order your strict attention to the just treatment of Frenchmen under your command, handicapped by unfamiliarity with our language and customs. P.S. If these men insist on leaving regardless of their commitment to continue to Boston, concede to their wishes but deny them wages and prize money.⟩

To James Lovell

LS:[5] National Archives, American Philosophical Society; copy and transcript: National Archives; copy: Harvard University Library

Sir,   Passy, July 22. 1778.
  I received your Favour of May 15. and was glad to find that mine of Decr. 21. had come to hand. Mr. Deanes Brother writes that it was not signed, which was an accidental Omis-

3. Published in Taylor, *Adams Papers*, VI, 311.
4. In the hand of WTF.
5. The first of these, from which we print, is in WTF's hand; the other, although signed, is labeled "Copy."

sion.[6] Mr. Deane himself is I hope with you long before this time, and I doubt not but every Prejudice against him is removed. It was not alone upon the Proceedings of Congress I formed my Opinion that such Prejudices existed.[7] I am glad to understand that Opinion was groundless, and that he is like to come back with Honour, in the Commission to Holland, where Matters are already so ripe for his Operations, that he cannot fail (with his Abilities) of being Useful.[8] You mention former Letters of the Committee by which we might have seen the Apprehensions of the Resentment of Foreign Officers, &c. Those Letters never came to hand. And we on our Part are amazed to hear that the Committee had had no Line from Us for near a Year, during which we had written I believe five or six long and particular Letters, and had made it a Rule to send triplicates of each, and to replace those that we happened to hear were lost, so that of some there were 5 Copies sent:[9] and as I hear that Capt. Young is arrived who had some of them, I think it probable that one at least of each must have come to your hands before this time:[1] Mr. Deane's Informations however, may supply the Want of them; whose Arrival, as he went with a strong Squadron of Men of War, is more likely than that of this Vessel, or any single one by whom we might send more Copies. The Affair with Mr. Beaumarchais will be best settled by his Assistance after his return. We find it recom-

6. BF's letter and Lovell's reply are above, XXV, 329–30; XXVI, 461–3. We have not found Simeon Deane's letter, apparently written after his arrival in America in mid-April: XXVI, 300.

7. Silas Deane had reached Philadelphia only ten days before: *Deane Papers*, II, 471–2. BF had defended him in his earlier letter to Lovell; the response here to a comment of Lovell's seems to be a reference to Arthur Lee's hostility to his former colleague.

8. See Lovell's May 15 letter. Deane's proposed commission to the Netherlands disappeared during the lengthy controversy in Congress over his finances.

9. See, for example, XXIV, 514–15 n, describing the fate of the five copies of the commissioners' letter of Sept. 8, 1777. Other letters not received include those of March 15–April 9, May 25, May 26, October 7 and November 30, 1777 (XXIII, 466–76; XXIV, 73–7, 79–82; XXV, 40–3, 207–14).

1. Young arrived although his ship was lost: XXIV, 514–15 n; XXV, 214 n.

mended to us, but we know too little of it to be able to do it well without him.

There has been some Inaccuracy in sending Us the last Dispatches of the Committee. Two Copies of the Contract with Mr. Francy, and the Invoices, came by the same Vessel, Capt. Niles.[2] And tho' one of your Letters mentions sending inclosed a Resolution of Congress relative to two Articles of the Treaty, that Resolution is not come to hand.[3] There are Circumstances in the Affair of those Articles, that make them in my Opinion of no Consequence if they Stand, while the proposing to abrogate them, has an unpleasing Appearance, as it looks like a Desire of having it in our Power to make that Commercial kind of War, which no honest State can begin, which no good Friend or Neighbour ever did or will begin, which has always been consider'd as an Act of hostility that provoked as well as justify'd Reprisals, and has generally produced such as have render'd the first Project as unprofitable as it was unjust. Commerce among Nations as well as between Private Persons should be fair and equitable, by *Equivalent* Exchanges, and mutual Supplies. The taking unfair Advantage of a Neighbour's Necessities, tho' attended with a temporary Success, always breeds ill Blood. To lay Duties on a Commodity exported which our Friends want, is a Knavish Attempt to get something for Nothing. The Statesman who first invented it, had the Genius of a Pickpocket; and would have been a Pickpocket if Fortune had suitably plac'd him. The Nations who have practis'd it have suffer'd for it fourfold, as Pickpock-

2. Jean-Baptiste-Lazare Théveneau de Francy, Beaumarchais' secretary, had signed, on his master's behalf, a contract with the commerce committee. It was intended to resolve the dispute over payment to Beaumarchais' company, Roderigue Hortalez & Cie., for arms supplied the United States: XXII, 454; XXVI, 475. Francy became acquainted with most members of Congress. In a breach of confidentiality Lovell handed him all the letters sent by the commissioners to the committees of secret correspondence and foreign affairs between Dec. 6, 1776 and Feb. 16, 1778. Francy made extracts which he sent Beaumarchais: Morton, *Beaumarchais Correspondance*, IV, 180, 208.

3. See commissioners to the president of Congress, July 20.

ets ought to suffer. Savoy by a Duty on exported Wines lost the Supplying of Switzerland, which thenceforth raised its own Wine; and (to wave other Instances) Britain by her Duty on exported Tea, has lost the Trade of her Colonies. But as we produce no Commodity that is peculiar to our Country, and which may not be obtained elsewhere, the Discouraging the Consumption of ours by Duties on Exportation, and thereby encouraging a Rivalship from other Nations in the Ports we trade to, is absolute Folly, which is indeed mixed more or less with all Knavery.[4] For my own Part if my Protest were of any Consequence, I should Protest against our ever doing it even by way of Reprisal. It is a Meanness with which I would not dirty the Conscience or Character of My Country. The Objections stated against the last of the two Articles had all been made and consider'd here; and were sent I imagine from hence by one who is offended that they were not thought of weight sufficient to stop the signing of the Treaty, 'till the King should in another Council reconsider those Articles, and after agreeing to omit them order new Copies to be drawn, tho' all was then ready engross'd on Parchment as before settled.[5] I did not think the Articles of much Consequence; but I thought it of Consequence that no Delay should be given to the signing of the Treaty after it was ready. But if I had known that those Objections would have been sent to the Committee I should have sent the Answers they received, which had been Satisfactory to *all* the Commissioners when the Treaty was settled and untill the Mind of one of them was alter'd by the Opinion of two other Persons.[6] 'Tis now too late to send those Answers. But I wish for the future if such a Case should again happen,

4. The proposed articles would have prohibited France from putting export duties on molasses shipped from the West Indies to America and America from putting export duties on any goods shipped to the French West Indies. BF's long-standing advocacy of free commercial exchange is discussed in George Stourzh, *Benjamin Franklin and American Foreign Policy* (2nd ed.; Chicago, [1969]), 108–10.

5. Arthur Lee's objections had threatened to delay the signing of the treaties: XXV, 559, 563–4, 570–1.

6. William Lee and Ralph Izard, who influenced Arthur Lee to raise his objections; Izard was still exercised over the treaties: Wharton, *Diplomatic Correspondence*, II, 661–3.

that Congress would acquaint their Commissioners with such partial Objections, and hear their Reasons, before they determine that they have done wrong. In the mean time this is only to you in private: It will be of no use to communicate it, as the Resolution of Congress will probably be received and executed before this Letter comes to hand.

Speaking of Commissioners in the plural puts me in mind of enquiring if it can be the Intention of Congress to keep *three* Ambassadors at this Court; we have indeed *four* with the Gentleman intended for Tuscany, who continues here, and is very angry that he was not consulted in making the Treaty which he could have mended in several Particulars; and perhaps he is angry with some Reason if the Instructions to him do, as he says they do, require us to consult him.[7] We shall soon have a *fifth*, for the Envoy to Vienna not being received there, is, I hear returning hither.[8] The necessary Expence of maintaining us all, is, I assure you enormously great: I wish the Utility may equal it: I imagine every one of us spends nearly as much as Lord Stormont did.[9] It is true he left behind him the Character of a Niggard; and when the Advertisement appear'd for the Sale of his Household Goods, all Paris laughed at an Article of it, perhaps very innocently express'd, *Une grande quantité du Linge de Table,* QUI N'A JAMAIS SERVI— *Cela est très vraisemblable,* say they, *car il n'a jamais donné à manger.* But as to our Number whatever Advantage there might be in the joint Counsels of three for framing and adjusting the Articles of the Treaty, there can be none in managing the common Business of a Resident here. On the Contrary, all the Advantages in negociation that result from Secrecy of Sentiment, and Uniformity in expressing it, and in common Business from Dispatch, are lost. In a Court too where every Word is watched and weighed, if a Number of Commissioners do not every one hold the same Language, in giving their Opin-

7. A strained reading of Izard's instructions: *JCC,* VIII, 521.
8. William Lee left in July for Frankfurt after his rebuff: Karl A. Roider, Jr., "William Lee, Our First Envoy in Vienna," *Va. Mag. of Hist. and Biog.,* LXXXVI (1978), 167.
9. David Murray, Lord Stormont, the British ambassador who had left Paris the preceding March.

ion on any publick Transaction, this lessens their Weight; and where it may be prudent to put on or avoid certain Appearances, of Concern, for Example, or Indifference, Satisfaction or Dislike, where the utmost Sincerity and Candour should be used and would gain Credit, if no semblance of Art shewed itself in the inadvertent Discourse perhaps of only one of them, the Hazard is in Proportion to the Number. And where every one must be consulted on every particular of common Business, in answering every Letter, &ca. and one of them is offended if the smallest thing is done without his Consent, the Difficulty of being often and long enough together, the different Opinions, and the time consumed in debating them, the Interruption by new Applicants in the time of meeting, &c. &c. occasion so much postponing and delay, that Correspondence languishes, Occasions are lost, and the Business is always behind hand. I have mentioned the Difficulty of being often and long enough together: This is considerable where they cannot be all accommodated in the same House: But to find three People whose Tempers are so good, and who like so well one anothers Company, and Manner of living and conversing, as to agree well themselves, tho' being in one House; and whose Servants will not by their Indiscretion quarrel with one another, and by artful misrepresentations draw their Masters in to take their Parts, to the Disturbance of necessary Harmony, these are Difficulties still greater and almost insurmountable. And in consideration of the whole I wish the Congress would separate Us.

The Spanish Galleons which have been impatiently expected are at length happily arrived. The Fleet and Army returning from Brasil is still out, but supposed to be on the Way homewards. When that and the South Sea Ships are arrived, it will appear whether Spain's Accession to the Treaty has been delayed for the Reasons given, or whether the Reasons were only given to excuse the Delay.[1]

The English and French Fleets of nearly equal Force are

1. The fleet and army were returning from the 1777 expedition against Portuguese Brazil: Dull, *French Navy*, pp. 63, 75, 127 n.

now both at Sea. It is not doubted but that if they meet there will be a Battle. For tho' England thro' Fear, Affects to Understand it to be still Peace, and would excuse the Depredations she has made on the Commerce of France by Pretences of illicit Trade &c. yet France considers the War as begun from the time of the King's Message to Parliament complaining of the Insult France had given by treating with Us, and demanding Aids to resent it, and the Answers of both Houses offering their Lives and Fortunes, and the taking several Frigates are deem'd indisputable Hostilities. Accordingly Orders are given, to all the Fleets and arm'd Ships to return Hostilities, and Encouragement is offered to Privateers &c.[2] An Ambassador from Spain is indeed gone to London, and joyfully received there in the Idea that Peace may be made by his Mediation. But as yet we learn nothing certain of his Mission, and doubt his effecting any thing of the kind.[3]

War in Germany seems to be inevitable, and this occasioning great Borrowings of Money in Holland and elsewhere, by the Powers concerned, makes it more Difficult for us to succeed in ours. When we engaged to Congress to pay their Bills for the Interest of the Sums they should borrow, we did not dream of their drawing on Us for other Occasions. We have already paid of Congress Drafts to return'd Officers 82,211 Livres and we know not how much more of that kind we have to pay, because the Committee have never let us know the Amount of those Drafts, or their Account of them never reached Us, and they still continue coming in. And we are now surprized with Advice of Drafts from Mr. Bingham to the Amount of 100,000 more.[4] If you reduce us to Bankruptcy here, by a Non Payment of your Drafts, consider the Consequences. In my humble Opinion, no Drafts should be made

2. These orders (July 10 on the part of France, July 19 and August 2 on the part of Britain) were the closest either government came to a formal declaration of war: *ibid.*, p. 120 n.

3. This ambassador, the marqués de Almodovar, had just held his first interview with secretary of state Weymouth: Manuel Danvila y Collado, *Reinado de Carlos III* (6 vols., Madrid, 1891–96), v, 10–11.

4. Above, XXVI, 300.

on us, without first learning from us, that we shall be able to answer them.

Mr. Beaumarchais has been out of Town ever since the Arrival of your Power to settle with him. I hope he will be able to furnish the Supplies mentioned in the Invoice and Contract. The Settlement may be much better made with the Assistance of Mr. Deane; we being not privy to the Transactions.

We have agreed to give Monsr. Dumas 200 Louis a year, thinking that he well deserves it.[5] With great Esteem, I have the honour to be, Sir, Your most obedient and humble Servant

B FRANKLIN

Mr. Lovell Honle. James Lovell Esqr.

Endorsed: July 22d 1778 to JL Doctr. Franklin recd. July 31st 1779. answd Aug 6th[6]

5. See Dumas to commissioners, July 17, and commissioners to the president of Congress, July 20.

6. Lovell had already received a copy of this letter (now missing) on July 27, which apparently bore the notation, "forwarded by J. Williams Nantes Feb. 25, 1779." Burnett, *Letters,* IV, 350, 353 n. On the basis of that notation, Lovell claimed that BF had "probably fabricated" his letter in the hope of vindicating Deane, whose inflammatory letter to the press of Dec. 5 had angered Congress: *Deane Papers,* IV, 41.

This accusation was unfounded, and seems especially unlikely in light of how little of the letter concerns Deane. But only part of the delay in sending it can be explained with certainty. BF, perhaps intending to reconsider some of its contents, did not forward it to JW until early November. At that time, the beleaguered JW was planning his return to America and intended to carry the letter himself. By Feb. 16, 1779, his plans had changed and JW entrusted BF's dispatches to Matthew Ridley, who was to sail "in about 10 Days," *i.e.* Feb. 25. JW to BF, Nov. 5 and Feb. 16, 1779 (APS).

142

James Moylan to the American Commissioners

ALS: Historical Society of Pennsylvania

Honorable Gentlemen L'Orient 22d. July 1778
Mr. Bingham of Martinico inclosed me the letter that accompanys this, which I received this post.[7] As I presume he gives you the necessary information of his department, it is needless for me to trouble you with the copy of his letter to me. I have therfore only to add that I am with respect Honorable Gentlemen Your assurd humble Servant   JAMES MOYLAN

The Honble. Plenepotentiary Ministers of the United States of America at Passy

Addressed: A Messieurs / Messieurs Les Ministres Plenepotentiaires / des Etats Unis de L'Amerique / à Passy

Notation: James Moylan. July 22. 1778.

From George McCall[8]

ALS: American Philosophical Society

Sir Glasgow July 22d. 1778.
I take the liberty to address you with a true Account of the situation of the Bearers Messrs. Lawrance and Robert Brooke, Sons of Richard Brooke Esqr. of Smithfield Virginia; He was pleased in the year 1770 to send these young Gentlemen to my care here for their Education, and they have applied with that attention to their studies, and behaved so remarkably well since that time that they will be a comfort and Credit to their Parent and Friends, and an honour to their own, or any other

---

7. Bingham's last three letters to the commissioners are those of March 5, May 29 and June 16 (XXVI, 49–51, 538–9, 627). Lacking his cover letter to Moylan we cannot be sure which letter Moylan was forwarding.

8. A member of a prominent mercantile family in Glasgow who became a burgess of the city in 1766 and was currently engaged in the tobacco trade. He had recently signed a merchants' petition urging settlement with America. Hardy B. McCall, *Memoirs of My Ancestors* ... (Birmingham, 1884), pp. 10–12; Theodore M. Devine, *The Tobacco Lords* ... (Edinburgh, [1975]), pp. 118, 182; Stevens, *Facsimiles*, XI, no. 1060.

country. And as they have now finished their Studies here are desirous to return to their Native Country via France as the most proper plan.[9]

My Sincere regard and duty to them demands my best services in their behalf, and as you have it most in your power to favour their intentions, I have ventur'd tho a Stranger to you (but having had the pleasure to enjoy some evenings in company with you in Virginia many years ago)[1] to give the foregoing just Acct. of Messrs. Brook as they may be almost without Acquantances in Paris.

This Address from a Person to whom you may be an utter Stranger at this time requires evidence of the verasity of what I write, and the only security that at present occurs for this not being fictitious, Is, that William Alexander late of Edinburgh and William Lee Esqrs. are acquanted with my handwrite and may have Opportunity of ascertaining this, and whether the Charecter I sustain be sufficient for you to trust my representation respecting Messrs. Brooke, the Bearers; taking for granted that you will be satisfied of the above I have only earnestly to recommend these Gentlemen to your favour for promoting their safe return to their Friends in Virginia or

9. The Brookes, who matriculated at the University of Glasgow in 1773 and are said to have studied in Edinburgh, had noteworthy careers. According to family records, BF appointed Lawrence surgeon on the *Bonhomme Richard*; he served under Jones in 1779 and 1780 before returning to Virginia in 1783 to practice medicine. His brother Robert was later prominent in Virginia politics, serving as governor and attorney general in the 1790's. St. George Tucker Brooke, "The Brooke Family," *Va. Mag. of Hist. and Biog.*, XVIII (1910), 454–5; XIX (1911), 320–4, 435–7; William I. Addison, *The Matriculation Albums of the University of Glasgow* . . . (Glasgow, 1913), p. 105; Morison, *Jones*, p. 203; Robert Sobel and John Raimo, eds., *Biographical Directory of the Governors of the United States, 1789–1978* (4 vols., Westport, Ct., [1978]), IV, 1624–5.

1. Presumably during one of BF's two visits on Post Office business, in 1756 and 1763.

doing them any other Service which they may Merit. I have
the honor to be Very Respectfully Sir Your most obedient Servant   GEORGE MCCALL
Honble. Benjamin Franklin Esqr.

Notation: Geo McCall Glasgow concg. Messrs Brooke July 22
1778

The American Commissioners to S. and J.-H. Delap

AL (draft): Massachusetts Historical Society; two copies: National Archives

Sir   Passy July 18 [*i.e.,* 23] 1778[2]
   Having the fullest Confidence in the Security you offer for
Captain William Hill Sergeant, We herewith enclose a blank
Bond for you to fill up, sign and return to us:[3] We enclose also
a Letter for Captain Sergeant with his Commission and In-
structions. We have the Honour to be with great Esteem &c.
                                                    F. L. A.

Messrs S. & J. H. Delap.

Franklin and John Adams to Arthur Lee

L:[4] Harvard University Library

[July 23, 1778][5]
Mr. A. Lee is desired to sign and return the enclosed if he
approves it.

2. The date as written (and repeated in the copies) is an obvious slip of
the pen; this letter is written in answer to Sargeant's of July 18, and en-
closes the commissioners' reply of the 23rd.
   3. The completed bond, dated August 19 and signed by Sargeant and
J.H. Delap is at the APS; for further details see Taylor, *Adams Papers,* VI,
305–6 n.
   4. In WTF's hand.
   5. Dated by its enclosure, the commissioners' letter to the president of
Congress, immediately following.

Addressed: A Monsieur / Monsieur Lee M.P.D.E.U.⁶ / a sa Maison / A Chaillot

Endorsed: Recd. from a Commissionaire on my way from Challiot to Paris, between 6 & 7 OC. in the Eveng., containing a Paper of which the enclosd is an exact Copy. A Lee July 24th. 1778. Returned unsignd at 8 OC. next morng.

Franklin and John Adams to the President of Congress⁷

LS:⁸ National Archives; copies: Harvard University Library,⁹ South Carolina Historical Society (two); transcript: National Archives

⟨Passy, July 23, 1778: We are informed by the Count de Vergennes that the British cabinet plans to offer independence to the United States if it will make a separate peace.¹ M. de Vergennes requests us to inform Congress that war between Britain and France, though not formally declared, is considered as having begun with the mutual withdrawal of ambassadors and hence the treaty with the United States is in full force.² He expects Congress's answer will be the same should a separate peace be proposed. We have expressed the opinion that you will unhesitatingly give such an answer even though you may not have been informed that war has begun and the treaty become binding.⟩

6. Ministre plénipotentiaire des Etats-Unis, a courtesy title.
7. Published in Taylor, *Adams Papers*, VI, 312.
8. In WTF's hand. Lee refused to sign: see the preceding document.
9. In Arthur Lee's hand.
1. A false rumor also prevalent in America: Weldon A. Brown, *Empire or Independence: A Study in the Failure of Reconciliation, 1774–1783* (University, La., 1941), p. 282.
2. A half-truth. Although with the withdrawal of ambassadors in March, 1778, both Britain and France prepared for military operations against each other, neither side wished to bear the diplomatic consequences of appearing the aggressor. This was the reason France had made her treaty with the United States eventual rather than immediate. In reality open hostilities had begun only in June. Jonathan R. Dull, *A Diplomatic History of the American Revolution* (New Haven and London, [1985]), pp. 97–9.

The American Commissioners to William Hill Sargeant

AL (draft): Massachusetts Historical Society; two copies: National Archives

Sir   Passi July 23. 1778

We herewith Send you the Commission you desire, and wish you good Success with it being your very humble servants   F. L. A.

To William Hill Sirgeant Commander of the Brigantine Dispatch, from Virginia

From the Comte de Conway[3]

ALS: American Philosophical Society

Sir   Paris rue vendome au marais ce 23 Juillet 1778

Your excelency will find here the weight and prices of the two pieces of brass Canon I had the honour to Speak to you off[4] which are to be Seen at Chevalier Darcy's[5] in your neighbourhood at fauw bourg du Roulle. I could wish as they are of the best kind and have been proved before his late Majesty that they may shute [suit] your need. As to the price I shall come into any measures you think proper.

I shall be much obliged to your excelency if youde let me know if you had any late news from america and when any Ship parts for that continent.

3. Gen. Conway's father, an Irish officer in the French service: Bodinier, *Dictionnaire*. "He seems," JA said of him, "a venerable Personage": Butterfield, *John Adams Diary*, II, 302–3.

4. The details, in a different hand, are on another sheet. One of the cannon was a four-pounder weighing 1,265 lbs. and the other an eight-pounder weighing 2,310; the cost of the copper, tin, and workmanship was also specified. The total price was 6,475 *l.t.*, to which Conway added in his own hand a 900 *l.t.* commission.

5. Comte Patrice d'Arcy (1725–79) was, like Conway, an Irishman, who came to Paris in 1739 and served in the War of the Austrian Succession and the Seven Years' War. He had been a member of the Académie royale des sciences since 1749, and became known for his *Essai sur l'artillerie* (1760) and other tracts. He was a close friend of J.-B. Le Roy. See also XXIII, 287.

My daughter[6] begs her kind Compliments to you your family and mr. adams and is as youle easily imagin impatient to know if there be any late acount from her husband. The favour of your answer Sir by my Servant bearer hereof will greatly oblige Sir your excelencys most humble and most obedient Servant   CONWAY

Endorsed: Conway Offering Cannon

Notation: 24. Juillet 1778.

To Champigny   ALS (draft): American Philosophical Society

Sir   Passy, July 24 1778

I have received your Letter of the 9th Instant, wherein you reproach me with breaking my Engagements to you, in not having paid you twenty one Ducats which you say I owe you, reminding me that while I charge Breach of Faith on the King respecting my Constituents I ought not to break mine to you, as private Engagements are more sacred than those of Sovereigns. I hold myself always ready to pay my just Debts, and shall pay this as soon as I am convinc'd it is of that kind. But as you have not favour'd me with your Account I know not how it arises. I have not here my Books [*interlined:* and Receipts relating to] that contain my Money Transactions and Expences while in England: But I remember that many years since a Gentleman of your Name, to whom I was entirely a Stranger, apply'd to me for a Subscription to a History of England which he propos'd to write. I consider'd the Affair as one of those genteel Methods by which Men of Letters are assisted when their Circumstances require Assistance, without being put to the Blush in being oblig'd to ask it as a Benevolence. In that Light I gave him perhaps two or three Guineas (I do not exactly remember the Sum) and took his Receipt promising the History, but without the least Expectation of ever seeing it. Accordingly I never enquired after it, I never

6. In fact his daughter-in-law, the Comtesse.

ask'd him for it. I had by me at the time near a Dozen such Receipts, for Books not yet printed, and many of them I believe never intended to be written. I have however lately received 2 *Volumes*, as they are Called of that History, and four Volumes of Histories of Sweden and Denmark which I never desired or heard of before. They are badly printed and so thin, as not to make more than two sizable Quarto Volumes when bound together, so that I cannot conceive them worth more than I have already paid. Nevertheless[7] I do not on that Account desire to keep them. Had you publish'd Your History of England within the Time you first promis'd to your Subscribers, I might possibly have lived to read it. But you broke your Engagement with me, and that long before you could have the least Pretence for accusing me, as you now do, of the same Crime, and I never complain'd of it. You have since made another Promise,[8] that from the Month of September 1777, (when the two first Volumes appear'd) two more should be publish'd every 5 Months. Ten Months are since elaps'd, and not one of the four Volumes due[9] has yet been heard of; so that I can have no Dependance on ever seeing the Work compleated. Besides I am now grown very old, have but little time left, and that is occupy'd with too much public Business to allow me any Leisure for the private Amusement of reading History. I request therefore that you would direct your Correspondent here to call for and receive back the 6 Volumes of different Histories you have sent me;[1] and I desire you would

7. BF wrote and deleted a different conclusion: "Nevertheless if you are the Person, and will be so good as to send me a Copy of my Subscription that I may know what I stand engag'd for, I shall take care to comply with it: But I request you would take again the Histories of Denmark and Sweden, and not put them into your Account; for my little Estate in America being in the Hands of our Enemies, I am now too poor to pay for all the Histories you may be capable of writing and translating; and that at so high a Price as 21 Ducats for two 4to Volumes unbound. I am, Sir, Your &c."

8. Apparently in a letter now missing.

9. Champigny had spoken of four volumes (XXIV, 399) and Quérard of a planned fifteen (*France littéraire*); but only the two ever appeared.

1. Presumably the three vols. of the *Histoire des rois de Dannemark*, the one-vol. *Histoire abrégée de Suède*, and the two vols. of the *Nouvelle histoire générale d'Angleterre*. See above, XXIV, 400 n.

accept what you formerly had of me, and believe me your
Welwisher and very humble Servant   BF

I return enclos'd your Receipts.[2]

Dumas to the American Commissioners[3]

ALS: American Philosophical Society; AL (draft): Algemeen Rijksarchief

⟨The Hague, July 24, 1778, in French: It is reported that
France has declared war on England,[4] causing the British
stocks to decline in Amsterdam. It is also reported the British
have released the Dutch ships they captured. Thank you for
forwarding me the packet from the committee of secret correspondence. I will continue to do all I can to add to our friends
and weaken the enemy. On Monday[5] I may perhaps deliver
the treaty to the Grand Pensionary; I will also send it to Amsterdam. Two copies are being made; on French instructions
articles 11 and 12 will be eliminated.[6]⟩

2. If BF thought that this bristling rejoinder would bring matters to a
close, he was wrong. Champigny wrote him three more times. The first
letter, of Aug. 10, reaffirmed that BF was honor-bound to pay at least for
the history of England. If he chose to return the history of Denmark, his
debt—to be paid to the bearer—would amount to only 12 ducats. Later
that day, Champigny, claiming to have just received this letter, wrote again
and stressed that far from having extended mere charity, back in England,
the American had pledged himself to become a subscriber. On Oct. 22, a
last attempt was made to extract the 12 ducats Champigny still felt were his
due. The outcome is unknown. All three letters are at the APS.
3. Published in Taylor, *Adams Papers*, VI, 313–15.
4. Neither France nor Britain ever issued a formal declaration of war.
5. July 27.
6. The two articles of the Treaty of Amity and Commerce that the
United States and France had agreed to drop.

From de Reine ALS: American Philosophical Society

Monsieur le docteur   a versailles le 24. juillet 1778.

A l'instant je recois une lettre de la nouvelle Orleans en date du 29. mars dernier, par laquelle le chevalier d'Erneville[7] le premier capt. du tems que nous avions cette colonie me mande.

"M. Willinge depéché par le congrés avec trente hommes vient d'Enlever toute la rive gauche du mississipi et un navire mouillé manchak portant 16. canons et autant de mortiers, il a tout devasté et a fait pour un million de butin et fait tort de plus de deux a la vielle angleterre. Notre gouverneur M. de galvey a protegé l'une et l'autre et a observé une grande neutralité."[8]

Si vous savez cette nouvelle Monsieur Le docteur, je vous prie de Regarder ma Lettre comme non avenue. J'en retireray un precieux avantage puisqu'elle me procure l'occasion de vous assurer que j'ai l'honneur de vous assurer que je suis avec Respect Monsieur le docteur Votre tres humble et tres obeissant serviteur   DE REINE

ancien capt rue Sataury aux 4. bornes

a M. Le docteur franklin a passy.

Endorsed: M. La Reine Versailles

To Vergennes   ALS: Archives du Ministère des affaires étrangères

Sir,   Passy, July 25. 1778.

We have just received another Copy of the Ratification. We understand the Congress have sent five by so many different Conveyances.[9] The Vessel now arriv'd left Boston the 16th

---

7. See the biographical note on him in Winston DeVille, *Louisiana Troops 1720–1770* (Fort Worth, [1965]), 123.

8. For Willing's expedition see XXVI, 377–8.

9. Six copies were sent, of which at least four had arrived by July 29: *JCC*, XI, 463; Wharton, *Diplomatic Correspondence*, II, 673.

June. There was then no News there of Count D'Estaign.[1] I send enclos'd a Letter from Dr. Cooper to me, the latest Newspaper, and an Account of the Cargo of the Duchesse de Grammont, of whose safe Arrival we have now first the good News.[2] I am, with great Respect, Your Excellency's most obedient humble Servant   B FRANKLIN

[*In the margin*:] Mr. Adams and myself were at Versailles to day, with an Intention to pay our Respects to your Excelly. but receiving Notice while there of the Arrival of Dispatches for us, we hasten'd back to see if there was any News of Importance.

M. le Comte de Vergennes

1. The vessel was the schooner *Dispatch*: XXVI, 600–1; Taylor, *Adams Papers*, VI, 315. D'Estaing's fleet reached the Delaware Capes on July 8: see RB to BF, above, July 14 and W.M. James, *The British Navy in Adversity: A Study of the War of American Independence* (London, 1926), p. 97.
2. Cooper's letter is above, June 1 (XXVI, 562–6). The *Duchesse de Grammont* was one of the ships sent by JW (XXV, 494 n); her cargo list, at the AAE, reads as follows:
Etat du Chargement du Navire la duchesse de Grammont
arrivé a Portsmouth dans la nouvelle Hampshire le commencement de Juin 1778.
13,433 Habits de Soldats complets
13,000 paires de Bas
80,000 Livres pesant de Cuivre
32 Futailes de pierres a fusil
2 petite pieces d'artillerie de Fonte
1500 Fusils de Rampart
775 musquetons ⎫
800 paire de pistolets ⎪
1400 paire de Fonts ⎬ pour la Cavalerie
100 Cartouches ⎪
100 Pelles ⎭
176.200 Bouchons de Liège distribues parmi les Fusils etc.
Le tout pour le Compte du Congress dont le prémier achat en France est d'environ 800.000 Livres Tournois.

From ——— Guichard[3]

ALS: American Philosophical Society

Monsieur   a Marennes Le 25 Juillet 1778.

Je Pris La Liberté de Vous Ecrire Le 6. de ce mois pour vous prier de Vouloir Bien Me faire compter la somme de 720 *l.t.* düe a augustin Guichard Mon frere Embarqué En qualité d'officier sur un Bâtiment des Etats unis appellé Lexington, commendé Par M. Johnson, pour un an de Gage à Compter du 12. May 1777. au 12 may 1778. ainsy que Les deux Parties qui Luy Reviennent sur les Prises qu'ils onts faittes. Je vous observay, Monsieur, que Mon frere ayant Eté Pris[4] et se Trouvant avoir Besoin D'argent a Eu Recours a moy, que luy en ayant fait Passer, Il me donne ordre De Retirer Les Gages et Parties de Prises dont s'agit. Je me Persuade, Monsieur, que vous voudrés Bien m'entendre a Cet Egard, et Rendre Justice a la demende que Je vous fais. Mon frere à servi avec assés de distingtion et d'aplausiment [applaudissement] les Etâts unis Pour en Esperer du Retour par le payement d'un L'Egitime dû.

Tout s'acorde a Rendre Justice a Mon frere, M. Wilk comis de feu M. Moris De Nantes agent du Congrés M'en a parlé dans les Meilleurs Termes, et M'assure qu'il Luy est dû ce qu'il Reclame. M. odeas fils subdelegué de pimbeuf[5] me dit par sa Lettre du premier de ce mois qu'il L'a Parfaittement connu

3. The brother, as he says here, of Augustin Guichard, quartermaster on the *Lexington* and prize master of the *Sally of Baltimore* in June, 1777: Clark, *Wickes*, pp. 203, 226. This letter and the one of the 6th (now missing) produced no response. Neither, as far as we know, did his subsequent letters, two to BF (Aug. 12 and Nov. 21) and one to Arthur Lee (Sept. 1), in which he repeats the story with increasing frustration: he allows for BF's difficulty with the French language, but finally threatens to take his case "au Ministre" if BF continues to be silent. APS.

4. Guichard was captured in the *Lexington*'s encounter with the *Alert*, Sept. 19, 1777: Clark, *Wickes*, p. 381.

5. M. Odea, in Paimboeuf, had been used by JW as an interpreter the previous July; by December he was helping outfit the *Ranger*. JW to Odea, July 11, 1777 (University of Pa. Library); Charles Henry Lincoln, ed., *A Calendar of John Paul Jones Manuscripts in the Library of Congress* (Washington, 1903) p. 34.

Lors qu'il y conduisit une prise du Capne. Johnson, nommée La Salle de Baltimore. Je pence, Monsieur, que vous daignerés Me Repondre et accorder ce que Je vous demande, D'autant mieux, que c'est pour adoucir Les Peines d'un Malheureux qui s'est Livré Tout Entier pour Le Bien du Congrés. Ce n'a eté Ny Libertinage ny L'apas du Gain qui L'a fait agir mais Bien Le désir de combatre pour une Cause Juste quoy qu'elle ne le Regardât Pas. Je suis avec Respect Monsieur Votre tres humble et Tres obeissant serviteur GUICHARD AINÉ

Commis aux Classes de La Marine

Notation: Guichard July 25 / 78

To ———[6]   Draft:[7] American Philosophical Society

Passy ce 26 Juillet 1778

Les affaires dont je suis chargé, Monsieur, ne me permettent pas de quitter paris et par consequent d'accepter vostre invitation; je vous prie de croire cependant que j'y suis tres sensible, et que c'est avéc reconnoissance que je suis, Monsieur, vostre tres humble et tres obeissant serviteur.

Notation: Le Veillard

From Genet[8]

ALS: American Philosophical Society; incomplete copy:[9] Library of Congress

Monsieur   A V[ersai]lles ce 26. juillet 1778.

Je suis bien faché que le n° 49 ait paru hier. J'y aurois inséré avec le plus grand empressement le § 1er de la lettre du Dr. Cooper, que j'ai l'honeur de vous renvoyer ici en original, et

6. Possibly to Richelet who had invited BF on July 18.
7. In Le Veillard's hand.
8. In response to BF's letter to Genet's superior, Vergennes, July 25.
9. Containing that portion of the letter from "Je vois, Monsieur . . ." to the complimentary close.

tous mes lecteurs à Paris et dans le Royaume y auroient vû avec plaisir la cargaison de la Duchesse de Grammont, heureusement arrivée a sa destination, et dont le prix coûtant en France, a eté de huit cents mille livres. Personne ne doute ici de l'avantage que nous procure le commerce de l'amérique, mais ce sera toujours faire plaisir à notre nation que de lui en articuler les détails, pour lui donner la jouissance de s'applaudir de ce qu'Elle a fait. Le n° 50. ne tardera point à paroitre, et vous y verrés cette cargaison, avec l'extrait *convenable* de la lettre du Dr. Cooper et les passages interessans de la gazette, que vous avés aussi communique a Msgr. le Cte. de Vergennes, et que vous trouverés pareillement ici.[1] J'attens au surplus ceux qu'il vous plaira encore de m'envoyer. Je vois, Monsieur, dans la lettre du Dr. Cooper que deux imprimeurs de Boston veulent y faire une gazette pour laquelle ils compteroient principalement sur des articles de France capables d'entretenir l'union et la satisfaction des deux nations. Je me félicite d'avoir conçu ici un projet tout semblable, dont j'ai déja eu l'honeur de vous parler plusieurs fois. Je ne l'ai pas encore mis formellement sous les yeux de Msgr. le Cte. de Vergennes, du ressort de qui seroit l'execution, et qui me paroit disposé à y consentir. Je serois infiniment flatté que sa derniere détermination fût motivée par le suffrage des Honorables plénipotentiaires et l'encouragement particulier que vous daigneriés y donner. Je prens la liberté de mettre le plan en substance sous vos yeux[2] et d'y ajouter

Premierement que le privilege me rendant le Chef de l'entreprise, je puis répondre aux honorables deputés que ce ne

1. A French translation of most of Cooper's letter of June 1 (xxvi, 562–6) appeared in the *Affaires de l'Angleterre et de l'Amérique*, vol. xi, part ii, cahier l (dated July 30), pp. cxlix–clii. The cargo list of the *Duchesse de Grammont* immediately followed; the same issue contained information on the Carlisle peace commission and its rejection by Congress, as well as a translation (on pp. ccx–ccxiii) of Cooper's letter to BF of July 2.

2. The enclosure, "Projet d'une gazette en langue angloise, imprimée à Paris sous ce titre *The American Correspondant in france*," is at the APS; an English version of it, dated July 20, 1778, and signed by Genet, is in the Genet Papers at the Library of Congress. As far as we know nothing came of the idea.

sera point tant une affaire de marchandise, que de sentiment, c'est à dire

2° que tout y sera calculé pour cimenter l'union des deux Païs, et le contentement qu'ils doivent avoir l'un de l'autre

3° pour promouvoir entre eux l'industrie et le commerce jusqu'au plus haut dégré possible, et surtout du coté de la France pour reduire le monopole, et établir le concours qui assure la bonne foi etc.

4° que cette gazette angloise sera vendue à l'amérique presque pour le prix du papier, qui encore ne sera pas de la plus chere qualité.

J'entens que j'ai la parole des libraires imprimeurs mes associés, qu'ils ne chercheront le profit par le débit en Amérique que sur le grand nombre, et que par conséquent le prix sera d'un bon tiers au dessous de ce qu'il seroit en France, s'il s'y en place quelques exemplaires ce qui est croyable dans les circonstances actuelles

5° que ce sera le seul papier de cette espece qui sortira de France, ainsi que le garantit le privilege exclusif qui me sera donne; d'où doit résulter

6° que l'amérique n'en recevra que ce qui est nécessaire pour donner une nouvelle vie a ses propres gazettes, qui pourront réimprimer, commenter, répondre etc. et augmenter par là la curiosité de leurs lecteurs, sans que le débit de cinq ou six mille copies, de la notre, fut presque sensible sur toute l'étendue de ce vaste continent et leur porte préjudice.

Je souhaite, Monsieur, que ce plan vous soit agréable [et] à vos honorables collègues, et je recevrai avec reconnoissance ou vos observations pour le changer, ou votre agrément donné sous la condition du bon plaisir du Ministre. Je suis avec un profond respect Monsieur Votre très humble et très obeissant serviteur   GENET

P.S. Je songe Monsieur, que vous pourriés avoir régulierement les deux gazettes que vous désirés,[3] par ce moyen ci. Il faudroit que vous eûssiés la bonté d'écrire à un de vos amis à Londres,

3. The *London Evening Post* and the *London Chronicle*, requested by BF on June 29: XXVI, 696. See also Genet's letter of July 2.

de mettre à la poste les dites deux gazettes par chaque ordinaire avec addresse, à moi, en ces termes—à Monsieur *Monsieur Genet à Versailles*. Sans autre chose. Je connoitrai en ou-
vrant le paquet qu'elles sont pour vous et je vous les enverrai
sur le champ. Recommandés qu'on n'en envoye pas d'avantage, parce que je reçois déja des paquets, francs de port
comme le seront ceux là. Vous payerés à Londres les de-
boursés de votre ami et vous n'aurés rien à me rendre. Mais
cela ne durera qu'autant que les ports de Douvres et de Calais
resteront ouverts pour la correspondance. Il faudra après un
autre arrangement par Ostende.

P.S. 26 july. As it is seriously my résolution that the paper
shou'd be sold to the Americans at the lowest price possible,
and that with that view, it shall be printed upon a very cheap
sort of paper, that contrafaction may not take place in america,
unless with disadvantage. Your Honour will oblige me particularly, if you don't think the quantity of five or six thousand
in the whole continent won't find a sale, to let me know your
fears and apprehensions on the subject. Besides I must tell
your Honour that we intend only to try with three or four
numbers and let it alone till we receive answers from america
with orders to the printers, and if there is no hopes of a large
Sale, and that on the contrary we find the americans disposed
to get the Sale intirely for themselves by reprinting we'll give
it over.

The Booksellers are agreed to receive the returns, not in
money, but in goods of the country such as find a vent in ours,
and they'll chuse to have five or six Booksellers in the principal Seaport towns along the coast to be their retailers. I beg a
thousand pardons for this further importunity. You'll surely
approve of the motive, which is the want of being here to save
ourselves on the quantity, by contenting ourselves with the
smallest profit.

Notation: Genet Juillet 78

From Johann Rodolph Valltravers

ALS: American Philosophical Society

Sir!   Rockhall, Bienne, in Switzerland, July 26. 78.

Being ignorant of the Fate of my 2. last Letters, of April 14th. and May 17th.,[4] directed from this Place to yr. Exccy. by the Poste: I am at a Loss, to learn, whether they were received at all, in due Time? and, if come safe to Hand, whether they have been welcome, or no? This Uncertainty, and Fear of being indiscretly troublesome, whilst I sincerily wish to be Serviceable, has prevented my conveÿing to Your Excy., the inclosed Sketch of a few Principles, Whereon to build a lasting Foundation of Friendship, and of mutual good offices, between the two Sisters, the 13. republican States of N. America, and of Switzerland, much sooner, than I now do, by a trusty Friend of mine, Mr. de Grüffy the Bearer of this Packet.[5] I humbly submit it to Yr. Excy.'s Judgment and Corrections, if thought deserving of your Consideration. When improved, and approved of by Yr. Excy., I then shall recommend it to your further Protection in conveÿing it to the Congress, previous to its being imparted to the Ministry of his most christian Majesty; and at last, by his Ambassador, to our several Cantons. My good offices, if accepted of by the Congress shall not be wanting, in paving the Waÿ toward a good Reception of its consequential Overtures, provided I be duly impower'd thereto and suported.

Should a similar Connection between the N American confederate States, and the naval Republicks of Venice, and of Genoa, be thought of, before, or after the proposed Alliance with Switzerland; there also I am at their Command, and yours. My vicinity with those States, and Knowledge of their Language, as well as of their mutual Constitutions, Interests, and Connections, will greatly facilitate my Negociation, and assist my Zeal, in promoting the Liberties and Prosperities of both States, on both Sides the attlantick.

4. See xxvi, 292–4, 495–7.
5. The enclosure, in six parts and in French, is also at the APS and bears the notation "M Valtravers Rocoll 17 may 1778." For de Gruffy see xxvi, 42 n.

The Copy of Your Excellency's Treaty with France, kindly promised me last april, is not yet come to hand. I much long to See it, with the Sequel of the french Pamphlets on English and american affairs, from No. XXIII. down to the present Time.

I have taken the Liberty to adress a Letter the 21t. of May, to Your Excellency's Landlord, Mr. Chaumont, on a commercial Subject; which, I hope, he has received. My sincere Respects waite on him, and on his Ladies; as also on Your Colleague and Grandson; being with infinite Veneration, true attachment, and neverceasing Gratitude, for all Favors Shewn to my Friends, and Self—Sir! Your Excellency's Most faithfully devoted humble Servant   RODH. VALLTRAVERS

Addressed: A Son Excellence Monsr. B-n Frankling, Envoyé extre. et Ministre Plénipote. des Louables 13. Etats confederés de l'Amérique Septentrionale, Auprés de S.M.T.C. A Passy.

The American Commissioners to Schweighauser

AL (draft):[6] Massachusetts Historical Society; two copies: National Archives

Sir   Passy July 27. 1778
We recd. yours of the 22d Inst. acquainting us that Capt. Reed in the Baltimore has bro't from 40 to 50 hhds. of Tobacco consigned to you by the Committee of Commerce. We have advice of the same from the Committee,[7] who let us know that the Qty. is 49 hhds. which they have order'd to be sold and the Money held at our Disposition. But as we have long since enter'd into a Contract with the Farmers General for Tobacco's[8] we desire this may not be sold but deliver'd to their Agent at Nantes or whoever may be appointed by them to receive it in part of whatever we are to furnish. We thank

6. In Arthur Lee's hand.
7. The commerce committee, in its letter of May 28 (XXVI, 537). Schweighauser's letter of the 22nd is missing. For Capt. Thomas Read see the *DAB.*
8. XXIII, 514–17.

you for your care in forwarding Capt. Barnes to paris[9] and are Sir your most Obedient &c.

Mr. Schweighauser

Exchanges with Anne-Louise Boivin d'Hardancourt Brillon de Jouy: Six Letters *circa* July 27, 1778

(I) AL: American Philosophical Society; (II) AL: American Philosophical Society; (III) AL: American Philosophical Society; (IV) AL (draft) and autograph copy or press copy: American Philosophical Society; (V) ALS: American Philosophical Society; (VI) ALS: American Philosophical Society

As is often the case with the Doctor's much-admired neighbor in Passy, chronology hangs on tenuous clues. Franklin, who sometimes showed irritation toward people who did not date their letters, slipped into that habit himself when addressing her. In this instance, where a number of documents obviously belong together, only one of them provides a month and a day, July 27, but no year. We have opted for 1778. Whereas July, 1777, seems too early in their acquaintance for such frivolous banter, anything later than 1778 would be too late, since after September of that year their roles as father and daughter had been solidly established.[1]

For all the tender jesting, these letters reveal a relationship in crisis. The man is demanding what the woman is not willing to yield. The woman demands an emotional monopoly that the man, under the circumstances, is not ready to grant. Some four years later, Franklin will evoke the longing he had felt for her, calling it "une jolie Passion." That longing, to the best of our knowledge, remained unfulfilled.

The first two exchanges of letters seem perfectly in place from a psychological point of view, setting the stage, as they do, for the

9. Corbin Barnes was captain of the recently arrived *Dispatch*: XXVI, 600–1; BF to Vergennes, above, July 25. He reached Passy on the 25th: Taylor, *Adams Papers*, VI, 315.

1. See the headnote on BF to Mme. Brillon, Sept. 1. In a letter of March 20, 1782 (APS), Mme. Brillon referred to their private "peace treaty" (letter VI, below) as having been concluded in 1776—an obvious slip of memory, since she and BF had not yet met, but an indication of how early in their relationship it seemed to her. For an analysis of Mme. Brillon's role in BF's life see Lopez, *Mon Cher Papa*, pp. 29–121, 313–21.

exchange that follows. There is a possibility, however, that the second pair belongs to a later period. Franklin's copy of his letter (IV) may have been made on a letterpress, an instrument that was not in use before 1780. We have decided to print them here, anyway, on the assumption that this correspondence was such a *jeu d'esprit*, with many hands and translators taking part, that an early letter may well have been translated and copied on the letterpress at a later date.

I.

ce jeudi matin

Vous m'avés délaissée hiér mon chér papa, et pendant ce tems la, je m'occupois de vous, et de vos plaisirs; je demandois les livres que vous avés désiré et que je vous envoye; toute la bibliothéque de mr. du Bospin est a votre sérvice, il est de mes amis: je ne vous vérrai donc que samedi? Vous vous passés donc aisaiment de moi un mércredi? Et vous dirés aprés cela, *je vous aime furieusement, trop*: moi mon bon papa qui ne vous aime pas *furieusement*—mais trés *tendrement*, pas, *trop*; je vous aime assés pour éstre fâché de ne vous pas voir toutes les fois qu'il m'est, ou a vous possible de le faire; qui aime le plus, et le mieux de nous deux? Jugés cela mon bon ami non en homme intéréssé dans cétte affaire, mais en homme juste, en docteur Franklin.

Addressed: A Monsieur / Monsieur Franklin / A Passy

II.

J'ai été bien mortifié hier au soir de n'avoir pas pû me rendre chez ma chere Amie. J'avois une *Visitation* qui à durée jusqu'à onze heures.

Bien des Remerciements pour votre soin obligeante en me procurant ces livres. Je les retournera bientôt en bon ordre. Je suis bien obligé aussi à M. de Bospin.

C'est vrai que j'ai souvent dit que je vous aime *trop*, et j'ai dit la verité. Jugez vous, après une Comparaison que je va faire, qui de nous deux aime le plus. Si je demande d'un Ami, J'ai besoin de vos Chevaux pour faire une Voyage, pretez les à moi; et si il repond, je serois bien aise de vous obliger, mais je crains qu'ils seront gatées par cette Voyage et je ne peux pas me resoudre de les preter à personne;—ne dois-je pas conclurre que cet homme aime ses chevaux plus qu'il ne m'aime? Et si dans le meme Cas je voudroit volontairement hazarder mes chevaux en les pretant a lui, n'est il pas clair que je l'aime plus que je n'aime[2] mes chevaux, et aussi plus qu'il m'aime. Vous sçavez que je suis pret a sacrifier mes beaux et grands chevaux.

III.

Sçavés vous mon bon papa que vous m'avés joué un mauvais tour, vous demandés votre voiture a huit heures, et a sept et demie vous vous envollés pour me punir de m'estre énnuyée a promener des *dames*, tandis que je me serois amusée a rester avec vous; le grand *voisin*[3] aussi nigaud que le grand *cousin* n'a pas eu l'ésprit de vous offrir des *dames de bois*[4] en m'attendant, je suis remonté, je me suis mise en colére, j'ai juré contre les *dames*, contre le *voisin*, contre *vous* contre *tout le monde*, contre *moi*, contre tout ce qui m'a privé du plaisir d'estre avéc vous que j'aime du fond de mon coeur. Une autre fois songés que c'est un gros péché de causer du mal a son prochain et restés jusqu'à huit, neuf, ou dix heures.

Notation: Madame Brillon

IV.

[Vendredi matin][5]

2 { Vous aviez tort, ma chere Amie, de vous mettre en colere et de jurer contre tout le monde pour ce que je m'ai oté une demie-heure plutôt qu'á mon ordinaire. Une demie-heure avec un Viellard qui ne peut pas en faire la meilleur Usage, est une très petite chose, et on ne doit pas se mettre en colere pour des petites choses. Sammedi au soir, je resterai jusques vous souhaiterez ma depart, et malgré votre politesse usuelle en phrase de mots, je sçaurai le tems par votre refus d'un Baiser.

2. From the beginning of the paragraph, "C'est vrai . . . ," until this point, BF imitated Mme. Brillon's writing.
3. Le Veillard.
4. To play chess, one of BF's favorite pastimes.
5. Supplied from the final version, where BF also reversed the paragraphs as indicated here, running them together, and added a new beginning: "Ce n'est que hier au soir que votre Billet est venu a main. Voici la

1 {

J'avois été debout Mecredi Matin[6] a quatre heures, je n'avois pas fait mon post-scriptum, j'avois travaillé beaucoup, j'avois diné à Paris, et j'étois très fatigué, et fort disposé à dormir après votre descente dans le Jardin, et je commençois à le faire sur le banc pendant qu'on parloit à moi. Ainsi je le trouvois plus decent de me retirer: et je m'etois couché devant huit heures. Il faut donc pardonner le grand Voisin et tous les autres et avouer que

V.

ce 25 a passy

Vous me demandés la liste de vos péchés mon chér papa; elle seroit si longue, que je n'ose entreprendre ce grand ouvrage; vous n'en faittes pourtant qu'un; mais il a tant de branches, il se répétte si souvent, qu'il faudroit des calculs infinis pour en trouvér le nombre juste; et vous voulés aprés cela que je vous pardonne, moi qui suis votre diréctrice:[7] si j'etois homme, c'est tout ce que je pourrois faire; mais je ne puis en vérité suivant ma consçience, et mon intérest surtout, tolérér le systéme dangereux "que l'amitié qu'on a pour les fémmes, est divisible a l'infini." C'est ce que vous cherchés a prouvér tous les jours mon chér papa, et ce dont je ne m'accomoderai jamais: mon coeur capable d'aimér beaucoup a choisi peu d'objéts pour reposér sa tendrésse; elle les a bien choisi, vous éstes a la teste: en éparpillant votre amitié comme vous faittes mon amitié ne diminuera pas, mais j'essayerai d'estre un peu plus sévére sur vos fauttes que par le passé, pour voir si je rattraperai par la une partie de ce que je crois devoir m'appartenir pour prix du sentiment que j'ai pour vous; voila mon sistéme a moi; guérre

---

veritable Cause de ma Retraite." A few spelling corrections are too insignificant to note; even so, the French is obviously his own. We are deviating in this case from our usual practice of printing the revised version rather than a draft, because this draft provides a rare glimpse into Franklin's struggles to impress his female correspondent.

6. Mme. Brillon's receptions always took place on Wednesdays and Saturdays.

7. An echo of their March flirtation along theological lines. See xxvi, 75–6.

ouvérte la dessus[8] je ne vous passerai plus rien. J'y suis décidé, oui tout aussi décidé qu'a vous aimér toujours: j'ai l'honneur d'éstre mon chér papa: Votre trés humble et trés obéissante sérvante D'HARDANCOURT BRILLON

Addressed: A Monsieur / Monsieur Benjamin Franklin / A Passy

VI.

Passy, July 27

What a difference, my dear Friend, between you and me! You find my Faults so many as to be innumerable, while I can see but one in you; and perhaps that is the Fault of my Spectacles. The Fault I mean is that kind of Covetousness,[9] by which you would engross all my Affection, and permit me none for the other amiable Ladies of your Country. You seem to imagine that it cannot be divided without being diminish'd: In which you mistake the nature of the Thing and forget the Situation in which you have plac'd and hold me. You renounce and exclude arbitrarily every thing corporal from our Amour, except such a merely civil Embrace now and then as you would permit to a country Cousin; what is there then remaining that I may not afford to others without a Diminution of what belongs to you? The Operations of the Mind, Esteem, Admiration, Respect, and even Affection for one Object, may be multiply'd as more Objects that merit them present themselves, and yet remain the same to the first, which therefore has no room to complain of Injury. They are in their Nature as divisible as the sweet Sounds of the Forte Piano produc'd by your exquisite Skill:[1] Twenty People may receive the same Pleasure

8. This is the expression that links this letter to BF's "peace treaty" below.

9. There are two French translations of this letter in the APS, one probably in her husband's hand (a), the other by her cousin, Mme. Melin-Dutartre (b). They both render the meaning faithfully, though in different language. In (a), "Covetousness" has been translated as "taquinerie," which Mme. Brillon has corrected to "avarice." She also added a notation at the bottom: "léttres écrittes en anglois."

1. Mme. Brillon was among the first Parisians to have a piano; hers was an English-made instrument sent by J. C. Bach sometime before 1770. Charles Burney who visited her that year described her considerable talent

from them, without lessening that which you kindly intend for me; and I might as reasonably require of your Friendship, that they should reach and delight no Ears but mine.

You see by this time how unjust you are in your Demands, and in the open War you declare against me if I do not comply with them. Indeed it is I that have the most Reason to complain. My poor little Boy,[2] whom you ought methinks to have cherish'd, instead of being fat and Jolly like those in your elegant Drawings, is meagre and starv'd almost to death for want of the Substantial Nourishment which you his Mother inhumanly deny him, and yet would now clip his little Wings to prevent his seeking it elsewhere![3]

I fancy we shall neither of us get any thing by this War, and therefore as feeling my self the Weakest, I will do what indeed ought always to be done by the Wisest, be first in making the Propositions for Peace. That a Peace may be lasting, the Articles of the Treaty should be regulated upon the Principles of the most perfect Equity and Reciprocity. In this View I have drawn up and offer the following, viz.

Article 1.

There shall be eternal Peace, Friendship and Love, between Madame B. and Mr. F.

Article 2.

In order to maintain the same inviolably, Made. B. on her Part stipulates and agrees, that Mr. F. shall come to her whenever she sends for him.

---

and proficiency, and was particularly struck by her sight-reading ability. He could not persuade her, however, to play with the stops on; "ç'est sec," she had said, and as a result, all the notes were "like the sound of bells, continual and confluent." BF, who favored the harp and his own bell-like armonica, seems to have shared her taste. From Bruce Gustafson, "The Music of Madame Brillon: A Unified Manuscript Collection from Benjamin Franklin's Circle," *Notes*, XLIII (1987), 526–7.

2. Rendered as "petit enfant" in (a), and "petit amour" in (b).

3. The theme of the starved Cupid will be picked up again in 1781, in another exchange of gallantries.

Art. 3.

That he shall stay with her as long as she pleases.

Art. 4.

That when he is with her, he shall be obliged to drink Tea, play Chess, hear Musick; or do any other thing that she requires of him.[4]

Art. 5.

And that he shall love no other Woman but herself.

Art. 6.

And the said Mr. F. in his part stipulates and agrees, that he will go away from M. B.'s whenever he pleases.

Art. 7.

That he will stay away as long as he please.[5]

Art. 8.

That when he is with her he will do what he pleases.

Art. 9.

And that he will love any other Woman as far as he finds her amiable.[6]

Let me know what you think of these Preliminaries. To me they seem to express the true Meaning and Intention of each Party more plainly than most Treaties. I shall insist pretty strongly on the eighth Article, tho' without much Hope of your Consent to it; and on the ninth also, tho I despair of ever finding any other Woman that I could love with equal Tenderness: being ever, my dear dear Friend, Yours most sincerely

BF

4. A footnote in (b) adds: "bien entendu, ce qu'il pourra faire."
5. Articles 6 and 7 are mistranslated in (b); they imply that BF will stay at Mme. Brillon's as long as he pleases.
6. A footnote in (b) adds: "Les femmes peuvent aller se noyer."

Thomas Simpson to the American Commissioners[7]

ALS: American Philosophical Society

⟨Brest, July 27, 1778: I wrote you from Nantes that I was planning to sail on the *Providence*. Mr. Livingston arrived from Paris informing me that you had appointed him to command the *Ranger*, but gave that post to me when Capt. Jones delivered up my parole. Your letters to Capt. Whipple and Mr. Schweighauser also arrived; Whipple ordered me on the 24th to go immediately to Brest and ready the *Ranger* for sea with no less than three months' provisions. Mr. Schweighauser provided a letter for a friend here who could supply me with every necessary. I left Nantes the evening of the 24th and arrived here the 26th; the ship seems nearly ready, wanting some stores and her bottom cleaned, which will take only a few days.[8] Capt. Whipple and Mr. Schweighauser recommended that I take 30 or 40 of the prisoners to serve on the *Boston*, which I shall do. I will send an accounting of the *Ranger*'s stores as soon as possible. The prizes are not yet sold, but if their value can be determined Mr. Schweighauser has kindly agreed to advance the money to the crew. I am pleased to inform you that your appointment of me met with the greatest satisfaction of the officers and men.⟩

Dumas to the American Commissioners[9]

ALS: Harvard University Library; AL (draft): Algemeen Rijksarchief

⟨The Hague, July 28, 1778, in French: I enclose summaries of twelve pages of diplomatic correspondence.[1] It is reliably reported that there will be a suspension of arms in Germany

---

7. Published in Taylor, *Adams Papers*, VI, 324–5.
8. Simpson's letter to Whipple, informing him of the same, arrived on the 31st: see Whipple to the commissioners, July 31.
9. Published in Taylor, *Adams Papers*, VI, 328–30.
1. Dispatches from Vienna and Ratisbon: *ibid.*, p. 330 n.

until August 1 and it is generally thought peace will follow.[2] This morning I took a copy of the treaty, omitting articles 11 and 12, to the Grand Pensionary, who promised not to circulate it until you give permission for publication. He agrees with me that the chances of the British peace commissioners are very poor and that the Spanish negotiations in England are the Bourbons' final attempt to preserve the peace. I told him perfect harmony exists between Congress and the states, that there is no misunderstanding between it and General Washington and that America would not make peace unless France was included. I also sent a copy of the treaty to Mr. van Berckel.)

From Isaak Iselin[3]
ALS: American Philosophical Society

Monsieur   Bâle en Suisse ce 28 Juillet 1778

Disciple et confident de la nature vous avés devoilé aux mortels étonnés ses secrets les plus sublimes; vous leurs avés enseigné a la desarmer de ses feux les plus terribles et a les conduire d'une maniere bienfaisante dans le sein de la terre. Vous avés fait plus. Vous avés introduit vos compatriotes dans le sanctuaire de la liberté, vous les avés initiés dans les mystères sacrés, vous leurs avés appris a manier sans en abuser, un feu plus délicat encore et souvent plus destructeur, que le feu électrique, celui de l'autorité. Cette derniere qualité est le titre qui m'encourage á m'adresser a vous, Monsieur.

Je travaille depuis quelques années a un ouvrage périodique destiné a éclairer mes compatriotes sur les besoins et sur les droits de l'humanité, et a les instruire des bonnes choses qui

2. These reports proved false, although negotiations did occur: Paul P. Bernard, *Joseph II and Bavaria: Two Eighteenth-Century Attempts at German Unification* (The Hague, 1965), pp. 112–17.
3. Philanthropist and student of law, Iselin (1728–82) founded in 1777 the Société d'utilité publique de Bâle. He also was the editor of the *Ephemeriden der Menschkeit. Dictionnaire historique et biographique de la Suisse.*

se font par ci par la. Je suis dans la persuasion que l'humanité porte en elle un germe de perfection dont le développement peut et doit être accéléré par le soin d'eclairer et d'adoucir les hommes. C'est dans ce point de vue que je travaille et que je tâche de recueillir partout des faits instructifs et dignes d'être imité. Votre heureuse patrie doit, comme une terre défrichée nouvellement en fait de politique, doit en fournir un grand nombre et de bien interessans. C'est un spectacle bien ravissant pour l'humanité qu'un peuple qui a sû se delivrer de toutes les entraves qui l'empechoient de marcher vers la perfection tant morale, que politique et économique. Je serois enchanté de pouvoir en présenter de tems en tems a mes compatriotes quelques parties. J'ose recourir a vous, Monsieur, pour vous prier de me procurer soit a Philadelphie soit ailleurs, une personne qui se charge de m'en fournir de tems en tems des notices, soit en anglois, en françois ou en allemand. Je sens que ma demande seroit très indiscrète, si elle n'avoit pour bût que de satisfaire ma curiosité, mais comme elle tend a répandre et a faire fructifier en Allemagne et en Suisse le bien qui se fait en Amérique, j'ose me flatter que vous ne la désapprouverés point. La maniere la plus naturelle de me faire parvenir ces notices seroit de les envoier a votre Consul a Nantes Mr. Schweighouser qui est mon concitoien et qui aura sans doute la bonté de me les faire parvenir par la voie la plus convenable. J'ai l'honneur d'être avec un parfait respect, Monsieur, vôtre très humble et très obeissant serviteur

Isaac Iselin

Secretaire du Conseil de la république de Bâle qui est la patrie des Bernoullis[4]

Addressed: Monsieur / Monsieur le Docteur Franklin / ministre plenipotentiaire de / la Republique des XIII Provinces / unies de l'Amérique auprés de S.M.T.C. / à Paris

Endorsed: M. Iselins / 28 Juillet 1778. / Proposition

4. The Bernouilli family has several illustrious mathematicians among its members.

From Plombard & Legris[5]

ALS: University of Pennsylvania Library

Nantes Le 28 Juillet 1778

Nous Vous remettons cy joint Monsieur, une Traitte sur Vous de £900 par Le President Henri Laurens a 30 Jours de Vüe, passée a L'ordre de nos Messieurs du cap par Monsieur Colson que Nous Vous prions de Nous renvoyer acceptée. Comme Notre maison du cap français a St. Domingue a de fortes Liaisons d'affaires avec L'amerique Septentrionale, que Nous avons meme une maison Etablie a charlestouwn Notre Sieur Plombard y Estant actuellement et Tres connu dans Le pays,[6] pourrions-Nous Monsieur Nous flatter que Vous Voulussiez aggréer L'offre de Nos Services, dans Notre Ville de Nantes, pour Les Expeditions que Vous pouvez avoir a faire faire Pour Votre pays. Nous Nous ferions un vray Plaisir de Vous Etre de quelqu'utilité et de Vous donner de frequentes preuves de Notre zele et de Notre Devouement. Nous avons L'honneur d'Estre avec une haute Consideration Monsieur Vos tres humbles et Tres obeissans Serviteurs

PLOMBARD ET LEGRIS

Addressed: A Monsieur / Monsieur Benjamin franklin / agent des Etats unis de L'amerique / A Paris

Notation: Plombard et legris / Nantes 28. Juillet 1778.

From Nicolas Moreau

ALS: American Philosophical Society

Monseigneur   Cadiz 28 juillet 1778

La declaration que notre Roy tres Chrétien a fait faire a la Cour de Londres par son Embassadeur Monsieur Le Marquis de Noailles ou on i voit un traitté d'amitié et de commerce avec les etats unis de l'amerique septentrionale que votre

5. A firm only slightly involved, by Nantes standards, in American trade. See Villiers, *Commerce colonial*, p. 406.
6. In November he was appointed French consul in Charleston: Howard C. Rice, "French Consular Agents in the United States 1778–1791," *Franco-American Review* 1 (1936–37), 369.

Grandeur represente m'a toujours donné esperance que les Marchandises qui etoient chargée en angleterre sur les navires francois pourroient naviguer avec sureté et sans interumption. Cepandant avec peine je vois que le Navire la fortune Capitaine Y. Bertrand Kenguen sorti de londres pour cadiz portant des mdises [marchandises] pour compte de francois a qui elles sont consignés par le connoissement, le dit navire a eté pris par les americains et conduit a Boston suivant la lettre du Capitaine du Navire la fortune arrivé a Brest datté du 28 juin ecrit a Monsieur Gregoire alvares verjusti Negt Espanol dont inclus V.G. [Votre Grandeur] a la Copie.[7] Il paroist que l'on a rendu que les deux objets la sienne et mdises apartenant a Messieurs desomberger Reiter et Compagnie qui sont allemans etabli a Cadiz. Comme il paroist par la lettre du Capitaine qu'il a eté debouté de ses demandes en reclamation dans les tribunaux inferieurs et qu'il reste notre recours au Conseil du Congré j'espere que votre Grandeur voudera bien etre mon protecteur aupres de ce Conseil pour que le montant de mes mdises me soient payé. Elles concistent en deux Caisses Bas de laine marque joseph ma coni compris Comme justice lb. 1. 2. chargé a londres par Mr. denison sur le Navire la fortune et signation. Ils montent a £st.391:17 les frais de Chargement a Londres. Votre Grandeur est protecteur de la entre les americains et notre Nation française je fairay la justification de la proprieté de la mdise ou elle l'ordonnera ou si Votre Grandeur veut bien me le permettre je lui envoirai les lettres et factures qui constent que la mdise est de mon Compte. J'espere que le traitté d'amitié et de commerce que vous avez signé avec sa Majeste s'etendera aussi sur ces sujets qui commercent hors du Royaume et son etablis chez les allies a qui on a rendu, ou payé le Montant de Leurs Marchandises. Je crois que la Loix doit être Egal pour

---

7. The copy, dated June 26, is in the APS. The *Fortune*, carrying both Spanish and French cargo, had been taken the previous October, causing the commissioners considerable embarrassment. In a memorandum to the French and Spanish courts, they had promised the owners full restitution of the cargo's value. See XXV, 70, 184–7, 211.

les francois. J'ay l'honneur d'etre avec un tres profond Respect
Monseigneur Votre tres humble et obeissant serviteur

NICOLAS MOREAU

Notation: Nicholas Moreau Cadiz 28 Juillet 1778

The American Commissioners to the Committee of Commerce[8]

AL (draft): Massachusetts Historical Society; two copies: National Archives

⟨Passy, July 29, 1778: We have received your letter of May 28[9]
by Captain Reed [Read]. We rejoice at the arrival of even 49
hogsheads of tobacco, but wish for more. As we are under
contract with the farmers general to furnish 5,000 hogsheads,
for which we have already received a million livres, we have
consigned this small amount to them, rather than disposing of
it at private sale.[1] We have no further directions for Capt. Reed
other than your orders to receive goods from Schweighauser.
Your orders of May 16 will be attended to.[2] We learn from Mr.
Lovell's letter of April 16 that Mr. Bingham is authorized to
draw on us for not more than 100,000 livres. We will honor
his drafts whenever we receive the order of Congress, but are
anxious about our funds.[3]⟩

8. Published in Taylor, *Adams Papers*, VI, 331.
9. See XXVI, 537.
1. See the commissioners' letter of July 27 to Schweighauser.
2. To liquidate accounts with Beaumarchais: XXVI, 475.
3. See BF to Lovell, July 22.

The American Commissioners to the Committee for Foreign Affairs[4]

AL (draft): Massachusetts Historical Society; three copies and one transcript: National Archives

⟨Passy, July 29, 1778: We received your letters of May 14 and 15.[5] We congratulate you on the general good appearance of our affairs and are happy you are determined to accept no peace terms contrary to our alliance with France. We have not received from Congress the authorization we need to remove articles 11 and 12 from the treaty; the count de Vergennes has expressed complete willingness to agree to the change.[6] We have not yet seen Mr. Beaumarchais but shall attend to the business with him as soon as possible.⟩

The American Commissioners to the Eastern Navy Board[7]

AL (draft): Massachusetts Historical Society; two copies: National Archives

⟨Passy, July 29, 1778: We have received your letter of June 8[8] by Captain Barnes of the *Dispatch*, as well as the packets forwarded by the Massachusetts Council. We have given orders to Mr. Schweighauser to provide for the captain's return voyage[9] and have ordered our banker to give a month's pay to him and his crew and an additional one hundred dollars to him in lieu of primage, as you instructed. P.S. We are surprised at the monstrous sum you want advanced to them here, in silver and gold. If it is really your intention, we wish you had specified the sums to be paid each individual.⟩

---

4. Published in Taylor, *Adams Papers*, VI, 332.
5. XXVI, 448–9, 461–3.
6. As the committee must have expected: *ibid.*, 448–9 n.
7. Published in Taylor, *Adams Papers*, VI, 333.
8. XXVI, 600–1.
9. Below, of this date.

The American Commissioners to the Massachusetts Council

AL (draft): Massachusetts Historical Society; two copies: National Archives

Gentlemen, Passi July 29 1778

We have received the Honour of your Letter of June 9,[1] by Captain Corbin Barnes of the Schooner Dispatch together with three Packetts, directed to Us. We shall leave the Captain to his own Discretion concerning the Port he may return to. It is at present a Time of Scarcity of News, but We expect hourly important Intelligence from America, as well as from the french and English Fleets, which are both at Sea, and very near each other. The War is commenced in Germany between the Emperor and King of Prussia, but no Event of great Importance has yet taken Place. We are informed that the British King and Council have determined to offer Independance to America, provided she will break her Treaty with France, which We look upon to be a symptom of Despair and the last Effort of Deception, Seduction and Division. We have the Honour to be

The Hon. Council of the Mass Bay.

The American Commissioners to the President of Congress

AL (draft):[2] Massachusetts Historical Society; three copies and one transcript: National Archives

Sir Passy July 29 1778

Mr. Livingston received a Commission from us as first[3] Lieut. of the Boston and made a Cruise in her in which she had the good Fortune to take four prizes. He is now obliged

1. XXVI, 602–3.
2. In the hand of Arthur Lee.
3. This word was dropped from the copies; Livingston had been second lieutenant of the *Boston*.

174

to leave the Ship, but we have the pleasure of a Letter from Capt. Tucker[4] in which he gives us an handsome Character of Mr. Livingston and of his Conduct during the Cruise. We have also a good Opinion of him and recommend him to the Favor of Congress. We are &c.

Honble President of Congress

The American Commissioners to Thomas Read

AL (draft): Massachusetts Historical Society; two copies: National Archives

Captain Read,   Passi July 29. 1778
You will take on Board your Vessell such a Cargo, as you shall receive from Mr. Schweighauser, out of such Merchandises belonging to the Public as he has in his Hands. You will get loaded and to sea with all possible Dispatch and return to such Part of America as you shall judge safest. We propose to send Dispatches by you, which We shall forward in season, but dont wait, after you are ready to Sail for any Dispatches from Us, without further orders from Us. We are &c.

Captn. Read of the Baltimore

The American Commissioners to Schweighauser

AL (draft): Massachusetts Historical Society; two copies: National Archives

Sir   Passi July 29. 1778
We have directed the Captain's Read and Barnes to apply to you for such Cargoes as they can take for America, and for such Necessary supplies as they may demand, which We desire you to do with all possible Expedition and Frugality. We are &c.

Mr. Schweighauser.

4. Addressed to JA: Taylor, *Adams Papers*, VI, 259–60; see also Tucker to the commissioners, July 3.

To William Carmichael   Copy:[5] National Archives

Dear Sir   Passy, July 29. 1778

Yours of May 14. gave me great Pleasure, as it inform'd me
of your safe Arrival and Welfare.[6] And I hope that as soon as
you have seen your Friends and settled your Affairs, You will
return again to Europe, where your Abilities may be greatly
useful to your Country.[7] I continue in the same or rather in a
more uncomfortable Situation than that in which you left me.
If ever any Man was most cordially hated and detested by
Persons whom he never desired to offend, I am so by two of
our Countrymen here, for which I can give no kind of Account, unless it be that I am too much respected, complimented and caress'd by the People in general, and a Deference
a little too particular paid me by some in Power, the whole
indeed far above my Merit, but which I do not seek and cannot
help. By these Gentlemen I am reviled and abused wherever
they can get any body to hear them, and I have received from
them near a Dozen very angry and provoking Letters, some
very long and very bitter, all which I lay aside without Answering, and oblige my private Feelings to give way to the
Calls of Publick Character, showing nearly the same Civilities
to their Persons when we meet in Public as if we lived on good
Terms; because I know that an open Quarrel would grieve and
hurt our Friends and our Cause, and please none but our Enemies.[8]

I thank you for the curious Facts you observed relating the
Sucker Fish and the dead Whales. I suppose the Oil of the
Whale was diffus'd on the Surface of the Sea, either by means
of Sharks tearing its Skin and Flesh, or by their dissolution.[9]

5. In BF's hand and with his signature.

6. XXVI, 450–2.

7. This sentence is underlined and marked with "x" in the copy, probably by a later hand; the document eventually was used by Carmichael's
widow in obtaining compensation from Congress (DAB).

8. He is referring, of course, to Arthur Lee and Ralph Izard: see XXV,
432–3, 535–8, 550–1, 667–8, 710–11; XXVI, 187–8, 207–8, 215–6, 220–3,
229–35, 342–3, 491–2, 640–53.

9. The calming effect of oil upon water was a subject of longstanding
interest to BF; see, for example, XX, 30–1.

Every thing goes well at this Court. The Fleets of the two Nations are at Sea, and we hope soon to hear good News from ours.¹ With great and sincere Esteem, I am, Dear Sir, Your most obliged and most humble Servant   B FRANKLIN

M. Carmichael

W. Carmichael Esqr

Copy

John Ayres to the American Commissioners²

ALS: American Philosophical Society

⟨Bordeaux, July 29, 1778: I arrived yesterday in 26 days from Boston with a packet for you which ill health prevents me from delivering personally. Mr. Texier,³ a friend of Mr. Bondfield, has agreed to deliver it. I trust I shall soon recover and will be glad to serve in my capacity as captain in the continental navy. If not, I will await your orders. P.S. Mr. Texier disappointed me by not going to Paris, so Mr. Pauly is the bearer.⁴⟩

Sartine to the American Commissioners

LS: Harvard University Library; copies: Massachusetts Historical Society, Library of Congress, National Archives; two transcripts: National Archives

A Versailles Le 29 juillet 1778

J'ai recu, Messieurs, La Lettre que vous m'avés fait l'honneur de m'ecrire Le 16 De Ce mois. Sa majesté compte beaucoup

1. A revealing use of the possessive pronoun; BF hoped for good news from the French fleet.
2. Published in Taylor, *Adams Papers*, VI, 333–4. Ayres is identified in XXVI, 681.
3. Probably the merchant Pierre Texier, for whom see Taylor, *Adams Papers*, VI, 63.
4. On Nov. 6 a Jh. Dl. Pauly forwarded, on behalf of Bondfield, Richard Peters' letter of Aug. 13.

177

sur les secours en vivres que Le gouvernement de la Baye de Massachusset pourra procurer aux isles St. pierre et Miquelon.

Les difficultés que les Corsaires des Etats unis ont Éprouvées jusqu'a ce jour dans les ports de france soit pour la vente de leurs prises, soit pour la garde de leurs prisonniers doivent cesser par le changement de circonstances. Je ne doute pas, d'un autre Côté que Les Etats unis ne procurent dans Leurs ports les memes facilités aux Corsaires françois. Pour remplir ce double objet j'ai fait rediger un projet de Reglement que je m'empresse de vous communiquer.[5] Je vous prie de L'Examiner, et de me marquer ce que vous en penserés, ou meme de m'indiquer d'autres moiens pour atteindre Le meme But, afin que je puisse prendre Les ordres de sa majesté. J'ay L'honneur d'Etre avec un sincere attachement, Messieurs, votre très humble et très obeissant serviteur   DE SARTINE

Messrs. Les deputés des Etats unis de L'amerique

Philip Hancock: Receipt

ALS: American Philosophical Society

Amsterdam 29 Juillet 1778
Recu de Messieurs Horneca Fizeaux & Cie.[6] d'ordre et pour Compte de Messieurs Les Commissionaires du Congrés La somme de deux Cent florins Argent Court d'hollande fait a double ne Servant que pour une   PHILIP HANCOCK

5. A translation of the new French regulations is printed in Wharton, *Diplomatic Correspondence*, II, 685–7. Congress failed to reciprocate, burying the matter in committee: Taylor, *Adams Papers*, VI, 334.

6. For this prominent Amsterdam banking house, of which the Grand brothers were behind-the-scene directors, see XXVI, 135 n, 338–9 n. Apparently Horneca, Fizeaux & Cie. acted on its own initiative, perhaps with collaboration from Ferdinand Grand, whose letter of Aug. 27 below reveals his own sentiments respecting Hancock.

From ———— Pelletier[7]   ALS: American Philosophical Society

Monsieur   A Paris ce 29 Juillet 1778.

Quoique ces essais ne contiennent que des idées très simples, l'utilité dont je crois qu'elles pourroient être à vos compatriotes et l'intérêt que leur courage inspire à tous ceux en qui la corruption n'a point éteint les sentimens de la nature, m'engagent à les mettre sous vos yeux. Si elles étoient adoptées, le tems actuel est peut être celui dans lequel il seroit le plus important de former les établissemens que je propose. Ce seroit le moyen de porter le crédit public à son plus haut dégré, par la confiance qu'inspireroit une telle administration et par la facilité avec laquelle l'Etat obtiendroit les finances qui lui seroient nécessaires. Cette administration pourroit n'être qu'agréable aux peuples et ne pourroit que leur assûrer encore plus cette liberté inestimable qu'ils défendent si généreusement. Les Asyles augmenteroient certainement l'attachement et le courage des Troupes, et seroient des moyens assûrés pour attirer les étrangers, par la certitude dans laquelle chacun seroit d'avoir toujours des retraites honnêtes, et de ne jamais manquer du nécessaire. Ce seroit enfin un moyen sûr pour établir des manufactures dans toutes vos Provinces, et pour rendre en peu d'années votre Etat le plus fort, le plus heureux, le plus peuplé et le plus florissant de la terre.

J'aurai l'honneur de passer chez vous d'ici à quinzaine, et si vous jugez que mon travail ne soit bon à rien, je vous serai obligé de vouloir bien me le faire remettre.[8] En attendant, Per-

7. All we know about the author is his address, rue neuve de Richelieu, given in his memoir.

8. Endorsed by BF "Memoire de M. Pellethier Azyles pour les Indigents," the thirteen-page memoir is at the APS. Its first part is the outline of a taxation plan for America based on a system of districts and the division of the population in three classes—the first of which is called "les nobles," an indication that the author is still thinking in French terms. His scheme, however, tends to lift the burden of taxation from the poor. The second part deals with ways of procuring housing to the indigent, in the form of military-type barracks to be run by the inmates themselves who will cultivate the adjacent land. Children will be raised in common and instructed in the military arts by the older residents. No one can enter the asylum for

mettez que j'aie l'honneur d'être avec la plus grande estime, Monsieur Votre très humble et très obéissant serviteur

PELLETIER

John Emery to Arthur Lee[9]   ALS: Harvard University Library

Sir   Bilbao 29 July 1778

I have at length got the Liberty of Cap. Allen and his Crew who are now here with some more Sailors which have been taken and sett onshore in Spain.[1] I have a schooner here which is a remarkable fine Sailor and these people seem disposed to make a Cruize this Summer before they go home therefore I am preparing to Arm the Vessell as a Privateer. If you can send me a Commission by return of Post you will oblige me very Much as the Vessell will be ready by that time and wait only for that. There have been no Arrivals here for some months past from America consequently No News. The Schooner is Calld the Newbury John Allen Comr. mounts 8 Carriage Gunns and 8 Swivels and 30 hand.[2] Am sir your Most Obedient Servant   JNO EMERY

Arthur Lee Esqr Chaillot

Notation: Messrs. Franklin & Adams If there is no objection be so good as to send a Commission &c wch I will dispatch Augt. 9th. 1778 A Lee[3]

---

less than one year. After six years, all private possessions will belong to the community. The clergy should be kept out at all costs. Such a system, concludes Pelletier, would offer respectable and productive alternatives to those men and women whose only choices would otherwise be prostitution and thievery.

9. We include this because of Lee's notation to BF and JA. For Emery, a transplanted Newburyport merchant, see above, XXV, 499 n.

1. For Allen's difficulties see *ibid.*, pp. 430–1.

2. Her bill of lading, dated Jan. 26, 1779, is at the National Archives.

3. We have no record of a response; presumably BF and JA complied with Lee's request.

From Johann Reinhold Forster[4]

ALS: Franklin Library, Franklin, Massachusetts

Dear Sir   London July the 30th 1778.

Give me leave to present You with a Copy of the Observations made during my late Voyage round the World,[5] and I hope You will favour me with the acceptance of them. These Observations contain a variety of Philosophical Subjects, and the last Chapter contains useful Directions for preserving the lives of mariners on long Voyages. Humanity prompted me to publish them, and as I consider mankind everywhere as my Brethren, I hope they may by Your means, become useful to my Brethren in America, who are obliged to go on long Voyages. I envy the good luck of my Son,[6] who so often enjoyed the pleasure of being in Your company during his Stay at Paris. My Daughter at Vienna[7] has likewise the pleasure of

---

4. For the famous naturalist (1729–98) see above, xv, 147–8.

5. *Observations Made during a Voyage Round the World, on Physical Geography, Natural History and Ethnic Philosophy* . . . (London, 1778). For an account of this work see Michael E. Hoare, *The Tactless Philosopher, Johann Reinhold Forster* (Melbourne, [1976]), pp. 183–6. The *Jour. de Paris* announced on July 9 that Forster's book was available at Pissot's bookshop.

6. Johann Georg Adam Forster (1754–94) was the writer's oldest son, who had accompanied his father on Cook's second voyage. The father had expected to write the account of this voyage but since Cook was determined to do it himself, Forster was forbidden from doing so by the Admiralty. He complied with the letter of the order but encouraged his son to write it instead. A short time before Cook's narrative appeared, Georg Forster's account was published under the title *A Voyage Round the World, in His Britannic Majesty's Sloop, Resolution* . . . (London, 1777). The resulting furor led to Johann Reinhold's imprisonment for debt and his son's departure from England. *DNB*.

7. Forster had four daughters. This one was most likely the second, Antonia Elisabeth Susanna (1758–1823). We are told that she left home at the beginning of September, 1776, having inherited her father's roving spirit. She worked as a governess, first in Vienna, later in Copenhagen, Hanover, Courland, and Berlin. According to Hoare (*op. cit.*, 8th prelim. leaf and p. 164), "she was respected as a highly intelligent, informed companion and educator, although few failed to notice her fiery pride, and refusal to bow to the social conventions of the times."

being often in company with Mr. Lee;[8] and I wish ardently Providence may bless You with health Contentment of mind and long life and that You may be long useful to Mankind and be an honour to Your Age and Country. I am with the duest regard Dear Sir Your most obedient humble Servant

JOHN REINOLD FORSTER

Dr Franklin

From Philip Hancock   ALS: American Philosophical Society

Honored Sir   Amsterdam July 30: 1778
   The Reason I have Presum'd to take the Liberty To Address you, was to Inform you My Motive for Comming with M. Welsh[9] Was By the Advice of many Friends To That Noble Cause you Are Engaged In, to Inform you of those Past Proceedings And Glad to have Your Instruction How to Act for The feauter [future]. Therefore As we Could not give your Honor Any Information By Letter without Danger Thought it the most Prudent method for one of us to Come to Parris and Beg the favour of a Personal Interview Which if your Honor will Pleas to grant me hope Shall Be Able to Inform Your Honor of Som Things That wont make my Visit at Parris Desagreeable.[1] I Remain with Due Respect Your Exelency Most Obedient Servant   PHILIP HANCOCK

Addressed: Honb. Benjman Franklin / Parris

Notation: Philip Hancock Amsterdam July 30 1778.

8. William Lee, who was in Vienna from the end of May until July: Karl A. Roider, Jr., "William Lee, Our First Envoy in Vienna," *Virginia Mag. of History and Biography* LXXXVI (1978), 163–8.
   9. David Welsh: see his letter above, July 2.
   1. BF not only granted an interview, he also rewrote Hancock's petition: below, [after Sept. 2].

From John Holker[2]

ALS: American Philosophical Society

Monsieur et Respectable ami   Rouen le 30 Juillet 1778

Mr. Lalanne negociant au havre, mon ami, et encore plus l'ami de mon fils, m'a recommandé d'une maniere particuliére Monsieur Le Baron de Reuschenberg qui vous remettra la Presente.[3] Il désire passer en amérique, pour y trouver de l'employ et y finir sa carriere et m'a demandé une lettre de Recommandation pour vous, digne et Respectable ami. Je n'ai pu la lui refuser surtout m'etant presenté par un aussi bon ami que M. Lalanne, c'est ce motif qui me fait prendre la Liberté

2. The prominent Rouen businessman and father of Jean Holker: above, XXIV, 357 n.

3. Jean Lalanne was apparently part of the clan that had a branch in Bayonne and included Pierre Lalanne, the Paris banker: Lüthy, *Banque protestante*, II, 703 n. About the Baron we know nothing except that he had large ideas and was persistent in advancing them. On Aug. 7 he sent from Paris a verbose memorandum, which BF endorsed "Reflection sur la Guerre." In it Reuschenberg suggests that he go to the U.S. and settle there; he would be useful in war or peace. His idea is to raise a legion by instalments, some 900 men a year for four years, and then further legions like the Roman. Even a quarter-legion, with experienced officers, could hold its own against an enemy regiment; for its strength would come from hard living, strict discipline, and the fear of God. The U.S., after it wins the war, will need a strong militia to guard against a British return, Canada as a dangerous neighbor, or Indian attacks on the frontiers. Legions would serve the purpose; each would be a military colony, where the children were brought up in common and trained to be tireless soldiers.

The writer would not in peacetime be useless baggage. He has been raised in courts and public affairs, has helped to govern two provinces, and has had diplomatic experience. He speaks French, German, and Latin, and knows enough Spanish and English to translate; he is familiar with agriculture, forestry, manufacture, and smelting. He would prefer to live in Pennsylvania because it is, he is told, full of Germans. But even if he never sets foot in America he will be glad to contribute indirectly to upholding that bastion of liberty.

On Aug. 14, having apparently heard nothing, he writes BF again at great length to expatiate on the advantages of his legion. This time he longs to be an aide to Lafayette, and asks to have his ideas forwarded to Congress and Washington. Once more he had no reply, for his efforts ended, as far as we know, with an undated appeal for some word of response to his two previous letters. APS. His only personal contact with BF, it seems, was when he delivered Holker's letter.

183

de vous prier d'éclairer Monsieur Le Baron de vos Bons avis et de l'honorer de votre Protection pour le succès de son Projet. Je suis avec Respect Monsieur et Respectable ami Votre tres humble et tres obeissant serviteur   J HOLKER

Addressed: A Monsieur / Monsieur Le Docteur franklin / Ambassadeur des Etats unis de / l'amerique en son hotel / Passy

Endorsed: Holker July 30. 78

From ——— Sieulanne

Copy: American Philosophical Society

⟨Ste. Croix de Teneriffe, July 30, 1778, in French: Having captured and brought into Palma, one of the Canary islands, the English brigantine *The Countess of Mouton*, Capt. Conyngham, of the *Revenge*, asked me to bring her to Martinique. We settled on conditions. As I was about to sail on July 19, I was accosted by an armed sloop sent by the Governor of Palma acting on orders from Marquis de Travallosos, Commander-in-Chief of the Canaries. The instructions were to stop my ship and arrest me, as well as Capt. Conyngham who was still in sight of the port. I was abused and eventually told to address myself to an English merchant in Orotava, named Thomas Cologan.[4]

His answer, enclosed, proves that my arrest was really a reprisal against Conyngham.[5] Could you please obtain from the court of Spain a reimbursement for the five hundred piastres this delay is costing me? The sum should be remitted

4. In the enclosed copy of his letter to Cologan, July 27, Sieulanne suggested that they settle the affair amicably even though he was aware that Cologan had requested his arrest.
5. Cologan's answer, of July 29, denied that he sought the arrest: he had never heard of Sieulanne and had no grievance against him. But Conyngham, behaving like a pirate, had seized a Swedish ship laden with cargo belonging to inhabitants of the Canaries and that cargo should not be allowed to proceed. (The *Countess of Mouton* did eventually reach Martinique: Neeser, *Conyngham*, facing p. 152). By 1783, Mrs. Cologan, living in Paris, was on friendly terms with BF to whom she sent some wine grown on their Teneriffe estate.

to the French consul who will forward it to me. As to the insult to the flag, I am certain you shall obtain redress.⟩

Jacques Barbeu-Dubourg[6] to the American Commissioners

AL: American Philosophical Society

[before July 31, 1778]

Dubourg attendra vendredi 31ᵉ juillet Messrs. Franklin, Lée et Adams chez Esprit Libraire au Palais royal[7] a deux heures precises, pour avoir l'honneur de les conduire en une maison du voisinage, ou on sera tres flatté de les recevoir.

Dumas to the American Commissioners

ALS: American Philosophical Society

Messieurs   La haie 31 Juillet 1778

Je viens de recevoir les doubles des deux Lettres du Committé des affaires étrangeres, que vous avez eu la bonté de m'envoyer.[8]

Voici quelques Extraits des Depêches ministériales pour ce qu'il y avoit de plus essentiel.[9]

6. BF's old friend and former translator. This note was written on the verso of a letter from Genet of July 23 which, we are convinced from internal evidence, was to JA.

7. A bookstore specializing in new books: *Almanach des marchands*, pp. 369–70.

8. Presumably the committee's letter of May 14 to Dumas (Wharton, *Diplomatic Correspondence*, II, 580) was one; the other could have been the committee's letter of May 15 to the commissioners (above, XXVI, 461–3) or Lovell's to JA of April 29 (Taylor, *Adams Papers*, VI, 69–73), both of which mention Dumas.

9. Dumas enclosed excerpts from Dutch diplomatic dispatches from Berlin and Vienna about the armies of Emperor Joseph and King Frederick, from Madrid about the arrival of the Vera Cruz treasure fleet at Cadiz, from St. Petersburg predicting a Russo-Turkish war, from Paris about the operations of the French navy and from London reporting the arrival of the Carlisle commission, General Clinton's entry into New Jersey, and the sailing of an American squadron. For a further description see Taylor, *Adams Papers*, VI, 330 n.

Ici rien de nouveau, si ce n'est que la désertion est très forte parmi les troupes de la république. Pas moins de 1500 déserteurs pendant ces 2 mois de Juin et de Juillet. Cela vient de ce qu'on n'a permis à personne d'aller en semestre.

Vous verrez, Messieurs, par les Imprimés ci-joints, l'usage que je fais des dernieres Nouvelles que vous avez eu la bonté de me faire parvenir. L'article où j'ai mis un *M* est concerté.[1] Je suis avec le plus respectueux dévouement, Messieurs, Votre très humble et très obéissant serviteur   C.G.F. DUMAS

Paris à LL.EE. M. les Plénipotentiaires des Etats-Unis de l'Am.

Addressed: à Leurs Excellences / Messieurs les Plénipotentiaires / des Etats-Unis de l'Amérique / Paris

Notation: Dumas July 31 La Haie—78

Abraham Whipple to the American Commissioners

ALS: American Philosophical Society; copy: Yale University Library

On board Continental Frigate Providence Paimbeuf
Honoured Gentlemen   July 31 1778
Have the pleasure of acquainting you, that my Ship has been in readiness for the Sea ever since the 25 inst. only wait for a favourable wind, the wind has been to the westward this fifteen days past, which makes it absolutely impossible to get out. These winds blowing directly up the River added to this the water is so exceeding shoal, we are obliged to sail on the tide of flood. Your Honours Letters dated the 13th came to hand the 18th, in these you were pleased to Order Captn. Tucker of the Boston Frigate to join me in my Cruize to America and to get to sea with all possible dispatch; acquainted Capt. Tucker with these instructions and wrote him to repair to the mouth of this river as soon as might be. As yet the

1. These enclosures have become separated; the *Ga*ζ. *de Leyde* of July 31 carried a variety of American news probably provided by Dumas.

Boston has not joined me, and if she does not arrive here shall proceed the first fair wind and touch at L'Orient for Capt. Tucker; the 22d recieved your Letters of the 16th acquainting me that Lt. T. Simpson was appointed to the Command of the Ranger and in his destination for America was to obey my Orders, accordingly dispatched Lt. Simpson the 24th by land for Brest with express instructions to fit the Ranger for the seas with all possible dispatch. This morning recieved a Letter from him, informing me that he doubts not to be ready very soon and in compleat Order. After having joined Captn. Tucker at L'Orient shall both proceed for Brest the first oppertunity wind and weather permitting and if your honours have any Orders to Communicate in future be pleased to forward them for Brest. Have taken on board a quantity of Goods Arms and Ammunitions for the United States which Mr. Schweighauser will inform you of. My Prisoners are Delivered to the Agent agreable to the Orders recieved. At Present have on board Two hundred and Forty Men and Boys included all in good health and high spirits, Many of whom are Gentlemen Volunteers belonging to America, Masters of Ships &c. who have had the misfortune to be made Prisoners. With four months provisions on board, my Officers and People well Cloathed my Ship in Compleat Order, and all hands contented doubt not shall be able to pay my respects to the Guernsy and Jersy Privateers; with the most Agreable hopes that before I arrive in America I shall do honour to the Command with which I am entrusted, Permit me to assure your Honours that I am with all imaginable respect Your most Obedient and most humble servant ABRAHAM WHIPPLE

Notation: Capt. Whipple Paimbeuf July 31 1778

From Joseph-Mathias Gérard de Rayneval[2]

Two copies: Library of Congress

A versailles 31 Juillet 1778

M. Le Comte de Vergennes étant surchargé de travail, Monsieur, il m'a chargé de vous faire part de la bonne nouvelle que nous venons de recevoir.

Un premier Avis qui nous étoit parvenu ce matin, nous avoit annoncé un Combat entre M. Le Comte D'Orvilliers et M. L'Amiral Keppel. Deux couriers qui viennent d'arriver, confirment cette importante nouvelle. Le Combat s'est engagé lundy dernier 27. de ce mois vers midy, et a été général et des plus vifs.[3] M. d'Orvilliers ayant de l'avantage, apres plusieurs heures de Combat, a reviré sur son Ennemi pour le serrer de près, mais le vent étant devenu favorable à M. Keppel, celui cy l'a mit a profit pour éviter le Combat que notre Flotte s'efforçoit de rengager; il a éteint tous ses feux tandis que tous les notres étoient allumés, et il a profité de la nuit pour fuir et pour laisser à M. D'Orvilliers le Champ de Bataille et l'honneur du Combat. Notre flotte est rentrée dans Brest pour se reparer. Nous n'avons encore que peu de Details sur cette glorieuse affaire, mais nous ne tarderons pas d'en avoir. Je suis certain, Monsieur, que vous partagez la satisfaction qu'elle nous donne, car notre Cause est commune. J'ai l'honneur d'être avec un parfait attachement, Monsieur, Votre tres humble et tres obeissant Serviteur

(signé) GERARD DE RAYNEVAL
secrétaire du Conseil d'Etat.

P.S. Les Anglois avoient 32. Vaisseaux de ligne[4]

2. Vergennes' undersecretary in charge of American correspondence: XXVI, 376 n.

3. On July 27 the fleets had fought west of the island of Ushant (Ouessant); the battle was indecisive, d'Orvilliers' suffering more casualties, Keppel's worse material damage: W. M. James, *The British Navy in Adversity: a Study of the War of American Independence* (London, 1926), pp. 128–36.

4. In fact 30 on the day of the battle, as against 27 French: *ibid.*, pp. 432–3.

From Julien-Alexandre Achard de Bonvouloir[5]

ALS: American Philosophical Society

Monsieur   [July, 1778]

Je suis a paris depuis deux jours, et si je n'eusse pas été incommodé et extremement Las, j'aurais deja eu l'honneur d'aller vous presenter mon Respectueux hommage et vous rendre compte de mon voyage. Il a été on ne peut plus malhureux, j'ai été pris par la fregate La galathée, a quinze lieues de Charlestown, et conduit a st. augustin ou j'ai eprouvé les plus affreux traitements. Ils m'ont tout pris, j'avais viron [environ] 12000 *l.t.* sur le Batiment; ils ne m'ont pas même laissé ma montre, ny mon epée ny mes effets d'usage journalier. J'ai trouvé dans la même prison Mr. de bretigny, Keranguais et beaucoup d'autres officiers francais, qui gemissaient dans les fers.[6]

Vous m'aviez, Monsieur, confie des Lettres je les ai regardées comme un Depôt sacré confie a mes soins, et je les ai conservées malgré vent et marée; j'ai l'honneur de vous les envoyer.

J'ose esperer, Monsieur, que vous voudrez bien etre mon protecteur, et chercher a m'indamniser de mes pertes. Il est question d'un avancement tres avantageux pour moy, l'on me demande un Certificat, comme je me suis bien conduit chez vous, et que j'ai cherché a vous rendre quelques services. J'ai eu l'honneur, Monsieur, d'etre connu de vous à philadelphie, ma conduite, et ma bonne volonté vous etaient connues.

Ce certificat, conçu a peu près dans ces termes;

5. The ill-fated young man who had met in 1775 with the Committee of Secret Correspondence (XXII, 310–18). He returned to France in June, 1777 and then, subsidized by his brother, went back to America in hopes of becoming a merchant. Captured by the British, he landed in France once again in July, 1778: Joseph Hamon, *Le Chevalier de Bonvouloir* . . . (Paris, 1953), pp. 78–89.

6. For Brétigney, Keranguez and their companions see XXIV, 96–7, 205–6. The *Affaires de l'Angleterre et de l'Amérique* of July 12, vol. XI, part II, cahier XLIX, pp. cix–cxi, carried a letter from Bonvouloir to Sartine recounting their sufferings. The letter was also printed in the Aug. 5 issue of the *Mercure de France.*

Je certifie, que le Chevalier Achard De Bonvouloir, officier au Regiment du Cap, que j'ai connu a philadelphie, c'est bien conduit et qu'il a cherché a nous rendre service. En foy de quoy etc.

Ce certificat dieje [dis-je], Monsieur, ne vous enguage a rien et me peut procurer mon avancement. J'attends cette grace de vous, Monsieur, j'en serai a jamais recconnoissant, j'irai vous en faire mes tres humbles Remerciments et vous offrir le profond Respect avec lequel j'ai L'honneur [d'être] Monsieur Votre tres heumble et Tres obbeissant serviteur

DE BONVOULOIR

Si vous m'envoyez ce certificat, je vous prie de le faire par le porteur, j'en aurai besoin ce soir vous voudrez bien y mettre votre cachet.[7]

Notation: M. Bonvouloir

From James Brehon[8]   ALS: Historical Society of Pennsylvania

May it please your Excellency   Forton, July. 1778

Having addressed you twice before which I imagine have never reached you from my receiving no Answer and nothing but distress could have induced me to trouble you so often which distress has indeed of late been allevated in a great Measure by the Generosity of the British People which I believe you have already been informed of and the sums which the [they] so generously Voted for our Support[9] is as we are Informed almost expend'd owing to the great number of other Prisoners added to our number since that time, and our former distress begins to stare us and we already anticipate the hor-

7. Bonvouloir also sent BF an undated note asking for the return of a letter, perhaps prior to his 1777 departure for America. APS. As we mentioned in vol. XXII, he did eventually obtain a naval commission and died while serving in India in 1783.

8. A native of Cambridge, Maryland, Brehon had been surgeon of the sloop of war *Hornet*, captured April 27, 1777: Robert H. Elias and Eugene D. Finch, eds., *Letters of Thomas Attwood Digges (1742–1821)* ([Columbia, S.C., 1982]), p. 11; *Naval Docs.*, VIII, 454.

9. XXV, 350 *et seq.*

rors of our former situation, and In order to remedy in Some measure the wants which I am likely to feel I make bold to demand of you a small sum of Money which I should not do were I not intitled thereto by being in the Continental Service as you are already Informed by a list carried over by Mr. Thornton from hence and the Number of Prisoners committed Since his departure amount to 78 Amoungst which is Capt. Hindman of the Cont. Ship Alfred and four of his Officers which Joyned to the four of us belonging to the Hornet are all the Continental Officers which are in this Prison.[1]

From your Natural Love of the rights and Liberties of Mankind and your well know Sympathy for those who tho Unfortunate are still Suffering in the Same glorious Cause by which you are Animated will I hope Influence you to grant the Assistance which I write for which will be allways Acknowledged as an Eternal Obligation and Chearfully Allowed in Account by your Excellencies Most Obedient Humble Servant

JAMS BREHON

Addressed: His Excellency / Benjamin Franklin Esqr. / Paris

Notation: Brehon Prisoner

From ———   AL: American Philosophical Society

[before or during July, 1778][2]

On a appris par un officier francois lieutenant dans les troupes aux ordres du général Gates que Klinton avec un corps de 4000 hommes, etant en marche pour se réunir a Philadelphie au général Howe a été attaqué en chemin par le general Gates, et qu'apres un combat très opiniâtre les anglois ont été tous

---

1. For the capture of the *Alfred* see XXVI, 539. John Thornton had visited Forton in December, 1777: XXV, 414–19. One of the *Hornet's* officers soon escaped, as did Hinman: see Leveux's letter of Aug. 10 and Hinman's of Aug. 19.

2. By the end of July news had reached Paris of the evacuation of Philadelphia: *Courier de l'Europe*, July 28, 1778 (IV [1778], p. 61). This false rumor must predate that time.

ou tués ou blessés ou prisonniers de guerre. Le Genéral Klinton s'est sauvé preque seul a Philadelphie.

L'auteur de cette lettre a ete blessé, elle est ici entre les mains des parens de ce jeune homme.

On peut prendre la dessus des informations aupres de M. l'abbé Radix chanoine de Notre dame[3] qui a donné a plusieur personnes un extrait de cette lettre. Elle est écrite a un de ses neveux par le jeune homme lieutenant dans les troupes américaines.

Addressed: A Monsieur / Monsieur Benjamin Franklin / A Passy

Peter Collas to the American Commissioners[4]

ALS: American Philosophical Society

Gentlemen,   Passy, August 1, 1778

As I late master of the brigg Triton belonging to the United States of America which was Captur'd by the Enemy within bell Isle, On my Return here from England, I Protested Against the Said Captur's therein Showing where And by whom taken and the Value of the Said brigg and her Cargo, which Protest you have been Pleased to Present to the Minister, Requesting of him to Stop the Value of the Triton and her Cargo to the Amont of the Sum Mantioned in the Protest.[5] Out of Such Vessells belonging to the English Nation as are or My be Stop in france. As I am going to America by ferst opportunity I hereby Inpower you the Said Commissioners to do, Act and Transact in my Stead and behalf and every thing, Relative to the Said brigg and her Cargo also of a Small Sum

3. One of 40 priest-canons of the cathedral: *France ecclésiastique* for 1778, p. 350.

4. The husband of Jane Mecom's daughter Jane. For an account of his disastrous voyage see xxv, 459 and xxvi, 259–60. Collas' letter to jw, March 22, 1778 describing his misfortunes is in the APS. BF had already advanced him 96 *l.t.* on July 21 and later noted that Ridley had given him the same sum in London. On Aug. 5 BF gave him another 312 *l.t.*: Waste Book (above, XXIII, 19, account I).

5. These papers do not appear to have survived.

which was my Property and which is Mantioned in the Above Said Protest. I Remains with Due Respects your Most Obedeint and humble Servant   PETER COLLAS

Honorable Banjamin Franklin Arther Lee and John Adams Esqrs Commissioners for the therteen United States of America.

Notation: Capt Peter Collas power to the Commrs Passy 1. Aug. 78

James Moylan to the American Commissioners[6]

ALS: American Philosophical Society

⟨Lorient, August 1, 1778: The *Boston* and her three prizes sailed this morning. Captain Tucker accidentally mentioned to me your orders to load some goods, but as the wind was fair he decided not to wait for them. I can freight them for you at reasonable terms on a French ship I am sending to America next month. I am much obliged to Mr. Franklin for advancing Mr. Ogden 8 guineas which I desire my friend in Paris to repay him.⟩

From Barbeu-Dubourg   ALS: American Philosophical Society

1er aout 1778

Je vous prie, Mon cher Maitre, de faire tenir ces trois petites lettres, par autant d'occasions differentes a mesure qu'il s'en presentera, a Mr. d'Arcel à Boston,[7] afin qu'il en arrive plus surement une; ce que l'on desire d'autant plus qu'il a marqué n'en avoir encore reçu aucune de son frere qui lui en a ecrit neuf, depuis qu'il est dans ce pays là.

Je vous reïtere aussi, et à Monsieur Lee, ma supplique de

---

6. Published in Taylor, *Adams Papers*, VI, 343.

7. D'Arcel reappears below in Dubourg's letter of Sept. 1 as Jean Darcel. We know nothing about him, but five years later a man of that name was working for BF: Darcel to WTF, June 26, and S. Vaughan to BF, Dec. 27, 1783, APS.

faire tenir une douzaine de Louis, (d'or,) au fils de Mme. de Foucherolles, beaufrere de M. Brisson, pris sur le navire le d'Argentré, et detenu prisonier à Oak-hampton en Devonshire, à 30 miles de Plimouth, et qui a pris le nom de La Mote Du Pin, et cinq louis d'or à son compagnon de captivité mon petit neveu, qui est appellé Dubourg de la Blanchardiere dans la même ville, qui peut en avoir besoin quoiqu'il doive en avoir reçu par le correspondant d'un Negociant de Nantes.[8] Mme. de Foucherolles et moi sommes prêts a consigner d'avance, dès aujourd'huy meme, cette somme à remettre, et ce qu'on peut presumer qu'il pourra y avoir de frais occasionnés par cette remise, dont il est trop juste de tenir compte, et meme des faux frais inevitables en pareil cas, comme ports de lettres, commissions etc.

Quant à leur echange, je compte toujours sur vos bontés, pour le tems le plus prochain, où elle pourra avoir lieu. Tous les deux avoient des brevets de sous Lieutenans du premier regiment d'infanterie de la nouvelle Georgie à l'armée continentale. J'ai l'honneur d'etre avec un tendre et invariable attachement, Monsieur et cher Ami, Votre tres humble et tres obeissant serviteur DUBOURG

Notation: Dubourg Augt. 1. 1778

8. Foucherolles had tried to get into the American army. Brisson had asked Dalibart to intercede for the young man with BF, and had described him as twenty-three, well set up, in good health, and full of zeal, vigor, and the desire to be useful: Brisson to Dalibart, undated, APS. De La Plaigne recruited him as well as young Dubourg, about whom we know nothing, for the Georgia regiment; they were all captured and imprisoned together. Mme. de Foucherolles paid BF twelve guineas for her son: Cash Book (above, XXVI, 3), entry dated only August. By the following February the prisoner was at home again; he wrote BF, still under the name of La Mothe du Pin, to request a letter to the president of the Georgia legislature: Feb. 5, 1779, APS. See also Bodinier, *Dictionnaire*, pp. 492–3.

From the Comte de Bussy-Dagoneau[9]

ALS: American Philosophical Society

Monsieur   Enclos du temple ce 1er aoust 1778.
Mes Ennemis vouloient m'éloigner de la france, J'aurois désiré combâttre ceux d'un peuple qui vous doit en partie ses vertûs, son Energie, et son Bonheur. Des maladies et des procés me retiennent encore, Monsieur. J'arriveray peutêtre un jour a Boston, trop tard pour ma gloire, a temps pour admirer celle de Vos Concitoyens et de mes compatriotes. Garcilasse De Lavegá mourant, chantoit les Victoires De Charles Quint.[1] Malade, j'ay ôsé, Monsieur, celebrer celle que l'amour de la liberté fit remporter. Daignés recevoir avec complaisance, l'hommage que je rends a votre patrie, et a vous. Je suis avec Respect Monsieur Votre tres humble et tres obeissant serviteur
    LE COMTE DE BUSSY-DAGONEAU
    Colonel cydevant Commandant les hussards chasseurs
    Gardes de Limbourg

From Patrick Clear (or Cleary)[2]

ALS: American Philosophical Society

Most Excellent Sir   Lisbon the 1st August 1778
    Emboldened by your Excellencies universal character both in public and particular station, I presume to address myself to

9. Born in 1735 into a well-known Burgundian family, the count served in the musketeers until 1761. Bodinier. That something went wrong in his life after that is shown by his address. The *enclos du Temple* was inhabited by three categories of people: rich aristocrats, small artisans, and impecunious debtors protected by asylum privileges. He obviously belonged to the third. See J. Hillairet, *Dictionnaire historique des rues de Paris*, II, p. 547.
    1. Garcilassó or Garcias Lasso de La Vega (1530–1568) was a Peruvian historian.
    2. The name is spelled both ways in *The State Records of North Carolina* ... (26 vols., Goldsboro, N.C., 1886–1907), where his brother Timothy appears frequently as a merchant and prominent citizen of New Bern: VI, 211, 852, 914–15, 963; VII, 35–6; VIII, 508, 510. What little more we know of Patrick comes from an undated memorandum in French in the third

your Excellency, and implore your Excellencies protection in the present affair. I have had a Brother by name Timothy Clear, or Cleary, who resided a long time in Newbern North Carolina in America, where he was married to a woman of the Campbells: he and she died some time in September, One Thousand Seven Hundred and Seventy Five, possessed of a tolerable good fortune, he died without making a Will; but she who survived him four days, made her Testament, bequeathing to her Nephew what belonged to her, the rest for the Heirs of her deceased husband Timothy Clear, or Cleary. One of the Executors by name David Baron, wrote to Ireland to the Heirs of said Timothy, by name are, Patrick, Simon, Esther, Margaret, and Mary, Clear or Cleary, all which are duely and legally authenticated before the Lord Mayor of Dublin; and the aforesaid Coheirs gave me their Brother, a full power and commission to act in the affair, as shou'd seem to me most adviseable. I for the execution of said Commission, determin'd to go to Spain, and from thence to America; but on the way fell sick in Lisbon, and was thereby prevented to continue my journey, having been lately inform'd that there was an act passed by the Provincial Congress of North Carolina, whereby the Lands and effects of all those who were absent, and did not appear, or put in their Claim, before the expiration of October of this present Year, wou'd be confiscated;[3] and I was also told that our being Roman Catholicks, and my being a Clergy-Man of the Roman Catholick Church, rendered me incapable of enjoying what our Brother acquir'd by fair dailing and unblemished character. My Author for this is one Owen, from North Carolina, who has been outlawed there; in consequence of which, I appeal to your Excellency, not doubting but the justness of the cause will meet with your Excellen-

---

person, probably by Cleary himself (APS). What it adds to his letter is that abbé Patrick Cleary is a native of Ireland who for a number of years has resided at Cadiz, pursuing his studies and an ecclesiastical life. BF endorsed it "Memoir given me & recommended to me by the Portuguese Ambassador Cleary's Affairs."

3. This law which was passed in November, 1777 is discussed in Isaac S. Harrell, "North Carolina Loyalists," *N. C. Hist. Review* III (1926), 581.

cies protection, who is Pater Patriae, Restorer of freedom and liberty. I was offer'd several Letters for the first Nobility of Paris to entercede with your Excellency on this affair, but thought them unnecessary as uprightness, and integrity, are the distinguishing characteristicks of your Excellency; I remain Your Excellencies most faithful and Most Humble Servant   PATRICK CLEAR OR CLEARY

P.S. If your Excellency shou'd be pleas'd to answer this Epistle, vouchsafe to order it to be directed to me at the Irish College of Lisbon.[4]

Addressed: To / His Excellency B. Frankland / Embassadour Plenipotenty. / from the United States of / America / Paris

Notations in different hands: Patrick Clear or Cleary Lisbon 1. Aout 1778 / Patrick Clear or Cleary

From Leslie Grove[5]   ALS: American Philosophical Society

Dear Sir   London. 1st. Augt. 1778
    From the honor I had of your acquaintance at My Lord Le Despencers at W. Wycomb in 73,[6] I am Induced to flatter myself the request I have to make for the Enlargement of a particular Friends Brother now a Prisoner onboard an American Vessel in Brest Road will be comply'd with, the person solicited for is a Brother of Mr. John Trumans an Irish Factor in this City. He was a Passinger on board the Lord Chatham a Merchant Vessel from hence to Dublin, that was taken off Wicklow the 16th April last by the Revenge Privateer belonging to Piscataway.[7] You will I am satisfied be more readily be

4. BF apparently obliged since in 1784 the governor of North Carolina mentioned a letter from him on Patrick Cleary's behalf; the state eventually passed an act to remove all his disabilities: *State Records* ... , *op. cit.,* XIX, 750–1; XXIV, 696–7, 889–90, 988.
    5. Formerly the captain, as he says here, of the *Thynne.* An article in *The Public Advertiser,* Aug. 14, 1776, spells his name "Groves," and his ship *Tyne.*
    6. BF was a frequent visitor to Lord Le Despencer's West Wycombe home during the summer and fall of 1773; see XX, *passim.* No evidence of an acquaintance with the Groves has survived.
    7. For the *Lord Chatham*'s capture by the *Revenge,* see XXVI, 321–2 *et seq.*

led to comply with this request when I tell you the young man Mr. Thos. Truman has a wife and three young Children much distressed and Unhappy at his Absence and Unpleasent Situation. I shall therefore hold myself Exceedingly Obliged If you will as soon as possible give the Necessary orders for his being set at liberty to return to his Family as I am much Interested for him on his Brothers account.

I resigned the Command of the Thynne Packet, (which you did me the honor to see Launched) about a year ago and have Commenced a manner(?) of business in partnership with my late most worthy Father in laws partner Mr. Knox in this City.[8] And when our Unhappy disputes with America are at an end, which I hope will be the case Er'e long, I hope I shall have the honor of seeing you here in the mean time Mrs. Grove begs to Join me in best Compliments to you, I am with great Regard and Esteem Dear Sir Your Most Obedient Humble Servant   LESLIE GROVE

If I am to Expect the honor of a line please to direct to No: 4 Crosby Square

Doctor. Franklin

Addressed: Doctor Franklin

Endorsed: Capt Grove about an Eng. Prisoner London 1. aout 1778.

Notation: recd. Sunday and opened according to Dr Franklins Desire.

---

8. The father-in-law was probably Mercer. Ralph Knox was director of the Royal Exchange Assurance, and the firm of Knox & Mercer was located at the address Grove provides below, 4 Crosby Place: *Kent's Directory* for 1778, p. 103.

From the Chevalier Thomas O'Gorman[9]

ALS: American Philosophical Society

Monsieur   a Paris ce lr. Aout 1778

N'ayant appris que ce matin que Monsieur Williams votre neveu etoit aupres de vous, il m'etoit impossible de l'avoir invité l'autre jour à etre de votre partie lundi prochain, c'est pourquoi je vous supplie, Monsieur, de vouloir bien l'engager à vous accompagner ce jour la. Il me fera un honneur et plaisir tres sensible. Recevez les assurances très sinceres de mon profond respect et les sentimens distingués avec lesquels j'ay l'honneur d'être Monsieur votre tres humble et très obeissant serviteur   LE CHEVR. O'GORMAN

Endorsed: Chevr. O Gorman / 1. Aout 1778.

From Veuve Jean Martin Smets

ALS: American Philosophical Society

Monsieur   Anvers le ler Aout 1778

La presente etant uniquement pour avoir l'honneur de vous prevenir de vous avoir Expedié par la diligence ordinaire un pacquet a votre adresse reçu de Monsieur Aychmayer de Rotterdam, esperant que vous l'aurez deja Reçu bien Conditionne, charmez que cette occasion me procure Celle de vous offrir mes Services, vous priant de disposez de moi, et de me Croire avec un profond Respect Monsieur Votre tres humble et tres obeissante Servante   VEUVE JEAN MARTIN SMETS

Addressed: A Son Excellence / Monsieur Le Docteur franklin / Ministre Plenipotentiaire de LL.hh.PP. / les Seigneurs Etats unis de Lamerique / Pres de S.M.F. / a Paris

Endorsed: Veuve Smets Packet never receiv'd Anvers ler aout 1778

---

9. BF's winegrowing friend is identified above, XIX, 86 n.

From Johann Rudolph Tschiffelÿ[1]

ALS: American Philosophical Society

Berne en Suisse ce 1er d'Aout 1778

Daignes Monsieur permetre que mettant de coté vos eminentes dignites politiques, je ne m'addresse qu'au Philosophe, qu'au précieux ami de l'humanité.

La passion pour l'Agriculture m'a fait passer touts les moments de loisir a l'etudier et a la pratiquer. J'en ai fait renaitre le gout parmis mes concitoÿens, et puissament soutenu par plusieurs d'entre eux, nous osons croire que nos efforts ont contribué de quelque chose au bienêtre phisique de nos compatriotes. Vieux aujourdhui et ne pouvant plus prêcher d'exemple, mon plus grand desir aujourdhui seroit de rendre utiles le peu d'heures qui me restent au bonheur politique de la Societé.

A mes ÿeux rien n'ÿ contribuera plus efficacement, que de repandre aussi loin qu'il me sera possible les nouvelles constitutions des divers peuples dont Vous etes le Pere. Je viens d'en voir Monsieur une Collection partielle traduitte en françois par Mr. Regnier, qu'il a eu l'honeur de Vous dedier. En la lisant il m'a semblé qu'il n'avoit pas toujours sous les ÿeux son original, ou que du moins avec une organisation monarchique il n'a pas partout egalement saisi le sens d'un sistème entierement nouveau pour lui.[2]

1. Also known as Tschiffeli (1716–80), he was founder of the Economic Society of Bern, and author of several books and memoirs on economic and agricultural reform. *Dictionnaire historique et biographique de la Suisse*; Quérard, *France littéraire*. He was also known in France as a man of integrity and literary acumen; Voltaire wrote that he possessed "baucoup de savoir, un bon esprit, et un bon coeur," and Rousseau had warmly recommended him as an editor to the Parisian book publisher, C.-J. Pancoucke, in 1764. Theodore Besterman, *Voltaire's Correspondence* (51 vols., Geneva, 1968–77), XVI, 294; R. A. Leigh, *Correspondance complète de Jean Jacques Rousseau* (44 vols., Geneva, 1965–85), XXI, 74.

2. Tschiffelÿ was perceptive in his criticism of Regnier's work (see above, XXVI, 529–30). The so-called Swiss edition was nothing more than a pirated reprint of already published documents. See Gilbert Chinard, "Notes on the French Translations of the 'Forms of Government or Constitutions of the Several United States' 1778 and 1783," APS *Year Book 1943*, pp. 89–96.

Je me propose de faire connoitre incessament ces belles Loix, non seulement a ma patrie mais a l'Allemagne et a l'Italie; la traduction pour ce dernier Païs se fera sous mes ÿeux, et l'allemande sera de ma main; Persone ne la feroit avec plus d'attention et plus de zêle.

J'ose donc Vous supplier Monsieur qu'en faveur de motif Vous voulies bien permettre a un de vos Secretaires, de me faire parvenir par la Messagerie touttes ces nouvelles constitutions en Anglois, soit imprimées soit exactement copiées, quel qu'en puisse etre le prix, au quel je ne m'arrêterai jamais. Cette faveur obtenue ajoutera a mon profond Respect pour votre personne la plus parfaite reconoissance. J'ai l'honeur d'etre a jamais avec la plus grande veneration Monsieur Votre tres humble et tres obeissant Serviteur

   Tschiffelÿ

  Secretaire du Supreme Consistoire de la republique

Endorsed: Tschiffeley would translate American Constitutions

From Benjamin Vaughan

ALS: American Philosophical Society

     Morning, Augt: 1st: 1778.

Your letter, my dearest sir, was heavenly to me and filled me with the utmost transports. I dare not tell you what I had feared; but I thought *your* mind must see into every little corner and expectation of my heart, and would acquit me of every thing but the true motive. It has done so, and has only if possible raised you higher in my conceptions.

As I know nothing of this opportunity, I shall only add that the leaves you wrote for, were sent per post last night, directed to Mr. Chaumont, Passy near Paris.[3] The rest will be conveyed

---

3. That note to Chaumont, written in French, is at the APS. It mentions a small piece of paper to be remitted to that "venerable friend who always wears glasses on his nose and kingdoms on his shoulders." More is to follow soon.

to you by the bearer of this; together with a book from Dr. Forster,[4] intended he says for your *country*.

The accounts with Johnson[5] I had settled, and charged them to Mr. Jonathan Williams. But in consequence of your letter, I shall get the money from Mrs. Hewson and have it paid to Johnson; which will leave 4 ½ guineas more to W's credit. There were some additional articles at Johnson's, besides those ordered by myself; the whole together amounting to £8 or £10. I believe I sent Mr. Ws the particulars; if not, they *shall* be sent.

I told you of the firmness of a certain character which you so covered with benedictions; by *that opportunity* I did not choose to add, that there is reason to think his successor has been alike firm; which gave me infinite joy, and will give you some little satisfaction. Many men think they know the foibles of the last; I am sure however they know not what his virtues are, or the *turn of his talents*. I shall soon give you some anecdotes; but not by this or the next opportunity of writing. I say next, because Mr. W: Senior[6] pretends to have made his mind up about going. I have used all my little eloquence to persuade him, and hope with appearance of success, but Jonathan must not even yet thoroughly depend upon him. The party is fooled and amused here, and will get nothing. With increased gratitude and veneration, I am, my dearest sir, your most devoted and affectionate   BENJN. VAUGHAN

You will hardly conceive which of the papers in your packet I turned to first: It was the paper about Baxter.[7] When I have

4. Johann Reinhold Forster, *Observations Made during a Voyage Round the World* ... (London, 1778). See above, Forster to BF, July 30.

5. Probably the bookseller and publisher Joseph Johnson (1738–1809) who published BF's *Political, Miscellaneous and Philosophical Pieces* ... (London, 1779). *DNB*.

6. Jonathan's uncle, John Williams, the customs inspector.

7. For BF's letter to [Thomas Hopkinson?], Oct. 16, 1747, which Vaughan frequently referred to as "Vis Inertiæ," and thought was addressed to Andrew Baxter see above, III, 84–89, 91, 166, 273 and BF's *Political, Miscellaneous and Philosophical Pieces*, pp. 478–86. The book referred to in that letter was Baxter's *An Enquiry into the Nature of the Human Soul* ... (3rd ed.; 2 vols., London, 1745).

thought more ripely about it, I shall perhaps send you a *very short* line on the subject. I am most thankful for that and the rest some of which I never saw before, and are therefore new treasures. Johnson however advises me to wait some very short space before we begin anew. I expect your other promised boon with prodigious impatience. My messenger was quite delighted with his second reception. We think him here a blunt, independent, faithful man, with a great portion of good sense and management. He governs in a variety of things. No news I believe.

Endorsed: Vaughn Augt. 1. 78

John Paul Jones to the American Commissioners[8]

Copies: United States Naval Academy Museum, National Archives, University of Virginia Library

⟨Passy, August 2, 1778: Captain Jones requests the commissioners to supply him with copies, or allow him to copy, the following letters: M. de Sartine's letter to the commissioners about Capt. Jones, their answer, the commissioners' letter to Lieut. Simpson resulting from Capt. Jones's proposition in his favor,[9] and Capt. Jones's memorandum of July 4.⟩

From Hannah Sowden   ALS: American Philosophical Society

Sir   Rotterdam August the 2d 1778

Excuse the liberty I take in acquanting you with the decease of one who during his life was honored with your occasional correspondance, The Revd. Mr. Sowden who died on the 22d of june last my worthy and honored parent, after a residence of 30 years in this City.[1] How much his sudden and almost momentary death is publicly or privately regretted, does not

8. Published in Taylor, *Adams Papers*, VI, 343.
9. Of July 5, 11, and 16, respectively.
1. Benjamin Sowden, minister of the English Presbyterian church in Rotterdam, had last written BF on June 1: XXVI, 568–71.

become me to mention, nor am I certain whether he was personally known to you. Be that as it may, with his character as a man of Letters, and a friend to both civil and religeous liberty you were well acquanted and will therefore excuse my troubling you with this information, and with the enclosed as I know of no other way of communicated the melancholy intelligence to Mr. Gordon, whom the Public papers cannot reach and from whom I have just received a letter address'd to my Dear Father, who desires him to convey his answer by your means, and I the more readily rely on your goodness in this particular, as I have had the honor of enclosing some of Yours to Mrs. Macauley to whom I am not unknown.[2] Permit me Sir the additional one of subscribing myself with all possible consideration and respect Your Very humble and obedient Servant   HANNAH SOWDEN

Addressed: A Monsieur / Monsieur le Docteur Franklin FRS / a / Paris

Endorsed: Miss Hannah Sowden Rotterdam

From the Marquise de Lafayette

ALS: American Philosophical Society

[before August 3, 1778]

Mde. De la fayette a recu des nouvelles d'amerique, et la relation d'une petite affaire ou s'est trouvé mr. De la fayette.[3] Elle

2. William Gordon had been the intermediary in Sowden's correspondence for some time; he is identified in XXIII, 391 n. Catherine Macaulay, the English historian, had visited BF in Passy the previous year (XXV, 203, 264–5). None of BF's letters to her have been located.

3. The "petite affaire" must have been the skirmish on May 20 at Barren Hill, Pa., in which Lafayette suffered a slight wound: Idzerda, *Lafayette Papers*, II, 77–9. Our guess is that the "relation" she sent BF is the one that appeared in the *Affaires de l'Angleterre et de l'Amérique*, vol. XI, part II, cahier L, pp. ccxvii-ccxix, right after an excerpt from a letter from Washington to Congress dated May 24. Since a variety of American news appearing in that cahier was received on Aug. 3 (Taylor, *Adams Papers*, VI, 346–7, 349),

n'ose y ajouter foy, jusqu'a ce que monsieur franklin ait eu la bonte de lui confirmer. Elle espere qu'il voudra bien lui mander ce qu'on peut en croire, et lui envoye cette relation. Les nouvelles qu'elle annonce sont bien bonnes et elle le prie d'en recevoir tous ses complimens ainsi que messieurs adams et lee etc.

Mde. De la fayette joint a cette relation plusieurs lettres dont on l'avoit chargée pour mr. De la fayette une qu'elle vient d'ecrire et une autre pour un prisonnier que sa pauvre mere prie de lui faire passer.[4] Mde. De la fayette avoit deja parle a monsieur Deane en faveur de ce prisonnier, et elle le reccommande de nouveau avec infiniment d'interet et d'instance aux bontés de mr. franklin (la lettre de la mere est decachetée son adresse est dessus la lettre) cette pauvre mere est bien malheureuse sa situation est cruelle et elle interessera surement la sensibilite de monsieur franklin.

Mde. De la fayette lui presente ses hommages et le conjure de l'avertir de la premiere occasion d'ecrire en amerique parceque, quoiqu'elle lui envoye cette lettre elle aimeroit mieux que mr. De la fayette eut de ses nouvelles les plus fraiches possibles. Elle reitere a monsieur franklin les assurances de sa reconnoissance et ose meme dire de tous les sentiments qu'il lui connoit   NOAILLES DE LA FAYETTE[5]

---

we date this letter on the assumption that Mme. de Lafayette received her news somewhat before that day.

4. Possibly Mme. Dauber de Peÿrelongue who had pleaded for her son on June 25: XXVI, 148.

5. The marquise sent BF another note, dated merely "mercredy," (APS) asking him to give letters of recommendation to Congress in favor of her relative, the baron Pierron, who was setting off for America with a passport from Montbarey, minister of war. We have found no trace of Pierron.

The American Commissioners: Receipt for an Installment of a French Loan[6]

DS: American Philosophical Society

A Paris le 3 aoust 1778

Nous avons reçu de Monsieur d'harveley Garde du Trésor Royal[7] sept cent cinquante mille Livres

B FRANKLIN
ARTHUR LEE
JOHN ADAMS

From Antoine Borel

ALS: American Philosophical Society

Monsieur,   Pierefitte[8] Ce 3 août 1778

J'aurai encore recours a vous pour vous prier de me donner une heure vendredi matin. La planche qu'on grave sur le dessein, que j'ai eu l'honneur de vous presenter est fort avancée, et je me rendres de la campagne que j'habitte depuis six semaines a passi pour refaire quelques choses d'apres vous si vous voulés bien le permettre.[9]

Je serai chez vous Monsieur entre huit et neuf heures du matin. J'ai l'honneur d'etre avec respect Monsieur Votre tres humble et tres obeissant serviteur   BOREL

Addressed: A Monsieur / Monsieur Franklin / A Passi

6. The third quarterly installment of a 3,000,000 *l.t.* loan extended by the French government the preceding November (XXV, 207–8). The previous payments were made on February 28 and May 19: account XII (described in XXV, 3).

7. Joseph Micault d'Harvelay, keeper of the Royal Treasury: XXIII, 199 n.

8. On the Aire near Bar-le-Duc.

9. See XXVI, 560, 678–9.

From Louis Clouet[1]

ALS: American Philosophical Society

Monsieur   Paris le 3 aoust 1778.

Je viens de recevoir une lettre dattée d'york towne en pensilvanie du 7 fevrier de cette année du sieur Fouquet maitre poudrier au service de france qui est passé en 1776 à celui des Etats unis de l'amerique. Sa lettre est accompagnée de trois effets sur vous montant à 1460 *l.t.* qui lui ont été fournis par les Etats. Ayez la bonté de me mander quelle est la personne chargée de les acquitter et dans quel lieu et à quelle heure je peux en envoyer recevoir le montant.

Le sieur fouquet se loue Beaucoup des Bontés et de la confiance qui lui sont accordés par les Etats et il fait tout ce qu'il peut pour s'en rendre digne.[2] C'est parce que je le connoissois pour un homme sage, tres honnete et tres intelligent que la regie des poudres de france à cru faire un bon present aux Etats unis en lui accordant un congé. Ce particulier a laissé en france sa femme avec deux enfans. La femme est morte il y a six mois il n'en est pas encore instruit. La regie prend soin du plus jeune des enfans et j'ay pris l'ainé chez moi. Vous sentez Monsieur combien il est important pour ce pere qu'il recoive de mes nouvelles, et qu'il puisse me faire passer les fonds qui proviendront de ses Économies. Permettez moi de vous adresser les lettres que je serai dans le cas de lui ecrire afin que j'aye plus de certitudes qu'elles lui parviendront.[3]

---

1. One of the original members, with Lavoisier, of the *Régie des poudres* established by Turgot in 1775 to control the manufacture of gunpowder: Schelle, *Œuvres de Turgot*, IV, 366, 371; Denis I. Duveen and Herbert S. Klickstein, "Benjamin Franklin (1706–1790) and Antoine Laurent Lavoisier (1743–1794) . . . ," *Annals of Science*, XI (1955), 273, 277 n.

2. Nicolas Fouquet and his son Marc went to the U.S., as Clouet says, in 1776; they were commissioned captain and lieutenant respectively in the U.S. army in November, 1777, and remained until October, 1779. From their base in York, Pa., they traveled extensively through New England to improve domestic powder-making, and left behind treatises on the subject and models of machinery: *ibid.*, pp. 276–7, where the date of their arrival is confused with that of their commissioning.

3. BF agreed to forward the letters, which Clouet sent with a covering note on Aug. 25. The letters contained instructions about Fouquet's work

AUGUST 3, 1778

J'ay lieu de croire que vous ne me refuserez pas ce service et que vous voudrez bien etre persuade de celui que j'ay cherché à rendre aux Etats unis aujourd'huy nos alliés. J'ay l'honneur d'etre avec les sentimens de consideration d'estime et de respect qui vous sont dus, Monsieur, Votre tres humble et tres obeissant serviteur   CLOUET

regisseur général pour le Roy des poudres et Salpêtres à l'arsenal

Addressed: Monsieur le Docteur Franklin à Passy

Endorsed: Closse abt a Powder Maker

Notation: 3. Aout 1778.

From the Comte de Conway

AL: University of Pennsylvania Library

Ce 3. Aoust 1778.

Mr. le Comte de Conwai est venu pour avoir l'honneur de voir son excellence monsieur franklin, sa famille et monsieur Adams, et leur presenter mr. de Brion beaufrère de messieurs le Marquis et le Chevalier Alexandre D'Hanache:[4] mr. de Brion va partir très incessamment pour St. Domingue, il desirerait être chargé des commissions de monsieur franklin s'il en a pour ce pays la, et d'une lettre pour le Comte Alexandre parent de sa femme, avec lequel il compte aller faire connaissance.

and news of his family; Clouet also enclosed for BF copies of the *Régie*'s recent pamphlet on manufacturing saltpetre. At about the same time a brigadier of artillery by the name of Soleirol wrote BF, with no date, to enclose his own letter to Fouquet informing him of his wife's death; this event would doubtless induce him to prolong his stay, the writer added, and that would be beneficial. APS. Soleirol's name and the year he wrote are misstated in *Annals of Science, op. cit.*, p. 277.

4. Brion was perhaps a son or grandson of François de Brion de Combronde (*Dictionnaire de la noblesse*), but we know nothing more about him. For his brothers-in-law and their relationship with Lord Stirling (the "Comte Alexandre" who appears at the end of the sentence) see XXV, 114.

208

Mr. de Conwai desirerait sçavoir si les deux pieces de canon, dont il a parlé a son Excellence, peuvent lui convenir.[5] Son adresse est rüe de Vendôme au marais, chez mr. le Chevalier de Mezières Marechal de Camp.

Si son excellence voulait bien marquer en même temps a mr. de Conwai le jour qu'il sera sûr de le rencontrer a Passy.

Notation: Le Cte. de Conway

From François-Marie Fyot[6]

ALS: American Philosophical Society

Monsieur   Ce Lundi 3e. aoust 1778.

M.M.Les Comtes de Langeron[7] et de Lastiques[8] m'avoient conseillés il y a environ six mois d'avoir L'honneur de vous voir de leur part pour vous démontrer plusieurs découvertes utiles a L'humanité; L'incertitude de vous rencontrer dans un temps que vous n'eussiez pû me donner une heure d'audience, joint aux embaras de transport d'instrumens et autres mechaniques qui rendent palpables mes differentes découvertes, ont fait que j'ay hésité jusqu'a ce jour a vous proposer de vouloir bien jetter un coup d'oeil sur ces decouvertes pour en decider de l'utilité.

Vous sçaurez Monsieur que je suis l'inventeur de la poulie mechanique et simple de laquelle vous n'avez vû seulement

5. See his letter of July 23.
6. A mathematician and inventor of some note in his day. He had published his *Mémoire des avantages que procurera la géométrie sublime* . . . (Orléans, 1770), and the next year had participated in a royal French expedition to study the determination of longitude at sea, where his contribution had been a "chaise marine" to facilitate accurate observations: *Histoire de l'Académie royale des sciences* for 1773 (Paris, 1774), pp. 300–1. He subsequently published a *Précis sur les longitudes résolues tant sur terre que sur mer* (London, 1785). For his mechanical pulley see G. Touchard-Lafosse and F. Roberge, *Dictionnaire chronologique et raisonné des découvertes . . . en France . . . de 1789 à la fin de 1820* (17 vols., Paris, 1822–25), XIV, 207–8.
7. Charles-Claude, comte de Langeron (b. 1720). See *Dictionnaire de la noblesse* under Andrault, I, 482.
8. Possibly François, comte de Lastic (b. 1729): *ibid.*, XI, 648–9.

que l'effet vendredy dernier a l'assemblée de la societé d'Emulation a laquelle vous vous êtes reunis comme je l'ai vû ce même jour sur la feuille de cette assemblée; J'ay L'honneur de vous informer que j'ay fais disposer pour la Societé d'Emulation une nouvelle poulie mechanique qui renferme les deux Effets; sçavoir Celui de la poulie qui suspend la planche a dessigner de votre Societé d'Emulation[9] et celuy de la manivelle moyen qui peut [meut?] par le Cabestant et devenir très avantageux pour lever l'ancre du navire en construisant cette poulie proportionnellement a la Masse qu'on veut qu'elle enleve. Je compte presenter Cette poulie demain a l'assemblée.

M. Millon[1] Conseiller qui est aussy de la même Societe D'Emulation et qui est un de mes commissaires pour decider de l'inscription des poligones reguliers tant pairs qu'impairs dans un cercle par le seul usage des parties egales du compas de proportion, a qui J'en ai demontré la precision, et qu'il a verifiée luy-même en ma presence, Ce M. a trouvé cette découverte simple et utile pour les mechaniciens. M. Millon n'a que trop éprouvé combien de pieces de mechanique les Ingenieurs en instrumens luy ont perdues faute d'avoir des moyens mechanique pour opperer avec precision; J'ay joint à cette decouverte celle de la trisection de l'angle tant géometrique que mechanique et une nouvelle methode pour former une table par l'addition pour avoir tous les nombres qui representent les cotes des quarrés et des diagonalles en nombres entiers et que quelqu'immenses soyent ces nombres l'exces ou la difference selon la geometrie ne different ou n'excedent jamais que d'une seule unité. Ce Commissaire a trouvé ces decouvertes exactes et utiles a la mechanique et m'a en même temps promit de me menager deux heures de temps pour venir chez moy examiner mes autres decouvertes; Je vous prie Monsieur de me marquer le jour et L'heure que vous voudrez venir voir ce que je compte avoir trouvê d'utile. J'espere que vous amenerai d'autres connoisseurs. Vous obligerai Infiniment Celuy qui a

9. BF had previously attended meetings of this Society for which see above, XXIII, 451 n.
1. See XXV, 301–2.

L'honneur d'être avec un très profond respect Monsieur Votre très humble et très obeissant serviteur
    FYOT
    professeur de Mathématiques
    rue de la vieille monnaye 2e porte Cochere a gauche entrant par celle des [*missing.*]

Endorsed: Fyot Invention

Notation: 3 Aout 1778

From Genet   ALS: American Philosophical Society

Monsieur   A V[ersai]lles ce 3 août 78
    Je travaille fortement à la traduction des très interessantes gazettes de Pensylvanie du 30. mai et du 20. juin. Comme j'attends d'un moment à l'autre les relations angloises du Combat du 27. je ne puis point m'absenter, mais si vous voulés bien me communiquer des articles pour le numero 50. des affaires de l'angleterre qui paroitra jeudi ou vendredi, je vous supplie de me les envoyer ici sans délai, par la poste.[2] Je suis avec respect Monsieur Votre très humble et tres obéissant serviteur   GENET

Addressed: M. Franklin

Notation: M. Genet 3 Aoust 78

Intelligence from Toulon and Other Places

D: National Archives

According to practice we summarize here the nine other intelligence reports which fall within the period of our volume. All were written in French; the final two are in an unknown hand, while the first seven (and the one we print) are in the hand of the chevalier de

2. For this cahier of the *Affaires* see Genet's letter of July 26. News of Ushant appeared in the following cahier, dated Aug. 14.

Kéralio, the military inspector who was the general source of the reports.[3]

(I) Brest, August 10, 1778: M. d'Orvilliers has received orders to sail again as soon as possible,[4] but I doubt he will be able to leave before the 20th. Repairs are proceeding day and night on his damaged ships. No English ships have been encountered in the Channel; it is likely Keppel has been damaged more than us and it appears we will be ready before him.[5] The *Neptune*, 74, will be launched on the 23rd. Evidence mounts that Admiral Byron's squadron has been dispersed.[6]

(II) Brest, August 12, 1778: d'Orvilliers hopes to sail on the 16th. M. Duchaffault's wound continues to heal.[7] Since the *Ville de Paris* needs an overhaul, M. de Guichen will take over the *Couronne*.[8] A convoy has arrived from Martinique.

(III) Paris, August 12, 1778: The comte d'Aranda provides news of the arrival at Cadiz of the Buenos Aires fleet.[9] The Spanish fleet is arming. Admiral Keppel had several vessels dismasted and is having difficulty repairing them. It is believed our fleet will embark troops and cannon at St. Malo. Byron's fleet no longer exists, at least for practical purposes. A prize worth £60,000 has been brought into Toulon. The King of Prussia has refused an armistice;[1] 50,000 Prussian troops have entered Bohemia and another 48,000 are screening Saxony.

(IV) Brest, August 17, 1778: The fleet, 24 or 25 ships of the line, has sailed; the remaining ships except for the *Ville de Paris* are almost ready. The *Neptune* will be launched the 20th.

(V) Brest, August 19, 1778: The ships left behind by d'Orvilliers rejoin him in perfect weather. In addition to the *Neptune*, two ships

3. See xxv, 413 n.

4. D'Orvilliers' fleet had returned to Brest after the battle of Ushant: Rayneval to BF, July 31.

5. They were: d'Orvilliers sailed again on the 17th, Keppel six days later (Mackesy, *War for America*, p. 211).

6. By a storm while en route to America: *ibid.*, p. 212.

7. Louis-Charles, comte du Chaffault de Besné, commander of the French vanguard at Ushant, had been wounded in the shoulder: Larousse.

8. Luc-Urbain de Bouexic, comte de Guichen, who had commanded the center division of the French fleet: Larousse.

9. Aranda, the Spanish ambassador, has appeared in previous volumes. The Buenos Aires fleet had served in the 1777 Spanish campaign against Brazil: see BF to Lovell, July 22.

1. See Dumas to the commissioners, July 28.

of the line will be launched here this month and three others at Rochefort.[2] Ships have arrived from Bengal and China not knowing we were at war. M. de Kéralio presents his respects and will return *La population de la France* to M. de Wimpfen.[3]

(VI) Paris, August 21, 1778: Six vessels should leave today to join d'Orvilliers, leaving only two in port.

(VII) Brest, September 4, 1778: d'Orvilliers will have 31 ships of the line when he is joined by the *Neptune*, which will be ready in a few days. The *Ville de Paris* will begin her overhaul in two or three days. The construction of a 100-gun ship has been ordered, as have overhauls to three more ships of the line. A prize has been brought in by the frigate *Iphigénie*.

(VIII) Rochefort, September 8, 1778: A frigate was launched yesterday, but there were difficulties. Two more are in construction and four others ordered. A huge shipment of wood is expected. The Lisbon packetboat has been captured. Two frigates and a corvette are preparing to go on cruise.

(IX) Brest, September 25, 1778: A ship from Virginia reports encountering the *Ranger* and two American frigates[4] with a number of prizes. The frigate *Oiseau* has captured an English frigate and the *Aigrette* a privateer. Presently only one ship is being constructed but a number are being overhauled. D'Orvilliers has detached several ships to the Channel to free some of our blockaded frigates. At Rochefort construction has begun on three ships of the line.

De Toulon le 3 Aout 1778

La frégate *la Gracieuse*, commandée par M. de Violis est entrée hier dans ce port, convoyant deux prises faites par l'escadre de M. le Chevalier de Fabry[5] dans les parages de Mahon: Une

2. Dull, *French Navy*, pp. 352–5, provides information on French ship construction.

3. Either of two brothers, each a distinguished soldier, the baron Louis-François de Wimpfen-Bornebourg (1732–1800) or the baron Félix de Wimpfen (1745–1814). Larousse.

4. The *Boston* and *Providence* which sailed with the *Ranger* for America from Brest in late August: Taylor, *Adams Papers*, VI, 383 n.

5. Louis de Fabry de Fabrègues, *dit* le chevalier de Fabry for whom see Georges Lacour-Gayet, *La marine militaire de la France sous le règne de Louis XV* (2nd ed.; Paris, 1910), p. 508 n. He commanded a squadron of four ships of the line which cruised in the western Mediterranean from July 26 to Oct. 27: Archives de la marine, B³657: *passim* and B⁴135: *passim*. Mahon was the port of British-held Minorca.

d'elles chargée de velour d'Angleterre et de bijouterie, aiant du plomb et de l'etain pour lest est estimée a 1400000 *l.t.* L'autre est une tartane chargée de Toiles et de Draperie.

La Corvette *l'Eclair* commandée par M. de Flotte a amené aussi trois prises en revenant du Levant, que l'on dit très riches, cette Corvette a combattu un Corsaire anglois et l'a forcé de se refugier a Nice. Il y a environ 150 hommes sur ces 5 prises.

On travaille avec beaucoup d'activité à l'armement des frégates, *L'Aurore, La Mignone* et *l'Atalante.* On n'en met pas moins à la Construction des trois Vaisseaux qui sont sur les chantiers.

La frégate *la Magicienne* a été lancée à la mer avant hier, *la Précieuse* le sera à la fin du mois.

Addressed: A monsieur / Monsieur Franklin, chés / Mr. de chaumont / à Passy

Notation: Intelligence from Tulon aug. 3d. 1778.

Dumas to the American Commissioners[6]

ALS: Harvard University Library

⟨The Hague, August 4, 1778, in French: M. van Berckel has responded to my letter.[7] The Grand Facteur strongly recommended I send you a copy. P.S.: Congratulations on d'Orvilliers' victory over Keppel; a letter sent to the chevalier [Georges] Grand by his brother informed us of it.⟩

6. Published in Taylor, *Adams Papers,* VI, 344–6.

7. Dumas included a copy of van Berckel's letter of July 31 asking him to convey to the commissioners the gratitude of the regents of Amsterdam for having communicated the Franco-American treaty of commerce. Van Berckel expressed the regents' hope for ties of amity and commerce with America and blamed the inactivity of the States General on the pro-England faction.

From William Parsons[8]

ALS: American Philosophical Society

Sir   London August 4th, 1778.

I am at a loss in what manner to address you, more particularly as I fear I appear in a very unfavorable light to Doctor Franklin, but my situation and my distracted state of mind, bordering almost upon despair, on account of my poor unhappy Wife will I hope plead my excuse, whose wretched Situation Chevalier Hickey, the Bearer of this, will inform you of. I, Sir, will trouble you with but a few words more. When I left this with a resolution to offer my services to the united States of America, I was made to beleive I shou'd not meet with the least difficulty in my services being accepted of. Therefore, sanguine in the cause I was going to embark in and certain of ending my life at the other side of the Atlantic, I wrote my friends and particular connexions, letting them know my purpose, with my reasons for it. When I went to pay my personal Compts. to you, Sir, at Paris, my poor unhappy Wife met me there. Indeed my hopes flatter'd me with a beleif that we shou'd not be there a week before we embark'd. What my disappointmt. when my offers were rejected! I had embark'd too far to recede, and distress staring me in the face; yet I hop'd I might still succeed. In fact, I was afraid to return. I wrote home, but my letters were treated with disdain and Resentment for what I had done, or not Answer'd at all. I had £250 in the hands of my Cousin-germain, Sir William Parsons, which I left a power to have lodg'd in the hands of Messrs. Nesbitt[9] in this Town for my use, and which I thought had been paid in, when I ventur'd to give you, Sir, the draft I did; but this has been cruelly and most inhumanly with-held

8. See his letter in xxv, 693–5.

9. Arnold Nesbit (1721–79), formerly banking and business partner of his uncle Albert Nesbit (d. 1753), took his nephew John into partnership in 1778. Described by contemporaries as "a shockingly wicked fellow always," Arnold was by this time in serious financial difficulty, and when he died left debts in excess of £100,000. Namier and Brooke, *House of Commons*, pp. 194–5 for all three; Lüthy, *Banque protestante*, II, 423, 425, where the firm is still listed as Arnold & Albert Nesbit.

in Resentment to me,[1] but contrary to every idea of justice. I still continued to write home, but with similar success. All this time our distress encreasing, ('tho Capt. Hickey can answer for the very recluse life we led) our debt at the Pension where we liv'd accumulating, 'till at last threat'ning succeeded. Thus dreadfully circumstanc'd in a strange Country, friendless and unknown, I ventur'd to come home to endeavor to extricate us from this misfortune, but I have met nothing but insults and threat'nings. I have been afraid to stir out of my Room, and, so help me God!, I have often, since I came to Town, been twenty-four hours together without Eating a morsel or having wherewithal to procure it. This, or more I cou'd bear, but to think what may happen to my Wife by a set of unfeeling Wretches, in whose house she is, that stings me to the quick. I have, for many years preserv'd her, with tenderness and care, from the most distant idea of distress, and, oh, that such a Woman shou'd ever meet with any! Sir, she will stand the test of enquiry or scrutiny, and will be found to possess whatever is deem'd desireable in a Woman, with an understanding equall'd by few. Excuse, oh! excuse a fond doating Husband, whose heart is this moment ready to burst. If ever merit in distress found freind, for pity's sake!, be one to a poor, forlorn, and deserving Woman. If ever Charity was deem'd a Virtue, it surely, surely must in this instance. In return, may you and your's never meet with any misfortune or disappointment in this life, but, here and hereafter, enjoy the blessings, ever the consequence of humanity, charity and benevolence. If ever I can prove my gratitude, I will go to the farthest part of the World to do it. If my services will not be accepted of by you, Sir, I have wrote to Mrs. Parsons to come home, if enabled by your generous humanity, 'tho I wou'd rather prove my gratitude in America than elsewhere.

1. In the letter cited above he described Sir William as strongly opposed to the administration and therefore, by implication, well inclined toward his cousin's joining the Americans. Parsons had drawn on BF for 15 guineas but when BF tried to use the bill for the relief of American prisoners in England he found that it was worthless: to Mrs. Parsons, under Aug. 12.

Pardon this trouble and ease a tortur'd and afflicted heart, and, as you are one of the greatest, be also one of the best of Men. With misery, beyond Conception, beleive me, Sir, with the truest Respect, Your most Obedient and Most Devoted humble Servant   WM. PARSONS

Addressed: A Monsieur / Monsieur Franklin / a Passy

Notation: Wm Parsons

William Bingham to the American Commissioners

Two LS: American Philosophical Society

Messieurs   a st. Pierres le 5 aout 1778

Suivant Les Intentions Du Congrès j'ay L'honneur De Vous Donner avis que j'ay faits Traitte ce jour sur vous ordre De Monsieur aubin Bellevue Pour la somme De Mil Livres Tournois Payable a Trois Mois De Vue que je vous Prie D'avoir La bonté D'accueillir favorablement et en passer le Montant a L'acompte Des Etats unis De L'amerique.[2] J'ay L'honneur D'etre très Parfaitement Messieurs Votre très humble et très obeissant serviteur   WM BINGHAM

A Messrs. Benjn. franklin et Jean Adams Commiss. Des Etats Unis De L'amerique a Paris.

Addressed: A Messieurs / Messieurs Benj. franklin / et Jean Adams Commiss. Des / Etats Unis De Lamerique / a Paris

2. For Bingham's authorization to draw on the commissioners see BF to Lovell on July 22. During the remainder of 1778 there are four similar letters in French from Bingham (APS): Aug. 6 for 2,666 *l.t.*, 13 *s.*, 4 *d.*, payable to de Moriac, merchant at Bordeaux; Aug. 10 for 15,000 *l.t.*, payable to Jh. François Majastre of Marseilles; Sept. 1 for 2,200 *l.t.*, payable to [William?] Lee, and Sept. 17 for 22,705 *l.t.*, 17 *s.*, payable to Les Cousins Pascal, merchants at Marseilles. These are the first extant letters from Bingham not written in English. At the APS are also two lists sent by Bingham on Aug. 26 and Sept. 6 of "sundry Setts of Exchange" drawn by

From the Abbé de Tristan-Brision

ALS: American Philosophical Society

Monsieur   Ce 5. aoust 1778.
Il m'est tombé entre les mains une Lettre à vous adressée.
Je vous prie de l'envoyer querir par un de vos gens, de maniere
à m'assurer qu'elle vous sera remise en main propre.

La personne dans les paquets de qui elle est venüe est toute
royaliste et malgré Les Egards qu'elle doit à Celui qui la lui
recommande il étoit decidée à la jetter de côté.

Je m'en suis emparé et je me depêche de vous en donner
avis. Je la Joindrois à cellecy mais la manière dont on demande
qu'elle vous soit remise en main propre me decide à ne la
Ceder que quand Je Serai sure qu'elle vous sera remise. Je Suis
Monsieur avec respect Votre Tres humble et tres obeissant Serviteur.   L'ABBÉ DE TRISTAN-BRISION
                     Maison du Sieur Hugot Serrurier rüe de Clery
                     on entre sur la gauche par la rüe M. Martre.

Endorsed: L'abbé de Tristan Brision

From La Blancherie   ALS: University of Pennsylvania Library

                    Ancien College de Bayeux rue de la Harpe Paris
Monsieur le Docteur,   le 5 Août 1778
     L'Intéret que vous voulez bien prendre à l'établissement que
je dirige, me fait espérer que vous apprendrez avec plaisir
qu'enfin je vais bientôt changer de logement, graces aux soins

---

him. On the back of the latter BF wrote "Recd. Nov. 18. 1778. Had accepted
before

One presented by Bernier	600.0.0
Beauvais	6600.0.0
Do	4400.0.0
Bailly	10000.0.0
De Perpigna	1682.4.8
des Hommets	4144.18.0
Lee	22000.0.0
Antin Bellerce	1000.0.0
Majastre	15000.0.0"

généreux de m. Elie de Beaumont. Ce qui me flatte en cela
c'est d'être a même de recevoir un personnage aussi distingué
que vous et plus convenablement et plus souvent que je ne l'ai
fait.

Je Compte beaucoup sur votre bonté et votre indulgeance
Monsieur le Docteur. C'est pourquoi j'ai l'honneur de vous
prier de nous accorder celui de votre présence à l'assemblée de
demain. Plusieurs circonstances pourroient se réunir qui la
rendroient en effet très précieuse pour nous.[3] Je vous supplie
monsieur le Docteur, de continuer encore par ces témoignages
de votre complaisance à être le bienfaiteur de notre établissement. C'est avoir des droits éternels sur mon coeur et sur celui
de toutes les personnes qui aiment les Sciences et les Arts.
Mes très humbles respects, s'il vous plaît, à M. Adams,[4] Mes
civilités les plus respectueuses à M. Votre fils. J'ai l'honneur de
mettre à vos pieds les assurances de la vive reconnoissance, de
la plus grande admiration, et du tres profond respect avec lesquels je suis Monsieur le Docteur Votre très humble et très
obéissant Serviteur   LA BLANCHERIE

Notation: La Blancherie 5 Aout 1778

3. BF did not attend that meeting or those that followed; they were
clearly not high among his priorities. On Aug. 12 La Blancherie wrote to
urge him to come the next day: "aurions-nous eu le malheur de vous de-
plaire vous ne nous mettez plus à même de vous faire la cour." University
of Pa. Library. No result. A third letter, on Sept. 2, bewailed the time that
had passed since BF had last honored him with his presence. Tomorrow's
gathering, the last until November, will have several matters of interest,
and M. de Marolles also wants him to come. APS. This was the chevalier
de Marolles de Lucé (xxv, 12 n), who also wrote on Sept. 2 and explained
one of the matters of interest: he will show the assembly the picture of the
temple of liberty that he designed the year before; BF sent the original to
Congress and will, he hopes, be on hand to approve the work and do justice
to the artist's talent. The design was exhibited, and BF evidently was not
there: *Jour. de Paris*, Sept. 4, p. 999. On Oct. 21 the chevalier wants cash as
well; he is ill and indigent, and says that Elie de Beaumont urged BF to help
him. Another appeal from him, undated, is substantially the same. These
three letters are in the APS. In the summer BF gave Marolles 43 *l.t.*: account
V (above, XXIII, 20), entry of Aug. 19.

4. He had attended an assembly on June 27, when La Blancherie mistakenly referred to him as a member of the APS: *Jour. de Paris*, June 28, p. 713.

From William Lee

ALS: American Philosophical Society

Sir.   August 5th: 1778

I have received a letter from Robert Morris Esqr. informing me that he has impower'd Mr. Ross to settle the affairs of his late Brother Thomas Morris Esqr.[5] and I presume he has also authorized Mr. Ross to receive and take into his possession the papers of the late Mr. Thos. Morris. Therefore if Mr. Ross shou'd apply to you on this Subject and you think the powers he has are sufficient to warrant the delivery to him of those papers, you will please to deliver to him all those papers of the late Mr. Thomas Morris of a private nature or that relate to the house of Messrs. Willing Morris & Co. which were left by me in your Custody, take a receipt from Mr. Ross specifying the number of peices of paper that he so receives. Those papers of the late Mr. Thos. Morris that concern or relate to the Public business you will no doubt still continue to keep in your custody.

There must be among those papers a few letters of my writing which please to deliver to my Brother The Honourable Arthur Lee Esqr. for me. I have the Honour to be with great Consideration Sir Your most Obedient and most Humble Servant   W. LEE

To The Honourable Benjamin: Franklin Esqr Passy near Paris

Endorsed: Recd the 11th

Notation: W. Lee August 5, 78. to BF

---

5. Presumably the letter of May 22 mentioned in Smith, *Letters*, IX, 740 n. BF had reluctantly been drawn into the dispute between Lee and Ross over the papers of Thomas Morris: see above, XXV, 541–3 ff. and XXVI, *passim*.

Alexander Fowler[6] to the American Commissioners

ALS: American Philosophical Society

London 6th. Agust 1778.

The Petition of Alexander Fowler Esquire late an Officer in His Brittannick Majestys Service. Humbly Sheweth.

That your Petitioner served His Brittannick Majesty *Eighteen Years* with Honor and Reputation as will be seen by the Annexed Testimonials of His Conduct and Character.[7]

That in the year 1773, your Petitioner being then quartered in the City of Philadelphia, when it was no longer doubtfull that the British Legislature had formed a Plan to entail Slavery on the Inhabitants of North America, and when the liberal part of the British Soldiery spoke the language of Britons and openly expressed their Indignation against so Unconstitutional a System, among Whom Was your Petitioner, Who in Consequence thereof soon became deserted by His Brother Officers, Who declared Him a Son of Liberty. His former Bosom Friends soon became His Worst Enemies; the Confidence of Friendship was sacrifised, and every effort tryed to prejudice the Commander in Chief (General Gage) against your Petitioner, Which by the duplicity of *False Friends* was soon effected.

Your Petitioner at this time had been above *Four Years* at the head of the list of Lieutenants, and as an Augmentation of Two Companies to each Regiment was to take place He was every day in expectation of His Company; but of this your Petitioner was prevented by the Unjust Conduct of *General Gage* and left in such a Condition at Boston as Would have touched the Heart of the most obdurate—Cooped up in that

6. Fowler (d. 1806) served as an officer in the British army from 1757 to 1775, and as of 1767 in various parts of America: see the American commissioners to Read, Aug. 22, and Margaret P. Bothwell, "Devereux Smith, Fearless Pioneer," *Western Pennsylvania Hist. Mag.*, XL (1957), 289.

7. He enclosed copies of two laudatory letters from his former officers: one, dated 1767, from Lt. Col. William Masters of the 74th regiment, the other, 1773, from Maj. Isaac Hamilton of the 18th or Royal Irish.

City Come Servitude, and too Weak to bear the Inclemency
of Winter Without Pay, Lodging, Fuel, or Provission; and had
it not been for the Attention and assistance of a Brother in the
38th. Regiment,[8] He must with His Wife have then perished
for Want for Money was not to be had but from Paymasters of
Regiments Who did not dare to supply Him, nor were Fuel or
Provissions to be had but from the Commissaries who would
not furnish Him with any. Thus Situated, your Petitioner Was
Prohibited from going to Pensylvania, or any other part of the
Continent, nor would *General Howe*, (after *General Gage* left
Boston) allow Him a Passage on Board of a Transport to England. Your Petitioner However with much difficulty, at last
procured a Passage on Board of a *Victualler*, sailed from Boston the 5th. December 1775, and Arrived in England the 27th.
of same Month, when after advising with His Friends, He took
the Opinion of *Mr. Serjeant Glynn*,[9] and Accordingly brought
an Action of Damages against *General* Gage for £5000. But a
certain Secret Influence pervades every Court of Justice in
Great Britain: The tryal was quashed Your Petitioner was not
Allowed a Hearing. A Middlesex Special Jury was directed by
the Partiallity of a *Judge* to find a Verdict for Defendent thereby
Involving your Petitioner in Tenfold Affliction. Your Petitioner
thereupon with the Assistance of a Friend got a Letter conveyed to the Honorable *Silas Deane*, who from the Contents of
a Letter Intercepted by the *Continental Congress* in 1775, and
your Petitioners Intimacy With *Mr. Wharton*, *Mr. Bache*, *Mr.
John Baynton*, *Mr. John Bayard*, *Dr. Morgan*, and Mr. *George Morgan* &c.[1] became fully acquainted with His Sentiments, and
thereupon humanely forwarded said Letter to Your Petitioner

8. George Fowler, a quartermaster and ensign in that regiment: Worthington C. Ford, *British Officers Serving in the American Revolution* ...
(Brooklyn, 1897), p. 72.

9. John Glynn, sergeant at law and M.P. for Middlesex: see XXI, 89 n.

1. Samuel Wharton and Richard Bache need no introduction. John
Baynton, Dr. John Morgan and George Morgan are identified in XI, 187 n;
XII, 126 n; XIII, 400 n. John Bayard (1738–1807) was a prominent merchant,
soldier and political leader (*DAB*). Fowler presumably met all these Phila-
delphians while he was stationed there.

to Guard him against the Consequences, a Copy of which He has herewith Annexed.[2] And Mr. *Deane*, knowing the Situation of your Petitioner, on the Receipt of His Letter from London immediately procured Him a Passage and acquainted Him *by Letter* therewith,[3] which Unfortunately for your Petitioner on Account of the Embarrasment of His Private Affairs He had it not in His Power to Embrace, of which Mr. *Samuel Wharton* is fully acquainted, as well as with your Petitioners line of Conduct since His Arrival in England, and the Anxiety he has been Under to get to the United States of America. The treatment of your Petitioner he Will presume to say is without a precedent in the Annals of this or any other Civilized Nation; But He will not presume to trouble your Excellencys with a more Circumstantial detail of it, flattering himself at the same time that Your Excellencys are not Unacquainted therewith.

As an oppressed and suffering Friend of Liberty; As an Injured and Ruined Individual for His Attachment to the Cause of America, your Petitioner has thus presumed to Appeal to the Humanity of your Excellencies, And Humbly Prays that your Excellencies will procure Him and His Wife a Passage to any part of the United States of North America, and for such other protection and Countenance as to your Excellencies may seem Most Meet.[4]

For Which your Petitioner as in duty Bound shall ever Pray.

A. FOWLER.

2. It is from Capt. Benjamin Charnock Payne, of the 18th regiment, to Capt. John Shee, April 19, 1775, accusing Fowler of a connection with "the most violent Sons of Sedition" and recommending that he be removed from office. For Payne and Shee see Ford, *op. cit.* pp. 142, 160. Fowler's point of view is explained in his series of letters published in *The General Advertiser, and Morning Intelligencer*, June 18, 22, 27; July 7, 10, 11, 14, 16, 18, 25, 30, 31; Aug. 1 and 17, 1778.

3. We have not located Deane's letter but they clearly knew each other. See *Deane Papers*, 1, 45, 380.

4. The commissioners were moved by his petition. See their recommendation to Capt. Read below, Aug. 22.

To the Honorable Benjamin Franklin, Arthur Lee & John Adams Esquires Commissioners Plenipotentiary of the united States of North America.

Notation: Mr A Fowler Letter lately in the B Army. 6 Aout 1778.

John Paul Jones to the American Commissioners[5]

ALS: American Philosophical Society; copy: United States Naval Academy Museum

⟨Passy, August 6, 1778: By a resolve of Congress the seamen engaged on the *Ranger* were given forty dollars each, and the landsmen twenty dollars advance in continental bills. They have also been supplied with slops, and received a small cash advance at Nantes last winter. I consider it my duty to represent these circumstances to you. I hope that you will order receipts for my indemnification, and have my stores, furniture, etc. delivered. Please recommend to Congress the men who landed with me at Whitehaven, as you promised.[6]⟩

Jonathan Williams, Jr., to the American Commissioners
ALS: University of Virginia Library

Honorable Gentlemen.   Passy Augt 6. 1778.

In the Extracts from Mr. Deans Letters to me, which I had the honour to give in to you some time since, I refered to the whole Letters of the following Dates, June 27. July 19. July 28. Augt. 1. Augt. 7 and Nov. 15, all in 1777. I have now the honour to inclose Copies of the whole of these Letters, and shall be happy if they are of any use to you.[7]

---

5. Published in Taylor, *Adams Papers*, VI, 352–3.
6. Jones's account of the Whitehaven raid is above, XXVI, 535.
7. The first five of these letters are at the University of Va. Library, and the sixth (printed in *Deane Papers*, II, 224) is at the Connecticut Historical Society. The July 19 letter is in fact the joint one from BF and Deane published above, XXIV, 332–3. Extracts of all six are at the National Archives.

I propose to sett off for Nantes tomorrow or next day, unless your Commands should require my longer Stay.[8] I have the Honour to be with the greatest Respect Honourable Gentlemen Your most obedient servant JONA WILLIAMS.

The Hon. The Ministers Plenipotentiary of the United States.

Endorsed: rcd the 8th A Lee

Notation: Jonan. Williams to Hon: Comrs. U.S. (6 Augt. 1778.)

From Antoine-Louis Brongniart

ALS: American Philosophical Society

Monsieur   6 Aoust 1778.

Les experiences que j'ay annoncées dernierement dans les papiers publics, sur l'augmentation du fluide electrique, dans les Machines exposées au Soleil, ont excitées une certaine sensation chez les Phisiciens. J'ai répété hier et avant hier ces Experiences nouvelles, en presences de Plusieurs personnes et Medecins Electrisans, et J'ay obtenu les mêmes effets.

J'avois invité Monsieur Dubourg a me faire l'honneur d'y assister, des affaires l'ont empeché d'y venir.[9] Je me propose de les annoncer Lundi Prochain a Plusieurs amateurs, et a quelques Personnes de qualité qui voudront bien se reunir chez Moy vers les cinq heures et demie du Soir; Je joindrai a ces Experiences, celles que nous procurent Les Emanations Elastiques.

Je n'ose vous inviter a me faire L'honneur d'augmenter Le Nombre des Personnes de Consideration que je recevrai, Je sens combien vos instants sont Pretieux; Cependant Si vous pouviez vous derober un moment, et me L'accorder, il deviendroit pour moy Le Plus flatteur et le plus Glorieux. Agrées

---

8. For jw's stay in Passy see his letter of July 17.

9. BF and Dubourg had already witnessed some of Brongniart's experiments the previous spring. See XXVI, 253.

L'homage du Profond Respect, avec Lequel J'ay L'honneur d'Etre Monsieur Votre tres humble et tres Respectueux Serviteur   A. L. BRONGNIART
demonstrateur de Chymie et de Physique
Rue et hotel Serpente

Notation: Brongniart Philosophe

Endorsed: Paris 6 août 1778.

From Genet   ALS: American Philosophical Society

Monsieur   A V[ersai]lles ce 6 août 78
J'ai l'honneur de vous remettre la lettre du Dr. Samuel Cooper que vous avés bien voulu me communiquer et a laquelle je joins quelque gazettes angloises arrivées aujourdhui. Le no. 50. doit paroitre après demain.[1] Je suis avec respect Monsieur Votre très humble et très obéissant Serviteur
GENET

Notation: M Genet 16. Août 1778[2]

From ——— Lecavelier fils

ALS: American Philosophical Society

Monsieur   Caen le 6 aout 1778
J'ay L'honneur de vous donner avis que trois Matelots parlant anglais ont entré avec Leur chaloupe dans un petit port a 4 lieue de Cette ville.[3] On les a amenés icy et Conduit Chez

---

1. We discuss this cahier in Genet's letter above of July 26. The date we give there (July 30) is that of the purported letter from a London banker which opens the cahier, not that of the actual publication.

2. The notation does not correspond to the date Genet wrote, which, although written over another number, clearly appears a 6.

3. Doubtless the three prisoners whose letter to BF appears below, Aug. 7.

Monsieur Le Commissaire de la marine ou L'on m'a fait venir pour Les interroger. Ils se declarent americains de Boston ou des environs qu'ils ont eté pris Sur un Navire américain Venant a nantes et Conduits a Portsmouth; que S'etant engagés Sur un Navire de Transport qui alloit en amerique Dans l'espoir de Se Sauver lorsqu'ils y Seroient Arrivés qu'ayant Trouvé le quart d'heure favorable ils en ont profité pour Se Sauver en france avec La chaloupe du transport ce qui Leur a heureusement Reussy; il m'ont paru assez unanimes dans L'interrogatoire d'hier pour me persuader qu'ils disent La verité; on les a par precaution Consignés au chateau de Cette Ville et monsieur Le Procureur du Roy de Cette amirauté a donné des ordres pour Leur Subsistance, Sans quoy J'y aurois pourvu preferant de rendre Service a un anglois en Supposant qu'ils Soient des imposteurs (ce que Je ne Crois pas) Plustost que de laisser Manquer des habitans des colonies unies de ce qu'ils pourroient avoir Besoin. Ils m'ont prié hier de vous ecrire pour Reclamer Votre protection a l'effet de Les faire Retourner Dans Leur pays et leur faire donner Ou procurer Les moyens de S'embarquer dans quelqu'un de nos ports; Je leur promis que Je ne manquerois pas de vous instruire a cet effet.

Ils vont encore Subir un interrogatoire ce Matin afin de voir S'ils sont reellement des Sujets des etats unis de l'amérique.

Sy Je puis a leur occasion Vous etre de quelque utilité icy J'en ressentiray un vray Plaisir etant depuis Longtems attaché de Sentiment a la prosperité des Etats unis. J'ay L'honneur D'etre avec la plus parfaite Consideration Monsieur Votre tres humble et tres obeissant Serviteur   LECAVELIER FILS

Endorsed: Suavelier has relieved some Prisoners Caen 6 aout 1778.

From Robert Niles   ALS: American Philosophical Society

Sir   Nantes Augt. 6. 1778

I arived at Paimbeauf on the third Instt. and shall make all possible dispatch to proceed on my Voyge. Inclos'd you have a Bill to the amount of the Money remitted for the purchase

of Types.[4] I am Sir Your very Humble Servant   ROBT NILES
Amt. of the Bill £1364. 13 s.o[5]

Addressed: The Hble Benjamin Franklin Esqre. / Paris

Endorsed: Capt. Niles and Watson about Types

From ———— Stadel[6]   ALS: American Philosophical Society

Monsieur   à Paris ce 6 Août *1778*

J'espere que vous auroit Monsieur du depuis examiner les Echantillons des Couteaux et fourgette que nous vous avons Laisses Dimanche et qu'en consequence vous auroit eu La bonté de faire dessiner sur un Pappier la façon come Elle doivent être faitte.

Cy joint encorre Le Detail au sujet de L'acier pour que vous Pussioit Monsieur faire votre Speculation. Monsieur Honsberg partant samedy au soir, vous suplie Monsieur de faire Connoitre s'il doit se trouver demain au soir ou samedy matin pour prendre vos ordres. J'ai L'honneur d'être avec La Consideration La plus parfaitte et distingué Monsieur Vostre tres humble et tres obbeissant serviteur

STADEL
à L'hôtel au nom de Jesus
Cloître St Jacques de L'hopital

4. For the use of Connecticut printers; see XXVI, 547 n.

5. Following this is the computation 1364.13 minus 470.13.0 totaling 894.0.0.

6. A merchant from Strasbourg. He brought with him François Honsberg, from Lemscheide in Germany, who had supplied the enclosed list of prices for different qualities of steel. According to G. Anquetil Brutière, Stadel called on BF again the following month: see XXVI, 598 n.

[Edward Bancroft] to [Franklin and John Adams]

Two copies and transcript:[7] National Archives

In early 1778 Silas Deane and his friend Edward Bancroft had used their inside knowledge of the Franco-American treaty negotiations to wager on the London stock market.[8] Unfortunately for them, Musco Livingston, a young ship captain, saw a letter written by Bancroft to a Mr. Wharton (probably Samuel Wharton, Bancroft and Deane's partner, but perhaps Samuel's brother Joseph, who was also involved).[9] On April 11 Livingston informed the commissioners of what he had seen.[1] The present letter was written by Bancroft to shift the blame onto John Thornton, Arthur Lee's secretary, who so far as we know was not guilty of any involvement in the stockjobbing. Ironically, however, unknown to Lee and perhaps also to Bancroft (himself a British spy), Thornton too was a British agent.[2] Bancroft's stratagem worked, at least in part; Franklin remained convinced that his friends Bancroft and Deane were innocent.

[before August 7, 1778][3]

Some time in March last Mr. Samuel Wharton informed me by Letter that he feared his Brother Joseph Wharton (who had lost near £10,000 Sterling by the Bankruptcy of the House of Richard Ford & Co.) was disposed to endeavour to repair his losses by Insurance on Political Events, and that Mr. Thornton

---

7. The copy from which we print is in Arthur Lee's hand (as is another copy, from an unidentified repository, in *Lee Family Papers*, reel 5, frames 565–8); we have used the transcript to help decipher it. His covering letter, discussed below, is published in Wharton, *Diplomatic Correspondence*, II, 679–80.

8. See XXIII, 202 n; XXV, 417 n.

9. Edward Bancroft and Silas Deane, Abstract of Accounts, [c. May 1779], Connecticut Historical Society. Joseph Wharton, Jr. (1733/4–1816), suffered reverses during and after the war which led him to retire from business: *PMHB* I (1877), 457–8.

1. XXVI, 256 n, 652 n.

2. XXV, 26–7.

3. On Aug. 7 Arthur Lee wrote the committee for foreign affairs enclosing this letter: "The enclosed paper, letter A, was communicated secretly by Dr. Bancroft to Dr. Franklin and Mr. Adams, the latter of whom delivered it to me." Lee then attempted to exonerate Thornton and to place the blame back on Bancroft.

229

was as he suspected encouraging and misleading him into that kind of speculation.

A few weeks afterwards Mr. Austin[4] informed me that Mr. Thornton had shewn him a note of hand for £500 Sterling Payable by Mr. Jos. Wharton to Mr. Thornton on condition that war shoud be declared before a certain day in April; this note I understood to have been obtained by Mr. Thornton from Mr. Wharton as a Consideration for some intelligence which the former had sold to the latter, and I concluded that Mr. Wharton in order to have enabled himself to pay the Sum of £500 in case of War, must have given considerable Premiums upon the ground of Mr. Thornton's supposed valuable intelligence. About this time Mr. Joseph Wharton intimated to me in a letter and under injunction of secrecy that he had found a most valuable channel of intelligence and as a proof of it mentioned that among other important secrets he knew that a Certain power had engaged to *declare war at farthest before the 1st of May*. Soon after that a Letter sent me from Dr. Franklins with several others that were for me and having hastily opened it, without attending to the fictious name it was addressed to, I found it to be a Letter from Mr. Joseph Wharton severely reproaching Mr. Thornton for having Cruelly led him into heavy Losses by falacious intelligence. Mr. Thornton the next day sent for this Letter, describing the address and I sent it with an excuse for having mistakenly opened it. At the same time from a motive of humanity wrote a Letter to Mr. Jos. Wharton imparting that tho' I considered Mr. Thornton as a well meaning man, I thought him an indiscreet Chatterer and so little informed of the private intentions or transactions of men in power, either here or anywhere else that in my opinion it was not prudent in any Body to risk money on his intelligence, nor honorable in him to take money for giving it. In answer to this Letter Mr. Wharton wrote me on the 20th of April as follows:

"In regard to Thornton I agree with you that he is a very

4. Jonathan Loring Austin, who had brought to Europe the news of Saratoga and had undertaken a mission to England to meet with leaders of the opposition: xxv, *passim*.

indiscreet Chatterer, and I have often wondered such a man was entrusted with such State Papers, and so I do still. Indeed it is really wonderful that such Copies of such papers should be taken and carried from Paris to London, from London to Portsmouth &c. &c. Surely no good can come of this. And if he would shew them to me a stranger to him woud he be less communicative to others? My Lord North I shoud think woud have given £20,000 for them. On the other hand if they were not real and official papers, what Character does the man deserve who woud use Honorable names to sanctify perhaps his dishonorable intentions?"

Astonished at these observations and a repetition of them afterwards in another Letter of May 15th which I cannot now find, I desired by Letter that Mr. Wharton woud give me some account of the State Papers here alluded to, and in consequence of this desire I received a Letter dated the 1st of June the original of which will be herewith delivered No. 1.[5] I had no ill will towards Mr. Thornton. I certainly had wished to do him good and not harm. But after full reflection I coud not but think it my Duty to Communicate the Letter to Dr. Franklin. I did so and he thought it my Duty likewise to Communicate it to the other Commissioners. I promised to do it, though I did not know and am still uncertain whether Mr. Wharton might not blame my proceeding thus far. A journy into Flanders and my hurry since that Journy have retarded the proper Communication until the present time.

In answer to Mr. Wharton's Letter of the 1st of June I wrote that the papers shewn to him by Mr. Thornton appeared to me to be forgeries and forgeries which coud not have been made with so much art and pains unless for a purpose of considerable moment and that I did not conceive any purpose Mr. Thornton coud answer by them, unless it were to sell them to the British Ministry, or to dupe some person into Insurances or other gaming speculations. In reply to this Mr. Wharton wrote on the 16 of June as follows "Your last acknowledges the receipt of my information respecting Thornton, and I am

5. This letter, now at the National Archives, was also enclosed by Arthur Lee in his to the committee for foreign affairs.

glad you shewed it to the old Gentleman. It is high time such a *forgerer* shoud be *discarded*. Your conjectures are right, he either must have used the papers with Ministry or employed them to *Gull* others and in the latter number I must include myself having suffered but too *much by him.*" This Constitutes the most important Charges against Mr. Thornton. Reports of his imprudence have been numerous. Capt. All and many others coming from England have repeated conversations held by Mr. Thornton at Mr. Hartleys and in other places suited indeed to flatter the prejudices of Englishmen, but very unfit to be held by any man known to be employed by one of the American Commissioners. There have been also accounts of indiscretions of another nature. A Correspondent of mine wrote on the 12th of May as follows, "Thornton arrived here again the 8th instant in the Evening. His friends or himself must surely be engaged in Stocks insurances. He called on me this morning and what was only doubtful before he arrived he makes certain by every where declaring that the Toulon fleet are gone to America, under orders to attack all English Vessels there. I think him an odd character and connected as he is with certain people here I shall avoid him."

Mr. Ridley[6] and others in their Letters have enquired concerning Mr. Thornton in terms which imply that they think his Language and Conduct extraordinary and suspicious.

Some time about the 20th of May Mr. Samuel Wharton sent me the Copy of a Letter to him from Mr. Thornton desiring Mr. Wharton to discount a Bill which he said woud be drawn by him on Mr. Grand for account of Arthur Lee Esqr. That Mr. Lee's name coud not indeed be mentioned in the bill. That he Mr. Thornton durst not take a Credit from any Banker in Paris or any Banker in London because that woud have blown all, but that he had been recommended for supplies of money, to a Mr. Bridgen who was going to Bath &c. The Copy of this Letter was left with Dr. Franklin and has not since been returned or it woud have been cited at large. Mr. Wharton did not chuse to discount Mr. Thorntons Bill, but in compliment

6. Matthew Ridley, a Maryland merchant: XXVI, 227 n.

to Mr. Lee he lent Mr. Thornton twenty pounds or Guineas I forget which; and some weeks after I received from him a Letter of which the paper marked No. 2 is a part and in the handwriting of Mr. Samuel Wharton.[7]

It can scarce be necessary for me to say that I am actuated by no enmity towards Mr. Thornton in this relation. I have entered into it reluctantly, from a sense of duty and after delays which a mind influenced by ill will or resentment woud not have permitted to take place.

Notations in different hands: True Copy M. Livingston True Copy M. Livingston / A Lee's Aug 7 1778 Informatn. respectg. Thornton

From John Atwood, Jacob Vere, and Nathan Chadwick[8]

ALS: American Philosophical Society

Dr. Franklin Sir   August the 7th year 1778

We take Leave to write to your Honour to Let you know We are amaricans taken prisoners By the English and Endangered our Lives to get to france Expecting to get our Liberty and the people are suspicious of our Being English and we Desire the favour to Come Before your honour to answer for our Selves. We are your honours most humble and obedient Servents   JOHN ATWOOD
                                     JACOB VERE
                                     NATHAN CHADWICK

Major Kauchÿ [?]

Addressed: To / the Right Honourable / Dr. franklin Ambasin-

7. This letter too was enclosed by Lee.
8. The sailors mentioned above by Lecavelier on Aug. 6. John Atwood had been on the *Dalton*, Capt. Eleazer Johnson, when it was captured Dec. 24, 1776. He made an unsuccessful escape attempt Aug. 27, 1777. Nathan Chadwick subsequently was a seaman on the *Susannah*. *New-England Hist. and Geneal. Register*, XXXII, 308; Kaminkow, *Mariners*.

der / for / the United States / of Amarica / [*in another hand:*] a Paris

Notation: 3 Americans to Dr. Franklin

Endorsed: Prisoners

John Gibson[9] to the American Commissioners

ALS: American Philosophical Society; copy: National Archives

Gentlemen   Treasury Office Philadelphia August 8th 1778

In pursuance of an order of the Board of Treasury, I inclose you the following Resolutions, and beg leave to inform you, that notwithstanding the order of Congress for immediately striking Bills of Exchange to a greater amount, the Interest of the Continental Loan Office Certificates Issued to the 10th of March last will not exceed the sum of Two Millions and a half of Livres Tournois Annually; which agreeable to the Resolution of Congress of the 10th Septr. last is to be paid by Bills of Exchange on the Commissioners of the United States in Paris.[1] I am also to inform you that many of the Lenders will be entitled to the Interest on the 10th Sept., and others at different periods between that and the 10th March, next; The Resolution for paying Interest in Bills of Exchange expired in March last, and has not been since renewed. I am with very great Respect Your Honors Most obedient and Very humble Servant   JOHN GIBSON
                                                         Aud Genl

By Order

To the Commissioners of the United States Paris

9. The Auditor General, elected by Congress in 1776: Ferguson, *Morris Papers*, I, 269 n. He was probably the Virginian of that name (1729–82) who moved to Pennsylvania and was for a time mayor of Philadelphia: Geneal. Soc. of Pa. *Pub.*, XIV (1942–44), 67, 70–1.

1. Interest on loan office certificates issued between that date and March 1, 1778 (which Gibson for some reason gives as the 10th) might be paid in bills of exchange on the commission: above, XXV, 210 n. On May 19, 1778, Congress resolved to print immediately 6,300,000 *l.t.* in such bills, but

From Barbeu-Dubourg

ALS: American Philosophical Society

Monsieur et cher Maitre   Paris 8e. Août 1778

Je suis chargé de vous recommander ce memoire, quoique j'en augure peu favorablement; on auroit pris mon refus pour mauvaise volonté. Je vous prie de vouloir me faire au moins a ce sujet un mot de reponse ostensible.

Si vous avez, comme on le dit, de bonnes nouvelles, je vous prie aussi de m'en faire part; et de compter toujours sur le plus fidele attachement de Votre très humble et tres obeissant serviteur   DUBOURG

Notation: Dubourg Augt. 8.78

From Granville Sharp[2]

ALS: American Philosophical Society

Dear Sir   Old Jewry 8 August 1778

Permit me to recommend to your friendship and good Offices Mr. Laurence Brooke of Virginia, who came to Europe some Years ago, on account of Education; and tho' he has since resided chiefly in Scotland, I cannot find that he has imbibed the least prejudice of that unhappy Country, but on the contrary entertains a most perfect regard for the natural Rights of Mankind and the sacred cause of liberty in general. You will also find him, in every other respect, (I trust) highly worthy of your esteem; and as he is desirous of returning to his native Country, together with his Brother Mr. Robert Brooke, and Mr. Robert Nicholson (both natives of Virginia, and very amiable young Gentlemen in their conversation and behaviour) I must request that you will be pleased to favour them with your advice and good offices to forward their in-

---

printing was held up; a second resolution, July 11, modified the wording of the bills: *JCC*, XI, 513, 683. They were for the loan offices to issue, and Congress had authorized more than enough; Gibson's estimate of 2,500,000 was doubtless based on his knowlege of how many loan certificates had been issued before March 1.

2. The famous English reformer, scholar, and publicist; in 1774 BF had helped publish and distribute one of his pamphlets: XVII, 38 n; XXI, 263 n, 453.

tended voyage,[3] by which you will also confer a particular favour and obligation on, Dear Sir, Your affectionate friend and obedient humble Servant GRANVILLE SHARP.

Endorsed: Granville Sharpe Messrs Brooke

From Antoine-Laurent Lavoisier

ALS: Historical Society of Pennsylvania

Monsieur le 9 aoust 1778.

M. le Roy m'apprend que malgré les grands objets dont vous etes Occupé vous voulés bien nous donner votre avis sur la reconstruction du magazin des poudres de l'arsenal[4] et que vous me faitte l'honneur d'accepter a diner pour mardy prochain ainsy que M. votre petit fils. Permettes moi de vous temoigner toute ma reconnoissance et de vous assurer de tout le plaisir que nous aurons de vous recevoir. Tous les instans de votre existence sont consacrés, ou a l'instruction, ou au bonheur de vos semblables et il faut que la posterite sache qu'au milieu du tourbillon de la politique, tandis que le grand franklin ebranloit et mettoit en mouvement toutes les puissances des deux mondes, il savoit encore trouver le tems d'assurer la tranquilite des habitans de Paris en construisant un magazin a poudre a l'abri de tous evenemens. J'ay l'honneur d'etre avec un proffond respect, Monsieur, Votre tres humble et tres obeissant Serviteur LAVOISIER

Addressed: A Monsieur / Monsieur Franklin membre du Congrés des Etats de lamerique / A Passy

Endorsed: Lavoisier

Notation: Augt. 9. 78

3. For the Brookes see George McCall's letter under July 22. Robert Nicholson attended William and Mary in 1776 and finished his education in Scotland after the war. *W&MQ*, 1st ser., 1 (1892), 25. He served as surgeon for the Virginia state artillery from 1783 to 1798: John H. Gwathmey, *Hist. Register of Virginians in the Revolution* (Richmond, 1938), p. 585.

4. On Aug. 12 the régisseurs des poudres et salpêtres, of which Lavoisier was inspector general, asked the Académie royale des sciences to name

The American Commissioners to John Paul Jones[5]

LS: National Archives; AL (draft): Massachusetts Historical Society; two copies: National Archives

⟨Passy, August 10, 1778: We are not authorized by Congress to allow deductions from the seamen's prize money or their advances. As for your stores and furniture, M. Simpson will undoubtedly deliver your private property upon request. We cannot advise you regarding your indemnification, but we hope you will be furnished the proper receipts upon request. We shall recommend to Congress the men who landed with you at Whitehaven. Should our letter miscarry, recommend them yourself and include an extract of this paragraph. The *Ranger*'s men have merited such honor that Congress may approve of deductions from their wages to be paid in America, so that they may have their prize money here.

We have received a letter concerning some prize plate you placed in the hands of a gentleman who awaits your orders to deliver it, which you will of course give.[6]⟩

Sartine to the American Commissioners[7]

LS and copy: Library of Congress; copy: Massachusetts Historical Society

⟨Versailles, August 10, 1778, in French: Since I wrote you on July 29 the *commissaire des classes* at Nantes informs me the American agent there has entrusted him with some British prisoners. M. de la Porte, intendant at Brest, has written me

---

a committee to advise on the construction of the magazine; BF, Lavoisier, Le Roy, and three others were appointed: *procès-verbaux*, XCVII, fol. 284. They delivered their report on March 26, 1779: procès-verbaux, XCVIII, fol. 83–5.

5. Published in Taylor, *Adams Papers*, VI, 363–4. A notation on the draft explains that Lee, being at Versailles, was unable to sign.

6. The gentleman eludes us; the plate was Lady Selkirk's, taken during the Whitehaven raid: XXVI, 502. It was not returned until after the war was over: Morison, *Jones*, 154–5.

7. Published in Taylor, *Adams Papers*, VI, 364–5.

237

that the cargo of the *Ranger*'s prize is spoiling. I await your reply in order to conclude a mutually advantageous agreement.[8]⟩

From Jacques Leveux[9]   ALS: American Philosophical Society

Monsieur   Calais le 10 aoust 1778

Deux americains se sont presentés chez moy il y a deux Jours et ont fait leur raport ainsy qu'au commandant de la ville qu'ils s'étoient sauvés des prisons d'angleterre ou ils avoient été conduits apres avoir été pris par les anglois. L'un est le Sieur Edward Leger lieutenant a bord du Navire le Hornit Cap. John Nicholson au service du Congrès et L'autre le Sieur thomas Barns Chirurgien a bord du Brigantin americain hampden Cap. Burroughs.[1] Ils sont partis ce matin par la voiture publique pour avoir l'honneur de se presenter chez vous et comme il leur manquoit de l'argent je leur ay fourni a chacun quatre guinés pour subvenir aux frais de leur voyage. J'ose me flatter, Monsieur, que vous voudrez bien approuver ma conduite qui n'a pour but que de remplir le devoir dont vous m'avez chargé icy qui est de rendre service a vos compatriotes; je vous prie de me dire si je peux agir de meme avec ceux qui pouroient venir par la suite. Soyez persuadé que vos ordres Seront executés avec la plus grande ponctualité. J'ay l'honneur d'etre avec respect Monsieur Votre tres humble et tres obeissant serviteur   JES. LEVEUX

Notations in different hands: Leveux Calais / 10. Aout. 1778.

8. The proposal in Sartine's letter of July 29. Arnauld de la Porte (1737–92) had been named intendant at Brest in 1776, and rose to the rank of minister of the marine, briefly, in 1789.

9. For this Calais merchant and agent of the commissioners, see XXVI, 515 n.

1. Edward Leger escaped from Forton on July 23: Kaminkow, *Mariners*, under Lashire. He was paid 240 *l.t.* by the commissioners on Aug. 14, as was Thomas Barnes (or Barns): Alphabetical List of Escaped Prisoners. For the disposition of Barnes's case, see below, BF to JA, *c.* Aug. 26.

From John Murfey [Murphy]

ALS: American Philosophical Society

Sir   August th 10 1778

You'l Exscuse the Liberty I take in Righting as Necesity oblidges me to Do it and ask your advice in my Present Situation. I Saild from the State of Rhode Island the 26 August 1777 In the Sloop Swallow Privateer Belonging to that State and had the misfortune to Be taking By one of King Georges frgates on the 12 of Septmr. following and sent to Jamica from that by Admiral Gaytons orders was sent to England in Irons where we arived on the 17 January and on the 23 was Commited to fortune Prison and there have Been Ever Since till the 28 July when I with 9 more maid my Escape and on the 9 of August Arrivd in Boulogne And Shall stay here a few Days. If you Please to favour me with an answer Direct to Mr. Merten lieutenant de marechausseé a Boulogne.[2] The Letter I have Inclosd is one I Received from admiral Gayton when a Prisoner in Jameica as the North side of that Island was to have Been my Randevoze.[3] I am Sir Your most Obedient and Humble Servant   JOHN MURFEY

To His Exelency Benjamin Franklin

Notation: James Murphy 10 Aug. 78.

---

2. Murfey was paid 240 *l.t.* on Aug. 20. Alphabetical List of Escaped Prisoners. See also Kaminkow, *Mariners,* where his escape is dated July 23.

3. For Admiral Clark Gayton (1720?–1787?) see the *DNB.* The enclosure, dated Oct. 10, 1777, signed by Thomas L. Yates and passed through a number of hands, explained Murfey's deportation to England as an alternative to execution. APS.

Peter Frederick Dobrée to the American Commissioners[4]

ALS: Harvard University Library

Honourable Gentlemen   Nantz 11 August 1778

My Father in law has just now comunicated me the Honorable Mr. Lee's Letter of the 4 Instant, which he received Yesterday, together with sundry extracts which would greatly alarm me, was not I consious of my Innocence. I will not take too much upon those precious moments which you so laudably dedicate to your Country, to refute the false accusations contained in the anonimous Letter, but beg you would judge whether or not a Merchant happy in his situation in life and free from any kind of conscern in Vessells as is my Father would for the sake of others send his *only* Son as a Spy in so well an administered a Kingdom as is France? And whether it is probable, that I who have my Establishments here, my Wife, Child and Relations would sacrifice my all to give advices to People who are almost Stangers to me, as I was sent very Young to School in England, and at my return staid but a very short time at Guernsey before I came here, where I have now been three Years. As to Jersey I have laid there one night by stress of Weather and hardly know any body in that Island. Is it possible that I should have carried on the treachery I am accused of, so long unpunished? Is it not natural that if I found success in this dirty business that my Relations aught to have reaped the benefit wheras none of them have armed any Privatiers as you may yourselves learn if you would be indulgent enough to make inquiries. The Chevaillier de la Poterie and the Chevaillier de Villevocque arrived Yesterday from thence and gone of this morning for Paris. They have been recommended to you by Mr. Schweighauser and are very proper Persons to question on that subjet. You know Honourable Gentlemen what it is to be falsely accused and that at my time of life a stain on ones Reputation is of the greatest consequence. I must then earnestly entreat you to discover me the

4. The background of this letter is discussed in our annotation of Chaumont to BF, July 5.

author of that anonimous Letter, (which to my sorrow has been so easily believed by Monsieur Le Ray de Chaumont) as I am determined not to leave one Stone unturned 'till I have found the inventor of such Calumnies for neither my life or fortune will ever put a stop to my inquiries.

My Worthy Father in law's nomination to the Agentcy (altho' he never asked it) has created him a number of deceitfull Ennemies who through the vilest Jealousy have since constantly endeavoured to hurt him, but his well established reputation and his unstained upright Character have set him above all their Machinations and having none to find but the Place of my birth that one has been attended to. The Continual hurry of Business and above all my Father in law's Rheumatism hinders my setting off for Paris, nevertheless I would do it imediately was I persuaded that it might help to set things in their true light. If you indulge me with an answer be obliging enough to give me your much valued opinion and if so I will gladly and instantly take Horse to undergo any examination and if culpable ask to be dealt with with the utmost severity. But if on the contrary I shall insist upon a publick Reparation of Honour from the Wretch who has so scandalously slandered mine, fully persuaded how ready you are to lend your helping hand to injured Innocence.[5] I have the honor to be with the utmost veneration and respect Honourable Gentlemen Your most humble most obedient most devoted Servant   PETER FREDERICK DOBRÉE

To the Honourable Ministers Plenipotentiary of the United States of America at the Court of France residents at Passy

---

5. The commissioners made no further effort to discover the writer, as far as we know, and let the whole matter drop, even though Dobrée wrote them again along the same lines on Aug. 20 (APS). On Jan. 22, 1779, below, Capt. Niles reported that Dobrée's father was co-owner of a privateer attacking American shipping from a base in Jersey. The reputation of Schweighauser's son-in-law survived unimpaired, however: XXVI, 330 n.

From David Hartley[6]

AL (draft): M.D.A.F.H.H. Hartley Russell (1955) on deposit in the Berkshire County Record Office; transcript: Library of Congress

Dear Sir   Golden Square August 11 1778

I writ to you as long ago as the 14th of last month to tell you that the administration here had given their consent to the exchange of prisoners at Calais and that they would agree to give any ship on your part a free passport from Brest to Calais upon your sending me a similar assurance that any British ship going to Calais for the purpose of the exchange should have free entrance without molestation and free egress with the prisoners in Exchange. I have again received a confirmation of these assurances from our board of Admiralty here and we are now waiting for your answer after the receipt of which the Exchange will be forwarded with all expedition.

We have just received in this Country the report of the answer of the Congress to the Commissioners.[7] After the conversations which I had lately with you upon the Subject it was no surprize to me to find the Answer of the congress such as it has been. You may easily imagine that an explicit acknowledgement of the independence of America must be somewhat grating in this Country and yet this Country is very far from being in a state of exasperation against america. I judge likewise from the answer of the Congress that America is not disinclined to a return of friendly disposition upon safe and honorable terms.

I remember a phrase of yours in a letter some time ago that a little time given for cooling on both sides would have excellent effects.[8] I allways did and still do perfectly agree with this sentiment and If I were to mediate between the two Countries it should be upon a principle conformable to that sentiment.

6. Hartley rewrote this letter three days later, retaining the first paragraph but thoroughly revising the remainder for reasons that he explains there.

7. Congress on June 17 demanded an acknowledgement of independence as a precondition of negotiations with the Carlisle commission: *JCC,* XI, 615.

8. In his letter of Oct. 3, 1775: XXII, 216.

My first proposition should be to withdraw all the fleets and armies.

2dly to proclaim a cessation of hostilities both by sea and land for 5 years.

3dly all prisoners on either side to be immediately discharged.

4thly A free and open trade without any molestation on either side whatsoever.

5thly All mutual intercourse and mutual naturalization to be restored as formerly between G[reat] B[ritain] and N[orth] A[merica].

6thly A Treaty of Peace alliance and Commerce to be negotiated between the two Countries.

I think these terms would give all practical and effectual security to America, and by giving time to cool on both sides might afford a golden bridge to both parties. I know the sincerity of your disposition to restore peace upon equitable and honorable terms. I should heartily rejoice to concur with you in any measures towards that most desireable end. I shall be very glad to hear soon from you. I am &c.

To Dr F Aug 11 1778

James Moylan to the American Commissioners

ALS: American Philosophical Society

Honorable Gentlemen   L'Orient 12th August 1778

The forgoing is extract of a letter I this day received from Lisbon dated 21st July.[9] It may happen, the information may be of some utility to you, which is the reason I forward it,

9. It reads: "The Albion 74 Gun Ship arrived here yesterday, she was one of Admiral Byrons Squadron, and parted them about 400 leagues to the Westward of this place, having carried away her Main Mast in a Gale of wind." For the dispersal of Byron's fleet see the headnote on intelligence reports above, Aug. 3. The storm, besides damaging the rest of Byron's fleet, also drove the ship of the line *Russell* back to England and the *Invincible* to Newfoundland: W. M. James, *The British Navy in Adversity: a Study of the War of American Independence* (London, 1926), pp. 110–11. For a complete list of Byron's ships see *ibid.*, pp. 431–2.

AUGUST 12, 1778

being with due respect Honorable Gentlemen Your assur'd
humble Servant   JAMES MOYLAN

The Honble. Plenepotentiary Ministers of America at Passy

Addressed: The Honorable / Plenepotentiary Ministers / of the
United States of / America / at / Passy

Notation: Mr Moylan L'Orient 12 Augt 78

From R. Parsons   ALS: American Philosophical Society

                 Mr: Pernet's Maitre de Pension, Clotre de Jacobius
Sir   Rue St: Jaques 12th: August 1778
    I hope you will Pardon a liberty which nothing but the
deepest distress cou'd induce me to take. I feel the indelicacy
of importuning a Perfect stranger to afford that relief, which I
have no right to demand, and which goodness of heart alone,
can Prompt you to bestow; but indeed, Sir, a Situation such as
mine, is an excuse for any impropriety there may be in thus
addressing you.
    I have not words to express the astonishment and horror I
was struck with to day, upon the return of Captain Hickey
from delivering my Unhappy Husband's letter to you.[1] He informed me, that you Sir, had declared you never gave Mr:
Parsons the least encouragement to go to America; but, that
on the contrary, you had taken pains to disswade him from it,
and represented it as very improbable that he shoud be received into the service of the United-States. Mr: Parsons coud
have no inducement for coming over here, but the hopes of
obtaining your Protection and recommendation to the Congress; and I understood from him, that you had received his
offered services, and th'o you cou'd not give him an appointment, you woud recommend him to those who might; and
that we were to go from Nantz to America, the first favorable
opportunity. This is what I have thought to be the case, ever
since I have been in Paris, and Mr: Parsons openly declared
here, that he was going to America under your Patronage: but

    1. His letter of Aug. 4, clearly sent to BF in her care.

244

sure he must strangely have deceived himself, and me, to answer no end, if in reality, he has never had any countenance from You. If his first offers were absolutely rejected, Tho' we were at a great expence in making seperate Journeys to this Kingdom, yet we coud have gone back with credit, and with no farther suffering than that of being disappointed in our hopes. But now, as we are unfortunately and miserably circumstanced, if you Sir do not extricate us, ruin must inevitably Ensue. If Mr: Parsons, as I all along thought, had hopes of putting his American Scheme in execution, I can account for his staying here so much longer than he ought. He was in constant hopes of soon going, he was in expectation of receiving money from England, in which he has been disappointed; he was told that you always gave a certain sum to every one you sent out; and what was still more, the Idea he had formed, from the Character he always heard of Doctor Franklin, in England, (where he is by numbers almost adored as a Deity) might perhaps have flatter'd him, that as he was going to offer his life and services in the American cause, he woud be assisted, if he stood in need of it, by the Principal Supporter of that cause. All these circumstances have combined to plunge me into the Scene of wretchedness to which I am now exposed. I cannot accuse my self of any one extravigance since I have been here, we have both lived quite retired, from a Prudential motive, and the same motive made us chuse A Pension-house, tho we have found it much dearer than it ought to be. When Mr: Parsons found he cou'd not pay what was oweing, he thought the only method to extricate us, was to go to England, and try to get money from his freinds. I advised him to it, as the properest step I coud think of. The People of the house consented upon condition I joined as security; (for it seems a married woman's security is as good as any other, in this country) I signed the security, and Mr: Parsons set out. He has not been able to get any money; for those who woud assist him at another time, have refused him upon knowing his intention of going abroad. The People here are very Poor, the time is elapsed in which they expected to be paid, they have it in their Power to send me to Prison, and tho' all they can get by that, will be only hastening me into another

245

world, yet they perhaps think otherwise. In short Sir, you cannot have an Idea of the horrors of my unhappy situation— A stranger in a foreign land, without a freind, without a shilling, even almost without the wretches last resort, hope— Threatned with all the miseries of want, and a jail; Indeed, indeed Sir, the very Idea almost deprives me of reason. I have nothing but my little Wardrobe, which I woud with pleasure dispose of to the last article, and go to England, if it woud answer the Purpose, but tho' it cost me more than I owe, it woud not fetch the quarter of it, and besides I am such a total stranger here, that I shoud be quite at a loss how to dispose of it. Thus Sir, I have given you a true relation of my dreadful situation, and if you will have the goodness to Assist me you will save an unfortunate fellow-creature from the worst of human miseries, and perhaps a very short time may put it in our power to return with gratitude and thanks, whatever you are pleased to give. At present I can only pray the Almighty to recompence my Benefactor, and if he has an Ennemy, to make him a freind. I have the honor to be Sir Your Most Obedient Humble Servant   R: PARSONS

I once more beg leave to apologize for this trouble, and shall hope for your Answer, with a degree of anxiety which none but the unhappy can experience.

Notation: Mrs Parsons

To R. Parsons   ALS (draft): American Philosophical Society

Madam,   [on or after August 12, 1778][2]
    I did truly tell Capt. Hickey as you mention that I had never given Mr. Parsons the least Encouragement to go to America.

---

2. This is unquestionably in answer to Mrs. Parsons' letter of the 12th, which immediately precedes it. But in her next to BF below, Aug. 17, she says that she has heard nothing from him, and her later pleas, Oct. 2 and Nov. 2, do not mention any word from Passy. Furthermore, BF's accounts show no trace of the guinea he promises her here. The best explanation of her receiving no reply is that BF did not send this.

Your good Opinion of your Husband, which is very natural and laudable, induces you to think there is some Mistake in this, and you express your Doubt in these Words, *"If* IN REAL- ITY *he has never had any Countenance from you,"* &c. You also intimate that if his first Offer had been absolutely rejected, you and he could then have gone back with Credit, and that my having accepted his offered Services, and promised him a Rec- ommendation that might procure him an Appointment in America, had occasioned his Stay here till by the Expence you were brought into your present Difficulties. It gives me Pain, Madam, to repeat it to you; But as such a Representation of the Affair affects my Character, I am oblig'd to assure you, that in truth I told him plainly on his first Proposing his Project, that I could not encourage him in it, that our Armies were fully officer'd, and that Numbers of very good Officers who had been to seek Service in America were actually return'd, not being able to find Employ there. In his own Letter to me, just received, after mentioning the Hopes he had conceived in England, he speaks of our first Interview in these Terms: "When I went to pay my personal Compliments to you Sir, at Paris, what my Disappointment when my Offers were re- jected!" Indeed Madam, I am not capable of deceiving a Gentleman, giving him Expectations, and keeping him in Suspence on a Point wherein I know I can not serve him.

Mr. Parsons came to me some time after,[3] and acquainted me, that he was going to England, that his Money fell short, that he had no Credit with any Banker here, but that he had £250 in the Hands of Messrs. Nesbit & Co. in London, and he requested me to advance him Fifteen Guineas, for which he would give me his Bill on those Gentlemen, which he as- sur'd me would be immediately honour'd. I was weak enough to comply with this Request. And having Occasion soon after to remit such a Sum for the Relief of some of my distress'd Countrymen Prisoners in the English Goals, I sent over that Bill for the Purpose, not having the least doubt of its being paid. I am now surpriz'd to find by his Letter, that Messrs.

3. In March: xxv, 693 n.

Nesbit had no Money of his in their Hands, and that the Bill is therefore not paid. Nevertheless, he desires me to pay his Debts in Paris.

This is too much for one Stranger to expect of another.

I must be content, I suppose, to lose what I have lent him; for I have not the smallest Imagination that so imprudent a Man will ever be able to pay any Debt he has contracted. But my Fortune is not equal to the Extricating every body from their Difficulties that may think fit to apply to me. I commiserate however your Misfortunes, as by your Letter you appear not to have merited them; I have never seen, and perhaps never shall see you; but as you tell me you have not a Shilling, I send you a Guinea, with my Wishes that you may be soon in a happier Situation. I am very respectfully Madam, Your most obedient humble Servant   BF.

The American Commissioners to Sartine[4]

AL (draft):[5] Massachusetts Historical Society; two copies: National Archives

⟨Passy, August 13, 1778: We are sorry for the delay in answering your letter of July 29. We are of opinion that the regulations are very good but wish to make the following observations. We propose that judges of admiralty in America because of the size of their jurisdictions be permitted to delegate their authority.[6] We also wish permission to store captured merchandise until it can be exported to America so as to avoid paying heavy customs duties.[7] We suggest that the expenses attendant on these regulations and fees be made public. Inconveniencies may possibly arise once the regulations go into ef-

4. Published in Taylor, *Adams Papers*, VI, 368–70.
5. In JA's hand with a notation by Arthur Lee which reads, "Dr. F concurs with us in these sentiments but as he is absent we are obliged to send the letter without his signature."
6. To examine prizes—see articles 2 and 4 of the proposed regulations: Wharton, *Diplomatic Correspondence*, II, 685.
7. See article 14: *ibid.*, p. 687.

fect; we beg leave, in that case, to call them to your attention and to request His Majesty to make necessary alterations.⟩

To William Lee[8]   AL (draft): American Philosophical Society

Sir,   Passy Augt 13. 78
    You left a Trunk in my Care seal'd up, and took my Receipt attested by four Witnesses, wherein I promis'd to deliver that Trunk to you or your Order in the same State wherein I receiv'd it.[9] This I am ready to do whenever you please. But I am not willing to have any Concern in the Opening of it, or in examining and Sorting as you desire, the Papers it is said to contain. For this I have my Reasons. And I do not see any Necessity for my being the Person, as here are two other Commissioners, your Brother and Mr. Adams, either or both of whom can do what you desire as well or better than myself. You will be so obliging therefore as to excuse me in this, and command in some other Service Your most obedient and most humble Servant   BF
Honble. Wm Lee Esqr

From Jean-Rodolphe Perronet[1]

ALS: American Philosophical Society

ce 13 Aoust 1778.
Mr. Perronet assure de son Respectueux attachement Monsieur Francklin et lui envoy un Plan du Combat Entre la flotte anglaise et l'Armée du Roy, persuadé qu'il pourra lui faire plaisir.

8. In response to Lee's letter of Aug. 5.
9. See XXVI, 40–1.
1. This is the only letter we have to BF from his fellow member of the Académie royale des sciences. Perronet (1708–94) was the leading engineer in France: Schelle, *Œuvres de Turgot*, IV, 123; see also Larousse. The enclosed plan, now lost, was of the first naval engagement of the war, the indecisive Battle of Ushant on July 27.

From Richard Peters[2]   ALS: American Philosophical Society

Dear Sir   Philadelphia Augt. 13th. 1778
    Let me beg of you to endeavor at sending the enclosed Letter to my Father if he be still in England. I fear all Letters to him are examined at the Post Offices and therefore presume you can contrive the Matter so as that it shall not pass thro' them. It contains Information of absolute Necessity to him but perhaps it might be of Disservice to him if publicly known. I know it ought not to be but the British may with Truth (I mean those of them who go to Church) declare that they do and have done the Things they ought not to do and ought not to have done. I repeat my Request to you to supply my Father with some Money thro' Apprehension that my other Letters may have been prevented from arriving to your Hands.
    We expect daily to hear of the Recovery of Rhode Island and of Course of the Capture of the British Troops there.[3] General Clinton with the Main Body is still besieged in New York by General Washington and his Misfortune at Monmouth has taught him not to be adventurous.[4] I wish you every Happiness and am with great Truth and Esteem Your obliged and obedient Servant   RICHARD PETERS.

The Count D'Estaing is at Rhode Island with his Squadron.

Honble. B Franklin Esqr

Addressed: Honble Dr Benjamin Franklin / one of the Commis-

---

2. For Richard Peters (1744–1828) see XXIII, 274–5 and XXVI, 553–5. William Peters, his father, was eventually located by Thomas Digges. Robert H. Elias and Eugene D. Finch, eds., *Letters of Thomas Attwood Digges (1742–1821)* ([Columbia, S.C., 1982]), pp. 45–6.
3. On July 29 Admiral d'Estaing, having failed to capture Howe's fleet at New York, arrived off Newport. The British garrison was faced by units of the continental army and Rhode Island militia commanded by Gen. John Sullivan. In early August Newport was placed under siege. Willcox, *Portrait of a General*, pp. 242–4; Christopher Ward, *The War of the Revolution* (2 vols., New York, 1952), II, 588–90.
4. The indecisive Battle of Monmouth, fought on June 28 by the armies of Washington and Clinton.

sioners from the United / States of North America / Passi / near / Paris per the Dolphin Capn. Sanfort

Endorsed: Richd Peters

Notations: Richard Peters Philadelphia 13 août 1778 / forwarded By your Honour Most humble and Obedient Servant for Mr. J. Bondfield Jh. Dl. Pauly Bordeaux 6. November 1778

Barbeu-Dubourg to the American Commissioners

ALS: American Philosophical Society

Messieurs,   Paris 14 aout [1778]

Je prens la liberté de vous adresser M. de Vic dont le fils M. de Bois Bertrand etoit passé en Amerique vers le mois de juin ou de juillet 1776 a la recommandation de M. Penet[5] qui lui avoit fait esperer le grade de Lieutenant Colonel ou même de Colonel. Nous avons appris depuis qu'en arrivant au Continent ses services y furent agréés, mais qu'il fut pris quelques jours apres avec M. Le General Lee.

Je vous supplie de vouloir ecouter favorablement M. de Vic qui vous informera de la suite,[6] et qui compte que vous voudrez bien que son fils aine dont il a fait le sacrifice a votre patrie y retourne incessamment, repandre son sang si l'occasion s'en presente pour affermir la liberté de la nation a laquelle il desire de rester a jamais incorporé. J'ai l'honneur

5. Pierre Penet, the enterprising merchant settled in Nantes, first appeared in vol. XXII.

6. The father was Etienne-Henry Gaiault de Vic, provost of the maréchaussées in Berry: Bodinier, *Dictionnaire* under Gayault. He presumably wanted to bring the commissioners up to date on what had happened since his son, Boisbertrand (XXII, 469 n; XXIII, 452–3) had escaped from Forton Prison, and thereby pave the way for the latter's memorandum to the commissioners below, Sept. 5. De Vic had already called on BF, probably some weeks earlier, for Hutton knew of the visit by the time he wrote BF from the Netherlands on Aug. 16.

d'etre avec un respectueux devouement Messieurs Votre tres
humble et tres obeissant serviteur   DUBOURG

Endorsed: Dubourg 14. aout

From David Hartley

ALS: American Philosophical Society

Dear Sir   Golden Square Aug 14 1778

I writ to you as long ago as the 14th of the last month to
tell you that the administration here had given their consent
to the exchange of prisoners at Calais, and that they would
agree to give any ship on your part a free passport from Brest
to Calais, upon your sending me a similar assurance that any
British ship going to Calais for the purpose of the Exchange
should have free entrance without molestation, and free egress
with the prisoners in Exchange. I have again received a confirmation of these assurances from the board of admiralty here,
and we are now waiting for your answer, after the receipt of
which the exchange will be forwarded with all expedition.

I had writ thus much to you by the last post, and then as
you know that peace with America is allways uppermost in
my thoughts, my pen ran on with some ideas and propositions
to that end, which led me insensibly beyond the hour of the
post. I see so little probability in my attempt in the present
state of things that I confess I am quite disheartned, tho I
cannot keep my thoughts from the subject, but I think it not
worth while to trouble you with any further propositions at
present.[7] I am confident that the wishes of both nations are for
peace, but the moment any proposition is reduced into shape
or texture its virtue ceases, and instead of drawing parties together it excites jealous repulsions between them. If more suc-
cessfull or more promising times should come, my thoughts
will ever be upon the watch. These sentiments are suggested
to my mind upon the report of the late negotiation between

7. Hartley's original version of this letter, which contained six explicit
peace proposals, has appeared under Aug. 11; the first paragraph is repeated here.

the Congress and the Commissioners. If I can judge of the disposition of the two nations I think that terms of safe and honorable mediation might be offered between them, but we must wait for the favorable moment. A premature anxiety repels instead of inviting its object. Peace will ever be my object. When the opportunity offers favorably then will be the time to strike. A man of feeling can not be indifferent at such a critical time especially when the parties seem nearer together than they think themselves. Jealousies and punctilios make the greatest difficulties. If instead of the distance of 3000 miles, the treaty were set on foot only at the distance of 300, and conducted with Confidence, a more fortunate end might be expected. I shall be glad to hear from you soon. Believe me ever Yours most affectionately   DH

To Dr Franklin

Notation: D.H. Augt. 14. 1778.

From Honoré-Sébastien Vial du Clairbois[8]

ALS: American Philosophical Society

Monsieur   A Brest le 14 aoust 1778
   Je vous suplie d'agréer un exemplair de mon livre sur l'architecture navale.[9] C'est un homage que je crois devoir au Philosophe-homme d'état: Et d'ailleurs il est independant de toute raison particuliere. Je suis avec respec Monsieur Votre très humble et très obeissant Serviteur
                     VIAL DU CLAIRBOIS
                     Ingenieur de la marine au Departement de Brest

M. Franklin à Paris

---

8. Clairbois (1733–1816) became a noted authority on naval architecture; during the Revolution he was in charge of the installations at Lorient, and under the Consulate headed the engineering school at Brest. Larousse under Vial.
   9. *Essai géométrique et pratique sur l'architecture navale* (Brest, 1776).

253

Endorsed: Vial du Clairbois with a Book on Naval Architecture
Notation: 14 Aout 1778.

The American Commissioners to —— Berubé de Costentin[1]

Copy:[2] National Archives

Sir,   Passi Augt. 15th 1778
  We desire you will allow Mr. Thomas Wilkinson,[3] one of the Prisoners made by the Ranger, and now in your Hospital, to go into the Country for the benefit of his health, on his parole. We are Sir your most obedient Servants Signd
                                                                                       A L. J A.
                                                                               Dr F. being out

Monsr. Beroubé de Constantine Negt. a Brest

John Paul Jones to the American Commissioners[4]

ALS: American Philosophical Society; copies: National Archives (two), United States Naval Academy Museum

⟨Brest, August 15, 1778: I have been here five days and have neither seen nor heard from Lt. Simpson; but Mr. Hill[5] reports the general rumor that I have been turned out of the service,

  1. The man Schweighauser had put in charge of American vessels and prizes in Brest. See Costentin to BF, Aug. 24.
  2. In Arthur Lee's hand.
  3. He had been the pilot of the *Drake.* See Comte Sutton de Clonard to BF, March 15, 1779. APS.
  4. Published in Taylor, *Adams Papers,* VI, 372–3. Jones reinforced his case against Simpson with an 8-page, exhaustive, undated memorandum intended for BF but sent, we are convinced, in a letter of Aug. 14 to Bancroft (Library of Congress). Jones asked Bancroft to forward the enclosure if he thought fit, and explain that he "was afraid of giving [Franklin] too much trouble." An incomplete copy of the memorandum is at the APS; a fuller version is at the Library of Congress. It is summarized as [to the commissioners] under the date [Aug. 15], in Charles Henry Lincoln, comp., *A Calendar of John Paul Jones Manuscripts in the Library of Congress* (Washington, 1903), pp. 45–6.
  5. Benjamin Hill, midshipman on the *Ranger.*

that Simpson has replaced me with a captain's commission, and that my letter to you of July 16 was only in obedience to your orders. These are not conjectures but melancholy facts. Since the *Boston* and *Providence* are about to arrive, I demand redress by a court martial which can now be summoned with the assistance of Capt. Hinman who has the unquestioned right to succeed me in the *Ranger*'s command. I have faithfully served the dignified cause of human nature ever since the American banner first waved. I conclude by requesting you to question Edward Meyrs,[6] at the house of the Swedish ambassador, about my conduct at sea.[7])

From Jane Mecom   ALS: American Philosophical Society

Dear Brother   Warwick August 15 1778
I wrot you concerning the Enemies being in posesion of Philadelphia.[8] I now congratalate you on there Evacuation of it, and that they have done so Litle Damage to the Real Estates in the City, as I hear from a Transient person for I have had no Leter from your children yet to Inform me of particulars; no doute you have saffered much in movables but Since they have got rid of them I hope never more to Return that

6. Jones seems to be confusing two of his crew members. Edward Myer, boatswain's mate, had signed the petition of June 15 against Jones (XXVI, 621–3). The captain undoubtedly meant Lt. Jean Meÿer, the Swedish volunteer who had been introduced to BF by the Swedish ambassador in July (above, De Baër to BF, July 13). Meÿer's allegiance had been proven: he had warned Jones of a mutiny plot just before the Whitehaven raid, and had saved Jones from being stranded on the beach, as his men had intended, once the raid was over. Meÿer's certification, April 14, 1780, National Archives.

7. The commissioners drafted a reply on Aug. 22, which survives in both Lee and JA's hands (National Archives; Mass. Hist. Soc.). It acknowledges receipt of this letter, which they mistakenly date Aug. 16, and says that they were requesting Whipple to summon a court martial: Taylor, *Adams Papers*, VI, 385. This reply was never sent and, as far as we know, the letter to Whipple never drafted, undoubtedly because Whipple's letter to them of Aug. 19, with its news that Hinman would refuse to serve, arrived in the meantime.

8. Missing.

will be the Easeier to be borne, what suckses we shall have hear in Expelling them from Rhoad Island is uncertain. They have Fortified themselves Strongly and it is said burnt and sunk all there Shiping since the French Fleet came in which looks as if they Intended to fite as they have no way to Escape. Our Armie is gone on, what number I dont hear, but there is many volinters. My Grand-son and two of His Brothers are of that number, there Brother the General is also there.[9] Mr. Hancock Heads an Independant Company from Boston of which it is said there is not a man among them worth les than ten Thousand pounds Sterling; I hope they will have there desiered suckses for the sake of the whol comunitie and a litle for my own for I have lived in constant Jeperdie since the Spring when my children removed from Coventry to this place where we are much Exposed and have been under constant Aprehensions. I have been Part of the time at the Governers[1] but it was full as bad there for they offered a reward for Takeing him, you will Acknolidg this is Rather wors than being harried about by wons Friends,[2] yet I doubt not but that is Troblesom to you who are so desierous of Retierment, I fear you will never be suffered to Injoy it. I had a hint from Mr. Williams[3] at the time we recved your Leters by Mr. Dean that gave me hopes of your Return but it is all blown over now. I was in hopes of a leter by the other Brother[4] but sopose There was none or Mr. Bache would have sent it Ere now. I do not wonder if you are discuridged from writing to me for I Fear you have never recved any of my leters but the won you

9. Elihu Greene, the husband of her granddaughter Jane Flagg (XXII, 496 n). The brothers must have been William (1743–1826) and Christopher (1748–1830). See Louise B. Clark, *The Greenes of Rhode Island ...* (New York, 1903), pp. 210–12. The latter is not to be confused with Col. Christopher Greene (1737–80), son of Philip Greene (XXII, 647 n). The brothers probably belonged to the Rhode Island militia that took part in the siege of Newport. Their brother the general was Nathanael.

1. Gov. William Greene (1731–1809), husband of Catharine Ray Greene.

2. "I feel a little myself the Inconvenience of being driven about by my Friends," BF to Catharine Greene, Feb. 28, 1778: XXV, 733.

3. Jonathan Williams, Sr.

4. The brothers Silas and Simeon Deane.

mention that was to have gon by my son Collas and I think I have sent seven, I all-ways sen them throw the hands of Mr. Beach, or Mr. Williams, but two of them hapened to go by my son Collas[5] and we sopose he is Taken again. He has had nothing but Misfourtun and the sicknes but it is very disagreable to me to write trobles and Dificulties and I have in other leters Informed you of His being a prisner at New york a long time. Has since been twice taken wonce drove back in port by storm to refit which was the means of his haveing two of my leters to you. I had wrot many things about your children and there children which I knew you would be glad to hear. I cannot now so much as say they are well, I wrot you of our Friend Greenes being Governer, that Ray was at Mr. Moodys scool[6] and comes on bravely with His Larning, that ther Eldest Daughter was married to Major Ward.[7] What I had to write concerning I have Injoyed many blesings my own Perticular Famely has been as was comon to me all my life mostly distressing. Poor Benjamin[8] Strayed a way soon affter the batle at Trenton and has never been heard of since, I can hear nothing of His Famely tho I have wrot several times to Inquier, but what now distreses me much now is that the woman that keeps my son Peter[9] in the Country Demands five Dolars a week for takeing care of him to comence September 1777 or she would send him to boston. I wrot to Mr. Williams to git Him Put in to the Alms house there but he says there is no provision for such persons there. I have sent a second Leter to Urge it but have had no Ansure. I write this with grat Reluctance but as you desiered me to Inform you of my circumstances as well as helth and Situation it will not be confideing in you as Such a Friend as you have allways been to me and prehaps the only disintrested won I have in the world to keep

5. Jane's son-in-law, Peter Collas.
6. Dummer Academy in Byfield, Mass., established in 1763. The Reverend Samuel Moody (1726–95) was its first master: *Sibley's Harvard Graduates*, XII, 48–52. See also above, XXV, 118.
7. XXVI, 403–4.
8. Her eldest surviving son: I, lxi. See Lopez and Herbert, *The Private Franklin*, pp. 108–12, and her letter below, Feb. 14, 1779. APS.
9. Peter Franklin Mecom (I, lxii) was insane: see X, 355, 384.

it back. I did some time ago writ you that my Expences from Philadelphia had cost me seventy dolars[1] that the Price of won pare of shoes hear was as much as I could by Seven pair for of the same sort when I was in boston but I then wrot a mistake, for they asked me six dolars for a pair such as I used to bye for half a dolar a pair by the doz in Boston but I bye as litle as posable. I also wrot you that what mony I had a mounting to four hundrid Dolars I had put to Intrest only reserving for nesesary use, that I Live comfortable with my Grandchildren and have my Helth but no Income but what that litle money Produces which however I should do very well with were it not for this dredfull affair of Peter which you see will take the most I have if I am forced to pay it and if Mr. Williams cant git Him in to the Alms House. God only knows what I shall do with him in future. I think you cant disaprove of my En-devouring it. I was in hopes to have bee able to Informed you it was done but haveing opertunity to send this to Mr. Wil-liams by Mr. Hubard[2] I would not Neglect it.

I Intended to have said a grat deal to you about many other things but my spirets feel so deprest and I have such horrid pens and paper I shall only add my love to your grand sons from your affectionat Sister   JANE MECOM

If we have the good fortune to Drive the Enemie from New-port I hope to be Able to be won of your first Informers & write in a nother maner

Prehaps Mr Williams may prevail with the overseers to take in poor Peter paying the Rent of the House you used to alow me which I know you will have no objection to. I had forgot to mention that to Him but shall now   JM

Addressed: Dor Franklin / Paris

Notation: Jane Mecom Warwick 15. aout 1778.

---

1. See XXVI, 403–4.
2. Either Thomas Hubbart (1717–96), husband of Judith Ray and brother-in-law of Catharine Ray Greene, or his brother Tuthill (1720–1808?), the Boston postmaster.

The American Commissioners to Jacques Paulze[3]

L (draft):[4] Library of Congress

Sir,   Passy, August 16. 1778.

Several Ships have been sent to North America as french Property with Clearances for the French Islands, loaded with Supplies for the United States. Mr. Peltier Du Doyer[5] has accordingly been obliged to make a Submission at the Offices at Nantes to return the *acquits à Caution* for their Cargoes duely discharged, which was impossible to be done. We therefore beg leave to request of you an Order to your Officers at Nantes to give the said Mr. Peltier a general Discharge from his Submissions for the Cargoes of all the Ships that have been fitted out by him to the United States, under the Appearance of being sent to the French Islands.[6] We have the honour to be, Sir, with great Respect, Your most obedient and most humble Servants.

Mr. Paulze

Notation in Franklin's hand: Farmer Gener

John Bondfield to the American Commissioners[7]

ALS: American Philosophical Society

⟨Bordeaux, August 17 [*i.e.*, 16][8], 1778: Captain Ayres's poor health probably precludes his return voyage with your dis-

3. The commissioners' liaison with the farmers general and director of their tobacco department: XXIII, 130 n.

4. In WTF's hand, with BF's emendations.

5. Jean Peltier-Dudoyer was the agent of Beaumarchais and Montieu; the commissioners had had frequent dealings with him since their arrival in France.

6. These submissions were a longstanding problem for ships trading secretly with America: see XXV, 253.

7. Published in Taylor, *Adams Papers*, VI, 373–4.

8. In his letter below of Aug. 17, Bondfield says this letter was written the previous day. We therefore elect to publish it under Aug. 16. It is also possible that the latter letter was misdated, and that the two were written on Aug. 17 and 18.

patches.[9] Instruct me concerning his successor. Ships like his could transport goods to America quickly; if financial considerations permit, I could execute a partial order. I do not wish to seem presumptuous but I am herewith submitting a plan designed to restore confidence in the inflated American currency.[1] P.S. I send this by M. Le Normand of the House of Le Couteulx & Cie. of Cadiz, to whom I draw the commissioners' attention for his extensive connections and ability to provide information.[2]⟩

Sartine to the American Commissioners[3]

LS: Harvard University Library; copies: Massachusetts Historical Society, Library of Congress, National Archives; two transcripts: National Archives

⟨Versailles, August 16, 1778, in French: In answer to your letter of the 13th on the question of prizes and prisoners, I enclose a copy of the regulations with revisions to articles 2 and 14.[4] I will at all times receive with pleasure your representations on any inconveniencies attending the execution of the regulations and you may be assured His Majesty will always be disposed to grant Americans every facility compatible with his financial interests and his subjects' commerce.⟩

9. See his letter of July 29; also, William James Morgan, *Captains to the Northward: the New England Captains in the Continental Navy* (Barre, Mass., 1959), p. 150.

1. To BF, on or before Aug. 16, below.

2. The Cadiz branch of this Parisian house was called Le Couteulx, Le Normand & Cie. Simon-Emmanuel-Julien Le Normand (or Normant) subsequently became receiver general of finance in La Rochelle: Lüthy, *Banque protestante*, II, 458 n, 700. For Le Couteulx & Cie. see above, XXVI, 467 n.

3. Published in Taylor, *Adams Papers*, VI, 374–5.

4. The text and amendment to the regulations are published in Wharton, *Diplomatic Correspondence*, II, 685–7.

From John Bondfield

ALS: Historical Society of Pennsylvania

Sir,   [on or before August 16, 1778][5]

As every plan for publick use ought to be laid down in the most simple and uncomplicated State, the following I presume will justify the Ideas of that I had yesterday the Honor to lay before you.

A plan for sinking the paper money and Loan office Certificates without remaining a Debt to the publick or a private Loss.

All the paper money and Loan Office Certificates to be calld in and as recceived the Treasurer to deliver in Exchange a note or Certificate to the proprieter for the Amount conceived in the following terms:

The Note Anext with the indorsments of the sums liquidated in proportion to the reduction.

The new Issued Notes or Certificates to be made from 10 to 1000 Dollars in equal sums of tens for the greater facility of the publick Books. The calculations of the reductions and the renewd Certificates.

The Calculation of the reduction or discompts to be printed on the back of the Notes leaving a blank for the Indorser so that the holders may not lay under any difficulty to assertain exactly the value of the Bill or Certificate on paying it nor the receiver at receiving both values being exprest.

The Certificates stand subjected on every indorsment to a reduction of half per Cent which half per Cent takes place neither in favor of the receiver nor to the prejudice of the payer but in favor of the Note itself becoming thereby a personality of real representation. That is the Note is decreased in value in virtue of every indorsement half per Cent so that in the progression of 21 payments (as is laid down on the anext Certificate) the Note is reduced in Value One Tenth and so on by a further progression to its entire discharge.

To explain in which manner loss is not to ensue to the payer nor Receiver the first proprieter who issues the Note makes good ½ per Cent over the Amount of the Certificate which

5. Enclosed in Bondfield's letter to the commissioners summarized above, Aug. 16.

suffices to indemnify all the succeeding proprieters each paying and receiving the said ½ per Cent to the term of the negotiation as will appear on an Arithmatical proof here the first proprieter is reduced only to a sacrifice of half per Cent and all the succeeding possessors freed from Loss.

Here no time is loss as no term of payment takes place it is as Gold in the Pocket. Its true it is not a growing fund nor is it a sinking fund to the Holder.

In all Mercantil Negotiations a discompt of half per Cent is allowd per month on Bills put in Circulation and not due. There the holder loses or sustains a real Loss of [½ ?] per Cent which on a long term amounts to a great share of the Capital. With this Certificate an Estate may as well be purchased as with Gold. Let us carry the parelels: Gold is an Earth dugg which carries a value by the consent of Nations to form a Medium in Exchange. Return it to the Mine its value returns to its source. Paper Money in its present State is as Gold in the Mine. [*In the margin:* the holders of the present paper money is the Mine] Give it a consistence by a resolve of Congress that it shall under certain regulations be Legal tender it will operate the same effect to its total Extinction.

This simple Brief discription may lead to more enlarged and better digested Explainations. It appears to me there is Matter for Speculation. With due respect I have the honor to be Sir your most Obedient and Obliged Humble Servant

JOHN BONDFIELD

To His Exellency D. B Franklin

From Robert Cochran[6]   ALS: American Philosophical Society

Sir,   Charles Town So: Carolina Augt: 16: 1778
Having been repeatedly inform'd of the friendship and kindness with which you have favourd my dear little Son,[7] I

6. A South Carolina shipyard owner and ship captain: XXIII, 38 n.

7. BFB's best friend Charles B. Cochran, later a lawyer and South Carolina legislator: James D. Tagg, "Benjamin Franklin Bache and the *Philadelphia Aurora*" (2 vols., Ph.D. diss., Wayne State University, 1973), I, 44; Taylor, *J. Q. Adams Diary*, I, 34 n.

should accuse myself of ingratitude was I not to acknowledge the satisfaction it gives me, his being so situated as to be noticed by you, and to have your Grandson for an acquaintance: permit me Sir to send you my sincere thanks, and I should be very happy to have an oppertunity to make a more suitable return. I hope his behaviour is such as to merit your approbation. The length of time which elapses without hearing from him, makes me very anxious, if Sir you will extend your goodness so far as to desire him to write when you hear of an oppertunity, it will be conferring on me An additional obligation, as I am inform'd his Tutors have it not in their power to assist him in sending letters.

I think to take a voyage to France in the Winter. In the mean time Most Worthy Sir I am with the Greatest Respect Your Most Obedient Hble Servant   ROBT: COCHRAN

His Excellencey Benjn: Franklin Esqr:

Notation: Robt. Cochran Charlestown 16 aout 1778.

From ——— Durand de las Bordas[8]

ALS: American Philosophical Society

Monsieur   Paris le 16e août 1778

J'ay vû naitre Les pretentions de L'amerique, j'ay vû triompher Ses armes et Sa cause etoit Si Belle, que La regardant comme personnelle, j'ay joui Sincerement de tous ses avantages. Le Succés Le plus Brillant a couronné Ses hauttes Entreprises, Ses voeux sont remplis et quoiqu'il vous importe peu de Savoir La part que j'y prends, je ne peus resister plus Longtems a L'envie que j'ay de vous La faire connoitre.

Cette revolution fait sans doutte Le Bonheur de L'amerique, La France le partage et chaque Cytoyen fait Eclater sa joye. Ma Satisfaction est d'autant plus grande, que Le Roy de France, m'ayant nommé Son consul a cagliary et autres ports du Royaume de Sardaigne, je trouveray peutetre des occasions

---

8. His name appears this way in the list of French consuls in Italy provided by the *Almanach Royal* for 1778, p. 501. He kept the post until 1784.

dans ce département a me rendre utille aux Sujets de L'amerique; je les saisiray avec Empressement et dans tous les tems,
je Leur Seray dévoué Sans reserve: cet interet que je Sens plus
vivement que je ne L'exprime est commun a toutte ma famille;
M. Gabriel Durand mon pere, m'ecrit de Barcelone En Cata-
logne, ou il reside depuis Longtems, et me charge de vous
demander pour Luy Le consulat des Etats reunis de L'amerique dans cette principauté; Si vous n'avez point disposé de
cette plasse, je vous en Demande La preference, Lorsque Les
circonstances vous permettront d'y nommer; vous ne Sauriez
en charger personne de plus Zélé pour La prospérité d'une
puissance dont vous faittes La gloire et L'ornement. Je suis
avec respect, Monsieur, Votre tres humble et tres obeissant
Serviteur   DURAND
                        Hotel D'artois rüe Guénégaud

Mr Franklin ministre plenipotentiaire des americains a Passy

Endorsed: Durand Consul

From James Hutton

ALS: American Philosophical Society

My dear old Friend   Zeist. Aug. 16. 1778
    The mariage of one of the loveliest men in the world to as
lovely a Woman, both of whom look upon me as their own
and I them as my own, has brought me to Holland. I do not
remember whether I ever mentioned to you a friend who in
your time was Sub Preceptor to the P. of Wales, a Mr. de Salgas. This is the name of the man and his Lady was widow of
a rich Mr. Bicker [*and*] Daughter of Mr. Boreel formerly Embassadour to us from Holland.[9] These dear people were expected over in England this Summer: they were married last

9. Claude de Narbonne Pelet Salgas, a Protestant Swiss, was tutor to the
Prince of Wales and then to the Duke of York; before that he had been
secretary to Jacob Boreel for the decade, 1764–74, when the latter had been
the Dutch envoy to St. James's. Boreel's daughter Catharina (born 1736)
had married Jan Bernd Bicker in 1758. *Gent. Mag.*, LXXXIII (1813), part I,
285; Johan E. Elias, *De Vroedschap van Amsterdam* ... (2 vols., Harlem,
1903), I, 538.

Sunday at Amsterdam, but instead of going to England, they go to Switzerland and Nice on account of the Health of a fine Child of the Lady. I had never seen the Lady, but have had many Letters of friendship from her, and as she can not come to England till next year, I could not wait till then as perhaps I may not be alive to that time. So I arrived here in Holland last Tuesday at 8 in the morning. Shall stay with them till they set out and then return to England: or rather go with them as far as Brussels perhaps, and then go to England from thence.[1] I lay at the Hague at the Sister's of my Daughters [Daughter's], for so the new married Lady will be called. From the Hague I came to the new married people at Amsterdam the next day Aug. 12. The 13th. I spent in Amsterdam. The 14th I came to Mr. Boreel's House the Brother of the Bride,[2] near *Zeist, at which place* I write this, at 5 in the morning. Shall return by and by to Mr. Boreels and then go with my Son and Daughter. I passd the night at Mr. Boreels and dined there yesterday, spent the afternoon and night here and go by and by to dinner to Mr. Boreels where I hope to find my Son and Daughter. I lodge here at the Revd. Mr. Seyffert's Minister at Zeist to whom I desired you to send the Passport for our Vessel going to Labradore. By some fatality it never came to hand[3] and our Vessel is gone without that mark of your Love and kindness to me which I make not the least Doubt of. If it should be taken our poor people will perish with hunger very probably and there are 22 of them there whose main and almost whole Dependance is on the food we send them from England, from year to year. I sent you twice the Description of the Vessel. As you know the tender personal friendship and Love I ever had and ever will have for you, I am certain it is owing to any thing else rather than unwillingness to do me a pleasure.

If you recollect there was a French Officer taken with General Lee, who had been imprisoned and illused about whom I

1. In fact he accompanied the newlyweds to Valenciennes and then went to Calais; in early September he was about to cross to Dover: to Ferdinand Grand, Sept. 8, 1778, APS.
2. Jacob Boreel was an official in Amsterdam: Elias, *op. cit.*, p. 539.
3. BF, after a long delay, had sent the safe conduct for the ship with a covering letter in late June: XXVI, 667–8, 674.

spoke to you, whose Father waited on you to try to get him exchanged.[4] With this Gent. I corresponded while in Prison, and tried by Representations repeated and even teazing to our Ministry, that He might be exchanged or at Liberty on Parole not to serve till exchanged, but all without effect. 4. or 5 days before I set out, He wrote me word He had broke Prison, of which I was most glad. He came to me and I hope he is got to France. I should be vex'd if He was retaken. His Intention was to go to Deal to a Smuggler's and thence run over in the night. I was glad that He was free and that I . . .[5]

My dearest Friend you and I have pleasures that many do not take, we try to serve mankind, in their Distresses. I always found you such, and honour your heart for it.

I wish to hear whether this Mr. Gaiault de Boisbertrand is got safe over to France. D'Antic is his particular friend and so is Court de Gebelin.[6]

Any Letter to me sent directed thus, chez Madame Fagel neè Boreel a la Haye will find me surely and will not be open'd at our office. The Lady will take care of any such Letter.[7]

We have some of our people going soon to Bethlehem, if they can get thither; I wish I could get your Passport for them. Their Names that I know of are, as already fixed, the Revd. Mr. Reichel and his wife, Mr. de Marshall and his Lady and Daughter and a Miss Watteville, Grand Daughter of Count Zinzendorffe and 3. or 4 single Brethren. Mr. Reichel goes on a Visit, but the rest intend staying there. Mr. de Marshall was chief of our North Carolina settlement and I suppose returns

4. For the father see Dubourg to the commissioners, Aug. 14.
5. Suspension points in the original.
6. For Boisbertrand and his vicissitudes see his memorandum for the commissioners below, Sept. 5. For Hutton's friend, Court de Gébelin, see XIX, 342 n. Paul Bosc d'Antic, a physician, chemist, and glassmaker, was a friend of Hutton and Dubourg. The former had tried to get him to England more than two years before, and Dubourg had urged BF to recruit him to promote the arts in America: XXII, 463.
7. The sister of Catharina Salgas, Agnes Margaretha Fagel, was now a widow; her husband had belonged to one of the most distinguished families in the country: Elias, op. cit., p. 538; above, XXI, 35 n; Hutton's letter to Grand cited in note 1.

thither.[8] As there is nothing upon Earth that I could do with any kind of Propriety, which I should decline doing [at yo]ur Request, I am persuaded you will not [disapprove?] this Request, if you can grant it with Propriety. Sir John and Dr. Ingershausen were well when I left London, and Dolly too.[9] The same good Girl you ever knew her.

I beg my Compliments to my kind Landlord, Mr. de Chaumont and his Family, and to all my friends near you. I am with great Respect and attachment your most obliged and most affectionate   JAMES HUTTON

If you can give me such a Passport I wish you could do it soon and if sent to that Lady at the Hague will come certainly safe. Perhaps at your Request Mr de Sartine would give you also a Similar Pass.

To Doctor Franklin

Endorsed: M. Hutton wants Passports Augt. 16. 1778.

John Bondfield to the American Commissioners

ALS: American Philosophical Society

Sirs   Bordeaux 17 Augt. 1778

By Monsieur Le Norman[1] who left this yesterday I had the Honor to advise you of the ill State of Health of Cap. Ayres and of my apprehendtion of his incapacity to proceed. I am more confirmd in my doubts his Physicians assuring me it will be imposible for him to resist the sharpness of the Air and the fatigue of the Passage, and of which he appears himself convinct by his conversation to me last Evening. The Vessel[2] will be off the Waies this evening and by Saturday will have her

8. The directing board of the Moravians sent this party, led by Bishop John Frederick Reichel, to curtail the increasing independence of the Bethlehem community. For the companions of Anna Dorothea de Watteville, granddaughter of the Moravian leader, see Joseph M. Levering, *A History of Bethlehem, Pennsylvania* . . . (Bethlehem, 1903), pp. 506–7.
9. Sir John Pringle, Ingenhousz, and Dorothea Blunt.
1. For whom see Bondfield's letter of the previous day.
2. The packet *General Arnold.*

provissions Water &c. on board ready to proceed. The Captain has on board a few Hogsheads Tobacco and other triffles given him by Genl. Warren[3] and others his Freinds in Boston the proceeds to be laid out in Family Stores for themselves. There is no Goods on Board on Account of the States.

Permit me to refer you to mine of Yesterday with regard to my favorite Plan which I should be happy to find correspond with your Ideas of its Utility. I have the Honor to be with due Respect Sirs Your most Obedient Humble Servant

JOHN BONDFIELD

Paris The Honbles the Commissioners

Addressed: The Honble. Benj Franklin / Arthur Lee. John Adams Esq / Commissioners from Congress / at / Paris

Notation: Mr Bondfield Bourdeaux 17 August. 78

James Moylan to the American Commissioners[4]

ALS and copy:[5] American Philosophical Society

⟨Lorient, August 17, 1778: The brig *Lady Washington*, Captain Rowntree, arrived yesterday from the James River with a cargo of tobacco, having sailed July 8. The captain tells me the two armies were in New Jersey and the British transports still in the Delaware. Washington's army amounted to 18,000 men, the people were in high spirits and money was appreciating in value. D'Estaing's fleet is expected daily.⟩

---

3. James Warren, the Eastern Navy Board member and Massachusetts politician.

4. Published in Taylor, *Adams Papers*, VI, 375–6.

5. The copy is endorsed by BF: "Moylan News."

From Georges Grand[6]

ALS: American Philosophical Society

Monsieur,   Paris le 17 aoust 1778

Mr. Boggiano[7] de cette ville est chargé de procurer une introduction auprès de vous à la Personne a laquelle je prens la liberté de remettre cette lettre, pour que vous ayez la bonté de luy donner audience. Je suis avec beaucoup de respect, Monsieur, Vôtre très humble et obeissant serviteur   GRAND

Addressed: A Monsieur / Monsieur le Docteur / Francklin / a Passy

Endorsed: Billets

From R. Parsons

ALS: American Philosophical Society

Mr: Pernet's Maitre de Pension Rue St: Jaques 17th:

Sir   Augst: 1778

Th'o I was not so fortunate to receive any answer to my last letter, I venture once more to address you upon the same melancholy subject. Pray Sir, forgive my presumption, forgive the reiterated trouble my distress forces me to give you. I am almost distracted, and I know not which way to turn for relief. I am under the humiliating necessity of deviating from Truth to the People of the house where I am, in order to screen myself from the effects of their resentment shoud they know how I am really circumstanced. I was obliged Sunday sen'night to say that I had no letters, th'o it was the day I received that, I took the liberty of sending to you;[8] and yesterday, I was obliged to pretend I had one, from Mr: Parsons mentioning his being ill, as an excuse for his not sending some money for them. Indeed Sir, I detest a falshood and as I shall answer to

6. He resided in Amsterdam but made frequent visits to his brother Ferdinand in Paris.

7. Nicolas Boggiano was a Parisian banker: *Almanach royal* for 1778, p. 511.

8. The Sunday was the 9th, when she received her husband's letter to BF from London of the 4th. Her own to BF, mentioned in the first sentence, was on the 12th.

that being who is pleased to afflict me thus severely, I do not exaggerate a single circumstance of my unhappy case, nor tell you a word that is not litterally true. If I knew of any honest means on earth, of Alleviating my Present distress, I woud not presume to importune you in this teizing manner, but Alas! Sir, what can I do, where shall I apply for succour? I cannot expect the Almighty shoud work a miracle in my favour; and freinds I have none, not one here that woud lend a saving hand to snatch me from impending ruin. Those who can form no Idea of that distress they never felt, woud perhaps laugh at my sufferings, others woud despise me for wanting that, which is too often bestowed on the unworthy. But you, Sir, are an Englishman, and a *good* Man, 'tis your Universal character, and what every one says, must be true. Do not therefore worthy Sir, let me be the only one who sues to you in vain; do not deprive me of all hope, for indeed I have no present hope, but a reliance on the goodness and benevolence of your mind. If you coud know the painful anxiety, the continual uneasiness, the complicated misery I have endured these eight days past, I am sure your generous heart woud be affected, and you woud be induced to lessen those sufferings which have almost drove me to dispair. I am not so ridiculous or unreasonable as to expect that you shoud entirely extricate me from my difficulties, but if you woud be so good as to enable me to do something for the Present, I shoud be restored to the right use of my reason and be able to try every endeavour for the settling this unhappy affair. At Present, I am incapable of either thinking or acting to any purpose, and the letters I attempt to write to Mr: Parsons, are more calculated to deprive him of his senses, than to point out any means of relieving our Misfortunes. Had I foreseen what has happened, I shoud have been far from advising him to leave this, we woud at least have suffered togather, but I did it for the best, th'o God help me, it has turned out for the worse. I am at this moment so ill that I am scarce able to hold a Pen, I have kept my bed all day, nor shoud I have quit it, but to write this; and I most solemnly declare, I am so very wretched, than [that] an assurance of Death within the next four and twenty hours woud make me infinitely happy, compared to what I am at this moment. I will only add, that I most humbly entreat you Sir, to commiserate my unhappy case, and to grant me some little assistance, just to put it in my Power to shew my creditor, that I can do something for him, that I may have a little tranquillity of mind, to turn my thoughts towards the best means of extricating myself from this dreadful dilemma. If you are pleased to do this, I shall ever look upon you as a saving Angel sent from Heaven to administer consolation to the Afflicted mind, and may that being who rewards every humane action grant you every happiness you can wish for, here and hereafter. On reading what I have wrote, I am almost ashamed to send it, but I am not able to attempt a better, and hope the severe affliction I am involved in will plead my excuse for any impropriety this may contain. I have the honor to be, with the greatest respect Sir Your Most Obedient Humble Servant   R: PARSONS

Notation: Mrs. Parsons

The American Commissioners to Sartine: Two Letters

(I) AL (draft):[9] American Philosophical Society; (II) AL (draft): Massachusetts Historical Society; two copies: National Archives

I.

Sir,   Passy, Aug. 18. 1778
    The Administration in England have agreed to an Exchange of Prisoners with us, and propose that it shall be made at Calais.[1] They will accordingly[2] furnish us with a Pasport for a Vessel to bring the Prisoners from Brest to Calais,[3] if we procure a similar one for their Vessel which is to bring the Prisoners from England.[4] As our People may languish in their Confinement, and when recover'd, may be of Use to Capt.

---

9. In BF's hand, with his own deletions as indicated.
1. Deleted: "if that Place is approved by Government here."
2. Deleted: "If there is no Objection to this, we pray your Excellency."
3. Deleted: "on our procuring them a."
4. See above, Hartley to BF, July 14. BF here deleted: "If this Proposition is approved by Government here, we pray your Excellency to give us such a Passport."

Jones, or in some other Enterprise, we wish the Exchange may be made as soon as possible, and therefore request your Excellency would take the Affair into Consideration, and afford us your Advice and Determination upon it. We are, with the greatest Esteem and Respect, Your Excellency's most obedient and most humble Servants

His Excy M. de Sartine

Notation by Arthur Lee: The Minister has already agreed to give a Passport for the english vessel whenever we inform him it is necessary for Brest and therefore I presume he will have no objection to give it for Calais.

Notation by Franklin: Rough To M. Sartine Passport[5]

II.

⟨Passy, August 18, 1778: In answer to your letter of the 16th we believe the alterations to the projected regulations will remove the difficulties we apprehended. We thank you for your readiness to discuss the matter further should inconveniencies arise in the execution of these regulations, which we hope will not occur.[6]⟩

Dumas to the American Commissioners[7]

ALS: American Philosophical Society

⟨The Hague, August 18, 1778, in French: Nothing worthy of writing has occurred since I last wrote. I visit the French ambassador daily and, through him, received the *Gazette de Yorktown*[8] that Mr. Franklin had entrusted the Chevalier

5. This, one of the few letters of the period drafted by BF, was apparently not sent, perhaps because of Lee's objections. Instead the commissioners requested the passport from Vergennes in their letter of Aug. 28.
6. Published in Taylor, *Adams Papers*, VI, 376. The new French prize regulations went into effect on Sept. 27: *ibid.*, p. 334.
7. Published in Taylor, *Adams Papers*, VI, 377–8.
8. The *Pennsylvania Gazette*, published in York during this period: Clarence S. Brigham, *History and Bibliography of American Newspapers 1690–1820* (2 vols., Worcester, Mass., 1947), II, 933–4.

Marianne Camasse, comtesse de Forbach and duchesse
douairière de Deux-Ponts, and her sons Christian and
Wilhelm von Zweibrücken (Deux-Ponts)

[Georges Grand] to forward to me. Today's *Gazette de Leide* is filled with its contents. I'm enclosing a copy of a letter I sent yesterday to Mr. van Berckel. My friends' vessel has left.⁹⟩

John Ross to the American Commissioners[1]

ALS: Harvard University Library; three copies, National Archives

⟨Nantes, August 18, 1778: I wrote on July 16th and 23rd[2] respecting public business and have received no reply. Mr. Delavile has applied to me once more with bills of Mr. Ceronio on the public account.[3] I need an answer for him. Likewise I require the funds owed Willing, Morris & Co. from the public account to terminate their private accounts. French authorities here have sold Mr. Thomas Morris' private effects. As representative of Mr. Robert Morris I herewith notify Mr. William Lee, commercial agent, through the commissioners in whose name he claims to exercise his unprecedented and extravagant authority, irrespective of the reputation and credit of Willing, Morris & Co.⟩

From the Duchesse de Deux-Ponts[4]

ALS: American Philosophical Society

Forbach *le 18 aoust 1778*

Avant toute chose mon cher et respectable amis permettez moi de vous demander de vos nouvelles? J'en recevois indirecte-

9. Dumas' associates Hendrik Fynje and Jacob de la Lande; for their plan to send a ship to America see above, July 17. Dumas also enclosed a copy of a letter to van Berckel, described in Taylor, *Adams Papers*, VI, 378 n.

1. Published in Taylor, *Adams Papers*, VI, 379–80.

2. Not found.

3. Delaville, apparently a merchant and ship owner in Nantes: JW to WTF, June 18, 1783, APS. The American agent Stephen Ceronio at Cap Français, identified in XXII, 664 n, had been amassing debts: see XXVI, 218–20.

4. For BF's great friend, also known as the comtesse de Forbach, see XXV, 313 n; Lopez, *Mon Cher Papa*, 189–94.

273

ment par M. de Keralio[5] mais sa Maladie m'en a privée depuis pres de deux mois. Je ne veut pas que vous m'ecriviez vous meme je scait que vous ete trop occuppés, mais vous avez un petit fils, qui me paroit aussi obligeant qu'aimable, qui peut vous servir de secretaire. Je me recomande a lui, en lui faisant Mille amities pour scavoir coment se porte son respectable grand pere dont la Conservation et le bonheur, M'interesse au dela de toute expression.

Apres Cela Mon cher Monsieur franclin permettes moi de vous demander des Nouvelles de mon jeune neveux M. de fontevieux?[6] Vous aves bien eut la bonte de me faire dire que *La Duchesse de grammont* etoit heureusement arrivée a boston, mais scavoir si ce pauvre jeune homme n'est pas mort en chemin? Scavoir ce qu'il est devenus depuis son arrivee? Et si Là republique et le général Wassington l'ont admis a L'honneur de Les servir? D'aillieurs je suis inquiette de scavoir coment il subsistera, et je ne scait coment m'i prendre pour lui faire toucher la pension de 1800 *l.t.* que je lui fait? Je desirerois mon cher Monsieur que vous me procureries quelq'un qui Lui paya Cette pension par cartier, et j'en ferois remettre La totalite a vos banquier a paris, mais en attendant je meur de peur que le pauvre jeune homme ne manque de tout. Je voudrois aussi lui ecrire, mais je ne scais coment Lui fair passér ma Lettre. Je suis desoller de vous importunér Mon cher monsieur franclin par la multitude de mes questions, mais a qui pourois-je avoir recour si ce n'est a vous? Qui d'aillieur etes si bien fait par votre humanite, exelant homme pour inspirér la plus grande confiance; La Mienne en vous est sans borne, Mon respectable amis, parce qu'elle derive de la plus tendre et de la plus juste veneration, dont vous m'avez penetree. Recevez en le fidel homage mon cher monsieur franclin et Souvenez-vous quelques

5. Chevalier Agathon Guynement de Kéralio, identified in xxv, 413 n, had been her sons' tutor and was still her confidant.
6. Jean-Baptiste Georges de Fontevieux was doing well: see xxv, 314 n.

fois, de la personne du Monde qui vous aime Le plus, et qui fait le plus grand cas de votre amitie.⁷

M: DOUAIRIERE DU DUC DE DEUXPONTS
CTESSE DE FORBACH

Endorsed: Comtesse de Forbach

Notation: 18. Aout 1778

From Antoine Faillieux le Jeune⁸

ALS: American Philosophical Society

⟨Paris, August 18, 1778, in French: I delivered a letter to you from one of your correspondents in Amsterdam and have left my address that the answer may be returned to my care.⟩

The American Commissioners to John Bondfield

AL (draft):⁹ Massachusetts Historical Society; two copies: National Archives

Sir   Passi Augst 19 1778
   We have considered your plan¹ and think it will be proper to send it to Congress for their Approbation.
   We desire you will purchase and ship on public Account in the best and cheapest Manner 28 Iron Cannon of 24 pound Ball and 28 of 18 lb.² You will be so good as to send one set of Bills of Loading to us and another to the Marine Committee of Congress. We are Sir &c.   BF. AL. JA
Mr Bondfield

---

7. On Sept. 1 she told BF she was expecting his visit the following day. APS.
8. He signs himself, "Negt. rüe des petis champs St Martin."
9. In Arthur Lee's hand.
1. See Bondfield to BF, Aug. 16.
2. In response to a request from the marine committee: XXVI, 609.

The American Commissioners to Schweighauser

Draft: Massachusetts Historical Society; copies (two): National Archives

Sir   Passi August 19 1778

We desire you will furnish Lieut. David Walsh with twelve Guineas taking triplicate Receipts from him payable to the president of Congress or his order.[3] We are Sir Your most Obedient   BF AL JA

Mr Schweighauser

Elisha Hinman[4] to the American Commissioners

ALS: American Philosophical Society

Gentlemen,   Brest August 19 1778

I have the pleasure of acquainting you, that I arrived here the 17th and am happy in finding the Providence Frigate Captn. Whipple, ready to part for America I have embarked on board, and flatter myself with a Speedy and safe passage.[5] After Compliments of Respect I have the honour to be Gentlemen Your most Obedient very humble Servant

E. HINMAN

Addressed: Honble American Commissrs / Messrs Franklin, Lee & Adams / Paris

Notation: E. Hinman. Aug. 19. 78.

3. On Oct. 8 Franklin accepted a draft of Welsh's for 176 *l.t.*, dated July 22: Taylor, *Adams Papers*, VI, 361.

4. Hinman, captain of the *Alfred*, had been captured in March and confined to Forton prison on July 18. Five days later he bribed the guards and walked out. Kaminkow, *Mariners*, p. 90; William J. Morgan, *Captains to the Northward* . . . (Barre, Mass., 1959), p. 124. He had made his way to Dunkirk by Aug. 11, when he received 720 *l.t.*: second account of payments to prisoners described in xxv, 4.

5. Whipple had discussed with Hinman the possibility of attending a court martial for Thomas Simpson, which he refused; see Whipple to the commissioners, below, of the same date. After the war Whipple sought reimbursement for the "extra Stores laid in for Eleven Gentleman Passengers Recommended by Doctr. Franklin and Mr. Schweighauser," including

Abraham Whipple to the American Commissioners[6]

ALS: American Philosophical Society; copy: National Archives

⟨On board the *Providence*, Brest, August 19, 1778: I wrote you from Paimboeuf on July 31; since then the *Boston* joined me and on Aug. 8 we proceeded in company to Brest, delayed by unfavorable winds until the 14th. I found here that Lt. Simpson had obeyed my orders of July 24th in quickly preparing for sea. But I was surprised to find that none of the *Ranger's* prizes had yet been sold, nor had the crew received a single sou for all the time they had been in France; I allowed them a day or two to try and settle the matter. This might have been sufficient had not Capt. Jones interfered in an extraordinary manner, blocking the sale and producing obstacles "as frivolous in their natures as hurtful in their effects."[7] When a man is blinded by self-interest and acts in opposition to the interests of his country, it is my duty to represent his conduct with candor and leave the determination of its pernicious tendency to my superiors.

I enclose a copy of a letter Capt. Jones sent me yesterday, along with my answer.[8] Tomorrow I shall sail, wind and

---

Hinman; BF denied authorizing the expense. Whipple to BF, Oct. 25, 1786, APS; BF to Whipple, Nov. 16, 1786, Library of Congress.

6. Published in Taylor, *Adams Papers*, VI, 381–3.

7. Jones told another story. Berubé de Costentin had informed him on the evening of Aug. 16 that the *Drake* and *Lord Chatham*, with their merchandise, would be sold the following afternoon. Since the *Patience* was still being used to confine prisoners, she was exempt. National Archives. Jones attended the sale, he wrote Bancroft on the 21st, despite his strong objections because it had not been sufficiently advertised; the *Lord Chatham* and her cargo were sold separately, he heard, for 50,000 *l.t.* The *Drake's* stores had previously been plundered—he had even seen officers' uniforms publicly sold on shore and worn by sailors—and her sale was postponed. His personal items had been thrown ashore from a boat and left broken in the dirt. U.S. Naval Academy Museum.

8. Jones asked Whipple to summon a court martial for Thomas Simpson. Whipple's refusal, dated Aug. 19, was unequivocal: Jones could not muster the three necessary captains since Hinman, who was awaiting his own court martial in America, declined to sit; furthermore, Simpson had

weather permitting, with or without the *Ranger*, although I shall try to settle her unhappy affairs as best I can.⟩

From Benjamin Chew[9] ALS: American Philosophical Society

Honored Sir   Bourdeaux 19th. August 1778

I hope you will Excuse the liberty I take in Writeing to you in the fameliar Stile I am about Respecting my brother Sufferers in forton Prison who are Really Distresst for the Necessaries of Life Which Could they Get a Small Part of what is due them from the Commissioners would in a Great Measure Relieve them from their Present Distresst Situation If not from bondage, among Whom of them Gentlemen is One Mr. Alexander Dick, who was A Captn. in the 1st. Virginia Redgiment. He is a Gentleman of Considerable fortune in Virginia, not only his Pay Due him Sir but his other Circumstances in America Will Enable him to Repay you any Sum You may Please to Remitt him there, and I believe His noble Disposition will Urge him to Give you a true Sense of his Gratitude for your favours.[1] Your Assistance to him would be Very Condusive to his Health, as he is in a Very bad State of Health and a long imprisonment is Apt to Give Some Uneasiness to the Mind, as also nothing but Boild Beef for a Person

---

been released from his parole by Jones's own letter of July 16, and was therefore not subject to examination. Copies of both letters are in the APS.

9. A lieutenant on the *Sturdy Beggar* out of Maryland, he was committed to Forton on Jan. 23, 1778. He escaped July 23. *New-England Hist. and Geneal. Register*, xxx (1876), 348 n.

1. Dick had been captain of the marines for John Harris on the *Mosquito*, captured early in 1777. He was committed to Forton on Aug. 8 or 9: *ibid.*, xxxiii (1879), 36, xxx (1876), 345. See also Harris' letter above, July 14. The commissioners sent him 480 *l.t.* on Sept. 17: Taylor, *Adams Papers*, vi, 360. By May, 1779, Dick was in France, dining with JA among others, who spoke of his "good family and handsome fortune in Virginia:" Butterfield, *Adams Diary*, ii, 370–1, 379. In August he sailed with Jones on the *Bonhomme Richard* as liaison officer with the French marines: Morison, *Jones*, 204.

is [in] his State of Health, and not a farthing to Purchase the least Nourrishment that would be Suitable for a person in his State. I hope you will Excuse Me the liberty I take in behalf of that Gentleman as I have a true Sinse of his Distress from my being a Prisoner myself in health I Conceived myself Misrable. Wherefore I am Acquainted with the true Colours of his Distress in his Present State of health, your Assistance to him Sir would Induce him and family to be under the Strongest ties of Obligation to you, So you will Please to Excuse Me as an Individual and believe that I am a true Subject to Congress. Honored Sir Your Most Obedient Humble Servant

BENJAMIN CHEW

Addressed: To / Benjamin Franklin Esqr. / Plenipotenciary for the Thirteen / United States of America / at / Paris

Notation: Benjamin Chew Bordeaux 19 Augt. 78

From Philip Hancock   ALS: Historical Society of Pennsylvania

Most Honored Sir   Amsterdam Augast 19; 1778

As you have Been so good to Premitt Me to have the Honour to Pay you a Visit, Thought it my Duty to Aquint you that I Set out from hence in Two or Three Days. Would Have Come Amatley [immediately] on Recipt of your Letter To Mr. Le Grand only waits for the Arivell of the Englesh Post By which I Expect to Recive Some Letters. Mr. Le Grands Behavour to Me has not Onley Been that of a Gentleman But a friend.[2] I am with Due Respect your Excenelecy's Most Obedient Servent   PHILIP HANCOCK

Addressed: Honnourable Benjn. Franklin parris

Endorsed: P. Hancock

2. As indeed was the case: see Georges Grand's of the following day.

From Claude-Valentin Millin de la Brosse[3]

ALS: American Philosophical Society

⟨Paris, August 19, 1778, in French: As you certainly remember, I tried to join the American forces two years ago under Mr. Deane's sponsorship. I failed and was subsequently treated by Mr. Deane and yourself with a severity I am now disposed to forget. My wish at present is to cross to America, a country I love, not as an officer but as an eager citizen. I am not a nobody. I might convince Florida and Canada to revolt. I ask you for some land in Pennsylvania or Maryland, the kind of help the British government used to grant colonists, free passage for myself and a servant, and some letters of recommendation. All this is in keeping with the rank of lieutenant-colonel I would have received, had I been able to join your army.[4]⟩

From Jean-Pierre Bérenger

ALS: American Philosophical Society

Monsieur   Lausanne, ce 20 Aoust 1778
  Vous aviez parlé de moi et de mon Histoire de Genève avec bonté; vous offriez de m'aider dans mon projet de faire l'Histoire des 13 Etats-Unis,[5] et je crus devoir vous écrire, vous remercier, vous demander des conseils: j'ai fait tenir ma Lettre à un ami alors à Paris, qui devait vous la porter: vous ne m'avez point repondu et sans doute, ou vous n'avez point reçu ma Lettre, ou vous avez renoncé à m'être de quelques

3. For his previous misadventures and his problems with the commissioners see xxv, 297, 698–9.
  4. He did not reach his goal: on March 6, 1782, he was still writing from Paris. APS.
  5. For the *Histoire de Genève* and the projected history of the United States see Bérenger's earlier letter above, xxvi, 4–8. As mentioned there, BF acquired thirteen sets of the former; this suggests that he intended to send one to each of the American states, and we know that North Carolina and Rhode Island received theirs the following spring: Walter Clark, ed., *The State Records of North Carolina* (26 vols., Raleigh, N.C., 1886–1907), xiv, 35; William Greene to BF, Oct. 5, 1779, APS.

Secours dans l'execution de mon dessein, ou peut-être encore, la multitude des affaires ne vous a point permis de penser à celle qui m'interesse. Nul homme ne craint plus que moi d'être importun, et surtout de l'être pour vous, mais il s'agit d'un trop grand intérêt, d'un projet trop cher à mon coeur, pour ne pas me hazarder à vous distraire un moment. Je vous écris donc, Monsieur, et je vous envoye ma Lettre directement. Daignez me dire, ou me faire dire si vous daignez penser encore à moi, à mon plan, et si vous voulez y cooperer. Voici ce que je puis, ayez la bonté de me dire ce que vous pouvez y ajouter.

J'ai un ami à Londres, homme deja connu par divers ouvrages estimés qui s'occupe à me faire une collection de tous les ouvrages qui ont paru en Angleterre et relatifs à mon plan: je n'en ai excepté que ceux qui sont absolument mauvais. J'en ai un à Goettingue[6] qui me fait une Collection semblable de tous ceux qui ont été publiés en Allemagne: j'aurai tous les Livres français qui ont trait à ce sujet, et deja j'en ai plusieurs. J'ai aussi l'espece de Journal qui a pour titre *Affaires de l'Angleterre et de l'Amerique.* S'il était quelques Manuscrits qui pussent me servir et que vous pussiez me procurer, c'est en cela que vous pourriez principalement m'obliger. Et lorsque j'aurai assez de materiaux pour commencer, je vous enverrai mes cahiers l'un après l'autre. Vous jugerez de ce qui y manque, et me direz ce que vous en desaprouvez. Voila, Monsieur ce que je desire: votre reponse sera pour moi l'oracle qui doit decider de l'emploi de ma vie. Oui, je la croirai remplie quand mon but le sera dans l'étendue que je lui donne.

J'aurais bien voulu aussi que vous m'eussiez dit si les cartes de l'Amerique qu'on vend à Paris comme étant un relevé des arpenteurs des differentes Provinces, sont bonnes, ou s'il en existe ailleurs de telles. Pour l'Historien qui ne connait pas un Pays par lui même, d'excellentes cartes sont absolument necessaires.

Notre Société vous avait envoyé les Histoires de Genève que vous demandiez: elle les avait adressé à Mr. Bastien Li-

6. August Ludwig Schlözer, mentioned in Bérenger's letter just cited, was a keen observer of the North American scene. See Horst Dippel, *Germany and the American Revolution 1770–1800* (Chapel Hill, 1977), pp. 56–7.

braire à Paris,[7] et n'en a point eu de reponse. Ne les auriez-vous point reçu?

J'y avais joint deux Lettres imprimées dont l'une m'a privé de ma Patrie, et l'autre est la seule justification, la seule vengeance que je me sois permise. J'étais flatté que vous fussiez mon Juge. . . .[8] Mais bientot tout sera oublié, les Genevois m'ont temoigné souvent leurs regrets, et dans le Code des Loix auquel ils travaillent, celle qui m'éloigna de ma Patrie doit être aneantie.[9]

Pardon, Monsieur, si je vous parle avec plus de liberté que je ne le devrais peut-être. Je sais que j'écris à un homme celèbre et respectable par ses talens et par ses écrits, au Législateur, au Père des Americains, mais j'ai cru que vous parler en homme libre, c'était vous connaître et vous rendre hommage. D'autres peuvent se servir d'expressions plus respectueuses; nul n'aura dans son coeur un respect plus vrai, plus profond que celui avec lequel j'ai l'honneur d'être Monsieur, Votre très humble et très obéissant Serviteur

BERENGER,
de la Société Typographique
et Litteraire de Lausanne

A Mr. Le Docteur Franklin

Si vous voullez bien me repondre, vous pouvez le faire en Anglais que je puis lire.

Notation: Berenger *Historien* 20 Aout 1778

7. Actually, the Society, of which he gives the title at the end of this letter, had sent the sets to another bookseller in Paris, Duplain ainé, on March 1. Noted in an enclosure to Bérenger's letter of that date.
8. Suspension points in the original.
9. This was not done, as mentioned in the headnote on his previous letter, until 1781.

From Georges Grand

ALS: American Philosophical Society

Monsieur   Amsterdam le 20 Aoust 1778
  J'ay receu la Lettre que vous m'avés fait l'honneur de m'é-
crire le 7 de ce mois, et suivant Vos ordres,

j'ay payé à la Veuve Macgrath   f.76.3
pour la dépense de M. Welsh;[1] suivant le
Compte que Je vous ai remis Je luy avais fourni
en deux fois 4 Ducats............................   21
et J'avais payé a M. Hancock dont Vous avés le
Receu..   200
                                         Cf297.3s.

Pour le Compte de Messieurs Les Commissionnaires du
Congrés dont ma maison se rembourse sur eux, chez mon
frere, par sa Traitte de £646.17.3 qui au change de 52¾ et 4½
pour cent d'agio ballance cet objet.[2]
  J'ay de plus payé à M. Hancock suivant Son Receu, pour
Votre compte particulier Cf200 tant pour sa dépense, et habil-
lement que pour son Voyage, dont ma Maison se rembourse
de même en £435.7. Aussi sur Vous chez mon frere, auquel
Vous voudrés bien donner Vos ordres pour acquiter ces deux
Traittes.
  Le bon Hancock avait été laissé tout nud par Welsh, à qui il
avait donné jusques à sa derniere chemise, Je n'ai Jamais
connu un meilleur et plus honnête homme. Je luy ai donné
de bonnes recommendations pour Anvers, et Bruxelles, pour
l'aider dans sa route, il ne sçait pas un mot de français.
  Il n'y à point de difficulté pour acheter icy les 28 canons de
24 lb. et les 28 de 18 lb. dont Vous avés besoin,[3] non plus que
pour les expédier pourvu que ce soit par petites parties, que

---

  1. Grand enclosed a note by David Welsh, identifying himself as he had
to H. Godet; see Godet's letter of Sept. 2. Macgrath was Welsh's landlady.
  2. Agio means the difference between the nominal and real value of cur-
rencies or between one country's currency and the other's. F indicates a
florin, Cf a Carolus florin.
  3. The commissioners had entrusted Bondfield with an identical order
the day before. The supplying of cannon has been discussed in xxiv, 75 and
xxv, 132 n.

les Vaisseaux prennent à fond de Calle dans leur Lest; on ne demande Jamais de Permission pour ces Sortes d'importations, sur lesquelles l'Etat ferme les yeux en facilitant le Commerce, et il n'est pas besoin de déclarer leur destination reelle, à nos Amirautés, pour obtenir des Passeports; le plus grand risque, est de la part des Anglais, qui sont en Droit de prendre tout ce qui est armes, munitions et articles de contrebande désignés dans le Traitté d'Utrecht.

Il n'en est pas de meme de Toute autre espece de Marchandise que vous pourriés nous demander, et que nous Vous envoyerions librement dans aucun Port de France, ou de nos Colonies à portée de l'Amérique. Nous trouverions même à la faire assurer solidement. Si vous prenés la peine de me désigner le genre, et la quantité de ces marchandises, Je vous donnerai Tous les renseignements nécessaires sur leur prix, et les moyens de les expédier; nous chercherons à les acheter avec le Papier, que Vous m'annoncés, au lieu d'argent comptant, et ce serait un moyen de le mêtre en Circulation sur notre Plaçe.[4]

Voicy une Lettre que Votre Amy, le bon Hutton, m'a envoyé hier de Zeist, en me la recommandant beaucoup; cet Ange de Paix n'aura pas reçeu celle que Je luy addressé de Votre part à Londres, d'ou il etait parti pour venir dans ce Paÿs. J'espère que Vous me donnerés enfin des nouvelles de *nos Amys* et qu'elles seront aussi bonnes que je le souhaite; vous en avés receu de Dumas, qui Vous auront prouvé, que Vous avés aussi des Amys icy, ou je serais bien charmé de vous voir, pour en augmenter le nombre; car en imposant des Loix au Tonnere vous y ajoutés le Talent de subjuguer les coeurs. J'ay l'honneur d'etre avec le plus respectueux attachement Monsieur Votre tres humble et tres obeissant serviteur   GRAND

Honorable Doctor franklin

Endorsed: Sir Geo Grand

Notation: amsterdam 20 aout 1778

4. An allusion to the books of promissory notes which the commissioners finally sent at the end of the month. See the commissioners to Horneca, Fizeaux & Cie., Aug. 31.

From Jean-Baptiste Mailhe[5]

ALS: American Philosophical Society

Monseigneur   A Castel-nau de magnoal ce 21. août 1778.

L'horreur qe j'ai conçue dès long-temps pour la Tyrannie des Anglois, et la justice de la cause américaine, m'ont inspiré cette piece de vers.[6] Que n'ont-ils la vertu d'entraîner quiconque n'est pas partisan du Congrès? Ce nombre est pourtant bien petit. On ne parle plus que de Vashington et de Franclin. L'Amérique, pour secouer le joug anglican, avait besoin d'un général tel que le premier, et d'un ministre tel que vous, Monseigneur. Après avoir éclairé le monde par vos lumieres et par les recherches et les decouvertes que vous avez fait dans la physique, il ne manquait plus à votre gloire, que d'être choisi par toute une nation, pour plaider sa cause devant les puissances de L'Europe, et de remplir son attente avec ce patriotisme et cette sagesse qui vous caractérisent. Puisse la revolution qui se prepare, être bientôt achevée! Puissiez-vous bientôt, Monseigneur, revenir dans vôtre patrie, pour y recueillir le fruit de vos travaux! Et s'il m'est permis de faire des voeux pour moi-même puissiez-vous jetter un regard favorable sur mon ouvrage. J'ai l'honneur d'être avec un très-profond respect de vôtre altesse Monseigneur Le très-humble, le très-obéissant serviteur   MAILHE
avocat au parlement de Toulouse

5. The young lawyer (1754–1839) made a name for himself during the French Revolution as one of the most rabid anti-royalists, a stand for which he spent fifteen years in exile during the Restoration. Larousse.
6. Missing.

The American Commissioners to James Moylan

AL (draft): Massachusetts Historical Society; two copies: National Archives

Sir   Passi August 22. 1778

We had the favour of yours of the seventeenth of August, and are obliged to you for this and several other Instances of your Attention to Us, in furnishing Us with early Intelligence.

It is somewhat remarkable that a Vessel from James River should have brought no Letters. But We are happy to hear that affairs were in so prosperous a Train.

We are very anxious for further Intelligence from America, as We have received none as yet of the Compte D'Estaing.

We have Reports that the French Fleet is gone out, but none as yet of the English.[7] We are, Sir with respect, your most obedient Servants.

Mr James Moylan at L'orient

The American Commissioners to Thomas Read or Any Other Captain of Any Vessel Bound to America

AL (draft): Massachusetts Historical Society; copies: National Archives (two), University of Virginia Library

Sir   Passi August 22. 1778

Mr. Alexander Fowler with his Wife being bound to America, where he has heretofore resided as an officer in the British Army;[8] and it having been represented to Us, that his Friendship to America occasioned his quiting that Service and has occasioned him some hardships, and Inconveniences, We recommend him to you for a Passage to America, he paying your

---

7. The French fleet had sailed and the British was about to: see (I) in the collection of intelligence reports under the date of Aug. 3, above.

8. Fowler had petitioned the commissioners on Aug. 6. After reaching America, he offered his services to Congress on Jan. 18, 1779, and was appointed auditor for the Western district of the Continental Army. Smith, *Letters*, XI, 504 n; *JCC*, XIII, 177, 217. He eventually settled in Pittsburgh where he became a prominent citizen.

Demands for the same, and that he and his Wife may be treated with Respect. We are your humble Servants.[9]

To Captain Read at Nantes or any other Captain of any Vessell bound to America.

The American Commissioners to Schweighauser[1]

AL (draft):[2] Massachusetts Historical Society; two copies: National Archives

⟨Passy, August 22, 1778: We received yours of the 18th. Tell Mr. Bersolle[3] he must send us his accounts and vouchers before we will pay him; we hope for his sake as well as ours that he will not proceed to the indecent violence you apprehend. Dispose of the saltpetre as speedily and inexpensively as possible. Mr. Hall must also provide a receipt for the beef delivered to the *Ranger* before he can be paid. As for captains and other Americans not actually in the service of the thirteen states, do not advance them any public money when they are at Nantes, and capable of providing for themselves.⟩

9. The commissioners attached to this recommendation a certificate, written by Fowler and dated Aug. 23, testifying to his British birth and current American allegiance. University of Va. Library.

1. Published in Taylor, *Adams Papers*, VI, 385–6.

2. In Arthur Lee's hand.

3. Emmanuel-Yves Bersolle, a Brest merchant whose refusal to furnish supplies to the *Ranger* had elicited complaints both from John Paul Jones and from Lt. Elijah Hall, acting commander of the ship in Jones's absence: XXVI, 535, 579. In June, as part of the general policy of greater financial rigor introduced by JA, the commissioners had refused to pay Bersolle's drafts until he sent proper accounts: *ibid.*, 620–1. Lacking Schweighauser's letter of the 18th we do not know the exact nature of Bersolle's threats.

George Finlay, Thomas Anquetil, Wm. Allan and Brown Bencor to the American Commissioners[4]

ALS: American Philosophical Society

⟨Ancenie, August 22, 1778: We are prisoners taken by Capt. Tucker of the *Boston*. From Nantes we were sent to this town. We beg you to grant us liberty or supplies, since we have done nothing different from other captains who have been freed. Commanders of American vessels have gained their liberty.⟩

From Madame Herbaut de Marcenay

ALS: American Philosophical Society

Epinay ce 22 aoust [1778]
Je me flatte monsieur, que vous serez persuadé du regret que j'eprouve d'avoir passé tant de tems sans avoir l'honneur de vous voir. Beaucoup de voyages à la campagne sont causes de cette privation. Mais je n'ai point oublié que vous avez eu la bonté de m'engager a vous aller demander à diner à passy, et que vous m'avez chargée de vous mener ma soeur. Cette partie monsieur m'est trop agreable pour n'être pas tres empressée de l'executer. Si donc vous voulez bien de nous, j'aurai l'honneur d'aller diner avec vous dimanche 30. aoust, et je vous menerai mr. et md. de breget mr. de la marre et mr. de carmontelle, à qui nous savons bon gré chaque jour, de nous avoir fait un portrait charmant, que nous regardons sans cesse avec un nouveau plaisir.[5] Si cependant monsieur, le jour que je

---

4. Published as "British Prisoners of War to the Commissioners" in Taylor, *Adams Papers*, VI, 386.
5. We cannot identify De la Marre. The Brégets, as mentioned before, were her sister and brother-in-law. Louis Carrogis, known as Carmontelle, served the duc d'Orléans as dramatist, designer, and artist. His portrait of BF that delighted the Marcenays was either an earlier version or the original drawing, supposedly executed several years later, that is described in Charles C. Sellers, *Benjamin Franklin in Portraiture* (New Haven and London, 1962), pp. 214–15, and is reproduced on the facing page.

Benjamin Franklin: engraving by François-Denis Née after
Carmontelle

vous propose vous etoit importun, je vous prie de me le mander et de m'en indiquer un autre. Malgré le desir que j'ai de passer des momens avec vous, je ne veux pas être indiscrete. Mr. le roy à qui je m'adresse pour vous faire tenir cette lettre, voudra bien se charger de votre reponse.[6] Je l'attendrai avec l'impatience du plaisir que j'aurai toujours à vous renouveller les assurances des sentimens que vous m'avez inspires et avec lesquels j'ai l'honneur d'etre monsieur votre tres humble et tres obeissante servante   MARCENAY

Addressed: A Monsieur / Monsieur Franklin / a passy

Notation: Me Marcenay 22 Augt

From Vergennes

L (draft):[7] Archives du Ministère des affaires étrangères; two copies: Library of Congress

à Versailles le 22 aoust *1778*

J'ai communiqué à M. de Sartine, Mr. le memoire par lequel vous avez demandé la liberté d'un forçat de Brest nommé Marc François Gautier;[8] je joins ici la réponse de ce Ministre; vous

---

6. She went on using Le Roy as go-between, and on occasion he acted as one without consulting her. In an undated note he invited BF to attend with him a musical evening at Epinay; the ladies would have asked BF if they had not feared to seem importunate, and would be happily surprised to see him. On Oct. 5, her last letter, Mme. de Marcenay wrote BF that she had been trying to arrange a dinner, either with them at Epinay or with him at Passy, but that Le Roy had not answered her letters. She did not then know of his loss (his son Basile had died in September), and was now applying directly to BF. Would he come to Epinay with his "son," and with Le Roy if his grief permitted? They could then settle on a return engagement at Passy. APS.

7. In Rayneval's hand.

8. BF's memorandum is missing, but the background is explained in Gauthier's letter above, July 5. One of the copies includes Sartine's letter, which explains that the King, in consideration of Gauthier's good conduct in his fourteen years of confinement, has ordered him released to be a gunner in the American service.

y verrez que S.M. a bien voulu accorder la grace que vous avez sollicitée.⁹

M. franklin

Notation: [Liberté?] accordée à un [forçat] nommé Gautier [de] passer au Service [des] Etats-unis

John Bondfield to the American Commissioners

ALS: American Philosophical Society

Sirs,   Bordeaux 23 Aug 1778
    Since the Letter I had the Honor to write you the 17th Inst. the Liberty Captain Reed arriv'd at this Port from Edenton which place he left the 7 July. He brings no confirmation of the French Fleets arrival such report prevaild but gives it only as french report. As per my last the Cutter General Arnold is all ready and attends the arrival of your instructions. Captain Ayres will not be able to proceed. Captain Hatch by Captain Ayres's desire has requested me to mention him to you should you be unprovided. Permit me to add that he appears a Seaman and desireous to be employ'd in the American Navy, which he flatters himself should he meet your approbation to the command would be a step at his Arrival on the other Side. I have the Honor to be with due respect Sirs Your most Obedient Humble Servant   JOHN BONDFIELD
Paris The Honble. Benj Franklin Arthur Lee John Adams Esqr

Addressed: The Honble Benj Franklin / Arthur Lee John Adams Esqr. / Commissioners from Congress / at / Paris

Notation: Mr Bondfield Bordeaux 23 Augt 1778

9. This act of clemency was later used as a precedent by other convicts, as will be described in Vol. XXVIII.

From ——— Meschinet de Richemond fils[1]

ALS: American Philosophical Society

Sir,   Rochell, August 23d. 1778
In expectation of Your honored answer to my last, I have the honour to inform You that the Privateer of Boston named General Mifling, MacKnill Master has taken and Sent into this harbour the Ship the hunter of two hundred tuns loaded with 19 hogsheads Sugar and 5 tuns of Steels, going from Yarmouth to Archangel with a Crew of 11 Men.[2] The Leftenant told us that it is their 11 Prize.

As the Post Sets off I have but the Time to subscribe myself respectfully Sir, Your most humble and most obedient Servant
                              MESCHINET DE RICHEMOND FILS

Addressed: A Monsieur Monsieur Le Docteur / Franklin / A Passy près / Paris

Endorsed: Meschinet de Richmond fils Rochelle Augt 23. 78

Musco Livingston to the American Commissioners[3]

ALS: American Philosophical Society

⟨Nantes, August 24, 1778: My illness since Capt. Tucker's departure prevented my writing you concerning three prizes he sold to M. Puchelberg of Lorient, for Mr. Schweighauser's account. Puchelberg advised Tucker of the high duty on the prize cargo of fish. Consequently Tucker permitted sale of the fish and the three vessels for 30,000 livres, a sum far short of the true value had provisions of the treaty with France been

---

1. An outfitter in La Rochelle: John G. Clark, *La Rochelle and the Atlantic Economy during the Eighteenth Century* (Baltimore and London, 1981), p. 52. His only previous letter extant is in XXIII, 186; to the best of our knowledge, this is his last.
2. The *General Mifflin*, Capt. Daniel McNeill, arrived at Lorient on Aug. 25 after a four-month cruise in which she captured 13 prizes. See Bondfield's and Moylan's letters below, Aug. 26, and for McNeill's distinguished career, the *DAB*.
3. Published in Taylor, *Adams Papers*, VI, 387.

observed. Acting for Tucker, I am inquiring for information about the possibility of redress.⟩

Puchelberg & Cie. to the American Commissioners[4]

ALS: American Philosophical Society

⟨Lorient, August 24, 1778: We are herewith forwarding a letter given us yesterday by Mr. Lee, living at Schweighauser's.[5] Please acknowledge its receipt. As associates of Schweighauser in this town, we offer our services and would appreciate your patronage.⟩

James Smith to the American Commissioners[6]

ALS: American Philosophical Society

⟨Paris, August 24, 1778: When I reached Calais on May 4 the customs officers detained part of my luggage, consisting of household linen and plate, as contraband. Soon after arriving in Paris I mentioned the matter to Mr. [Arthur] Lee, who told me that I had no remedy; his brother, though a public minister, had had to pay fifteen guineas. Public officials may have to live in a splendor unsuited to new republics groaning under financial burdens; private individuals fleeing from the tyranny of old governments are in a different position, however.

I spoke to M. Grand, who promised to use his good offices. When I did not hear from him I told Dr. Franklin on July 4. He said he would make the necessary application, but some time later he had forgotten the whole business and asked for a memorandum. Aware that memory fades in the evening of life, I sent the memorandum by young Mr. Franklin so that he

4. Published in Taylor, *Adams Papers*, VI, 388.
5. Thomas Lee, identified in Berubé de Costentin's letter of this date, below.
6. Published in Taylor, *Adams Papers*, VI, 389–92. For Smith, the physician and former professor at King's College, see above, XXVI, 387 n.

might compensate for the imbecility of old age. He answered with expressions unfit for any one who serves constituents.[7])

From Berubé de Costentin

ALS: American Philosophical Society

Monsieur   a Brest le 24 aoust 1778

Je me trouve depuis un peu de tems chargé par Mr. J. D. Schweighauser de Nantes de la direction a Brest des Vaisseaux et des Prises appartenant aux Etats unis de L'amerique, et c'est ce qui me procure l'honneur de vous ecrire affin de recevoir vos plus prompts ordres pour me mettre a Lieu de me débarasser s'il vous plait de 140. a 150 prisonniers qui restent en cette rade depuis plusieurs mois a bord de la prise de la fregate le Ranger, nommée *La Patience*.

Pendant que cette fregate a resté icy, son Equipage prenoit soin de leur faire la chaudiere,[8] de les contenir et netoyer, mais depuis 5 a 6. Jours qu'elle a party en compagnie de La providence et du Boston[9] ces prisonniers abandonnés a Eux mêmes et a une foible garde de soldats qui n'y sont même pas regulie-

7. In his letter to WTF, Aug. 14, Smith assumed that Americans had a right to free passage for their goods through France, and that the commissioners had the duty to secure that right. He had spent all his time in his country's cause "while Boys are receiving Places of Profit and Emolument under the Congress." He appended a list of the missing articles: a parcel of table linen and another of silver-handled knives and forks, "etc." WTF's answer on the 16th pointed out that BF could not act without a written statement of the particulars, which he had never received; Smith's complaint to his grandson was therefore ill-founded, improper, and indecent: University of Pa. Library. Smith replied on the same day: he had called on BF upon arrival, but had been ignored until the 4th of July party, though he had a right to attention as an American and a gentleman. He had explained the particulars to BF when dining with him at Passy, had been promised action, and then had discovered that "he had *intirely forgot the Transaction*"; reminding WTF of it did not constitute impropriety or indecency. Copies of these letters, except as indicated, are in the APS.

8. To supervise the cooking.

9. The *Ranger*, along with the *Providence* and *Boston*, had left the harbor on Aug. 20: Taylor, *Adams Papers*, VI, 383 n.

rement etablis, ces prisonniers disje se sont revoltes il y a Deux Jours et eussent enlevé un autre Navire moüillé aupres d'eux dans la Rade s'il n'etoit promptement venu du secours d'une fregate du Roy qui se trouva heureusement a proximité. Cela arriva dans la Nuit, et il y a tout a craindre, pour la sureté même des Batiments du Roy et du payis a la Côte que ces gens n'entreprennent des hostilités de moment a autre et n'y reussissent. Depuis environ 15. Jours, Mr. Th. Lee fils[1] et moy nous sommes presentés plusieurs fois a M. Le Commandant et a M. L'Intendant[2] en les suppliant de se charger de ces prisonniers dans les prisons du Roy et que nous en payerions la depense. Ils nous ont toujours repondu qu'absolument ils ne le peuvent faire et j'en ay informé M. Schweighause auprès duquel Mr. Lée vient de se rendre en poste pour hâter de plus en plus un party a prendre sur des dangers aussi inquietants et autant de Consequence.

C'est a cette extremité que j'ay crû ne pouvoir manquer de vous supplier d'apporter le remede que vous Jugerés Bon et promptement s'il vous P. Si les prisons de Brest sont trop Bornées pour n'y pouvoir recevoir les prisonniers des Etats, Le Roy en a de plus Vastes a Dinan. Il y en a aussy a Josselin qui

1. Thomas Lee (1758–1805), eldest son of Richard Henry and nephew of Arthur and William Lee, was nineteen when, early in 1777, his English studies were interrupted and he was sent to France where he remained until 1780. Thomas went to Nantes to live with Schweighauser and become his clerk, learning business practice and French. Oliver Perry Chitwood, *Richard Henry Lee* (Morgantown, 1967), p. 228; James Ballagh, *The Letters of Richard Henry Lee* (2 vols., New York, 1911), I, 280, 287, 307; Idzerda, *Lafayette Papers*, I, 36.

On Aug. 20 Jones, hearing that the prisoners were unguarded, threatened Thomas Lee, who was assisting Costentin at Brest, that if they were not secured that very afternoon they would surely escape, and Thomas would be held personally responsible. Jones to Lee, Aug. 20, National Archives.

2. Pierre-Bernardin de Thierry, marquis de la Prévalaye (d. 1786) had entered naval service in 1729; in 1776 he was named director general of the arsenal at Brest, and in this capacity acted as *commandant de la Marine* in 1778–79 while d'Orvilliers was at sea. Didier Neuville, ed., *Etat sommaire des archives de la Marine antérieures à la Révolution* (Paris, 1898), pp. 133–4. The intendant was Arnauld de la Porte.

est au centre de la province et peu eloigné du port Loüis. Vos prisonniers coûtent icy plus de 24.s. par Jour châque de depense. C'est un double motif de les retirer, mais la sureté publique surtout l'emporte. Je suis avec Beaucoup de Respect Monsieur Vôtre tres humble et tres obeissant serviteur

BERUBÉ DE COSTENTIN

Endorsed: Berubé de Costutier about the Prisoners at Brest to be answered Brest 24 aout 1778

From John Channing[3]　　　ALS: American Philosophical Society

Honorable Sir　　　　　　London August. 24. 1778

The Bearer of this is one of our Particular friends, Capt. Tristram Barnard[4] An American, who has distinguishd himself by his Generossity towards the unhappy Prisoners who have fellen this way. I therefore Recomend him as one Worthy your honors Notice. I am with due Respect, Your honors Most humble Servant　　　　　　JOHN CHANNING

Addressed: To / The Honbl. Benm. Franklyn Esqr. / Paris / favd. per / Capt. Barnard

Notation: Jno. Channing London. Aug. 24. 78.

3. An escaped prisoner, not to be confused with the South Carolinian living in London and mentioned by Hezekiah Ford on July 21, above. This man identified himself as a lieutenant in the continental navy in his petition to BF below, under [Sept. 4]. He may have been the Channing appointed second lieut. for Whipple's *Providence* by the marine committee on July 8, 1776; but his captivity proves he could not have actually sailed on her. *Naval Docs.*, v, 856 n; Alphabetical List of Escaped Prisoners.

4. A whaling captain from Nantucket, anxious to leave England and rejoin the American cause, he did not cross the Channel until the first days of October. He then presented himself to the commissioners: below, Oct. 9 and 13.

From James Hutton   AL: American Philosophical Society

My dear old Friend   Hague Aug. 24. 1778
   I recd. to day from London your kind Letter of June 23.[5]
which inclosed the Paper you was so kind to send me. It did
not get to my Wifes hands till Aug. 17. The Vessel sail'd in the
very first days of July.
   If you can let me know the name of the Vessel in which that
monument is gone to America, I certainly will and with all my
heart do the best I can.[6] I love that gallant man's memory and
many a Tear was dropt over him in England, so that I hope if
that vessel be taken, that monument will be restored. I hope
that monument will come safe. I am much obliged to you for
your great kindness of Intention about our Labradore Ship.
Whatever Mr. Grand of Amsterdam sends to me under
Madam Fagel, (nèe Boreel's) Cover à la Haye will come *sure*
and *safe* to the hands of your thankful old friend. I am at the
Hague for a few days to see some dear friends who are going
to Nice for the Health of a Lovely Child. I wrote to you last
week under Mr. Grands Cover. I hear to day that Mr. Marshall
about whom I wrote to you in that Letter will probably bring
his Daughter with him to America.

Addressed: Dr. Franklin

Notation: Hutton 24 Augt 1778

   5. This letter (XXVI, 674) granted a passport to a Moravian ship carrying
supplies to their mission in Labrador.
   6. Hutton asked first Ferdinand Grand on Sept. 8, then Georges Grand
on Oct. 27, for the same information. APS. In the former letter, Hutton
hoped that his friends going to Bethlehem (for whom see his letter to BF,
Aug. 16) might look after Montgomery's monument. BF appears only to
have known that the vessel carrying it ultimately arrived in North Carolina:
BF to John Jay, Oct. 4, 1779, National Archives.

From John Paul Jones

ALS: American Philosophical Society; AL (draft): National Archives; copies: United States Naval Academy Museum, Library of Congress

Honored and Dear Sir   Brest August 24th. 1778.

Had I indulged my inclination since my return here I should have already troubled you with sundry letters. I must not however abuse the indulgent liberty which you gave me at parting. And I have therefore been the more troublesome to my good Friend Doctor Bancroft.[7]

I wish not to be thought too impatient, but you know my dear Sir, that this is the nice moment when I ought either to be in search of Marine Knowlidge with Count D'Orvilliers or in search of honor in attempting some private Enterprize. Before I was at liberty to go the good old Count pressed me much to Accompany him. But since Doctor Bancroft has informed me that it would be agreeable to the Minister that I should go I have been precluded from following the Fleet, as the present Commandant has no Orders for that purpose.

Thus circumstanced, without Employment and in appearance cast off, I have written the within letter to the Prince De Nassau, which I leave open for your perusal.[8] Should you find the whole, or any part of it improper I beg of you to withhold it.

After all my disappointments I am yet persuaded that the Court had from the beginning and still have intentions in my favor, since you know the connection is not of my seeking. I am with the highest sense of your Friendship and Goodness Honored and Dear Sir Your truely Obliged very Obedient very humble Servant   JNO P JONES

7. Three surviving letters to Bancroft of Aug. 14, 21, and 24, are summarized in Charles Henry Lincoln, comp., *A Calendar of John Paul Jones Manuscripts in the Library of Congress* (Washington, 1903), pp. 45, 47, 48–9.

8. Jones's friend Charles-Henri-Nicolas Othon, prince de Nassau-Siegen, has been identified above, XXVI, 558 n. The letter repeats Jones's litany of complaints and begs the prince to use his influence with the King to secure him a ship. It is printed in John Henry Sherburne, *The Life and Character of John Paul Jones* . . . (2nd ed.; New York, 1851), pp. 72–3.

AUGUST 24, 1778

NB. I have engaged part of the porter and will send some round to Havre de Grace for you & for Mr. Adams.[9]

His Excellency Doctor Franklin

Endorsed: Augt 24 78 de Brest. Capt Jones

From Henri-Charles, comte de Thiard[1]

ALS: American Philosophical Society

Boulogne sur mer le 24 aoust 1778.
J'ay l'honneur de vous adresser monsieur un anglois que j'ay trouvé a boulogne et qui desire passer a boston. Comme il ne scait pas un mot de francois et qu'il pourroit dans ce moment etre inquieté dans son passage en France je luy donne un passeport pour qu'il ne luy soit rien fait de facheux sur sa route. Il desire que je le recomende a vos soins paternels; je consens avec d'autant plus de plaisir que cela me fournit une occasion de vous assurer des sentiments d'estime et de veneration avec les quels j'ay l'honneur d'etre monsieur Votre tres humble et tres obeissant serviteur LE CTE DE THIARD

Endorsed: Comte de Thiaud

9. Largely invisible in our documents, the story of this prize porter which Jones freely offered to BF, JA, JW and Bancroft illustrates another aspect of his frustration and reflects the power struggles among the American factions in France. Before the *Lord Chatham*'s cargo was sold on Aug. 17, Thomas Lee had promised to reserve Jones 100 hhds. of its porter. After the sale, Jones was told he could have only half that amount. For the next three weeks, the captain made repeated applications for its delivery, to no avail. Finally on Sept. 6 Berubé de Costentin, acting for Schweighauser, told Jones his credit was worthless and the porter would not be delivered unless paid for in cash. The same day, an indignant Jones demanded that Schweighauser explain to JW his position regarding Jones's prize property and, in particular, the porter. The answer came on Sept. 13 *via* Thomas Lee: Berubé de Costentin had that day been ordered to deliver the porter whenever convenient. Jones to Schweighauser, Sept. 6, and to JW, Sept. 11, 1778, National Archives; Thomas Lee to Jones, Sept. 13, 1778, U.S. Naval Academy Museum.

1. The comte (1726–94) was a great favorite of the King, made *commandant en chef* of Provence in 1782 and later of Brittany. Larousse. We have found no trace of an earlier career in Boulogne.

298

From Griffith Williams[2]

ALS: American Philosophical Society

Sir London August. 24. 1778.

By favour of Captn. Channing[3] send you few lines Aquainting you that matters in this Country are likely to take a very diffrent turn to What was expected by the favourers of despotism to the West'ard of London.

All men agree (Confesedly) that the Conquest of America is now utterly inpracticable; the most Bloody invoakers of the destruction of that Country are now reduced to wish for peace at any rate, a very diffrent language to their Boasting threats few years ago.

I need not enlarge. Captn. Channing will fully inform you of particulars have the Honour to Remain Yours very Sincerely G.W.

Notation: G.W. London Aug 24 78.

Ralph Izard to the American Commissioners[4]

ALS: American Philosophical Society; copies: National Archives, South Carolina Historical Society; two transcripts: National Archives

⟨Paris, August 25, 1778: I lately received a letter from Florence recommending we attempt to involve the French court as security in any attempt to procure a loan in Genoa. Should I apply to the count de Vergennes on the subject or do you believe the application should first be made by you?

2. In a note on Williams' letter of Oct. 2, BF identified the writer as a surgeon who had been helpful to Americans escaping from English captivity. His first name is supplied from an undated list, in his hand, at the Pennsylvania Historical Society, entitled "Friends to American Liberty are friends to Mankind," and concluding with the note: "all the Crew of the Southern Whale Fishery have been very Generous to American prisoners in distress."

3. John Channing was not a captain but a lieutenant. See his letter to BF on or before Sept. 4. On subsequent occasions, Williams referred to him as "Mr."

4. Published in Taylor, *Adams Papers*, VI, 392–4.

Captain Woodford[5] who intends to command a vessel from Leghorn fears meeting cruisers from the coast of Africa. By Article 8 of the Treaty of Commerce the King of France engages to use his good offices with the Barbary States to protect our inhabitants, ships and effects from such attacks. Please inform me whether the French court has taken any steps in the matter.⟩

The American Commissioners to Ralph Izard[6]

AL (draft): Massachusetts Historical Society; copies: National Archives (three), South Carolina Historical Society; two transcripts: National Archives

⟨Passy, August 25[–27], 1778: We will propose tomorrow to the count de Vergennes the subjects of the loan in Genoa and the interposition of His Majesty with the powers of Barbary. P.S.:[7] The count de Vergennes gave us no encouragement in the affair of the loan. The other matter will be the subject of a proposed written memorial.⟩

Thomas Read to the American Commissioners[8]

ALS: American Philosophical Society

⟨Nantes, August 25, 1778: I received yours by Capt. Barnes.[9] I am recovering from an illness, and should be ready for sea in a few days. I request leave to sail for three months; I have sufficient provisions for that long, and, having brought thirty-one men, need only two more, for whom I request expenses. The men belonging to my vessel are willing to relinquish their

5. Thomas Woodford (b. 1736), the younger brother of Gen. William Woodford: see *Virginia Mag. of Hist. and Biog.*, XXXIII (1925), 34. He visited Paris, where on Aug. 20 he signed an oath of allegiance (APS); see also Salucci et fils to BF, below, Feb. 5, 1779. APS.
6. Published in Taylor, *Adams Papers*, VI, 394.
7. Dated Aug. 27 and in Arthur Lee's hand.
8. Published in Taylor, *Adams Papers*, VI, 396–7.
9. The commissioners' instructions to Read were written July 29; their most recent letter was Aug. 22.

high wages and sail for continental pay. My cruising in the Mediterranean, which I know very well, could more than re-pay all expenses. It will soon be the season for Newfoundland ships bringing fish to market; we need carry but a small quantity of provisions. I would like an answer as soon as possible.[1]⟩

From Peter Collas ALS: American Philosophical Society

Honorable Sir Nants August 25th 1778

It is with honour, pleasure and Satisfaction I here by Im-form you of my going to take my Departure from this place to boston On board of Captn. Barnes[2] where I hope if fortune favour to meet with your worthy Sister and her Amaible Darther;[3] Same time geaving you thanks for the Numberless favours Showed to the familly of whom I have the honor (by Mareage) to be Conected and Perticulerly for the last Showed me at Passy, Same time Endeavor to geave Satisfaction to all my beneefacters, not withstanding my Repeeted mesfortunes. I Remains with due Respects your most Humble and Obed-eint Servant PETER COLLAS

To the honorable Benjamin Franklin

Addressed: Honorable / Benjaman Franklin / at / Passy

Endorsed: Peter Collas

Notation: 25. August. 1778.

From ———— Trottier ALS: American Philosophical Society

⟨From La Breteche, near Tours, August 25, 1778, in French: Rumor has it that some Americans have been so taken with the beauty of Tours and surroundings that they would like to own or rent property near the river. The lovely house I have

1. None has been found.
2. Captain Corbin Barnes, of the *Dispatch.*
3. Jane Mecom and her daughter Jane Collas, his wife.

to offer will soon be connected by a new bridge to the center of town. It was lived in for a year by the Ogilvie family, relatives of the Duke of Richmond.[4] Tours is a commercially very active town, famous for its textiles. I hope to be of service to you.[5]⟩

From Valltravers

ALS: American Philosophical Society

Rockhall, at Bienne, in Switzerland,
Sir! Augt. 25th. 1778.

Since no Letter is dispatched from the Post-office at Paris, to any Part of Switzerland, except Genève, which has not been Free'd to the Frontier-Town of Pontarlier; and I may very possibly have forgot, to inform Yr. Eycy. of this Circumstance: I now beginn to attribute my Misfortune in not hearing from You, in Answer to my 3. last Letters, of april 14th. May 17th. and July 26th., not to your silence; but to yr. Letters being detained in the Post-office at Paris, for Want of their being free'd by yr. servant. Yr. Excy., whose Punctuality and Kindness I have So often experienced, will certainly thank me for this Hint, and order the Recovery of what Letters may have been stopt in their Way from Passy to this Place; and which I Much long to receive.

Since my last, I have been sollicited by my old good Neighbour, Baillif de Graffenried, Baron of Worb, a Gentleman of Rank and of Ingenuity, a Lover of planting and gardening and a Grandson of one of the chief settlers of N. America, who has already 4. Children from his Wife, an amiable young Lady, of his own Rank and Name: to obtain some Information, on the few queries, contained in his inclosed Memorial.[6] The first of

---

4. The family's headquarters were in Aubigny (Berry). See Lewis, *Walpole Correspondence*, VI, *passim*.

5. BF endorsed this: "Trottier Maison à vendre."

6. Enclosed was a third copy of the memorial relating to his American cousin Tsharner, the possibly illegitimate son of Christopher, which Karl Emanuel Graffenried had first sent BF on Jan. 16, with no result; see that

these Queries may easily be answered by the Deputy of the Province of N. Carolina to the general Congress. As to the second, concerning the Use of all his Grants and Title-Deeds, inherited by his Grandfather, perhaps some satisfactory Answer may be Kindly given him, by Yr. Excy. self? In which Case your Kind opinion shall be esteemed a particular Favor. My own he has already, as far as I could conjecture. Vizt. That the Baron should send his Répresentatif, with full Powers and Instructions, to each of the Provinces, where his Inheritances are situated; with legal Copies of all his Title-Deeds, and Filiation; to claim in his Name all such Lands, as have not been vacated, sold, ceded seized for Debts, or Non-Payment of Taxes, Contributions and to renew the Grants thereof by the present new Legislative Power; To setle, what Parts may turn to best Account, by Emigrants from Europe; and to act in his and his Family's Behalf, as a Faithfull, active, and intelligent Agent, under adequate support and Encouragement.

With my best Wishes for Yr. Excy's. Health, and For the Prosperity of our respectable sister-Republicks in N: America, and with due Respects to your Colleagues and Grandson, I beg Leave to remain for ever Sir! Your Excellency's Most obedient humble servant   RODH. VALLTRAVERS.

Notation: M. Valtravers [*illegible*] 1778

letter above, xxv, 483–4. The first copy, as Graffenried explained to Valltravers on Aug. 19, had been forwarded through Necker; the second copy through a Swiss guard. The memorial asks first for any information relative to Tsharner's activities, whereabouts and progeny, and second, whether Graffenried still has claims to their common grandfather's land titles. APS.

To John Adams[7]   ALS: Massachusetts Historical Society

Sir   [c. August 26, 1778]
   If you write to this Mr. Barnes, please to acquaint him that
the Reason he had no Answer from me to his Letter[8] was
because he did not send word where he lodged. I agree to the
5 Guineas.   BF.
To Mr. Adams

John Bondfield to the American Commissioners[9]

                         ALS: American Philosophical Society

⟨Bordeaux, August 26, 1778: Last evening arrived one of Captain McNeill's prizes, the brig *Archangel,* taken at latitude 72°
N. longitude 25° E. while en route from Archangel to London.[1] A boat from Boston belonging to Basmarein & Co. has
arrived but brings no news.[2] Captain Ayres continues to decline; I have sent him to the country but the doctor believes

   7. Written on the back of Thomas Barnes's letter to JA of Aug. 25, which
had been sent care of "Monsieur Franquelen a passis."
   8. That letter, now missing, was written on Aug. 24 and requested 5
guineas. Having heard nothing, Barnes repeated his story the following day
to JA: he had escaped from Forton prison, been given assistance, but doc-
tors' bills had claimed half of it. He had perhaps been presumptuous in
writing directly to "a gentleman of [Franklin's] qualety." Taylor, *Adams Papers,* VI, 394–5. JA, who gave him the 5 guineas on Aug. 26, evidently explained BF's silence; Barnes begged the Doctor to forgive his carelessness,
in his reply to JA of Aug. 27: *ibid.,* 400–1. See also Leveux to BF, Aug. 10.
   9. Published in Taylor, *Adams Papers,* VI, 397–8.
   1. The *General Mifflin* had captured eight ships off the North Cape of
Norway, sinking four, keeping three as prizes and loading eight British
captains and 43 seamen aboard the last. This last ship arrived off Murmansk
in wretched condition in late July. Empress Catherine was outraged at the
Americans who reportedly also boarded Russian fishing boats and fired on
some Dutch ships. She proposed to the Danes that the two countries fit out
squadrons to protect their commerce. For this minor diplomatic crisis see
David M. Griffiths, "An American Contribution to the Armed Neutrality of
1780," *Russian Review,* XXX (1971), 164–72. McNeill proceeded to Lorient
via the English Channel where he captured five more prizes.
   2. Reculès de Basmarein & Raimbaux had long been involved in American trade: see XXIII, 47 n.

he is too far gone. The ship [*General Arnold*] is ready for sea on short notice.⟩

James Moylan to the American Commissioners[3]

ALS: American Philosophical Society

⟨L'Orient, August 26, 1778: Capt. Daniel McNeill arrived here yesterday on the *General Mifflin*, privateer. He left Portsmouth May 8, cruised the north seas, and captured thirteen prizes there and at the mouth of the Channel. Five he sunk, the rest he sent to America or France; one [the *Isabelle*] arrived here. He also has some fifty prisoners. Can they be exchanged for Americans imprisoned in England?⟩

Puchelberg & Cie. to the American Commissioners[4]

ALS: American Philosophical Society

⟨L'Orient, August 26, 1778, in French: We refer to our letter of the 24th and to the arrival of the *General Mifflin*, Captain Daniel McNeill. McNeill wishes to sell the recaptured French ship [*Isabelle*]. Since his commission and those of his officers conform to Captain Tucker's, it may be necessary for him to report his captures to Tucker and divide the proceeds accordingly. We request instructions.⟩

From Jean-Baptiste Le Roy

ALS: American Philosophical Society

De Paris ce mercredy [August 26?, 1778] au Soir
Je vous tourmente toujours mon Illustre Docteur mais c'est par contrecoup parcequ'on me tourmente aussi. Je vous ai demandé une lettre de recommandation pour un negociant de St. Brieuc M. De La Lande Robinot qui doit envoyer un vaisseau

3. Published in Taylor, *Adams Papers*, VI, 398.
4. Published in Taylor, *Adams Papers*, VI, 399–400.

richement chargé en Amérique. Vous m'avez dit qu'il falloit que vous seussiez quelle sorte d'homme etoit ce négociant. Je vous ai donné une lettre que m'a écrit un Maitre des requêtes à son sujet et ce maitre des requetes est un homme de merite et très estimable.[5] Vous avez bien voulu me promettre la lettre et je crains que vous ne m'ayez oublié. Cependant ce vaisseau doit partir sous dix ou douze jours et n'attend véritablement que votre Lettre. Permettez donc que je vous renouvelle la requête que je vous ai presentée à son sujet. Pour vous dé-dommager de cette importunité, je trahirai un petit secret que l'on m'a confié c'est qu'une belle Dame doit vous aller de-mander à dîner Dimanche et cette Dame est Mde. De Mar-cenay. Vous inspirez des passions de tous les côtés. Ne trahis-sez pas le traître. Mr. De Caraman de qui j'ai recu une lettre ce matin et qui me charge de vous dire mille choses pour lui m'a envoyé un petit papier pour vous faire une demande de la part de M. Le Baron de Wimpfen.[6] Je les joins ici. Recevez Mon Illustre Docteur mille assurrances des sentimens d'attache-ment que je vous ai voués pour la vie   LE ROY

From Leveux   ALS: American Philosophical Society

Monsieur   Calais le 26 aoust 1778
Le 10 de ce Mois J'ay eu l'honneur de vous prevenir que deux americains sauvés des prisons d'angleterre s'etoient pre-sentés chez moy a leur arrivée icy et que je leur avois fourni a chacun quatre Louis d'or pour se rendre a Paris.
Le 13 du meme mois Le sieur John Murfey cy devant Commandant le Navire le Swallow pris près du Cap francois par la fregatte L'eole, apres s'etre sauve de prison est arrivé

5. See our note on Le Roy's letter of July 6.
6. For Mme. de Marcenay see her letters of July 12 and Aug. 22. In the latter she invited herself and others to dine with BF at Passy on Sunday, Aug. 30. We assume that Le Roy is referring to that occasion, and is there-fore writing on the previous Wednesday. For Caraman see XXVI, 302. What-ever of his Le Roy enclosed is missing, and without it we cannot identify which of the two Wimpfen brothers, both barons, had written, or what he requested.

icy et apres m'etre venu faire sa declaration de ce qui luy etoit arrivé, m'a declaré vouloir aller a Paris pour avoir l'honneur de vous Saluer et comme il se trouvoit sans argent je luy ay aussy fourni quatre Louis pour son voyage.[7] Aujourdhuy J'ay eu la visite de Mr. Rolandeau officier du 5eme Regiment le refleman de Charlestown et qui en retournant a l'amerique a été pris dans le vaisseau la Victoire parti de Bordeaux pour charlestown.[8] Comme il avoit été obligé d'emprunter une guinée pour son passage je luy ay fourni six Louis d'or pour se rendre à Paris.

J'ay jusqu'aujourdhuy, Monsieur, taché de me rendre utile et d'aider les Sujets americains. Je vous prie de me mander si je peux continuer sur le meme pied et fournir le meme secours a ceux qui aprés s'etre echapé des prisons d'angleterre viendroit les reclamer icy. Un mot de reponse de votre part me servira de loy et je vous suplie de me l'accorder. J'ay l'honneur d'etre avec respect Monsieur Votre tres humble et tres obeissant serviteur

JES. LEVEUX

Endorsed: J Leveux, Calais 26 Augt. 1778

From Jonathan Williams, Jr.

ALS: American Philosophical Society; copy: National Archives

Dear and honored Sir,   Nantes Augt 26. 1778.

Mr. Porter of Connecticut who was lately at Paris applied to me in distress for Money and said you desired him to do so: I advancd him four Guineas as per the inclosed Receipt relying on his word that you would not object to it.[9]

Mr. Leger Capt. Jno. Nicholsons first Lieutenant is arrived here and has no money, the 10 Guineas he received at Paris being spent in living there and coming hither.[1] He has applied

7. See Murfey's letter of Aug. 10.

8. Louis-François Rolandeau had already been a source of trouble to BF by returning to France without leave from his S. Carolina regiment. See XXV, 87–8, 279–80, 409–10.

9. This former prisoner received 96 *l.t.* from JW on Aug. 20: BF Accounts with JW, May 31, 1781, National Archives.

1. Another former prisoner: see Leveux's letter of Aug. 10.

to Mr. Schweighauser who has no orders therefore did not supply him. He requests me to write to you and asks your assistance to enable him to pay for his support here during the Time he is obliged to stay, and to furnish him with some necessarys for his voyage. If you think proper to comply with his request please to limit the Sum. Many other americans are here in similar Situations without prospects of paying their necessary Debts, which daily increase by their Stay.

Please to remember me with Gratitude to all the agreeable Circles at Passy particularly to Madame Brillon and her amiable Family.

My Love to Billy, I thank him for the letter he sent me under a *blank* Cover.

Capt. Collas goes in a day or two, I write to aunt mecom by him. I am with great Respect Your Dutifull and obliged Kinsman
                                                          J WILLIAMS J

Addressed: A Monsieur / Monsieur Franklin / Ministre Plenipotentiare / des Etats unis / en son Hotel / a Passy / prés Paris

Endorsed: Jonathan Wms. about supplying Money

Notations in different hands: Nantes 26 aout 1778 / referred to the other Commissioners.

The American Commissioners to John Bondfield

AL (draft):[2] Massachusetts Historical Society; two copies: National Archives

Sir   Passi August 27 1778.

We have before us yours of the 23d Inst. and are very sorry that Capt. Ayres is so indisposed as to prevent his return to America in the General Arnold. We wholly refer the appointmt. of a Master for this Vessel to you and Capt. Ayres and doubt not you will find a good Seaman and a person in whom you can confide. We are &c.

Mr Bonfield

2. In the hand of Arthur Lee.

From Georges Grand ALS: American Philosophical Society

Monsieur   Amsterdam le 27 Aoust 1778
   Depuis la Lettre que J'ay eu l'honneur de vous ecrire le 20
de ce mois M. Hancok à attendu les 3 malles qui sont arrivées
d'Angleterre sans avoir receu les nouvelles, et les remises qu'il
attendait.
   Dans l'idée que les Lettres de son frere sont intercéptées, il
s'est décidé à partir ce matin pour se rendre auprés de Vous,
ou Je compte qu'il arrivera dans la huitaine.
   Je luy ai fourni des recommandations, avec une dirêction
pour sa route aprés luy avoir procuré un Passeport, et comme
sa dépense à augmenté par son séjour, il à eu besoin d'un
suplêment de 10 Ducats, dont voicy son reçeu. Vous voudrés
bien les rembourser à mon frere, sur le Mandat de ma Maison
de £115.2.9. argent de france.
   Voicy une Lettre qui m'a eté addressée pour vous, par le
bon Mr. Hutton,[3] toujours Anglais Pacifique, Votre Amy et le
mien, mais encore plus celuy de George III. J'ay l'honneur
d'etre avec la plus parfaite Considération Monsieur Votre tres
humble et tres obeissant serviteur   GRAND

Honble. Doctr. Franklin

Addressed: To / The Honble. Doctor Franklin / Paris.

From de Reine ALS: American Philosophical Society

Monsieur Le docteur   a versailles le 27 aoust 1778
   Hier a l'hotel De joui j'ai eu l'honneur de vous parler d'un
topique de plus merveillieux pour la reunion des os pour toute
les fractures.
   Cette objet est trop interressant pour l'humanité pour être
négligé: autant il paroit extraordinaire vérifié par nombre
D'Experiance appuyée de certificat les plus autentique. Cependant je vous Supplie, Monsieur le docteur, d'avoir la bonté
de vous donner la peine d'Examiner par vous même cette important objet pour reconnoitre la verité!

3. Of Aug. 24.

Pour cette effet Si vous voulez accelerer et profitter du sejour a paris de la personne qui possede cette découverte, vous pouvez Ecrire de ma part directement *a Madame la veuve detoujan rue St andré des arts au caffé militaire a paris*, et avoir la bonté de donner vos ordres pour le Jour et l'heure que vous serez visible elle se rendra chez vous.

J'auray beaucoup de Satisfaction si ma prévoiance peu devenir utile a votre patrie! Et je seray surpayé d'avance par le plaisir de vous assurer de toute ma vénération avec laquel j'ai l'honneur d'Etre Monsieur Le docteur Votre tres humble et tres obeissant serviteur

DE REINE
ancien capt. rue Sataury aux 4. bornes.

a M. Le docteur franklin a passy

Endorsed: De Reine

[Ferdinand Grand][4]: Memorandum for the American Commissioners

AD (draft): American Philosophical Society

[before August 28, 1778?][5]

Le Congrés a authorisé ses Comissionaires a emprunter en Europe 2 millions Stl. soit 46 millions argent de france remboursable dans 10 ans a l'interret de 6 pct. tous fraix faits.[6]

Les Comissionaires ont en consequence commence par faire imprimer pour 4 millions de promesses. Quoyqu'ils n'en ayent pas encorre fait usage ils ont tout lieu d'esperer que la bonne opinion que l'on a generalement et avec fondement de la fidelité et de la solidite de leur Pays, facilitera beaucoup cet

4. Identified by the handwriting.
5. Presumably composed in conjunction with the commissioners' letter of Aug. 28 requesting further financial assistance from Vergennes. Another clue is the reference to the printing of promissory notes; we assume these were for the loan the commissioners hoped to float in the Netherlands. As of late August the notes had been printed and signed but not yet sent to the commissioners' Dutch agent: see their letter of Aug. 31 to Horneca, Fizeaux & Cie.
6. The proposed loan of £2,000,000 first appears above, XXIII, 56.

emprunt et nuira meme à ceux que L'angleterre sera obligée d'ouvrir dans peu.

La simplicité de cet emprunt ajoute a l'economie de l'inter-ret celle des fraix, et son utilité pour nos manufactures doit non seulement le favoriser mais meme le proteger puisqu'il pourroit etre utille au Gouvernement[7] de s'en charger et de proffiter des moyens qu'il a de faire usage de ces promesses pour les faire gouter du public de sorte que sans paroitre, c'est a dire sans faire usage de son credit, le Gouvernement peut se procurer des ressources utiles par la d'autant que si les ar-rangements que le Congres a pris ont lieu, il n'aura besoin que de la plus petite partie de cet emprunt, et le surplus seroit une jouissance pour l'administration qui pendant cet Intervalle menageroit ses moyens directs et seroit en effet le moyen le plus heureux et le plus sur de retablir la confiance et de la porter à son plus haut degré que de ne point faire paroitre d'emprunt pendant que les autres puissances font à qui mieux mieux. Il suffiroit pour cella que les Comissionaires ameri-quains fussent asseurés de trouver au tresor royal les secours necessaires au fur et mesure de leurs besoins sans etre dispen-sés de travailler come si de rien n'etoit au debouché de leurs promesses dans l'Etranger surtout et que les fonds qui en pro-viendroyent fussent versés au tresor Royal.

The American Commissioners to James Smith

AL (draft): Massachusetts Historical Society; two copies: National Ar-chives

Sir,   Passi Aug 28. 1778

We received your Letter dated Paris Hotel de Saxe Aug. 24. and, altho We are altogether of a different opinion from yours respecting your Right of passing with your Effects Americans being intituled by the Treaty, no more than the Subjects of any other state in Europe in Amity with France, to pass with their Effects Duty free; yet having the Honour, on the 26 of seeing

7. The French government; the commissioners in their letter of the 28th asked permission to solicit subscribers in France.

the Compte De Vergennes, We mentioned your Case to him and requested of him as a Favour that you might be permitted to pass with your Effects.[8] His Excellency desired us to commit it to writing, which We have done this Day; but We wish you had furnished Us with an Invoice, which We suppose would have rendered the Business less difficult. We have however contented ourselves with the general Description of your goods contained in your Letter. We wish you Safe to America, and are your Countrymen and humble servants.

Dr James Smith Hotel de Saxe. Paris, Rue de Columbie

The American Commissioners to Vergennes[9]

LS: Archives du Ministère des affaires étrangères; AL (draft):[1] Massachusetts Historical Society; two copies: National Archives

⟨Passy, August 28, 1778: We have several subjects that we must lay before you. One, unfortunately, is money. The nature of the war has necessitated far more emissions of paper currency than would ordinarily have been wise; to limit them Congress has borrowed extensively, with interest to be paid in Europe, great sums of which are now due. The financial assistance so generously furnished us is almost spent, and our expenses here have been so great that our resources are exhausted. We hope that His Majesty's quarterly payment of 750.000 *l.t.* may be continued. Congress authorized us to borrow two million sterling,[2] and we request permission to raise such part of it in this kingdom as may be possible. We are willing to limit the interest to that given by His Majesty, to whom most will prefer to lend; but the desire to establish commercial connections may induce some to serve the Americans in this way.

8. The commissioners' written request to Vergennes is contained in their letter to him below of this date. Smith's description of his goods is in his above of the 24th; he was slightly more precise in the letter to WTF summarized there.

9. Published in Taylor, *Adams Papers*, VI, 401–5.

1. In JA's hand with emendations by Lee.

2. See Ferdinand Grand's draft memorandum, before Aug. 28.

We understand that ships of ours in Italy wishing to return home, and Italian merchants wishing to trade with America, are deterred by the danger from Barbary corsairs. We therefore request assistance through His Majesty's good offices with the Barbary states, as stipulated in the Treaty of Commerce.[3]

Many Americans in England and on the Continent want to return home but fear difficulties in removing their property. We submit to His Majesty's wisdom whether some way may be found for them to pass through this kingdom with their personal effects, not for sale, without paying duty. Dr. Smith informs us that part of his baggage, consisting of household linen and plate, is detained in Calais as contraband.[4] We should be grateful if you could secure him permission to take his effects home with him duty free. We also request a passport for the English ship that is to land our prisoners as close to Brest as possible.⟩

John Paul Jones to the American Commissioners[5]

ALS: American Philosophical Society; draft: National Archives; copy: United States Naval Academy Museum

⟨Brest, August 28, 1778: M. de la Prévalaye, who commands here in the absence of the comte d'Orvilliers, has just told me that he can no longer furnish a guard for the *Ranger* prisoners detained aboard the *Patience*. Unable to depend on the *Ranger*'s officers, I had arranged for a guard with the comte d'Orvilliers; he furnished twelve soldiers with officers, relieved daily and altogether supported at the expense of France. Not a single prisoner has so far escaped. Were d'Orvilliers still here, I am sure he would order the guard continued. I entreat you to apply immediately to the French minister so that a cartel may not be lost.⟩

3. See xxv, 602–3.
4. See Smith's letter of Aug. 24.
5. Published in Taylor, *Adams Papers*, vi, 405.

From Pierre-Joseph Odolant-Desnos[6]

ALS: University of Pennsylvania Library

Monsieur   a Alencon en normandie ce 28 aoust 1778

Comme pere d'une famille particuliere et de plus pere d'un grand peuple pour le bonheur duquel, dans un âge tres avancé vous avés fait tant de sacrifices particuliers, j'ose esperer que vous voudrés bien user d'indulgence pour un pere malheureux qui cherche de tous cotes un enfant cheri qui ne lui a jamais donné jusqu'à ce moment que des sujets de satisfaction tant du côté de la Conduite que du coté des études. J'avois elevé dès L'enfance avec Le plus grand soin deux fils pour tâcher d'en faire des citoyens utiles à la patrie: L'ainé est mort a paris dans Le moment ou il alloit prendre un état; Le second âge de dix neuf ans et demi après avoir fini son cours de trois années d'etudes en medecine dans L'universite de Paris me demande la permission d'aller soutenir ses theses et prendre le bonnet de docteur a Rhims: je Lui fais passer les fonds necessaires. Il m'ecrit le 13 juin dernier qu'il part pour s'y rendre. Effective-ment il fait emporter une male contenant ses meilleurs effets et entre autre beaucoup de Livres de Medecine, quitte en meme temps La maison de M. Levacher De La feutrie mede-cin de Paris chés lequel il demeuroit depuis trois annees,[7] en disant également qu'il part pour Rhims. Quinze jours après j'aprends qu'il n'a point paru a Rhims. Je m'adresse à tous les Bureaux des messageries qui y conduisent sur touttes Les routes, mon enfant n'y a point paru. J'ay fait chercher a Mont-pellier. Je me suis adressé a M. Le Lieutenant general de Police de Paris, au secretaire de la marine: je n'ay pu rien decouvrir.

Je soubconne qu'il Lui a monté dans La tête de passer chez les insurgents Pour Les quels je L'ai [ré]entendu plaider avec enthousiasme La derniere fois que je L'ai vû. Faittes moi La grace de m'indiquer La façon de m'assurer si mes soubçons

---

6. A doctor and antiquary, an associate, like BF, of the Société royale de médecine, and a writer on medicine and local history. Larousse; Quérard, *France littéraire.*

7. On the rue St. Antoine. *Almanach Royal* for 1778, p. 421.

314

sont fondes,[8] et, dans Le cas où ils le seroient, Les moyens surs de fournir à ce malheureux enfant les secours qui lui deviendront bientot necessaires pour le soustraire a La misère ou il va être reduit. Il n'aura osé me faire part de son projet; il aura senti que je ne lui aurois jamais conseillé d'abandonner une petite fortune honête dans sa province pour courir après une chimere: Il savoit que je me flatois qu'il fermeroit Les paupierres a un pere accable d'infirmités par le travail et qu'il succederoit a la confiance dont on m'honore dans mon canton. Il n'aura donc osé attendre a être recu medecin, il s'est seulement muni de son extrait de bapteme en regle. Il a Levé à L'université ses inscríptions pris ses certificats des professeurs des trois années d'etudes de medecine et profite du petit argent destiné a sa reception pour s'embarquer. Je crains seulement qu'il ait eu L'imprudence de changer Les noms sous Lesquels il étoit connu de crainte d'être arrêté dans sa course par quelqu'un de ma connoissance. Ses noms de famille sont Odolant Desnos de Lazerie natif de la ville d'Alençon en normandie.

Daignes Monsieur faire donner un mot de renseignement a une famille dans la consternation dépuis L'evasion d'un enfant qui en faisoit toute la consolation. J'aurois pu employer auprès de vous M. Dubourg medecin de Paris avec La famille duquel j'ay des Liaisons d'alliance et a La quelle j'ay eté souvent utile; mais j'ay cru n'en avoir pas besoin. Le coeur d'un pere et d'un chef d'une grande nation ne peut se refuser à La pitié paternelle. J'ay L'honneur d'etre avec un profond respect Monsieur Votre tres humble et tres obeissant serviteur

Odolant desnos correspondant
de la Societé Royale de medecine de Paris.
Secretaire perpetuel de la Societé d'agriculture
de la generalité d'Alençon, membre de
differentes accademies

Notation: Odolant 28 Aout 1778

8. They were, but his anxiety was not. On June 10 the young man had written bf to ask for free transportation to America; he wanted to go as a

From Dumas

ALS: American Philosophical Society; AL (letterbook draft): Algemeen Rijksarchief

Monsieur,   La Haie 28e Août 1778.

Les Lettres que j'ai reçues, et les Dépêches que j'ai pu voir depuis quelque temps, ne me disent rien de plus que ce [*que*] publient en même temps les Gazettes, et surtout celle de Leide, qui est la meilleure, et laquelle je suppose que vous voyez regulierement. J'ai craint, depuis ma derniere du 18, d'abuser du précieux temps de l'honorable Commission en écrivant ce qui ne valoit pas la peine d'être lu. Je vois cependant tous les jours Mr. le g—— F——.[9] Je crois qu'il n'a pas non plus des choses fort importantes et pressantes à apprendre à sa maison. Tout est absent, et voltige dans les champs, comme des papillons, pendant ce bel Eté. Nous faisons pourtant toujours la guerre à l'oeil;[1] et en attendant plus grande partie, nous pelotons toujours quelque petite occurrence, dont le détail, d'ailleurs inutile, ne se fie pas trop au papier. En voici pourtant une qui me fait mettre la main à la plume, parce qu'elle pourra vous intéresser. Mr. Hutton, le Morave, qui, dit-on, vous a porté des propositions d'accommodement, est ici depuis quelque temps, logé, d'abord chez Mad. Fagel née Boreel, et depuis 15 jours à une campagne près d'ici, chez son ami Mr. de Salgas, qui vient d'épouser Mad. Bicker, née Boreel, et pour les noces duquel il paroît être venu. Cependant, nous n'avons pas laissé de croire à la possibilité de quelque négociation secrete, cachée sous ce voyage; et j'ai profité de l'occasion, toute naturelle, qui se présentoit, d'aller féliciter Salgas. Celui-ci tire une pension de 600 L.St. et porte la clé du R—— G——,[2] pour avoir été précepteur de ses enfans pen-

---

volunteer and serve wherever he might be accepted: XXVI, 32. If he had any answer, which as far as we know he did not, it would certainly have been negative.

9. For G—— F—— see our annotation of Dumas to the commissioners, July 3.

1. Meaning *gratis*.

2. "Roi Georges," in whose household Claude de Narbonne Pelet Salgas had been a tutor; see the note to James Hutton's letter of Aug. 16.

dant quelques années. Je crois donc qu'il l'aime mieux que nous. Cependant, comme je me suis apperçu que sa prospérité ne lui a pas fait méconnoître ses anciennes connoissances, j'ai continué de l'estimer et de le voir. Nous observons seulement, l'un avec l'autre, une discrétion vraiment Pythagorique sur les affaires du temps. J'y ai vu Mr. Hutton. Il m'a paru un Ange. Je le voudrois seulement d'une autre secte, s'il est si nécessaire que l'homme en ait une: car la sienne est celle de toutes dont les connoisseurs se défient le plus. Leur Communauté parfaite de biens (et peut-être de f—— [femmes]) qui fait que de Hispahan à Zeist, et jusqu'en Amérique et au Groenland, ils ont le compte exact de la recette et dépense commune; leur despotisme absolu sur les esprits, qui prescrit à chaque classe, depuis la plus bête jusqu'à la premiere moins une, ce qu'elle doit savoir sans plus; leur nombre, beaucoup plus grand qu'on ne sait et qu'on ne pense: tout cela la rend plus redoutable encore que celle des Jésuites. Pardonnez-moi la digression, si elle est de trop.[3] Dans la conversation Mr. Hutton me demanda si je connoissois Mr. le Chevalier Grand d'Amsterdam. Je lui dis qu'oui. Il se mit tout de suite à lui écrire une Lettre, qu'il me pria de remettre à la poste en rentrant en ville. Je l'ai fait. Demain, je compte de lui faire une visite de civilité, pour lui offrir mes services de la part de Mr. Grand, de qui je me le suis fait écrire. Si j'observe quelque autre chose d'extraordinaire, je vous en ferai part, Monsieur; sinon je n'en parlerai plus car il doit s'en retourner la semaine qui vient par Bruxelle en Angleterre. Le g—— F—— est instruit de cela, et me fait agir.

Voici quelques dépêches. Conservez, s'il vous plait celle de Paramaribo,[4] pour la retrouver au besoin: car quand le g—— F——, qui vient d'aller pour huit jours à Amsterdam, etc. sera de retour, je le consulterai, si l'on ne pourroit pas saisir cette occasion, pour faire quelque démarche, qui mît cette République dans la nécessité de parler. Je fais bien des voeux pour

3. For the communal aspects of the Moravian sect see Gillian Lindt Gollin, *Moravians in Two Worlds: a Study of Changing Communities* (New York, 1967).
4. In Dutch Guayana (Surinam).

la conservation de votre santé, et suis avec un très respectueux attachement, Monsieur, Votre très humble et très obéissant serviteur   DUMAS

Vous verrez, dans le bout de Gazette ci-joint, le but de l'article marqué X.

Paris à S.E.M. le Dr. Franklin Esqr., Min. Pl. des E.U. de l'Am.

Notation: M. Dumas / 28 Aug. 1778

John Bondfield to the American Commissioners[5]

ALS: American Philosophical Society

⟨Bordeaux, August 29, 1778: I have received your letter of the 19th commissioning the purchase of 56 pieces of cannon. I suspect it will be November before I can collect them. I presume they are for naval use; let me know where to send them. I am without instructions for the *General Arnold*; the delays cause very heavy expenses which are charged to me. Another of the *General Mifflin*'s prizes bound from London to Archangel has arrived at the address of my friend Jean Baptiste Nairac[6] at La Rochelle. The privateer *Oliver Cromwell* was met north of the Azores. Merchants here are alarmed that the West India ships were abandoned by their convoy escort off Bermuda.[7] Future instructions for the naval captains providing convoy will probably be changed and hopefully our ships will share the protection accorded America-bound French ships.⟩

5. Published in Taylor, *Adams Papers*, VI, 406–7.
6. One of the port's major outfitters of ships in the West Indian trade: Villiers, *Commerce colonial*, p. 333.
7. The failure of the French navy to provide convoy protection from port of departure to port of arrival left merchantmen easy prey to British privateers. By the end of the year an improved convoy system was begun. *Ibid.*, pp. 212–18, 296–7.

From ——— Guigon[8]

ALS: American Philosophical Society

⟨Agde, August 29, 1778, in French: I am sending you a modest work on engineering and make bold to congratulate your country on its alliance with France, that generous protector of the weak. May America prove a faithful daughter!⟩

From ——— Hill[9]

ALS: American Philosophical Society

A Paris Ce 29 Aoust 1778

J'ai recu de Mr. Franklin la somme de Cinq Cent Livres a Compte, de ce qu'il me doit de Memoire que je luy ai donné,

HILL

Notation: Hills Rect for 500 Livs

The American Commissioners to Sartine

AL (draft): Massachusetts Historical Society; two copies: National Archives

Sir   Passi Aug. 30. 1778

We have just received a Letter from Brest[1] relating to the insecure State of our Prisoners there a Copy of which We inclose and request your Excellencys Aid in Securing them more effectually, till they can be exchanged. We also beg Leave to remind your Excellency of the Passport we desired for the English Cartell ship which is to bring the American Prisoners

---

8. He signs himself *Maître de Chapelle* de la Cathédrale d'Agde.

9. A tailor who had been serving the members of the commission for at least a year; he appears sporadically throughout WTF's Accounts (see XXIII, 19), and F. Grand's Accounts with the Commissioners (XXIV, p. 3) where this transaction, and one with JA, are recorded on Aug. 30. Taylor, *Adams Papers,* VI, 359.

1. Presumably Jones to the commissioners, Aug. 28. Jones also complained of the lack of security for prisoners in his Aug. 21 letter to Bancroft (U.S. Naval Academy Museum).

from England to Calais or Brest, or such other Port, as you may think most proper.[2] We are, with great Respect.

M. De Sartine

John Paul Jones to the American Commissioners[3]

ALS: American Philosophical Society; draft: National Archives; copy: United States Naval Academy Museum

⟨Brest, August 30, 1778: My friend M. de la Porte, intendant, has now agreed to furnish a vessel and send the *Ranger*'s prisoners to England, if you consent. This offer is too generous to refuse.[4]

The guard will be discontinued unless you procure an order from the minister.[5] As for the exchange, perhaps M. de Sartine will agree to the transport of prisoners by water to Calais; transportation by land would be expensive. If a direct exchange can be effected, this will be the way of least risk, trouble, and expense.⟩

From François Teissedre de Fleury

ALS: American Philosophical Society

Monsieur a St. hipolitte ce 30 aoust *1778*

Je viens d'etre informé par un de mes amis a qui je m'etais adressé pour qu'il me procurat s'il lui etoit possible des nouvelles de mon fils n'en ejant [ayant] pas eu depuis un fort long-

2. For the minister's promise see Lee's notation to the commissioners' letter to Sartine, Aug. 18. They had requested a passport from Vergennes on Aug. 28.

3. Published in Taylor, *Adams Papers*, VI, 410.

4. The offer was in response to Jones's urgent letter to de la Porte earlier that day, beseeching him to secure the prisoners; Jones claimed that poor health prevented him from delivering the letter in person, and sent it by Mr. Amiel. National Archives.

5. They were in the process of doing so: see the commissioners to Sartine, Aug. 30.

temps, il me mande par le courrier d'aujourdhui qu'il a appris qu'il avoit ete fait prisonnier avec pleusieurs autres officiers francais sur la delavare, et conduits a St. augustin dans la floride.[6] Je m'adresse a vous monsieur dans la confiance ou je suis que vous ne refuseres pas a un pere et a une mere avances dans l'age, et qui n'ont que ce seul enfant pour toute consolation de leur en donner des nouvelles et leur dire si ce qu'on leur a ecrit est bien vray persuadé que nous sommes que vous en etes instruit. Je ne me borneray pas monsieur a vous demander cette seule grace, je vous prieray encore de vouloir bien faire tout ce qui dependra de vous aupres du congré pour qu'il soit echangé et qu'il lui soit fourni tout ce qui peut lui etre necessaire et etre assuré du remboursement des avances qu'on lui aura faites. Je voudrois bien monsieur trouver quelques occasions a vous donner des preuves de ma sensibilite a touts vos biens faits et de l'attachement respectueux avec lequel je suis Monsieur Votres tres humble et tres obeissant serviteur   DE FLEURY

Veuilliés monsieur m'honorer dune reponse pour la tranquilité d'un pere et d'une mere qui sont dans les plus grandes allarmes sur le conte de leur fils et que l'on vous en donne des nouvelles lorsque vous ecrires a l'amerique. Mon adresse est a M. de fleury cosseigneur de la ville de St. hipolitte par montpellier a St. hipolitte en cevennes

Notation: Defleury St. Hippolite 30e mars [*sic*] 1778.

6. His son, François-Louis, had already been the object of inquiries on the part of Mme. de Flavigny and Father Bertier. See XXVI, 329 n. The news of his capture was false: it may have arisen from a confusion with the capture of a group of French officers for which see XXIV, 206 n.

The American Commissioners to Horneca, Fizeaux & Cie.[7]

Copies: Massachusetts Historical Society,[8] National Archives (two), University of Virginia Library[9]

⟨Passy, August 31, 1778, in French: We send by Mr. Whitall[1] a book of promissory notes and interest coupons, for 205,000 florins payable on January 1, 1788.[2] You will fill in the blanks in each with the number and date of delivery, likewise the counterfoils, and keep an exact record. Sell the notes only for cash, as soon as possible and with due prudence. We are allowing you one percent to cover expenses. Correspond with us or our successors to arrange the prompt remittance of funds received.⟩

7. Published in Taylor, *Adams Papers*, VI, 411–13; see also p. 327 n.

8. In Arthur Lee's hand.

9. With an emendation by Ferdinand Grand, who probably drafted the letter.

1. Joseph P. Whitall of Philadelphia. He had the packet on the 24th, when he gave WTF a receipt for it: APS. For some reason he carried it without this covering letter, which did not arrive until mid-September; see the firm to the commissioners, Sept. 17.

2. Our previous discussion of this loan carried the story through June: XXVI, 338–9 n. BF's handling of the details delayed matters, according to Arthur Lee, who complained on July 1 that the bills were not yet printed: Wharton, *Diplomatic Correspondence*, II, 638–9. In fact they were: on that day the printer reported to Ferdinand Grand that he had sent the day before the first of five volumes that BF had ordered; three were enclosed, and the fifth promised for the next day. Boudet to Grand, July 1, 1778, University of Pa. Library. By the end of July the commissioners were signing the notes: Wharton, *op. cit.*, p. 671. If they delayed for another month sending the material to Amsterdam, as they seem to have, the reason may lie in Lee's strenuous objections to dealing with Horneca, Fizeaux & Cie., for which see Taylor, *op. cit.*, p. 413 n.

The American Commissioners to Musco Livingston

AL (draft): Massachusetts Historical Society; two copies: National Archives

Sir   Passi Aug. 31. 1778

We are favoured with yours of the 24, and are not able to give you any certain Directions concerning the Duties upon C. Tucker's Prizes.[3] We have heretofore taken a great deal of Pains concerning the Subject of Prizes, and the Duties which must be paid upon them. Mr. Schweighauser of Nantes has obtained, as We understand, from M. Necker, a List of the Duties that must be paid, untill a general Regulation can be made. M. De Sartine has for some Time been employd in preparing a system of Regulations, concerning Prises and Prisoners, which We expect every day to see determind by public Authority.[4] We shall write to Mr. Schweighauser on the Subject, and must refer you to him for the present, and are &c.

Mr Livingston at Nantes.

The American Commissioners to James Moylan[5]

AL (draft): Massachusetts Historical Society; two copies: National Archives

⟨Passy, August 31, 1778: We are pleased to hear from you of the good success as well as the adventurous and patriotic spirit of Capt. McNeill. When the prisoner exchange we have been promised is accomplished, his prisoners can be exchanged for a like number of our suffering countrymen. We will inform you when the necessary passports arrive. We expect in a few days new French regulations on prizes and prisoners; orders

---

3. The commissioners seem to be missing the point of Livingston's protest which was not against the duties but rather the low purchase price by Puchelberg for Tucker's prizes.

4. Sartine first wrote on the subject on July 29.

5. Published in Taylor, *Adams Papers*, VI, 414.

have already been sent to keep the prisoners in French prisons.[6] Officers' paroles have been generally taken.⟩

From John Holker

ALS: American Philosophical Society

Cher Monsieur   Rouen 31 Aoust 1778
    Je prends la liberté de vous recommander encore la Maison de Mr. Le Couteulx de Cadix:[7] leur Scituation, leur richesse, la considération dont ils jouissent en Europe et Surtout a la Cour d'Espagne, avec leur façon de penser pour la noble cause, mérite réellement votre attention. Mr. Le Normand[8] leur associé doit vous remettre cette lettre et vous me flaterés infiniment de l'accüeillir et de lui donner votre confiance, ainsi que de vouloir bien les recommander a l'occasion a vos dignes Compatriotes; Je réponds que vous serés très satisfait de leur connoissance, n'estant point au hazard que je vous demande votre estime pour cette famille, que j'ai l'avantage de connoistre et de chérire depuis que je suis en France. J'ai vu naistre et élever ceux qui sont a Cadix, ayant été intimement lié avec feu leur respectable Pere, Député du commerce de la ville de Paris, qui a été générallement regretté. Je présume que dans la circonstance présente, que le commerce d'Amérique pouvant tourner de leur costé, cette maison peut vous estre d'une grande utilité. Toutes ces considérations m'ont engagé a vous faire cette démarche et a vous prier de m'excuser et de me croire avec l'assurance de mon respectueux attachement Cher Monsieur Votre très humble et très obeissant Serviteur
                                                              J HOLKER

a Mr. D. Franklin

Endorsed: Holker recommending the House of Couteulx at Cadiz Rouen 13.[*sic*] aout 1778.

---

6. As earlier requested: commissioners to Sartine, July 16.
7. The Parisian house of Le Couteulx & Cie. had branches in both Rouen and Cadix; the latter was called Le Couteulx, Le Normand & Cie. Lüthy, *Banque protestante,* II, 458 n.
8. Identified above, Bondfield to commissioners, Aug. 17.

From John Paul Jones

ALS: American Philosophical Society; AL (draft): National Archives; copy: United States Naval Academy Museum

Honored and dear Sir,   Brest August 31st. 1778.

Since my return here I have written several letters to Doctor Bancroft, to none of which I have yet received any Answer, tho' the first was dated the 14th. and left Brest by the next mornings Post. This has made me Apprehend that he is absent from Paris as I know he purposed going to Holland upon hearing from Mr. Deane. I am therefore induced to trouble you with the foregoing and inclosed, the Originals of which were made up in one of my letters to Doctor Bancroft.[9] If my letter of the 15th. to the Commissioners has not been presented before this reaches your Hands, I beg you to Suppress it, the Frigates having Sailed the 22d.[1]

It is reported here this morning that the Jamaica Fleet of 70 Sail under Convoy of the Portland and four Frigates passed in sight of the Brest Fleet and got clear, because Comte D'Orvilliers would not break his Line in the Chase. I wish to disbeleive this Account because I had written to him that such a Fleet was expected, And I should be exceedingly sorry to find it true as it would give his Enemies such an Opportunity of talking.

I endeavour to Console myself with the Reflection that my own situation cannot well be altered for the worse: I must Acknowlidge however that I have need of some of your Philosophy, yet ardently wishing for Opportunities to Merit the Continuance of your Friendship and Good Opinion, I am Honored and dear Sir Your very Obliged very Obedient very humble Servant   JNO P JONES

His Excellency Doctor Franklin.

Endorsed: Capt. Jones Brest. Aug. 24. 78

---

9. The "foregoing" was a copy of Jones's letter of Aug. 24 (which explains BF's endorsement); it, in turn, included a copy of Jones's letter to the Prince de Nassau.

1. The *Boston*, *Providence*, and *Ranger*.

From Barbeu-Dubourg

ALS: University of Pennsylvania Library

Mon cher Maitre   [August?,[2] 1778]

Je prens la liberté de vous recommander encore diverses affaires dont j'ai eu l'honneur de vous parler.

1° Celle de M. Coder qui est tres interessante et qui requert celerité.

2° Celle des toiles a voiles et autres marchandises que l'on offre de fournir aux prix courants soit au Congrés, soit aux armateurs particuliers, et de recevoir en payement des papiers du Congrés.

3° De la place sans emolumens de Consul des Etats unis en Normandie pour M. Gregoire, homme tres honnete et tres recommandable.[3]

4° N'y auroit-il pas moyen de faire echanger mon petit Neveu fait prisonier par les Anglois sur le navire le d'Argentré, dans son passage pour l'Amerique avec un brevet d'officier dans les troupes de la Georgie? N'est il pas consequemment reputé Americain, et dans le cas de l'echange, en vertu

---

2. Dubourg raises four points. The first probably has to do either with his and Coder's scheme of attacking British commerce, which is explained above, XXVI, 655–6 n, or with their plan to raid the English and Irish coasts (for which see our annotation of Coder's letter of Sept. 15, below). The second is unidentifiable. The third is a recommendation that he made intermittenly until August, 1779, and therefore is no help in dating this letter. The fourth gives a clue, though a faint one: his plea for his great-nephew sounds like a fairly immediate sequel to that on Aug. 1. Hence our tentative dating.

3. The Grégoire brothers submitted an undated memorandum arguing that their firm, Veuve Grégoire & fils, should represent the U.S. in Normandy. They offered to serve without reward in money or privileges, to be responsible for U.S. subjects who found themselves in trouble, to uphold the rights of the nation with local authorities, and to keep the American minister in Paris informed of whatever he should know. Dubourg reintroduced the application on a number of occasions (see below, Oct. 21), and sent an undated reminder to the commissioners mentioning that France had appointed a consul in the U.S., which Gérard indeed had done in July: XXV, 238 n. Dubourg finally explained his recurrent insistence on the matter of the Grégoire firm in a letter to BF of July 29, 1779: Grégoire was a close relative of Dubourg's friend Agatange Le Roy, to whom he was obligated. All these documents are in the APS.

du cartel, pour un officier de même grade, c'est à dire sous lieutenant des troupes Angloises? Vous m'obligeriez et toute la famille tres sensiblement. Je suis de tout mon coeur avec un attachement inviolable Monsieur et cher Ami Votre tres humble et tres obeissant serviteur   DUBOURG

Cyjoint une notte pour Monsieur Adams et une lettre pour M. de la Balme et des vers de M. Quillan.[4]

From Charles-Armand Flöbergue de la Motte de la Rocatelle[5]   ALS: American Philosophical Society

⟨Toul, [August?,[6] 1778], in French: On the 28th of last June I addressed a memorandum to Congress and to M. Washington and sent the packet to M. Williams to forward. He did not reply, and I have heard nothing from America; the packet, I fear, was lost. I send you enclosed the same memorandum, in which I propose to head a school to teach young Americans all that is requisite for engineers and artillerymen. I shall need

4. Quillan we cannot identify, but Col. Augustin Mottin de la Balme was among the Frenchmen then serving with the U.S. army: XXIII, 36–7 n.
5. Since his only previous appearance, mentioned below, we have learned his full name and a little more about him. His dates were 1727–94; he was an artilleryman in the Bavarian service and then an engineer in the French, and from 1769 to 1772 was stationed in Guadeloupe. He retired perforce on Jan. 1, 1777, charged with misconduct both in the West Indies and after his return; he fought the charges without success. Bodinier.
6. The letter is impossible to date precisely. It looks at first glance like a product of the chevalier's effort to make his project known in America in the summer of 1777, the effort to which he refers at the start. He wrote his memorandum on June 28, 1777, we take him to mean ("last" can be stretched to cover more than a year), and then sent it with a covering note that JW forwarded to the commissioners on Aug. 15. Above, XXIV, 438 n. That note, dated Aug. 5, gives no hint that the writer knew any one on the commission. Yet here he speaks of seeing BF in Paris about a year ago and being promised recommendations; he also says that Duportail and his companions have had one campaign in America. Hence he is undoubtedly writing in 1778. Our guess of August rests on a testimonial to him from the minister of war, dated July 30, 1778, which with an undated covering note of his own is among BF's papers in the APS. We assume that these were intended to supplement the present letter.

as assistants an expert mathematician and a cartographer-draftsman.[7]

When I saw you in Paris about a year ago I showed you all my papers. I speak German well, having as I told you been in the service of the Emperor Charles VII. I was recalled to the French service in 1745 and was in all the campaigns from 1741 to 1748, and again in 1760. In 1763 I became a chevalier de Saint-Louis at the age of thirty-six, was promoted to major in 1774, and retired in 1777. If fortune had favored me I should have gone to America last winter with the recommendations that you offered me. I still have in me twenty years of useful service, and promise to learn English within a year of emigrating; my family will go with me, a wife, son, and three daughters. M. Duportail is fourteen years my junior, M. de La Radière fifteen, and Messrs. Laumoy and Gouvion nineteen; thus I deserve a higher rank than M. Duportail. They are good officers, but have not experienced war except in their American campaign last year.⟩

From Jean-Baptiste Le Roy

AL: American Philosophical Society

Dear friend   Thursday Morning [August, 1778?][8]

I send you Dr. Forster's *Observations made during a voyage round the World* and I have marked the page wherein he explains the formation of Those Ilands I spoke to you of and That are hardly higher than high water mark.[9] I have marked

7. He goes into considerable detail about the curriculum and his subordinates' duties.

8. On July 30, Forster sent his book to BF who must have received it some time in August, and lent it to Le Roy, who is now returning it. See also Vaughan to BF, Aug. 1.

9. The formation of what Cook called the "half-drowned islands," known today as the Tuamotu Archipelago, was the subject of lively scientific speculation. Forster's son George, who accompanied his father on Cook's expedition, wrote: "It remains a subject worthy the investigation of philosophers, to consider from what probable principles these islands are so extremely numerous, and form so great an archipelago to windward of

equally The page wherein he speaks of that curious observation They made aboard a ship at Tahity where they saw the fire running down the chain into the water &c.[1] Since I left you my Dear Doctor I reflected on your explanation of the splitted wood in sundry pieces by the Lightning but Tho' it seemed to me at first to give a good reason of that curious Phaenomenon nevertheless in considering afterwards more attentively of it I thought there was two very strong objections against it.

1st That it splits not only trees but even dry very dry wood such as laths and Beams of roofs in which there seem to remain but very few particles of Water.

2dly That in the wood the water is so disseminated and so spread amongst all its particles of it That the action of that Water must be very Weak and So little able, to produce such violent effects for if the force of the water reduced in Vapour is very strong it is when there is a certain collection of particles together as the Canon Powder of which a certain number collected in a Heap and lighted at once may blow up a House for instance but when spread and disseminated if I may say so, in the whole Mass of the House so that There be a grain of powder there and There you might light the whole I believe without a great effect and I have some notion that amongst the different fire Works there are some made upon that Principle viz. to produce a great fire but with a small explosion.

---

the Society islands...." George Forster, *A Voyage Round the World* ... (2 vols., London, 1777), II, 46. The father's theory, offered on pp. 150–1 of his *Observations*, was that they were fundamentally the product of coral-like animals called lithophytes, and that decomposing organic material from the sea had formed on them a thin layer of soil sufficient to sustain vegetation.

1. "The isles in the South-Sea are ... subject to lightening and thunder storms; for we experienced some at different places and seasons, in the several parts of our voyage over this ocean; and we were now and then obliged to fix the electric chain, to prevent fatal accidents. Once at O-Taheitee, the man who was sent up to the main top-gallant mast head, had scarcely fixed the chain, and another man was still clearing it of the main-chains and shrouds, when the latter received an electric shock, and the fire

You know furthermore with what force the water freezing spreads and Breaks Glasses, earthen and China Pots, and even green Barrels and that those violent effects are produced only by the different particles of the air disseminated in the water that unite together and by that Mean acquire The force of Breaking and tearing all that opposes Their action. And a great proof of this is That if you lett the small particles of air go out as they are expelled of the intervals of the particles of water all Those violent effects of the water freezing do not take place and the freezing goes on quietly without any explosion. But your Superior Genius My Dear friend will may be answer these objections and Dispell The Cloud that This Seems to spread upon your Explanation.

Addressed: A Monsieur / Monsieur Franklin deputé / du Congrès / à Passy

Vergennes and the American Commissioners: An Exchange of Declarations

(I) D (draft):[2] Archives du Ministère des affaires étrangères; two transcripts: National Archives; (II) D (draft):[3] Harvard University Library; copy: Historical Society of Pennsylvania; two transcripts: National Archives; (III) AD (draft):[4] Cornell University Library; two transcripts: National Archives

On August 3 the commissioners finally received the anticipated permission to delete articles 11 and 12 from the Treaty of Amity and Commerce.[5] Vergennes' undersecretary drafted both a French and an American declaration to serve the purpose (documents I and II);

---

was seen running down the chain into the water, without doing any damage." Forster, *Observations,* p. 119.

2. In the hand of Gérard de Rayneval. It carries a later notation that a copy was sent in June, 1780 to La Luzerne, the French minister in Philadelphia. In August of that year BF sent a copy, apparently no longer extant, to James Lovell: Wharton, *Diplomatic Correspondence,* IV, 27; II, 699.

3. Also in Rayneval's hand.

4. In BF's hand.

5. Taylor, *Adams Papers,* VI, 347. See also the commissioners to the committee for foreign affairs, July 29.

Franklin then prepared an English translation of the latter (document III). For some reason, however, the formal exchange of declarations did not occur until November.[6]

I.

A Velles [Versailles] le ler jour du mois ler. de 7bre.
1778.

Le Congrès-général des Etats unis de L'Amérique septentrionale ayant representé au Roi que l'exécution de l'article 11. du traité d'amitié et de commerce signé le 6 du mois de fevrier dernier pourroit entrainer des inconvénients après soi, et ayant desiré en conséquence que cet article demeurat suprimé, consentant en échange que l'article 12. soit également regardé comme non avenu, S.M. [Sa Majesté] pour donner aux Etats-unis de l'Amérique Septentrionale une nouvelle preuve de son affection ainsi que de son desir de consolider l'union et la bonne correspondance établies entre les deuxs Etats, a bien voulu avoir égard à leurs representations; en conséquence S.M. a déclaré et déclare par les presentes qu'elle consent à la suppression des articles 11. et 12. susmentionés, et que son intention est qu'ils soient regardés comme n'ayant jamais été compris dans le Traité signé le 6 fevr. dernier.

II.

Declaration
[on or after September 1, 1778]

Le Roi Très-chrêtien ayant bien voulu avoir égard aux representations que lui a faites le Congrès-général de l'Amerique Septentrionale relativement à l'article 11. du traité de commerce signé le 6. fev. de la presente année, et S.M. ayant consenti en conséquence que le dit article demeurât supprimé a condition que l'article 12. du même traité fut également regardé comme non-avenu; Le Congrès général a declaré de son coté et declare qu'il consent à la suppression des articles 11. et 12. susmentionnés, et que son intention est qu'ils soient regardés comme n'ayant jamais été compris dans le traité signe le 6 fev. dernier.

6. See Vergennes to the commissioners, Oct. 31.

III.

Declaration

[after September 1, 1778]

The most Christian King having been pleased to regard the Representation made to him by the general Congress of North America, relating to the 11th Article of the Treaty of Commerce signed the 6th of February in the present Year, and his Majesty having therefore consented that the said Article should be suppress'd, on condition that the 12th Article of the same Treaty be equally regarded as of none Effect. The above-said general Congress hath declared on their part, and do declare, that they consent to the Suppression of the Eleventh and Twelfth Articles of the abovementioned Treaty, and that their Intention is that these Articles be regarded as having never been comprised in the Treaty signed the 6th of February. In faith whereof, &c.

To Madame Brillon   LS: American Philosophical Society

September saw a turning point in the relationship between Madame Brillon and the Doctor, and we outline here our tentative reconstruction of their correspondence during that month.

It is obvious from the exchange published under July 27 that, "peace treaty" notwithstanding, an impasse had been reached. The solution they adopted, certainly one of the lady's devising, was to turn the would-be lover into a well-loved father, thus confining within the realm of *amitié amoureuse* a rush of feeling that was becoming embarrassing all around. The mutual "adoption," offering deep emotional commitment, was discussed at Madame Brillon's summer residence in Anet, near the Normandy frontier, in the course of the stay Franklin made there on September 6 and 7.[7]

A week later [September 13], possibly in anguish at the thought of having lost her admirer altogether, she urged him to come on another visit or at least to send her a message in French since she could not read English.

---

7. On the morning of Sept. 6, BF wrote John Paul Jones that he would be out of town for a few days.

Franklin tried to oblige. In a somewhat melancholy vein, he agreed to consider her henceforth as a daughter. Unable, however, to convey in a foreign tongue the exact nuances of his meaning, he did not finish the letter nor did he send it.[8] We are publishing it under the tentative date of [*c.* September 15]. When Madame Brillon heard from their common friend Le Veillard that Franklin was indeed planning a second visit, she was overjoyed and sent him two letters of excited anticipation [September 17 and 20]. This meeting took place from September 26 to the 28th.[9] The principle of reciprocal adoption was definitely accepted and from then on Madame Brillon would frequently refer to herself as "votre fille."

Franklin had barely left when she was already telling him of her letdown after the exaltation of the previous days [September 29]. Only on the 30th, we believe, did she discover the letter in French that he had not mailed but probably left in his room: her reaction to it is one of immediacy.

Another manuscript Franklin may have brought to Anet is that of the *Ephemera*, a gracious tribute to his hostess. See our annotation to it under September 20.

Ce Mardy [September 1, 1778] à Versailles[1]

J'accepte avec bien du Plaisir, mon incomparable Amie, votre agréable Invitation. Je me rendrai, ainsi que mon Petit Fils (qui est on ne peut pas plus flatté de l'honneur que vous voulez bien lui faire) chez vous Dimanche dans l'Après midy, nous y passerons la Nuit et nous reviendrons l'Après midy de Lundy, ayant des Engagements pour le Mardy. Je vous embrasse en attendant mille et mille fois, et vous reitere les Assurances de mon inviolable et respectueux Attachement

B FRANKLIN

8. His French was forceful and even ingenious (his creation of *enfante*, for instance, to designate a female child) but decidedly ungrammatical.

9. BF told JA on Saturday Sept. 26 that he would be out of town until Monday.

1. The date is in BF's hand, the text in WTF's, and the signature looks like a playfully clumsy imitation of BF's by his grandson.

333

From Barbeu-Dubourg

ALS: American Philosophical Society

Mon cher Maitre   Paris 1er 7bre 1778

Je vous prie de me mander par la petite poste ce que valent a Boston quatre-mille piastres en papier;[2] si on peut les placer sur les fonds publics des Etats unis, et quel interet on en pourroit tirer icy annuellement. Cela m'interesse beaucoup.

En 2e lieu, je vous prie, lorsque vous aurez occasion d'ecrire a M. Williams a Boston de vouloir lui recommander tres particulierement M. Jean Darcel actuellement en cette ville qui est mon bon, et fidele correspondant, homme plein de zele et d'activité, eleve de M. Breffaut que vous connoissez; je vous en serai fort obligé. Je compte que je vous l'avois deja recommandé l'année derniere,[3] mais vous pouvez l'avoir oublié. Je suis de tout mon coeur, Mon cher Maitre, Votre tres humble et tres obeissant serviteur   DUBOURG

Notation: M. du Bourg 1 sept. 1778

Addressed: A Monsieur / Monsieur Franklin / A Passy

From ——— Oster[4]

ALS: University of Pennsylvania Library

Monsieur   [c. September 1, 1778][5]

Apres avoir combatu longtems dans la crainte de vous importuner je prends pourtant le party de m'adresser a vous pour vous prier de me donner quelques consolations. Mon déséspoir l'emporte sur ma volonté. Depuis 6 mois que mon

---

2. The piasters in question were doubtless the famous Spanish dollars, which were silver coins; "en papier" probably means in the form of a draft.

3. Possibly he had, but more probably he was thinking of his letter above, Aug. 1.

4. The wife of Martin Oster who served three years as Holker's record keeper in Philadelphia and became vice-consul when Holker resigned in 1781. He later served in Virginia but never reached the rank of consul he so often requested. Abraham P. Nasatir and Gary Elwyn Monell, *French Consuls in the United States* . . . (Washington, 1967), pp. 566–7.

5. Six months after the date she ascribes to her husband's departure with Holker. For Holker's mission see above, xxv, 238–9 n.

mari est party je n'ay reçu aucunes de ses letres parce qu'il lui a été defendu de m'ecrire, je sais a la verité qu'il ne s'est embarqué que le 29 fevrier et qu'a cette epoque par consequent il n'etoit pas mort, mais depuis ce tems quoi que je sache a n'en point douter qu'on a recu des nouvelles de l'arivée de Monsieur olker avec lequel il est, et que j'en aye demandé a Monsieur de chaumont il m'en a refusé malgré qu'il sache ma situation, elle est si peinible que j'espere tout de la bonté de votre ame, elle ne peut etre insensible a mes meaux.

Je suis sans fortune par des circonstances qu'il seroit trop long de detailler, mais l'inclination et l'estime ayant eté la base de notre union monsieur oster et moi, je me contentois du peu d'aisance qu'il me procuroit, enfin nous vivions et il me suffisoit, dans cette tranquilité je comptois bien passer ma vie avec lui et on m'en a separé sans m'en avoir même prevenu la surveille, ny sans m'informer de l'endroit où il alloit, a quoi on l'employoit, quels seroient ses apointements, pas même la plus petite chose de ce qui devoit m'interesser. Je m'étois acquise la confiance de mon mary et je la meritois mais on lui avoit fermé la bouche il étoit lié par son serment. J'ignore encore aujourdhui tous ces details et ne m'en suis informé de rien par prudence et ne m'interressant qu'a ses jours. Je demande donc qu'il me marque s'il se porte bien et s'il m'aime, seroient il des raisons de politiques qui le deffendroient, d'ailleurs s'il faut se taire il me sera bien plus aisé de le faire quand je n'auray point a me plaindre. Par grace Monsieur procurez moi de ses nouvelles, ou les moyens de le rejoindre s'il ne doit pas revenir, me refuserez vous cette satisfaction? Je me jette a vos pieds pour vous en suplier ayez pitié de moi; il vient d'arriver un vaisseau qui n'a été que 20 jours en route on sait le resultat des nouvelles qu'il contenoit il a du en aporter de mon mary, il m'aimait il n'a pas pu m'oublier j'en suis sure. Si je suis assez heureuse pour que vous vouliez bien vous interresser a Mon sort vous voudrez bien donner votre reponse au comissionaire qui vous remetra ma letre il ne comprometra persone. Je suis tres respectueusement Monsieur Votre tres humble et obeissante servante   F[EMME] OSTER

From John Bondfield   ALS: American Philosophical Society

Sir   Bordeaux 2 Sept 1778
   At the repeated Instances of La Marquise de La Fayette that
I would give in charge some dispatchs or packets that she
might have the pleasure to deliver to you in person I cannot
decline her obliging attention and esteem the oppertunity of
acquainting you that as your Agent I have been honor'd by Le
Marchal and La Mar[échale] de Mouchy Governor of the
province La Duchess de Duras La Marquisse de La Fayette,
La vicomtess de Noel and the dependants of the Family with
particular Civility and consideration.[6] I have the Honer to be
with due respect Sir Your most Obedient Humble Servant
                                                    JOHN BONDFIELD

The Honble. Benj Franklin

Notation: Bondfield 2nd. Sept. 1778.

From Margaret Cavendish[7]

                                ALS: American Philosophical Society

⟨Calais, September 2: Having had no answer to my two previous letters, I suspect you did not receive them. I implore the
protection you promised me, so that I may be allowed by the
Court to import my brother's work[8] to this country. Please
answer me before I depart for England in a fortnight.⟩

---

   6. All the people Bondfield mentions were relatives of BF's friend
Adrienne de Noailles, marquise de Lafayette: Philippe de Noailles, the maréchal duc de Mouchy (1715–94) and his wife Anne (1718–94) were her
great-uncle and aunt; Louise de Noailles, duchesse de Duras (1745–1822)
was her second cousin; and Louise, vicomtesse de Noailles (1758–94) was
both her younger sister and wife of another second cousin. See Idzerda,
Lafayette Papers, I, [xliv–xlv] and *passim*.
   7. Better known to BF as Margaret Stewart. See XXIII, 302 n where we
discuss her many appeals to BF. We omitted this one because we had been
thrown off track by her signing herself Cavendish.
   8. *The Senator's Remembrancer*, by John Stewart. For a description of this
remarkable work, see XVIII, 36 n.

336

D'ESTAING.

D'Haisne Pinx.ᵗ   Geldar Sculp.

Charles-Henri, comte d'Estaing

From Silas Deane   ALS: American Philosophical Society

My Dear sir   Philadelphia 2d Sepr 1778
    I wrote You by Capt. Cummins who sailed a few Days
since, and I have been so particular to Docr. Bancroft who will
communicate my Letter to You that I have very little to add.[9]
Genl. Sullivan by Accts. of the 25th Ulto. was endeavoring to
make good his Retreat from Rhode Island, which it is thought
he will hardly effect without some Loss.[1] The Country and
Army enjoy a good Share of health and are tolerably supplied,
but Our Finances are in a most deplorable situation Exchange
Five, Six, or at Times Seven for one, the Value of the Currency
still depreciating tho not so rapidly as formerly, Congress are
taking measures to regulate their Treasury and Finances but it
is a Work of Time, and the Evil in the mean time increases.
The People are excessively irritated at the Conduct of the
Count *D'Estaing*, and complain loudly, while Our internal
Enemies take the Advantage of it to depreciate Our Alliance.[2]
I have contented myself with stating the Facts in my Letter to
Docr. Bancroft, and to Mons. Beaumarchais, and am of Opin-
ion nothing else is necessary to be done to the Ministry to
enable them to form their Judgment and take their Measures.
The going to the southward, by which he miss'd the Jamaica
Fleet, and suffered the Enemy to Escape from the Delaware
was the first and capital misstep—and the finishing one was

9. Possibly John Cummings of Philadelphia: Charles H. Lincoln, ed.,
Naval Records of the American Revolution 1775–1788 (Washington, 1906), p.
444. We have not found Deane's letters to Bancroft or to Beaumarchais,
mentioned below.
    1. For the siege of Newport see Peters' letter of Aug. 13. Soon after it
began, d'Estaing's fleet put to sea to meet Admiral Howe's fleet and was
subsequently damaged in a storm. This damage and the reported arrival of
British naval reinforcements led the French admiral to sail for Boston on
Aug. 21/22. Gen. Sullivan managed a successful retreat a week later. See
Christopher Ward, *The War of the Revolution*, (2 vols., New York, 1952), II,
590–3 and Emery's letter of Oct. 7.
    2. This dispute was quelled by Washington and others: Freeman, *Wash-
ington*, V, 73–6; William C. Stinchcombe, *The American Revolution and the
French Alliance* (Syracuse, [1969]), 51–7; Smith, *Letters*, X, 636–7.

his quitting the harbor of New Port to go out after Lord Howe just at the Instant when Genl. Sullivan was ready, in Consequence of an express Agreement with the Count, to Attack the place. By this last measure he has left Genl. Sullivan exposed to suffer exceedingly in his retreat which will at best be disgraceful, and excessively Mortifying. I have not to this Moment settled any Measures with Congress, but I hope to Soon and that I shall have the pleasure of embracing You in Paris early Next Winter.[3] My Compliments to Freinds. Mr. Beach, and Family, are still in the Country. Be assured that in whatever part of the World I am I shall never cease to be with the greatest respect, and Esteem Your sincere Freind and Most Humble servant   S Deane

his Excellency Dr Franklin

Addressed: To / his Excellency / Benja Franklin / Minister for the United / States of America / at / Paris

Endorsed: Mr Deane Sept. 2. 1778

From ———— d'Urbainville[4]

ALS: American Philosophical Society

Monsieur,   à Toulouse ce 2. 7bre 1778
    Je rends avec plaisir cet hommage à une Nation naissante, qui offre à l'Univers le Modèle d'un des plus beaux gouvernemens politiques qui aient eû lieu. Puisse votre Constitution nationale ne recevoir Jamais aucune atteinte; et accélérer l'heureuse révolution que le progrès des lumières semble annoncer comme prochaine, en faveur du Commerce des Na-

---

3. An expectation shared by BF: see his letter to Lovell, July 22. Deane had testified to Congress on August 17 and 21 about "his whole transactions in France": *JCC*, XI, 801, 802, 826. His hopes of quick congressional approval were soon frustrated: see his letter to BF below, Oct. 21.

4. Director of the *Journal du Languedoc* in Toulouse, as he identifies himself at the end of the 109-line long "Diatribe en vers sur le Peuple anglois" which he enclosed. See Anne-Marie Chouillet, *et al.*, *Dictionnaire des journalistes (1600–1789) . . . Supplément . . .* (4 vols. to date, 1980–), II, 16, 19.

tions! On l'aura dûe, Monsieur, en grande partie, aux principes lumineux que votre Congrès met en pratique dans ses traités.

Si (ce dont Je n'ose me flatter) vous jugez que cette Diatribe mérite L'impression, en françois, ou en traduction angloise, qui pourroit être beaucoup meilleure que l'Original; je vous supplie de m'en addresser quelques Exemplaires. Je suis avec autant d'admiration, que de respect, Monsieur, Votre très humble et très obéissant Serviteur   D'URBAINVILLE

Philip Hancock to the American Commissioners

(I) ALS: Historical Society of Pennsylvania; (II) AL (draft): American Philosophical Society

On the supposition that these memoranda were written on the same day, we are publishing together the petition of Philip Hancock to the American Commissioners and the version Franklin rewrote for him in clear, forceful English. Franklin, like Georges Grand, was moved by the plight of this man of good will and his commitment to the Americans imprisoned in England.

I.

[after September 2, 1778][5]
The Reason of my Addresing His Excellance and you Honnourd Sirs Is to Inform you that Being an Inhabatant of Plymouth Dock ware a great many of the Subects of the United States are In Prisond And Being Convinced of the Rectude of the Conduct of the Ammericans In Revfuten the Iniquetas Accounts of the British Ministrey was willing to Contrubet My Mite According to my Privet Station in Life to Promote that glourse Cause they was Engaged in. I therefore Shall give your Honnours a small Spaceman [specimen] of what I have Done not Being able to give your Honnours a Perfect Account

5. On that date he was in Brussels, where he borrowed 124 *l.t.*, en route from Amsterdam. The commissioners' accounts with F. Grand, entry of Nov. 18, in Taylor, *Adams Papers*, VII, to be published under Nov. 12; Georges Grand to BF, Aug. 27.

not haveing any Books hear To Refore to only what I Can at Present Recllect.

When I sett out from home it was fare from my Intention to ask any favours from his Exellency or you, But to settle some Plan for the Relife of the Unhappey Suffers that for the feauter might fall in my way on that Account Sirs By the advice of many friends to the Cause was the Reason of my Jurney to Parris.

But Being So Unlucky to Relese an Ungrateffull Villin[6] has Been the Cause of Laying me under the Imbrasment of Beging the asistance of His Exellency and you to Enable me to Return home. I hope Therefore That His Excellency and you will take My Cause In to You Conserdation and any Favour Received will meet with the most gratefulst Return from Your most Obligd and Obedient Servant   PHILIP HANCOCK

To his Excellency Benj. Franklin and the Honourable Commisonrss of the United States of Ammerica.

II.

Gentlemen,   [after September 2, 1778]
   I beg leave to inform you, that being an Inhabitant of Plymouth Dock, where a great many of the Subjects of the United States are imprison'd, and being convinc'd of the Rectitude of the American Cause, and compassionating the Sufferings of those in Confinement, I was willing to contribute my Mite to their Relief, and to assist them in escaping to serve that just Cause, which I did according to my Ability at first, but was thereby gradually brought on to do more than I could afford, of which I give you herewith a sketch from Memory, having when I set out from home no Intention of asking the Favour of anything in Return. My Purpose was, at the Request of some Friends to the Cause, to make a short Trip to Paris, to concert with you some Method of assisting the Prisoners, (as we durst not write upon the Subject,) and of providing for the Expence which was become too heavy to be continued by pri-

6. David Welsh.

vate Persons. I am ready to give your Honours all the Information I can respecting the Matter; and I offer my Service to
execute any Orders you may think fit to give me, in behalf of
the Prisoners. But having the Misfortune to be accompanied
into Holland by an ungrateful Villain, whom I had reliev'd,
and who after plundering me left me sick there, I have not
wherewith left to pay my Expences back without your kind
Assistance.[7] Be pleased, Gentlemen, to consider this, from
Your most obedient humble Servant

To the honourable the Commissioners of the United States of
America.

Notation in Franklin's hand: Draft of Memoire for Mr. Hancock

A Page from the Visitors' Book

D: American Philosophical Society

[after September 2, 1778][8]

Mr. Me. et Mlle. Defouchy sont venus pour avoir l'honneur de
voir Monsieur franklin.[9]

Comte de Mac Donald Colonel.[1]

P. Hancock, from England au Caffe anglais Rue st. honore du
sergent.

Hemery fondeur en carataire d'ainprimery Rue st. jaque che
Mr. Canon Cordonier visavi le notaire.

<hr/>

7. Hancock received 600 *l.t.* from BF and JA on Sept. 22: Taylor, *Adams Papers*, VI, 360. He presumably returned to England.
8. See the preceding document.
9. Jean-Paul Grandjean de Fouchy, an astronomer, had been *secrétaire perpétuel* of the Académie des Sciences from 1743 to 1776. *DBF*.
1. See XXIII, 168 n, where MacDonald's rank was that of captain.

To David Hartley

Transcript: Library of Congress

Dear Sir   Passy, Sept. 3. 1778.

I received duly your Favours of July 14. and August 14. I hoped to have answered them sooner, by sending the Passport. Multiplicity of Business has I suppose been the only Occasion of Delay in the Ministers to consider of and make out the said Passport.[2] I hope now soon to have it, as I do not find there is any Objection made to it. In a former Letter I propos'd to you that the Exchange would in my opinion be preferable at or near Brest, and I expected some time your Answer on that Point, but perhaps you have not received my Letter, for you say nothing of it.[3]

I wish with you as much for the Restoration of Peace, as we both formerly did for the Continuance of it. But it must now be a Peace of a different kind. I was fond to a Folly of our *British Connection*, and it was with infinite Regret that I saw the Necessity you would force us into of breaking it: But the extream Cruelty with which we have been treated has now extinguish'd every Thought of returning to it, and separated us for ever. You have thereby lost Limbs that will never grow again. We too have suffered greatly but our Losses will soon be repair'd, by our good Government, our Industry, and the Fertility of our Country. And we now see the Mischievous Consequences of such a Connection, and the Danger of their being repeated if we should be weak enough again to enter into it: We see them too plainly ever to listen in the least to any such Proposition. We may therefore with great Propriety take leave of you in those beautiful Lines of Dante to the late Mistress of his Affections, [. . .][4]

---

2. The commissioners had sent requests for the promised passport on Aug. 28 and 30.

3. BF's letter is missing; his last extant one on the subject, July 13, still discussed using Calais as the transfer point.

4. The quotation was not transcribed. He may have had in mind Dante's last words to Beatrice in Canto XXXI of *Il Paradiso*: "O lady in whom my hope takes its root . . . / Thou has brought me, a slave, to freedom's state, / Through all those roads, by use of every means / Which thou didst have the power to employ . . . " *Divine Comedy*, Thomas Bergin, trans., (New York, 1955), p. 99 of third pagination.

I receiv'd the Thermometer safe, and thank you for your kind Care in sending it.[5] You have not mention'd to me whether Parsons's Bill on Nesbit was accepted and paid.[6] By some Circumstances I suspect it was not, and that I was cheated. Please to present my Respects to your amiable Sister,[7] and believe me ever, my dear Friend Yours most affectionately

B FRANKLIN

Notation: Benjamin Franklin to David Hartley

Penet, D'Acosta frères & Cie.[8] to the American Commissioners
ALS: American Philosophical Society

⟨Nantes, September 3, 1778, in French: We are enclosing a letter for you brought from Boston by our ship *Le Courier de l'Europe* and renew our offer of services.⟩

From Dumas
ALS: American Philosophical Society; AL (draft): Algemeen Rijksarchief

Monsieur,   La haie 3e Sept. 1778.

Le sujet de la présente est une affaire très délicate, qui me fait prendre le parti de vous l'adresser en particulier, afin de laisser à votre sagesse toute la liberté de la peser, et de voir ce qu'il sera à propos de laisser connoître et faire.

There is a blank space in the manuscript in which someone has written, "Mr. Newby must get some Italian scholar to point out those stanzas and have them placed here."

5. The thermometer was not mentioned in any of Hartley's prior extant letters.

6. See BF to Mrs. Parsons, [Aug. 12].

7. Mary Hartley, David's half-sister, for whom see George Herbert Guttridge, *David Hartley, M.P., an Advocate of Conciliation, 1774–1783* ([Berkeley and London, 1926]) p. 235.

8. Penet's new partners in Nantes. D'Acosta frères were a Nantes merchant firm which was engaged to a significant degree in transatlantic trade: Villiers, *Commerce colonial,* p. 405.

Les Etats sont rassemblés depuis hier. J'ai vu *notre Ami*.⁹ Il a commencé par me faire part de la démarche suivante qu'il vient de faire. Un Marchand d'Amsterdam est venu lui parler, pour savoir si la Régence d'Amsterdam seroit disposée à faire favoriser les liaisons naissantes directes entre les sujets de cette Rep. et celle des Etats-Unis de l'Amérique, qu'il s'étoit trouvé *par hazard* à Francfort avec Mr. Lee, *l'un des Plénipotentiaires des Etats-Unis de l'Am.*, chargé de faire un emprunt d'environ 700,000 florins à Amsterdam, et que lui, Marchand, seroit bien aise de contracter pour avoir le débit de ce papier, si la Régence d'Amst. vouloit témoigner, par une déclaration qu'il feroit parvenir à Mr. Lee, ses dispositions de favoriser, en tout ce qui dépendroit d'elle, l'amitié et le commerce entre les sujets réciproques.¹ Mr. V. B.[van Berckel], bien aise de profiter de l'occasion qui se présentoit pour faire déclarer la Régence d'Amsterdam, s'est fait autoriser par elle à donner une telle déclaration, pour être envoyée à Mr. Lee comme à un Plénipotentiaire compétent, dans la persuasion que le Marchand étoit véridique, jointe à la supposition qu'il étoit bien instruit. Après ce récit, Mr. V. B. m'a sommé de lui dire mon sentiment sur le tout, et ce que j'en savois. J'ai répondu, que je ne connoissois d'autres Plénipotentiaires que ceux qui, comme il le savoit lui-même, sont à Paris, à la tête desquels est Mr. Franklin, auxquels je rendois compte en détail, ainsi qu'à l'hon. Congrès en substance, de tout ce qui passoit par mes mains, pour remplir les devoirs de l'Agence et de la Confiance,

9. Van Berckel was in collusion with Jean de Neufville, the banker sent to meet in Frankfurt with William Lee: Jan W. Schulte Nordholdt, *The Dutch Republic and American Independence* (trans. Herbert H. Rowen; Chapel Hill and London, [1982]), pp. 64–6; Taylor, *Adams Papers*, VII, under Sept. 4.

1. On Sept. 4 the two met again at Aix-la-Chapelle (Aachen), where they drafted a treaty of amity and commerce between the Netherlands and the United States: Wharton, *Diplomatic Correspondence*, II, 787–98; Samuel Flagg Bemis, *The Diplomacy of the American Revolution*, rev. ed. (Bloomington, Ind., [1957]), 157–61. Neither man possessed diplomatic standing for such an action and they did immense harm. In 1780 the British captured Henry Laurens while en route to a diplomatic post in the Netherlands and thereby procured a copy of this draft treaty. They subsequently were able to use it as an excuse for opening war on the Dutch: Ian R. Christie, *The End of North's Ministry 1780–1782* (London, 1958), pp. 243–50.

dont le très-hon. Congrès m'avoit honoré directement depuis 1775, dont il m'honorait encore, et dont j'osois croire que je serois toujours digne; qu'à la vérité j'étois en correspondance amicale avec Mr. Wm. Lee, dans laquelle j'avois tâché de lui rendre des services personnels, tels que je serois toujours prêt à en rendre à tous les Américains, et à lui sur-tout, comme au frere de Mr. A. Lee Plénipotentiaire, et de Mr. R. H. Lee Membre du Congrès et l'un des Membres actuels du Committé des affaires étrangeres; mais que je n'étois point instruit de la nature de sa mission et de ses opérations;[2] que quant à une négociation d'emprunt, je croyois devoir lui dire en confidence que le dessein en étoit formé et seroit, selon toute apparence, bientôt exécuté; que le domicile de cette négociation étoit ar- rêté, et les contractants, qui s'en chargeroient à Amsterdam, choisis; que je savais cela de la bouche de ces contractants, de la véracité desquels il m'étoit impossible de douter; que quant à la déclaration remise au Marchand pour Mr. Lee, il convenoit que Mr. V. B. m'en remît une tout pareille, dont j'enverrois une Copie de sa part aux Plénipotentiaires à Paris, et une autre Copie dans le premier paquet que j'expédierois pour le Congrès. Il m'a donné parole de le faire, dès qu'il sera de retour à Amsterdam. Enfin il m'a témoigné s'interesser pour le Marchand qui a fait l'ouverture, comme pour un homme qui ne devoit pas souffrir du mal-entendu, s'il y en avoit. Je lui ai donné parole à mon tour, que dès qu'il en sera temps, j'adres- serai ce Marchand aux personnes qui seront chargées de la négociation de la part du Congrès par Messrs. les Plenipoten- tiaires afin qu'il puisse souscrire pour telle somme qu'il jugera à propos, et Mr. V. B. est content de cela; comme aussi, de vous faire parvenir, Monsieur, à l'avenir, directement, par mes mains, et point par d'autres, tout ce qui pourra contribuer à cimenter les liaisons desirées de part et d'autre: chose qu'il m'a avoué après cela lui avoir été conseillée comme convenable et

2. So far Dumas had been talking about the negotiation between W. Lee and Jean de Neufville, meeting in Frankfurt. From here on (up to the words: "quant à la déclaration remise au Marchand ... ") he addresses himself to the loan William Lee planned to float in Amsterdam: see the following document.

importante, par une personne de grand poids, à qui il avoit eu occasion de parler de la déclaration accordée.

J'ajouterai à tout cela, que s'il y avoit dans cette démarche un peu de précipitation, il ne faut l'attribuer qu'à la peur salutaire que je n'ai cessé d'imprimer, et à l'empressement, qui en est une conséquence naturelle, de Mr. V. B., de saisir les occasions, pour prévenir toute impression désavantageuse que les Anglois voudroient donner des Hollandois, afin de les faire exclure, ou traiter moins favorablement, dans un Traité de paix.

Le très-hon. Congrès a dans ses dépôts mon serment de fidélité dans la premiere dépêche que j'ai eu l'honneur de lui écrire. C'est en conséquence de ce serment, et par conséquent sans acception de personne, que je crois remplir mon devoir, en vous rendant le compte ci-dessus. Du reste, je me repose, quant à mon sort, avec une parfaite confiance, sur la justice et sur la magnanimité des Etats-unis, que j'ai le bonheur de servir, et sur votre affection, que je mériterai toute ma vie par le respect et l'attachement avec lequel je suis véritablement, Monsieur Votre très humble et très obéissant serviteur

DUMAS

Paris à S. E. Mr. le D. Franklin, Min. Plenip. des Etats-Unis de l'Am.

Dans ce moment, je viens de recevoir avis de notre bon Chevalier [Georges Grand], que les titres nécessaires pour ouvrir la négociation, sont en chemin, et attendus tous les jours, et qu'il m'informera du moment de leur arrivée. Tant mieux. J'ai compris par quelques mots échappés, que bien des gens, et des premiers d'Amst. prendront de ce papier avec avidité. Mais une concurrence dans cette conjoncture, sans réussir au gré de ceux qui l'entreprendroient, ne feroit que nuire au tout. Permettez-moi, Monsieur, d'espérer, que lorsqu'il sera temps de faire des Eclats, ce sera vous que je verrai venir ici recueillir la gloire de mettre la derniere main à la grande oeuvre.

Notation: Dumas Sept 3. 78

346

From Georges Grand

ALS: American Philosophical Society

Monsieur   Amsterdam le 3 Septe 1778

J'ay eu l'honneur de vous rendre Compte, des manoeuvres de M. W. L. et de ses propositions, pour ouvrir icy une négociation particuliere de F 700/m pour la Province de Virginie.[3]

Je m'etais flaté que mon Refus et les raisons dont je l'ai apuyé l'auraient détourné de suivre un projet aussi contraire aux Interets des Etats Unis que nuisible à leur Credit.

Mais Vous verrés par la Lettre cy Jointe, que je viens de recevoir de M. Dumas,[4] que bien loin de se rebuter, il s'est arrangé avec un autre Maison d'icy avec laquelle il à fait un programme, ou Traitté par main de Notaire, qui engage non seulement la Province de Virginie, mais les Treize Etats unis ce que Je ne crois, ni praticable, ni possible, Sans Votre concours et celuy de Messieurs Vos Collègues.

Il faut espérer que le Livre[5] que Vous m'avés annoncé nous parviendra assés Tot, pour prévenir l'effet de toutes ces menées. J'ay l'honneur d'etre, avec l'attachement le plus respectueux Monsieur Votre tres humble et Tres obeissant serviteur

GRAND

M. Le Doctr. Franklin

Addressed: To / The Honble. Doctor Franklin / Paris.

Endorsed: Mr. Grand Amsterdam Projects of Mr. W Lee

3. Governor Patrick Henry of Virginia had sent William Lee authorization to obtain for his state 2,000,000 *l.t.* of war supplies or to borrow money for their purchase: Boyd, *Jefferson Papers*, III, 90–1. The 700,000 florins Lee proposed to raise in the Netherlands were roughly equivalent to 1,650,000 *l.t.*

4. On Sept. 2 Dumas wrote two letters informing Grand of Lee's plan. In the first he told Grand that he had attempted to discourage the plan; in the second he said he believed it an intrigue aimed at supplanting Grand. Both letters are at the APS.

5. The book of promissory notes was on its way.

From Thomas Mante

ALS: American Philosophical Society

This writer, author of the *History of the late War in America* ... (London, 1772), was an English military historian of some note.[6] The bizarre episode referred to in this letter and five subsequent ones belongs to a later and unfamiliar period of his life. Two quite different versions of the events leading up to the man's imprisonment are available.

One, highly subjective, is to be found in an undated memoir he sent to Antoine-Jean Amelot, Ministre de la Maison du Roi, or secretary of the interior. It explains that, born English but eventually naturalized French, he entered in July, 1777, into a verbal agreement with the comte de Boisgelin[7] to raise English sheep on the count's estate in Brittany, for which he was to receive a salary and various perquisites. Within two months, on his return from a brief absence, Mante found that Boisgelin had seized his papers and planned to drag him to court, presumably to avoid fulfilling his own part of the contract. Before Mante could lodge a counterclaim, he was thrown in jail and left there against all rules of law. He demanded his release.[8]

The other version, pieced together from a number of messages about Mante that crisscrossed the Channel during 1777 and 1778, implies that he was a spy working either for France or for England, possibly for both, and distrusted equally in Paris and London.[9]

A final puzzling touch is that BF sent this man some money. An entry of 48 *l.t.* for Mante, dubbed ChY [Charity] is recorded under the date of August 19, two weeks *before* this appeal.[1]

---

6. See XXIII, 255 n; *DNB*.

7. Louis-Bruno de Cucé, comte de Boisgelin (1733–94), a member of the Ordre du St.-Esprit, had been made Master of the Wardrobe the previous February, around the time of Mante's arrest. Lewis, *Walpole Correspondence*, VII, 14, and *passim*.

8. This memoir is at the APS. Mante argued that he had already imported 176 of the agreed 200 sheep; his perquisites were to include a house, land, and 12,000 *l.t.* a year.

9. Stevens, *Facsimiles*, XIV, no. 1413; XVI, nos. 1587, 1594. See also Frank Monaghan, "A New Document on the Identity of 'Junius,'" *Journal of Modern History*, IV (1932), 68–71; Claude-Anne Lopez, "Benjamin Franklin and William Dodd: A New Look at an Old Cause Célèbre," APS *Proc.*, vol. 129, no. 3 (1985), 260–7.

1. BF's Accounts as Commissioner: Account V (XXIII, 20).

Au Fort L'Eveque[2] ce 3d. Septemr. 1778.

I have no other title, Sir, to implore assistance from you but that which those who are oppressed with injustice may be permitted to claim from humanity. In a stranger even this may be thought presumption. Yet to solicite aleviation of affliction is a privilege accorded to distress. Seven months the iron hand of power has kept me in a prison, deprived me of all that I possessed: the wretchedness of this situation is encreased by the torments of the stone, whilst I am destitute of the smallest means to procure the least aleviation to my misery. Dare I hope that in this state you will humanely grant me some relief.

M. Le Comte de Boisgelin is my persecutor, though at this moment he is indebted to me 1,500 l.t. The humanity of M. Turgot has ineffectually endeavoured to soften the obduracy of this Tyrant.[3] The parliament must then judge between us, but in the mean time I perish for want, literally, not having bread to eat.

I beg your acceptance of the book[4] which accompanies this letter, as a feeble mark of my hommage to your distinguished Character: Having the honour to be with respect, Sir, Your most obedient most humble Servant   THO. MANTE

The Bearer may be entrusted with any reply that You may chuse to honour me with.

Endorsed: Mante

2. Generally spelled For-l'Evêque, this Parisian jail was reserved mostly for actors and debtors. It was demolished in 1780, shortly after Mante's release.

3. Turgot and Mante may have met in 1776, when the latter tried to interest the French government in a new method for purifying salt and was referred to Turgot in his capacity as Comptroller General. Stevens, *Facsimiles*, IX, no. 907. On March 19, 1778, Turgot wrote his friend Pierre-Samuel Du Pont (later known as Dupont de Nemours) that Mante was a consummate crook who had defrauded Boisgelin out of 24.000 l.t. Schelle, *Œuvres de Turgot*, V, 546–7. Nevertheless, Turgot subsequently tried in vain to soften Boisgelin's attitude: *ibid.*, p. 575.

4. His *Traité des prairies artificielles* (Paris, 1778). BF's copy is in the Yale University Library.

From ───── de Perygnon

ALS: American Philosophical Society

Monsieur   Paris ce 3. 7bre. 1778
   La réputation d'homme obligeant dont vous jouisséz m'enhardit à oser vous demander quelques instants. C'est un fait
arrivé à Philadelphie qui donne matiere à un procès considerable par sa nature et les suites qu'il aura.
   On a eu occasion de Soutenir au Conseil Supérieur du Port
au Prince, isle et côte françoises de St. Domingue, la validité
d'un mariage contracté à Philadelphie dans l'Eglise Catholique
entre Alexis Le Blanc et anne Tendon,[5] l'un et l'autre natifs de
Beausejour en Acadie. Ce fut vers la fin de la derniere Guerre,
pendant la Translation des acadiens en Carroline et à Philadelphie, que ce noeud se forma. Le mariage fut célébré par le
Reverend Pere Ferdinand Farmer,[6] qui a délivré l'acte de célé-
bration cijoint. Anne Tendon passat à la Paix avec ses pere et
mere et son mary à St. Domingue; Les premiers Morts, elle
chercha à se soustraire au Second, Le renia pour époux. Pendant un Voyage de cet homme, elle se remaria à un autre, son
premier existant. On plaide sur la nullité du Second mariage,
comme formé avec empéchement dirimant.[7] Cette femme a
fait appelle comme d'abus de son premier mariage 1°. Sans

   5. The Feb. 10, 1763 marriage of Alexis LeBlanc and Anna Tendon (misspelled Dendon) is listed in Francis T. Furey, "Father Farmer's Marriage
Register, 1758–1786, preserved at St. Joseph's Church, Philada.," American
Catholic Historical Society of Philadelphia *Records*, II, (1886–88), 282.
   6. Ferdinand Farmer, né Steinmeyer, (1720–86), a Swabian, entered the
Society of Jesuits in 1743, arrived in America in 1752, and settled in Philadelphia in 1758. During the British occupation he was asked to serve as
chaplain for a regiment of Roman Catholic volunteers. When the University of Pennsylvania was reorganized in 1779 he became a trustee under the
provision that the trustees should include the senior pastors of the six principal denominations. See Martin I. J. Griffin, "Rev. Ferdinand Farmer S.J. of
Philadelphia, 1758–86," *The American Catholic Historical Researches*, XIV
(1897), 2–5.
   7. A term of canon law meaning an obstacle that will, in the eyes of the
Church, invalidate a marriage.

consentement des pere et mère, 2°. Sans publication de bancs 3°. en Etat de minorité. 4°. Sans signature des parties et des témoins ni mention qu'ils ne savent signer, 5°. avec l'assistance de deux temoins seulement. Un premier arrêt a jugé qu'on ne pouvoit statuer sur ces moyens d'abus, que par le voeu des Loix angloises, et a demandé à cet effet un acte de Notoriété de Philadelphie sur tous ces points et sur la tenue des Registres. On a pu se procurer cet acte de notoriété à St. Domingue, et on se propose de s'adresser d'ici au Congrès pour se le procurer.

J'ai l'honneur de vous observer que le consentement des pere et mere est établi par la Cohabitaion des deux époux chés eux, qu'anne Tendon avoit 21 ans lors de son mariage, et vous verrés par l'acte cijoint, que le reverend Pere Farmer dit avoir observé les regles et usages de l'ancienne Eglise Catholique de Philadelphie. Je vous Supplie de daigner me donner Votre Avis au pied de l'acte ci joint, de marquer si le défaut de publication de bancs opere la nullité d'un mariage.[8] 2°. Jusqu'à quel âge le Consentement des Parens est nécessaire, et quel est celui de majorité pour les filles. 3°. Combien il faut de témoins, s'il faut qu'ils Signent ainsi que les parties, ou s'il faut faire mention qu'ils ne le savent. 4°. Sur la tenue des Registres à Philadelphie. Enfin, si d'après l'assertion du Missionnaire, devant insérer qu'il a observé les regles et usages, ce premier mariage ne seroit pas à Philadelphie un empechement invincible à la formation d'un Second noeud, le premier existant.

J'ose croire, Monsieur, que vous ne dedaignerés pas rendre ce Service à un Citoyen honnête qui vous le demande avec la

8. In Father Farmer's marriage records the dispensation of the banns is sometimes noted. This was not the case in the record of the LeBlanc-Dendon (Tendon) marriage.

derniere instance. Je suis avec respect, Monsieur, Votre très humble et très obeissant serviteur

DE PERYGNON
Chés M. de Chanseru
membre de la société royale de Médecine
rue Ste. anne butte St. Roch[9]

Endorsed: De Perygnon abt a Marriage[1]

Berubé de Costentin to the American Commissioners[2]

ALS: American Philosophical Society

⟨Brest, September 4, 1778, in French: In accordance with your request of August 15, Thomas Wilkinson left yesterday for St. Pol de Léon. I await your orders regarding the prisoners here.⟩

Dumas to the American Commissioners[3]

ALS: American Philosophical Society; AL (draft): Algemeen Rijksarchief

⟨The Hague, September 4, 1778, in French: Mr. van Berckel and I propose an ambitious initiative[4] for which we need supporting papers. Please send either a proposal for a general treaty of amity and commerce or a declaration that you desire the Netherlands to conclude with the United States a treaty similar to the American treaty with France. The Grand Facteur approves this plan and thinks no time should be lost. If

9. Roussille de Chamseru was in fact a member of the Société royale de médecine: *Almanach Royal* for 1778, p. 603.
1. De Perygnon also sent a copy of a June 12, 1776 deposition of Father Farmer that he had performed the marriage according to the rules and usages of the Catholic Church.
2. Published in Taylor, *Adams Papers*, VII.
3. Published in Taylor, *Adams Papers*, VII.
4. That of obtaining from the regents of Amsterdam a declaration in favor of a Dutch-American commercial treaty.

sent at once it will arrive just as the Assembly of the States of Holland adjourns and van Berckel will be able to begin immediately proceedings with Amsterdam. This plan is very auspicious because it would no longer be America soliciting, but the city pressing for it. Our friend is as enthusiastic about it as I am. He has composed an important document on Dutch politics. The merchants of Amsterdam have agreed to equip fifteen warships at their own expense. Several merchants have asked for compensation for vessels seized by the British. If the republic tolerates such seizures France threatens to exclude Dutch coastal shipping from her ports.[5] This has reduced an important personage [the Stadholder?] to silence. A new 54-gun ship has caught fire under suspicious circumstances.⟩

From John Channing   ALS: Historical Society of Pennsylvania

Honorable Sir   [on or before September 4, 1778[6]]

I Leave A List of Americans who made their Escape from England, myself who had a Leuitnts Commission for the Continental Navy.[7] We are desitute of money for to Repair to America therefore request your assistance and am with Respect Sir Your very humble Servant   JOHN CHANNING

PS We will wait on yr honor at 9 oClock
Wm. Knapp
Wm. Daniels
James Spencer
David Lymon
Joseph Pulford[8]

5. A diplomatic tactic which eventually proved very successful in stimulating Dutch resistance to the British: see Samuel Flagg Bemis, *The Diplomacy of the American Revolution* (rev. ed.; Bloomington, Ind., [1957]), 138–40.
6. When BF and JA gave them 10 louis apiece: commissioners' account with Ferdinand Grand, Taylor, *Adams Papers*, VI, 360.
7. See his previous letter, Aug. 24.
8. Channing and these five men appear both in the Alphabetical List of Escaped Prisoners, and in the second memorandum summarized in XXV, 4.

From David Williams[9]　　　ALS: American Philosophical Society

Dear Sir,　　　London Meard Street Soho Sept 4th 1778.

You will see by these Proposals that I persevere in the prosecution of a Plan, which you seemed willing to support while in England. I have apprized you of the various Steps I have taken in my Letters to you in America; some of which I am told you have received. And I sent you two of the Liturgies, but by such conveyances that I doubt of their having reached you.[1]

On your departure, my affairs wore a very discouraging aspect. I was assured of a large subscription by a Society consisting mostly of my provincial Neighbors and Acquaintance; some of whom accompanied me to your house. On your departure I lost them wholly; as well as several others who had appeared sanguine in supporting the Design. Some of the Gentlemen who met at the Coffee-house, and at your Room to read the Liturgy,[2] were disposed to become Subscribers, if I chose to hazard the Undertaking. I opened the Chapel therefore, on the seventh of April as an Adventure. Great Numbers came to it out of Curiosity; some behaved indecently; and all with a shy timidity; excepting two or three of my particular friends. I conducted the service for some time, with a subscription only of eight Guineas; the greater part of which was given by two or three persons of our Club at the Coffee-house. My expences continued much above my Income for two years. But the Design is gradually succeeding, for those who have continued to attend at the Chapel have formed themselves into a Society this year; have engaged to defray all expences; and to allow me a small salary.[3]

9. The dissenting preacher; see above, XXI, 119–20; XXII, 173–4.
1. "These proposals" are discussed later in the letter. The overall "Plan" doubtless had to do with the promotion of deist doctrine and order of worship. While in London, BF had been interested in these projects, especially in liturgical reform. The "Liturgies" were probably copies of his *Liturgy on the Universal Principles of Religion and Morality* (London, 1776). We have no evidence that they were received.
2. BF's fellow members of the Club of Thirteen.
3. Williams, originally a dissenter and by now an outright deist, had withdrawn from his Highgate congregation in 1773. He is reporting here

My old Friends, seeing I have not ruined myself, have made proposals to open another Chapel for me; and the Plan is now under consideration. But my Instructions are to keep it secret till the beginning of the Winter.

The present Managers of our little ecclesiastical affairs are of opinion that I should publish the Lectures I delivered in the first two Years; and I have taken their advice as to the time and manner of publication.

If, in the Intervals of your more important business, you can attend to such an affair as this, and will procure me any subscribers, I shall be much obliged to you. If not, you will be so good as to leave those Proposals which are *signed* at Mr. Pissot's Bookseller, who will probably have some of my Proposals to return in April or May.

I am afraid it is in vain to ask for that little *moral work* which you had thoughts of finishing when you left England; to which there was *not much to be done*; and which you wished to have distributed with the Liturgy at the Chapel. It was written in a little Pocket-Book.[4] If you could send it it would be very acceptable and useful to many people here. I am Sir with great regard your much obliged humble Servant   D WILLIAMS

I have sent 20 Proposals signed.

Addressed: Dr. Franklin

Endorsed: D. Williams, Revd. Subscription Sept. 4 1778

---

on the establishment of a deist congregation, using his liturgy, which opened a chapel in Margaret Street on April 7, 1776. *DNB*; David Williams, *Incidents in My Own Life* . . . (ed. Peter France; [Brighton], 1980), pp. 17–18. This congregation was beset with such financial difficulties and internal disputes that Williams eventually "relinquished" the undertaking. *Ibid.*, pp. 18–22. The subscription mentioned here was intended to rescue him from financial ruin. It led to the publication of his lectures under the title of *Lectures on the Universal Principles and Duties of Religion and Morality* (2 vols., London, 1779).

4. Our best guess is that the little moral work is BF's long-contemplated but never completed *Art of Virtue*, which he had apparently discussed with English friends as early as 1760. He first mentioned it in a letter to Lord Kames and described it at some length: IX, 104–5, 375. He promised Kames

René-Etienne Henry Vic Gaiault (or Gayault) de Boisbertrand:[5] Memorandum for the American Commissioners

ADS: Archives du Ministère des affaires étrangères, Harvard University Library; copies: University of Virginia Library, National Archives

⟨September 5,[6] 1778, in the third person, in French: At the beginning of May, 1776, Dubourg and Penet asked him to join the U.S. army; he was then a lieutenant colonel in the French cavalry. He would carry dispatches about the ministry's attitude toward the Americans, Dubourg told him, and be welcomed by Congress; 300 louis would be deposited for him in Paris. He chose two junior officers to accompany him, and soon received a two-year leave. Then Dubourg said the money was not available but that his passage would be repaid in America. Filled with admiration for those who were defying a mighty empire, he accepted.

He and his companions were put to the expense of waiting two months at Nantes for their ship, while Penet assured them that they would be reimbursed. During their wait, at Dubourg's request, he inspected and reported on some arms furnished by Montieu and La Tuillerie; the weapons were bad, he found, and Penet was being deceived. The deal was cancelled, thereby saving Congress more than £12,000.[7] The party sailed on September 10 in the *Hancock and Adams* which was captured, strangely enough, by a Rhode Island privateer; his servant and companions were kept on board, while he was sent a prisoner to New Bedford, where the committee released him; he went to Boston, and the authorities paid his way to

---

that a return to America would give him the leisure to complete it, but it evidently did not: XII, 162; XIV, 71. Part of *The Art of Virtue* BF appears to have incorporated into his autobiography: *Autobiog.*, pp. 148–60.

5. We have summarized the vicissitudes of this young Frenchman up to the end of 1776: XXII, 469 n.

6. So dated in another hand in the ADS in the AAE. The ADS at Harvard is dated in the same way the 7th, which must have been when the commissioners received the document with Sartine's second letter of the 6th.

7. See XXII, 459, 464 n.

Philadelphia. Near Morristown he fell in with Gen. Lee's army, which was in a major crisis, and joined it in hope of being useful; his dispatches he delivered to M. Couleaux, an associate of Penet, to take to Congress. Three days later Boisbertrand was captured with Lee and, wounded as he was, consigned to a frightful prison in New York. Not allowed to send for his servant or baggage, he slept on the floor for two months without blankets or change of clothing, and was fed on short rations of mouldy biscuit and salt pork.

The captain of the privateer put Boisbertrand's companions on an Irish prize, to be released ashore. But she was retaken; they were confined for a month in a dark cell on Rhode Island, then dispatched to his prison in New York. The party, thus reunited, was sent to England on February 14, 1777, and eventually committed to Forton, whence he escaped on July 23, 1778; the others are still there. It would take a volume to detail their sufferings.

Boisbertrand, back in France, is unemployed; the length of his imprisonment was unknown when his leave ran out and his place was filled.[8] In twenty-nine months since he was first given the dispatches for America he has spent 10,000 livres of his own money, and has lost an equal amount with his French position. He is also forced to replace the costly horses and baggage lost in America. Please take into consideration his zeal and his deprivations.[9] He asks for a brigadier general's rank in the U.S. army; Gen. Lee assured him that he would obtain it, and he now has even more claim to it. He will leave when ordered, and wishes to establish himself in America.)

8. By his brother: Bodinier, *Dictionnaire* under Gayault.
9. For the response see our note on Sartine's second letter of Sept. 6.

Abraham Whipple to the American Commissioners

Copy: Yale University Library

On board American Contin Frigate Providence
Gentlemen   Latt 47.30 Long 35.00 Septbr 5 1778.

This Oppertunity by a French Vessel[1] permits me to Acquaint you, that I am at present on my passage with the Boston and Ranger, have Captured a Brig laden with Provisions for the British forces at Pensacola, Ordered her for America Cargo, Beef Pork Flour, Butter &c. &c.

The Ships Crews are in general healthy and Officers and Mens in high Spirits.

Capt. Hinman who favours me with his Company for America is well on board, and Presents his respectful Complimts. Have the honour to remain Gentlemen Your most Obedient humble servant   AW

Honble Amer Commisrs Paris.

From Pierre-Augustin Caron de Beaumarchais

AL: American Philosophical Society

ce Samedi 5 7bre 1778.

Mr. De Beaumarchais a l'honneur de présenter son très humble hommage a Monsieur franklin. Il le prie de vouloir bien lui mander, par le postillon porteur de cette lettre, quel Jour il poura conférer avec Lui et Mr. Lée, Sur l'objet de la Théréze. Les lettres de Nantes exigent que Mr. De Beaumarchais donne promptement des ordres pour la vente, que le moment favorise.[2]

---

1. A note in the margin reads, "AW to Commissrs. Sent in a French Brig which we spoke with."

2. The *Thérèse* appears frequently in vol. XXIII; she was one of the ships chartered by Beaumarchais' trading company, Roderigue Hortalez & Cie. For the last year the commissioners had debated whether the firm (which had been established with funds loaned by the French and Spanish governments) was entitled to reimbursement for the goods it had supplied the United States; see especially XXV, 341–2. In May they had been ordered to

veille Rue du temple

Notations in different hands: M. De Beaumarchais 5 7bre. 1778 /
M. Beaumarchaises Card 5. Septr. 1778 / John Gilbank John
Gale[3]

From Rodolphe-Emmanuel Haller[4]

AL: American Philosophical Society

Hotell Colbert Septbr. 5. 1778
Mr. Haller Presents his most respectful Compliments to the
Right Honourable Doctor Franklin and shall be very glad of
his company at dinner on wednesday next the 9 inst.

PS Pray answer iff you Please

Addressed: To / The Right Honble. Doctr. Franklin Esqr / chez
Mr. Le Ray de / chaumont / Passy / hotel Colbert

---

liquidate accounts with Beaumarchais (XXVI, 475, acknowledged in the
commissioners' letter of July 29 to the committee, above). Now at issue
was the cargo the *Thérèse* had brought back from America. For further details about the dispute see Taylor, *Adams Papers*, VII, under Sept. 10, and
Morton, *Beaumarchais Correspondance*, IV, 229–30 n, 286.

3. The latter notation has nothing to do with Beaumarchais; Gilbank
and Gale were assisted by the commissioners on Sept. 12: Taylor, *Adams
Papers*, VI, 360. The first of these gentlemen, detained at Jersey, has appeared before: Ford to commissioners, July 21.

4. Born in Bern, son of the famous Swiss intellectual Albrecht von
Haller, Emmanuel (1747–1833?) married into a prominent Dutch merchant
family and moved to Paris in August, 1777. There he joined with Jean
Girardot de Marigny to take over, under the name of Girardot, Haller &
Cie., what used to be the Necker family bank. The new firm tried unsuccessfully to become primary bankers to the American commission. Known
as a brilliant though not always scrupulous businessman, Haller used his
contacts in Holland, England and Paris to speculate broadly on the war. He
was a long-standing associate of Thomas Walpole, whose Paris correspondence was forwarded through the firm (see above, under July 14). In August, 1778, Haller arranged a clandestine transfer of £50,000 in English
funds from Bancroft to Walpole. Lüthy, *Banque protestante*, II, 406–7, 603–6,
619–23.

To John Paul Jones   ALS: National Archives

Dear Captain   Passy, Sept. 6. 1778 5 AM.
    I received your Favours of the 24th and 31st of August. I
am told by Mr. C. that Mr. S.[5] is sorry you did not go with M.
D'Orvilliers. He had sent Orders for that Purpose, and your
staying at L'Orient occasion'd your missing the Opportunity.[6]
Your Letter was sent to the Prince de Nassau.[7] I am confident
something will be done for you, tho' I don't yet know what.
Dr. Bancroft has been indispos'd, and I have not lately seen
him, but hear he is getting better, and suppose he has written.
I go out of town early this Morning for a few Days,[8] but the
other Commissioners will answer your Letter. I am glad you
have procur'd a Guard for the Prisoners. It is a good Piece of
Service. They have concluded in England to send us an equal
Number of ours, and we expect to morrow to send the Passport for their Cartel Ship, which is to bring them.[9] If we are to
deliver theirs at Calais, I should be for accepting thankfully
the Offer you mention. We have no News from America but
what comes thro' England. Clinton's Letter is in the London
Gazette, and for Stile and Colouring is so like Keppel's, that I
cannot help thinking neither of them Originals, but both the
Performance of some underSecretary, whose Business it is to
cook the News for the Ministers.[1] Upon the whole we learn,
that the English Army was well worried in its March, and that
their whole Fleet and Forces are now block'd up in New-York
by Washington and Gates on the Land Side, and by Count

    5. Chaumont and Sartine.
    6. Jones, who had left Lorient in plenty of time, was both baffled and
enraged by this news. He fired off letters to the Prince of Nassau and later,
Sartine; copies of these were enclosed in his reply to BF of Sept. 14. The
enclosures are summarized there.
    7. Enclosed in Jones's of Aug. 24.
    8. He was going to Mme. Brillon's summer home in Anet.
    9. Sartine sent the passport to Vergennes that very day; see his letter to
the commissioners, Sept. 6.
    1. Keppel's letter, describing action with the French fleet, appeared in
The London Gazette, Aug. 3. Clinton's appeared in the Aug. 24 issue. It was
a copy of a genuine one written to Lord Germain on July 5, describing the
battle at Monmouth on June 28; the original is reproduced in Stevens, *Facsimiles*, XI, no. 1114.

D'Estaign by Sea, and that they will soon be in want of Provisions. I sympathise with you in what I know you must suffer from your present Inactivity, but have Patience. I am ever, with great Esteem, Dear Sir, Your most obedient humble Servant   B FRANKLIN

Addressed: A Monsieur / Monsieur le Capitaine Jones / dans le Service des Etats Unis / de l'Amerique Septentrionale / à Brest.

Endorsed: From His Excelly. Doctr. Franklin Passy Septr. 6th. 1778 Recd. Brest Septr. 8th. 1778 No. 4. & 5. Cartel

To Jacques Le Maire de Gimel[2]

Copy:[3] Library of Congress

On March 18, 1778, Capt. Jacques Le Maire de Gimel had set sail for his native France with letters from Patrick Henry to Franklin and William Lee. Lee's orders were to procure arms and ammunition for the state of Virginia. Le Maire, with the cooperation of the American agents, was to assist Lee in procuring and inspecting those military supplies.[4] What Le Maire encountered from the Lee brothers, rather than cooperation, was evasion and abuse, provoking a flurry of desperate letters to Franklin in the fall of 1778.

Le Maire's misadventures began in late May when he presented himself at Passy. With William Lee in Germany, Franklin immediately located three merchants each of whom was willing to undertake the whole order and give the desired credit. When Arthur Lee then insisted on taking charge of the business, the three possibilities vanished: one merchant flatly withdrew his offer; a second insisted that any agreement be co-signed by Franklin and Adams, which Lee refused; the third offer was rejected for reasons Franklin never knew.[5] Thereafter, Arthur kept the negotiations secret from his col-

2. We have found no trace of a letter to which BF is responding. However, Le Maire had discussed his situation with BF before leaving for Nantes, as he reminded him on Sept. 19 and Oct. 3, below.

3. In BF's hand.

4. See above, XXVI, 34–5 n, and our annotation of Grand's letter of Sept. 3.

5. See BF to Patrick Henry, Feb. 26, 1779 (APS), and to Le Maire, [after Oct. 15], below.

league, and sent Le Maire to Frankfurt to see his brother William.

William Lee had gotten wind of his orders before Le Maire arrived. He heard he was to purchase 1,000,000 *l.t.* worth of goods, but was concerned that the state had sent no authority to borrow money.[6] (In fact, Virginia was hoping to barter with tobacco.) As soon as Le Maire arrived, he was sent on what turned out to be a fruitless tour of Germany. Several of the manufacturers he contacted wrote directly to Franklin that they would supply the arms on Franklin's approval. The Doctor scrupulously turned over this correspondence to Arthur Lee who, to the best of our knowledge, let the matter drop.[7]

The Lees, in the meantime, had begun their own campaigns to quietly procure supplies directly from the French court. On June 3 Arthur requested brass cannon from Vergennes; he enlisted the prince de Montbarey, the French army minister, to follow up this request two days later with a list of Virginia's military needs and recommendations for supplying them. Vergennes replied to Lee on June 9 with a partial grant of guns.[8] William Lee was working through local French officials. He had persuaded the baron de Breteuil, French ambassador to the Austrian court, to deliver Vergennes the extensive list of desired articles which presumably had come with Le Maire. William's plan, as he wrote to his brother on June 24, was to convince the French court to make an outright loan of the 1,000,000 *l.t.*[9]

Le Maire continued his travels throughout the month of June, periodically sending progress reports to William Lee. He had gotten some firm proposals in Strasbourg; Lee, however, found the prices excessive, and answered that a contract was out of the question.[1] At some point before the beginning of August, Le Maire returned to Paris.

For reasons which remain unclear, Arthur Lee signed an agreement with Penet, d'Acosta & frères on July 1, providing for arms to be sent to Virginia no later than September.[2] This was done without

6. To Richard Henry Lee, May 30, 1778: Ford, *Letters of William Lee*, II, 443.

7. BF to Patrick Henry, Feb. 26, 1779 (APS).

8. Stevens, *Facsimiles*, VIII, nos. 830, 831, 833.

9. To Arthur Lee: Ford, *Letters of William Lee*, II, 448–51.

1. To Arthur Lee, June 27: *ibid.*, p. 461.

2. Lee to Penet, d'Acosta & frères, Nov. 10, 1778, a copy of which was enclosed in the firm's letter to BF, April 3, 1779 (APS).

the knowledge, or ultimate approval, of William, who maintained a long-standing animosity towards the firm. On August 4, Arthur Lee sent Le Maire to Nantes with authorization to examine and approve the arms and munitions.[3] The captain engaged five specialists in arms, and by mid-month they had begun to examine and test each piece. Le Maire's new problem, as becomes clear in this and the ensuing documents of this volume, was that Arthur Lee, having refused to answer his letters, now refused to honor his drafts. As the months wore on, Le Maire continued his work, exhausted his personal resources, and turned desperately to Franklin, who felt duty-bound not to interfere. Finally on October 15, Le Maire wrote to William Temple Franklin. The grandfather now seized a diplomatic opportunity for responding: he drafted an apologetic letter to the Frenchman, and apparently directed Temple to send it.[4] The entire incident, which continued well into 1779,[5] reveals another aspect of the brittle protocol observed between Franklin and his Chaillot colleague, and its effect on the individuals who were unlucky enough to fall between the cracks.

Sir   Passy, Sept. 6. 1778

As Mr. Lee has undertaken to furnish the whole of what was required by the Government of Virginia, I cannot with Propriety interfere in any Part of that Business, or give any Advice to purchase of other Persons than those he has agreed with. Otherwise I have a very good Opinion of Mr. Gruel, and am satisfy'd that if he engag'd in it, he would execute it with Honour; I would have you write again to Mr. Lee for the Money necessary for your Support. Perhaps Multiplicity of Business has occasion'd him to forget it. If Mr. Tessier shows

3. Lee to Penet, Aug. 4, 1778, a copy of which was enclosed in *ibid.*
4. See below, [after Oct. 15].
5. Thomas Jefferson was ultimately responsible for getting Le Maire compensated. The agent had "executed his Commission with a zeal and assiduity which we have rarely met with," Jefferson wrote Benjamin Harrison on Oct. 29, 1779: Boyd, *Jefferson Papers,* III, 124.

the Letter I gave him to the Governor,[6] it will do as well as if I wrote another. I am, &c.

To Capt. Lemare

Copy

Notation in Franklin's hand: Copy of Lett. to Capt. Le Maire from BF. Sept. 6. 78.

Sartine to the American Commissioners: Two Letters

(I) Copies: Library of Congress (two), Massachusetts Historical Society; (II) copies: Library of Congress, National Archives

I.

⟨Versailles, September 6, 1778, in French:[7] I have received your letter of August 30 last, and have sent M. de Vergennes the passport for the British ship involved in the exchange of prisoners; I shall order your prisoners at Brest kept under closer surveillance until exchanged.⟩

II.

Versailles, 6.7bre. 1778

Je joins, Messieurs, un Mémoire du S. Gaiwal [Gaiault] de Boisbertrand qui demande de l'emploi et de l'avancement dans les troupes des Etats Unis de l'Amerique, ainsi qu'il le lui avoit été promis.[8] Le cas particulier où il se trouve pour avoir cedé aux Instences qui lui ont été faites de passer au Service des Etats Unis, semble meriter quelque Consideration. Je ne peux refuser a l'intérêt que je prends à ce qui le regarde de vous le recommander et de vous prier de lui accorder des Lettres pres-

6. Missing. BF had also recommended this surgeon to Benjamin Rush: XXVI, 699–700.

7. Published in Taylor, *Adams Papers*, VII.

8. The memorandum is above, Sept. 5.

santes pour qu'il puisse être placé à son arrivée.⁹ J'ai l'honneur d'être avec beaucoup de Considération, Messieurs, Votre très humble et très obeissant serviteur. (Signé)   DE SARTINE.

From John Adams[1]   AL (draft): Massachusetts Historical Society

⟨Passy, September [6?]–13, 1778: In order to understand our affairs and to be able to account to our constituents we should decide which expenses we will pay jointly and which separately. I think we should pay jointly for the rent of the house and furniture, hire of coachman, horses, and carriage, wages of maitre d'hôtel and cook, and table expenses. We should pay separately for our clerks and servants, clothes, books, newspapers, and other expenses. I also feel we should keep an account of our common expenses and take receipts and that each of us should have a copy monthly. Memoir, September 13: This letter, written a week ago, was never sent. This morning, while Mr. Austin was present, Mr. W. T. Franklin brought the accounts for his family and offered that I should in future keep them.[2]⟩

9. Sartine expects Boisbertrand to return to the U.S., which he did not do. Two undated documents in the APS throw a little light on subsequent attempts to help him in Paris. One is a memorandum, endorsed by BF, in which the Frenchman repeats the salient points of his earlier one. The other is in two parts. The first appears to be a French draft prepared for BF by Le Veillard; it is a certification, doubtless meant to be signed by the commissioners, that the details of Boisbertrand's captivity are understated rather than exaggerated, and that his obtaining what he asks would be a great satisfaction to the U.S. The second is a note in BF's hand and signed by him as minister: "I am of Opinion that the Sufferings of M. de Bois Bertrand occasion'd by his Endeavours [in] their Service, being made known to the Congress, it will be very agreeable to them to understand that he has met with Consideration here on that Account." Both, we believe, were part of an effort to secure him some sort of compensation from the French authorities.

1. Published in Taylor, *Adams Papers*, VII, where the dating is explained.

2. Listed as Account III above, XXIII, 19. WTF's last entry is Aug. 24, 1778; he closed it as of Sept. 14, with a balance (later corrected) owed the com-

From Joan Derk van der Capellen tot den Pol[3]

Translations: Public Record Office,[4] National Archives; incomplete ALS: American Philosophical Society; incomplete copies: National Archives, Connecticut State Library, Massachusetts Historical Society (two)

Sir   Zwol September 6. [-after December 14] 1778.

I took the liberty to write you a Letter dated Zwol April 28. this year, and I was about writting you a second to inquire if you had received the first, when I found myself honoured with a Letter from His Excellency Mr. Jonathan Trumbull Governor &c. of the State of Connecticut dated at Lebanon June 27. 1777.[5] inclosed in another dated Philadelphia July 22. of the same year which a Dutch Gentleman settled in America named Gosuinus Erkelens[6] directed to me at the request (according to his own words) of the President and Members of

---

mission of 286 *l.t.* 4 *s.* Subsequent entries are actually copies of those made by JA, beginning Oct. 1: Taylor, *Adams Papers*, VII.

3. The great Dutch supporter of the American cause. His previous letter was actually written on April 26: XXVI, 349–54. For the dating of the final portion of the present letter see below.

4. Captured by the British from Henry Laurens in 1780 and published in Stevens, *Facsimiles*, X, no. 935. We publish from it because, like the other translation and unlike the ALS and copies, it contains the second postscript which comprises the bulk of the letter. However, it lacks a brief first postscript which we note below.

5. Trumbull's letter is a defense of the American cause, apparently intended for publication. National Archives. A Dutch translation is in *Brieven van Hunne Excellenties de heeren Jonathan Trumbull en William Livingston . . . aan Johan Derk baron van der Capellen . . .* (Amsterdam and elsewhere, [1779?]), pp. [1]–12.

6. Erkelens (whose name is spelled in various ways) was a native of Holland, a sometime resident of Connecticut, and the brother-in-law of a friend of van der Capellen. He had become convinced of the justice of the American struggle and had written an account of the cruelties of the British army, which Governor Trumbull thought might sway Dutch opinion: Trumbull to Hancock, April 14, 1777 (National Archives). Further details about him are given in Jay's letter of Jan. 3, 1779, below. His letter was being sent to van der Capellen to be publicized; see van der Capellen to Trumbull, Dec. 7, W.H. de Beaufort, ed., *Brieven van en aan Joan Derck van der Capellen van de Poll* (Utrecht, 1879), pp. 84–94.

the honourable the Congress. The originals of those Letters were sent by Congress undercover to you, the Duplicate and triplicate by the West Indies, this one I only received last tuesday, some accident must have happened to the two others. Not being able now to comply with the request of Mr. Erkelens without first speaking to some persons whom I must go to out of this Province and to whom I can not write having no correspondence with them, and that only in a few days I can execute the Plan I have form'd, I beg Sir that as soon as possible you will be so kind as to inform his Excellency the Governor that his Letter which fully rewards me for what I have suffered by meddling with the American affairs, and that of Mr. Erkelens have at last reached me and that I shall not delay my answer in the manner directed by Mr. Erkelens, vitz. the orriginal to you and the 2d. and 3d. by way of the West indies. I have the honour to be with the highest veneration

J D VAN DER CAPELLEN

Second Postscript.[7] After having a few days ago dispatched the first and second of the above, one by way of Paris the other by the West Indies and altho I had seald this third, I can not help adding this Postscript.

I had in order to give example placed about 20000 livres french Money in the Negotiation for the United States in the hands of Messrs. Horneca & Fizeaux, I had succeeded in persuading some people of my Province, and I expected to have the same influence in others where I have connections: the Credit of America can only gather strength by degrees and as the numbers of persons inclined to trust them ogments, so that in my opinion it would be more advantagious in the actual conjoncture to procure one hundred thousand Livres furnished by 50 persons of different parts of the Country, than even a Million furnished by one single person. I began to rejoice on the perspective which appeared very flattering, but

7. The first postscript, here missing, reads: "P.S.: Si je m'abuse dans votre addresse, ayez la bonté de me le pardonner et de me donner la veritable. J'ignore la denomination du Caractere dont Vous étes revetû a Paris. Addresse J.D.: Baron Van der Capellen Seigneûr dû Pol Membre du Corps des Nobles de la Province d'Overÿssel a Zwol par Amsterdam." (APS).

the Letters lately arrived from London threw the alarm on all sides.

The People in America are disgusted with the New Congress. Of 32000 Elects is only 600 were found willing to take the Oath of abjuration, the number of the Royalists ogment daily. It is Governor Johnston who has asserted this in the House of Commons.[8] The Ministers assure that all the news received from America coincide in giving the greatest hopes that this campaign which will begin with all imaginable vigour will be attended with more success than the preceeding, and the Newspapers aid [add], (from Letters from New York) that discord begins to reign between the French and the Americans, and amongst those last with one another, that *several* of the United States are on the point of following the Exemple of Georgia, the Carolinas, and CONNECTICUT who they say have acknowledged obedience to the King. What can I do or what can I say in the midst of such perplexing incertitudes—they do not cease in holland to observe that the Americans instead of persuing their advantages already gained on Burgoins Army, advantages that this very General in his report to Lord Germaine *thought was of a nature to put an end to the War*, have notwithstanding remain'd inactive. They ask me every moment "is it want of strength or of courage? Why at a time when France makes an open Diversion in their favour, dont the Americans drive their Enemies from the only two places they possess in their Country &c." For want of information I can only answer to those questions by another, "Why dont the Spaniards who are a powerfull and established Nation why dont they drive the English from Gibraltar?" I remind them that New York and New Port are two Gibraltars, but they allways conclude by saying "That the Americans do not defend themselfes with the same animosity and fury that the Dutch

8. This second postscript was written well after the letter itself: Johnstone, a member of the Carlisle commission, asserted in Commons on Dec. 14 that only 600 or so of the 32,000 Pennsylvania electors from the last election had sworn the necessary oath to qualify them to vote for Pennsylvania's next delegates to Congress. *Parliamentary Register*, XI (1778), 156; Cobbett, *Parliamentary History*, XX, 77.

did when they revolted against the Spaniards, and the Switzers against the Germains, that nothing has yet been done in America comparable to the sieges of Harlem Leiden and several other of our Cities, or to the Battle of Morgarten in Switzerland."[9] I repeat Sir that I am sorry to find such objections dayly made to which I cannot answer for want of information, I beg not with an indiscreet curiosity (but with Zeal for the interests of a People for whose Liberty I would willingly give my life) that you will inform me as soon as possible of the *true* situation of affairs in America. I wish Congress could quiet the minds of the Dutch with a certitude that *whatever turn* affairs may take, or *whatever Treaty* they may make with England, One of the *first articles* shall be the *Security* of the principal and Interest of the *Debts contracted during the troubles*. Believe me Sir, Congress to succeed in holland must condescend to cure my country Mens uneasiness which whether Ideal or real are still incompatible with its credit, and can only retard the happy event so much desired by the Friends of both Nations vitz. the acknowledgement of the Independence of America by this Republic. I am capable of secrecy. Trust my discretion.

One idea more and I will finish.

If a Pamphlet was published and circulated in America reciting the manner in which some people particularly amongst the moderns have heroically defended this Liberty, the sieges of Harlem of Leiden of St. John de Lone [Losne] (in france) the ardour with which the Genoes drove off Genl. Botta (in 1742) if I am not mistaken, and particularly the famous Battle of Morgarten which is found in SEMLER DE REPUBL: HELVETIORUM an Esteem'd author, some of whose most remarkable Pages I have sent you read Sir what is contained in the 70th. and the following.[1]

Are there no true Heroes in America as in Switzerland, amongst a Nation who possess such shining principles and

9. These famous sieges and battle occurred, respectively, in 1572, 1573 and 1315.

1. Rodolphe Valltravers had sent BF a copy of this celebrated work: xxv, 243.

virtues are there not to be found a sufficient number who preferring glory to Death, *by a coup d'éclat*, would put an end to a War which endangers their Liberty and Destroys their Dear Country by Ravage and Plunder? Why should not America have its sacred Phalanx as well as Thebes? Certainly they ought.

Notation: The Baron J.D. Vander Capellan to Dr. Franklin, dated Zwol 28th April 1778. & 6th September

From [Benjamin Vaughan]

AL: American Philosophical Society

My dearest sir Essex, Septr: 6, 1778.

I waited three days for an opportunity of sending the *leaves* you wrote for by a private hand; but not meeting with one, I sent them by post, directed to Mr. Chaumont.[2] The remaining leaves, with a letter, I gave to Mr. *Williams*,[3] upon his promising to convey them; but you know the man, and there they rest. He is a good natured, well disposed character; but I cannot move him so fast as Jonathan wishes: and I believe I must get my packet back again from him. While it is on my mind, give me leave to mention that the *enclosed* are for the president of C[ongress]'s son whom I remember to have made known to you; and who is Gen: W:'s aid de camp, and consequently about his person. His wife and daughter are in our village as inhabitants: and his brother is now at our house drinking tea; and a very fine fellow he is, and will make a very worthy character in *any* situation in his country.[4] Thus much for private matters.

2. Above, Aug. 1.

3. John Williams, the customs inspector.

4. Henry Laurens' son John (1754–82) was married to the former Matilda Manning (*c.* 1754–81), daughter of the senior Laurens' London business agent; their infant daughter's name was Frances Eleanor: Sara B. Townsend, *An American Soldier: the Life of John Laurens* . . . (Raleigh, N.C., [1958]), pp. 47–53. For John's younger brother Henry Laurens, Jr. (1763–1821) see David D. Wallace, *The Life of Henry Laurens* . . . (New York and London, 1915).

As to the public, it is not easy to describe the state of it. People seem very strong inclined on all sides to make peace with *you*, and the bulk of the people to make war with *France*. As to ministry, there are very few but their direct dependents, who do not wish to have them changed; some only secretly, others openly; and there is no confidence in their ability, their attention, or their honesty. Some quarrel with them for going back, others for beginning; and between both sets they are left in the lurch. However in the present state of things, I meet with nobody who is *now* inclined to conquest. The country people, who are not so nimble in changing their opinions as the court and city, are very much shocked with the duplicity of Lord North and Ld. G: Germaine in disavowing their former intentions and declarations respecting America:[5] But being at a distance from the centre of news, are not yet *warmed*.[6] However they have burned the above gentlemen in effigy at Durham; and a certain *Welch* dignitary (your friend)[7] writes me that he sees a great, almost a total change of opinion, in the country gentlemen there. They are changing at Manchester and in Scotland, from different causes; which will readily occur to you. Even the American refugees, having hints given them that their pensions may hereafter be discontinued, begin very much to look dissatisfied. There was something very like a crisis in the *spring*, which has now passed over for the present. Had opposition not divided and the parliament continued sitting, I think it would have been difficult to have avoided a surrender almost at discretion, on the part of the court; as indeed was in part indicated by offers to Lord C: and *afterwards* to Lord S:[8] But first of all Lord Sandwich won the king by his review of sights in the dock yards, and by his flummery;[9] (though very much against the inclinations of

5. An apparent reference to the concessions embodied in North's conciliatory bills: see xxv, 689–91.
6. Underlined by a series of dots.
7. Bishop Jonathan Shipley.
8. Lords Chatham and Shelburne.
9. The king and queen visited the dockyard at Portsmouth on May 2–4 with the Earl of Sandwich, First Lord of the Admiralty: *General Advertiser and Morning Intelligencer*, May 1, May 4–5, 1778.

the Scotch; but the king having been left a good deal to *himself* of late, through Ld. B.:'s timidity,[1] this did not so much matter; as there was no deep party made.) Next the French have been very inactive, and still more so the Spaniards. The fleets also have arrived; and money got more plentiful, and the burthen of the loan of last year over in a great measure for the present.[2] But as next year will have outstanding fleets again, and still heavier loans than the present, and as more energy may appear in Europe than at present, and as parliament also must meet again and in rather more disatisfaction because they will have talked with their constituents; you may easily guess that the coming winter will have a crisis again in it. In this summer season, news spreads very slowly and imperfectly, at least through London; but we shall soon get together again. However I cannot possibly tell you the obligations we have to those, who have furnished our newspapers lately with American news; the effect has been *prodigious*. But people have grown almost callous to national honor like people who have once got dirtied, they do not so much mind more dirt: and though this may be recovered, yet the present consequences are singular. But unless circumstances mend very much beyond present appearances, I think some part of the next winter may exhibit a little ferment. As to manufactures, many of them are standing still; but there is rather murmer than outcry from it. War makes a trade, and it takes off some of the artisans; it also by captures occasions many orders to be often executed over again, sometimes more than once; some circuitous trade by foreigners and others, still subsists; speculators too arise and give orders for goods, and answer for bad debts as far as their capital goes, to the clemency of the manufacturer; the merchant if *he* meets a loss, holds his tongue, to save his credit, and by incroaching on his principal in trade makes out the vulgarly supposed case of the cattle feeding on its own fat; the

1. Lord Bute.
2. The fleets were the incoming convoys from the West Indies and elsewhere: Mackesy, *War for America*, pp. 208–11. For the increased circulation of money and the government's favorable financial situation see the *London Packet; or New Lloyd's Evening Post*, July 6–8, 1778.

merchant has usually been the addresser, and has accordingly been the sufferer rather than the manufacturer, but as they have not struck their bad debts out of their books, they do not know how deeply they are cut; and they keep up a great deal of their old state, as being indeed necessary as they find to their *credit*. Should add with respect to manufactures, that though some have dropped, others have increased; and that workmen in some cases have their wages *very usefully* reduced. Landed estates and villas and town houses too, are all fallen, especially the former two. Estates must keep low while public interest is high, but I think we shall have a trade soon open very probably to America again; more or less open and direct according to circumstances. It will be contrary to most of the cases I have seen, if we refuse trade with you; for even if our quarrel is meaned to lie open, it will be difficult to reject present gain for the sake of public form or future views. Things are so dull here, that people itch (to use the phrase) for new mercantile enterprizes; and will run into them headlong I believe, whenever government affects to be asleep, or whenever the frigates are in any degree withdrawn.

I forgot to mention about D'Estaing and Clinton: But The circular letter about Byron's destination appears a hint to D'Estaing to make quick work.[3] If he has left New York, as they think he has, Byron's three ships and the Cork provision fleet[4] may get in; if not, every thing wears the worst aspect, and the chances against them: The consequence of which *may be*, that infinite blood may be spilt at a moment when it was least necessary; for Clinton will be found perhaps more enterprising than Howe, and is likely to prove a lion in toils if there is opportunity and as far as his ability goes. If the commissioners would have consented, they say he meditated and had laid a foundation for a brilliant stroke before leaving Philadelphia! I think there are four characters that seem to have been formed for the present epocha: The K-, and Gen. Howe, for

3. The commissioners' circular letter of May 18 (above, XXVI, 499) was printed in the *London Packet* of Aug. 26–8.

4. Provisions convoys were sent from Cork in May, June and July, all arriving safely by late October: R. Arthur Bowler, *Logistics and the Failure of the British Army in America, 1775–1783* (Princeton, [1975]), p. 117 n.

English war and English politics; and a certain master of mine, and General Washington, for American Ditto. However if the whole force in America goes, many Englishmen, from affection to America, will rejoice in the crush: not very wisely, as we shall both agree, provided (as seems likely from everything) they are otherwise withdrawn. If not, the shortest work and shortest expence is the best for this side, situated as the matter seems now to be. Every information however agrees that a detachment was going to the West Indies;[5] and Clintons last letter alludes to the most convenient spot for an *embarkation* I think, of a part at least.

I believe I never told you what had made me warm against the Rockinghams. It was first four or five of the chiefs getting in a circle and laughing, the day Ld. C. fell which these eyes beheld. Next, some very cruel insinuations of the Duke of Richmonds on the day of his annuity bill,[6] which shocked many besides myself. Next their expressions, that Ld. C and S should "both be hung in the same halter, &c."; yet their *own* conduct very much a measure to *cut* the Gordian knot of the declaratory bill,[7] and to form a new ground for attack on ministry for not removing the *cause of war* with France. I could go on much farther; but I have not wholly cooled, having been at times of late a little in earnest about it in conversation to clear up misapprehensions of my friends and then let them rest. They are good men, but they want common sense often under their *present leaders,* and in *internal* politics their measures and principles are not *strong enough* for the people, which will tend to make [*them*] unfriendly to popular men, unless low enough to be tools to work with.

5. As indeed it was, to attack the French island of St. Lucia: Mackesy, *War for America,* pp. 181–6. For the detachment's departure see Deane to BF, Sept. 15.

6. For Richmond's criticism of Chatham during the third reading of the Chatham Annuity Bill (June 2, 1778) see Cobbett, *Parliamentary History,* XIX, 1236–7, 1249, 1253–4. Vaughan's quotation is a garbled version of a comment by the earl of Abingdon about the present ministry: *ibid.,* p. 1236. Chatham had been stricken in the House of Lords on April 7.

7. *I.e.,* to repeal it; a bill to that effect had been brought in April: Cobbett, *Parliamentary History,* XIX, 1010–12.

I must now conclude with telling you that I avoid all communications, but such as shew the temper of the times and the general posture of affairs, as far as occurs to my mind at the moment: Particular facts cannot remain hid to you. But I am not so blind as to what has passed, as not to see the mildness of your politics, and to know the use you will make of these slight hints.

I turn with impatience to hear from you, your last letter having given me more comfort and heartfelt pleasure than perhaps any letter I ever shall again receive in the course of my life.[8] It allayed a thousand fears about misapprehensions &c. which would make me of all men the most dejected, being my dearest sir, with the most ardent devotion and thanks your ever attached and most affectionate

P.S. We are going to work directly.

Notation: Vaughn Sept. 6. 78

Horneca, Fizeaux & Cie. to the American Commissioners[9]

LS: American Philosophical Society

⟨Amsterdam, September 7, 1778, in French: We have just received by Mr. Whitall the book of notes and coupons. To begin the negotiations we need only your orders about the expenses and allowances above the stipulated five-percent interest.[1]⟩

John Bondfield to the American Commissioners[2]

ALS: American Philosophical Society

⟨Bordeaux, September 8, 1778: The privateer schooner *Success* arrived this morning. Her master, Captain Attwood of Vir-

8. BF's letter is missing.
9. Published in Taylor, *Adams Papers*, VII.
1. The commissioners' covering letter of Aug. 31 apparently had been separated.
2. Published in Taylor, *Adams Papers*, VII.

ginia, reports d'Estaing sailed from Chesapeake Bay for New York on July 9, leaving behind five frigates. When English prisoners are brought here by privateers, your authority is not invoked as to whether they should be set free or not, and the French government doesn't interfere. Neither do their courts recognize cases between masters and their seamen. I suggested earlier the advantages of all American vessels being required to report to you.[3] I am attentive to procuring as authentic reports as I can on my own.⟩

From Dumas

ALS: American Philosophical Society; AL (draft): Algemeen Rijksarchief

Monsieur,   Lahaie 8 Sept. *1778*
    Je n'ai aujourdhui qu'une demi-heure (entre une visite faite, et une autre à faire), pour vous confirmer ma Lettre particuliere à vous seul, du 3; et celle du 4 incluse. J'ai oublié de vous dire, Monsieur, que le g—— F——, en revenant d'Amst—— le 3, lorsque je lui rendis compte le 4 au matin de mon entretien avec notre Ami, étoit déjà instruit par celui-ci de la déclaration envoyée à Mr. L. par le Marchand, mais non de l'emprunt projetté, qui avoit fait demander et accorder la déclaration; que l'affaire avoit paru si sérieuse au g—— F——, qu'il en avoit écrit à sa maison, et averti que ces canaux de traverse ne valoient rien. Depuis qu'il sait l'affaire de l'emprunt projetté, il n'a nullement changé de sentiment. Quant á notre Ami, il ne savoit rien de la négociation dont Mr. G. est chargé:[4] il le sait à présent. Il m'a dit que le Marchand correspondant de Mr. L—— est actuellement à Aix La Chapelle avec lui; ils s'y étoient donné rendez-vous. Le g—— F—— m'a dit de vous écrire, qu'il ne seroit pas mauvais, dans la Lettre que vous m'écrirez, de faire sentir délicatement, si vous le jugez propre, qu'avec toute la bonne volonté pour cet Etat qu'ont le

3. Possibly a reference to Bondfield's July 7 suggestion of monthly shipping reports.
4. Georges Grand. Van Berckel had indeed been informed that W. Lee held no congressional power: see Dumas' letter of Sept. 3.

Congrès, les principaux dans les divers Etats-unis, et vous Messieurs, vous n'êtes pas sûrs que le peuple Américain en général n'accordât quelque privilege aux Anglois et aux François pour l'amour de la paix, s'il continuoit de ne voir faire aucun pas à la rep. pour les rencontrer, eux qui se sont tant avancés. Je suis avec un vrai respect et attachement, Monsieur, Votre très humble et très obéissant serviteur   D

Paris à S.E.M. le Dr. Franklin M.P. Des E.U. de l'A.

Addressed: à Son Excellence / Monsieur le Dr. Franklin, Esqe., / Ministre Plénipotentiaire des / Etats-Unis de l'Amérique &c. &c. / en son particulier et en mains / propres / à *Paris.*

Endorsed: M. Dumas private Sept. 8. 1778

From Robert Ellison[5]   ALS: American Philosophical Society

Dear Sir,   London the 8th September 1778
    I hope that my former acquaintance with you will be a Sufficient apology for the request which I have to make of you.
    Having an Interest which requires authentic proof of the date of the Treaty made the beginning of this Year between France and the Thirteen United States of North America I take the liberty of troubling you on that occasion.
    It appears by a Pensylvanian Newspaper publish'd by Order of Congress,[6] that the Treaty in question was Sign'd on the 6th of Febey. last: But such a proof not being deem'd of sufficient authority I have no other way of ascertaining the fact

---

5. Ellison (1737?–83), a London merchant, was associated in the schemes of Deane, Bancroft and Samuel Wharton to use their inside knowledge of the commissioners' affairs to play the London stock market (discussed in Bancroft's letter of Aug. 7): Robert Surtees, *The History and Antiquities of the County Palatine of Durham* . . . (4 vols., London, 1816–40), II, 79; Bancroft and Deane, abstract of accounts, [c. May, 1779] (Connecticut Historical Society). His letter was forwarded by Bancroft on Sept. 14 and presumably, like Bancroft's letter, circulated to the other commissioners.
    6. See *JCC*, XI, 468–9 for the congressional order to publicize the Treaty of Amity and Commerce.

than by requesting the favour of your assistance for that purpose.

What I venture to propose is that a Notary Public may be permitted to have Such a Sight of the Treaty above-mention'd, as may enable him to certify it's Date.

I have the less difficulty in making this Request as what I desire is only the Authentication of a Fact, which is already of common notoriety; a consideration which will, I hope, at least be Sufficient to acquit me of Impropriety in making the application.

If this proof was not necessary to me, (in the way I have stated, or in any other which may be more agreeable to you) I should not have presum'd to give you this trouble; from which, however, I am glad to have an opportunity of assuring you of the Sincere respect, with which I have the Honour to be, Your Excellency's most obedient humble Servant

ROBERT ELLISON

Notations: Robert Ellison. 8 Septr. London. requesting the date of the Treaty.[7] / 8. 7bre. 1778

From Jean-Baptiste Le Roy

AL: American Philosophical Society

[before September 9, 1778[8]]

M. Le Roy est bien fâché de s'en aller à Paris sans avoir eu l'honneur de voir Monsieur Franklin depuis son retour. Il a envoyé hier deux fois chez lui pour aller lui gagner une partie d'échecs mais toutes ces deux fois là il n'y étoit pas. Il lui fait demander s'il a recu des nouvelles de M. D'Estaing. Il lui renouvelle les assurrances sincères de tout son attachement.

Addressed: A Monsieur / Monsieur Franklin / Deputé du Congrès

7. In JA's hand.
8. Dated on the assumption that the inquiry at the end is about whether d'Estaing has reached America. The Count passed the Straits of Gibraltar on May 16, was sighted off the Delaware Capes on July 8, and anchored off

The American Commissioners to Dumas[9]

LS:[1] William N. Dearborn, Nashville, Tennessee (1962); copy: National Archives

⟨Passy, September 9, 1778: We received yours[2] hinting that some of your friends wish the commissioners should propose a treaty to your government. It really would be a pleasure thus to cement a union between the two republics, but having received no answer to their letter sent some months ago on the subject to the Grand Pensionary[3] they apprehend any further motion would not be agreeable. They are ready to enter on such a treaty whenever it shall seem good to their High Mightinesses.[4]⟩

The American Commissioners to the Massachusetts Council

ALS (draft):[5] American Philosophical Society

Honourable Gentlemen   Passi September 9. 1778

The inclosed Letter was delivered to Us by the Person intrusted with it for Inspection. We did not think it proper that a Letter should go through our Hands to America, from Mr. Hutchinson, without Examination. We accordingly broke the seal and found the two Powers of Attorney, and the Letter inclosed, of which Letter We have taken a Copy.[6] We think it

New York harbor on July 11. News of his arrival reached Paris by Sept. 9. Butterfield, *Adams Correspondence*, III, 88.

9. Published in Taylor, *Adams Papers*, VII.
1. In WTF's hand.
2. Above, Sept. 4.
3. See XXVI, 267–8.
4. The States General; see our note on Dumas to the commissioners, July 3.
5. In JA's hand. We do not know why Lee failed to sign this letter.
6. The copy of former Massachusetts governor Thomas Hutchinson's letter, dated Aug. 10 and attested by Jonathan Loring Austin, is at the University of Pa. Library; it is also printed in the *Magazine of American History*, XII (1884), 462–3. It asks Dr. James Lloyd of Boston to oversee the family's Massachusetts estates. See Sabine, *Loyalists*, II, 23–4. The powers of attor-

proper to send it to you, rather than Dr. Lloyd. You will judge what is proper to do with it. It requires no Comments of ours, who have the Honour to be with great Consideration, Your most obedient humble servants   B FRANKLIN
                                         JOHN ADAMS

The Hon. Council of Mass. Bay.

The American Commissioners to [John Ross][7]

AL (draft): Massachusetts Historical Society

⟨Passy, September 9, 1778: We acknowledge yours of August 29. We are authorized to discharge neither your private nor your public debts. If you purchased goods with money sent you by the commissioners and had given us an account, we could have given you orders. As it is, any goods you have belonging to the United States should be delivered to Mr. Schweighauser. You have failed to account for large sums entrusted you by the commissioners. Reconsider your conduct in conscience and send no more letters until they are in keeping with public service.⟩

Dumas to the American Commissioners[8]

AL: Harvard University Library; AL (draft): Algemeen Rijksarchief

⟨The Hague, September 9, 1778, in French: The Assembly of Holland yesterday debated Amsterdam's proposal opposing an increase in the size of the army. I will translate and send

---

ney are those of Hutchinson and his sister-in-law Grizell Sanford, for whom see Bernard Bailyn, *The Ordeal of Thomas Hutchinson* (Cambridge, Mass., 1974), p. 30.

7. Published in Taylor, *Adams Papers*, VII, where the identity of the intended recipient is explained notwithstanding the absence of an Aug. 29 letter. This letter was marked "not sent"; sections of it were deleted on two different occasions.

8. Published in Taylor, *Adams Papers*, VII.

you a copy of the proposal. Mr. van Berckel criticized the Grand Pensionary and suggested I press him for an answer to your letter.[9] I told him I could not do so without your orders. I await an answer to mine of the 4th. The Pensionaries of Harlem and Dort are two very capable men, good republicans and friends of our friend.⟩

From Vergennes

AL (draft):[1] Archives du Ministère des affaires étrangères; copies:[2] Massachusetts Historical Society, Library of Congress (two)

A Versailles le 9. Septembre 1778.

Vous avez demande, Mr. un passeport pour le bâtiment anglois qui doit amener vos prisonniers en france; vous trouverez cette piéce cyjointe;[3] elle indique Nantes ou L'orient pour le lieu de débarquement.

M. francklin

The American Commissioners to Beaumarchais[4]

AL (draft): Massachusetts Historical Society; two copies: National Archives

⟨Passy, September 10, 1778: The cargo of the *Thérèse* has been assigned to us. We do not know how you claim her as your vessel since Mr. Montieu claims her as his and demands the remainder of our payment for her hire.[5] We request your attention to our powers and instructions from Congress. Until

9. Of April 10 in which the commissioners had promised to forward a copy of the Treaty of Amity and Commerce with France: see XXVI, 268.
1. In Gérard de Rayneval's hand.
2. These indicate that this letter was addressed to the commissioners.
3. A copy is at the Library of Congress.
4. Published in Taylor, *Adams Papers*, VII and Morton, *Beaumarchais Correspondance*, IV, 226–30.
5. See Beaumarchais' letter of Sept. 5. Jean-Joseph Carié de Montieu chartered ships to Beaumarchais' Roderigue Hortalez & Cie.: XXIII, 200 n; Taylor, *Adams Papers*, VII.

the accounts of Roderigue Hortalez & Cie. are settled we cannot send you the proceeds of the sale of the cargo. We will give orders that they be reserved to be paid the firm or its representative as soon as the accounts are settled or the contract between Congress and the company is ratified by the company and us. We are ready to confer with the firm or its representative at whatever time or place they or you wish.⟩

The American Commissioners to Sartine[6]

AL (draft): Massachusetts Historical Society; three copies: National Archives

⟨Passy, September 10, 1778: Captain Daniel McNeill of Boston retook a French vessel [the *Isabelle*] held by a Guernsey privateer more than three days. He brought her into Port Louis where he has met with difficulties selling her and her cargo. In keeping with His Majesty's interest and the treaties between our two nations, we ask your attention to this case.⟩

The American Commissioners to Vergennes[7]

ALS:[8] Archives du Ministère des affaires étrangères; AL (draft): Massachusetts Historical Society; two copies: National Archives

⟨Passy, September 10, 1778: On April 13 Congress resolved that the commissioners should settle with Roderigue Hortalez & Cie. on a compensation for the supplies they provided. The commerce committee sent us the contract made with Beaumarchais' agent Théveneau de Francy and ordered us to liquidate the affair. Congress on May 16 resolved to send us an invoice of additional articles to be ordered from the company. We enclose copies of the contract between the Committee and

6. Published in Taylor, *Adams Papers*, VII.
7. Published in Taylor, *Adams Papers*, VII.
8. In Arthur Lee's hand.

Mr. Francy, his powers, and the list of articles to be furnished.⁹ We do not know who the persons are who constitute the house of Roderigue Hortalez & Cie., but we, the Congress and the American people understand we are indebted to His Majesty for the goods furnished by the company.¹ We cannot discover a contract between any American agent and Roderigue Hortalez & Cie. nor do we know of any witness or evidence as to the terms of such a contract. We are sure it is the wish and determination of the United States to discharge as soon as possible their obligation to His Majesty; in the meantime we are ready to settle and liquidate the accounts at whatever time and in whatever manner His Majesty or you wish. We ask your advice whether it is safe or prudent to ratify the contract with the company and for Congress to depend on it for supplies.)

To de Perygnon²   AL (draft): American Philosophical Society

Sir   Passy, Sept. 10. 1778
I have not with me here the Book of Laws of Pensilvania, and therefore can only give such an Opinion in Answer to your Questions as my Memory, perhaps imperfect, may furnish me with. 1. The want of Publication of Banns does not nullify a Marriage; it only gives a right to any Person injured by the Marriage to prosecute the Clergyman in Law for Damages who marries without such Publication or a special Licence. 2. I know not at what Age the Marriage of a Girl with-

9. For the contract see BF to Lovell, July 22; for the resolutions, *JCC*, x, 342, and xi, 505; and for the commerce committee's covering letter, xxvi, 475.

1. For the relationship between the company and the French government see xxii, 454. On Sept. 16 Vergennes forwarded the contents of this letter to Gérard, stressing that the King had not directly provided the arms to Congress, but rather had allowed Beaumarchais to take from the royal arsenals the necessary quantities under the proviso of replacing them later: Meng, *Despatches of Gérard,* pp. 293–5.

2. In answer to his inquiry of Sept. 3.

SEPTEMBER 10, 1778

out Consent of Parents would be null: but I think if she was above 14 the Want of that Consent would not nullify the Marriage; tho' as the Law requires the Consent of Parents or Guardians, if the Girl is under 18 and the Man under 21, the Minister who marries them without that Consent would be subject to a Prosecution. 3. I do not know that any Witnesses are absolutely necessary, Faith being given to the Minister's Register and Certificate; tho' Marriages are rarely celebrated so privately. 4. I suppose every Minister of every Religion in Pensilvania keeps such a Register: and lastly I think the Certificate of Mr. Farmer sufficient to prove the Marriage in question, and that the same join'd with Proofs of Cohabitation as Man and Wife would confirm the Marriage in that Country, and prevent a new Match during the Life of the two Parties. I am Sir, Your most obedient humble Servant

To de Perygnon

Jonathan Williams, Jr., to the American Commissioners[3]

ALS: American Philosophical Society

⟨Nantes, September 10, 1778: M. Montaudoüin[4] has learned from Mr. Kergariou, commander of the French frigate *Oiseau*,[5] that the Guernsey and Jersey privateers which infest this bay provision in Bilbao under pretense of being American. I hope this practice can be stopped.⟩

3. Published in Taylor, *Adams Papers*, VII.
4. This prominent Nantes merchant, identified above, XXIII, 195 n, had been in frequent contact with JW and with the commissioners.
5. De Kergariou Loc Maria, wounded in battle with the British frigate *Magician* in 1783, became a member of the Order of the Cincinnati and a victim of the French Revolution: *The Order of the Cincinnati in France* (Newport, 1905), p. 137. For the *Oiseau* see the headnote on intelligence reports, above, Aug. 3.

384

From Charles Gadd[6]   ALS: American Philosophical Society

⟨Marstrand, Sweden, September 10, 1778: American vessels have been coming here, and there now remain only a brig commanded by one Capt. Child, and a ship, Capt. Loweth, both from South Carolina. These addressed themselves to merchants in Gothenburg which is not a free port, and where an English consul named Erskine is active. When they need protection I can only assist them in secret, and at a distance. This port is the only safe one for American commerce with Sweden, Denmark, Russia, Poland, and a part of Germany. I therefore wish you would appoint a consul here who could openly declare himself a protector of Americans and obtain the approval of the king of Sweden. The king, I hope, would not refuse protection to any one in the free port of Marstrand, which has a different status from the rest of the country.[7] Please consult the Swedish ambassador to France, count Creutz. I humbly offer my services, and am willing to serve without pay for as long as necessary.[8]⟩

From the Chevalier de Kéralio[9]

ALS: American Philosophical Society

à L'Ecole Royale m[ilitai]re, Le 10. 7bre 1778.

Je pars demain, Monsieur, pour aller voir celles de nos écoles militaires de province qui n'ont pas été inspectées L'année derniere. Ce sera un voyage de Deux mois. Pendant mon absence j'ai pourvu à ce que vous ayés Les nouvelles que je pourrai recevoir. C'est mon frere qui vous Les fera parvenir.[1] S'il n'y a

6. He calls himself French vice-consul in Marstrand, a small island north of Gothenburg.

7. Marstrand was, indeed, the only port open to all belligerents: Adolph B. Benson, *Sweden and the American Revolution* (New Haven, 1926), p. 20 n.

8. The endorsement reads: "Charles Gadd Marstrand Sweden Offers services as Consul."

9. For Agathon Guynement, chevalier de Kéralio, see the intelligence reports of Aug. 3.

1. Louis-Félix (1731–93), known as Kéralio-Luxembourg because he had received from Monsieur, the King's brother, the use of the petit

point d'indiscrétion, je supplie Mr. votre fils que j'embrasse de tout mon coeur de vouloir bien adresser celles que vous recevrés à *Mr. de Keralio, au Luxembourg, cour des Fontaines, a paris*; il me Les fera passer partout ou je serai et partout je serai flatté de recevoir de nouveaux bienfaits de votre part. Partout je publierai les bontés dont vous m'avés honoré et La Vénération que vous m'avés inspirée.

Notre Bonne et céleste amie[2] m'a chargé de vous présenter son tendre hommage et de vous prévenir que dimanche prochain elle se fait une grande fête d'aller causer avec vous.

Donnés-moi votre Bénédiction, monsieur, il n'en est point dont je fasse plus de cas et recevés Les assurances bien sinceres du dévouement inviolable et Respectueux avec Lequel je suis, Monsieur, votre très humble et très obéissant Serviteur

LE CHR DE KERALIO

Notation: de Keralio 10. Sept. 1778.

From Le Maire
ALS: American Philosophical Society

Monsieur   Nantes Le 10 7bre. 1778

Je n'ai rien de plus pressé que de vous envoyer Le procès verbal de L'inspection que j'ai faite des fusils, en méme temps pour vous faire voir mon éxactitude.[3] Vous verrez par ce procès verbal que j'ai apporté tous les soins pour procurer à la Virginie la meilleure qualité possible d'armes, et comme j'ai eu l'honneur de vous dire qu'il manquoit quantité d'autres objets que le Gouvernement de cette province a demandés et dont elle a besoin, je vous réitere toujours ma priere, en vous sup-

---

Luxembourg. He had served as a diplomat in Scandinavia and Spain. Larousse.

2. The duchesse de Deux-Ponts.

3. The report was dated Sept. 10 and signed by Le Maire as well as his five specialists in arms. After meticulous testing, which lasted twenty-five days, they now certify that of the 8,000 fusils purchased by Arthur Lee from Penet, D'Acosta & frères, only two percent were found defective. The others are packed and sealed with the inscription, *"government of Virginia."*

pliant de m'accorder votre approbation en cas que je sois à même de pouvoir traiter avec quelqu'un; M. Gruel ne peut remplir mon objet par le retard d'un navire qu'il attendoit de St. Domingue. L'objet devient maintenant bien moins consequent: avec environ 200 mille livres je remplirai la totalité de ma mission. Ces fonds ne seroient payés à celui avec qui je traiterois, qu'avec Les Tabacs de virginie qui passeroient en France. J'ai l'honneur d'etre avec le plus profond respect, Monsieur Votre très humble et très obéissant serviteur

J. LE MAIRE

P.S. J'ai communiqué à M. Tessier L'intérêt que vous prenez a ce qui le regarde, il est Très reconnoissant de vos bontés, il remettra à M. Le Gouverneur de la Virginie la lettre de recommandation que vous avez bien voulu lui donner.

Monsieur Franklin Escuyer

Notation: Lemaire Nantes 20. 7bre 1778

The American Commissioners to John Bondfield[4]

AL (draft): Massachusetts Historical Society; two copies: National Archives

⟨Passy, September 11, 1778: We have received yours of the 5th[5] and wish better health to Captain Ayres. His ship should sail forthwith if it has not already done so. We will honor the draft for the account you enclosed, but you must distinguish the sums advanced to Mr. Adams in a private capacity as well as those advanced him, Captain Palmes and Dr. Noël for their stay at Bordeaux and journey to Paris.[6] Mr. Adams will pay you for the articles you forwarded to his family; for the remainder draw on the commissioners. This does not settle your account as we feel the 5% commission you charge is too high; many persons would be willing to do the business for 2%.⟩

4. Published in Taylor, *Adams Papers*, VII.
5. Missing.
6. Palmes and Noël were respectively an officer and a fellow passenger on the *Boston*: Butterfield, *John Adams Diary*, II, 269–71, 289–90.

Dumas to the American Commissioners[7]

AL (draft): Algemeen Rijksarchief

⟨[The Hague], September 11, 1778, in French: Tomorrow the Amsterdam merchants as a body will present to the Assembly of Holland an address requesting protection from the British. All trade at Amsterdam is at a standstill because no one wants to give insurance. I still await what I requested on the 4th.⟩

From the Abbé Chalut[8]

AL: American Philosophical Society

ce vendredi matin [September 11, 1778]

L'Abbé Chalut présente ses civilités à Monsieur le Docteur Franklin: il le prie de lui faire l'honneur de venir manger sa soupe demain samedi 12 7bre. avec M. L'Abbé de Mably qui doit être de la partie.[9]

Addressed: A Monsieur / Monsieur Franklin / ministre plenipotentiaire des / Etats unis d'Amerique / A Passy

From Dumas

ALS: American Philosophical Society; AL (draft): Algemeen Rijksarchief

Monsieur,   Lahaie 11e 7bre *1778*

J'ai eu l'honneur de vous écrire deux Lettres particulieres, du 3 et du 8, et deux autres à LL. EE. Messrs. les Plenipts. en commun, du 4 et du 9 de ce mois. Notre ami me dit hier, qu'il avoit reçu une réponse du Marchd. qui est revenu d'Aix-la-Chapelle à Amst., par laquelle il lui marquoit que Mr. L. lui avoit caché la Négociation qui est présentement entre les

---

7. Published in Taylor, *Adams Papers*, VII.

8. For this jolly abbé see XXV, p. 382.

9. Gabriel Bonnot, abbé de Mably (1709–1785) was a publicist, historian and philosopher whose vast output included *Observations sur le gouvernement et les lois des Etats-Unis d'Amérique* (Amsterdam and Paris, 1784): Butterfield, *John Adams Diary*, II, 315 n.

mains de Messrs. Horneca, Fizeaux & Comp.,[1] et domiciliée dans cette Maison au nom des XIII Etats-Unis; mais qu'il lui avoit fait voir qu'il étoit Commissionaire du Congrès. Sur les questions que notre Ami m'a faites là-dessus, je lui ai répondu candidement, que je ne savois pas de quelle nature étoit la Commission de Mr. L., qu'il étoit possible qu'elle fût directement du Congrès, pour quelque objet particulier; mais que, si elle n'étoit pas subordonnée à l'hon. Commission Plénip. établie à Paris, je ne concevois pas qu'il fût possible de supposer, qu'elle s'etendît jusqu'à croiser celle-ci, nuire à ses opérations, ou lui être égale en tout et par-tout. Il m'a demandé si Mr. L. ignoroit donc la Négociation des Etats-Unis? J'ai répondu que non.

Pour ne vous laisser, Monsieur, aucun éclaircissement à desirer sur ma propre correspondance avec Mr. L., je crois devoir vous dire, que je m'y suis borné à lui rendre les services particuliers qu'il me demandoit, avec le même bon coeur avec lequel ils sont voués à tous les Américains unis, que dans sa Lettre de Francfort, du 4 Avril dernier, il m'a dit *You will be so good as to avoid mentioning any thing about me to any person whatever*; et que je me suis conformé à ses desirs, tant qu'il m'a paru qu'il ne s'agissoit que de ses propres affaires: que par sa derniere, du 27 Août, il me dit, *Should you have occasion to write to me at Paris, you may put yr. Letter under cover to Mr. Grand as formerly, only desiring, under the direction to me, that the Letter may not be delivered into any hands, but my own;*[2] ce que je ferai, si le cas l'exige, si vous ne m'avertissez point qu'il y a quelque inconvénient à cela, et tant que je vous saurai persuadé, Monsieur, que le service des Etats-Unis, l'approbation et la protection du Congrès et votre affection pour moi, ont et auront toujours la préférence chez moi sur toute autre liaison: car

1. Of which Georges Grand was one of the directors.
2. There is a letter of similar purport in Ford, *Letters of William Lee*, II, 472–3, but we have found no copies of Lee's letters to Dumas of April 4 or Aug. 27, mentioned above, or of May 30, mentioned below. Lee subsequently complained of Dumas' not replying to his letters and suspected BF was responsible: Ford, *Letters of William Lee*, II, 504.

c'est véritablement que je vous respecte et aime, Monsieur, Votre très humble et très obeissant serviteur   DUMAS

P.S. Je viens de chez *notre ami.*

Le Marchand, non content de lui avoir écrit, est venu lui-même lui apporter une Déclaration de Mr. L. en réponse à celle que le Marchd. lui avoit remise de la part de notre ami, et pour lui garantir à son tour les bonnes dispositions réci-proques des Etats-Unis, et les vôtres, Messieurs, notre ami lui a répété, qu'il avoit à sa porte ce qu'il cherchoit loin; qu'il pouvoit contracter des premiers pour tout ce qu'il voudroit avec la Maison où se trouvoit domiciliée la Négociation et qu'il en étoit averti, et invité à cela, comme de la part de Messrs. les Plénipotentiaires, par une personne suffisamment qualifiée à pouvoir le faire: ce dont le Marchd. a témoigné être fort content, et résolu de s'adresser de la part de notre Ami à Messrs. H.F. & C.

J'oubliois, Monsieur, de vous dire encore, que par Lettre de Vienne du 30e. May, Mr. L. m'avoit demandé s'il y auroit moyen d'emprunter pour l'Etat de Virginie un million de Livres de France; que pour lui complaire, je consultai là-dessus Sir G. Gd et une autre maison amie;[3] et qu'en réponse je l'ai averti qu'une telle négociation ne pourroit se faire pré-sentement, sans porter coup à celle qu'il savoit. Comme depuis ce temps il ne m'en a plus parlé, j'ai supposé qu'il n'y pensoit plus.

NB. Le g—— F—— sait, et par consequent a vu tout ceci.

[*Illegible*] a Son Exc. M. le D. Franklin M.P. des E.U. de l'A.

Addressed: à Son Excellence / Monsieur le Dr. Franklin, Esqr. / Ministre Plénipotentiaire des Etats unis de l'Amérique / *en mains propres* / à Paris

Endorsed: Dumas Sept 11. 78

---

3. See Georges Grand's letter of Sept. 3. The other banking house may be Dumas' associates de la Lande and Fynje.

From Count von Sickingen[4]

AL: American Philosophical Society

Ce vendredi [September 11, 1778[5]]
a Paris Barriere du Roule
Mr: Leroy Et d'autres personnes de La Connaissance de Monsieur franklin, se rassembleronts Lundi 14 7bre chez Le Comte de Sickingen, et on s'y occuppera de quelques recherches sur la Platine; si Cette Societé et Le motif qui La rassemble pouvaient Engager Monsieur franklin a faire L'honneur au Comte de Sickingen de Diner ce jour Chez Luy, il En serait infiniment flatté; il a L'honneur de le saluer.

R.S.V.P.

Addressed: A Monsieur / Monsieur Francklin / A Passi

John Bondfield to the American Commissioners[6]

ALS: American Philosophical Society

⟨Bordeaux, September 12, 1778: I have received offers from every forge from Angoulême to Bayonne for the cannon you commission me to purchase. None will promise to complete delivery before February and the arsenals cannot loan any. Thus I have decided to contract with the forges of Petigore [Périgord]. No ships have arrived from America the last three days despite the westerly winds.⟩

---

4. Karl Heinrich Joseph, Reichsgraf von Sickingen, had been the Elector Palatine's minister to France since at least 1770: Lewis, *Walpole Correspondence*, IV, 442 n. The *Almanach royal* for 1778, p. 163, confirms the address given here. On Sept. 5 he had read a report on platinum to the Academy of Sciences: *procès-verbaux*, XCVII, fol. 305.
5. We assume that he wrote on the Friday before the gathering.
6. Published in Taylor, *Adams Papers*, VII.

From ——— Branche

ALS: American Philosophical Society

Monsieur, Paris 12. 7bre. 1778.

Monseigneur le comte de Vergennes m'a autorisé a réclamer vos bontés, et à me présenter à vous, à l'effet d'être chargé de faire les Médailles, sçeaux, Cachets, Timbres etc. pour la nouvelle République des Etats-unis de l'Amérique; Ce Ministre veut bien être mon protecteur auprès de vous, Monsieur, il a eu la bonté de me faire espérer qu'il vous en parleroit. La réputation que mes travaux pour la Cour m'ont acquise, est un motif bien puissant pour obtenir la grâce que je sollicite de votre bonté, je ferai tous mes efforts pour me la mériter par mes soins et mon application à remplir vos intentions et celles des Etats-unis de l'Amérique. J'ai l'honneur d'être avec des sentimens pleins de reconnoissance et de respect, Monsieur, Votre très humble et très obéissant serviteur

Branche
Graveur de Monsieur frere du Roy
Rue St. Louis du palais

Endorsed: Branche Graveur offers to make Seals 12. 7bre. 1778.

From Simon-Pierre Fournier le Jeune

ALS: American Philosophical Society

Monsieur, Paris le 12 7bre 1778

Je reçois à l'instant vos ordres pour la fonte de Petit Romain, d'ont vous me parlates dans le tems; j'y répond aussitot, afin de ne mettre aucunne lenteur à les exécuter lors-ce que vous auréz daigné m'éclairer sur les objets essentiels que j'ignore.

1° Quel est l'oeil[7] que vous auréz choisi? Je vous prie de me le désigner par son numéro, au livre des Epreuves, que j'ai eu l'honneur de vous présenter, 2° la quantité qu'il faudra d'italiques, 3° ce que signifie les lettres n, et m, figuré a l'article des cadrats, ainsi que les suivantes m's. Quand aux espaces, j'en-

7. Type face. In the absence of BF's instructions, we cannot elucidate the other queries.

tends qu'il en faut de quatre sortes dont la plus grosse du nombre de 15000, et les autres par gradation de plus mince, en plus mince.

4° S'il y a une hauteur particulliere pour ce caracterre, ou si il le faut simplement a la hauteur de Paris? Dans le cas contraire, vous auriez la bonté de m'envoyer des modelles.

Je vous suplie, Monsieur, de m'eclercir toutes ces choses et soyez persuadé du zêle, et de l'activité que je mettrai a vous servir. J'ai l'honneur d'être avec toute l'estime possible Monsieur Votre très humble et obeissant serviteur

FOURNIER LE JEUNE

Ma femme, Monsieur, qui a conçu pour vous tout le respect possible à l'honneur de vous le présenter.

From ——— Saint Sauveur fils[8]

ALS: American Philosophical Society

⟨Trieste, September 12, 1778, in French: No Frenchman venerates your qualities more than I. Born under the same sky as your Excellency, of a mother descended from a Franquelin, I submit the following along with my respectful sentiments.

My great-grandfather, a Franquelin, served the King in Canada. He married there, had children, and returned to France. He sent for his family, who embarked on a ship which was wrecked on an island in the St. Lawrence. M. Franquelin believed that none of his children had survived; but my grandmother, who had been ill, had remained in Canada under a nursemaid's care. Thinking herself an orphan, she married and never followed the traces of her father. From my own father's research, we learn that after he left his country, my great-grandfather was never seen again there.

8. He signs himself vice-consul in Trieste. His father, consul in that city, wrote on the same day in support of this letter. He, too, wishes a place in BF's esteem. He might have the good fortune of being known to him, having served in Canada as "secretaire du Gouvernement." He and his son owe their careers to M. de Sartine. APS. Father and son are listed under consuls in Trieste in the *Almanach royal* for 1778, p. 502.

Please excuse this minute detail. I offer it in hopes that the similarity in names might merit some title to your benevolence.)

From George Scott[9]   ALS: American Philosophical Society

Worthy Sir   Leeds the 12th. Sept. 1778

I arrived safe at home a fortnight ago. I staid in London a few days, and delivered punctually the messages committed to my care. Since my return I have thought much upon my project, and I continue determined to persevere; but I find I cannot Settle my dependencies, and concerns here, so soon as I could wish; for which reason I am obliged to solicit your friendly interference and assistance (if necessary) for a permission to return to settle my affairs here finally. If I can be accommodated with this indulgence, it will be a great convenience to me, and as a pledge of my sincerity, I will agree to deposit in the hands of congress, Five Hundred pounds Sterling, to be forfeited if I deviate from any engagement I may make with them relative to this subject. I will also agree (if required) not to carry any more Goods than what I carry over the first time; and these shall be to the amount of my own property as near as I can calculate, and may probably run to the amount of, from One to Two Thousand pounds Sterling. I would not sollicit such a favour if I did not see a necessity for it; and as I am sincere in my intentions, I hope this favour will not be denied me. I shall be glad to have your answer soon as convenient that I may regulate myself accordingly.

I beg you to accept my best thanks for the civillity with which you treated me at Passey, and I beg you to oblige me so far as to present my best compliments to Mr. Adams, Your Son and Mr. Austin, whose friendships, as well as your own I

9. This friend of Joseph Priestley resumed corresponding with BF in the winter of 1780 with other elusive references to either the export of goods, emigration or both. Although we are unsure about his identity, he was most likely a merchant in Leeds who, in 1774, contributed to a new White Cloth Hall: *The Publications of the Thoresby Society*, XLIV (1955), 15; XXII (1912–14), 140–1.

wish to secure. I am, with esteem Worthy Sir Your Most Obedient Servant   GEO. SCOTT

NB. When you write me, please put your letter under cover to
Mr. Thomas Squire Merchant in Amsterdam.

Addressed: The Honble. Benj: Franklin Esqr. / at Passey / near /
Paris

Notation: Geo Scott Duas [Leeds] 12. 7bre. 1778.

The American Commissioners to Schweighauser[1]

AL (draft): Massachusetts Historical Society; two copies: National Archives

⟨Passy, September 13, 1778: The *Thérèse*, whose cargo is assigned to us, has arrived at Nantes.[2] We wish to sell the cargo
and reserve the proceeds for a particular purpose. We request
and impower you to sell the cargo, transmit an account, and
hold the proceeds for our orders.

M. de Sartine informs us he has taken measures regarding
the prisoners. We have received from him a passport for a
cartel ship to come from England to Nantes and Lorient with
American prisoners. This ship should take off your hands and
ours all the British prisoners in France captured by American
warships and privateers. We sent this passport to England
yesterday.[3] We hope all these unhappy prisoners, British and
American, will soon have their liberty; if not, it will not be our
fault.

We want the *Baltimore* to sail as soon as possible, having no
particular orders to give about her.[4] We think the 5% commission you charge is too high and are willing to pay no more
than the customary commission, which we understand is 2%.⟩

1. Published in Taylor, *Adams Papers*, VII.
2. For the dispute over the *Thérèse*'s cargo see the exchange with Beaumarchais, Sept. 5 and 10.
3. Vergennes had told them on Sept. 9 that he was sending the passport;
BF did not actually forward it to Hartley until the 14th.
4. Sailing orders had already been sent to her captain, Thomas Read, on
July 29; see also Read's letter of Aug. 25.

Dumas to the American Commissioners[5]

ALS: American Philosophical Society; AL (draft): Algemeen Rijksar-chief

⟨The Hague, September 13[–18], 1778, in French: The Assembly of Holland has resolved to increase the republic's naval forces in Europe by 32 ships of the line as well as frigates and 8,000 crewmen. The address of the *bourse* of Amsterdam has arrived as has one from a number of Rotterdam merchants. The merchants of Dort are also complaining. The Dutch envoy in London reports three vessels have been returned, including one that a Dutch captain recaptured. The envoy has protested the English captures.

September 16: I have received your letter. The Grand Facteur was very pleased with it. I will leave a copy with our friend van Berckel.

September 17: A second address from Rotterdam describes the questioning which the masters of Dutch vessels taken to England must undergo. The issue of the captures will be discussed tomorrow. The Grand Facteur has made a copy of the address of the Amsterdam merchants.

September 18: The resolution taken today by the States of Holland to make stronger representations and to protect the country's trade is satisfactory.⟩

Vergennes to the American Commissioners

Draft:[6] Archives du Ministère des affaires étrangères; copies: Harvard University Library, Massachusetts Historical Society (two), National Archives, University of Virginia Library

A Versailles le 13 7bre *1778*

M. Lée m'a addressé le 12. du mois d[ernier], Messrs., un mémoire en faveur du Sr. Stevenson qui desiroit d'obtenir la permission de se rendre a la gadeloupe pour y recouvrer les sommes qui luy sont dûes;[7] M. de Sartine, à qui j'en ai fait

5. Published in Taylor, *Adams Papers*, VII.
6. In the hand of Gérard de Rayneval.
7. Stevens, *Facsimiles*, VIII, no. 846.

part, écrira aux administrateurs de cette Colonie pour qu'ils facilitent au S. Stevenson les moyens de faire ses recouvrements.[8]

From Madame Brillon

ALS: American Philosophical Society

ce 13 [September, 1778] a annét[9]

J'aimerois bien mieux prendre le thé avéc vous les mercredis et les samedis, et vous dire que je vous aime mon chér papa, que d'éstre reduitte a vous l'écrire; la maniére dont on dit qu'on aime; le ton qu'on y mest; un regard; éxpriment si bien et si viste—écrire tout cela, c'est difficil, c'est impossible! Cependant je n'ai que la ressource de l'écriture pour vous rappellér qu'au milieu des champs, vous avés laissé la fémme qui vous est le plus sincérement attaché; je m'en rapporte a votre coeur pour devinér ce que j'éxprimerai mal, ou trop foiblement. Nous menons ici une vie douce; avéc de l'occupation, et de la libérté, on ne s'énnuye jamais; mais avéc une áme tendre, il n'est pas un instant ou l'on ne sente qu'on est loin de ses amis! Oh mon chér papa, si jamais vous nous quittés tout a fait, je serai bien malheureuse ... mais éloignons cétte idée;[1] vous nous aimés, vous éstes avéc nous; vous viendrés peut éstre encore passér quelques moments dans ma chaumiére; oui vous viendrés nous rendre parfaittement heureux surtout si vous l'éstes avéc nous: il m'est si doux de vous soignér, de vous amusér, de cherchér a vous plaire; mon papa il fait encore beau, éstce que vous ne reviendrés pas: ne m'écrirai vous pas un mot en françois, car avéc l'anglois je serois pire que tantalle; une faim d'amitié me paroist la plus fascheuse de toutes. Adieu mon aimable papa, aimés moi tant que vous

8. *Ibid.*, XXII, no. 1945, where Stevenson's first name is given as William. He was the friend of Lee and rival courier to Carmichael: above, XXV, 406.

9. See our headnote to BF's letter to Mme. Brillon of Sept. 1.

1. One of several hints, that summer, to BF's possible departure. See Mme. Brillon's letter of Sept. 30.

voudrés, j'y répondrés tant que vous voudrés. J'ai l'honneur d'estre Votre trés humble et trés obeissante sérvante

D'HARDANCOURT BRILLON

Reçevés les hommages de toute ma société.

Addressed: A Monsieur / Monsieur Franklin / A Passy

From François Grasset & Cie.[2]

L: American Philosophical Society

A Lausanne en Suisse, dans le Canton de Berne,
le 13e. de Septembre 1778 et la 2de. de
l'Independance de nos bons amis
les Anglo-Americains.

Monsieur!

Nous vous prions d'excuser, avec votre bonté ordinaire, si nous prennons la liberté de vous ecrire pour vous offrir nos humbles et respectueuses obeissances en tout ce qui peut dependre de nous en ce Pays, ou nous sommes entierement a vos ordres: nous ne vous demandons pas moins la même faveur, pour celle que nous avons encore pris, de vous addresser le Catalogue general de notre librairie, qui contiennent environ dix mille articles differents, de livres en tous genres et facultés, en Latin, Anglois, François, Italien et Espagnols, avec les prix en argent de france, non reliez, a l'exception de ceux qui sont désignés tels sur nos dits catalogues. Et comme ils sont un peu considerables, nous vous les avons addresse par Diligence de Lyon a Paris. Nous desirons de recevoir bientôt vos ordres gracieux; en les attendant, nous vous suplions de nous permettre de nous dire, avec la plus grande veneration et le plus profond respect! De Votre Excellence, Les très humbles, obeïssants serviteurs

FRANÇOIS GRASSET ET COMP.

Libraires et Imprimeurs, a Lausanne en Suisse

2. François Grasset opened his business in 1753 and two years later his unauthorized edition of *La Pucelle* precipitated a famous controversy with Voltaire. For the past decade the firm had been publishing the *Almanach de Lausanne. Dictionnaire historique de la Suisse.*

a Son Excellence Monsieur Francklin, Ambassadeur du Congrès en son hotel à Paris

Notation: Grasset & Co Booksellers Lausanne

To David Hartley

ALS and transcript: Library of Congress; copy: Public Record Office

Dear Sir,   Passy, Sept. 14. 1778

I now send you the Passport required. I postpon'd answering your last[3] in hopes of obtaining it sooner; but tho' it was long since agreed to, much Business in the Admiralty Department here has I suppose occasion'd its Delay. The Port of Calais was not approv'd of, and I think the Ports mention'd (Nantes or L'Orient) are better for you as well as for us, not only as being nearer to Plymouth, but as many of your Sailors would probably have found Opportunities of deserting in the long March from Brest to Calais, they being afraid of the Press. I understand that upwards of 80 more of your People have been brought by ours Prisoners into France since the List I sent you, but I cannot now send you their Names.[4] You have not mention'd whether the Proposition of sending us the whole of those in your Prisons was agreed to. If it is, you may rely on our sending immediately all that come to our hands for the future; or we will give at your Option, an Order for the Ballance to be deliver'd to your Fleet in America. By putting a little Confidence in one another, we may thus diminish the Miseries of War. To make the Expence of these Exchanges more equal, if another Cartel Ship should be hereafter necessary, we hereby promise to send it to England at our Charge; and so it may continue to be done alternately as long as the

3. Of Aug. 14.
4. BF had sent his list on July 13. At least fifty of the new prisoners were McNeill's: see Moylan's letter of Aug. 26 and the commissioners' reply of the 31st.

War continues. With great Esteem and Affection, I am ever Dear Sir, Your most obedient and most humble Servant

B FRANKLIN

David Hartley Esqr

Endorsed: D F Sept 14 1778

From Edward Bancroft

ALS: Harvard University Library

Dear Sir   Monday Morning 14 Septr. 1778

Inclosed I send you an English News paper which though it Contains little, contains all the news I have received from London. I also send you a Letter which I have received from Mr. Ellison,[5] who with Mr. Saml. Wharton desire me to second the request it Contains; which however I would not do, did there appear any impropriety in it; but as it intends only to ascertain a fact, which is no secret, and which Congress has long since published, I do not see any harm that can result from it, and should you perceive none and be willing to comply with the request, I will according to Mr. Ellison's desire, engage a Notary to Call any morning that may be convenient just to see the Date in question.

I am not yet able to Walk as far as Passy or would have waited on you myself. I am ever Dear Sir Your most respectful and Devoted humble Servant   EDWD. BANCROFT

Addressed: To the Hon'ble / Benjamin Franklin / Passy

Notation by Arthur Lee: Gambg. Letter of Dr B. sent to the other Commissioners by Dr. Franklin

5. On Sept. 8 Ellison had asked which day the treaty was signed.

From John Paul Jones

ALS: American Philosophical Society; AL (draft): National Archives; copy: United States Naval Academy

Honored and Dear Sir,   Brest September 14th. 1778.

Your much esteemed favor of the 6th. at 5 AM. I received the 8th. That kind letter from your Hand at so early an Hour adds much to former Obligations, but more especially as it found me in need of such Cordials; for I have yet received no other letter from the Eastward since the 17th. before Doctor Bancrofts indisposition.

The Strange mistake of the Minister induced me to write the within letter to the Prince the 9th.[6] I sent it inclosed to Doctor Bancroft, as I apprehended that it would Appear before your return to Passy from the Country. It was submitted to his Criticism, therefore I am not sure whither it has or has not been delivered.

I yesterday took the resolution to write the inclosed explicit letter to the Minister. I still wish to think he meant to do me Service from the beginning, And in that Case I think a liberal Minded Man ought not to take offence at liberal Sentiments, Especially where there is no offence intended. I submit both the letters to You with Utmost deference and beg you will Suppress the last if you find it Amiss. I am sorry it is so long, but I could not be Sufficiently full, and more Concise.[7]

I should have made no Mention of my Rank had it not been hinted to me that it was proposed to send me from St. Malo under the Command of French Lieutenants, which I think I

---

6. Sartine, who claimed to have sent orders for Jones to sail with d'Orvilliers, had accused the captain of failing to arrive at Brest in time to meet the fleet (BF to Jones, Sept. 6). Jones was mystified, and begged the Prince de Nassau to "undeceive the Minister": he had been in Brest since Aug. 10 and had dined frequently with d'Orvilliers, who lamented having to leave without having received the authorization to take Jones with him. APS.

7. Jones's letter to Sartine, Sept. 13, reviewed the events which had so far led only to "tormenting suspense": John Henry Sherburne, *The Life and Character of John Paul Jones* (2nd ed.; New York, 1851), pp. 74–6.

ought not to Submit to, as Congress has never proposed to put me under the Command of Captains.[8] The Frigates from St. Malo[9] were sent in consequence of a hint which I furnished. Tho' I am myself neglected, I hope they have been very successful.

I have Written to the Marine Committee that the Court of France have requested as a favor by a letter to the American Plenipotentiaries, that I might be permitted to remain for some time in Europe. Of course no Command will be reserved for me in America. Yet it is more consistent with my Honor and Duty, However great the Mortification, to return to America unemployed before the Winter; than it would be to remain here Amused with Unmeaning Promises 'till the Spring, and then be disappointed.

It is in Vain for the Minister to pretend that he has not Ships to bestow. I know the contrary. He has bestowed the Renommée and others here since my return; and there are yet several New Ships Unbestowed at St. Malo and elsewhere: I know too that, unless the States oppose it, the Indean can be got afloat with a tenth part of the Difficulty that has been represented. If I was worth his notice at the beginning I am not less so now.

After all, You have desired me to have Patience. And I promise you that I will wait your kind Advice, and take no Step without your Approbation. If it were consistent and convenient for you to See Monseigneur de Sartine, I should hope that such an explanation would be the consequence as might remove every cause of Uneasiness. I am, with a Heart impressed with Sentiments of the truest Esteem and Respect,

8. Sartine, as Jones had understood it when at Versailles, had proposed to give him command of the 22-gun frigate *Lively* and join an expedition from St. Malo to the North Sea. The *Lively*'s command, in the mean time, was given to some one else. Jones, for once, was relieved: the ship turned out to be inadequate and, as the expedition was to be commanded by a lieutenant, he had been spared the insult of being asked to serve under an inferior officer. Jones to Louis XVI, Oct. 19, APS.

9. The *Gentille* and *Amazone*, along with the cutter *Guêpe*, cruised in the North Sea from Aug. 14 to Nov. 9: Archives navales B³649:229; B⁴138: 160–82; Didier Neuville, ed., *Etat sommaire des Archives de la Marine antérieures à la Révolution* (Paris, 1898), p. 195.

Honored and dear Sir Your very Obliged very Obedient very
humble Servant,   JNO P JONES
NB No News to be depended upon from the Fleet.

His Excellency Doctor Franklin.

Endorsed: Capt Jones Brest Sept. 14. 78

To Madame Brillon

AL: American Philosophical Society

[*c.* September 15, 1778][1]

J'accepte avec un plaisir infini, ma chere amie, la Proposition
que vous me faites avec tant de bonté de m'adopter pour vôtre
Pere. Je serai bienheureux en la Parenté d'une si bonne enfante; et comme en venant m'etablir ici, j'ai perdu la douce
Compagnie et l'Attention respectueuse d'une Fille affectionnée, cette Perte sera reparée, et j'aurai la Satisfaction de refle-
chir avec Confiance, que, si je passe ici les petites restes de
mes jours, une autre fille affectionnée me soignera pendant ma
vie, et fermera tendrement mes paupieres quand je dois prendre mon dernier Repos. Oui, ma très chere enfante, je vous
aime comme Pere, de tout mon Coeur. C'est vrai que je soup-
çonne quelquefois cet Coeur de vouloir aller plus loin, mais je
tache de cacher cela de moi-même.

Je ne pu pas passer en vue de cet sejour hôpitalier[2] ou j'ai
été si souvent heureux en vôtre Compagnie, et en votre amitié, sans être sensible de tout cet Regret, et ces Peine
d'Absence que vous sçavez si bien exprimer. Vos bons Voisins[3]
sont bien obligeantes, et ils font que les soirées des Mercredis
et des Sammedis soient aussi agreables à moi que possible
sans vous. Mais la Vue de ceux que j'ai été accoutumé de voir
avec vous, me fait apperçevoir continuellement que vous n'y
étés pas: ce qui tire de moi des Soupirs, que je ne blâme pas,
car quoique à mon age il ne convient pas de dire que je suis
amoureux d'une jeune femme, il n'y a rien qui me prohibe de

1. See the headnote to BF's letter to her of Sept. 1.
2. Her house in Passy.
3. The Le Veillard family.

confesser que j'admire et que j'aime une Assemblage de toutes les virtues femelles, et de toutes les Talens admirables; et que j'aime ma Fille parcequ'elle est vraiment aimable, et qu'elle m'aime.

John Bondfield to the American Commissioners[4]

ALS: American Philosophical Society

⟨Bordeaux, September 15, 1778: The cutter *Tartar*, Captain Southcomb, arrived yesterday from the York River, which it left on July 29.[5] Southcomb reports d'Estaing had taken five English frigates and that New York was closely blockaded and would doubtless fall. [*Postscripts*:] Captain Ayres died on the 13th; I had him buried as decently as is allowed to Protestants. I will forward Mr. W.T. Franklin's commission[6] this week.⟩

Richard Grinnell to the American Commissioners[7]

ALS: American Philosophical Society

⟨Guernsey, September 15, 1778: Captain Peter Collas and I sailed with Captain [Corbin] Barnes from Paimboeuf August

4. Published in Taylor, *Adams Papers*, VII.

5. This does not appear to be the Virginia State Navy vessel of the same name described in E.M. Sanchez-Saavedra, ed., *A Guide to Virginia Military Organizations in the American Revolution, 1774–1787* ([Richmond], 1978), p. 162.

6. Our best guess is that WTF was to serve in some capacity on the *Marquise de Lafayette*, a frigate being armed for privateering by Basmarein & Raimbaux: XXVI, 677 n. Bondfield was investing heavily in the venture: see his letter of July 24, 1779. APS. WTF never did take part in what turned out to be an unsuccessful cruise.

7. Published in Taylor, *Adams Papers*, VII. Grinnell described his recent history to the commissioners on July 9. For the information he provided on Guernsey's fortifications, see Butterfield, *John Adams Diary*, II, 320–22. See *ibid.*, 319–20, and below, Oct. 7, for his detailed account of the British whaling fleet which, together with that offered by Tristram Barnard, [after Oct. 9], formed the core of the commissioners' intelligence to Sartine of Oct. 30. JA recommended Grinnell for a place with Capt. McNeill to whom he proposed a cruise against the whalers: Taylor, *Adams Papers*, VII, under Oct. 9.

29. We were captured September 1 by Captain Abraham Bushall who treated us like brothers. We fell in with Captain Niles whose schooner *Spy* had been taken by a Jersey privateer. Niles and Barnes succeeded in throwing all papers overboard. Barnes is still on the privateer. You will receive this through the son of the Mr. Dobrée who resides here.[8]⟩

Daniel McNeill to the American Commissioners[9]

ALS: American Philosophical Society

⟨Paris, September 15, 1778: On my cruise in the *General Mifflin* I gave chase August 23 to three ships fifty leagues west and north of Ushant Island. I pursued the largest and brought her to at 2 p.m. She was the brig *Isabelle* from Guadeloupe bound for Bordeaux with a cargo of sugar, coffee and cotton; she had been captured by the *Prince of Orange*, commanded by Philip Amy of Guernsey, August 19 at 2 p.m. She was in English possession 80 hours.[1] Please apply to the French ministry for the vessel to be adjudicated or for liberty to sail with her or dispose of her.⟩

8. The father, Thomas, was a Guernsey merchant; the son, Peter Frederick, Schweighauser's son-in-law, resided in Nantes.
9. Published in Taylor, *Adams Papers*, VII.
1. The time factor is critical to the legal status of the capture, as correspondence on the following days between Sartine and the commissioners indicates.

From Henry Coder[2]

ALS: American Philosophical Society

Monsieur   paris ce 15e 7bre 1778

Je prends la Liberté de vous adresser la reponsse que m'a fait Le ministre a La notte que j'ai eu l'honneur de vous comuniquer.[3]

Je vous suplie de prendre conoissance, du memoire si joint et s'il vous interesse assés pour Le remettre ou du moins pour en parler a Mr. de Sartine, je vous devrai sans doute la fin d'une persecution, sous laquelle je suis a la vellie [veille] de succomber ainsi que mon frere.[4]

J'aurai Le plaisir d'aller a passi m'informer de l'etat de votre senté. Je suis avec veneration Monsieur votre tres humble et tres obeissent scerviteur   CODER

hotel dangletere rue de seine fb st germain

M. le docteur franklin

Notation: Coder Paris ce 15e. 7bre. 1778

2. The former infantry captain (identified in XXIII, 362–3) who had been furnishing uniforms to the Americans and who had concocted, with Dubourg, a plan for raiding the Mediterranean the previous spring: XXVI, 655–6 n.

3. Possibly a reference to the plan Dubourg and Coder had proposed, in an undated memorandum in Dubourg's hand now at the APS, and would resubmit to BF on Dec. 13. BF endorsed it "Project Descente sur l'Irelande," and some one has penciled on it "Coder;" it argues for raids on the English and Irish coasts. More than enough officers and old soldiers of all nationalities would leap at the chance of booty, and ships now fitted out as privateers might readily be borrowed. Congress could not invest in an enterprise that costs less or offers more. Coder is convinced that M. Jones or any other brave American—perhaps WTF—put at the head of such an expedition, "seroit un puissant aiguillon pour notre jeunesse avide de courses et de combats, de lauriers et de pillage." France is famous for such young men; why not use them?

4. Gabriel-Aphrodise de Coderc (b. 1743), an aide-major in the regiment of Port-au-Prince (St.-Domingue). Documentation of his travails fills a file at the Archives nationales (E 86 Colonies), and was forwarded by Jean-Claude David, Paris. Unless otherwise noted, details of the episode as given below come from that file.

Within two weeks of his arrival in St.-Domingue in mid-May, 1777 (*Naval Docs.*, IX, 124), the new governor of the Leeward Islands, comte Robert d'Argout (for whom see the *DBF*), propositioned Gabriel who refused to

From Silas Deane

ALS: American Philosophical Society

This is the first letter informing Franklin of his election as minister plenipotentiary to the court of France; the official notification was not sent for another six weeks.[5] The dissolution of the American commission was not the result of its internal dissensions and inefficiency, but rather of the dictates of diplomatic protocol. This demanded that the United States have a representative in France equal in rank to Gérard, who arrived in Philadelphia in July as minister plenipotentiary. Franklin was an obvious choice and apparently only Pennsylvania opposed him.[6] On September 11 Congress unanimously resolved that its interests required a minister in France and Franklin was elected to the new post three days later.[7]

---

compromise his honor "en se pretant a le favoriser dans ses redicules amours" (Henry Coder to Sartine, Oct. 4, 1778). Thereafter, the young officer, as he maintained, was persecuted by the governor. Exiled from the Court for reasons we do not know, Henry, in the fall of 1778, was trying to use all his connections on his injured brother's behalf. But BF, unwilling to be drawn into the personal claims of individual French citizens, would not go beyond assuring Coder orally on Sept. 29 ("mardi dernier") that he would seize the first opportunity of telling Sartine of his interest in both Henry and Gabriel. (*Ibid.*) During the following months, Henry tried to capitalize on his friendship with BF, who had given him reassuring words about Sartine's "justice et sagesse sans egard au rang et aux considerations." (Coder to Sartine, Nov. 19, 1778; see also his letter to Sartine, Feb. 18, 1779.)

Although Gabriel had come to France to present his own case, the King decided on Dec. 18 that a court-martial should be held in St.-Domingue. D'Argout, who had always maintained that the incident boiled down to a duel between Gabriel and another officer, acknowledged the order on April 26, 1779, and Gabriel was eventually vindicated: Coder to BF, Oct. 17, 1779, APS.

5. See BF's instructions of Oct. 26, below. In Smith, *Letters*, XI, 141 n, the editors speculate that Congress delayed because it wanted to draft instructions for BF, decide assignments for JA and Arthur Lee, and conclude its investigation of Deane. BF apparently received this letter from Deane in late November: Butterfield, *Adams Correspondence*, III, 122–4.

6. RB to BF, Oct. 22, below. The vote was secret.

7. *JCC*, XII, 901, 908. Copies of these resolutions, most probably sent with the Oct. 28 letter, below, of the committee for foreign affairs, are at Hist. Soc. of Pa. and Harvard University Library.

My Dear sir   Philadelphia Septr. 15th. 1778.

This is my fifth Letter since my arrival in this City and having sent Duplicates by three different Vessels I rely some one of them will arrive, and therefore in This only mention what has occurr'd since my last by Capt. Bell. Genl. Sullivan made a good Retreat from Rhode Island.[8] General Clinton with near One hundred Sail of Transports and about Five Thousand Troops arrivd the morning after he had left The Island. Byron's Fleet (supposed to be) has joined Lord Howe, and they appeared before Boston for a few Days. By the last Letters they were in Newport. Count D'Estaing is repairing in Boston the Damages received by the late Storm. Our Enemy is greatly superior at present by Sea, they landed at Bedford to the East of Rhode Island, burned a Number of Stores and Shipps, and it is said were actually entrenching At that place with Five Thousand Men. In the meantime from all Appearances, they are on the point of evacuating New York, their heavy Cannon and Stores are actually shipp'd and shipping, there are various Conjectures as to their Destination. I have no doubt that the main force is designed for the West Indies, and wish that Our Freinds in that Quarter may be ready to receive them.[9]

Congress yesterday chose You to be their Minister Plenipotentiary to the Court of France, and You will very soon receive their Letters, and Credentials. I am very happy on the Occasion, and the more so on Account of the Unanimity with which I learn it was carried; what other arrangements will take place I know not, nor do I much Interest myself on the Subject. I design to be in Paris next Winter when I shall relate to You many things, not proper to be committed to writing,

8. See Deane's letter of Sept. 2, the only one we have found of the five he mentions. Thomas Bell, a Philadelphian associated with Robert Morris and a frequent courier between America and France, carried one of the missing letters: Smith, *Letters*, VI, 161; *PMHB*, LV (1931), 227.

9. The attack on New Bedford was only a raid and the British did not evacuate New York (although in early November they detached 5,000 troops to reinforce East Florida and to attack the French Caribbean island of St. Lucia): Willcox, *Portrait of a General*, pp. 250–4; see also Vaughan's letter of Sept. 6.

especially in a Letter, at a Period like the present. Mr. Bache is
still in the Country with his Family, were your Freinds other-
ways than well, I should certainly hear of it. I send You the
papers of the Day by which and my former Letters You will
see what a foolish Game the Commissioners are playing, and
with how much boldness they assert what You and I, as well
as some others, know to be The most Absolute Falsehoods.[1] I
pray you to present my most respectful Compliments to Our
Freinds at Paris, and Passy, in particular to the Duke de *Roch-
faucaud*, and the Duchess *D'Anville*,[2] and to others in the Circle
of Our Acquaintance who may enquire after Me. I am very
impatient to be with You, on many Accounts, independant of
the esteem, and Freindship I shall forever have for You, and
shall exert myself to return as Soon as possible. In the meantime I am ever with the most sincere and respectful Attachment Dear sir Your most Obedient and Very Humble servant
SILAS DEANE

I have not received any Letter from You since my Leaving
France

His Excelly. Benja. Franklin

Endorsed: Mr Deane Sept. 15. 1778

From ―――― Gerard   ALS: American Philosophical Society

De Passy ce 15 7bre. 1778 à 9.heures du Matin.
M∴T∴C∴F∴[3]

Vous etes prié de la part de la R.L.D.St.P. des V. ffrs.[4] de
vous trouver jeudi. 17. de ce Mois de 7bre. 1778. à Midy
précises à la Loge d'adoption qui se tiendra au Ranelagh

1. The Carlisle commission's declaration of Aug. 26 accused the leaders
of the American cause of "blind Deference" to France: Stevens, *Facsimiles*,
XI, no. 1133, p. 2; Meng, *Despatches of Gérard*, p. 256.
2. The duke's mother, Marie-Louise-Nicole-Elisabeth d'Enville.
3. Mon très cher frère.
4. Respectable Loge de Saint Pierre des Vrais Frères, for which see Le
Bihan, *Francs-Maçons parisiens*, p. 22.

de Passy[5] près la Muette. Il y aura réception d'appsse. de Compgne. et de Maitsse.[6] avec Musique, Banquet ensuite et Bal.

La Cotisation est de 12 *l.t.* que vous êtes prié de faire remettre au f.·. Morisan à la grille du Bois de Boulogne et d'avertir sur le Champ si vous pouvez vous y trouver ou non.

Apportez s'il vous plait vos ornemens et votre glaive. Par Mandement   GERARD

Pour le secretaire

Loge d'Adoption au Ranelagh de Passy près la Muette

Addressed: A Monsieur / Monsieur de franklin / en son hôtel / a Passy

Endorsed: Gerard Free mason

Notation: 15. 7.bre 1778

From Yves-Joseph de Kerguelen de Trémarec[7]

ALS: American Philosophical Society

Monsieur   Saumur 15. 7bre. 1778.

J'ai appris que vous faites construire en hollande deux frégates tres fortes;[8] je serois au comble du bonheur si j'avais

---

5. The *loges d'adoption* were "paramasonic groups created ... to satisfy women's curiosity, silence calumny, and enliven Masonic fêtes." The Grand Orient de France had voted on June 10, 1774, to take them under consideration and impose rules and a ritual. Before 1789, they consisted mostly of ladies of high nobility. Information kindly provided by Prof. Gordon Silber. See also Pierre Chevallier, *Histoire de la franc-maçonnerie française* (4 vols., Paris, [1974–75]), I, 200–210. For the Ranelagh see XXVI, 697.

6. The feminine equivalents of apprentis, compagnons, maîtres.

7. This brilliant naval officer had been released on Aug. 25 from the jail in Saumur where he had been confined since 1775: Bodinier. See Kerguelen's memoir, XXIV, 279–81 and entry on him in Etienne Taillemite, *Dictionnaire des marins français* (Paris, 1982).

8. His information, perhaps not surprisingly, is badly out of date. The two frigates had become one, the *Indien*, and she had been sold to the French government in late 1777: XXV, 208–9.

L'honneur de commander un pareil batiment. On peut avec une frégate de ce genre se rendre maitre d'un vaisseau de Ligne surtout Lorsque la mer est grosse.

Si vous avez la bonté, Monsieur, de m'en confier une, j'ose vous assurer que je me conduirai de maniere a mériter votre estime, celle du Congréz, et de toute l'europe.

J'ai *43* ans, depuis l'age de 15 ans j'apprend le metier de la mer. J'ai commandé pendant 14 ans consécutifs dans toutes les mers. Etant capitaine des vaisseaux du roi la jalousie m'a fait eprouver des malheurs affreux. Il n'y a rien que je ne fasse pour les faire oublier et pour me venger de mes ennemis par des actions brillantes.

Je vous prie, Monsieur, de m'accorder le commandement d'une de vos frégates. Je vous en aurai une obligation infinie, et j'executerai vos ordres de la maniere la plus exacte et la plus glorieuse. Je suis avec respect Monsieur Votre tres humble et tres obeissant Serviteur   KERGUELEN

P.S. Si vous m'accordez, Monsieur, la faveur que je vous demande, je me rendrai sur le champ en hollande. Parcequil ÿ a boucoup de choses de détail a perfectioner dans la disposition d'un batiment pour le combat.

Endorsed: Capt. Kergueler Marine Offr.

From Jean-Baptiste Le Roy

AL: American Philosophical Society

AL: American Philosophical Society

M   [before September 16, 1778]
    Vous êtes prié d'assister au Convoy du fils de Mr. Le Roy qui sera Inhumé en la Paroisse Royale de Nôtre Dame de graces de Passy mercredy 16 7bre. 1778. a 8. heures du matin.[9]

Addressed: A Monsieur / Monsieur Franclin / A Passy.

9. This was "le petit Basile" mentioned in XXVI, 158 and in our annotation to Mme. de Marcenay's letter, Aug. 22.

Sartine to the American Commissioners[1]

Copies: Massachusetts Historical Society, National Archives (two), Library of Congress

⟨Versailles, September 16, 1778, in French: I have received your letter concerning the French ship *Isabelle* recaptured by the privateer *General Mifflin*. The naval ordnance of 1681 assigns captains of recaptured vessels a third of their value if retaken within 24 hours. American privateers in France benefit from these provisions assuming that conditions of reciprocity obtain for French privateers in American ports. Americans may prefer French to British law which awards a higher proportion to the original proprietor. The law, however, may not be applicable in the present affair of the *Isabelle*. The French proprietor claims his vessel as retaken from pirates; he offers to pay the American privateer one third its value. In all likelihood the Guernsey privateer had no letter of marque. The issue must be submitted to a court of law.[2] At any rate I await your opinion, in case our two nations are subject to different laws on the matter.⟩

From de Perygnon

ALS: American Philosophical Society

Monsieur   a Paris ce 16. 7bre. 1778

J'eus bien desiré vous exprimer verbalement combien je suis sensible à votre complaisance, mais ma maladie recule encore l'instant ou je pourrai jouir de cet honneur. Votre opinion en une matiere qui ne peut vous être inconnue mais Sacrée; c'est le plus heureux présage pour le succès d'une affaire bien intéressante. Votre bonté m'enhardit à vous supplier de m'accorder une nouvelle grace; je voudrois faire passer au Congrès l'arrêt du Conseil de St. Domingue qui demande un acte de notoriété de Philadelphie:[3] j'ai divers expéditions de cette

---

1. Published in Taylor, *Adams Papers*, VII.
2. As indeed it was. See Bachaumont, where a different and detailed version of the capture of the *Isabelle* is given, along with its legal implications. *Mémoires secrets*, XII, 186, 188–90.
3. This enclosure is at the APS.

piece, ma reconnoïssance sera sans bornes, si vous daignés me permettre de vous les remettre afin de faire tenir au Congrès l'arrêt et le Mémoire et en recevoir l'acte de Notoriété.

Je ne prendrois pas cette liberté si la route ordinaire étoit parfaitement sûr, mais je n'ose esperer, que par votre entremise, cet acte de notorieté qui Seul jugera la Cause. Daignés pardonner mon importunité. Votre bonté, plus encore que l'importance de l'affaire en est l'excuse. Je Suis avec respect Monsieur, Votre très humble et très obéissant Serviteur

> DE PEYRIGNON[4]
> chés M. De Chanceru,
> membre de la Société royale de medecine
> rue Ste. anne Butte St. Roch

Endorsed: De Pereygnon about a Marriage

The American Commissioners to the President of Congress[5]

AL (draft): Massachusetts Historical Society; three copies and transcript: National Archives

⟨Passy, September 17, 1778: Since our last letter, July 20, there has been an important naval battle in which, in our opinion, the French had a manifest and great advantage. Both fleets are again at sea. The British public is amused and the public funds supported by rumors of peace. We are in a state of suspense awaiting news of the comte d'Estaing.

We have taken measures to borrow money in Amsterdam but we cannot yet say with what success; we have had no answer to our request for permission to borrow money in France. We yesterday[6] applied [to the French government] for a continuation of the quarterly payments of 750,000 *l.t.* Because of the apprehension of a general war England, France,

---

4. Perygnon signs himself differently than he did in his letter of Sept. 3.
5. Published in Taylor, *Adams Papers*, VII.
6. In fact on Aug. 28; see their letter to Vergennes. The present letter was begun on Aug. 29: see the annotation of it in Taylor, *Adams Papers*, VII.

the Emperor, Spain and Prussia are borrowing money and offering better interest rates than we can.

We have administered the oath of allegiance and issued certificates to that effect to Mr. Moor, Mr. Woodford and Mr. Montgomery, have given naval commissions to Mr. Livingston and Mr. Amiel and have administered an oath of secrecy to one of our secretaries. We wish instructions about such matters, and about Englishmen wishing to emigrate to America, about certification of ship cargoes belonging to Americans, and about payments to escaped prisoners, a large segment of our expenses. The comte de Vergennes informs us he asked Mr. Holker to write him from time to time. We have sent orders to Bordeaux to ship you 56 cannon, but this will take perhaps two or three months.⁷⟩

The American Commissioners to Jacques Richard⁸

AL (draft): Massachusetts Historical Society; two copies: National Archives

Sir   Passi. September 17. 1778

We have written to Mr. Schweighauser of Nantes to receive the Cargo of the Therese and dispose of it as soon as may be. These are therefore to desire you will deliver the Cargo into his or his Agents Hands, whenever he shall demand it. We are, sir, your humble servants.

Captain Richards

7. Commissioners to Bondfield, Aug. 19.
8. The captain of the *Thérèse*: Morton, *Beaumarchais Correspondance*, III, 60 n.

The American Commissioners to Sartine[9]

AL (draft): Massachusetts Historical Society; copies: National Archives (three)

⟨Passy, September 17, 1778: We received today your letter of the sixteenth relative to the recapture of the *Isabelle*. We agree with your Excellency's sentiments on reciprocity between the two nations. Unfortunately we have no access here to United States' law. A copy of your letter and our answer will be sent to Congress and we assume Congress will extend to French privateers the advantages enjoyed by our privateers here. In the present case, depending as it does on a narrow construction of piracy and on a departure from the spirit of the laws of nations, we think it ill-advised of the owner to enter litigation.

We question the applicability of the royal ordnance of 1681: the Guernsey privateer was commissioned by the British king to cruise against American vessels and while no formal declaration of hostilities exists between England and France, these nations have in effect been at war since the mutual withdrawal of ambassadors. If it is admitted that the two nations are at war, it would be without precedent to judge the subjects of either one guilty of piracy for acts of hostility committed at sea against the other.⟩

Horneca, Fizeaux & Cie. to the American Commissioners[1]

Copies: National Archives, Massachusetts Historical Society

⟨Amsterdam, September 17, 1778, in French: Your letter of August 31 came only two days ago. Ours of the 7th acknowledged receipt of the book of notes and coupons signed by you. We will work on the arrangements with all possible zeal and prudence, and with all the skill we have acquired from fifty years of experience; your instructions will be scrupulously ob-

---

9. Published in Taylor, *Adams Papers*, VII.
1. Published in Taylor, *Adams Papers*, VII.

served. Because this loan is the first of its kind, we shall not know until we consult our brokers whether some authentication or other formality is needed. But we will approach them without loss of time, and try to get priority over the offerings of other powers, which are bringing money into short supply. The allowance you make should procure us this advantage. We will cover all expenses, including payment of interest, and take ten percent out of capital; for each thousand florins floated we remit you nine hundred. We hope that this arrangement will meet with your approval.[2]⟩

William Lee to the American Commissioners[3]

ALS: American Philosophical Society

⟨Paris, September 17, 1778:[4] I wish to confer with you on an important and profoundly secret subject;[5] I will wait on you at any hour tomorrow at noon or afterwards when you are alone.⟩

From Madame Brillon

ALS: American Philosophical Society

ce jeudi 17 [September, 1778][6] a annét

Comme je venois de vous écrire mon chér papa pour le thé de mércredi, comme je pensois bien fort a vous, comme je disois, óh surement si ce bon papa le peut, il reviendra nous voir; je

2. We have omitted a number of financial intricacies. The commissioners' reply below, Oct. 2, does not deal with them, but only with the firm's suggested ten-percent levy on capital; this applied only to the first year, and they would have none of it.

3. Published in Taylor, *Adams Papers*, VII.

4. Lee had been in Paris several days and planned to remain there no longer than three weeks: Ford, *Letters of William Lee*, II, 472, 473.

5. His meetings with de Neufville (discussed in Dumas' letter of Sept. 3). Lee had already told the committee for foreign affairs of his and de Neufville's draft treaty. He apparently left a copy with the commissioners: Ford, *Letters of William Lee*, II, 473–7.

6. See the headnote to BF's letter to her of Sept. 1.

reçois une léttre du voisin[7] qui m'annonce que vous viendrés tous le samedi 26, que le jour est pris, que vous viendrés disnér, et ne retournerés que le lundi 28 aprés disnér; qu'en attendant vous m'aimés toujours et que vous m'écrirés; vous exprimér le plaisir que m'a fait la léttre du voisin seroit bien difficile, si vous ne sçaviés déja a qu'él point je vous suis attachée; vous voir, vous voir chés moi mon chér papa, est un des plus grand bonheurs dont j'aye jamais joui, et que je puisse imaginér; mon áme faitte pour aimér bien fortement, pour sentir tout le prix du retour de la vostre, s'est si bien accoutumée a vous voir souvent, que vous lui manqués absolument, qu'elle vous chérche, vous appélle ... les mercredis et les samedis surtout sont d'une longueur a passér! L'éspérance au moins vá me soutenir; samedi je dirai, encore un mércredi, mércredi je dirai, samedi ce bon papa viendra; ce samedi la je dirai je suis heureuse; en attendant je penserai tous les jours, que le jour que je viens de passér, m'approche de celui ou nous nous revérons; et tous les jours je vous aimerai jusqu'a la fin de ma vie, et je croirai que quelquefois vous distes, madame Brillon est une amie de plus pour moi; j'ai l'honneur d'estre mon chér papa Votre trés humble et trés obeissante servante   D'HARDANCOURT BRILLON

Addressed: A Monsieur / Monsieur Franklin / A Passy

Francis Hopkinson[8] to the American Commissioners

ALS (three):[9] American Philosophical Society

Gentlemen   Philadelphia Septr. 18th. 1778
     I am directed by the Board of Treasury of the United States to transmit to you a List, shewing the Numbers the Bills of Exchange are to bear, which will be drawn upon you and is-

---

7. Le Veillard's country home was in Dreux, not far from Anet.
8. For BF's old friend, recently elected treasurer of loans, see XII, 125 n. The present letter is the first of many in which he reports on the distribution of bills of exchange to the state loan offices.
9. Marked "duplicate," "triplicate," and "quadruplicate."

sued from the respective Loan Offices. Agreeable to this Order I now enclose you an Invoice of such Bills as have been forwarded to each State from my Office, ascertaining their Numbers, Amount &c. The Design in giving you this Information, is that if any Bills should come to your Hands whose Numbers and Denominations will not correspond with the enclosed Invoice, you may know them to be Counterfeits.[1] I have the Honour to be Gentlemen Your most obedient humble servant FRAS HOPKINSON Treasurer of Loans

Addressed: To / The Commissioner or Commissioners / of the United States of America / at / Paris

Notations in different hands: Fr. Hopkinson Treasr. of Loans Sept. 18 1778. / [*in Hopkinson's hand:*] (on public service) (Duplicate) To be sunk if in Danger of falling into the Hands of the Enemy

Elisabeth-Angélique Lalouëlle to the American Commissioners

L:[2] American Philosophical Society

⟨St. Maio, September 18, 1778, in French: Bernard-Alexandre Lalouëlle, my son, embarked in January, 1777, on the *Reprisal,* Capt. Wickes, as second surgeon at the salary of 72 *l.t.* per month, plus two shares of the prizes.[3] He performed brilliantly

1. He was enclosing a list of the bills of exchange for payment of interest on loans between Sept. 10, 1777 and March 1, 1778 sent from his office to the state loan offices: see Gibson's letter of Aug. 8. At those offices, holders of the loan certificates could (at their option) accept them as payment of interest; the bills were payable on the commissioners at Paris. The list gives for each state the number of sets of bills, their serial numbers, and their denominations. Grand totals are $319,500 equalling 1,597,500 *l.t.* The majority of these bills had been accepted by the commissioners at least by 1785, most of them undoubtedly earlier: Thomas Barclay, Account of Bills drawn on the commissioners and paid by F. Grand, Aug. 24, 1785, Library of Congress.

2. Her brother, R.J. Faucon, acted as secretary.

3. Clark, *Wickes,* p. 375, lists him as surgeon's mate.

the amputation of the arm of the second officer in command.[4] When the *Reprisal*, having taken several prizes, docked in St. Malo in June of that year, my son visited me at home and came down with smallpox on the second day. Capt. Wickes came to see him, promised to pay all his expenses, and ordered him not to board the frigate until they were ready to sail because the French authorities were on the lookout for French officers. Yet my son received only 72 *l.t.* and a promise to be made first surgeon as soon as Capt. Wickes took the command of a larger ship.

The *Reprisal* sailed on September 14 and we never heard from my son since then. Rumor has it that the ship sank, without survivors, near Newfoundland.[5] If such is the case, I beg you to remit to me, through Messrs. Desegray & Beaugeard, the sum that was owing to him, *i.e.* his salary from January to September, minus 240 *l.t.* he had already received.)

From [Jean?] Chanorier[6]   L: American Philosophical Society

Ce Vendredy 18 [September?[7] 1778]
M. Chanorier présente mille respectueux Complimens a Messieurs franklin et a Monsieur adams et Les prient de vouloir bien se rapeller qu'ils se sont engagés à Lui faire L'honneur de diner chés Luy Demain samedy.

Addressed: A Monsieur / Monsieur Le Docteur / franklin / A Passy

4. For the treatment of the wounded officer, Lt. Robert Harris, see *ibid.*, pp. 131–2.

5. She did sink, with only one survivor: xxv, 205.

6. Probably the man of that name who was one of the *receveurs généraux des finances*: J. F. Bosher, *French Finances 1770–1795: From Business to Bureaucracy* (Cambridge, 1970), p. 323; *Almanach royal* for 1778, p. 497. A Chanorier signed himself by that title in writing to WTF on Feb. 14, 1783 (APS); the handwriting is different, but the present note may have been from a secretary.

7. The first time after JA reached France that Friday fell on the 18th of a month; the date might equally well be December of that year.

From T[homas] D[igges][8]

ALS: Historical Society of Pennsylvania

Sir   Bir[mingha]m Sepr. 18./78

My having an oppertunity to forward this under cover to
my freind Mr. I[zar]d,[9] induces me to obtrude a few lines on
You. Mr. Alex[ande]r Dick[1] and some companions of his
was lately with me, and their situation and circumstances demanded of me every alleviation of their wants that I had in my
power to afford them; in the doing of which I was obligd to
take Mr. Dicks bill on You dated Bristol Sepr. 8, ten days sight,
for twenty six pounds Sterling, which bill I shall keep until a
favourable oppertunity offers of remitting it to some freind in
France. As Mr. Dick promisd me to give You the earliest notice of this bill from the first port he might arrive at in France,
and to inform You for what it was drawn, who, and what His
circumstances were, and also to lodge the needful for its discharge, I make no doubt You are informd of it before this day,
and that it will be honord when presented to You.

I hope You will excuse me Sir for this unnecessary intru-
sion, but I am prompted from an ardent wish to be servicable
to You or Your Community, to go further, and make an offer
of my services to You. I am unavoidably prevented from giving my personal assistance to a cause I have extreemly at
heart, but I am so situated in this Country as to have it often
in my power to be servicable to those more actively and
openly employd; If You can point out any mode wherein I can
be useful, or will place confidence enough in me to transact or
do anything for You here, I promise You Sir it shall be done
with zeal punctuality secrecy and honor. It will not be prudent

8. This is the first letter of an extended correspondence. Digges (1742–
1821) was from Maryland; he lived in England where, before the revolution, he had acted as agent for various shipping companies. For the most
complete account of his life see Robert H. Elias and Eugene D. Finch, eds.,
Letters of Thomas Attwood Digges (1742–1821) (Columbia, S.C., 1982), pp.
xxiii–lxxvii.

9. The ellipses within proper names have been expanded according to
ibid., pp. 18–19.

1. For Alexander Dick see John Harris and Benjamin Chew's letters of
July 14 and Aug. 19. On Sept. 17 the commissioners had ordered the payment of 480 *l.t.* to him.

in me to be further explicit, Mr. I[zar]d, Messrs. L[ee]s, Mr. Jos. W[harto]n, Mr. C[a]rm[ichae]l whom I have reason to expect is returnd to You, or any other confidential Freind who has lately gone from England, Mr. R[idle]y, or Mr. J. J[ohnso]n,[2] can satisfy You who and what I am; The two first mentiond Gentlemen, and Mr. R[idle]y, can give You my name and direction, and I have lately wrote to the three, to mention a circumstance to You about our people in this quarter, that is deserving Your attention, for I begin to fear their situation will soon be again deplorable. I have the honor to be Sir Your very Obedient servant   T.D——

From John Paul Jones

ALS: American Philosophical Society; AL (draft): National Archives; copy: United States Naval Academy Museum

Honored and dear Sir,   Brest Septr. 18th. 1778.

The Fleet hath this day returned here, having been absent a Month and done nothing; for I call taking a small Tender and a small Privateer Nothing. A Frigate, the Juno, of 32 Guns 12 pounders is also Arrived and has brought in the English Frigate the Fox that was formerly taken by our Frigates the Hancock and Boston. This last Engagement lasted 2 hours and an half, in which time the Fox lost all her Masts.

The Fox mounts 24 Nine pounders, is Sheathed with Copper and said to sail pretty well. If the Minister will give me nothing better, I would rather accept that Ship with the Alert as a Tender than remain Idle: but I hope he has before this time determined to do more. I have shewed my letter of the 13th. to the Duke De Rochfaucault, who sets out in the Morning for Paris, but will not appear there 'till the first Ultimo. He commends the letter and thinks the Minister will be pleased with it.[3] They say the Alert did not sail well, but I am persuaded it is because they did not know her Trim. I have yet received no letters. I will perhaps send a Duplicate of my letter to M. De Sartine by the Next Post; as the Count De Gen-

2. For the brother of the Maryland governor see XXI, 157 n.

3. A copy of Jones's letter to Sartine, Sept. 13, enclosed in his to BF above, Sept. 14. The duc de la Rochefoucauld continued to help Jones communicate with Sartine throughout September and October.

leese,[4] whom I have Just now seen at the Levee, tells me that the Duke De Chartres can make it servicable at Court. If I write to the Duke I will inclose the letter for Your inspection. I am with the truest Esteem and Respect Honored and dear Sir Your very Obedient and Obliged Servant   JNO P JONES

His Excellency Doctor Franklin

Addressed: His Excellency / Doctor Franklin / American Plenepotentiary at the Court of France. / à Passy.

Endorsed: Capt. Jones Brest Sept. 18. 78

The American Commissioners to American Prisoners in England[5]

Draft: Massachusetts Historical Society; copies: National Maritime Museum,[6] Public Record Office,[7] National Archives (two); transcript: Library of Congress

⟨Passy, September [19], 1778: We have not written you for a long time but have been engaged in negotiating a cartel of exchange, and have assurances from England that an exchange will take place. The government of this kingdom has provided a passport for the purpose. We now sincerely hope you will obtain your liberty. Since we do not have an equal number to exchange, those among you in captivity longest will be considered first. So long as the British government refused an exchange, we did not discourage the escape efforts of our countrymen and provided them with small sums of money. However such escapes at the present time could undermine British commitment to the cartel. We now have permission to

4. Charles-Alexis Brulart, comte de Genlis (1737–93) was a friend and travelling companion of the duc de Chartres. Lewis, *Walpole Correspondence*, XXV, 348 n.

5. Published in Taylor, *Adams Papers*, VII.

6. Enclosed with a covering letter of Oct. 19 to Admiralty Secretary Philip Stephens from the Office of Sick and Hurt Seamen, indicating that it had been read aloud at Forton prison.

7. Enclosed with a covering letter of Oct. 23 from Stephens to Undersecretary William Fraser, prohibiting the reading of letters to prisoners from the commissioners without express approval by the Admiralty.

make use of French prisons for British captives. Keep us informed on the precise conditions of your captivity so we may enforce the same provisions here.⟩

Jonathan Loring Austin to the American Commissioners[8]

ALS: American Philosophical Society

⟨Passy, September 19, 1778: On Tuesday [September 22] I will leave for Holland and then for America. I would appreciate letters of recommendation to Congress, the Massachusetts Council and other assemblies or individuals. Had I the money myself or had I not exceeded the credit with Pliarne, Penet & Cie. given me by the Board of War in Boston, I would not ask compensation for my time and expenses. I will be answerable to you or to Congress for any sum you advance me. P.S.: Please recommend our commercial house whose address I leave.[9] I expect soon to report in French to the public about my activities, despite my lack of time here for study.⟩

Daniel Blake and John Lloyd to the American Commissioners[1]

Copy:[2] National Archives

Nantes Sept. 19. 1778.

Being informd that some malicious person, or persons, have been, and are still endeavoring, by the most infamous means, to deprive Mr. J. D. Schweighauser of his good name, and

8. Published in Taylor, *Adams Papers*, VII. In a covering letter to JA, Austin asked him to lay the present letter before the commissioners (APS).

9. Before coming to France with the news of Saratoga, Austin had been an active merchant in Kittery and Portsmouth: *Sibley's Harvard Graduates*, XVI, 303.

1. Daniel Blake (1731–80) was a brother of William Blake (XXVI, 40 n) and like him had married into the Izard family and was presently a merchant in Nantes: *S.C. Hist. and Geneal. Mag.*, II, 228 n, 231 n; *Laurens Papers*, VI, 55 n; Lloyd *et al.* to the commissioners, Jan. 7, 1779. APS. For Lloyd, another merchant, see Livingston's letter of July 21.

2. Included by William Lee in his letter to John Jay of March 8, 1779 (National Archives). The entire letter is published in Ford, *Letters of William Lee*, II, 540–84; see in particular pp. 580–1.

being apprehensive that the intention is to prejudice him in the estimation of the Honorable Commissioners,[3] we think it an act of Justice due to injurd Merit, to acquaint you, that we have employd, and are now employing that Gentleman to transact for our friends and ourselves to a very large amount. The satisfaction that they and We have receivd from his assiduity, honor, and integrity will induce us to pursue every means in our power, after our arrival in America, to serve him; being confident that as a Merchant he most justly deserves public and private confidence. He has had, and continues to transact a very considerable part of the business to and from America, and we have always heard the Americans, who have had any Connection with him, speak of him in the most respectful Terms.   (signd) DANL. BLAKE

JOHN LLOYD

S. and J.-H. Delap to the American Commissioners

ALS: American Philosophical Society

Gentlemen   Bordeaux 19th Septr. 1778.

We received the Letter you did us the honor of writing us the 18th July last[4] covering one for Capt. Wm. Hill Sargeant[5] and a Blank Bond for him to fill up and sign; inclosed we return you said Bond[6] executed by him and us for £1000 lawful Money of America, which is from what we could learn, the Security usually given for a Vessel of Cap. Sargeant's Burthen and Force. However, as you omitted mentioning the Sum and that we may be mistaken in what is filled up, we hereby engage ourselves to answer for the surplus that may be required.

Inclosed we hand you two Packets that came to hand for you from Martinico.

3. The attack on Schweighauser was a result of his relationship to Dobrée: see John Lloyd to Lee, Sept. 19, 1778, *ibid.*, p. 580. See also Chaumont's letter of July 5 and Dobrée's of Aug. 11, above.

4. Actually July 23.

5. A privateer captain identified in his letter to the commissioners of July 18.

6. Dated Aug. 19.

A Vessel arrived Yesterday from Baltimore that parted the 1st August. The Captain does not bring any News but what you must have learned some time ago. We have the honor to remain Gentlemen Your most obedient humble Servants

S & J H DELAP

To The Honble Benja Franklin & John Adams Esqrs.

Addressed: To / The Honble Benjamin Franklin / & John Adams Esqrs. / Ministers Plenipotentiary from the / United States of America, at the Court / of Versailles / Paris

Endorsed by John Adams: Mr Delap with a Bond.

Notation: 19 Sept. 1778

From —————— Christin[7]   ALS: American Philosophical Society

⟨Carlsruhe, at the residence of the Margrave of Baden-Durlach,[8] September 19, 1778, in French: Born in the canton of Bern, Switzerland, I have traveled through France, Holland, and Germany and devoted myself to clock-making and other works of precision. My ambition now is to submit to your judgment some of my inventions.

One of them is an oar for high free-board ships, designed in such a way that six of them can bring a vessel out of any port, away from currents, shoals and shallow waters, a mighty advantage in a war situation.

Another discovery I made concerns a machine for piercing metal: it would accelerate considerably the production of cannons.

Finally, I devised a new machine for cutting through steel and making files of all sizes by using the power of water, wind, or counterweights. A man operating it by himself could manufacture as many files as if he employed thirty workmen.

If you think it proper, I am ready to present my findings to

7. He signs himself "Horloger de la Cour."
8. Karl-Friedrich, whose reign (1728–1811) was one of the last and most distinguished in the history of patriarchal absolutism. *ADB.*

the academies of Paris or London. The first one seems particularly important.⟩

From John Emery

ALS: American Philosophical Society

Sir   Bilbao 19 Sept. 1778

By you kind favours with which you honourd me the 23d March last I was Informd that the King of France had orderd the Payment of 400,000 Livers in America for the use of the Owners and Captors of the Two Prizes taken by Cap. Babson last year and Confiscated at Nantes.[9] Last week arrived here one of the Officers of Cap. Babsons Ship and informs me No Order has appeard in America for the Payment,[1] therefore your further Interposition in this affair and Instructions how we are to Apply for it will be gratefully acknowledg'd by Your Most Obedient Servant   JNO EMERY

Should an Order be sent for the Payment Pray let it be to me as agent to Owners & Captors.

Honle Benjamin Franklin Esqr.

Addressed: Honbl. Benjamin Franklin Esqr / Commissioner of Congress / at Passy / Near Paris

Endorsed: Emery about the Prize Money Bilbao 9. Sept 1778.

9. See XXVI, 154; France's compensation for the prizes which had been returned to the British was announced by the commissioners in their letter to the committee for foreign affairs of Feb. 28: XXV, 728.
1. Jean Holker, whom Vergennes had authorized to make the payment, did not do so until October: XXV, 238–9 n; Smith, *Letters*, X, 195 n.

From the Marquise de Lafayette[2]

ALS: Dartmouth College Library

A Paris ce 19 7bre 1778

Permettés moy, monsieur, de joindre ma reccommandation a celle de mr. le Cte. Dossun, en faveur du nomme Rolleandeau, qui ce me semble ne doit pas en avoir beaucoup besoin auprès de vous, meritant vos bontés par ses services et son zele pour la liberte des etas unis. Après avoir recu plusieurs blessures il etoit revenu en france chercher ses freres pour les attacher au service des americains, et c'est en retournant en amerique qu'il a ete pris et a perdu tous ses titres. Je ne doute pas monsieur que vos bontes ne reparent ses pertes et que vous ne le reccommandiés dans votre patrie de maniere a lui faire rendre l'etat qu'il a perdu par son zele en amenant a la liberté de nouveaux defenseurs. Quoique je croye ma reccommandation superfflue avec de tels droits a vos bontes, j'en [aurai] une veritable recconnoissance. Receves monsieur je vous en supplie mes complimens et l'assurance de ma joye des bonnes nouvelles que nous recevons d'amerique dont les interets me sont bien chers, meme independament de ceux de mon coeur, et receves l'hommage des sentimens avec lesquels j'ai l'honneur d'être, monsieur votre très humble et très obeissante servante   NOAILLES DE LA FAYETTE

2. Included in Rolandeau to BF, below, Sept. 21.

From Le Maire   ALS: American Philosophical Society

Monsieur   Nantes Le 19. 7bre 1778

Je prends la liberté de vous envoyer cy incluse, la Copie de la lettre que j'écris à M. Lée,[3] ainsi que celle des propositions que M. Gruel fait de son navire pour conduire à bien tous les articles que le Gouvernement de virginie a demandé;[4] Je ne doute nullement, Monsieur, que vous n'approuviez le parti que je propose, S'il veut que tout arrive à Sa destination. Payer, pour payer, il est plus prudent d'avoir un navire de force, pour éviter les incursions des pirates qui sont en grand nombre et qui couvrent les mers. Il n'y auroit donc que des vaisseaux de ligne à craindre, ce qui n'est point probable qu'on en rencontre Car vous Scavez que les Anglais ont besoin de tous leurs navires pour former leur flotte et pour se mettre en force contre celle de France. D'ailleurs la saison de 9bre. et xbre. où je compte partir n'est pas un temps où les navires sont au large, raison de plus pour decider M. Lée. Vous verrez également, Monsieur, tout ce qu'il faut pour le Gouvernement de virginie et qui n'est point traité; ce qui m'afflige beaucoup, ayant à coeur de bien remplir la mission dont le Gouvernement m'a honoré, ainsi que de sa Confiance. Excusez moi, Monsieur, si je prends la liberté de vous fatiguer si souvent, mais un zele sans borne et le desir que j'ai de retourner promptement en virginie, me determine à m'adresser à vous pour en accelerer mon retour, étant persuadé du vif intérêt que vous voulez bien y prendre.

Je n'ai, Monsieur, encore reçu aucune nouvelle de M. Lée. Je lui ai écrit deux fois depuis que j'ai reçu l'honneur de la vôtre;[5] il scait cependant que j'ai besoin d'argent, il est à croire qu'il ne m'en enverra point et je suis dans la situation la plus precaire, ainsi que j'ai eu l'honneur de vous le marquer. J'aurois esperé qu'il m'auroit envoyé de quoi solder ma depense, pour

3. Of the same date, in which he gives an extensive list of the equipment he had procured for Virginia, including, among other items, components for military uniforms, foot gear, sheaths and other accoutrements, riding equipment, plus various mathematical and drafting instruments. APS.
4. An apparent reversal from Le Maire's letter of Sept. 10.
5. Of Sept. 6.

continuer mes operations, d'autant que je ne lui demande rien que de fournir à mes besoins indispensables. Si J'osois vous prier, Monsieur, de me faire toucher 600 *l.t.* pour payer ou je dois, je ne vous interromperois pas de sitôt; pardonnez, Monsieur, Mon indiscretion, mais examinez ma position, vous verrez qu'elle me force d'avoir recours à vous; d'ailleurs vous me l'avez permis, lorsque j'eus l'honneur de vous voir. Toute mon ambition est de pouvoir être assez heureux de vous convaincre que je suis un vrai et zelé Compatriote Americain. Penetré de ces sentimens, j'ose me dire avec le plus profond respect Monsieur Votre très humble et très obéissant serviteur

J. Le Maire

Je vous Supplie, Monsieur, de m'honorer d'un mot de reponse. Ne vous refusez pas à la prière d'un homme honnête qui vous en conservera pour la vie, la plus vive reconnoissance.

P.S. Je crois devoir, Monsieur, vous observer que Je crains que toutes les affaires ne transpirent. M. Lée a fait delivrer Toute la liste qui est au chateau de nantes à M. Schweighaucel. Je ne scai pas si vous savés que M. son gendre est un grenezien et que le pere de ce dernier est un commissaire anglais a guernezay et qu'il est interessé dans diferends corsaires.[6] Je ne puis cependant Rien Imputer à ces Messieurs ne les connoissant qu'indirectement. Je desirerois même que ce que je vous marque ne soit que de vous à moi, parce qu'en fin il ne faut accuser personne qu'apres de bonnes raisons. Je comptois recevoir des nouvelles de M. Lée par le courier d'aujourd'huy, j'ignore le motif de son silence: il sait cependant qu'il faut payer les ouvriers et Experts qui m'ont aidé a l'inspection des fuzils, qui se monte a la somme de 776 *l.t.* 16 *s.* y compris le plomb et la poudre. J'esperois Egalement qu'il m'en auroit envoyé pour pouvoir Suivre mes operations avec facilité. Permettéz monsieur que je vous réitere ici ma priere a cet Egard.

Monsieur franklin Ecuyer à Passy

Endorsed: Capt. Lemaire Nantes Sept. 19 1778

6. Thomas Dobrée and his son Peter Frederick.

To Madame Brillon: "The Ephemera"[7]

AL (draft): Cornell University Library; French translations: American Philosophical Society (three),[8] Bibliothèque de la Société Eduenne, Autun,[9] Institut de France; copy or transcript: Yale University Library;[1] incomplete copy: Huntington Library

The following piece, originally published as "Lettre à Madame B." but better known as "The Ephemera," strikes a rare note in the canon of Franklin's writings: a note of melancholy. In its bittersweet brooding over the brevity of life and the vanity of human endeavor, it does not try to instruct or reform, but merely to create a mood. That Franklin should have felt old and somewhat discouraged in

7. A facsimile of the original published version, in French, appears in *The Bagatelles from Passy* (The Eakins Press, New York, [1967]), pp. 143–6. This famous essay has been the subject of many studies. For the most extensive discussion of its background, and a detailed comparison of extant versions, see Gilbert Chinard, "Random Notes on Two Bagatelles," APS *Proc.*, CIII, 1959, pp. 740–60. A literary analysis can be found in J.A. Leo Lemay's chapter on Franklin in *Major Writers of Early American Literature*, E. Emerson, ed., (Wisconsin, 1972), pp. 234–8. See also Alfred Owen Aldridge, *Franklin and His French Contemporaries* (New York, 1957), pp. 167–8, and Lopez, *Mon Cher Papa*, pp. 50–2.

8. The earliest translation, dated Sept. 20, 1778, and probably made for Mme. Brillon, pre-dates BF's corrections and does not include his addition in praise of the French government. It is clearly the work of an English-speaking person whose French was good but far from perfect, and who knew Mme. Brillon well enough to translate "tune," in the last sentence, as "sonate."

The second APS manuscript, which bears no date but incorporates BF's additions, corresponds to the text published in his Bagatelles: it offers an introductory "Avertissement" which is virtually identical (with minor variations in capitalization) to the one BF printed. It also bears his endorsement: "Les Ephemeres." As in the printed copy, this translation lacks BF's original footnote saying "Caesar." It does contain the three footnote markers given in the printed text, but only gives two of the footnotes: the quotation from Horace, and "La Riviere de Seine," explaining "Ocean" in the text.

The third APS manuscript is similar to the second. It, too, contains the "Avertissement," although it is in a different hand from the text. The only two footnotes provided in this version are the quotation from Horace, and the attribution "Hipocrate."

9. This is the most florid of the translations; it does not include BF's footnotes or the "Avertissement."

1. Faithful to BF's text, but the French words are misspelled. The hand, it seems to us, is Carmichael's.

430

the summer of 1778 is hardly surprising. He was seventy-two. Flanked by the brisk and efficient Adams, not quite forty-three, and by the restless, hostile thirty-seven-year-old Arthur Lee, infatuated with the equally young Madame Brillon who was ever-so-gently rejecting him, he may well have thought that with the signing of the treaty of alliance in February his mission in France was coming to a close.[2]

The visit to Moulin-Joli that triggered "The Ephemera" may have taken place on August 13, one of the few occasions on which Franklin absented himself from Paris.[3] He composed the fantasy in the course of the following weeks, dated it September 20, not long before his second visit to Anet, and probably took with him a French translation for the benefit of Madame Brillon who did not read English.[4]

Two years later, he described "some few Circumstances" of the piece's composition and dissemination in a letter to William Carmichael:[5]

> The person to whom it was addressed is Madame Brillon a Lady of most respectable Character and pleasing Conversation Mistress of an amiable family in this Neighbourhood, with which I spend an Evening twice in every Week. She has among other Elegant accomplishments that of an Excellent Musician, and with her Daughters who sing prettily, and some friends who play, She kindly entertains me and my Grandson with little Concerts, a Dish of Tea and a Game of Chess. I call this my Opera; for I rarely go to the Opera at Paris. The *Moulin Joly* is a little Island in the Seine about 2 Leagues from hence, Part of the Country Seat of another friend, where we visit every Summer and spend a Day in the pleasing Society of the ingenious learned and very polite Persons who inhabit it.[6] At the Time when the Letter was written, all conversations at Paris were filled with Disputes about the Musick of Gluck and Picciny, a German and an Italian Musician, who divided the

2. BF had already hinted to Mme. Brillon that he feared he might soon be leaving France; see her letter of Sept. 13. See also her letter of Sept. 30 and the references cited there.
3. See the commissioners to Sartine, Aug. 13.
4. The first of the translations listed above at the APS.
5. To William Carmichael, June 17, 1780 (Library of Congress).
6. The owner, Claude-Henri Watelet, and his *amie*, Mme. Marguerite Lecomte, are identified in XXIV, 171 n. A number of their letters, undated and in the APS, discuss social engagements. Mme. Lecomte wrote Mme.

Town into Violent Parties.[7] A friend of the Lady having obtained a Copy of it under a promise not to give another, did not observe that Promise so that many have been taken, and it is become as publick as such a thing can well be that is not printed. But I could not dream of its being heard of at Madrid.[8] The Thought was partly taken from a Little Piece of some unknown Writer which I met with 50 years since in a newspaper, and which the sight of the Ephemera brought to my Recollection.[9]

When shown the piece, the Doctor's old friend and translator, Barbeu-Dubourg, was so enthusiastic that, taking his cue from its theme, he urged prompt publication: "Il est bien essentiel de faire

---

Brillon about an upcoming party in honor of the "insurgens allies et amis," to which she plans to invite all the inhabitants "de la Pensilvanie francoise." The guest of honor, of course, is to be "le chef du congres de Passi." In another note, Watelet and Lecomte remind BF and WTF of a dinner "samedi au louvre" with Mme. Brillon. A third message expresses the pair's regrets at having missed BF's and WTF's visit.

7. Paris indeed was abuzz with the controversy between the partisans of Christopher Willibald von Gluck, a frequent visitor from Vienna, and those of the Italian Niccolo Piccinni (or Piccini), appointed court composer in late 1776. Gluck's *Armide* was admired for its tempestuous and tragic passages, a break from the over-stylized tradition, Piccinni's *Roland* for its *airs délicieux* which the Queen, however, out of loyalty to her countryman, refrained from applauding. For the above and the facetious way in which each faction defaced the other's posters with puns see Bachaumont, *Mémoires secrets*, XI, 78, 98. For the composers see *The New Grove Dictionary of Music and Musicians*, Stanley Sadie, ed., (20 vols., London, Washington, Hong Kong, 1980), VII, 465–72; XIV, 723–7. Talking about a "Cousin" and a "Musketo," two words for the same insect, BF is hinting that the raging debate is really a tempest in a teapot.

8. Where Carmichael was stationed as secretary to minister-designate John Jay.

9. The "Little Piece" in question was originally published in *The Free Thinker*, April 24, 1719 under the title, "The Vanity and Ambition of the Human Mind," and was reprinted in the *Pa. Gaz.*, no. 366, Dec. 4–11, 1735, during BF's tenure as editor. Aldridge, *op. cit.*, p. 167, 250–1; Chinard, *op. cit.*, p. 751. Chinard also speculates that BF was influenced by Réaumur's treatise on "Mouches qu'on appelle Ephémères," published in the 1745 volume of the *Histoire de l'Académie Royale des Sciences*, a copy of which he owned. The famous naturalist, fascinated by the insects, also drew moral lessons suggested by the brevity of their lives. *Ibid.*, p. 754.

Observing the Ephemera by Night

paroitre *tres promptement* la traduction de ce petit morceau exquis qui perdroit chaque jour, pour ne pas dire chaque *heure*, beaucoup de sa valeur."[1] Franklin, who at first had shied away from publication, as he told Carmichael, changed his mind and printed, as a bagatelle, a French translation called "Lettre à Madame B." on his Passy press.[2]

Passy. Sept 20. 1778.

You may remember, my dear Friend, that when we lately spent that happy Day in the delightful garden and sweet Society of the *Moulin-Joli*, I stopt a little in one of our Walks, and staid some time behind the Company. We had been shewn number-less Skeletons of a kind of little Fly, called an Ephemere, all whose successive Generations we were told were bred and expired within the Day. I happen'd to see a living Company of them on a Leaf, who appear'd to be engag'd in Conversation. You know I understand all the inferior Animal Tongues: my too great Application to the Study of them is the best Excuse I can give for the little Progress I have made in your charming Language. I listned thro' Curiosity to the Discourse of these little Creatures, but as they in their national Vivacity spoke three or four together,[3] I could make but little of their Dis-course. I found however, by some broken Expressions that I caught now and then, they were disputing warmly the Merit of two foreign Musicians, one a *Cousin*, the other a *Musketo*; in which Dispute they spent their time seemingly as regardless of the Shortness of Life, as if they had been sure of living a Month. Happy People! thought I, you live certainly under a wise, just and mild Government, since you have no public Grievances to complain of, nor any Subject of Contention but the Perfections or Imperfections of foreign Music.[4] I turned

1. From Barbeu-Dubourg, undated (APS).
2. Only two bound copies of the collected Bagatelles have survived; one in the Franklin Collection at Yale University, the other at the Bibliothèque Nationale.
3. A gentle hint to the Gallic habit of interrupting one another.
4. This sentence, beginning "Happy People!", was a later addition in the margin, undoubtedly written when BF realized that multiple copies of the letter were being made and circulated. He would not have wanted to appear too critical of French society.

433

from them to an old greyheaded one, who was single on another Leaf, and talking to himself. Being amus'd with his Soliloquy, I have put it down in writing, in hopes it will likewise amuse her to whom I am so much indebted for the most pleasing of all Amusements, her delicious Company, and her heavenly Harmony.

"It was, says he, the Opinion of learned Philosophers of our Race, who lived and flourished long before my time, that this vast World, the *Moulin Joli*, could not itself subsist more than 18 Hours; and I think there was some Foundation for that Opinion, since by the apparent Motion of the great Luminary that gives Life to all Nature, and which in my time has evidently declin'd considerably towards the Ocean at the End of our Earth, it must then finish its Course, be extinguish'd in the Waters that surround us, and leave the World in Cold and Darkness, necessarily producing universal Death and Destruction.[5] I have lived seven of those Hours; a great Age, being no less than 420 minutes of Time. How very few of us continue so long! I have seen Generations born, flourish, and expire. My present Friends are the Children and Grandchildren of the Friends of my Youth, who are now, alas, no more! And I must soon follow them; for by the Course of Nature, tho' still in Health, I cannot expect to live above 7 or 8 Minutes longer. What now avails all my Toil and Labour in amassing Honey-Dew on this Leaf, which I cannot live to enjoy! What the political Struggles I have been engag'd in for the Good of my *Compatriotes*, Inhabitants of this Bush; or my philosophical Studies for the Benefit of our Race in general! For in Politics, *what can Laws do without Morals!*[6] Our present Race of Ephemeres will in a Course of Minutes, become corrupt

5. As early as 1749, the hypothesis that the end of the world would be due to the extinguishing of the sun had brought Buffon in conflict with the theologians of the Sorbonne. By 1777 he had theorized that the polar ice would ultimately extend to the equator, killing all life. Chinard argues persuasively that BF, aware of his friend's ideas, is giving them here an oblique endorsement: *op. cit.* pp. 756-7.

6. Footnote in text: "*Quid leges sine moribus*. Hor." The quotation is from Horace's *Odes*, III, 24:35.

like those of other and older Bushes, and consequently as wretched. And in Philosophy how small our Progress! Alas, *Art is long, and Life short!*[7] My Friends would comfort me with the Idea of a Name they say I shall leave behind me; and they tell me I have *lived long enough, to Nature and to Glory:*[8] But what will Fame be to an *Ephemere* who no longer exists? And what will become of all History, in the 18th Hour, when the World itself, even the whole *Moulin Joli*, shall come to its End, and be buried in universal Ruin? To me, after all my eager Pursuits, no solid Pleasures now remain, but the Reflection of a long Life spent in meaning well, the sensible Conversation of a few good Lady-Ephemeres, and now and then a kind Smile, and a Tune from the ever-amiable *Brillante*.

7. Footnote in text: "Hippocrates." The quotation is from *Aphorisms*, Sec. 1, I: "Life is short, the Art long, opportunity fleeting, experiment treacherous, judgment difficult." W.H.S. Jones, ed., *Hippocrates* (4 vols., Cambridge and London, 1923–49) IV, 99.

8. Footnote in text: "Caesar." Actually, the quotation is from Cicero's *Pro Marcello*, 25, and refers to a thought Caesar supposedly expressed.

From Amelia Barry

ALS: American Philosophical Society

My Dear Sir,   Tunis 20th Sepr. 1778

Pardon I beseech you, this one trouble more, which I am pained to give you; but being in the most perplexing suspence, I think it a duty to inform you of it. I besought you Sir, in the three last letters I had the honor to write you[9] to transmit your favors to Mr. Barry or me, under cover to Lewis Hameken Esq. Danish Consul at this place, and recommended to the care of Monr. Jean Baptista Fabré Negociant à Marsielle. Two vessels have arrived lately from that port one Venetian and one French. By the latter Consul Hameken has received several boxes of commissions &c. from Monr. Fabré but unaccompanied by a single line tho' every other neutral Consul in town has received letters by that conveyance: how to account for this circumstance, I am at the utmost loss: Should my revered Docr: Franklin have honored me with a letter, and it have miscarried, he may hereafter impute ingratitude or negligence to me for not acknowledging the receipt of it. The uncertainty of his having written or not, leaves me truly unhappy. All my hopes my dear Friend are in you. At Poverty I should not repine could I endure it alone but when I think of Mr. Barry and my Children's experiencing it, then indeed are my sensations exquisitely keen. Still, still do I hope my Doctor will set my heart at rest, and enable me to procure for my sweet Children the advantages of Education; of more real importance than Empires without it. If you should my dear Sir have written I must entreat you to inform me by a line, directed to me under cover to Monr. Molinare Sweedish Consul Tunis and recommended to the care of Monr. Paraut Negociant Marsielles. Should you not have written the other conveyance I should think must be safe yet the best conveyance of all must at presant be via Leghorn, as several neutral vessels (Venetian and Ragusa) are constantly employed in trading from that place hither. This address[1] must be safe. With the

---

9. See XXVI, 585–9.

1. Footnote in text: "under cover to James Traill Esqr. His Brittannic Majesty's Agent & Conl. Genl. Tunis to the care of Messrs. Gentil & Orr

most sincere and respectful attachment I have the honor to be Most Dear Sir Your ever-obliged and most devoted Humble Servant
A. BARRY

Endorsed: Mrs. Barry

Notations: Sept. 20. 78 / A Barry Sept. 20 78

From Madame Brillon
ALS: American Philosophical Society

ce 20 [September 1778][2] a annét
Mércredi vous prendrés encore le thé sans moi, samedi vous le prendrés avéc moi; si cétte idée vous cause seulement la centiéme partie du plaisir qu'elle me fait, vous devés estre bien content mon chér papa; il est un point dit on, ou l'amitié ne peut plus augmentér, je le crois, et crois en mesme temp que la miénne en est la pour vous; cependant chaques jours il me semble que je vous aime davantage; je crois que c'est tout uniement parce qu'il y a chaques jours, un jour de plus que je vous aime; nous approfondirons cette matiére ensemble samedi, oh mon chér papa samedi que je serai contente! J'ai l'honneur d'éstre avéc les sentiments les plus réspéctueux et les plus tendres, Votre trés humble et trés obeissante servante
D'HARDANCOURT BRILLON

Addressed: A Monsieur / Monsieur Franklin / A Passy

From François-Pierre de Vauquelin de Boisroger[3]
ALS: American Philosophical Society

the 20th. 7 r. 1778 au Château du Boisroger par
Sir   Noyer menars
Mr. St pierre a gentleman of this province was possessed of a plantation wich he had Called New bordeaux Seated in the

---

Mercts. Leghorn." Amelia Barry had first gone to Tunis in 1766 with James Traill as a governess in his family: XIII, 163 n.

2. See the headnote to BF's letter to her on Sept. 1.

3. Born in 1746 of an aristocratic Norman family. Bodinier.

Meridional Caroline upon the Side of a river wich discharge itself into the Savanah, and there he had been Killed by the indians about two years agone.[4] His heirs who Live at Caën, had Consented to give up all their rigths in My behalf. But I have not Ventured conclude that bargain, without knowing if the United States of america would allow the title of fellow Citizen to a french man. I have almost all my own, in my pocket book, Like as the greatest part of the other french protestants, and if the plantation above mentioned Does not fit me, my purpose were in that Case, to purchase another estate, according to my moderate fortune, if I Could hope increase it after wards, by ground's Comissions from the Congres. But as I should, overall, be pleased, to prove Serviceable to the States, I Should think myself much more happy, if I Could be both tiller and military. Therefore I have the honour to Lay before you, Sir, that I have Served ten years officer in the regiment of Metz Royal artillery. Having Left that Service after my mother's Decease,[5] I entered at that time, into the Light horses of the King's guards, by reform of wich I am Now without business. I have got hitherto the main Knowledge Necessary to the Officers of the Navy or artillery, even to a Naturalist, and tho' I am but thirty three years old, I know your Learned theory of electricity, Long Ago. I will Delay to buy the inheritence of mr. St. pierre, till I have received your answer. If you grant me your protection, Sir, by the Congres, I might embark, when I can do it with any Safety. Previously I Shall have the honour of Shewing you, plain proofs, of my Service, behaviour, birth or nobility. I pray you Sir to be indulgent to my importunity and to the mistakes wich I have, maybe, Done in a tongue, wich I have begun to Study these five months, alone and without master. I am with Respect Sir, Your most humble and most obedient Servant

DE VAUQUELIN DE BOISROGER

Notation: Vauquelin de boisroger to be answer'd

Endorsed: Offr. au Chateau Du Boiroger 20 7bre 1778.

4. For Jean-Louis Dumesnil de St. Pierre see XXIV, 337 n.
5. The archives at the War Office give a terse "destitué" (discharged) as the reason for his leaving his regiment. Bodinier.

438

Ralph Izard to the American Commissioners[6]

ALS: Archives du Ministère des affaires étrangères

⟨Paris, September 21, 1778: I have learned that the ship *Nile*, Captain Goldsmith, has been taken while bound from London to Leghorn and brought into Marseilles. She carried 20 packages of my baggage addressed to Monsieur Antoine Martinelli, merchant, to be delivered to the abbé Niccoli.[7] My name doesn't appear on them as this might have caused their detention at the London Customs House. Please take whatever measures you think proper, so they can be delivered to my authorized representative.⟩

Musco Livingston to the American Commissioners[8]

ALS: American Philosophical Society

⟨Bordeaux, September 21, 1778: I received yours of —— [August 31], and will answer on my return to Nantes where I have left the relevant papers. I have a very fine ship ready to sail immediately and will gladly take two or three hundred tons of the public goods now at Nantes. Since I am unfamiliar with the terms and conditions of shipment, write me your wishes by return post in care of Mr. Schweighauser.⟩

6. Published in Taylor, *Adams Papers*, VII.
7. Izard shipped his goods to Leghorn in anticipation of joining them in Tuscany. Meanwhile, he received from Florence a discouraging letter in which the abbé Niccoli (identified above, XXIV, 84–5 n) advised him against assuming his diplomatic post there: Wharton, *Diplomatic Correspondence*, II, 669–70. For Izard's reluctant acquiescence see *ibid.*, p. 714.
8. Published in Taylor, *Adams Papers*, VII.

Sartine to the American Commissioners[9]

Copies: Massachusetts Historical Society, Library of Congress (two), National Archives (two); transcripts: National Archives (two)

⟨Versailles, September 21, 1778, in French: I have received your letter of the 17th. I knew that the principle of reciprocity in the matter of recapture would meet with your approval. The regulations of Massachusetts of which Capt. McNeill informed you are different from the English and more like the French. The regulations of England, by allowing half the value of the vessel to the original owner, favor the interests of commerce. It would be important for the various American states to adopt a uniform law in this regard to preclude difficulties which owners of vessels might incur in their ignorance. With respect to the *Isabelle*, it is up to the courts of law, not the administration, to hear the owners' claim. Should the decision go against them, you will recognize that a third or a half the value of this vessel should be held by public officers until the two nations have agreed on a procedure regarding recaptured vessels.⟩

From John Paul Jones

ALS: American Philosophical Society; AL (draft): National Archives; copy: United States Naval Academy Museum

Honored and dear Sir   Brest Septr. 21st. 1778
    This serves only to cover my letters to the Duke De Chartres and his Squire as mentioned in my last.[1] Unless you entirely Approve of these letters I beg you to suppress them. If you Approve them I could wish it may be consistent and convenient for you to see, or Write a line to, the Duke about the time they are delivered, for there is such a Mystery in my situation that it is thought you have disapproved of my Conduct.

9. Published in Taylor, *Adams Papers*, VII.
    1. The two letters, to the duc de Chartres and comte de Genlis and dated Sept. 21, are a repetition of Jones's complaints and a plea for help; they are now in the Library of Congress.

440

The Alert was missing but is Arrived, And I having seen the Fox would wish to Accept of that Ship attended by the Alert in the Meantime, Unless something better is immediatly Offered and *Bestowed*. I shall with this Command expect Unlimited Orders. I am with the truest Esteem and Respect Honored and dear Sir Your very Obliged Servant   JNO P JONES

N.B. I am convinced that if an application is not Immediatly Made for the Fox, that Ship will be given away.

Endorsed: Capt. Jones Brest Sept. 21. 78

From Jean-Baptiste Le Roy

ALS: American Philosophical Society

à Viry ce 21 Septembre 1778

Au milieu de l'affliction[2] où nous sommes mon Illustre Docteur je ne puis m'empêcher de vous faire souvenir de la promesse que vous nous avez faite de venir nous voir ici à Viry chez mon frère. Nous lui avons parlé de cette promesse il en a été ravi et il desire vivement que vous l'accomplissiez. Vous savez combien un ami comme vous peut adoucir les maux d'un malheureux Pere et d'une malheureuse mère toujours livrés à leur douleur. Vous ferez je ne dis pas simplement une action conforme à vôtre bon coeur mais vous remplirez encore un devoir d'humanité. Quelle influence ne peuvent avoir sur nous la présence et les consolations d'un ami comme Vous. Daignes donc nous tenir votre parole cette espérance suffit seule pour apporter quelque soulagement à notre peine. Je n'ai pas besoin de vous prier d'amener Monsieur votre petit fils et de vous dire que mon frère sera fort aise d'avoir l'honneur de le recevoir. D'ailleurs toutes les personnes que vous amenerez seront bien recuës. Si vous voulez y coucher vous trouverez des appartemens bien clos et bien bons pour vous et pour Monsieur votre petit fils. Vous verrez certainement une des plus belles vuës et un des plus beaux pays qu'on puisse voir aux environs de Paris. Recevez les sincères assurrances des sentimens d'at-

2. Their son, Basile, had been buried on Sept. 16.

tachement d'un homme qui dans quelqu'etat que soit son ame ressent également l'amitié qu'il vous a vouée pour la vie.

LE ROY

Mde. Le Roy me charge de vous dire combien elle vous est attachée ayez la bonte de dire bien des choses pour nous à M. et Mde. De Chaumont. Nous n'oublierons jamais les marques d'amitié qu'ils nous ont donné dans cette funeste Occasion.

P.S. Si vous me favorisez d'une réponse, vous voudrez bien suivre l'adresse qui est ici dessous

a Monsieur Monsieur Le Roy maison de M. Le Roy à Viry sur Orge par Risse pour Viry

Addressed: a Monsieur / Monsieur Franklin / Député du Congrès / à Passy / près Paris

Endorsed: M. Le Roy

From Joseph Pine

ALS: American Philosophical Society

Sir   Josslin[3] Septr. 21th 1778

I hope your lord Ship will Take it in consederat[ion] Since it was my Mesfortune to be Taken by american Privatear as I was on my voyage to Newfoundland I was taken By the gennrell Putnan from Newlondon commanded by Thomas allen[4] whare of he Rancomd my vessell and Send me For England after my Sending two men for the Rancom. And as I was on my Passage to England was taken by a frinch frguate called the Servlent [*Surveillante*] and She keep me as Prissonears Ever Since the Sixteen Day of July and not Had the upertunety of writing to your ounner to acquent you of the faire which I hope it is in your Power to give Me my Leberty which I hope your ounner will Take It in consederation as I Rancomd my vessell to the american Private-teear. The franch had No Right

3. Near Vannes.

4. For the *General Putnam* and Thomas Allon of New London, see Louis F. Middlebrook, *History of Maritime Connecticut during the American Revolution 1775–1783* (2 vols., Salem, Mass., 1925), II, 98–9.

to take me Prissoner. I Should Take it as a great favour if your ounner will be So kind as to Send me and ancor [an answer][5] and Shall Be much oblige to your ounner. Sir I am your Huble Sarvent   JOSEPH PINE

Plese to Drect to Captn. Joseph Pine at Josslin grand Britune In France per care of Monsiure gautier.

Addressed: A Monsr. / Monsr. Frinkling / a / Paris

Notation: Josph Pine Sept. 21. 1778

From Louis-François Rolandeau[6]

ALS: American Philosophical Society

Monsieur   De paries ce 21 septambr 1778
Comme il y a 7 jours que je suis malade et que je me propose de jour en jour de vous aller voir et vous demander mon déportement (?) pour rejoindre [*mon régiment*], dans cet intervalle de ma maladie le marquis d'Ossun et Madame de la Fayette m'ont fait remettre deux lettres pour vous mettre en main.[7] Etant malade et ne pouvant que vous les envoyer, je vous prie d'avoir égard à leur recommandation pour moi et vous prie de me dire quel jour je pourrai avoir une de vos audiences. Vous m'obligerez infiniment vu l'envie que j'ai de

5. Pine was still making the same request to BF the following year, June 17 and Nov. 6, 1779. APS.

6. BF had been informed by J. Leveux on Aug. 26 that this irresponsible but well-connected young officer had been captured on his way back to his regiment in Georgia and was in France once again, seeking help. On Sept. 2, Rolandeau sent JA a list of his losses and on Sept. 4 the commissioners gave him 192 *l.t.:* Taylor, *Adams Papers,* VI, 360; VII, under Sept. 2. This letter is so garbled that we think it fit to offer a version of it in correct French.

7. The comte d'Ossun (XXV, 87 n), earlier referred to by Rolandeau as his protector, had sent BF an appeal on Sept. 12. He explained that Rolandeau had lost all his papers during his captivity but was eager to undertake the crossing once again, this time with two of his brothers. Ossun asked BF to furnish a new recommendation for Congress. APS. Mme. de Lafayette's letter is above, Sept. 19.

partir. Monsieur, je suis et serai toute ma vie votre très humble et très obéissant serviteur[8]   ROLANDEAU

To [the Marquise de Lafayette][9]

AL (draft): American Philosophical Society

[after September 21, 1778]

Wherever it is in my Power, I should certainly pay the greatest Respect to the Recommendation of Madame de la Fayette, but it is absolutely impossible for me to do what is desired for this M. Rolandeau. He was an Officer in the American Service; he left his Regiment without Leave and came to France. If he would return there it should therefore be at his own Expence. It cannot be thought reasonable that we should pay all the loss and Damage that arises from his Irregularity. Having been in America he must be known to the People there better than he is to me. If he has behaved well, a Recommendation from me is unnecessary; if ill, it would be of no Use to him, and I ought not to give it. His Letters to me, are so contradictory to one another, and so inconsistent with the Accounts he has given me of himself in Conversation, that I have no Confidence in any thing he says, nor any Faith in his Stories of being wounded in our Service. He has taken up Money on our Account without our Leave; and we have given him more to pay his Expence down to his own Country on his Promise to trouble us no farther but he has staid in Paris, and breaks that Promise by applying to us again after repeated Refusals and engaging your Goodness and that of the Count D'Ossun to solicit for him. But had I ever so good an Opinion of him, as I know his Place in America must be long since fill'd up, and

8. Rolandeau wrote again on Oct. 3 to inquire whether a certain letter addressed to him in BF's care has been received. He also requests a certificate of his services in the American army and of his having been taken prisoner by the British. APS. The correspondence ends there.

9. In answer to her letter of recommendation for Rolandeau, Sept. 19.

that there is no Vacancy there for him, and as the Congress have given us strict Orders to encourage no more Officers, the Armies being full and the Applications extreamly embarrassing, I dare not give him the least Encouragement to go thither, and if I were one of his best Friends I should advise him to stay where he is.

I rejoice with you on the good News from our Friends in America, and the Reputation your particular Friend has so deservedly acquired there. Continue your Prayers for us, and we shall do well. I am with sincere Respect Madam &c.

The American Commissioners to William Lee[1]

AL (draft): Massachusetts Historical Society; two copies: National Archives

⟨Passy, September [22–26],[2] 1778: We have considered the papers you submitted, including the project of a treaty between the Netherlands and the United States. As Congress has appointed no commissioner to deal with their High Mightinesses, we have taken and will continue to take all suitable measures to further friendship between our countries. We do not think it prudent for many reasons to express at present any decided opinion on the projected treaty you communicated to us. We however wish to express our disposition to treat on an object which promises to lay the foundation of an extensive commerce and to tend to prevent the continuation of war.⟩

1. Published in Taylor, *Adams Papers*, VII; see also Lee's letter of Sept. 17.
2. Because of its position in the letterbook, this must have been written between these two dates: Taylor, *Adams Papers*, VII.

The American Commissioners to the Massachusetts Council[3]

AL (draft): Massachusetts Historical Society; two copies: National Archives

Passi September 22 1778

Mr. Jonathan Loring Austin who was dispatched the last year by your Honours with the glorious News of the Convention of Saratoga,[4] being about to return home We think it proper to inform your Honours that his Behaviour since his arrival here has been entirely to our Satisfaction and to recommend him as a Gentleman of Abilities and Fidelity in Business, well attached to the Cause of his Country, and of exemplary Decency and Prudence. We have advanced him one hundred Louis for which he is to be accountable to Congress.[5] We have the Honour to be &c.

The Hon. Council of Mass Bay.

The American Commissioners to the President of Congress

LS: National Archives; AL (draft): Massachusetts Historical Society; copies: Massachusetts Archives, National Archives (two); two transcripts: National Archives

Sir,   Passy Septr. 22. 1778.

This will be delivered to you by Mr. Jonathan Loring Austin, who was sent the last Year express to France with the News of the Convention of Saratoga. He has resided chiefly in this Kingdom from that time, and has been employed, in the Service of the Publick, a part of the Time; and his Behavior from first to last has given entire Satisfaction to us. We think it our Duty therefore to recommend him to Congress as a

---

3. In response to Austin's request of Sept. 19.
4. See xxv, 97–9.
5. This sentence is interlined; there is an entry for that sum on Sept. 24: Taylor, *Adams Papers*, VI, 361.

Gentleman of Merit, of Ability and Diligence in Business, zealously attached to the Cause of his Country, and of exemplary Prudence and Decency. We have the Honour to be[6] with great Respect, Sir, Your most obedient and most humble Servants

B FRANKLIN
ARTHUR LEE
JOHN ADAMS

The Hon. President Laurens.

Notation: Letter from B Franklin Ar. Lee John Adams Sept 22. 1778 respecting Jona. Loring Austin Read May 10 1779. Referred with Mr Austin's memorial[7]

The American Commissioners to Vergennes

Copy: National Archives

Passi Sepr. 22d. 1778

We have the honor of enclosing to your Excellency a Letter to us from the Honble. Ralph Izard Esqr. Commissioner of Congress to the Grand Duke.[8] We beg the favor of yr. Excellency to give directions for the delivery of the Packages mentiond therein to Monsieur Etienne Cathalan[9] Mercht. at Marseilles, subject to the disposal of Mr. Izard. We have the honor of being with the greatest respect

To his Excellency Count de Vergennes

6. In WTF's hand up to this point; the complimentary close is in BF's.

7. See *JCC*, XIV, 567–8. Austin's undated memoir (National Archives) asked that he not be required to return the money advanced for his personal expenses since his return voyage had proved longer and more expensive than he had anticipated.

8. Above, Sept. 21.

9. Actually Cathalant: XXVI, 454.

[September 22, 1778]

We have, as you know, made Overtures to the Grand Pension-ary.[2] We took that to be the regular Course of Proceeding. We expect an Answer. If he gives us none, we shall naturally con-clude that there is no Disposition in their H. H. M. M.[3] to have any Connection with us, and I believe we shall give them no farther Trouble; at least that would be my Opinion; for I think that a young State like a young Virgin, should modestly stay at home, and wait the Application of Suitors for an Alliance with her; and not run about offering her Amity to all the World, and hazarding their Refusal.[4] My Colleagues have this Day proposed to me to go to Holland on this Business; but tho' I honour that Nation, having been frequently there,[5] and much esteeming the People, and wishing for a firm Union between the two Republicks, I cannot think of Undertaking such a Journey, without some Assurances of being properly received as a Minister of the States of America. Our Virgin is a jolly one; and tho' at present not very rich, will in time be a great Fortune; and where she has a favourable Predisposition, it seems to me to be well worth cultivating. Your State perhaps is not of that Opinion; and it certainly has a right to judge for itself.

You can judge better than we at this Distance, whether any farther Step can properly be taken on our Part, till some En-couragement is given on the Part of their H. H. M. M. Let me know your Sentiments.

1. The one which we print is an undated AL entitled "Extract from Mr. F's Letter to Mr Dumas." The other is quoted within Dumas' letter of Oct. 30, which provides its date. The recipient's copy of the letter apparently is no longer extant.
2. See XXVI, 267–8.
3. Their High Mightinesses, i.e., the States General.
4. A sentiment that BF previously expressed. See XXIII, 511.
5. In August-September 1761 and August 1766: see IX, 364–8; XIII, 383–5.

Jonathan Williams, Jr., to the American Commissioners[6]

ALS: American Philosophical Society

⟨Nantes, September 22, 1778: When I laid my accounts before you,[7] I left the general one open pending its completion; I now send it, closed and settled, up to May 30, 1778. You will also find accounts of the arms magazine, invoice of arms repaired, and the general account from June 1 to September 10, with a balance in your favor of 7,386 *l.t.* 18 *s.* 9 *d.*[8] I have subsequently received a bill for bayonet sheaths which, along with the articles at the bottom of the general account, leaves a balance of about 11,000 *l.t.* in my favor. I will draw on you for that amount and notify you. Duplicates of all my accounts have been sent to Congress.[9] The *Dispatch*, Captain Barnes, which sailed from here on August 29 has been captured and carried into Guernsey.[1]⟩

From John Adams[2]

AL (draft): Massachusetts Historical Society

⟨Passy, September 22, 1778: In examining our joint accounts I find some articles for which I have paid separately. For future planning I propose we pay jointly for the wages and expenses of the maître d'hôtel, cook, coachman and other servants, the hire of horses and carriage, postage and expresses, and other common expenses. If Dr. Franklin chooses to add the washerwoman's accounts or the expenses of a clerk for each of us I have no objection. Receipts are to be taken for payments and

6. Published in Taylor, *Adams Papers*, VII.
7. See JW to the commissioners, July 17.
8. Most of these accounts, beginning May 12, 1777, are at the University of Va. Library and are reproduced in *Lee Family Papers*, reel 3, frames 765–807. They were inadvertently omitted from the Editorial Note on BF's Accounts, XXIV, p. 3.
9. JW sent those accounts on Sept. 10 accompanied by a detailed narrative of his activity since leaving England, and a defense of his conduct in the face of Lee's charges. APS.
1. Grinnell had already reported the capture on Sept. 15.
2. Published in Taylor, *Adams Papers*, VII.

each party furnished monthly with a copy of the accounts, with an opportunity to see the receipts. Expenses for clothing, books, other personal items and pocket expenses are to be paid separately. If another plan is more agreeable to Dr. Franklin, Mr. Adams begs him to propose it. Accounts for our sons at school may be added or not as he chooses. I expected to pay my son's subsistence myself and will do so if Congress desires it, but as other gentlemen are maintaining, educating and enjoying large families here,[3] perhaps Congress may also allow it to us, whose duties, labors and anxieties may be greater.⟩

From George Anderson[4]   ALS: American Philosophical Society

Sir   Lisbon 22d: Septmr. 1778

I embrace this opportunity to inform Your Excellency, I was to have been the bearer of the Ratification of the Treaty between France and America together with a large Number of letters and papers from the Congress and the Governor and Counsel of Virginia (of the utmost consequence) to Their Excellencies The Ambassadors at paris; but was unfortunately taken (by The King George packet) with my Vessel and Cargo of Ninety Seven Thousand weight of Tobacco, within about Twenty Leagus of the Bay of Biscay, when I destroyed all the letters and papers having particular directions so to do in case I was taken. The only letters that were saved was four of recommendation, one of which was to Your Excellency, and Three to the rest of Their Exellencies The Ambassadors, from

3. Doubtless a reference to Izard and William Lee. JA had only his son John Quincy with him.
4. Anderson (1755–1816) had been entrusted with these documents by Patrick Henry, a fellow native of Hanover County, Va. He was the brother of Col. Robert Clough Anderson, later a prominent man in Kentucky political and military life. After the revolution George became a tavern keeper and plantation owner in Cumberland County. William T. Hutchinson, William M.E. Rachal *et al.*, eds., *The Papers of James Madison* (16 vols. to date, Chicago, 1962–), II, 33, 34 n.

the Secty., and The Governor of Virginia, which letters the English Consel here has taken from me, as I was set at liberty at this place; and was it not for the Civilities of Arnold. H. Dorman Esquire,[5] should be in distress for even Common Necessaries as they Strip'd me of everything except my Cloaths. He, Mr. Dorman, is kind enough to furnish me with Cash and tells me he will procure a passage either to France or america as soon as possible, if to the Former shall wait on Your Excellency.

As to News respecting The Two Armies, General Washington gave Sr. Henry Clinton (in his march to New York in June last) a handsome drubing, and had it not been for the Misconduct of Genl. Lee wou'd certainly have taken his whole Army, however from the best Accounts, he with the remainder must have Capatulated before this. I am Your Excellencies most Obedient Humble Servant   GEO ANDERSON

The Vessel in which I was taken was owned by Colo. Adams, Mr. Hylton, of Virginia & my Self, and was Commanded by Capt. Thoms Coleman, Called the Sally[6]

The Honble. Ben. Frankling Esqr.

Addressed: The Honble. Benj Frankling Esq. / a / Paris

Notations in different hands: Geo. Anderson Lisbon 22. Sept. 78 / Anderson Geo. 22d. Sept. 1778. / M Caccia Banquier à Paris rüe st. martin Vis avis la rüe aux Ours

5. Dohrman, a Lisbon merchant and consulship seeker, is identified in XXVI, 211–12 n; Anderson wrote a lengthy letter on his behalf to the commissioners on Feb. 16, 1779 (Harvard University Library).

6. Probably Thomas Adams, a Virginia delegate to Congress; Daniel L. Hylton, of Henrico County, Va., was a close associate of Thomas Jefferson who, with JA and others, supported the agricultural company of Philip Mazzei: Boyd, *Jefferson Papers,* II, 128 n; IV, 271–2; I, 158, 48–9. Coleman was probably the former pilot of the Virginia brig *Liberty: Naval Docs.,* V, 1299; VI, 1228, 1282; VII, 91.

From Marie-Laurence de Bonte de Kerguelen[7]

ALS: American Philosophical Society

Paris le 22 7bre 1778 a St. Thomas rue de seve F.b.
Monsieur   st g.m.[Faubourg St.Germain]
Des raisons de santé m'enpechent de me rendre chez vous
pour vous communiquer la lettre de mon marÿ qui desire
avoir le commendement d'une des fregate que l'on m'a assuré
que vous faite construire en hollande. C'est avec l'agrement de
m. de Sartine que je vous en fait la demande. Ce ministre
rendera justice a ses tallens et moi je me rend garrante de son
zele. C'est toute une famille qui s'unit a moi pour vous en
soliciter. C'est un des parents de m. de Kerguelen qui vous
remettera cette lettre et qui s'est chargé de touts les regrets
que j'ai de ne pouvoir aller moi meme chez vous. J'ai l'honneur d'etre Monsieur votre tres humble et tres obeissante servante   BONTE DE KERGUELEN

Endorsed: Made. de Kerguelin Ship.

From Le Maire

ALS: American Philosophical Society

Monsieur   Nantes le 22 Septembre 1778.
Je sens que je vous fatigue, j'en suis réellement confus; mais
la cruelle position ou je me trouve fait que j'ai recours à vous
pour vous prier de me faire toucher six cents livres, ainsi que
j'ai eu l'honneur de vous le marquer dans mes précédentes.
M. Lee vient de me marquer qu'il n'étoit point à son pouvoir de fournir à mes depenses pour suivre mes opérations
comme vous le verrez par la copie de sa lettre que je prens la
liberté de vous envoyer;[8] je dois déja ici quatre à cinq cens
livres, je voudrois, Monsieur que ma fortune repondît à mes
bonnes intentions, je ne vous importunerois point. Vous trouverez également ci inclus la reponse que je fais à Mr. Lee ainsi

---

7. She was born in Dunkirk in 1740. Bodinier. Since one of the charges
against her husband, Kerguelen de Tremarec, was the presence of a young
girl on his ship, the support of his wife and family was presumably designed to strengthen his appeal: see his letter of Sept. 15.
8. Dated Sept. 14.

que la copie du projet et prospectus de L'armement du Navire que je propose pour transporter tous les objets en Virginie, je vous envoie aussi la copie de la quittance des ouvriers que j'ai payés avec les fonds que j'ai touchés de M. Schweighauser de la part de Mr. Lee.[9]

Veuillez, Monsieur, preter toute votre attention à tous mes chefs de demande, votre belle âme ne pourra se refuser à la Solicitation d'un homme honnête qui n'a que pour but de bien remplir sa mission pour repondre à la confiance que le gouvernement de Virginie a bien voulu lui accorder. Si vous ne daignez venir à mon secours et que Le projet d'armement ne s'execute pas je crains que tout ne tombe entre les mains des Ennemis.

Tout mon Espoir est entierement en Vous, persuadé que vous voudrez bien y prendre le plus vif interet, vous supliant de m'honorer d'un mot de reponse et penétré de ce Sentiment, j'ose toujours me dire avec le plus profond respect Monsieur Votre très humble et très obeissant Serviteur   LE MAIRE

Monsieur *franquelin* Ecuyer à Passy.

Endorsed: Capt. Lemaire

Notation: Nantes 22. 7bre 1778

Engelbert François van Berckel to the American Commissioners[1]   Copy:[2] American Philosophical Society

⟨[Amsterdam, September 23, 1778], in French: The undersigned, counsellor pensionary of Amsterdam, informs the commissioners that the burgomasters of the city authorize the following declaration: assuming Congress will not enter into any agreement with the English commissioners that would be

9. Le Maire's reply, enclosing the prospectus and the bill for arms inspectors, was dated Sept. 22. Le Maire was urging Lee to engage and arm a vessel he had found, which was large enough to transport all the supplies and capable of eluding ships of war. All four of these copies are in the APS.

1. Published in Taylor, *Adams Papers*, VII.

2. In Dumas' hand and enclosed in his letter of Oct. 2.

harmful or prejudicial to Dutch trade in Europe either directly or indirectly, the burgomasters will work to facilitate a treaty of friendship between the Netherlands and the United States as soon as England recognizes American independence. The burgomasters authorize the use of this statement where it is deemed appropriate, not doubting this will be done with all the necessary precautions.[3])

Schweighauser to the American Commissioners[4]

Copy: National Archives

⟨Nantes, September 24, 1778: I received your letter of the 14th [13th] only yesterday covering one from Capt. Richard, together with the documents relative to the cargo of rice and indigo shipped by A[braham] Livingston of Charles Town.[5] The person in charge of the vessel, M. Peltier du Doyer, tells me that, on orders from M. de Beaumarchais, he has already sold the cargo except for a few casks of inferior indigo. I expressed suprise at this imprudent action. Until I receive further instructions from you, I will do nothing more. I am extremely happy to learn that an exchange of prisoners will soon take place. As to my commission of 5%, please consider the trouble and expense attendant on my situation. I must supply interpreters, outfitters and repairmen, and provide for the considerable needs of the prisoners. If I am to receive only 2% I must charge the travelling expenses of my representatives at Brest and Lorient. M. Penet and M. Thomas Morris offer precedents for my own demands which I do not think unreasonable.⟩

3. The editors of the *Adams Papers* speculate that van Berckel's declaration on behalf of the burgomasters was designed as a rationalization for the action taken at Aix-la-Chapelle by their representative Jean de Neufville. A covering letter from van Berckel to Dumas of Sept. 23 defended the burgomasters from the accusation of making their own foreign policy.

4. Published in Taylor, *Adams Papers*, VII.

5. Livingston, the commercial agent at Charleston, shipped the cargo on the *Thérèse*; he wrote to the commissioners on Oct. 20 with respect to other cargoes for France.

Vergennes to the American Commissioners

L (draft):[6] Archives du Ministère des affaires étrangères; copies: Library of Congress (two), National Archives

A Versailles le 24. 7bre. 1778.

Par la lettre que vous m'avez fait l'honneur de m'écrire le 28 du mois dernier, Messieurs, vous avez demandé l'entrée libre dans le Royaume et l'Exemtion de tous droits des effets de beaucoup d'Américains qui se trouvent en Europe, et qui sont dans le dessein de retourner dans leur patrie. J'ay communiqué votre demande à M. Necker, et je joins ici une copie de sa réponse; vous y verrez les justes raisons qui s'opposent à la grace que vous avez sollicitée, et les mesures qui pourront être prises pour favoriser l'entrée et la sortie du Royaume des effets que les américains voudront faire passer en Amerique.[7]

M. Francklin, Lée et Adams

Jonathan Williams, Jr., to the American Commissioners

ALS: American Philosophical Society

Honourable Gentlemen   Nantes Sept. 24. 1778.

I this Day compleated the Inventory of the magazine of arms and presented it to Mr. Schweighauser for him to sign the Receipt at the Bottom. We are agreed as to quantity and number but he declines engaging to receive the articles for Reparation remaining to be supplied without your orders.[8] I therefore request you to give your Directions accordingly that I may close the Business. These articles I am absolutely engaged to take and pay for on account of the Magazine, they

6. In Gérard de Rayneval's hand.
7. In his reply of Sept. 18 (Library of Congress) Necker pointed out that the request would violate all the regulations. An arrangement might be made, however, by which the goods would be charged a single duty at the point of entry, and then be sealed and sent without further charges to the point of departure. More favorable treatment could not be expected. Please let him know for whom it is intended so that he may issue the necessary orders.
8. For Schweighauser's comment on the receipt, see Sept. 26.

are necessary to the Reparation and would not have been ordered but for that purpose. You will therefore find them noticed at the bottom of the account I had the Honour to transmit per the last Post. I am with the greatest Respect Honourable Gentlemen Your most obedient Servant

JONA WILLIAMS J

The Honble The Ministers Plenipotentiary of the United States.

Addressed: The Honourable / The Ministers Plenipotentiary / of the / United States / Passy

Endorsed by John Adams: M. Williams Septr. 24 1778

From Cecilia Davies[9]

ALS: American Philosophical Society

Paris 7br. 24th 1778.

No words can express the Obligations we are under to our Dear and most Worthy Friend for his truly kind Letter, 'tis so great a proof of that Friendship which you have always shewn to our family that our Gratitude can only end with our Lives. How rejoiced we shall be to see you again Dear Sir, 'tis a happiness we shall hope to enjoy, and the very expectation of it will afford us some Consolation during our absence from a Person whom we shall ever Respect and Love most sincerely. My Mother and Sister join me in every wish for the continuation of your Health and Happiness, and I remain with the sincerest Attachment Dear Sir Your most Affectionate and most Oblig'd Humble Servant   DAVIES INGLESINA

Endorsed: Davies Inglesina

Notation: Sept 24 78

9. BF's friend, the singer known in Italy as "L'Inglesina," is identified above, XXV, 543 n.

From the Abbé Jacob Hemmer[1]

AL: American Philosophical Society

⟨Mannheim, September 24,[2] 1778, in Latin: Wishing to give you a token of its esteem, the Palatine Academy of Sciences has entrusted me with the pleasant task of sending you its *Transactions.* I rejoice in this chance to thank you again for the kindness you showed me and my friend Delor in Paris recently.[3]

Of the five volumes I am supposed to send you, the first two are made up of a mixture of history and natural science; the others deal with separate topics. The fourth, which I shall ship as soon as it gets off the press, is all physics.[4] It contains four of my essays—one on lightning rods in the Palatinate, one on memorable strokes of lightning, one on an electrical cure for paralysis that I performed, and one on the perpetual "electrophore" which I built here.

I will send you soon the by-laws of our own German Society, in the hopes that it will become the sister of yours.[5]⟩

From John Paul Jones

ALS: American Philosophical Society; AL (draft): National Archives; copy: United States Naval Academy Museum

Honored and dear Sir   Brest Septr. 24th. 1778.

Altho' the Ministers letter respecting me to Comte D'Orvilliers was not well timed, Yet I think it my Duty to thank him

---

1. For this prominent meteorologist and researcher in German philology (1733–1790), see the *ADB.* He was the first in the Palatinate to demonstrate the utility of lightning rods.

2. "8 calendas octobris."

3. In spite of frequent mentions of his work on electricity, Delor has remained a mystery figure: see IV, 315–16 n.

4. He sent it on Aug. 8, 1780. APS.

5. The "Catalogus librorum" that he enclosed contains the works of 44 authors for a sum total of 567 *l.t.* 5 *s.* BF endorsed the letter: "Hemmer Present of Books."

for his intentions.[6] It has been hinted to me that a Lieutenant who has been with the D. De C——[7] expects to Command the Fox thro' that Intrest. If this be true I am afraid the letters which I inclosed to you the 21st. will rather do harm than good, but perhaps it is rather that persons Wish than reasonable expectation?

Count D'Orvilliers tells me that the Fox is not and cannot be promised without an Order from Monseigneur De Sartine, therefore recommends that I should make application. The Minister need fear no difficulty here respecting the Alert. Count D'Orvilliers will readily remove and otherwise provide for the young Officer who now Commands that Vessel. This he expressly told me before the Fleet Sailed. One of the Gentlemen who should, agreeable to Monsieur De Chaumont, have Commanded under me from L'Orient may now Command the Alert unless a more fit Person should appear in the Meantime.

As I see no prospect of any thing better I am earnest in wishing for this Command for several Reasons. Both the Bottoms are Sheathed with Copper, The Ship will lodge 250 men compleatly, Carries for them Six Months Provision, and, with such a Tender, is well Calculated for a Project which I have in View. I have refered the Minister to you, and I wish it may be Suitable for you to See him.

The Prince De N——[8] has not Answered my letter.[9] Perhaps they are waiting to see what can be Effected at the Equinox. But even in that Case it is not very kind to remain Altogether Silent and leave me in all the torment of Indolence and

6. Jones had just seen the returning d'Orvilliers, who had received Sartine's orders only after he had been some time at sea. Jones immediately wrote to Sartine acknowledging the mishap, and repeating his request for a ship. U.S. Naval Academy Museum.

7. Duc de Chartres.

8. Nassau. He had been out of town, but was expected back soon: Bancroft to Jones, Sept. 23, 1778, National Archives.

9. A footnote in the draft reads: "respecting the Indien." The Prince de Nassau, who had gone to Amsterdam the previous spring to secure that ship, reported that she could not be launched and armed before the September equinox. Jones to Louis XVI, Oct. 19, 1778: APS. See also BF to Jones, June 1.

Suspense. The Minister has here an Opportunity of giving me a small Command without any inconvenience, and if he is now pursuing his first Plan, as it may fail at last, I beg that he may in the Meantime reserve for me the Ship and Tender which I have mentioned.

I have as yet received no letters from the Commissioners respecting the Prisoners. Doctor Bancroft too remains Silent, so that I am Afraid his indisposition is Relapsed. Tho' very troublesome to you at present I am with the truest Esteem and Respect Honored and Dear Sir Your very Obliged very Obedient very humble Servant   JNO P JONES

His Excellency Doctor Franklin.

Endorsed: Capt. Jones

Notation: Brest 24. Septembre 78

Vergennes to the American Commissioners

Copies: Library of Congress (two), Massachusetts Historical Society

A Versailles le 25. 7bre. 1778

J'ai reçu, Messieurs, la lettre que vous m'avez fait l'honneur de m'écrire[1] pour reclamer des Effets appartenans à M. Izarts qui ont été pris sur un batiment Anglois allant à Livourne. Je n'entrerai pas ici dans la question si le Navire Ennemi rend la marchandise Ennemie, les Capteurs l'éleveront certainement. Mais Comme cette question est du Ressort du Departement de la Marine, Je crois que vous ferez très bien de voir le plus tôt possible M. de Sartine. Ce Ministre est à Paris et y passera toute la Journée de demain. Je ferai volontiers ce qui dépendra de moi auprès de ce Ministre pour l'engager à vous procurer une prompte Decision. J'ai l'honneur d'être avec une parfaite consideration Messieurs, Votre très humble et très obeissant serviteur   (signé) DE VERGENNES

Messrs. Franklin, Lée et Adams

1. On Sept. 22.

The American Commissioners to Ralph Izard[2]

AL (draft): Massachusetts Historical Society; two copies: National Archives

Sir   Passi September 26 1778

Last Evening We had the Honour of an answer from the Comte de Vergennes to our Letter respecting your Goods. We inclose a Copy of it to you and believe it will be adviseable for you to wait on Mr. de Sartine. Perhaps he may not at first recollect the Article of the Treaty, as Mr. De Vergennes appears not to have done.[3] We have the Honour to be with great Respect, Sir your most obedient &c.

Hon. Mr Ralph Izzard

The American Commissioners to Sartine

AL (draft): Massachusetts Historical Society; two copies: National Archives

Sir   Passi September 26. 1778

The Honourable Ralph Izzard Esqr., Minister from the United States to the Grand Duke, having ordered his Baggage to Italy from London has had the Luck to have them taken in an English Vessell, and carried into Marseilles. We have written to the Compte de Vergennes on the subject who refers Us to your Excellency. We apprehend that by the sixteenth Article of the Treaty of Commerce Mr. Izzard has a clear Right to a Restitution of his Goods. But perhaps it will be necessary for your Excellency to transmit to Marseilles a Copy of the Treaty, or some orders relative to this Property of Mr. Izzard,

---

2. BF did not sign any of the commissioners' letters of the 26th: see the commissioners to Vergennes, of this date, below. He was in Anet visiting Madame Brillon.

3. It was article 16 of the Treaty of Amity and Commerce, which provided that goods belonging to French or American subjects put on board enemy ships up to two months before the declaration of war or without knowledge of it would not be liable to confiscation: xxv, 610–11.

which We have the Honour to request your Excellency to do. We have the Honour to be

M. de Sartine

The American Commissioners to James Smith

AL (draft): Massachusetts Historical Society; two copies: National Archives

Sir   Passi September 26 1778

On the 28 of the last Month We had the Honour of writing to M. the Comte de Vergennes, concerning your Goods, and in the same Letter, We requested that some Mode might be prescribed by which Americans, well affected to their Country, might pass through this Kingdom in their Way home with their Effects Duty free. The last Evening We received an Answer from his Excellency[4] inclosing Copy of a Letter from Mr. Necker upon the subject. A Copy of this Copy together with a Copy of his Excellency's Letter to Us We inclose to you, for your Government. We shall be ready to apply to Mr. Necker, in the Way prescribed by him, whenever you shall furnish us with the means of doing it, by sending us an Invoice of your Goods, and a note where they are, and for what detained, that We may inclose it to him. In the mean time, We are

Dr. Smith

The American Commissioners to Vergennes[5]

ALS:[6] Archives du Ministère des affaires étrangères; AL (draft): Massachusetts Historical Society; two copies: National Archives

⟨Passy, September 26, 1778: Last evening we received your letter of the 24th and shall observe the rules prescribed by M.

4. Above, Sept. 24.
5. Published in Taylor, *Adams Papers*, VII.
6. In JA's hand and signed by him and Lee. A postscript in Lee's hand reads, "NB. Dr Franklin is in the Country A. Lee."

Necker. We also received your letter of the 25th; article 16 of the treaty of commerce applies to Mr. Izard's goods as they were shipped before any declaration of war or at least within two months of the first appearance of war. We have referred him to M. de Sartine and following your advice will apply to that Minister ourselves as soon as possible.⟩

To John Adams[7]   ALS: Massachusetts Historical Society

Dear Sir,   Passy; Saturday Sept. 26. 78

I very much approve your Plan with regard to our future Accounts, and wish it to be followed.

The Accounts that have been shown you, are only those of the Person we had entrusted with the receiving and paying our Money;[8] and intended merely to show how he was discharged of it. We are to separate from that Account th Articles for which Congress should be charged, and those for which we should give Credit.

It has always been my Intention to pay for the Education of my Children, their Clothes &c. as well as for Books and other Things for my private Use; and whatever I spend in this Way, I shall give Congress Credit for, to be deducted out of the Allowance they have promis'd us. But as the Article of Clothes for ourselves here is necessarily much higher than if we were not in public Service, I submit it to your Consideration whether that Article ought not to be reckoned among Expences for the Publick. I know I had Clothes enough at home to have lasted me my Lifetime in a Country where I was under small Necessity of following new Fashions.

I shall be out of Town till Monday; when I return we will if you please, talk farther of these Matters, and put the Accounts in the Order they are hereafter to be kept. With great Esteem, I am, Your most obedient humble Servant   B FRANKLIN

I inclose a Letter just receiv'd from Mr Ross.[9] Some Answer

7. In answer to his of Sept. 22.
8. WTF: see JA's unsent letter of Sept. 6–13.
9. A now missing letter of Sept. 22, answered below on the 30th.

should be sent him. I have not had time. Enclos'd are his late Letters.

If any good News arrives my Servant may be sent Express to me with it.

J. Adams Esqr

Schweighauser to the American Commissioners[1]

Copy: National Archives

⟨Nantes, September 26, 1778: After I wrote you asking instructions about M. Peltier du Doyer's claim on the cargo of the *Thérèse*, I decided to put a stay on his action and demanded delivery of the goods to me to prevent his remitting the proceeds of his sales to Paris. The inventory of the arsenal is completed. Mr. Williams wants me to sign the annexed receipt which I will not do until you indicate that my draft on you for the remaining unfinished articles will be honored.[2] Please send the conditions of sale so that I may complete the account of the tobacco brought by the *Baltimore* and sold to the farmers general. The director of the farm has repeatedly requested it.⟩

Joseph Wharton, Jr., to the American Commissioners[3]

ALS: American Philosophical Society

⟨Paris, September 26, 1778: In order to lessen the scarcity of salt in America and to benefit myself I propose to send several

1. Published in Taylor, *Adams Papers*, VII.
2. JW said as much to the commissioners on Sept. 24. The receipt acknowledged arms, tools, keys to the magazine and transfer of its lease until Dec. 25, 1780, to Schweighauser, who would agree to "take what further articles for reparation which remain unfurnished, and which the said Williams stands engaged for giving him my draft on the Honourable the Commissioners for the same. . . ." A copy, dated merely "Sept. 1778", is at the National Archives.
3. Published in Taylor, *Adams Papers*, VII. For Wharton see Bancroft's letter under Aug. 7.

cargoes of it from Portugal this coming winter. As you informed me there is no congressional resolution against direct trade from Portugal to the United States, I ask passports for the vessels I may load there. Because of the supposed unfriendliness between the two countries these passports will be highly necessary both to remove the suspicions of Portuguese merchants and masters and to secure protection from American warships and privateers.[4]⟩

From William Alexander

ALS: American Philosophical Society

Dear Sir   Auteuil 26 Sept 1778
The inclosed Paper Contains a short sketch of Dr. Blacks Doctrine of Latent heat.[5] It is there applied only to a few phenomena but the Dr. has experiments to shew that it is also the Cause of vapour, and He Explains How Evaporation Generates Cold, and the whole Theory of fluidity. After you have red this short paper, When you meet with my B[rothe]r[6] He will give you the Extent of the Doctrine and Inform you of the Experiments by which It is supported.

This Paper I got from one of Dr. Blacks Students for the use of Monsieur De Morveaux.[7] I am with the most thorough Attachment Dear Sir Your most obedient humble Servant
W ALEXANDER

4. BF drafted such a passport in October (APS). He reused the draft later, lining out Wharton's name and substituting 1779 for 1778. It bears the notation "Passport for Mr. Whartons vessels. with salt."

5. Dr. Joseph Black (1728–99), professor of medicine and chemistry at the University of Edinburgh, and member of the eminent scientific societies of Europe, whose theory of latent heat formed the basis of modern thermal science. The theory was formulated as early as 1762, but never published; Black taught it in his lectures. DNB. BF had met him in Edinburgh in 1771 (XIX, 50) but there is no evidence that the two scientists corresponded.

6. Alexander John, for whom see XXIV, 199 n.

7. Louis-Bernard de Guyton de Morveau, the famous French chemist. Alexander had sent BF an advance copy of his most recent book the previous year: XXIII, 415, 440.

Addressed: A Monsieur / Monsr Franklin / a Passy

Endorsed: W Alexander

Notation: 26. Sept. 1778.

From Jean-Baptiste Machillot Desplaces

ALS: American Philosophical Society

Son Exelence   A Paris ce 26 7bre *1778*

Le nommé J.B. Machillot desplaces Valet de Chambre de Mr. le Mquis. de lafayette[8] suplie Son Exelence d'avoir la bonté de le faire payer de la somme de 400 *l.t.* qu'il a prêté a Mr. le Maire pour un mois seulement, le tems que Son Exelence devoit lui faire rembourcer les avances qu'il avoit fait pour Elle. Sans le connoître que pour l'avoir vû chez Mdme. La Mquise. de lafayette,[9] J'y ai été de bonne foie en lui accordant la demande qu'il me fit, aprésent je ne peu le ravoir sans le Scour [secours] de Son Exelence. Mdme. La Mquise. de la fayette m'a chargée de vous faire ses complimens. J'ai l'honneur d'être avec un très profond respect Son Exelence Votre très humble et trés obeissant Serviteur   MACHILLOT DESPLACES

tournés S'il vous plait

Je crain de fatiguer Son Exelence de lecture. Voila la Coppie du Billet qu'il m'a fait:

Je promet payer la Somme de quatre cent livres de france dans un mois datte de ce jour, a Mr. Machillot desplaces, Valet de Chambre de Mr. le Mquis. de lafayette a Paris

ce 30. Juillet 1778. Le Maire

bon pour 400 l.t.

Il m'a ecrit trois lettres depuis qu'il est a Nantes en reponces de mes demandes, pour obtenir du tems, auquel il n'a j'amais

---

8. Lafayette affectionately regarded him as "my dear Desplaces": Idzerda, *Lafayette Papers*, II, 176.

9. On Sept. 6 BF had declined to furnish personal support to Le Maire.

tenu parolle; j'ai toujour déférés a en donner connoissence a Son Éxelence crainte de lui auter la confiance qu'elle a en lui. C'est la nécessité qui m'y force crainte qu'il ne parte avant qu'il ne me paye parce que je voi qu'il abuse de ma bonté.

J'ai donné une léttre a Monsieur lee ce matin je crain de m'être mal expliqué voila pourquoi je prens la liberté de récrire celle cy.

Notation: Deplacé 26 Sept. 78

From Jean-Gabriel Montaudoüin de la Touche[1]

ALS: American Philosophical Society

Monsieur   Nantes 26 7bre 1778
Je profite de L'occasion de Mr. Blanchet qui va a Paris et qui a grande envie de vous rendre ses hommages pour me rappeller dans l'honneur de vôtre souvenir. Mr. Blanchet est eleve du celebre Agriculteur Tull.[2] Il parle Anglois. Il a traduit le *Commun-Sens*, il est fort zelé pour la cause Ameriquaine. C'est un homme sans faute. Il a les moeurs et la candeur du bon vieux tems, il a de L'esprit, et des connoissances. Il est connu de plusieurs personnes de distinction, entre autres de Madame La Duchesse d'Enville.

Il vous donnera des nouvelles de Mr. vôtre Neveu qu'il vit hier chèz moi, et qui partit peu de tems après pour La Rochelle. Je lui ai donné des lettres de recomandation pour Le Lieutenant General de L'Amirauté de cette ville là. Il est aussi recommandé au Beaufrere de mon frere.[3] Il y a quelque tems que Je le chargeai de vous informer que divers Corsaires Anglois qui croisent sur nos côtes alloient sous Pavillon Ameri-

1. Identified in XXII, 332 n.
2. Jethro Tull (1674–1741) had invented a celebrated planting "drill" and was the author of *Horse-hoing Husbandry*, much admired by Voltaire. *DNB*. Blanchet is a mystery to us; we have found no record of a French translation of *Common Sense* published prior to 1791.
3. His brother Arthur.

quain acheter des vivres en Espagne, notament a Bilbao.[4] On pouroit empecher cette Supercherie.

Ma femme vous dit mille choses honnetes.[5] Elle se retablit bien. Elle est accouchée a la fin du 7eme mois d'une fille morte. J'ai L'Honneur d'être avec une veneration sans borne et un tendre, et respectueux devouement Monsieur vôtre très humble très obeissant Serviteur MONTAUDOÜIN

Voules vous bien, Monsieur, embrasser pour moi Madame et Melle. de Chaumont, et faire agreer nos respects a Mr et a Mme Le Roy.

Addressed: A Monsieur / Monsieur Le docteur Franklin / Commissaire des Etats unis, membre / des Academies des Sciences de paris, / philadelphie, Londres, &c. / A Passy

Notation: Montaudoin 26. 7bre. 1778.

The American Commissioners to Sartine[6]

AL (draft): Massachusetts Historical Society; four copies: National Archives

⟨Passy, September 27, 1778: We received yours of the 21st relative to the retaking of the *Isabelle* by Captain McNeill. Since comte d'Estaing has probably retaken American vessels from the English, we should soon have intelligence on how this was handled. In the meanwhile we have advised Captain McNeill to turn over one third of the value of the *Isabelle* to a public officer whom you shall designate, to be repaid either to the Captain or to the original proprietor depending on the rule the two nations adopt. McNeill will deliver this letter to you and can take charge of any dispatches regarding this affair you wish to entrust to him.⟩

---

4. JW had transmitted the message on Sept. 10.

5. Catherine-Olive Hay de Slade, of Irish descent. She died in August, 1780. From information kindly communicated by Mme. Bertrand de Montaudoüin.

6. Published in Taylor, *Adams Papers*, VII.

Vergennes to the American Commissioners[7]

LS: National Archives; L (draft):[8] Archives du Ministère des affaires étrangères; copies: National Archives (three), Library of Congress (two), Archives du Ministère des affaires étrangères, Massachusetts Historical Society; transcript: National Archives

⟨Versailles, September 27, 1778, in French: In your letter of the 28th of last month you recalled the King's promise in article 8 of the Treaty of Amity and Commerce to employ his good offices with the regencies of Barbary on behalf of American trade. I have communicated your request to M. de Sartine. In his enclosed reply[9] he thinks the request well founded but needs further information, which I ask that you address to me. Be assured the King will do all in his power.⟩

From James Laurens, Jr.[1]

ALS: American Philosophical Society

Le Vigan-Cevennes-Languedoc: 27 September
Honour'd Sir   1778
Though I have not the pleasure of being personally known to you, I take the Liberty to address you as the Common friend of America and to request the favour of your assistance in procuring me a Pass, which may serve as a safe conduct for me and my Family in travelling from City to City through this Kingdom, which I am informd by the Commandant of this Town, will be absolutely necessary for me to carry about at

7. Published in Taylor, *Adams Papers*, VII.
8. In Gérard de Rayneval's hand.
9. A translation of Sartine's letter to Vergennes of Sept. 21 is published in Wharton, *Diplomatic Correspondence*, II, 731–2.
1. A prominent Charleston merchant (1728–84) and younger brother of Henry Laurens, whose daughters Martha and Mary Eleanor accompanied their uncle on the journey described here. James's illness began in 1774; he and his family left the following year for England. They went to southern France in April, 1778, and lived near Le Vigan during the war. David D. Wallace, *The Life of Henry Laurens* . . . (New York and London, 1915), pp. 57, 136, 226, 414–15, 418, geneal. table following p. 502; David Ramsay, *Memoirs of the Life of Martha Laurens Ramsay* . . . (Boston, 1812), pp. 16–21.

this Juncture.[2] It may be necessary to inform you that I am of Charles Town, South Carolina which place I Left in June 1775 merely in quest of health, which I have not yet been so happy as to obstain, though I have experienced much benefit from this Climate. I posted thro' France in Decemr. Last in Company with a friend who was perfectly acquainted with this Country and was so kind as to represent both our Families and do every thing that was necessary, by which means I never obtaind a Pass for my own Family, nor have I thought of one since the departure of that friend, till, the Commandant inform'd me of the necessity of having one.

As our Journey thro' france was in a severe frost and we hasten'd with our Families of Invalids to reach a milder Climate, I could not prevail on my friend to halt but one day at St. Denys (the 19th. Decemr.) when I embraced the opportunity of going to Paissy in order to pay my respects to you, but had the mortification to be inform'd by Mr. Dean, that you were engaged at Paris and would not return home till after Night and I was obliged to pursue my Journey the next Morning. I thought it necessary to trouble you with this minute Account of myself, as I have not the honour of being personally known and entreat you to pardon the freedom I have taken.

I Congratulate you with all my heart on the happy aspect of our American affairs in general, and on the success of your important negociation at the Court of France in particular, and hope that within a few Months our Country will enjoy perfect tranquility. I Remain with the most Profound respect, Honored Sir Your most Obedient humble Servant

JAMES LAURENS, JR.

P.S. It may be necessary to mention that my Family consists of five Persons Vizt. Mrs Laurens and myself, Mr. Petrie a Nephew of Mrs. L.[3] and two Young Ladies, daughters of my

2. BF obliged, in a letter of Oct. 23, now missing: James Laurens, Jr., to commissioners, Nov. 12, 1778, APS.

3. A sister of Laurens' wife Mary had married an Alexander Petrie; there is no record of children in the geneal. table cited above.

Brother Henry Laurens President of the General Congress in America

Addressed: A Son Excellance / Monsr. Le Docteur Franklin / Ministre Des Etats Unis / de L'Amerique a La cour / de France / Paris

Endorsed: James Laurens Esqr for a Pass / Mr Laurens Pass

Notation: Languedoc 27. 7bre. 1778

From ———— Hennessienne[4]

ALS: American Philosophical Society

⟨Vienna, September 28, 1778, in French: A friend and I have discovered a method for neutralizing gunpowder in such a way that it will not explode under any circumstances. We also know how to render it explosive again. Such a momentous secret is yours if you pay my collaborator a lump sum of 8,000 florins. As for me, I will rely on the well-known fairness of your country where I wish to settle. We can demonstrate our technique to anyone you will appoint in Vienna or come to Paris at your expense.⟩

From ———— Le Cordier[5]

ALS: American Philosophical Society

⟨Port Louis, September 28, 1778, in French: We are told here that you have asked the King to grant the Americans the use of four French ports and that His Majesty had named Dunkirk, Marseilles, Port Louis, and either Bordeaux or Nantes. If such is the case, I beg you to employ me here, where I have served the Compagnie des Indes since 1737. Dealing with

---

4. He signs himself "Docteur en Droit, Avocat, à la cour Souveraine de Lorraine et Barois, et Secretaire de L'Envoyer de france à la cour de Saxe. à l'hotel du Prince Esterhazÿ, à Vienne."

5. He signs himself "directeur des postes du Port Louis et pensionnaire du Roy."

merchandise and getting it ready for auction is my specialty and I have worked in that line for a number of shipowners in St. Malo and Lorient. I own commodious magazines in Port Louis.[6]⟩

Matthew Ridley to the American Commissioners[7]

ALS: American Philosophical Society; copy: Massachusetts Historical Society

⟨Paris, September 29, 1778: A number of years ago, in London, I came upon a manuscript book of the commissioners of the English navy. It contains accurate descriptions of the ships and their equipment then in commission as well as calculations for their repair and the duties of their officers. Conceiving this intelligence might be of use to those in the United States navy, I send it to you to present to Congress. I possess property in Maryland and consequently hope the navy of the United States will flourish.⟩

From Madame Brillon   ALS: American Philosophical Society

[September 29, 1778][8]

Je fus trop heureuse, samedi, dimanche, lundi; oui mon chér papa je fus trop heureuse, mon chagrin me le prouve a présent! Je n'ai pas voulu allér encore rangér votre appartement, parce que tout m'y disoit d'une maniére trop sensible que vous n'y éstes plus; mais j'ai été dans nos prairies, j'y ai vû partout la trace de vos pas; les arbres m'ont paru d'un vérd triste, l'eau de nos riviéres m'a semblé coullér plus lentement. Ce ne sont pas des compliments que je vous fais, c'est l'éxpréssion simple de mon coeur a laqu'elle je me livre: c'est

---

6. He enclosed a letter sent him in 1772 by various directors of the Compagnie des Indes, praising his zeal and fidelity. He also named nineteen important people who would vouch for him. BF endorsed the letter: "Le Cordier to be Agent at Port Louis."

7. Published in Taylor, *Adams Papers*, VII.

8. See the headnote to BF's letter to her of Sept. 1.

a mon pére, que sa fille tendre et aimante parle; j'eus un pére, le plus honnéste des hommes, il fut mon premiér, et mon meilleur ami; je l'ai pérdu avant le tems! Vous m'avés dit souvent: *ne pourroisje pas vous tenir lieu de ceux que vous regrettés*: et vous m'avés raconté l'usage humain de cértains sauvages, qui adoptent les prisonniérs qu'ils font a la guérre, et leur font prendre la place de ceux de leurs parents qui leur manquent; vous avés pris dans mon coeur la place de ce pére que j'aimois que je réspéctois tant; la douleur déchirante que j'éprouvois de sa pérte, s'est changée en une mélancolie douce qui m'est chére et que je vous dois; vous vous éstes acquis en moi, un enfant, une amie de plus; j'ai commencés par avoir pour vous l'idolatrie que tout le monde doit a un grand homme; j'ai eu la curiosité de vous voir, mon amour propre a été flatté de vous recevoir chés moi; ensuitte je n'ai plus vû en vous, que votre áme sensible a l'amitié, votre bonté, votre simplicité, et j'ai dit, cet homme est si bon qu'il m'aimera, et je me suis mise a vous bien aimér pour vous engagér a en faire de mesme; il est un moyen de me prouvér, si mon amitié vous est chére, si vous avés été content de la maniére dont je vous ai soigné chéz moi; c'est d'y revenir mon chér papa, avéc votre aimable fils avéc mon voisin;[9] j'espére que vous le pourrés, et que si vous le pouvés vous le ferés; j'ai l'honneur d'estre mon chér papa Votre trés humble et trés obeissante sérvante

D'HARDANCOURT BRILLON

Recevés les hommages de tous ceux que vous avés laissé chés moi.

Addressed: A Monsieur / Monsieur Franklin / A Passy

9. Le Veillard.

From ——— de Gruffy[1]

ALS: American Philosophical Society

ALS: American Philosophical Society

Monsieur   Paris 29 7bre 1778

Je viens de recevoir une Lettre de Me. La Comtesse de
Conway d'auxerre, qui est dans les inquietudes les plus
cruelles sur le sort de son mari, dont elle n'a aucune nouvelle,
et que la Gazette de divers endroits No 61 du 4 7bre dit avoir
été blessé dans une affaire qu'il a eu avec le Collonel Cadwallader.[2] Daignés Monsieur au nom de Dieu lui aprendre ce que
vous savés de cette affaire, et lui donner des Nouvelles de son
mari si vous en savés, quelles qu'elles puissent être; elles seront plus consolantes, que l'anxieté ou elle se trouve. J'ose
croire que vous voudrés bien par humanité, et par L'amitie que
vous avés pour Made. Conway que vous apellés du doux nom
de fille, avoir la bonté de lui écrire, ou me faire L'honneur de
me répondre, et je lui manderai tout ce qu'il vous plaira de
m'aprendre.[3]

Dans une Conversation que j'ai eu il y a environ 18 jours
avec Monsieur Adams, il me fit l'honneur de me dire que votre
patrie n'avoit pas besoin d'hommes, mais qu'elle avoit un plus
grand besoin d'argent. Je lui repondis que je pourrois peut être
faire quelques démarches avec succès, que la Republique de
Berne avoit un trésor Considérable, et que je savois qu'on
trouvoit facilement à faire des Emprunts à Genes. Comme j'ai
des rélations dans l'un Comme dans l'autre Endroit Je vous
offre avec sincerité et avec Empressement mes services, vous
n'aurés qu'à m'indiquer, quelle somme vous emprunteriés;
pour quel tems, quels sont les arrangemens que vous pren-
driés pour payer les Interets, et pour en faire le rembourse-

1. For this faithful friend of the Conway family see XXVI, 42.
2. Actually no. 71 of the *Gaz. de Leyde*, also called *Nouvelles extraordinaires
de divers endroits*: "Le Général Conway, qui a passé du service de France à
celui du Congrès, s'étant battu en Duel avec le Colonel Cadwallader de
Philadelphie, a reçu une blessure, qu'on espéroit n'être point dangereuse."
3. Countess Conway's brother, Major Denis-Jean Du Bouchet, wrote
the same day to WTF, urging him to communicate any news he had about
the duel and to forward a message to General de Kalb. APS.

ment.[4] Je ne doutte point de reussir. En tout cas, mon activité et les soins que j'y donnerai, vous prouveront le désir que j'aurois de faire quelque chose qui put vous être agreable et de vous voir agréer le profond respect avec lequel je suis Monsieur Votre tres humble et très obéissant Serviteur

DE GRUFFY
Rue du Temple

Notation: Gruffi about Me Conway Paris 29. 7bre. 1778.

From the Comte de Sarsfield

ALS: American Philosophical Society

Rennes le 29 7bre 1778

Voicy, Monsieur, une lettre que J'ecris a Made. Macaulay[5] et qui vous instruira suffisament de celle que J'ay recu d'elle. Je n'ay a y ajouter que le nom de celui a qui elle avoit confié ses livres. C'est Brewn ou Brown. Elle me mande qu'on lui a dit qu'il avoit eté pris par un armateur de Jersey et que vous comptiez les en retirer. Si vous avez quelque chose a lui faire savoir la dessus, ayez la bonté de lui ecrire. Vous etes interessé dans cet envoy pour le dernier volume de ses lettres et Made. de Chaumont pour un Exemplaire entier.[6]

J'espere etre bientot a Paris ou je me fais un grand plaisir

4. We have found no trace that the schemes were attempted.

5. Sarsfield's friendship with Catherine Macaulay dates back to her visit in November, 1777: XXV, 203.

6. In the absence of Sarsfield's enclosures, a letter from Thomas Digges to [Mr. Brown], dated merely "August," provides the background. In May, Mrs. Macaulay had asked Digges to forward, care of BF, a parcel of books for friends in Paris whom she had recently visited: one volume of her *History of England . . . in a Series of Letters* for BF, and four volumes each of her *History of England* for both Sarsfield and Mme. Chaumont. (See XXVI, 390 n.) Digges entrusted the parcel to "a friend" bound for America via France. En route from Guernsey to the French coast, the courier's baggage was seized and taken to the Guernsey custom house. Digges was trying to get the books released, but in the mean time Mrs. Macaulay, afraid her Parisian friends would accuse her of negligence, wanted BF apprised of these circumstances. Hist. Soc. of Pa.

d'avoir l'honneur de vous voir et de vous renouveller l'assurance des sentimens avec lesquels J'ay l'honneur d'etre Monsieur Votre tres humble et tres obeissant serviteur   SARSFIELD

Permettez vous Monsieur que je mette icy bien des choses
pour votre fils, Mr. Adams et Mr. Lee.

Endorsed: M. Sarsfield Rennes 29. 7bre. 1778.

From Anne-Robert-Jacques Turgot, Baron de l'Aulne

AL: American Philosophical Society

Ce Mardi 29 Septembre [1778].
Mr. Turgot fait mille compliments a Monsieur Franklin et le
prie d'ajouter au plaisir qu'il doit lui faire de diner demain chéz
lui, celui de proposer a Mr. Franklin le jeune et a Mr. Adams
de lui faire le meme honneur.

Addressed: A Monsieur / Monsieur Franklin / Ministre
plenipotentiaire[7] / des Etats unis / A Passi

The American Commissioners to John Ross[8]

ALS:[9] Detroit Public Library; AL (draft): Massachusetts Historical Society; copies: National Archives (four); transcript: National Archives

⟨Passy, September 30, 1778: We received yours of September
22. We have no authority to give you orders or advice beyond
what concerns the large sum of money advanced you by the
commissioners some time ago for which you refuse to account. We have nothing to do with your private affairs and
your relationship to Congress, nor can we be justified in advancing more money to someone whose refusal to submit accounts has been accompanied by circumstances of indecency.

7. One of the many instances of this title being given to BF before he
officially received it.
8. Published in Taylor, *Adams Papers*, VII. The letter it is answering is
missing.
9. In JA's hand.

Save yourself the trouble of writing us until those accounts are settled. P.S.[1] Mr. Williams' accounts indicate an advance of 20,000 livres to you as well.⟩

From Borel
ALS: American Philosophical Society

Monsieur   Ce 30. 7bre. 1778.

Vous me promites la derniere fois que J'eus L'honneur de vous voir de me faire passer les armes et les titres des etats independants de l'amerique.[2] Oserai-je vous prier de vous occuper un instant de cet objet dont j'aurai un extreme Besoin d'ici a tres peu de tems? J'ai L'honneur d'etre avec le plus profond respect Monsieur Votre tres humble et tres obeissant Serviteur

BOREL

rüe de Boucherat au Coin de celle de Xaintonge a Paris

Endorsed: Borel Armes & Titres du Congress

Notation: Paris 30. 7bre. 1778.

From Madame Brillon
ALS: American Philosophical Society

ce mercredi [September 30, 1778][3] a annet

Pourquoi ne vouliés vous pas me donnér votre lettre françoise, mon chér papa, votre coeur l'a dicté, et le mien l'eut sans doutte devinée si elle n'étoit pas claire, mais elle l'est parfaittement elle répond a tout ce que je desire; vous m'adoptés pour fille comme je vous ai choisi pour pére; vous aviés en amérique distes vous, une fille qui vous respectoit, vous chérissoit; je répare cétte pérte! Que pouviés vous dire mon cher papa

1. Added by Arthur Lee and signed by the commissioners.
2. He wanted the seal of Congress, not those of the states, for his engraving. He repeated his request on Oct. 22 (APS) and had it forwarded again through Comte de Tressan on Nov. 6. Eventually, BF obliged with two continental bills; see Borel's note to him, Feb. 3, 1779, APS.
3. See the headnote to BF's letter to her of Sept. 1. Since he left Anet on Sept. 28, her reference to what he said "avant hier" implies that she was writing on the 30th.

qui me fit autant de plaisir; pourquoi donc avés vous mécha-
ment gardé cétte léttre si tendre, ai aimable pendant si longtems; c'est qu'accoutumé a écrire parfaitement dans votre langue, vous n'avés pû supportér l'idée de la mediocrité dans la
nostre; rassurés vous mon chér papa comme vous ne pouvés
pensér et dire que d'éxcéllentes choses, a quélques défauts de
construction prés, vos léttres françoises moins parfaittes que
les angloises auront toujours un grand méritte.

Je retournerai prés de vous la semaine prochaine, puissiés
vous ne jamais quitter la france! Je repasse dans mon áme ce
que vous m'avés dit a ce sujét avant hiér au soir, et je la sens
se brisér, quand elle voit la possibillité prochaine de votre
départ[4]—si les amériquains consultent et sentent leur intérest,
il vous chargeront tout seul ici de les faire valoirs; nous ai-
mons nos alliés amériquains, mais nous révérons, idollastrons
leur chéf; l'amitié régnante entre les deux peuples subsistera
toujours parcequ'elle ne peut que leur éstre fort utile; mais si
l'on vous laisse ici, il se joindra a cétte union d'intérést, une
union d'ames qu'on vous adréssera, que votre présence entre-
tiendra et que vous finirés par faire partagér aux deux peuples
dans une grande révolution aussi importante que celle de
l'amérique; un grand homme bien placé, doit réstér a sa place,
ou l'équilibre juste et trouvé, peut manquér par la seule fautte
qu'on feroit de le déplacér; vous croyés peut éstre mon chér
papa que mon intérest pérsonél me fait voir comme cela, non!
Vous sçavés que je vous ai promis de vous écrire un jour ce
que je pensois de l'amitié, en attendant je vais vous dire ce
qu'elle est dans mon coeur. L'amitié, mon chér papa, fait la
plus grande part de mon éxistance, elle est répanduë sur peu
d'objets, que j'aime avéc idolastrie; je me sens toujours préste

---

4. Throughout the spring and summer BF was under the impression that
he might soon be returning to America: see Mme. Brillon's letter of Sept.
13 and his to her of Oct. 10. In November or early December he wrote to
Polly Hewson, who had asked to visit him, "I delay'd writing . . . from the
Uncertainty that I expected would have been remov'd in June or July, but
which still continues, in some degree. . . ." ([After Nov. 27], below.) By
Nov. 27 that uncertainty lifted somewhat with the arrival of the unofficial
news of his appointment as sole minister. *Adams Family Correspondence*, III,
122–3.

a sacrifiér mon bonheur au leur; je vous suis tendrement, fortement attachée; si je croyois que vous fussiés plus heureux en amérique qu'ici, je voudrois vous voir partir; votre départ me rendroit sans doutte bien malade, apporteroit une amértume, une douleur que rien ne pourroit dissipér dans mon coeur mais ce coeur aimeroit a souffrir, parceque plus il souffriroit, plus il sentiroit qu'il vous aime: adieu le meilleur des papas de la plus tendre des filles; aimés toujours cétte fille, n'oubliés pas si souvent que vous éstes son pére; vous sçavés ce que je vous disois dans la prairie, sur la médisance de ce pays; mon chér papa l'intention auroit beau éstre pure, on ne nous juge que sur les apparences, c'est une injustice j'en conviens mais les hommes sont souvent injustes; le sage les plaint et ne les corrige pas; soyons sages, souffrons leur injustice et conformons nous y; j'ai l'honneur d'éstre mon chér papa Votre trés humble et trés obeissante sérvante

D'HARDANCOURT BRILLON

Toute ma famille, et mes amis vous présentent leurs hommages. Maman[5] ne s'occupe plus que du plaisir de vous recevoir chés elle. Vous rappellés vous mon chér papa des mémoires, et une léttre d'un médecin nommé Roslin, qui vous sollicitoient pour une léttre de recomandation pour un jeune homme qui est a boston, si ce n'est pas une indiscrétion de vous la demandér, je vous la demande; on me pérsécutte pour l'a[ppuyer?] et je ne puis douttér que le jeune homme ne soit un trés bon sujet.[6]

Addressed: A Monsieur Monsieur Franklin A Passy

From the Chevalier De Coux[7]

ALS: American Philosophical Society

⟨Paris, September 30, 1778, in French: An outfitter from St. Malo has asked me to offer you a vessel loaded with cordage.

5. Mme. d'Hardancourt's maiden name was Marie Martin. Archives nationales, minutier central, XII, 897.
6. Not found.
7. He signs himself "officier d'Infanterie dans les troupes des Colonies."

His charges for freighting and insurance are enclosed. Please grant me an appointment to discuss this matter.⟩

From Joseph-Jerôme le Français de Lalande[8]

ALS: American Philosophical Society

Aigle de l'occident   Au college royal le 30 Sept. 1778

Je vous presente mes hommages, et ceux de M. Cerisier mon compatriote et mon ami, dont vous avés bien voulu accepter la dedicace, pour les 13 etats unis, d'un *Tableau des provinces unies.*[9] Il a eté attaqué en angleterre, il est bon que vous le Sachiés, il se justifie, et il est glorieux pour lui de mettre sa justification sous vos yeux. J'en profite avec empressement mon tres cher frere et illustre confrere pour vous assurer de mon plus tendre respect.   DE LA LANDE

Endorsed: Delalande Paris 30. 7bre 1778

From Edward Bancroft   ALS: American Philosophical Society

Dear Sir   Chaillot Tuesday Evening [September, 1778][1]

Inclosed I take the Liberty of sending you a Letter from Capt. Jones at Brest, and an English News Paper with an Extract of a Letter from London. These contain all the News I have recd. from that Quarter excepting that Mr. Walpole says he is informed that the British Ministry discouraged at their Prospects in America, think seriously of giving up their Claim

8. The Vénérable of the Loge des Neuf Soeurs, which is why he refers to BF as "brother:" XXVI, lxx and 697–8. On Nov. 28 he presided at a fête attended by BF in memory of Voltaire: *Gaz. de Leyde,* Dec. 11, 1778.

9. For Antoine-Marie Cerisier see XXVI, 408. The book dedicated to the United States was Vol. III (1778) of his *Tableau de l'Histoire générale des Provinces-Unies* (10 vols., Utrecht, London and Paris, 1777–84).

1. Dated on the basis of Bancroft's illness, which seems to have started around the beginning of September. He had been confined to his room for three weeks, Bancroft wrote Jones on Sept. 23; he apologized for not answering mail, but assured Jones that everything intended for BF had been forwarded. By early October he was completely recovered: WTF to Jones, Oct. 6. Both letters are in the National Archives.

of Dominion over that Country [*and*] of applying to you, to state Terms of Peace. I am very sorry that my Lameness prevents me from personally assuring you of the respectful Devotion with which I have the honor to be Dear Sir Your most Obliged and faithful Humble Servant   EDWD. BANCROFT

After reading the News Paper be pleased to give it to Mr. Adams with my Compliments.

P.S. Mr. Coffin desires me to inform the Commissioners that the three Americans who had escaped from England and embarked for St. Maloes as mentioned in his Letter of [the 24th?] have since been taken & sent into Dover.

Notation: Dr Bancroft

From [Pétronille Le Roy[2]]

AL: American Philosophical Society

[September, 1778?[3]]

Mils bonjour au cher et respectable papa. Sa petite famme de poche envoye savoire de cest [ses] nouvelle. Elle espere que sa chute ne l'aura pas incomode; elle luy demande par la meme ocasion se qu'il fait se soire parce que cest [ses] amis on le plus grand besoint de le voire pour calmer leur douleur il irois passe la soire avec luy car iere [hier] aux soire ils etoit aux despoire tout les deux.

---

2. "Petite femme de poche" was BF's nickname for the wife of his friend Jean-Baptiste Le Roy. See Lopez, *Mon Cher Papa*, 213–15, 222–24.

3. The allusion to their despair dates this letter fairly close to the death of their young son, Basile, who was buried on Sept. 16.

From Joseph-Etienne Bertier[4]

AL: American Philosophical Society

[before October, 1778][5]

Le P. Bertier présente ses respects et ce livre à l'illustre Mr. Franklin. Un de ses confrères est charmé de cette occasion pour avoir l'honeur de connoître personellement un homme qu'il connoît depuis long-tems par sa réputation et par ses écrits.

Addressed: Optimo Doctori / Franklin / A Passy

Franklin and John Adams to Ferdinand Grand[6]

Copies: Massachusetts Historical Society, American Philosophical Society

⟨Passy, October 1, 1778: Pay to John Adams 6,000 *l.t.* and charge the same to the commissioners' account.⟩

The American Commissioners to Vergennes[7]

ALS:[8] Archives du Ministère des affaires étrangères; AL (draft): Massachusetts Historical Society; three copies and transcript: National Archives

⟨Passy, October 1, 1778: We have received your letter of September 27 and its enclosure. Our instructions from Congress do not empower us to conclude treaties with the Barbary

4. Father Bertier was BF's *confrère* both at the Académie des Sciences in Paris and at the Royal Society in London: XXIII, 94 n. The book in question is probably his own *Histoire des premiers temps du monde* . . . (Paris, 1778). BF presented a copy of it, perhaps this one, to the APS in June, 1786.

5. A review of Bertier's book appeared in the October, 1778, issue of the *Monthly Review*, pp. 299–300.

6. This letter only exists as copied in the account books of JA and WTF. It is published in Taylor, *Adams Papers*, VII, under Oct. 1; it also appears in Account III described above, XXIII, 19.

7. Published in Taylor, *Adams Papers*, VII.

8. This, as well as the draft, is in JA's hand.

states but we request your help in obtaining passes from them for American ships and citizens. We agree with you that an acknowledgment of American independence and a treaty of commerce with those powers would be mutually beneficial. Should we, in your opinion, apply immediately for the passes or wait for powers to undertake negotiations towards a commercial treaty? Please inform us when we should apply directly to other ministers on subjects relating to their departments.⟩

Sartine to the American Commissioners[9]

Copies: Massachusetts Historical Society; Library of Congress (two)

⟨Versailles, October 1, 1778, in French: For certain reasons I am asking His Majesty to grant Mr. Fagan passports for three British ships to carry goods from France to England.[1] I request you to grant him whatever documentation he needs for protection against privateers. The merchandise involved consists only of goods belonging to French persons.⟩

From Isaac van Teylingen

ALS: American Philosophical Society

Monsieur   Rotterdam ce 1 octobre 1778
Les interessés dans le navire le chester, capitaine W. Bray, ont pris la liberté de vous exposer veridiquement la conduite injuste des americains en s'emparant d'un vaisseau, et d'une cargaison appartenant en propre et sans detour aux sujets de cette republique.[2] Ils vous en ont produit les pieces authentiques et justificatives. Votre reponce a eté claire et satisfaisante. Vous avez promis d'envoier ces papiers au congres, et

9. Published in Taylor, *Adams Papers*, VII.
1. According to a rumor reported in the *Courier de l'Europe*, Oct. 23, 1778 (IV, 258), Fagan's mission was to discuss an exchange of prisoners between France and England.
2. The misadventures of the *Chester*, a Dutch sloop captured by American privateers, have been abundantly related in vol. xxv.

de leur procurer le dedommagement qui leur etoit justement du. Ils vous ont remercié, comme de devoir, de votre declaration nette et positive, et se sont reposés entierement sur vos promesses et sur votre equité. Ils se sont flattés de jour en jour d'en recevoir des bonnes nouvelles, et ne les voiant pas arriver, ils se sont addressés de nouveau a vous et a Messrs. Dean et Lee le 18 de Decembre. Cette lettre etant restée Sans aucune reponce, ils m'ont priés d'interceder pour eux. Je n'ai pas pu refuser leur demande par des motifs, que j'ai exposés très amplement dans ma lettre du 16 Fevrier[3] a laquelle je n'ai jamais reçu reponce: la relation que j'ai avec mes concitoyens, l'adsistance que je dois a mon frere[4] qui travaille pour eux en commandite, et la justice de leur cause m'ont obligées de faire reiterer mes instances de bouche par messieurs van den yver de Paris,[5] et comme vous avez eu la bonté de les informer, que Mr. Dean avoit eté principalement chargé de cette correspondençe et qu'il est arrive en amerique, Sans que les interessés apprennent la moindre nouvelle de leur proprieté dont on les a privee il y a plus qu'un an; et ce qui est doublement dur pour eux, c'est que les americains aiant renvoiés l'equipage, et les aiant mis a terre a St. Eustache, ont empechés le capitaine de reclamer ce navire et sa cargaison, maniere d'agir aussi injuste que nuisible pour les interessés. Permettez donc, Monsieur, que j'ai l'honneur de vous recommander de nouveau cette malheureuse affaire, qui merite doublement votre attention, parce qu'elle est, comme j'ai eu l'honneur de vous exposer amplement dans ma lettre du 16 Fevrier, claire, sans détour, et sans aucune ambiguité. Que ce navire et sa cargaison appartient en propre sans le moindre reserve a des negocians Hollandois, qu'aucun etranger y a la moindre part, et que par consequent ils doivent etre dedommagés pleinement des pertes, qu'ils ont essuiées par cette prise, au moins, si on veut suivre le chemin de la droiture et de l'equité. Je vous supplie donc, Monsieur, de vouloir m'honorer d'une reponce satisfai-

3. Actually, the 12th: xxv, 657–9.
4. Pieter.
5. The Parisian branch of an Amsterdam mercantile firm: Lüthy, *Banque protestante*, II, 321–4.

483

sante afin de pouvoir calmer les esprits de mes concitoyens, et de les affermir dans la bonne idée qu'ils s'étoient formés par votre reponce, de l'equité du Congrés americain, aiant l'honneur d'etre avec une consideration distinguée Monsieur Votre trés Humble trés obeissant Serviteur   Is: VAN TEYLINGEN

Mon addresse est Isaac van Teylingen conseiller de la ville de Rotterdam

Addressed: A Son Exelence / Monsieur de Francklin / Ministre plenipotentiaire / Des Etats unis de Lamerique / a Paris

Notation: Van Teylingen 1. Oct. 1778.

The American Commissioners to Horneca, Fizeaux & Cie.

Copies: Massachusetts Historical Society; National Archives (two)

Messieurs,   Passi October 2d. 1778
    Nous voyons avec Plaisir, par votre Lettre du 17 Septembre, que vous avez bien compris L'arrangement proposé pour notre Emprunt et que vous y confirmerez,[6] a l'exception de la Retinüe que vous demandez pouvoir faire dans la premiere Année de dix pour Cent qui ne doivent vous entrer que par dixieme chaque Année. Nous ne pouvons admettre cette Proposition parce qu'elle nous feroit exceder LInteret de Six pour Cent auquel nous sommes limités, et auquel nous devons nous tenir. Nous ne pouvons donc rien changer a cet egard.[7] Nous sommes, Messieurs, vos tres humble et tres obeissants Serviteurs.[8]

Messrs. Horneca Fitzeaus & Co.

6. This should read: "et que vous vous y conformerez."
7. Dumas, that very day, was giving an optimistic assessment of the situation. See below.
8. The commissioners had no response to this letter and heard nothing more from the firm for months. On Dec. 6 they wrote to inquire what was happening (Mass. Hist. Soc.), and the reply on the 24th (APS) said that the

The American Commissioners to Sartine

AL (draft): Massachusetts Historical Society; two copies: National Archives

Sir   Passi Octr 2. 1778

We have the Honour of your Excellencys Letter of yesterdays Date, requesting Us to give to the Sieur Fagan all the Security in our Power, for three Vessells, to transport the Merchandises of France to England.

We have the Honour to acquaint your Excellency, that we have accordingly given the Sieur Fagan, three different Requests in Writing, to all Commanders of American armed Vessells to let the said Vessells and their Cargoes pass without Molestation, which was all the Security, that the Laws of our Country have empowered Us to give. We have the Honour to be, with the most entire Consideration, your Excellencys most obedient &c.

M. de Sartine

Joy Castle[9] to the American Commissioners

ALS: American Philosophical Society

Gentlemen   Bordeaux October the 2: 78.

This May Inform you That I have got My Ship Which I ham Much Obliged to you all for and Shall Sail for the Contanent Verey Soon. If there is aney thing In My power to Sarve you In I Should be glad To have the honner to Execute your Comand. I Shall Mack for the Caps. of Virginia if Posable. I Should a Sailed Before this But My Whife has Been Verey Bad I Shall be Obliged to Leve her In Bordeaux Un till I Return

---

loan was not yet filled. The correspondence dragged on from there, with no mention of how and how much the bankers were to be reimbursed for their services; the issue became moot as the project failed. The reasons for its failure are discussed in Friedrich Edler, *The Dutch Republic and the American Revolution* (Johns Hopkins University Studies in Historical and Political Science, XXIX, no. 2, Baltimore, 1911), pp. 78–80.

9. See XXVI, 528, 617, 669, 672–3, 686.

from the Contanet. The frinch pass you gave Me Was onley Tow Mounths and it Is out and as I Shall have a Valabel Carger On Board of Wolans Wines Cordage and Salt I Should be glad if you Will Send Me Another Pass or a Rigester or What you think proper For My Security from here to the Contanent In Case of Meting of aney thing to Intircep Me as It May Attend to a bad Consequence to Me and the Shipers. And In So Doing you Will oblige your Most Obliged and humbel Servant to Comand   JOY CASTLE

P.S. I here Inclose a Copey of a Contanentel Rigester And bag the favour if a greable to you to Sine It or Send Me What you think proper as it will Not be Safe for Me to Sail untill I have sumthing From Under your hands to prove My property.[1] It has been a handrance of Sum goods being Shiped With Me. My Ship is Called the Jane. Pleas to Deract to Me to the Care of Mr Bonfeld

Mursrs Benjm Franklin Ather Lee John Adams Esqrs. Commissiners from Congress

Addressed: Mursrs Benj. Franklin / Ather Lee John / Adams Esqrs / Commissiners from / Congress / at Paris[2]

Notation: Joy Castles Letter. Oct. 2. 1777

Dumas to the American Commissioners[3]

AL: American Philosophical Society; AL (draft): Algemeen Rijksarchief

⟨The Hague, October 2, 1778, in French: Since my last letter I have spent ten days in Amsterdam in the service of the United

1. The passport, for Castle, his family and servants, was issued under the commissioners' signatures on June 27. We do not know whether they returned the register Castle enclosed (*viz.*, a certification giving the name, ownership, etc. of the vessel—and in this case, clearly, of the cargo—as proof of nationality). The British must have captured the *Jane* on her voyage to America, for an English translation of the passport is in the Public Record Office.
2. A column of figures, seemingly unrelated to the letter itself, appears next to the address.
3. Published in Taylor, *Adams Papers*, VII.

States—one day with the Grand Facteur, two with our friend and seven writing 615 numbers, 2460 folios, 2255 times "A" and 2255 times "Passy 31. Aoust 1778" on your promissory notes. When I left Amsterdam they were being placed successfully; Sir Grand will tell you more, especially about the part our friend had in the success.

I am certain Britain will continue to evade our remonstrances; there is unrest at the exchange in Amsterdam. Enclosed are two pieces given to me.[4] Be so good as to send me a declaration I can forward to our friend on your behalf to calm Dutch fears of being excluded from American trade and to speed the eventual conclusion of a treaty of commerce. The aim is not only to have such a document ready but to involve the city of Amsterdam in these demarches. My role is to be an intermediary between you gentlemen and those of Amsterdam. The Grand Facteur is away; when he returns I will show him this letter. I forward you a copy of a letter from England for Samuel Stockton.[5]⟩

From Laurent Laffitte, François Mongin and Jacques Fraissignes
ALS: American Philosophical Society

Monsieur   A Alresford hampshire[6] le 2 8bre. 1778

Laurent lafitte francois mongin lieutenans et jacques fraissigner chirurgien du corsaire legust [*The Guest*] commendé par eduard mackaller de la nouvelle yorce[7] ayant eu le malheur d'etre pris le 14 du mois d'octobre mil sept cens soixante dix sept, apres un combat de trois heures et demy ou dix hommes ont perdeû la vie, et trente huit grievement Blessés, au nombre desquels ledit lafitte a reçu deux coups de fusil un a la figure et l'autre luy a cassé l'os du Bras gauche.

Mongin apres avoir ete pillé, reduit a la chemise ainsy que

4. Van Berckel's letters of Sept. 23 to the commissioners (above) and to Dumas (described in Taylor, *Adams Papers*, VII.)
5. William Lee's secretary: XXII, 198 n; XXVI, 518 n, 582–3.
6. About 15 miles N.E. of Southampton.
7. MacKellar wrote from Forton, along with Wuybert and Lunt, on the same date, below.

le reste de l'equipage a trainé les fers pendant sept mois conse-cutifs. L'humanite de l'amiral de la jamaique[8] ou on nous a conduits a fait metre les dits Blessés aux soins du chirurgien dans un Battiment servant de prison sans qu'il eut daigné faire donner de paille pour coucher ces Malheureux qui ont eté traites et fourny linge medicamens et autres ustancilles nesse-caires pour leur traitement au moyen de once cens livres que ce dernier a reçu d'un de ses amis de st. domingue; et de la conduits en engleterre ou nous avons aussy essuye toute sorte de cruaute jusques au premier du mois d'aout dernier, qu'on nous a envoyés a alresford comme prisonniers francais sur notre parole, et nous saisisons la premiere occasion qui se presante pour vous en instruire, et nous adresser a vous, comme embassadeur des treise provinces et a votre humanite pour secourir de malheureux qui manquent de tout a la veille de l'hiver et il ne nous sera pas dificille de donner des preuves de ces faits.

Notre capitaine a ete mis a forton prison ou on n'a pas voulu nous maitre parce qu'etant francois on ne nous regar-doit point comme prisonniers d'état. Nous avons l'honneur d'etre Votres tres humbles et tres obeissants serviteurs

L LAFFITTE
FS. MONGIN
FRAISSIGNES

Addressed: A Monsieur / Monsieur franklin / demeurant a passy ches mr. le ray de chaumont / A Passy

Endorsed: Laurens la Fitte Francois Mongin Jacques Frais-signes Frenchmen Prisoners in England[9]

8. An ironic reference to Rear Admiral Clark Gayton, for whom see Murphy's letter of Aug. 10.
9. Sartine subsequently intervened with the commissioners for Fraissi-gnes; see Nov. 5 and Nov. 16, below. C. February, 1779, Laffitte wrote a second, undated letter: he had been second in command on the *Guest*, a privateer armed at St.-Domingue by men from Baltimore. He had been wounded severely in the face and left arm. After his stay in Jamaica and transport to Portsmouth, he was kept in irons until his examination before the admiralty, then sent back to the roads rather than to prison, since he was French. On the "21e courant," after about four months, he managed to

Sir

Chez Monsieur Pernet Maitre. des. Pension Cloitre
des Jacobins Rue St: Jaques 2d: Octr: 1778

Notwithstanding the ill Success of my two former applications to you,[1] I am by dire necessity compelled once more to
address you. As a drowning Person will catch at the least twig,
so I am led by the last ray of hope, to solicit your Protection
before the finishing stroke is put to my calamity, which is already begun.

My Landlord yesterday seized all my cloaths, and wrote to
Mr: Parsons to inform him positively that if he did not in answer to that letter send him money, he woud immediately stop
my board &c. and proceed according to law; and from the
treatment I have lately received I am too sure he will put his
threats in execution. It is in vain I beg for Patience, he says he
will oblige me to find money to satisfy him, tho' he knows I
have no freind to whom I can apply for it, nor any means of
getting it till our affairs are settled. Mr: Parsons wrote some
time ago to Ireland to raise money upon his little Property
there, but it is so disagreably circumstanced that he will be
obliged to pay cent per cent for whatever he gets; and what is
still worse, as he is not able to be on the spot himself, it will
take up more time than this man's impatience will allow. I
know, sooner or later it will be done; but in the mean time I
shall be lost for want of a small sum to satisfy my Landlord.
Twenty Pound woud ensure my Peace, till this affair coud be
entirely settled; even half that Sum would be of infinite service
to me. I am very sensible Sir, that a Person in your situation,

---

escape and made his way to Calais; he begs BF to consider this case of a
wounded officer who has been continually tortured. APS.

BF's "Account of Cash paid out of private Purse," part of Account V
(XXIII, 20) reveals his personal commitment to several French prisoners.
Undated entries written at some point between Aug. 17 and when it was
closed on Oct. 4, 1778, show 48 *l.t.* for "Two french sailors who had been
in our service and taken prisoners, but escaped very naked," 12 *l.t.* for
"another," and 120 *l.t.* for a "french lieut. and Doctor who had been Prisoners."

1. On Aug. 12 and 17.

and line of life, is liable to frequent applications of this nature, and that it is impossible for you to Pay attention to them all. But if you will consider all the circumstances of my unfortunate case, and how unexpectedly, and (I hope I may say) undeservedly I have been involved, you will be convinced that no one ever asked a favor of this kind, that really stood in more need of it than I do.

Be assured Sir, I do not wish it for any Idle or unnecessary Purpose. I only want to Pacify my Landlord, if he is to be Pacified; or if not, to enable me merely to exist, till it shall Please God to put it in my power to pay the whole sum. No one that has not been in the Power of a strange creditor, can have an Idea of what I already suffer. One instance I will only mention. The weather is now cold, and my appartment which is on the ground floor is remarkably so, and yet these cruel People tho' it was in their agreement to find me in fire, will not allow me any, were I to Perish with cold; they know I have no redress, and they treat me accordingly. From this single circumstance, it may easily be judged how I suffer in every other respect. I woud not venture to affirm a thing that I was not sure of being able in some short time to Perform; and I do solemnly assure you Sir, that I shall be able, and most gratefully willing to repay you the small assistance I request, if you will be so good to lend it. I will engage myself in any manner you think proper, not to leave Paris till you are paid, and I shall be under an eternal obligation to you for such a Proof of your humanity and generosity. I am with all due respect Sir Your Most Obedient and Most humble Servant   R: PARSONS

I hope Sir, you will Pardon this reiterated trouble on account of the Melancholy cause, and be assured nothing coud induce me to this liberty, but such a Scene of real distress, as I want words to describe.

Endorsed: begging Letter

Notations in different hands: Mrs. Parsons / Paris 2. 8bre. 1778.

From Griffith Williams[2]

ALS: American Philosophical Society

Sir   London. Octr. 2. 1778.

The Bearer Captn. T. Barnard has been very liberal to the Unfortunate. You will readily Conceive my meaning without Mentioning particulars. His attachment to the Rights of Mankind Keeps Pace with his Benevolence. Whatever favour he may require (which I dare say will be not unreasonable) grant it if Possible.

The Papers by Mr. Channing[3] you Safely Received as he inform'd me by a letter from your Place of residence.

Captn. Collis and Barnard[4] will inform you of Particulars So need not enlarge. Few lines in return by favour of Captn. Barnard will much oblige a Sincere friend to freedom &c.

G. WILLIAMS

Addressed: The Honle. Benjamin Franklin / att / Pasa

Notation: G. Williams London. Oct. 2. 78.

From Antoine-Félix Wuybert, Joseph Lunt and Edward MacKellar[5]

ALS: American Philosophical Society

Sir,   Forton Prison (Gosport) Octor. 2d. 1778.

Having been Buoyed up with the hopes of an Exchange for Six, or seven Months, we began to surmise the Reason why it

2. His first name is supplied from an undated list in his hand at the Hist. Soc. of Pa. entitled "Friends to American Liberty are friends to Mankind." BF wrote on the bottom of this letter: "This Mr. Williams I understand to be a Surgeon who has been very charitable to the American Prisoners, conceal'd & reliev'd many of them, and furnish'd them with Money to get out of England. B F."

3. John Channing. See his letter of Aug. 24.

4. Captains Peter Collas and Tristram Barnard.

5. Wuybert's case had already been presented to BF the previous year; he had been chief engineer at Fort Washington until its capture by the British in August, 1776: xxv, 216, 268. Lunt was either a lieutenant or seaman on the *Rising States*: Kaminkow, *Mariners*. MacKellar had been captain of the privateer *Guest*, taken Oct. 14, 1777 in the West Indies after a fierce battle: above, L. Laffitte *et al.* to BF, Oct. 2.

491

was so long delayed was owing to a Nonconformity on the part of the British Ministry. Yet they disclaimd the charge; Alledging that they have complyed with every requisite on their part, and that the Completion of it rests wholly with you; yet as we put no great Confidence in them, we wish to hear the truth from yourself, which will give us infinite Satisfaction. The remembrance of our sufferings last Winter not being yet erased from our Minds, raises great Anxieties in us, as the ensuing Winter Approaches. We wish not to be continued another Winter if Terms for our relief can be accomodated. We the Subscribers are therefore Commissioned by the rest of our Brother Prisoners (Officers and Men) in the name and behalf of the whole to address you on this (to us) very Interesting Subject humbly begging a speedy, and official answer, as also your speedy Interposition, if any thing can be done to relieve us from our most disagreable Situation. In the greatest Confidence of your favour we have the Honour to Subscribe our selves your Most Obedient Humble Servants

Lt Col Wuibert
Joseph Lunt
Edward MacKellar

Addressed: To The Honble. Benjn. Franklin / Ambassador Plenipotentiary / From the Thirteen United States / of North America, at the / Court of France

Endorsed: Prisoners to be answer'd directly

John Bondfield to the American Commissioners[6]

ALS: American Philosophical Society

⟨Bordeaux, October 3, 1778: No ships have arrived from America; that none have come from [South] Carolina is to be expected because of the embargo on rice,[7] but many French

---

6. Published in Taylor, *Adams Papers*, VII.

7. Although Schweighauser reported a cargo of rice arriving from Charleston in his letter to the commissioners on Sept. 24.

vessels are in Virginia, Maryland and North Carolina, even if American ships are lacking.

A ship belonging to Mr. Ross was sold here. The crewmen who shipped for the round trip demand their wages, but Mr. Ross's agent insists they accept a reduction in pay because of the changed value of currency. The court of admiralty refers them to referees but no one will accept the task for lack of knowledge about American currency. I complained unsuccessfully to Mr. Delap to whom the vessel was sent and recommended to the crewmen they lay their cause before you.[8] I send you two hogsheads of Médoc wine for your inspection and can send you two more. I hope to transmit you some interesting intelligence in a few days.⟩

Thomas Grant and Joses Hill to the American Commissioners[9]

ALS: American Philosophical Society

⟨Bordeaux, October 3, 1778, with two paragraphs in French: We the first and second mates contracted on May 3 for us and eight other sailors of the snow *Nancy*, Edenton, North Carolina, James Morrisson master, to sail for Spain or France, load the ship and return to the united provinces. We were advanced a month's wages in dollars and in July, on arrival in Bordeaux, a second month's wages in French money. Mr. Delap, the owner's correspondent, sold the vessel contrary to the agreement and ordered us on shore. Capt. Morrisson left us in the lurch. Mr. Delap would pay us only 300 percent damages and put us on other vessels headed to America. That arrangement we refused. We sought help from an interpreter, the Admiralty Attorney, the Attorney General of the royal Admiralty, and Mr. Bondfield, consul for the Congress. The petition prepared by Mr. Bondfield and presented before the Admiralty Judge

8. See the following document.

9. Published in Taylor, *Adams Papers*, VII. Joses Hill subsequently commanded the Maryland schooner *Grampus*: Charles H. Lincoln, ed., *Naval Records of the American Revolution, 1775–1788* (Washington, 1906), p. 320.

argued that we be indemnified in the manner customary for sailors dismissed while in a foreign country, as well as given wages previous to our discharge. The case was decided in our favor, with the precise sums to be determined by an expert. We have been unable to secure an expert acceptable to all parties and consequently appeal to your honors.⟩

From Le Maire
ALS: American Philosophical Society

Monsieur   Nantes le 3. Octobre 1778
    Suivant les conditions que Mr. gruel a fait de son Navire sont arretées, je vous en ai envoyé cidevant copie, je vous enverrai par le courrier de mardi le Marché. J'ai enfin décidé M. L'ée a prendre ce parti, c'est à mon avis le plus sur moyen de reussir a faire parvenir tous les objets en Virginie que le gouvernement a demandés.

    J'ai recours a vous, Monsieur, pour vous prier de me faire toucher les six cent livres que je vous ai demandés par ma derniére. M. L'ée ne veut nullement m'en Envoyer, d'aignez je vous prie ne point me les refuser, car je ne sais plus ou donner de la tête; Rapelez vous, Monsieur, je vous prie, lorsque je pris vos ordres a Passy en partant pour Nantes, vous m'offrites généreusement vos Services au defaut de M. L'ée; voila deux mois que suis ici a suivre les ordres que le gouvernement de Virginie m'a donnés et n'ai touché le sou de qui que ce soit. Je dois et ne puis payer, d'aignez je vous suplie, m'honorer d'un mot de reponse. J'ai L'honneur d'Etre avec un profond Respect Monsieur Votre très humble et très obeissant serviteur[1]
                                                    LE MAIRE

Endorsed: Lemaire Nantes 3 octobre 1778.

---

1. He wrote again on Oct. 10. Having received no reply, he can only believe that his letters have been lost. He needs the sum previously requested, plus an additional 800 *l.t.* to cover his living expenses for the past two months and to see the project completed. APS.

From ——— Luet de Biscontin[2]

ALS: American Philosophical Society

⟨Venice, October 3, 1778, in French: I wish to apply for the post of American consul in Venice. My knowledge of this Republic's laws and customs, as well as the many personal connections I have formed over my fifteen years' residence here, will enable me to defend American interests efficiently. I shall, if needed, provide you with references.⟩

From [Turgot[3]]

AL: American Philosophical Society

Samedi 3 Octobre [1778].

Madame Helvetius me charge, Monsieur, de vous demander si vous serés libre samedi prochain 10 pour aller chéz Mr. De St Lambert avec elle.[4] Si vous n'étes pas libre, elle vous prie de me mander le premier jour où vous le serés, afin qu'elle propose ce jour la a Mr. De St Lambert.[5] Je me chargerai de lui faire savoir votre reponse. Vous connoissés, Monsieur, tout mon attachement.[6]

Addressed: A Monsieur / Monsieur Franklin / Ministre Plenipotentiaire / des Etats unis / A Passy.

2. He signs himself "Chancelier du Consulat de France a Venise."
3. Serving as amanuensis for Mme. Helvétius, whom he had courted when they were young: Lopez, *Mon Cher Papa*, pp. 244–5. BF and the 56-year-old widow were becoming fast friends.
4. For Jean-François, marquis de Saint-Lambert, see XXIV, 219–20 n.
5. The party, which was to include Turgot, did not take place on the proposed date. On Oct. 9, Mme. Helvétius, writing this time through abbé Lefèbvre de la Roche, announced that it was postponed until the following week because Saint-Lambert and the comtesse d'Houdetot (his *amie*) had to spend a few days in Paris. APS.
6. Under an unfathomable doodle on a separate sheet, BF began to draft his answer but did not get beyond the words: "I shall."

Franklin's Journal of His Health[7]

Oct. 4. 1778 [–January 16, 1780]

As my Constitution appears to have undergone some considerable Changes within the last 3 or 4 Years, it may be of Use
to make some Notes of the Changes past, and to continue
them, in order to ascertain what are hurtful or beneficial.

I had enjoy'd continu'd Health for near 20 Years, except
once in two or three Years a slight Fit of the Gout, which
generally terminated in a Week or ten Days, and once an in-
termitting Fever got from making Experiments over stagnate
Waters.

I was sometimes vex'd with an Itching on the Back, which I
observ'd particularly after eating freely of Beef. And sometimes after long Confinement at Writing with little Exercise, I
have felt sudden pungent Pains in the Flesh of different Parts
of the Body, which I was told were scorbutic. A journey used
to free me of them.

In 1773, being in Ireland,[8] I was, after a plentiful Dinner of
Fish the first Day of my Arrival, seiz'd with a violent Vomiting
and Looseness. The latter continued, tho' more moderate as
long as I staid in that Kingdom, which was 4 or 5 Weeks.

On my Return I first observ'd a kind of Scab or Scurff on
my Head, about the Bigness of a Shilling. Finding it did not
heal, but rather increas'd I mention'd it to my Friend Sir J.P.[9]
who advis'd a mercurial Water to wash it, and some Physic. It
slowly left that Place but appear'd in other Parts of my Head.
He also advis'd my abstaining from salted Meats and Cheese,
which Advice I did not much follow, often forgetting it.

In 1775 I went to America. On the Passage I necessarily ate
more Salt Meat than usual with me at London. I immediately
enter'd the Congress, where and with the Committee of
Safety, I sat great Part of that Year and the next 10 or 12 Hours
a day without Excerscise.[1] We lost 3 Members in those Years

---

7. The first section is largely a repetition of the description of ailments
BF had sent to Pringle, via Ingenhousz, in October, 1777. See our annotation of that document, xxv, 77–80.

8. BF's trip to Ireland was in fact during the fall of 1771.

9. John Pringle.

1. Arthur Lee echoed this in his journal: "Dr. Franklin assured me that

by Apoplexies, viz. Mr. Randolf, M. Bory, and Mr. Lynch.[2] I had frequent Giddinesses. I went to Canada. On the Passage I suffer'd much from a number of large Boiles. In Canada my Legs swell'd and I apprehended a Dropsy. Boils continu'd and harrass'd me after my Return, but the Swelling of my Legs pass'd off. The Boils however left round them a kind of dry Scab or Scurfiness, which being rubb'd off appear'd in the Form of white Bran. My Giddiness left me.

In my Passage to France Nov. 1776 I lived chiefly on Salt Beef, the Fowls being too hard for my Teeth. But being poorly nourish'd, I was very weak at my Arrival; Boils continu'd to vex me, and the Scurff extending over all the small of my Back, on my Sides, my Legs, and my Arms, besides what continued under my Hair, I apply'd to a Physician, who order'd me Bellosto's Pills and an Infusion of a Root call'd [blank in MS.] I took the Infusion a while, but it being disagreable, and finding no Effect I omitted it. I continu'd longer to take the Pills; but finding my Teeth loosning and that I had lost 3, I desisted the Use of them. I found that Bathing stop'd the Progress of the Disorder. I therefore took the Hot Bath twice a Week two Hours at a time till this last Summer. It always made me feel comfortable, as I rubb'd off the softned Scurff in the warm Water; and I otherwise enjoy'd exceeding good Health. I stated my case to Dr. Ingenhausz, and desired him to show it to Sir J.P. and obtain his Advice. They sent me from London some Medicines; but Dr. Ingenhausz proposing to come over soon, and the Affair not pressing, I resolved to omit taking the Medicines till his Arrival.[3]

In July the Disorder began to diminish, at first slowly, but afterwards rapidly; and by the Beginning of October, it had quitted entirely my Legs Feet Thighs, and Arms, and my Belly, a very little was left on my Sides, more on the small of my Back, but the whole daily diminishing.

I observ'd that where there was no Redness under the

upon an average he gave twelve hours in the twenty-four to public business." xxv, 101–2.

2. Peyton Randolph and Simon Boerum died of apoplexy in 1775, and Thomas Lynch in 1776. The third delegate was misidentified in xxv, 78 n.

3. See Ingenhousz's letters of March 6, May 12 and June 15: xxvi, 67–70, 439, 625.

Scurff, if I took it once off it did not return. I had hardly bath'd in those 3 Months. I took no Remedy whatever and I know not what to ascribe the Change to, unless it was the Heat of the Summer, which sometimes made me sweat, particularly when I exercis'd. I had five Boiles just before the Amendment commenc'd, which discharg'd a great deal of Matter. And once my Legs began again to swell. But that went off in a few Days, and I have been otherwise extreamly well and hearty.

The second Instant October I ate a hearty Supper, much Cheese, and drank a good deal of Champagne.

The 3d. I ate no Breakfast, but a hearty Dinner, and at Night found my Back itch extreamly near the Shoulders which continues to day the 4th. I ate some Salted Beef at Dinner yesterday but not much. I wish the Cool Weather may not bring on a return of the Disorder.

Oct. 4. The Itching continues, but somewhat abated.

Oct. 6. Drank but one Glass of Wine to day; the Itching almost gone. I begin to think it will be better for me to abstain from Wine. My Dinner to day was Mutton boil'd and Fowl, with a good deal of Fruit.

Oct. 12. I have lately drank but little Wine. The Itching has not return'd. The Scurff continues to diminish. But yesterday I observ'd my Ancles swell'd. I suppose my having us'd no Exercise lately may be the Cause.

Jan. 14, 1779. The Swelling above mention'd continu'd some few Weeks, being greatest at Night, my Complexion at the same time not fresh; at length the Itching return'd, and a new Set of Eruptions of scurfy Spots appear'd in many Parts of my Body. My Back had never been entirely clear'd and the Scurf began to increase there and extend itself. But it is not yet so bad as it has been, and it seems to spare the Parts that were before affected, except in my Back. The Swelling has left my Legs, which are now as dry and firm as ever, and I feel myself otherwise in perfect health, and have as much Vigour and Activity as can be expected at my Age. So that I begin to be more reconcil'd to this troublesome disorder, as considering it an Effort of Nature to get rid of Peccant Matter, that might if not so discharg'd, break up my Constitution.

Feb. 28. 79. The Disorder on my Skin has continu'd augmenting. On Monday the 15th I din'd and drank rather too freely at M. Darcy's.[4] Tuesday Morning, I felt a little Pain in my right great Toe. I bath'd that Day in the hot Bath, which I had long omitted. A regular Fit of the Gout came on, which swell'd my foot exceedingly, and I have had little in my left foot. It is now going off and I hope to get abroad in a Day or two. No remarkable Change in other Respects. In this Fit I had very little Appetite, which I do not remember to have been the Case in former Fits.

Jan. 16. 1780. I have enjoy'd good Health ever since the last Date. Towards the End of the Summer most of the Disorder in my Skin disappeared, a little only remaining on my left Arm, a little under each Breast, and some on the small of the Back. I had taken at different times a good deal of Dr. Pringle's Prescription; but whether that occasion'd the Amendment, or whether it was the Heat of the Summer as I suppos'd in October 1778, I am uncertain. The disorder seems to be now increasing again, and appears upon my hands. I am otherwise well; my Legs sound; To-morrow I enter on my 75th Year.

From David Hartley: Two Letters

(I) ALS: American Philosophical Society; transcript: Library of Congress (II) ALS: American Philosophical Society; transcript: Library of Congress

I.

My Dear friend   [October 4, 1778][5]

I thank you for yours of Sept. 3d inclosing those beautiful lines from Dante to the late Mistress of his affections, of which

4. Patrice d'Arcy, identified above in the comte de Conway to BF, July 23. He was a close friend of Le Roy, and several undated notes in the APS indicate that BF dined frequently with the two men during this period.
5. Supplied from the notation.

I feel the whole force. In return I send you another most pathetic Sonnet.[6]

Veteris vestigia flammae.

> When the Sheep were in the fould,
>> And the Ky at hame,
>> And all the world
>> To rest were gane.
> The waes of my heart,
>> fell in showrs frae my EE,
>> While my Gude man
>> lay sound by me.
> Young Jamie loved me weel,
>> and sought me for his bride,
>> but saving one crown,
>> He had nothing beside.
> To make that crown a pound,
>> My Jamie gang'd to sea,
>> and the crown and the pound
>> were both for me.
> He had not been awa'
>> a year and a day
>> ere my father brake his arm,
>> and the Cow was Staln away.
> My Mither she fell sick,
>> and my Jamie at the sea,
>> When auld Robin Gray
>> came a courting to me.
> My heart it said Nay,
>> I wishd for Jamie back,

6. The ballad "Auld Robin Gray" was written by Lady Anne Lindsay Barnard (1750–1825) in 1771. It was published anonymously in 1776 and various persons claimed its authorship. [David Herd, ed.], *Ancient and Modern Scottish Songs* . . . (2d ed.; 2 vols., Edinburgh, 1776), II, 196–7. The author acknowledged it two years before her death: see her *Lays of the Lindsays* . . . (Edinburgh, 1824), pp. [3]–6.

But the wind it blew hie,
and the Ship was a wrack.
The Ship was a wrack,
    why did not Jennie dee,
    o why was I spared
    to cry woe is me.
My father could na work,
    My Mither could na spin,
    I toild day and night,
    But their bread I could na win.
Auld Robin kept them baith,
    and with tears in his ee,
    said Jenny, for their sake,
    Oh would ye marry me.
My father loved me weel,
    My Mither could na' speek,
    But she look'd in my face,
    Till I thought I my heart would break.
So I gave him my hand,
    tho my heart was at Sea,
    and auld Robin Gray
    Is gude man to me.
I had na been his wife
    of weeks but only four,
    when sitting so mournfully
    out at the door;
I saw my Jamie's wraithe,
    for I did not think it he,
    till he said, I am come,
    Jenny, to marry thee.
Oh sair did we greet,
    and mickle did we say,
    He took but one kiss,
    and we tore ourselves away.
I wish I were deed,
    tho I am not like to dee,
    Oh why was I spared,
    to cry woe is me.
I gang like a ghost,
    for I canna sit to spin,

I may not think of Jamie,
for that would be a sin.
But I must do my best,
a good wife to be,
for Auld Robin Gray,
is very kind to me.

I have told you before that my heart is always set upon peace. In the present circumstances between the two Countries I can only think of one proposition to mediate. You may as easily imagine that the immediate and explicit acknowledgement of Independence, must be grating to this Country, as I can that America will not finally depart from it. The answer of the Congress to the Commissioners seems to imply this. What think you, of Suspending this point for five years, or seven years by a truce; and that nothing in the interim shall impeach their Independence. If such a proposition as this would bring the parties together, I think there would not be wanting a member of Parliament[7] to propose it in the house. When you put pen to paper again, tell me how you like *my* Dante; and match it if you can; and the sooner the better. Your affectionate   GB

Addressed: To Dr Franklin

Endorsed: Hartley

Notation: Oct 4. 1778

II.

My Dear Friend   October 4 1778
    I have received yours of the 14th of Septr. when I have any thing farther to communicate upon that Subject it shall not stop with me.
    I take this as my fundamental. The two *nations* are not exasperated against each other, therefore peace and friendship between them are still practicable. You know my earnest desire for peace as I know yours. You know likewise my Idea for

7. Probably Hartley himself.

getting over the chief Stumbling block that seems to me to be in our way. You likewise know *where* I would treat. If any such proposition would do, I would state the Matter thus. Supposing the ministry now sincerely desirous of peace; I think they would readily catch at any plan which might save the national honour. Supposing them not sincere, if any practicable proposition could be thought of, as I have suggested to you, it might be made in parliament. I have a strong opinion of the latent goodwill between the two Countries which makes me very earnest to take every chance for peace. But the Question still remains what is practicable? I know a friend of yours that would see you before the 26th of November,[8] if there were any the least chance of doing good. Is travelling in France as agreeable to an Englishman as it was, or if a friend were to bring an English cheese as a present, could you send any sort of Letter in the nature of a passport of hospitality, for the cheese and the bearer. Yours affectionately   GB

From Jonathan Williams, Sr.

ALS: American Philosophical Society

Honored Sir   Boston Octr. 4. 1778
    The Bearer Mr. Henry Bromfield[9] a Young Gentleman of this Town gose to France on Business as a Merchant and as he will be a Stranger in Paris your Civilities to him as such Will Much Oblige your Dutifull Nephew   JONA WILLIAMS
Doctr. Franklin

Addressed: Doctr Benjamin Franklin / Paris / Per Mr Bromfield

Notation: Williams Jonathan Oct. 4. 1778. Boston

    8. The fifth session of the fourteenth parliament opened on Nov. 26, 1778: Cobbett, *Parliamentary History*, XIX, 1277.
    9. Henry Bromfield, Jr. (1751–1837) was the son of the Boston merchant Henry Bromfield: XXII, 161 n; Daniel D. Slade, "The Bromfield Family," *New-England Hist. and Geneal. Register*, XXVI (1872), 141. Apparently he did not make immediate use of this recommendation; Samuel Cooper wrote a more detailed one for him on July 17, 1780 (APS), and we have no evidence that he was in France until that year.

Editorial Note on Franklin's Purported Address to the Irish People

The *Hibernian Journal: or, Chronicle of Liberty* published in its issue of November 2–4, 1778, an open letter "To the Good People of Ireland," signed by Franklin and dated Versailles, October 4, 1778. It was a long and uninspired diatribe against British policy, and ended with a promise that all restraints on Irish trade and manufacture would be removed. Publication in Dublin disturbed the Lord Lieutenant, who immediately wrote Whitehall for instructions.[1] The letter was reprinted the next year in Pennsylvania and elsewhere, and in the late nineteenth century appeared in pamphlet form as by Franklin.[2] Franklin, however, said that he was not the author: Jonathan Williams, Jr., when he received the American reprint, asked him whether he was, and he said no.[3]

From Jan Ingenhousz   ALS: American Philosophical Society

Dear Sir.   London Octob. 5th 1778

You will be surprised, that I did not keep my word or reather my resolution to come over to Paris. The reason was, that I undertook to finish a work upon the subject of the small pox and inoculation before I quitted this country, in which I was much interrupted by visitors and other avocations, which one can scarce avoid in a city as this, if a man has so many friends and acquaintances as I. I can scarce avoid to pay allmost every day a visit to our common friend, who seems to

1. Buckinghamshire to Weymouth, Nov. 4, 1778, Public Record Office.
2. *Pa. Packet*, Aug. 14, 1779; Paul Leicester Ford, ed., *An Address to the Good People of Ireland, on Behalf of America, October 4th, 1778. By Benjamin Franklin* (Winnowings in American History: Revolutionary Broadsides, No. 2; Brooklyn, N.Y., 1891). The editor, without citing his authority, says that BF probably printed the letter on his Passy press; copies were sent to Ireland, but were intercepted and eventually found their way to the Public Record Office.
3. JW to BF, Dec. 11, 1779, APS; BF to JW, Dec. 22, 1779, Library of Congress. The identity of the real author is still, to the best of our knowledge, a mystery; see Dixon Wecter, "Benjamin Franklin and an Irish 'Enthusiast,'" *Huntington Library Quarterly*, IV (1940–41), 209 n. A guess—but no more than that—would be Count Patrice d'Arcy.

find a kind of confort in my company, and who I respect too much for to not oblige him in any way in my power.[4] He excited me to make up some papers upon philosophical and medical subjects by form of letters. Having a good stock of such articles, I could do it, if I was left to my self. You know I am fond of this metropolis, as a place, in which I spended so many happy days. The place of my ordinary residence now affording me no confort equal to what I enjoy here, I can not quit this abode but with some reluctance, the more, as I suspect I will be obliged to take a farewell from it for ever. However I have some thaught of spending the next winter at Paris, without being able to tell it positively. In the mean time I hope your helth is very good. Your friend begins to linger some times and seems to be tired of his literary dignity, which he renounces. It is a pity he is not able to bear some vexations inseparable from an exalted situation. Some of his friends adscribe it to a degree of pride which he possesses; for my part I think it reader [rather] to be adscribed to a keen sensibility of temper, which makes him look with an eye of indignation upon those who obstruct him in what he is conscious of being right. I found out a manner of making in an instant as much inflammable air as I please and to shoot a leaden ball with it, which I will show you when I will be in Paris. Abbé Fontana[5] is here and occupyes my former lodgins at Mr. Pitter's in Northumberland Court Charing Cross.

I hope your family is well, and the business of Mr. Williams goes on prosperously.

4. Sir John Pringle had long been a close friend and admirer of the writer whom he had nominated for his appointment as physician to Maria Theresa. In 1778 Pringle's health began to fail, and he was obliged to resign the presidency of the Royal Society. *Biographie Universelle,* under Ingenhousz; *DNB.*

5. Identified in xx, 433 n.

Give my best respects to Mr. and Madame de chaumont.

I hear from Fontana the Vienna conjuror Dr. Mesmer[6] is at Paris, that he has been presented to the Royal academy, that he still pretends a magnetical effluvium streams from his finger and enters the body of any person without being obstructed by walls or any other obstacles, and that such stuff, too insipid for to get belief by any old woman, is believed by your friend Mr. Le Roy,[7] who protects him and will recommend him in London, where he has a mind to exercise his magnetical effluvia. I am very respectfully Dear Sir Your obedient humble servant   J. INGENHOUSZ

Addressed: a Monsieur / Monsieur Francklin / a Passi

Endorsed: Ingenhousz

Notation: sous couvert de Mr Tourton[8]

From Jean-François-Clément Morand[9]

ALS: American Philosophical Society

Monsieur et très honnoré Confrere   Paris ce 5. 8br. 1778.

Si le charmant poële de chauffage au charbon de terre, dont Vous avez eu la complaisance de me donner une gravure, etoit publié dans quelqu'un de vos ouvrages, il seroit actuellement a tout le monde, on en fairoit usage, et mention. Ayant envie d'en faire ce dernier usage, c'est adir, d'en parler, a la fin de

---

6. Friedrich Anton Mesmer (1734–1815) had left Vienna, where Ingenhousz had denounced him, and come to France in February, 1778. He and BF did not meet until the following year, but Mesmer had for some time been a proficient player on the glass armonica, and had been using the instrument in his séances of "animal magnetism" (x, 123). See also Robert Darnton, *Mesmerism and the End of the Enlightenment in France* (Cambridge, Mass., 1968).

7. Le Roy had read a letter by Mesmer on animal magnetism to the Academy of Sciences on Aug. 29. Condorcet, who kept the minutes, added, "J'ai été chargé de lui répondre que l'Académie ne doit point s'en mêler." *Procès-verbaux,* XCVII, fol. 291.

8. A banker under whose cover Ingenhousz had written previously.

9. For Dr. Morand's varied scientific interests, see our note in XXIV, 404; see also XXV, 457.

mon ouvrage, et de le faire graver dans une planche en Supplement, a celle que j'ai deja donné, il ne me conviendroit pas
de suivre a cet egard, la moindre de mes ideés, sans votre
Consentement.[1] Je vous serai infiniment obligé, de vouloir
bien me faire l'amitié, de me marquer sur cela Votre maniere
de penser; dans le cas, ou Vous me donneriez la permission
que j'ai l'honneur de vous demander, j'espere que Vous vou-
driez bien avoir une autre complaisance, scavoir de me donner,
une notice abregée, explicative de la planche, pour que Votre
ouvrage ne soit pas defiguré, devant etre donné, comme Vous
appartenant. J'ai l'honneur d'etre avec les sentimens de consideration et de devouement plus distingués, Monsieur et très
honnoré Confrere Votre très humble et très obeissant serviteur

MORAND DR.

Rue du vieux Colombier
fbg St germain

J'aurois besoin de scavoir a quoi m'en tenir dans ce moment.

M. franklin

Endorsed: Morand Oct 5. 78 Stove

From Charles-Hubert Moreau[2]

ALS: American Philosophical Society

Monsieur   A Versailles Ce 5 octobre 1778
    J'ai l'honneur de vous adresser deux lettres qui ont été re-
mises par un inconnu au Suisse de M. le Comte de Vergennes.

1. BF obliged. The "poële ingénieux du Docteur Franklin," a replica of
the engraving BF had also sent Dubourg in 1773 (see XX, xvii–xviii, 251),
became plate LVIII** in the third part of Morand's *L'Art d'exploiter les mines
de charbon de terre* (Paris, 1779). The accompanying text, on pp. 1585–6,
began: "Cette invention intéressante n'est pas encore publiée, quoique la
Planche en soit gravée; mais le célebre Auteur qui me l'a fait voir, a bien
voulu me permettre de la copier, et de lui donner place dans un Ouvrage
auquel il a contribué par l'envoi qu'il m'a fait des dessins dont j'ai formé les
trois Planches qui regardent les Mines de Charbon de Newcastle."
2. For a short biography of this civil servant (1732–1821), see Jean-
Pierre Samoyault, *Les Bureaux du secrétariat d'état des affaires étrangères sous
Louis XV* (Paris, 1971), p. 300.

OCTOBER 5, 1778

J'ai cru devoir vous les faire passer sans delai sous le Contre-
seing du Ministre. Je suis avec respect Monsieur Votre tres
humble et très obeissant serviteur

MOREAU

Secretre. de M. le Cte de Vergennes

Endorsed: Moreau Secr. de Cte Vergennes

Notation: Versailles 5. 8bre. 1778.

John Bondfield to the American Commissioners

ALS: American Philosophical Society

Sirs   Bordeaux the 6 8bre 1778
   I have only time to advise of the Arrival of a small Cutter
from Baltimore which place they left 14 Augt. and the Capes
the 23d. No advices when he left the Coast of Comte
dEstaings operations. Another Cutter is in the River from the
same port there probably may be letters on board. The fierre
Rodrigue from Virginia they left within a Days run of Rochefort to which port she was destind being the Vessel fitted by
Mons. Beaumarchais & Co. loaden with Tobacco.³ Many
french Vessels are arrivd in Cheasapeak Bay. I have the Honor
to be with due respect Sirs Your very humble Servant

JOHN BONDFIELD

The Honble. The Commissioners

Notation: Bondfield 6. October. 78.

From Charlotte Amiel⁴   ALS: American Philosophical Society

Honored Sir,   Auteuil, Octbr. 6th. 78
   From the known, and amiable character you bear, and from
the civilities Mr. Amiel and myself have had the honor to re-

   3. The *Fier Roderigue* arrived in Rochefort on Oct. 3 after a quick passage
of 39 days from the Chesapeake: Morton, *Beaumarchais Correspondance*, IV,
258 n.
   4. She and her husband had been guests of the commissioners in May
and were often in their company: see XXVI, 492.

508

ceive from you: thereon am I embolden'd to address you, and beg you would be so good to inform me whether you think there is any Prospect of Mr. Amiels succeeding in what he is gone upon, and at the same time, pray you will be so kind to push the matter on; and do him the favor to let him know, your real sentiments on the Subject; and if you think his long stay at Brest will be worth his while.[5] He has now been near two Months there, and with sorrow I know he is no more advanced in the business he went upon, than when he first set off. It will be hard upon Mr. Amiel if he does not succeed this time, doubly so, as in leaving England, he quited a certainty, for an uncertainty, in order to come here and try if possible to be of service to his Country. Hope, and am vain enough to flatter myself you will honor us with your friendship, and do me the pleasure to give me your sincere sentiments on the above. Mr. Amiel told me in his last, he wishes much to write to you and lay before you his (at present) disagreeable situation, but is fearful you would think him too presumptious was he so to do. Indeed my good Sir I am not a little uneasy at Mr. Amiels business being thus long delayed, and have apprehensions he will *be again disappointed as he was when he went to Dunkirk*, again permit me (and think me not troublesome in so doing) to entreat you will stand our Friend. *I know a great deal is in your power*, and if you will deign to favor us, I shall be exceedingly happy; and ever gratefully remember the same. Had the Weather not been so bad, I intended taking the liberty of asking you these questions in Person, as it is, hope you will not take my writing to you amiss, and honor me shortly with an answer. Permit me to subscribe myself, Honored Sir Your obliged Humble Servant ⁣ CHARLOTTE AMIEL

Addressed: Doctor Franklin / Passy

Endorsed: Mrs Amiel

5. Amiel was working for John Paul Jones inspecting ships, in anticipation of a commission. See C.H. Lincoln, comp., *A Calendar of John Paul Jones Manuscripts in the Library of Congress*, (Washington, 1903), pp. 54, 57. Samuel Eliot Morison claims that BF assigned Amiel to Jones as a bilingual secretary; he cites no evidence, and we have found none. Morison, *Jones*, p. 177.

From Dumas

ALS: American Philosophical Society; AL and partial AL (drafts): Algemeen Rijksarchief

Monsieur [October 6, 1778][6]
Honoré de vos deux Lettres du 22 Sept. et de la présence
agréable de Mr. Austin,[7] le desir de lui prouver tout le cas que
je fais de sa personne et de la main qui me l'a adressé, me fera
être aussi court aujourd'hui que je pourrai. J'enverrai demain
copie à notre ami de votre Lettre, où il s'agit de l'intrigue que
vous savez pour achever de le convaincre de l'irrégularité de la
démarche où l'on avoit cherché à l'engager.

Le passage en question de la Déclaration[8] dont j'ai eu copie
pour vous l'envoyer, Messieurs, avoit frappé mes yeux aussi:
mais accoutumé au langage qu'ils tiennent ici, et connoissant
la Carte du pays, j'avoue qu'il ne m'avoit point fait de peine.
Cette piece devant passer par diverses mains, entre autres par
celles du Marchand (et non Bourguemaître) Neufville; étant
une expression publique des desirs de la ville d'Amsterd., dé-
livrée par le Ministre et autorisée par les Bourguemaîtres de
cette ville (qui dans le fond ne peut traiter séparément du reste
de la Confédération), on s'est vu dans la nécessité d'y insérer
ce passage, pour obvier à tout prétexte de réclamation, et faire
néanmoins entendre ce qu'on souhaittoit d'effectuer, dès que
les circonstances quelconques où se trouve présentement
l'Etat le pourroient souffrir. Il s'agit donc d'une simple Lettre
ostensible à m'écrire, où, selon les desirs de notre ami, vous
approuveriez que notre ami fasse dresser un projet, lequel
puisse servir, par les soins de sa ville, à la double fin proposée
dans ma Lettre du 2 Oct. Cela, comme vous voyez ne vous
engage à rien, ni vous, Messieurs, ni l'Amérique.

Quant au G.P. (sans décider entre lui et nos amis à d'autres

6. Supplied from the drafts.
7. An extract from one of the two letters is given above. The other one
was presumably a recommendation of Jonathan Loring Austin; see the
commissioners' letters to the president of Congress and to the Massachusetts council of Sept. 22.
8. In Van Berckel to the commissioners, Sept. 23.

égards) on ne peut encore, à la rigueur, blâmer absolument sa retenue sur l'ouverture qui lui a été faite.[9] Il peut alléguer, 1°. que votre Lettre, Messieurs, laisse à sa prudence le choix du temps et des circonstances où il conviendra de communiquer l'ouverture à ll. hh. pp. 2°. que le Traité ne lui a été, d'abord exhibé, et puis remis, que sous la condition expresse de le garder par devers lui, et de ne pas le répandre, jusqu'à ce que vous m'auriez marqué qu'il pouvoit l'être; or, qu'il ne sauroit être communiqué à LL. hh. pp., sans par-la-même devenir comme public. Cette observation est de M. le g—— F—— même, et sans replique.

Je dois couper court ici, pour avoir l'honneur de présenter à S.E.M. l'Ambr. de Fr., Mr. Austin, qui vous assure de ses respects. Il n'est pas encore certain s'il partira d'ici directement pour l'Amerique. Je suis avec le plus respectueux attachement Monsieur Votre très humble et très obéissant Serviteur

DUMAS

Je répondrai Monsieur, au reste de votre Lettre le plutot que me le permettra une absence de 3 ou 4 jours que je dois faire à la fin de cette semaine.[1]

Paris à S. Exc. Mr. le Dr. Franklin

Addressed: à Son Excellence / Monsieur le Dr. Franklin / Minre. Plenipre. des E.U. / de l'Amérique / *Paris.*

Notation: Dumas sans date precis. Mois d'Octobre 78 Dumas

---

9. BF had complained in his letter of Sept. 22 of Grand Pensionary van Bleiswijk's ignoring the commissioners' overture of the preceding spring.

1. Dumas also enclosed a French translation of an Oct. 2 letter from Hamburg about the diplomatic repercussions of the hostilities between Austria and Prussia.

From the Vicomte Gaspard de Galbert[2]

ALS: American Philosophical Society

Monsieur   a brest le 6 8bre 1778.

Un événement qui vient d'arriver a un battiment de bordeaux sur lequel j'avois quelques bariques des sucres provenant de la guadeloupe ou est ma fortune m'engage a vous prier de vouloir bien faire accélérer la décision de cet événement dont vous ettes sans doutte instruit. Le navire l'isabelle de bordeaux venant de la guadeloupe a étté arrétté par un corsaire de grenesey et délivré par une frégatte amériquaine. Le capitaine du navire marchand prétend qu'il n'est pas de bonne prise, j'ignore si ces raisons sont valables. Mais me trouvant dans la circonstance présente avoir grand besoin de ce petit envoy qui est de 8 barriques des sucres, n'ayant aucun espoir d'en avoir d'auttres car il auroit peut ettre le sort d'ettre pris, je prend la libertté de vous prier de vouloir bien faire accélerer cette décision.[3] Je n'ai appris cet évenement qu'a mon arrivée ici avec l'armée ou je suis employé sur le vaisseau le solitaire.[4] Je vous aurai la plus grande obligation de vouloir bien vous en occuper. Je suis avec respect Monsieur Votre tres humble et obeissant serviteur

LE VTE DE GALBERT
enseigne des v[aisse]aux du roy

Endorsed: Le Cte de Galbert about 8 Barrels sugar

Notation: Brest 16. 8bre. 1778.

---

2. Galbert (1752–1807) had a brilliant career in the navy, distinguished himself in 1779 at the siege of Savannah, became an honorary member of the Society of Cincinnati, chevalier de St.-Louis, and eventually deputy from Guadeloupe to the States-General: *DBF*; Asa B. Gardiner, *The Order of the Cincinnati in France* . . . ([Providence], 1905), p. 218.
3. For the most recent effort of the commissioners to clarify the matter of the *Isabelle* with Sartine see above, Sept. 27.
4. The ship of the line *Solitaire* of 64 guns, commanded by de Briqueville: Amblard-Marie-Raymond-Amédée, vicomte de Noailles, *Marins et Soldats français en Amérique* . . . (Paris, 1903), p. 373.

Sartine to the American Commissioners[5]

LS: Harvard University Library; copies: National Archives, Library of Congress, Massachusetts Historical Society

⟨Versailles, October 7, 1778, in French: I have received your letter of September 26 supporting the request of Mr. Izard for the restitution of his belongings. I do not see how the commercial treaty applies in this case as Mr. Izard's name is not mentioned in the bill of lading and as there is no proof the baggage was not loaded by an Englishman for English use. Were it the government's decision, your assertion and that of Mr. Izard would carry very great weight, but the council on prizes has already assigned the King's proceeds to the ship's captors. In addressing himself to the courts Mr. Izard can expect the justice and consideration always accorded Americans.⟩

From John Emery

ALS: American Philosophical Society; copy:[6] Archives du Ministère des affaires étrangères

Sir   Bilbao 7th Octobr. 1778

By the Schooner Lively Cap. Dupuy[7] arrivd yesterday at this place from Newbury Port which he left the 27th. August I received the Inclosd Papers from my friend and Partner. I have taken the Liberty to forward them to you with the Postscript of my friends Letter.[8] By one youl find the dispositions made

5. Published in Taylor, *Adams Papers*, VII.
6. Lacking the complimentary close, but including the enclosure.
7. For Michael Dupuy and his ship see XXIV, 439–40.
8. Which BF had copied and sent to Vergennes. Dated Aug. 26 it reads:

> You will be much Surpriz'd when I Inform you that by all accounts the Expedition on Rhode Island must fail; soon after Genl. Sullivan had Landed his Troops and taken Possession of all the Island excepting the South End where Newport Stands, Count dEstaing who had Surrounded the Island with his fleet, hearing that Lord Howe with his Squadron was in Long Island Sound went out in Pursuit of him. Two days after he came up with him and both Admirals Engaged but an exceeding heavy Storm prevented any thing taking place that was decisive. This day week the

to attack Rhode Island and by the other the Cause of failure should they not Compleat their design. Perhaps Count dEstaing is unjustly Censured; the day Cap. Dupuy left New-bury he Saw the fleet going into Boston. The Counts Ship had lost the head of her foremast and her Missen Mast in the Gale. The rest of the Ships appeard in good order. I have the Honor to be Your Most Obedient Servant   JNO EMERY

Honble. Benjamin Franklin Esqr

Notation: Jno. Emmery Bilboa 7. Oct. 78

From Richard Grinnell: Memorandum[9]

ADS: American Philosophical Society

[October 7, 1778]

I Richard Grinnell of Newport Rhodeisland do heareby Sertify that on the Twenty third of Sept. 1775 I Sailed from Warren in Rhodeisland in the Ship George Aaron Sheffield master and that we went to the Coast of Braizels and obtained a bout Six hundread Barrells of oil and was bound for holland but was Taken and Carried Into Dover. There ware on the Coast this Preasen year a bout one hundread Sail from Different parts of amaraca and two or three Sail from London all Commanded and maned with amaracans. Except the Cooks Ship keepers and Boys.

Beeing in London and Distetute of money and friends I was obliged to Ship on Board the Brigg Dennis Jonathan Meader

---

Count returnd and Came up to Anchor under Point Judith. He Imediately acquainted Genl. Sullivan with his arrival but declin'd acting with him Urging that his Ships were disabled and that he must go to Boston to repair; the Most Perswasive arguments used by the General Officers Could not Perswade him to Tarry 24 Hours which time would have been Sufficient to reduce the Enemy. He Imediately saild for Boston—what a disappointment!

For further details see Idzerda, *Lafayette Papers*, II, 149–55; Freeman, *Washington*, V, 46–86.

9. See also his letter to the commissioners, July 9.

master[1] In the Capasety of Second mate harpooner and Surgan and that we Sailed from London on the 20th Sept 1776 went to the Coast of Braizels and obtaind a bout four hundread Barrells oil moostly Sparmycitty. There ware this year a bout twelve Sail from London all Commanded and maned with amaracans who was Protected for that Purpose otherwise the men must have been Impresed Into the Kings Servis.

NB: There was not one Sail on the Coast this year Belonging to amaraca.

On the 2d of June on our Return home to London I was Impresed on board the Belleisle man of war of Seventy four Guns John Brooks Esq Commander Beeing a bout one hundread Leagues from England in the Channell.[2] A few Days after I was Impresed we fell in with a fishing boat Neare I Reland. I Took this opertunity to write to London to Mr. Dennis De Burdt[3] marchant there who a plyed to the Lords of the admaralty and obtain my Discharge, and I Emeadeately made my Escape from London to Dunkirk and offered my Servis to Mr. Franklen. But after Wateing two months in Dunkirk and Beeing a Gain Distetute of money and not haveing an opertunity to Return to amaraca I was Prevailed upon to take the Charge of a Vessel and after Gitting from London a Number of amaracans Some of which went the Voige with me Namely James Buchanan John Wood Elias Porter[4] and a Bel[Abel] Tren, I Sailed from Dunkirk in the Brigg New Interprise, under my Command on the 5th of November 1777 went

1. A number of members of the Meader family were among the Nantucket whaling shipmasters who went to London during and immediately after the Revolution: Edouard A. Stackpole, *Whales and Destiny: the Rivalry between America, France, and Britain for Control of the Southern Whale Fishery, 1785–1825* ([Amherst, 1972]), p. 54; Butterfield, *Adams Diary*, II, 320.

2. Capt. John Brooks, R.N., had been ordered by the Lords Commissioners on April 26, 1776 to cruise with the *Belle-Isle* against all American vessels: *Naval Docs.*, VIII, 793–4.

3. Dennis De Berdt, Jr., (c. 1742–1817), son of the former Massachusetts agent in London, was New Jersey's last colonial agent, and managed the whale fishery for Robert Bartholomew who, with several others, controlled it in London: Butterfield, *Adams Diary*, II, 322; Smith, *Letters*, IV, 489 n.

4. Elias Porter, later a passenger on the *Spy*, was committed to Forton prison on Feb. 18, 1779: Kaminkow, *Mariners*.

to the Coast of Braizels and obtaind five Sparmycitty whals and a Rived in Dunkirk on the 17th June 1778.

This Preasant year was on the Coast of Brazils a bout fourteene Sail from London all Commanded and maned with amaracans. Wee alwasy Cruse of the River Plate In Lattitude 35 Degrees South and Longitude 63 Degrees west from London. Some times wee Go as fare South as forty Degrees South we always Keepe Neare upon Soundings and Sometimes in 60 and 90 fathom Waters. There is also Several Vessels Goes to forklands Island and Loade with Right whale and Sea Lion oil and five or Six Sail to Greeneland and Several Sail Last year and this year Go up the Streights and Loade with Right whale and Sparmycitty oil all Commanded and maned with amaracans. This Whaleing up the Strieghts is Keept a profound Secreet in London which Place I Left the 30th oct. 1778 [*i.e.* 1777]. There is this Preasent year a bout Seventeene Sail from London Bound to the Coast of Brazels. To the Truth of the a bove I am Ready to Sware to if Called upon Given under my hand in Pasy the 7th of oct. 1778   RICHARD GRINNELL

And whareas Last year I Read in the London Papers the Copy of a Letter from the Lords of the admaralty to Mr. Dennis De Burdt In Coleman Street Informing him that there was a Convoy apointed to Convoy the fleete to the Coast of Braizels. But when I a Rived on the Coast of Braizels from Dunkirk I made Enqurrey and found that there was no Convoy apointed and the Pretend Letter was all a Sham and as I have Read in one of the London Papers In Guernsey the Copy of a Nothers Letters from the Lord, of the admaralty to Mr. Dennis De Burdt Informing him that a Convoy was apointed and Should be Ready (if I mistake not) on the 20th Sept. to Convoy the fleet from London to the Coast of Braizels. But when I was In London I a Gain made Inqurrey and was Informd that there was no Convoy apointed and Several Vessels has already Sailed without Convoy and others Daly Sailing and that these Letters are all a Sham. But Should a Convoy Sail with the fleete it was Never ment that they Should Go any further than the Equater as they Could be of no Sarvis on the Coast Braizels as the Vessels are all Disparced and as Sone as one Gits Loded makes the Best of his way home.[5] Given under my hand In Pasy this 7th oct. 1778   RICHD. GRINNELL

Notation: Rich. Grinnell

From Robert Harrison[6]   ALS: American Philosophical Society

Honnorable Sir   Denan Prison[7] the 7 October 1778.

This Comes with my kind adress to youre Honnor, hoping you will take it in Consideration to wards me. I Was Borne in Newbery north ameraca and sarve my time to my unklle at the Ship Carpinter trade. I shipt in Newbery With one Captain foster Bound to nance. Wee had the fortune to be taking by the Wasp[8] Slope of Ware and Cared into Corke in Ireland. I Broak out of Prison there and maide the Best of my Way for Dublin and Ship on Bord of a Letter of marque Bound to Jemaca. If I had the good fortune to rech there Should make the Best of my Way for ameraca. Wee were takeing by a french frigate and Cared into Brest and from thence to Denan Prision here I remain. If youre honnor Would be so kind as to send me on Board some of the ameraca Ships or Privateers that I Could get to my one Contry one againe, I should for Ever be your humble and most sencere Sarvant,

ROBERT HARRISON
Carpinter of the Elliza Letter of marque

I hope youre honnor will not forgeet your Contry man. If your Honnor Would be so kind as to sent me a Pass to Saint Maloes I should get a ship Bound to Bardox. There is always

---

5. This paragraph, as well as some of the preceding statement, is noted by JA in his diary entry for Oct. 7, 1778: Butterfield, *Adams Diary*, II, 320, revealing the commitment to American whaling and fear of British usurpation which later characterized his tenure as first American ambassador to England: Stackpole, *op. cit.*, pp. 17–19.

6. See also his letter of Oct. 18, with John Lemon.

7. Dinan is in northwest France; the prison, a 14th-century castle.

8. Probably the *Wasp*, commanded by R. R. Bligh: *Naval Docs.*, VIII, 850.

Ships belonging to ameraca where I Should get home I hope your Honnor Will not forget me. ROBERT HARRISON

Addressed: To / The Honoble Docter Francklin / in, / Paris.

Notation: Rob. Harrison Prisoner in Dinant Castle. 7. Oct. 78 Ans. Oct. 15.

From ——— De Tournelle

ALS: American Philosophical Society

Monsieur   La Corogne le 7. 8bre 1778.
   J'ai l'honneur de vous remettre ci joint un paquet a Votre adresse que j'ai reçu des Isles Canaries. Le mauvais état de l'enveloppe m'a obligé pour plus de sureté a en mettre une seconde, et vous me pardonnerés d'avoir profité d'une occasion si naturelle de vous offrir et mes services et mon respect. Je suis avec tout celui qui vous est dû a tant de titres Monsieur Votre trés humble et trés obeissant serviteur

DE TOURNELLE
Consul de france

Endorsed: De Tournelle Consul de France a Corogne 7. 8bre 78

Domenico Caracciolo, Marchese di Villamaina[9] to the American Commissioners

Copies: Library of Congress, National Archives, Massachusetts Historical Society

Messieurs   Paris ce 8. 8bre. 1778.
   Je suis persuadé, qu'il est deja a votre Connoissance, que le Roy des Deux Siciles mon Maitre á ordonné de tenir ouverts

---

9. Caracciolo (1715–89) represented the courts of Naples and Sicily (the Two Sicilies) at the French court from 1771 to 1781: *Enciclopedia Storico-Nobiliare Italiana* (6 vols., Milan, 1928–32), II, 305; *Repertorium der diplomatischen Vertreter,* III, 423.

les Ports dans tous ses domaines au Pavillion des Etats Unis de L'Amerique au moyen de quoi pour eviter tous espece d'equivoque dans ces tems, que la mer est couverte des armateurs de differente Nations, et aussi des Pirates, je vous prie de me faire savoir les couleurs du Pavillon des états unis de l'amerique et aussi la forme des Expeditions de mer pour mieux connoitre la légalité des Patentes, qu'on á L'usage de presenter dans les Ports pour avoir l'entrée libre.[1] J'ai l'honneur d'Etre avec la plus parfaite consideration Messieurs Votre tres humble et tres obeissant serviteur

L'AMBASSADEUR DE NAPLES

Notation: Letter from the Neapolitan Ambassador 8: 8bre 1778 an[swere]d 9th

Peter Collas to the American Commissioners[2]

ALS: American Philosophical Society

⟨Passy, October 8, 1778: Last August 6 I left here for Nantes and sailed on the 29th for Boston on the *Dispatch*, Corbin Barnes, master. I was captured on September 1, and taken into Guernsey;[3] I made my way from there to England and finally to Calais. My trunk was searched and a number of articles were held on the supposition that they were made in England.[4] These articles are of French manufacture, purchased in Nantes. I need your assistance to recover them.[5]⟩

1. King Ferdinand IV, a son of King Charles III of Spain, had issued on Sept. 19 a declaration of neutrality: Dante Visconti, *Le Origini degli Stati Uniti d'America e l'Italia* . . . (Rome, [1940]), p. 135.
2. Published in Taylor, *Adams Papers*, VII.
3. See Butterfield, *John Adams Diary*, II, 321–2, for Collas' description of the Guernsey fortifications.
4. Collas lists some lengths of fabric, trimming, ribbon, thread, shoes, and "39 Neckleses," as well as a fan and some handkerchiefs, all items probably requested by his mother-in-law Jane Mecom whose modest trading ventures had always been encouraged by BF. See Lopez and Herbert, *The Private Franklin*, pp. 159–60.
5. The commissioners obliged; see their letter to Necker, Oct. 9. Collas and Barnes received 240 *l.t.* from them on Oct. 17, according to An Account of Payments to Prisoners [*c.* Dec. 31, 1778]. APS.

John Ross to the American Commissioners[6]

⟨Nantes, October 8, 1778: I have yours of September 30 indicating that I am to be deprived of the commissioners' advice beyond that concerning the money extended me. It has been my position all along that I am responsible only to Congress but I fail to see why you have charged me with indecency. Decency was also due to me. No decency was observed in seizing the private property of others. The money extended me by the commissioners has been accounted for in purchases by order of the committee of Congress. It will be replaced as soon as funds reach me. However I need instructions for shipping the remaining property, consisting in blankets, clothing, etc. Consider the ill consequences to the states of further delay. Wages to the officers and crew of *La Brune*[7] should not be considered advances to me. Mr. Williams knows how the 20,000 livres furnished me by order of Mr. Deane were disbursed. Mr. Hodge's disposal of the cutter *Revenge* followed Mr. Deane's instructions, as Mr. Lee is well aware.⟩

From Antoine-Alexis Cadet de Vaux[8]

ALS: American Philosophical Society

Monsieur   ce 8 8bre 1778
J'ai l'honneur de vous envoyer du pain de pommes de terre, fait sans un seul atome de farine et sans mélange d'aucune autre substance étrangere.

---

6. Published in Taylor, *Adams Papers,* VII.
7. For the sale of *La Brune,* renamed the *Queen of France,* by Ross to the commissioners, see xxv, 629–30, 648–9.
8. This celebrated chemist (1743–1828), who had started life as a pharmacist, became interested in public health after his encounter with Parmentier. He founded the *Journal de Paris* in 1777, directed it until 1789, campaigned for better hygiene in prisons and hospitals, and started a bakery school to propagate the new technique of "mouture économique." This is the first letter in what will be an extensive correspondence. *DBF.*

Cette decouverte si prétieuse, si intéressante est due a M. Parmentier mon confrere et mon ami;[9] tous deux réunis sur cet objet, nous cherchons maintenant à le porter au point de perfection dont il est susceptible, et a assurer par là dans les tems de disette une ressource à l'humanité.

Ce pain diffère peu du pain de froment par sa blancheur, sa saveur, sa légereté et a cet avantage qu'il ne faut ni moulins, ni meunier; je ne parle pas de la facilité avec laquelle la pomme de terre se cultive, du prix auquel revient ce pain; le blanc ne couterait pas ls 6d et le bis ne revient gueres qu'a 9 deniers.

Je me procurerai l'honneur de vous faire ma cour, monsieur, et d'entrer dans les détails que vous desirerés avoir sur cet objet qui ne peut qu'intéresser un philosophe, un ami des hommes et un legislateur tel que vous. Je suis avec le plus profond respect et la plus sincere admiration Monsieur, Votre très humble et très obeissant serviteur   CADET LE J.[1]
                                                                    Rue St Antoine

P.S. Ce pain-cy a été saisi au four, ce qui le rend moins agreable à l'oeil, inconvenient que previendrait l'habitude de le faire.

J'ai pris la liberté de joindre un second pain que Je prie Monsieur Franklin de faire passer a Madame Helvetius; il aura bien plus de mérite en venant de sa part.

Endorsed: Cadet Pain de pommes de terre

From Andrew Douglass   ALS: American Philosophical Society

⟨Senlis, October 8, 1778: I am a prisoner in the city jail. Born in the north of Ireland, I went with my parents at a young age to live in Pequea, Lancaster County, Pennsylvania, where I spent most of my life among the Douglass family. Last April I unfortunately accepted employment on a brig sailing from Boston to Cadiz. I was tricked "By A Spaniard through papish

9. Antoine-Augustin Parmentier, the well-known philanthropist (1737–1813), had also started out as a pharmacist. His vigorous campaign in favor of the potato was helped by BF: see Lopez, *Mon Cher Papa*, p. 161.
1. Jeune.

Treachery" into the house of the English consul Don Joshua Hardy. He took all my money, encouraged the British sailors lodging there to plunder my effects and charged me for food and drink that I never had. He sent me by boat to Portugal with a pass for Britain. I was ill-used in England, and found a cousin in Ireland who gave me money to get to Holland where I expected to find an American ship. I got a pass to France, intending to meet a ship, but after five days was committed to prison. I am certain you must have seen some of my relatives in Pennsylvania: Andrew Douglass, the justice, or his son George of Potsgrove Square, or John Douglass, assemblyman.[2] "I have Responsable Writing from Pensylvenia and Recomindations." I have wealthy cousins. If you would send me aboard an American privateer, my friends would redeem my passage. The French prisoners abuse me and I am at the jaws of death. You could grant me a pass to Holland where I know the language. Merchants in Philadelphia would not let me long lie here. I have seen no one who could read my papers.[3]⟩

From William Keating   ALS: American Philosophical Society

Worthy Sir   Dennant Castle October 8th 1778

Nothing but your distinguished Character for Remarkable Acts of Benevolence and Charity to the oppressed cou'd urge me to lay the following Sircumstances before you. I am a native of Virginia but Sarved my time in Willing & Morriss's Imploy out of Philadelphia and Sailed from thence some Years afterwards, During which time I had the pleasure of Hearing your Name often Repated. I returned to Virginia to see my friends, where I Marryed, and Sailed Master of A Packett Be-

2. John Douglas was commissioned a justice from 1759 to 1761 and served as a member of the General Assembly in 1763: *PMHB*, XLII, 17.

3. On Oct. 12 he wrote to the same effect, in even more vivid language, from the prison of St. Denis where he had been transferred. APS. He sent another appeal from St. Denis on Nov. 10. Hist. Soc. of Pa. BF apparently did intervene eventually and Douglass was granted his liberty: Necker to BF, Nov. 28 (Library of Congress).

tween Norfolk and Wmsburgh, wch Some of my Papers and the Certificates (or permits) I have with me will Testefy. In March 1775 I sailed from thence Mate of Captain Murphy, and we were takeing Servants on Board in Dublin, but was oblidged to put them A Shore, and Our Ship was laid up. Ever since I have been Sailing from thence in hopes of Meeting A favourable oppertunity of Returning home, but my Intentions were allways Frustrated it being A place of no great Trade, and the Town of Norfolk getting Disstroyed. I was taken on board the Eliza bound for Jamaica,[4] and I humbly beg you'll take my Distressed Situation unto your Tender Consideration, and forward me in my Just design of getting to my Family, or on Board some American Vessell, as you are the only Santurary under God I have to Rely upon for my Inlargement, for which as in Duty Bound I will ever Pray Worthy Sir I am with due Respect Your most Obedient and very humble Servant to Command WILLIAM KEATING

P.S. There is About Seven or Eight Americans here Who wou'd Gladly sarve their Country.

Addressed: Doctr. Franklin American Ambasador / At / Pariss

Endorsed: Wm Keating Prisoner Dennant Castle 8. 1778.

From the Maréchal de Merlet[5]

ALS: American Philosophical Society

Monsieur   A Paris le *8. 8bre. 1778.*

Je viens de Recevoir la lettre dont Copie cÿ Jointe, C'est la plus nouvelle de date qui me soit parvenuë de deux neveux que J'aÿ au service des États Unis et dont Le Sort m'inquiette, malgré la position honorable dans laquelle cette Dernierre me les peint.[6]

---

4. As was Robert Harrison: see his letter of Oct. 7.

5. For a brief sketch of his military career see *État militaire* for 1779, p. 98.

6. His nephews Louis-Pierre Penot Lombart, chevalier de La Neuville, and René-Hippolyte Penot Lombart de Noirmont were both to have suc-

L'Objet de celle cy est de suplier Votre Excellence, de me faire savoir ce qui peut Vous etre Revenu sur Leur existence et de permettre que l'Incluse Soit mise dans Vos paquêts. Ma Reconnoissance Egalera les Sentiments Respectueux avec lesquels J'aÿ L'honneur d'etre Monsieur, Votre tres humble et tres Obeissant Serviteur MERLET

> Mal. des Camps et Armées
> du Roy de france.
> Rue Beautreillis

M. Francklin Ministre Plenipotentiaire des Etats Unis de l'amerique. A Chaillot.

P.S. Noms des Deux Officiers qui font le Sujet de Cette lettre.

M. de la Neuville Chevalier de L'ordre Royal et militaire de St. Louis. Major au service de France.

M. de Noirmont, Capitaine Au Regiment de Royal Comtois Infanterie au Service de France.

Touts les deux passés en Amerique par Congé du Roy pour trois ans.

Le Premier est celuy qui mande avoir eté Nommé Inspecteur de l'armée du General Gates.

Le 2e. est celuy qui etoit aide de Camp du General Conwaÿ et que la Lettre dit devoir l'être aujourd'huy du General Leé.

Endorsed: Merlet Inquiry Paris 8e. 8bre. 1778.

---

cessful careers in the American army. See Lasseray, *Les Français,* II, 349–58. They befriended WTF after their return and will appear frequently in later volumes.

The enclosures are a letter sent from Yorktown on May 16 by La Neuville to his uncle and an excerpt of a congressional resolve dated May 14. The letter announces that he has been made inspector of Gen. Gates's army and his brother Noirmont aide-de-camp to Gen. Lee. The resolve fixes La Neuville's pay at 105 dollars per month and six rations per day. Both documents are at the APS. See also *JCC,* XI, 498–500.

The American Commissioners to [Domenico Caracciolo]

AL (draft): Massachusetts Historical Society; two copies: National Archives

Sir   Passy Octr 9. 1778

We are this Moment honoured with your Excellencys Letter of the Eighth of this Month, and We thank your Excellency for the Information that his Majesty the King of the two Sicilies, hath ordered the ports of his Dominions to be open to the Flagg of the United States of America. We should be glad to have a Copy of his Majesty's Edict for that purpose in order to communicate it to the Congress, who we are confident will be much pleas'd with this Mark of his Majesty's Benevolence.[7] It is with Pleasure on this occasion that We acquaint your Excellency, the Flagg of the United States of America, consists of thirteen Stripes, alternately red, white and blue;—a small Square in the upper angle next the Flag Staff is a blue Field, with thirteen white Stars, denoting a new Constellation.

Some of the States have Vessels of War, distinct from those of the united States. For Example, the Vessels of War of the State of Massachusetts Bay have Sometimes a Pine Tree, and South Carolina a Rattlesnake in the Middle of the thirteen Stripes.

Merchant Ships have often only thirteen Stripes. But the Flagg of the United States ordained by Congress is the thirteen Stripes and thirteen Stars as first described.

The Commissions of Ships of War belonging to the United States, as well as those of Privateers, are all signed by the President of the Congress, and countersigned by the Secretary. Each State may have a different Method of Clearing Merchant Vessells outward bound, and a different Form in the Papers given; We therefore are not able to give your Excellency certain Information respecting all of them. The Massachusetts

7. This sentence and the one below beginning, "The Commissions of Ships of War," were interlined by BF. He also added the phrase "on this Occasion" in the first paragraph, and "a different form of Papers given; We" in the fourth.

Bay, has only a Naval Officer in each Port who Subscribes a Register, a Clearance, and a Pass for the Castle in Boston Harbour. We have the Honour to be with the most perfect Respect, your Excellencys most obedient and most humble Servants.

His Excellency the Ambassador of Naples.

The American Commissioners to Necker

AL (draft): Massachusetts Historical Society; two copies: National Archives

Sir   Passi October 9. 1778

Captain Peter Collass of Boston in America, who has had the Misfortune to be thrice taken Prisoner in the Course of this War, by the Enemy, has made a Representation to Us of the Detention of a few Articles of his Property at Calais by the Customs house officers. Articles of the Manufacture of this Kingdom which he purchased at Nantes, in order to carry home to his Family, and which the Guernseyman had the Humanity to forbear to take from him. We inclose his Representation of his Case to you, and have the Honour to request in his Behalf, all that Indulgence, which may with Propriety be granted him. We have the Honour to be, with the most respectful Consideration, your etc.

Mr. Necker

Tristram Barnard to the American Commissioners[8]

ALS: American Philosophical Society

⟨[Paris], October 9, [1778]: For four years this humble petitioner, away from America, has been in English, though not in government, service. My only claim to supporting the Ameri-

---

8. Published in Taylor, *Adams Papers*, VII. Barnard identified himself in an oath before the commissioners, Oct. 13, below. His claim to generosity is documented in Channing's letter of Aug. 24 and Williams' of Oct. 2.

can cause is the relief I have given to many prisoners. I want to serve by transporting goods to the rising American states, and request a pass from London to Spain for this purpose. There are two gentlemen in London who would join me in procuring a vessel for sailing with the English convoy to Spain and thence to America.⟩

From David Hartley

ALS: American Philosophical Society; incomplete copy:[9] Library of Congress; transcript:[1] Library of Congress

Dear Sir   October 9 1778

You have a copy of my Letter to the board of Admiralty of the 15th of July last. I writ again upon the same subject on the 27th ultimo, saying that as you had so strongly expressed your desire to me to concur in every measure which might in any degree alleviate the miseries of war, I was in hopes that their Lordships would revise their first answer to mine of the 15th of July, and if possible concur with the proposition theirin contained upon some terms or other. I have recd. the following answer.

Sir   Admiralty office Oct 6 1778

Having laid before my Lds. Commrs. of the Adty. your letters of the 22d and 27th ultimo the former enclosing a french pass port for the Exchange of prisoners, with a copy of Dr. Franklin's letter to you; the other desiring their Lds. will reconsider the answer which you received to the proposition made in your letter of the 15th of July last, of clearing all the prisons at once of the American prisoners upon the condition of a number equal to the Surplus upon the exchange which is now proposed in a French port being to be delivered to Lord Howe or to his order in America, I am commanded by their L[ordshi]ps to acquaint you that they are of opinion it will be

9. Lacking the letter to the Admiralty.
1. Lacking the letter to the Admiralty, and with Hartley's notation: "Neither the letter nor the answer have been preserved."

prejudicial to his Majesty's service to exchange prisoners upon account of Debtor and Creditor. I cannot therefore consent to the exchanging them otherwise than man for man in Europe, and upon that Ground their L[ordshi]ps wish to know as soon as convenient the precise number of prisoners that are now in France ready to be sent to England in Exchange for an equal Number to be sent from hence. Yrs &c.   Ph Stephens[2]

To DH Esq

I wish that we may have now as little delay as possible. I hope one exchange of Letter more will finish the first Exchange of prisoners. I shall hope to hear from you soon. Your affectionate   D Hartley

To Dr Franklin

Endorsed: D. Hartley

Tristram Barnard to the American Commissioners[3]

ALS: American Philosophical Society

⟨[Paris, after October 9, 1778]: A valuable whaling business has been established by the English since the onset of hostilities with America. If you intend to destroy it I could give you adequate intelligence. I was involved in this business but quit, aware that I was doing wrong. Fifteen whaling ships, manned primarily by Americans who would gladly return home, sail in October, stop in the Cape Verde Islands and cruise between 26 and 38 degrees latitude south and 46 to 62 degrees longitude west. The fishery ends in April. The ships then moor at St. Helena to return home with the East India fleet. They carry no guns. Last season they brought 55 casks of oil worth £70 in England or £100 in America.[4]⟩

2. Secretary of the Admiralty (1763–1795): *DNB*.
3. Published in Taylor, *Adams Papers*, VII.
4. He also supplied the commissioners with information about the fleet of merchant ships loaded with provisions and war supplies to sail for the West Indies from Spithead: Butterfield, *Adams Diary*, II, 324.

The American Commissioners to Dumas

AL (draft):[5] University of Virginia Library; two copies: National Archives

Sir,   Passy, Oct. 10/16[6]. 1778

We have received yours of the 2d Instant, with the Declaration sign'd by Mr. Van Berckel, and his explanatory Letter to you, which give us much pleasure, as they show the good Disposition of that respectable Body, the Burgomasters of Amsterdam towards the United States of America, and their Willingness, as far as may depend on them, to promote between the Republick of the United Low Countries in Europe and the said States, "a Treaty of perpetual Amity containing reciprocal Advantages with respect to Commerce between the Subjects of the two Nations." As that Body must be better acquainted than we with the Methods of doing public Business in their Country, and appear to be of Opinion that some previous Steps can be taken by them which may facilitate and expedite so good a Work, when Circumstances shall permit its coming under the Consideration of their HH.MM. we rely on their Judgement, and hereby request they would take those Steps, as explain'd in M. Van Berckel's Letter. And they may[7]

---

5. In BF's hand, with marginal comments by Arthur Lee and a reply by BF. We print this in full because of its particular relevance to Franklin; it is also published in Taylor, *Adams Papers*, VII.

6. Originally drafted as "Oct. 10" and copied that way, BF changed the zero into a six after he had received Lee's remarks, dated Oct. 13. Lee's secretary Hezekiah Ford also changed the date from "10" to "16" in his letterbook (National Archives) and added, "In the above Letter (which was the one sent . . .) I find Dr. F. has altered it agreeable to the remarks made on it by the Honble. A. Lee. Esqr." In the absence of an LS, we are puzzled by Dumas' reference in his letter of Oct. 27, below, to theirs of the 10th.

7. Lee's marginal comment:

M. Vanberkle's Letter proposes to have the commercial treaty with France examined & accommodated to our present object, by some Merchants of Amsterdam. I submit therefore whether we can with propriety assure them that such a treaty wd be agreable before we have seen it; & whether it woud be better to say, They may be assurd that a treaty founded upon the principles of reciprocity and fair intercourse *woud at be assured that such a Treaty will be very agreeable to* the United States of America, who have great Esteem and Respect for your Nation; and that nothing will be wanting on our Part to accomplish the End proposed. We would only remark, that the Mentioning it in the Declaration as a Thing necessary to precede the Conclusion of such a Treaty *that American Independence should be acknowledged by the English,* is not understood by us, who conceive that there is no more Occasion for such an Acknowledgement before a Treaty with Holland, than there was before our Treaty with France. And we apprehend that if that Acknowledgement were really necessary,[8] England would *probably* endeavor to make an Advantage of it in the future Treaty of Pacification, to obtain for it some Privileges in Commerce, perhaps exclusive of Holland. We wish therefore that Idea to be laid aside, and that no farther Mention may be made to us of England in this Business. We are, Sir, Your most obedient humble Servants.

M. Dumas

Rough to Mr Dumas Treaty

Notation: The Commrs. to M. Dumas Oct. 16th 1778.

---

this time meet with no obstacle on the part of the United States. I put in, *at this time,* to leave room for them to apprehend that if delayed it may meet with obstacles. A. Lee.

BF countered at the top of the page: "The Remark in the Margin is not founded; the Words *such a Treaty* evidently refer to the foregoing Description of the Treaty which is taken from the Burgomasters own Declaration. B.F." He did, however, incorporate part of Lee's suggestion word for word. Following "such a Treaty," he crossed out "will be very agreeable to" and inserted, "as above described would at this time meet with no Obstacle on the part of."

8. Lee's marginal note:

Or *waited for,* England &c. It seems to me that this apprehension cannot be pressed upon them too often, or too much; & therefore I woud propose to add the above & leave out *probably* which weakens the argument. A Lee

To Madame Brillon AL: American Philosophical Society

Samedi [October 10, 1778?][9] a Passy

Comme il sera necessaire, ma chere Amie, que je pars un jour pour l'Amerique, sans Esperance[1] de vous revoir jamais, j'ai eu la Pensée quelquesfois qu'il sera prudent de me sevrer de vous par degrez, de vous voir premierement qu'une fois par semaine, aprés cela, qu'une fois par deux semaines, une fois par mois, etc. etc. afin de diminuer peu-a-peu le Desir immoderé que je sens toujours de vôtre Societé enchantante, et d'eviter par ce moyen le grand Mal que je dois autrement souffrir à la Separation finale. Mais, en faisant les Experiences en petit, je trouve que l'Absence au lieu de diminuer, augmente ce Desir. Le Mal que je crains est donc sans Remede, et je viendra vous voir ce soir.

——— Bailly aîné to the American Commissioners

ALS: American Philosophical Society

Messieurs   Nantes Ce 10. 8bre 1778

La Reponse que me Raportent par le Courier de ce jour mes Banquiers et que vous leur aves fait a de quoy m'etonner. En vous faisant passer la lettre D'advis de vôtre representant a la Martinique Mr. Bingham, que Je trouvay dans Celle de Mr. J.

I cannot help repeating my opinion that a personal interview to state & urge the Arguments for an immediate conclusion woud succeed, and that such a treaty woud prevent our Enemies from venturing upon another Campaign. A. Lee. Chaillot, Ocr. 13th. 1778.

BF consequently added the phrase "or waited for," at the footnote marker, and just following it changed "would probably" to "might."

9. This tentative date has been chosen because of the recurrent theme of BF's return to America. See our annotation of his letter to Mme. Brillon, Sept. 13. The last line implies that she is in Passy: she returned there in early October. But the letter could as well have been written some months earlier.

1. Above "Espérance," BF wrote "Espoir."

Hurlot[2] qui y est le mien, J'eus l'honneur de vous ecrire et de vous dire que je connoissois beaucoup M. Villiam Neveu de Monsr. Franklin a qui Il pouvoit mander de prendre chez moy Les informations que vous exigés et qui ne sont pas d'usage. Cependant quoique dans la lettre de 10.000 *l.t.* Je n'ay pas un sol D'interet Je me preté a ce que vous desirés En vous Remettant La lettre En original de M.J. Hurlot et qu'il vous plaira me Renvoyer soit sous couvert de M. de William ou de M. Schweighauzer si vous ne m'honores d'une Reponse. Mais je ne Renverray la lettre de 10.000 *l.t.* que quand vous m'aurés fait Scavoir que vous l'accueillerés d'une acceptation soit par vous ou par ceux que je viens de nommer cy dessus. J'ay l'honneur d'Estre avec Consideration Messieurs Votre tres humble serviteur   BAILLY AINE

Toute reflexion faite je joins icy Messieurs la lettre de Change tirée sur vous par Mr. Bingham de 10000 *l.t.*[3]

Endorsed: Bailly ainé Nantes 10. 8bre. 1778.

John Bondfield to the American Commissioners

ALS: American Philosophical Society

Sirs   Bordeaux 10th. 8bre 1778
    I have this day receivd from Mr. Livingston a Letter wherein he requests I would apply for a Letter of Mark for the Ship bought for him. I shall esteem the favor of you to forward one to me by the first Post I expect he will be ready for Sea by the first November.
    The Ship is called the Livingston, in Honor of Governor Livingston, the late Mr. P. Livingston, and the branches of that

2. In the enclosed letter J. Hurlot, a merchant in Martinique, explains to Bailly that the money in question is meant for the heirs of the late Gautier. Indeed, on Oct. 26, a Mme. Felix Desdodieres wrote to BF that she was one of those heirs and hoped he would promptly accept the bill of exchange. APS.

3. BF eventually accepted the draft: see our annotation of Bingham to commissioners, Aug. 5.

respectable family. The Master, Musco Livingston, is to mount ten Six Pounders, Swivels etc.[4]

I have just receiv'd a Letter from Mr. Louis Lizett late an Inhabitant in Canada. He writes me he has brought over his Family and Funds and proposes to retire and reside in this Kingdom. He was a respectable Cityzen of Quebec a Man of Considerable property. He requests me to become his Security as I apprehend he means to you I know not for what end unless to absolve him from his Oath of Fidelity by becomeing a Subject of France. If any Form of this Nature is requesit from my knowledge of him his Abilities and Probity I shall be ready to serve him with pleasure.

I have Letters from Carolina 14 August containing nothing interesting. I have the Honor to be with due respect Sirs Your most Obedient Humble Servant   JOHN BONDFIELD

The Honble. Benj Fraklin Arthur Lee John Adams Esqrs.

Adressed: The Honble Benj / Franklin Arthur / Lee John Adams Esqr. / Commissioners from Congress / Paris

Notation: Bondfield 10. Octr. 78

Ralph Izard to the American Commissioners[5]

ALS: American Philosophical Society

⟨Paris, October 10, 1778: Mr. Sartine's letter to you of the 7th, in which I am referred to the courts to recover my baggage, has just reached me. I disagree, since my claim is founded on an article of the treaty guaranteeing the return of American goods without delay and on demand. I am the more surprised as the minister, well aware that my name was not on the bill of lading, promised a few days ago that my goods would be

4. Musco was apparently related to "the respectable family" through William Livingston, governor of New Jersey and seventh son of Philip: Edwin B. Livingston, *The Livingstons of Livingston Manor* (New York, 1910), pp. 537–8.

5. Published in Taylor, *Adams Papers*, VII.

restored. I don't know what proofs are necessary; my name appears in many of the books and on a great number of papers. This should be sufficient proof, without the trouble and expense of a lawsuit. If necessary, I can procure the testimony of the merchant who shipped my baggage, the merchant in Leghorn and the abbé Niccoli. I fear the goods will be sold and urge you to speak to the minister about the matter when you go to Versailles tomorrow.⟩

From ———— Lesguillon

ALS: American Philosophical Society

Monsieur   Ce 10 8bre 1778

J'ay eu l'Honeur d'aller plusieurs fois chez vous Et entrautres le 29 avril dernier muni de deux actes pardevant notaires tels que vous Les aviez demandé pour faire payer un de mes anciens domestiques qui s'étoit attaché en me quittant au capitaine Jameson americain de nation qui ne lui a payé ny gages ny autres conventions.[6] Comme dans letand [le temps] vous me fites l'Honeur de me dire qu'il falloit environ six mois pour avoir reponse cet homme nommé *Frederik Foldé* me tourmente pour vous demander La reussitte de notre envoye. Differentes affaires m'empechant de sortir pour le moment j'ay l'honeur de vous l'adresser avec cette Lettre esperant que vous voudrez bien lui rendre reponse a sa demande et avoir pitié de lui suivant la reputation que vous avez de secourir les malheureux d'autant quil n'a pas beaucoup de tems a lui etant en service chez un maitre qui demeure a vincennes. Je compte sur vos bontes et suis Monsieur Votre tres humble et tres respectueux serviteur   Lesguillon

Endorsed: Lesguiller about Money due to his servant from Capt. Johnson 10. 8bre. 1778

6. We are inclined to believe BF's endorsement is correct and that "Jameson" was actually Henry Johnson, who appears frequently in volumes XXIII through XXVI.

From Alexander Niehaus

ALS: American Philosophical Society

⟨Haselünne in Westphalia, October 10, 1778, in German:[7] The famous tapestries of Osnabruck are made here. We also manufacture very good woollen stockings for soldiers, cheaper than elsewhere. Could you indicate how I should best start my trade and give me the name of a commercial agent?⟩

From Jacob Rieger[8]

ALS: American Philosophical Society

Honored Sir   Heidelberg Octr. 10th. 1778

According to your request I have taken the liberty in writeing to you haveing enclosd five letters directed to the care Mr. Parr[9] a particular friend of mine in Philadelphia. As my business oblidges me to tarry longer here then I first expected, and anxious that my friends should hear from me, I have taken this liberty of encloseing them to your care and if oppurtunity offers, I shall be under many obligations you will take the trouble of transmitting them to *America*. I was sorry I had not the happiness in seeing you before my departure from *Paris*. I waited on you to take my leave, but you had gone to *Versailes*. In regard of my object in comeing to this country which I informd you I am so far happy in hearing it is at interest and under the care of a wealthy Uncle, and I am assurd by my friends who I am with here, that it is undoubtedly secure. I am likewise happy to inform you that I am in this country amongst the midst of friends to our cause from the Lord to the Peasant.[1] I have been examind through every garrison I

---

7. A résumé of the letter, in French and in another hand, appears in the margin.

8. This surgeon, attached to a Philadelphia battalion, was introduced by RB on May 1 and by Thomas Bond, Jr., who outlined his mission on June 5: XXVI, 384–5, 589–90.

9. William Parr, a lawyer in Lancaster and in Philadelphia: *PMHB*, x, 414.

1. For other examples of pro-American feeling see Horst Dippel, *Germany and the American Revolution 1770–1800* (Chapel Hill, 1977), pp. 220, 228.

pasd but found no interruption in my rout. I daily carry my uniform, acknowledge my rank and support the character of an American *Officer*. In general the Germans have had but a feint Idea of the Strengh of our country and for what our glorious opposition was for. Many have visited me and are anxious for going to America. The *Elector* left this last week for *Bavaria* where he succeeds the late deceasd *Elector*.[2] Their appears to be a general discontent among the poeple here of the Protestant societies, about their rulers, who are chiefly of the Catholic Religion, which has made great partys, and seem to bear a great antipathy to each other particularly in this present war between the Emperor and King of Prussia, the former secretly praying for Prussian success, the other Emperial. As I now have given you a knowledge of my safe arrival and the disposition of the poeple in this part of the Globe towards us, I shall conclude not forgetting to return you many thanks for your friendly consul. I have the Honour to remaine with much respect your Honours most Obedient Humble Servant JACOB RIEGER

Addressed: The Hon. Benjamen Franklin Esqr / One of the Plenipotentionarys from / the United States—America / at the Court of France / Versailes

Endorsed: Dr Rieger from Heidelberg 10. 8bre. 1778.

From Jonathan Williams, Jr.

ALS: American Philosophical Society

Dear and honoured Sir.   Nantes October 10. 1778.

As I understand Mr. Schweighauser has informed the Commissioners of a Dispute that has happened between us relative to the Ship Drake which I have lately bought of him,[3] and as

---

2. Karl Theodor, the Elector Palatine (1724–99) succeeded Maximilian Joseph of Bavaria (1727–77). For issues surrounding the succession and the war attending it, see John G. Gagliardo, *Reich and Nation: the Holy Roman Empire as Idea and Reality, 1763–1806* (Bloomington and London, 1980), 68–72; see also xxv, 525–6 n.

3. The *Drake*'s sale had been postponed since August: see Whipple to the commissioners, Aug. 19.

you, being one of the Commissioners will of course hear the Story on his side, which may not be much in my Favour, I hope you will excuse the Trouble I give you by a Relation of the affair.

Capt. McNeill having directed me to sell one of his Prizes at Rochelle, and another being arrived at the same Port, of which he had not advice, I concluded to accept an advantageous offer for both, not doubting of his Confirmation. It turns out that Capt. McNeill wanted this 2d Ship for himself, and had taken measures accordingly. The Sale on every other Account would have pleased him, and my Ignorance of his Intention was the only cause of the misfortune. On his arrival he appeared determined to break my Bargain, which for my Reputations Sake I wished to prevent, it was therefore agreed to purchase the Drake and we sent to Mr. Schweighauser for the Inventory to judge of her value. At the Bottom of the Inventory are written these words "The above Articles are waranted in *Quantity* but not in quality." After examining the Inventory we in consequence of it offered twenty seven thousand Livres, Mr. Schweighauser refused this offer and told us that if we would give thirty thousand Livres we should have the Ship, on condition to take upon ourselves the Duties, which would amount to about 5 or six thousand Livres more, he at the same time promising to let the Vessell come under his name (tho' at Capt. McNiells Risque and Charge) to another Port where this Duty would not be payable, it being confined to Sales in the Port of Brest only. I then offered to Capt. McNiell to lose half of this Duty out of my own Pocket if he would buy the Ship, regarding that a small Sacrifice to the keeping my Word in the Sale I had made at Rochelle. Mr. Schweighauser then wrote an agreement in the following words:

"Je soussigné J Dl Schweighauser recconnois avoir vendu à Monsieur McNeill Le Navire Le Drake actuellement a Brest avec *ses agreez et appareaux conformement a l'Inventaire que moi McNeill reconnais avoir vu et accepté, et d'avoir en consequence* acheté du dit Sieur Schweighauser Le dit Navire pour la somme de trente mille Livres, payable a nantes en argent comptant aussitot que la Livraison m'en aura été faitte a Brest, moyennant deux pour Cent d'Escompte, et moi McNeill me chargeant de tous les droits qui pourraient etre exigés pour la vente du dit Navire, a Nantes le 7. 8bre. 1778 fait double et de bonne foi." Signé J. Dl. Schweighauser The Duplicate signed D. McNeill.

On the back of the Inventory Mr. Schweighauser required Capt. McNiell to write as follows. "J'accepte l'Inventaire de l'autre part dont il me sera fourni copie conforme a Nantes le 7. 8bre 1778." Mr. S then requested to have the Inventory untill the following morning to make the Copy, which was readily consented to: The Bargain being then finished each took the agreement which belonged to him and I came away.

Mr. Dobré, Mr. Schweighausers son in law, came to us the same Evening and told us that an article of the Inventory was *sold*. I then told him that he had only to replace the value and we would be satisfied, he then said the Article was the Iron ballast which ought not to have been put in the Inventory. We replied that it was the Inventory which induced us to make the purchase, and all the articles of it would be insisted on. The next Day Mr. Schweighauser refused to give either the Inventory or the order for delivering the Ship unless the Iron Ballast (an article as necessary to a Ship of War as her Masts) be left out. I told him as I had on the Evening before told Mr. Dobré that everything in the Inventory belonged to the purchaser and had induced Capt. McNeill to give so large a Price. By this Dispute the Ship will come 5 or 6000 Livres dearer than we expected, as in order to obtain Justice we shall be obliged to declare the Sale at Brest and of course be subject to the Duty, which Mr. Schweighausers verbal Promisse had given us hopes of Saving.

I have offered to leave it to the Merchants of this Change but Mr. S will hear no Reason but his own and I shall be under the disagreeable necessity of forcing him by legal Measures to comply with the Conditions of his own Signature for having Capt. McNiells affairs committed to me I shall be obliged to do my Duty. It appears that the Iron Ballast is not sold as was at first represented. I beg you will prevent any Interference from the Commissioners, unless it be to direct Mr. S to stand by his bargain which among merchants is or at least ought to be sacred, and this it was which determined me tho' I was not bound by the smallest scrip of Pen to lose 3000 Livres rather than undo my Bargain at Rochelle.[4] I am ever with the greatest Respect Your ever affectionate and dutifull Kinsman

J WILLIAMS J

Notation: Jonath Williams Scweighauser Nantes 10. 8bre. 1778.

From de La Plaigne *et al.*[5]

ʟs: American Philosophical Society

Honorables Messieurs   [after October 10, 1778][6]

Le Capitaine Emanuel pierre de laplaigne au service des Etats unis et Independans de l'amerique dans les troupes continentales au premier regiment de georgie; envoyé en france de la part du dit Etat de georgie, adressé a Son Exçellençe Mgr. franklin, ou a tous autres ambassadeurs ou commissaires des dits Etats chargés de pouvoirs aux fins d'acheter les munitions de guerre, artillerie, habillemens, et equipemens de troupes, marchandises propres pour traiter avec les indiens etc. specifiées dans ses instructions; aussi d'engager deux ou trois ingenieurs et autant d'officiers d'artillerie experimentés, ainsi que des canoniers, matelots, soldats, et des cadets volontaires que le susdit Etat s'engageoit a reçevoir et favoriser des traitemens usités dans l'armée continentale avec pouvoir au dit Capitaine de distribuer trois commissions en blanc dont il etoit porteur aux sujets qu'il auroit crû propres de recruter et fournir des soldats pour le dit service a l'honneur d'exposer a vos honneurs:

qu'ayant rempli autant qu'il a eté en son pouvoir les inten-

4. ᴊᴡ wrote to ᴡᴛꜰ the same day, asking for the commissioners' reaction to this letter. APS.

5. His last letter to ʙꜰ of July 11 was written as a prisoner in Plymouth. The captain was now acting as spokesman for a number of his comrades claiming compensation from Congress.

6. Dated on the basis of the statement toward the conclusion of this letter concerning their departure from Okehampton for France.

tions de l'honorable congrés de Georgie 1° Par son traité du onze deçembre dernier devant Gilbert notaire, par lequel les maisons garçon Bayard et Compagnie[7] se sont obligés entre autres articles *a faire porter "a leurs frais, perils et risques"* en Georgie les marchandises specifiées par les instructions du dit Capitaine pour y recevoir en denrées du payis le remboursement et qu'en effet en accomplissement du dit traité, la dite Société sous les raisons susdites a fait partir de Bordeaux en avril le navire le d'argentré et en Juillet les quatre navires nommés le adams, le consul de Cadix, le prince Emmanuel, et le vernet.

2° Par l'embarquement avec lui de deux ingenieurs connûs dix huit cadets volontaires independemment de ceux qu'il avoit embarqué sur la petite adelaide, sur le deain,[8] et cent cinq qu'il n'a pû embarquer faute de vaisseaux en qualité de soldats recrutés par les sieurs la plaigne de verine son frere, Barbeux dubourg de la blanchardiere et de foucherol dit Lamothe dupin,[9] que le dit Capitaine avoit reconnû propres a remplir les trois commissions dont il etoit porteur.

Le sixieme jour du départ du dit Capitaine avec les Ingenieurs, les cadets volontaires et les officiers susnommés c'est a dire le premier may dernier, ayant eté attaqué par le corssaire de gersai le lively, Capitaine John Kyrby, après un combat de deux heures et dix minutes soutenûs par les seuls Passagers destinés pour le service des Etats unis de l'amérique, l'equipage hors le capitaine et son second ayant refusé malgré les coups et les ménaces de se joindre ayant même eteints tous les feux, le capitaine du dit navire le d'argentré auroit eté obligé d'emmener les combattans mis aux fers, traduits a gersai, de là

---

7. Garson, Bayard et Cie., the Paris house which on Dec. 11, 1777 contracted to supply and transport to Georgia the goods de La Plaigne had ordered: Robert Rhodes Crout, "Pierre-Emmanuel de la Plaigne and Georgia's Quest for French Aid During the War of Independence," *Ga. Hist. Quarterly*, LX (1976), 180. Earlier in 1778 he had borrowed money from them, according to his letter to BF of March 7: XXVI, 77–8.

8. The *Deane*. For the fate of this and the other five ships, see Crout, *op. cit.*, 180–2.

9. See Dubourg's letter of Aug. 1 about the latter two.

a Plymouth a bord du Bleinheim, ensuite a oakhampton, d'ou enfin le dix octobre les soussignés suppliants ont eû la liberté de se retirer en france, ayant cachés leurs qualités sous le titre de passagers, ou marchands.

Les dits soussignés et suppliants representent humblement a vos honneurs q'outre la perte génèralle de leur pacotille, le pillage presque total des effets servants a leurs personnes, la captivité dans les fers ou dans les prisons, qu'ils ont souffert pour la cause de l'amerique, depouillés de tous secours, ils auroient eté obligés d'emprunter en angleterre pour leur passage en france dans la vüe seule de continuer le service qu'ils avoient embrassé service qu'ils suivent depuis l'epoque de leur embarquement; que le capitaine de la plaigne à en outre dix huit mois de ses appointements echus a reclamer, qu'ayant grandement alteré et quelques un même employé presque toute leur fortune, ils se trouvent en cette ville n'ayant de recours que dans les bontés de vos honneurs, et dans l'assistançe que les Etats unis rependent sur ceux qui souffrent pour leur cause, secours dont vous etes les sages distributeurs, honnorables Messieurs, secours auquel les soussignés suppliants ont tant de droits, secours enfin que vos honneurs ne peuvent accorder a personne de plus reconnoissant et qui fassent des veux plus sinceres et plus ardens tant pour la prosperité et gloire des Etats unis et independant, que pour la conservation et santé de vos honneurs, honnorable Messieurs, les tres humbles, tres obeissants et tres respectueux serviteurs

E.P. DE LA PLAIGNE capt au 1er de georgie
LA PLAIGNE DE VERINE Lieutenant au dit Regiment
RAYMOND DUVAL Cadet volontaire
LE CHEVALLIER DE ROMANEIX cadet id.[1]
BARDONNAUD DU BAUX cadet idem
CHEVALIER cadet volontaire
LEGER BENASSY soldat

1. His sister sent BF an appeal in his favor on Nov. 24 from Limoges (APS), saying that in order to reach Georgia he had borrowed more than he could pay back. In an undated note she asked de La Plaigne to introduce her brother to Turgot. APS.

à Son Exçellençe Mgr. franklin et les hbls. commissaires des Etats unis et Independants de L'amérique septentrionale

Endorsed: Memoire from M. DelaPlaine

Notation: Mr delaplen

The American Commissioners to Sartine[2]

AL (draft): Massachusetts Historical Society; two copies: National Archives

⟨Passy, October 12[–15], 1778: We received your letter of the 7th. We believe the article in the commercial treaty applies clearly, strictly and fully to Mr. Izard's case. The goods were shipped last April, when two months had not elapsed from the declaration of war. Mr. Izard assures us that his name is in many of the books and a great number of papers. He can procure additional testimony that the property is his. We understand that the captors have been granted the whole of it and while we wish them to enjoy the profits of their prizes, they must be aware that these goods belong to a friend and are not the King's to grant.

We beg leave to raise another subject. There are on board the *Fox* and *Lively*[3] a number of American sailors serving against their will. We ask that a list be made of them and that they be delivered to us.[4] We are desirous of attracting back as many American sailors as possible to their country. October 15: Since we wrote the foregoing we have received letters from four American sailors from the *Fox*, now prisoners in Dinan castle, asking for their release.[5]⟩

2. Published in Taylor, *Adams Papers*, VII, where the editors discuss why the letter was not sent until at least the 15th.
3. Two British frigates captured by the French: Dull, *French Navy*, p. 357.
4. The draft first included but then dropped a proposal to exchange them for American-held British prisoners.
5. Robert Harrison wrote on Oct. 7; John Lemon, Edward Driver and John Nichols on the 12th. The commissioners answered them on Oct. 15.

James Lovell to the American Commissioners

ALS and copy: American Philosophical Society; copies: National Archives (two), Library of Congress

Gentlemen   Philada. Octr. 12th. 1778

Congress having foreign Affairs now under Consideration, I shall not write to you on that Subject, more especially as it is quite uncertain how the present Papers will be conveyed to you. Nor shall I pretend to unravel to you the Designs of the Enemy. They are very inscrutable: The Printers know as much as I do about them, therefore I send a few of the last Prints of Dunlap,[6] which with the Boston Papers must decide you in Opinion. Your affectionate Friend and very humble Servant

JAMES LOVELL

Addressed: Honorable / Benjamin Franklin Esqr. / Arthur Lee Esqr. / John Adams Esqr. / Paris / To be sunk in Case of Danger / from the Enemy.

Notation: James Lovell Philada. Oct. 12th. 78.

Daniel McNeill to the American Commissioners[7]

ALS: American Philosophical Society

⟨Lorient, October 12, 1778: After my arrival I applied to the agent to receive my prisoners;[8] I sent them ashore but the commandant of the port refused them, lacking orders from the ministry. I cannot take them on board unless I send twenty Americans ashore. Since few opportunities for passage exist, this would be a great hardship for men who escaped English prisons and want to get home. Let me know what to do as soon as possible.

How do you think the lawsuit over the *Isabelle* will go? The

6. Probably John Dunlap's *Pennsylvania Packet,* published since 1771: Clarence S. Brigham, *History and Bibliography of American Newspapers 1690–1820* (2 vols., Worcester, 1947), II, 942.

7. Published in Taylor, *Adams Papers,* VII.

8. The agent in question is presumably Puchelberg.

former proprietors complicate the case with all kinds of deceptions. Another ship originally belonging to the same owners has arrived in Brest, recaptured by Capt. Pickerin under similar circumstances.[9] Hence it is important to establish a correct precedent.⟩

James Moylan to the American Commissioners

ALS: American Philosophical Society

Honorable Gentlemen   L'Orient 12th. October 1778
    Since the receipt of your favors 22d. and 31st. Augst. nothing occur'd worth troubling you with my letters.
    In consequence of your letter of 31st. August I apply'd to the Commissary of this port, to receive Cap. McNeill's prisoners, but he refused taking charge of them, as he had no kind of orders to that *effect* from Government. Cap. McNeill since his return from Paris, apply'd in consequence of your directions, to your Ajent here, who likewise refused to receive them, not having your orders for that purpose. Besides the inconvenience of keeping those prisoners on board Cap. McNeill's ship, the circumstance of their being insecure there, is an object of your consideration, four or five of which, have already made their escape. Cap. McNeill has received a proposal through the Admiralty, from the Original proprietors of the french reprisal to allow him one third thereof for his protection.[1] The danger of establishing a president that in the like future cases may be detrimental, has engaged him to let it go through a regular course of Law. For this end Mr. Le Ray De Chaumont will be furnished with the necessary credentials by the next post.
    As I suppose you have been inform'd from Brest of the arrival there of the privateer Hamden of Portsmouth and the

9. Thomas Pickerin, captain of the privateer *Hampden* of Portsmouth, N.H.; see Riou ainé to the commissioners, Oct. 23.
    1. Moylan is referring to the case of the *Isabelle*: "reprise," the French term for a recaptured ship.

news she brings from America, it is needless for me to say any thing further on that head. I remain with respect Honorable Gentlemen Your assur'd humble Servant   JAMES MOYLAN

Addressed: The Honorable Plenepoten / -tiary Ministers of the / United States of / America / at Passy

Endorsed: Moylan

Notation: Mr Moylan 12 Oct. 78

Sartine to the American Commissioners

Copies: Library of Congress (two), National Archives

A Marly 12. 8bre. 1778.

Je n'ai point oublié, Messieurs, l'intérêt que vous prenez à M. Jonet [Jones] et la Demande que vous avez faite, de lui accorder un Bâtiment armé qui puisse le transporter à l'Amerique. Le Roi à qui j'en ai rendu compte, est disposé a donner cette facilité à ce Capitaine, mais je desire prealablement de savoir, s'il sera possible de composer de Matelots americains l'équipage du Bâtiment qui seroit fourni à M. Jones, parce que l'article et le nombre des armemens de sa Majesté ne permeteroit pas de lui donner un équipage François. J'attendrai ce que voudrez bien me marquer à ce sujet, pour prendre les derniers ordres de Sa Majesté. J'ai l'honneur d'être avec la plus parfaite consideration, Messieurs, votre très humble et obeissant serviteur   DE SARTINE.

Messrs. Les Deputes des Etats Unis de l'A.

545

From [Pierre-Georges Cabanis][2]

L: American Philosophical Society

Lundy soir 12 8bre [1778]
Made. helvetius demande de la part de mr. hebert à mr. franklin si le Diné projetté avec mr. le maréchal de Duras[3] peut avoir Lieu samedy prochain ou mercredy de la semaine suivante. Mr. hébert chez qui doit s'exécuter ce diné, préférerait le samedy, mais toutes fois dans le cas où mr. franklin n'aurait aucun engagement pour ce jour là. Mde. helvétius sera de cette partie, et mr. franklin aura la bonté de la prendre en passant, et de lui mander par le porteur le jour qu'il a choisi.[4]

Addressed: A Monsieur / Monsieur franklin / A Passi

2. Twenty-one years old at the time, Cabanis was a medical student living at the home of Mme. Helvétius and often serving as her secretary. He gained considerable fame later on, both as a physician (Mirabeau was among his patients) and as one of the leaders of the school of the *idéologues*. Upon his hostess's death in 1800, he inherited the Auteuil estate where BF had spent many of his happiest hours in France. Cabanis published his reminiscences of those occasions in his *Notice sur Benjamin Franklin*: C. Lehec and J. Cazeneuve, eds., *Oeuvres philosophiques de Cabanis* (2 vols., Paris, 1956), II, 341–67; for a sketch of his own life, see *ibid.*, I, v–xxi. See also Lopez, *Mon Cher Papa, passim*; A. Guillois, *Le salon de Madame Helvétius* (Paris, 1894).

3. Emmanuel Félicité de Durfort, duc de Duras (1715–1789) managed to become *maréchal de France* without having ever commanded an army and member of the Académie without having written a line. In his capacity as First Gentleman of the Chamber, he supervised the royal theaters. Larousse. Antoine-François Hébert (b. 1709), *Trésorier Général de l'Argenterie, Menus Plaisirs et Affaires de la Chambre du Roi*, owned a beautiful house and garden in Auteuil. From information kindly provided by Jean-Claude David, Paris. See also J.F. Bosher, *French Finances 1770–1795: From Business to Bureaucracy* (Cambridge, 1970), p. 328.

4. Another note, undated, also in the hand of Cabanis, refers to a dinner party to take place "vendredy" at BF's. Turgot and the baron d'Holbach are to be among the guests. APS.

From the Duc de La Rochefoucauld

AL: American Philosophical Society

Lundi matin [on or after October 12, 1778][5]
Le Duc de la Rochefoucauld a l'honneur de faire ses complimens à Monsieur franklyn en lui envoiant une lettre qu'il a crû
convenable d'écrire au Capitaine Jones pour lui rendre compte
de sa conversation avec M. de sartine; la lettre est ouverte, et
Monsieur franklyn est prié de vouloir bien la lire.

Le duc de la Rochefoucauld se fera un grand plaisir de revoir Monsieur franklyn dans trois semaines et d'ici à ce tems
là, il lui souhaite l'arrivée de bonnes nouvelles.

From John Lemon, Edward Driver and John Nichols

L:[6] American Philosophical Society

Honored sir   Dunan Castle Octr. 12th, 1778
Not doubting but your goodness will pardon our Presumption in writing to your Honour we take this freedom upon us
to acquaint your Honour of the present Situation I am in. I
was taken in the Washington Privateer[7] brought to England
and put on Board a Man of War against our Will and now
taken in the fox Frigate by the French and [torn] Now confin'd
in Dunnan Castle as Prisoners. We therefore rely on your
Honours goodness to be assisting to us in geting our freedom
form our present Situation which if your honour shou'd succeed we shall be ever in Duty bound to pray and subscribe

---

5. The first Monday after Friday, Oct. 9, when Jones requested La Rochefoucauld's intervention in his dispute with Sartine: [Robert C. Sands,
ed.], *Life and Correspondence of John Paul Jones* ... (New York, 1830), pp.
134–6.

6. The signatures are in the same hand as the letter.

7. The *Washington*, fitted out by the continental army and commanded by
Capt. Sion Martindale out of Plymouth, was taken by H.M.S. *Fowey* in
December, 1775, making it the first British capture of an American warship.
Both Lemon and Nichols (Nicholas) are listed among the *Fowey's* prisoners;
Driver is not. *Naval Docs.*, II, 1288–91.

ourselves your Honours Most obedient and most humble Servants
JOHN LEMON
EDWD. DRIVER
JOHN NICHOLS

Answr from your honr. will add much to our happiness

Addressed: To / Dr. Franklin / Secretary of the united States / of America / at Passy

Notation by John Adams: Lemon Driver Nichols Oct. 12. 78. Prisoners in Dinant ansd. Oct. 15

From Necker

Copy: Library of Congress

Paris le 12. 8bre. 1778.

J'ai reçu, Monsieur, avec la Lettre que vous m'avez fait l'honneur de m'écrire le 19. de ce mois[8] la note des Effets retenus à la Douane de Calais sur le Capitaine Pierre Colas de Boston. Comme aucun des effets n'a conservé la marque de son Origine il n'a pas été possible de les considerer comme ouvrage de France. On n'a pû d'ailleurs en permettre l'entrée parce que [*le*] Vaisseau qui en étoit chargé, étoit anglois, mais je viens de marquer aux fermiers Generaux de les faire remettre au Capitaine dont il s'agit en payant les Droits sur un pied moderé et je vous prie d'être persuadé que je donnerai toujours la même attention aux objets qui vous interessent. J'ai l'honneur d'être avec un très parfait attachement, Monsieur, votre très humble et très obeissant serviteur. (Signé) NEKER

M. Franklin

8. Actually Oct. 9.

From [Henry] Pattullo[9]   ALS: American Philosophical Society

⟨St. Germain en Laye, October 12, 1778: Your reputation for knowledge, wisdom and virtue has made me long desire to meet you. Accidents prevented my being introduced to you in London seven years ago. I have some proposals to offer, based on a lifelong application to the study of rural and political economy. I am of a Scots family and was engaged "in a too remarkable character" in the unhappy affairs of 1745, after which I sought safety in travel. Since the expiration of the time limit on trials for treason, I have often gone to England and Scotland where I waited on the ministers of the time. I reside mostly in France, however, being used to the climate and attached to the engaging attentions of some of the best.

As it appears the United States will make good its independence, I wish, as a citizen of the world, to contribute to its wellbeing. In that view I enclose a summary of my proposals.[1] I will meet you with pleasure at the time and place of your choice.⟩

The American Commissioners to Ralph Izard

AL (draft): Massachusetts Historical Society; two copies: National Archives

Sir   Passi Octr. 13. 1778
    We have the Honour of enclosing to you a Copy of M. de Sartines Answer to our Application in Support of your De-

---

9. Although he doesn't give his first name we are convinced the writer is Henry Pattullo, author of *Essai sur l'amélioration des terres* (Paris, 1758) and *An Essay upon the Cultivation of the Lands and Improvement of the Revenues of Bengal* (London, 1772). He was a member of the academies of Auxerre and Villefranche: Quérard, *France littéraire*.
    1. The summary promised that the author would present a plan for the improvement of American land cultivation, which would lead to the increase of revenue and the establishment of all kinds of arts and industry. There is no indication that BF responded; he endorsed the letter (probably much later) "M. Patullo St. Germain en Laye 12. Oct. 1780."

mand of your Baggage taken on Board the Nile.[2] We have agreable to your last Letter written again to Mr. De Sartine requesting him to Stop the Sale of the Things till you can make your Objections to their being lawful Prize.

The Hon. Mr Izard.

The American Commissioners to Sartine

AL (draft): Massachusetts Historical Society; three copies: National Archives

Passi Octr. [13][3] 1778

We had the Honour of receiving your Excellencys Letter of the 7 Instant to which We shall take the Liberty of answering fully by another opportunity.[4] As you mention that the Prize was condemned on the 20th Mr. Izard is apprehensive that the goods in Question may be sold, before the ordinary Course of Law can prevent it. He therefore desires Us to request your Excellency to prevent that if possible. And We accordingly beg the Favour of your Excellency to do so. We hope there is no Impropriety in this, and that if there should be, you will impute it to our Want of Information, on the manner of such Proceedings here. We have the Honour to be &c.

M. De Sartine.

John Bondfield to the American Commissioners[5]

ALS: American Philosophical Society

⟨Bordeaux, October 13, 1778: We learn from an American privateer which arrived at Corunna on September 30 that Admiral Howe tried to relieve Rhode Island. His and d'Estaing's

2. Sartine's letter was of Oct. 7 but Izard, as he wrote the commissioners on Oct. 10, had already seen a copy.
3. Supplied from one of the copies.
4. Their answer, dated Oct. 12, was delayed: see above.
5. Published in Taylor, *Adams Papers*, VII.

fleets were severely damaged in a storm; he has returned to New York and d'Estaing regained his post off Newport.[6] The privateer took two packet boats from which he has brought into Corunna four colonels, four majors and eighty other prisoners. A French frigate sent a Lisbon packet worth £80,000 into Vigo. Two Spanish frigates from Ferrol are looking for an English privateer which engaged a Spanish privateer.

Please send me the letter of marque for the *Livingston* that I requested in my last letter. Mr. Livingston reports her well advanced; she is of 400 tons, will carry 20 guns and will be manned proportionately. The French merchants here are in a critical state because of the lack of convoys for their returning ships; the English have captured more than 50 of them.[7] This would present us an opportunity for our own trade with the West Indies, but there is such a stagnation here that no one has taken advantage of it. Four Virginia pilot boats are loading salt and a trifling amount of haberdashery. If I had your commissions I could immediately send to America 200,000 *l.t.* of woolen blankets and clothing.⟩

From Tristram Barnard: Oath

AD:[8] American Philosophical Society

⟨Passy, October 13, 1778: I, Tristram Barnard of Nantucket, swear I will proceed to England and, as soon as possible in a vessel of my own loaded with coal, to Spain. From thence, with a cargo of goods, I shall proceed to America to settle for life.[9] I will not use this pass from the commissioners in any way contrary to the interests of America or France.⟩

6. Within days news arrived that d'Estaing had abandoned the siege: see Vergennes' letter of the 19th.

7. See Bondfield's letter of Aug. 29.

8. In JA's hand, signed by Tristram Barnard, and attested by BF and JA.

9. He took an oath of allegiance the same day (APS). His subsequent service to his country included extensive privateering: Taylor, *Adams Papers*, VII, under Oct. 9.

From [Ferdinand Grand]   AL: American Philosophical Society

This is the earliest document in a correspondence that stretches over six weeks and gives an example of the way Franklin handled a diplomatic crisis.

Gustavus Conyngham was, once again, at the center of it. On May 31, his cutter, *The Revenge*, seized the *Henrica Sophia*, a Swedish ship laden with a Spanish cargo. The Swedish ambassador to Versailles, Count de Creutz, lodged a protest with Vergennes on October 1 but was told that, sorry as he was, there was nothing the King of France could do about the affair.[1]

It was Spain's turn to protest. Unwilling to communicate directly with a government it did not recognize, Madrid channeled its complaint through Ferdinand Grand. The banker, whose role often went way beyond financial matters, forwarded the message in this undated note written between October 2, when he heard of the Spanish displeasure,[2] and October 14 when Franklin penned the draft of a reply meant to placate the Spanish court (the following document). A fair copy of this reply was made the same day by his grandson Temple and submitted to Grand for comments, which he provided at the bottom of the page. Franklin in turn added some words of his own between Grand's lines.

Franklin then prepared a new draft, again in the form of a letter to Grand, but in a style more obsequious than his previous one. Grand translated it into French and in a note, undated as usual, urged him to prepare promptly the package going to Spain, the courier being about to leave (APS). Another courier left on November 9 or shortly thereafter, carrying a letter of that date from the Spanish ambassador, Aranda, to his Foreign Minister, Floridablanca, as well as the final French version of Franklin's letter to Grand, dated Nov. 3 (Archivo General de Simancas).

[before October 14, 1778]

La revanche Cape. Cunigham a pris le 31 may Le Batiment Suedois L'henriete Sophie Cape. P. held[3] allant de Londres à Teneriffe avec Cargaison de Draps et autres Effets pour Le Compte des Negocians des Canaries et Nommement pour

1. Neeser, *Conyngham*, pp. 133, 138–9.
2. In a verbal communication from the Spanish ambassador: *Documentos relativos a la independencia de Norteamérica existentes en archivos españoles* (10 vols. to date, Madrid, 1976–), VI, 145.
3. Capt. Peter Heldt: Neeser, *op. cit.*, p. 138.

celui de La Maison Cologan,[4] Come les Connoissements doivent le constater; ce Vaisseau ou plutot cette prise à Eté envoyée en amerique.

Cet armateur ne respecte rien et se conduit plustot en Pirate qu'en corsaire, il à obligé Le Cour d'Espagne de lui Interdire ses Ports dans lesquels Il s'introduit malgré cella.

Il est à observer d'apres le memoire de Cologan que ce meme Navire suedois avoit été arreté par un autre corsaire americain qui sur le vû de ses papiers l'avoit relaché. Il paroit aussy que cette meme prise a été reprise par les anglais qui l'ont conduit a halifax ou le Batiment a été relaché.

Endorsed: Note from the Spanish Ambassador through Mr Grand relating to Capt. Cunningham

To Ferdinand Grand

LS[5] and AL draft: American Philosophical Society

Sir,   Passy, Oct. 14. 1778.

I have considered the Note you put into my Hands, containing a Complaint of the Conduct of Capt. Cunningham in the Revenge Privateer. We have no Desire to justify him in any Irregularities he may have committed. On the contrary we are obliged to our Friends who give us Information of the Misconduct of any of our Cruisers, that we may take the Occasion of representing the same to our Government, and recommending more effectual Provision for suppressing, punishing and preventing such Practices in future. By the Papers I have the Honour to send you enclosed, and which I request you would put into the Hands of his Excellency Count d'Aranda, the Care of the Congress to avoid giving Offence to neutral Powers will appear most evident; first in the Commission given to Privateers, wherein it appears that Sureties are taken

4. Thomas Cologan & Sons had already crossed swords with Conyngham: see Sieulanne to BF, July 30.

5. In WTF's hand. For the background of this letter, see our headnote to the preceding document.

of their Owners that nothing shall be done by them *"inconsistent with the Usage and Customs of Nations,"* and those Sureties are obliged to make good all Damages: Courts of Admiralty are regularly established in every one of the United States for judging of such Matters; to which Courts any Person injured may apply and will certainly find Redress. Secondly, in the Proclamation of Congress,[6] whereby strict Orders are given to all Officers of armed Vessels to pay a sacred Regard to the Rights of neutral Powers and the Usage and Customs of civilized Nations, &ca. and a Declaration made, that if they transgress they shall not be allowed to claim the Protection of the States, but shall suffer such Punishment as by the Usage and Custom of Nations may be inflicted on them. Lastly, in the particular Care taken by Congress to secure the Property of some Subjects of Portugal (a Power that has not been very favourable to us) altho' no Reclamation had been made.[7] All these will shew that the States give no Countenance to Acts of Piracy; and if Captain Cunningham has been guilty of that Crime he will certainly be punished for it when duely prosecuted: For not only a Regard to Justice in general, but a strong Disposition to cultivate the Friendship of Spain, for whose Sovereign they have the greatest Respect, will induce the Congress to pay great Attention to every Complaint that is properly made and authenticated.[8] I have the Honour to be Sir Your most obedient and most humble Servant   B. FRANKLIN

Mr. F. Grand.

6. For the proclamation, issued May 9, see *JCC*, XI, 486.

7. BF is probably referring to the action of Congress respecting the snow *Our Lady of Mount Carmel and St. Anthony* and her cargo, property of Portuguese subjects, which was sent into Massachusetts as a prize, and whose owner did not claim her: *JCC*, XI, 487–9.

8. In the copy made by WTF, BF crossed out the phrase "that is properly made and authenticated" and substituted "publick or private that shall come from thence."

Grand's remarks and BF's interlineations read as follows:

"Ceci est trop General et meriteroit d'être particularisé surtout dans le Cas present et en faveur de l'Espagne. On pourroit en Consequence ajouter que vous allés (BF: "Nous allons") informer vous (BF: "nous") memes le Congrés des plaintes de la Cour et Le porter a Lui en donner la plus

Rockhall, at Bienne, in Switzerland, Octr. 14th.
Sir! 1778.
Apprehensive, by Your Excellency's Silence to my last Letter, of Augt. 25th., as well as to my three preceding Letters therein mentioned, of their not being as wellcome as heretofore, I shall cease troubling Yr. Excy. with my perhaps impertinent Zeal, For the good Cause which You so gloriously defend; and confine it to my sincere Wishes for its speedy Triumph over its unrelenting Ennemies, with consolidated Liberty, Peace and Prosperity.[9] It is not without Regret, that I percieve my good offices, for bringing on a happy Union of Friendship, between Yr. 13. confederate States, and our 13. Cantons, on those Principles, I had the Honor to lay before Your Excellency in my last, thwarted at Paris by my Ennemies, and by their Malice and Illwill, entirely Frustrated; as I could rationally promise myself a good success, with manÿ mutual advantages.

I am sorry your Troubles are not yet over. New Efforts are preparing against your Independency, by sea and by Land, which, it is to be hoped, will equally prove abortive, and defeated by yr. powerfull allies. That Liberty, Sir, which I have enjoyed this Twelvemonth past, and which I have been so desirous of sacrificing to Your Excellcy's, and to Your Country's service, is not likely to continue much longer. Endless Delays,

---

prompte et la plus complette Satisfaction (BF: "sur la Meconduite du Cape. Conyngham en desobeissant les ordres du Roy") attendu qu'il n'y a rien que les 13 Etats ne fassent non Seulement pour Eviter a La Cour d'Espagne tout ce qui pourroit lui etre desagreable mais au Contraire pour Lui prouver combien ils desirent de meriter Sa bienveuillance, et de parvenir a Etablir des relations qui ne lui Laissent Rien a desirer de leur part."

Our guess is that, starting with the words "Nous allons" BF planned to incorporate Grand's modified text into his draft. He must have meant this new letter to be addressed to d'Aranda, for he added "Excellency's" in the complimentary close, making it read: "I have the Honour to be Sir Your Excellency's most obedient and most humble Servant. . . ." Eventually, he returned to the idea of writing to Grand: see below, Nov. 3.

9. In fact he wrote again on Dec. 23.

and Difficulties, in calling in my many pecuniary advances, both to the Court I have so liberally served these ten Years past, and to several reputed Friends by their Professions, have rendered my Situation here very uncomfortable; and will oblige me soon to contract new Engagements, if not called forth by my two worthy Friends and Patrons, Your Excellency, and the present President Laurence, to dedicate my Time, and my Labours to the great Cause of the Liberties of Mankind, under Your Commands and Directions.

The inclosed Letter, on the Reception of which the Happiness of a worthy Family depends, craves Yr. Excy.'s Kind Protection. Col. Minning[1] I suppose very well known to Presidt. Laurence, who, I flatter myself, will see it put into the best and safest Channel of Dispatch.

The swiss have newly advanced considerable Summs of Money to the Duke of Deux Ponts, and to the Elector of Saxony in support of their Defence against the Emperor.[2] Why does not the American Congress avail itself, of our good Will towards its noble Struggle for solid Liberty? Yr. Papercurrency, You see, will not suffice, unsupported with cash and Credit! But I forget my incroaching too much upon Yr. Excy's Time, and adding still more to my former Indiscretions. I therefore conclude with never ceasing Prayers for Yr. Excy's Preservation, and best Success in yr. arduous Labors! And remain most respectfully Sir! Your Excellency's Most humbly devoted Servant   RH. VALLTRAVERS.

Dr. F———n.

Notation: Valtravers Rockhall 24. 8bre. 1778.

1. For Christian Minnick, see xxv, 554 n.
2. Both Karl August von Zweibrücken (Deux-Ponts) and the Elector of Saxony had claims on the Bavarian inheritance. As a consequence of the War of the Bavarian Succession (July 1778–March 1779), Austria reduced her claims to the part of Bavaria ceded to her by the heir, Karl Theodor of the Palatinate: John G. Gagliardo, *Reich and Nation: the Holy Roman Empire as Idea and Reality, 1763–1806* (Bloomington and London, 1980), pp. 70–2.

From Félix Vicq d'Azyr[3]   ALS: American Philosophical Society

Monsieur   [before October 15,[4] 1778]

J'ai l'honneur de vous adresser de la part de la société Royale de Médecine plusieurs exemplaires des Lettres Patentes que le Roi lui a accordées[5] et en même tems le Tableau des membres qui la composent, dont le Roi a confirmé la nommination. La compagnie avec L'agrement de Sa Majesté a inscrit votre nom en teste des associés Etrangers. Elle vous a rendu cet hommage avec bien de l'empressement.

La Société R. de Médecine tiendra une séance publique le mardy 20 du present mois dans la grande salle du Collège R. de france place Cambray rue Saint Jacques. Elle vous prie très instamment d'y assister comme vous avez bien voulu le faire au mois de Janvier dernier. Je vous envoie des Billets d'entrée qui serviront aux personnes auxquelles vous jugerez á propos de distribuer. Je [J'ai] l'honneur d'être avec le plus profond respect Monsieur Votre très humble et très obeissant serviteur

VICQ D'AZYR
secretaire perpétuel

Endorsed: Vicq. d'Azyr Société

Notation: Paris

---

3. The famous anatomist, who had been one of the founders of the Société royale de médecine and was its vice-director as well as secretary; BF's certificate of membership appears in XXIV, 176–7. BF's reply is below, on or after Oct. 15. For a detailed account of the meeting, which BF attended, see the *Jour. de Paris* of Oct. 21, pp. 1177–8.

4. Poissonnier's letter of that date renews the invitation in this one.

5. The King had created the Society in April, 1776, and confirmed it in letters patent of Sept. 1, 1778: *Almanach royal* for 1781, p. 517.

The American Commissioners to Americans Taken on Board of English Frigates

AL (draft): Massachusetts Historical Society; two copies: National Archives

Passy Octr. 15. 1778

We have received a Letter from Mr. Robert Harrison of the 7 Octr. and another from John Lemon, Edward Driver and John Nichols, of the 12, all Prisoners in Dinant Castle, all professing to be Americans who have been first compelled into the Service of their Enemies, and then taken Prisoners by the French.

You are not known to Us, but your Account of yourselves, considering the General Conduct of the English of late, is not improbable. We cannot but feel a Concern for all Persons in Such a Situation, of whom to the lasting Dishonour of the British Government and Nation, there are too many, on board almost every Man of War in their Service.

We have written to his Excellency, the Minister of Marine of this Kingdom upon the Subject: and Sincerely hope that Something may be done for your Relief, and that of all other Persons in your Situation.

But great Care must be taken, that neither We, nor more especially the Government of this Kingdom be imposed upon, by attempts to sett at Liberty, English, Irish, Scotch, or other Sailors disaffected to the American Cause or unprincipled in it. We therefore desire you to send Us a List and a Short Account of all the Sailors Prisoners with you, who were born in America, or have been in her Service, and are willing to Subscribe the Declaration and take the oath of Allegiance to the united States of America, and to live and die by her Cause.

Americans taken on Board of English Frigates.

From Pierre-Isaac Poissonnier[6]

ALS: American Philosophical Society

A Paris Ce 15. 8bre. 1778

La Société Royale de medecine Monsieur, m'a chargé de vous renouveller son invitation[7] a la séance publique qu'Elle doit tenir mardy prochain 20 du présent mois. Je seray fort aise d'avoir a luy apprendre que vous y viendrés surement. Je saisis cette occasion de vous répeter les assurances de la Consideration trés distinguée et de l'attachement inviolable avec lesquels j'ay l'honneur d'Estre Monsieur Votre trés humble et trés obeissant Serviteur   POISSONNIER

Endorsed: Poissonnier

Notation: Paris 15. 8bre. 1778.

From Jonathan Williams, Jr.

ALS: American Philosophical Society

Dear and honoured Sir   Nantes, Octor 15. 1778

Count Sarsfield having obligingly offered to take Charge of a Packet for you, I embrace the Opportunity to send you ten of your Cards which I found among my Papers.

Capt. Le Maire the officer appointed by the State of Virginia for the Inspection of military Stores, is frequently complaining to me of his hard treatment, and requests me to represent his Situation to you. I have at last told him I would mention him, but I was sure you would not interfere in the matter and I advised him to stick to his Duty, bear all that was said or done to him with Patience, and trust to the Candour and Justice of his Employers, for their Approbation and an adequate Reward.

---

6. A doctor and chemist, one of the leading figures in French public health, whom BF had nominated for the Royal Society five years before: XIX, 328 n. We have hitherto followed most of his contemporaries in misspelling the name as Poissonier.

7. Contained in Vicq d'Azyr's letter, [before October 15].

It is true the poor Fellow has no money to live on, and in addition is treated with such contempt and abuse as for the honour of human nature I hope but few Characters are capable of. I am ever Your dutifull and affectionate Kinsman

J WILLIAMS J

D Franklin

Notation: Jona Williams Nantes Oct 15—78

To Le Maire

AL (draft):[8] American Philosophical Society

[After October 15, 1778][9]

That Dr. F. has spoken to Mr. Lee in his Behalf, whose Answer was that he had furnish'd him with what he thought sufficient, and that he did not think he could be justifiable with the Government of Virginia in supplying him farther; that if after this Declaration of the Gentleman intrusted by that Government Dr. F. should advance Money to him it must be at the risque of being disown'd and refus'd Payment, especially as the Governor's Letter desires no such thing of him, but only requests that he would aid Mr. Lee by his Influence in procuring the things wanted. That Dr. F. had accordingly found three separate Merchants each of whom had offered to furnish the whole; but as Mr. Lee undertook the Business he perceiv'd

8. Written on the back of Le Maire's copy of his letter to Arthur Lee, Oct. 15; see the following note.

9. Having just received "une lettre outrageante de M. Lee," Le Maire wrote to WTF on Oct. 15 enclosing copies of their most recent correspondence, which he wanted forwarded to BF: Le Maire's letter to Lee, Oct. 6; Lee's "outrageous" reply, undated; and Le Maire's answer, Oct. 15. WTF endorsed the covering letter, "Capt. Le Maire . . . Ansd."; and the acknowledgement of that answer, dated Oct. 29, makes clear that WTF had written what his grandfather had drafted here.

The dispute involved a gun-carriage which had been supplied to use as a model for construction in Virginia. Lee had suddenly ordered the object removed from the arsenal. When Le Maire questioned the decision, Lee blasted him for disobeying orders, calling him a "simple et petit particulier" who was responsible for delaying the project. Hereafter, Lee would refuse to have anything further to do with him. All these letters are in the APS.

there was no Occasion for his Services. That the Commissioners are continually harass'd by Applications from poor Prisoners who have escaped for Supplies of Money and expect 250 more very soon whom their Duty obliges them to assist. That their Remittances having been much intercepted, it is with difficulty they can find Money for these purposes and to support their Credit. That Dr. F. is but one of the three, and as the others will not agree to it if he should propose it, there is nothing to be expected from the Commissioners. That he is extremely sorry for his Situation and he will speak again to Mr. Lee in his Behalf, and endeavour if possible to obtain what is necessary for him, but recommends it to his Consideration whether he had not better either quit entirely a Service which does not afford him Subsistance, or return to Virginia in the first Vessel.

To Vicq d'Azyr[1]

AL (draft): American Philosophical Society

Sir   [after October 15, 1778]

I received the Copies of the Charter, and the Tickets which you so obligingly sent me, in behalf of the Royal Society. I am extreamly sensible of the great Honour they have done me, in placing me at the Head of their foreign Members; and I shall not fail to attend their Meeting of the 20th Instant, which they so kindly invite me to.[2]

1. In answer to his invitation above, before this date.

2. BF originally wrote, and then deleted, "not only their Meeting of the 20th Instant, which they so kindly invite me to, but as many as I may of their subsequent Meetings during my Residence in France; being persuaded from the known Characters and Abilities of the Members that much Knowledge of the most useful kind may be gathered from their Communications. I have the Honour to be with great Respect, Sir."

Not everyone was so pleased with BF's appointment. Writing to his brother Arthur on Oct. 18, William Lee remarked, "Notwithstanding the late affectation of throwing aside the title of Doctor, I see your neighbor at P[ass]ly is among the list of M.D.'s lately incorporated by his most Christian Majesty for examining and licensing all quack medicines." Ford, *Letters of William Lee*, II, 505.

Sartine to the American Commissioners

Copies: Massachusetts Historical Society, Library of Congress (two)

Versailles 16 8bre 1778

J'ai l'honneur de vous envoyer, Messieurs, des Exemplaires du Reglement concernant les Prises que des Corsaires françois conduiront dans les Ports des Etats unis de L'Amerique; et celles que les Corsaires Américains ameneront dans les ports de France.[3] J'ai l'honneur d'être avec une parfaite Consideration, Messieurs, votre très humble et très obéissant serviteur

DE SARTINE.

Messrs. Les Ministres des Etats Unis de L'Amérique

From Dumas

ALS: American Philosophical Society; AL (draft): Algemeen Rijksarchief

Monsieur,   Lahaie 16e Oct. 1778.

De retour, et un peu incommodé d'un petit voyage fatiguant pour mes affaires particulieres, il me fut impossible d'écrire l'ordinaire dernier.

Je réponds aujourdhui à la fin de la respectée vôtre du 22e. 7bre. qu'il y [a] certainement des démarches à faire de votre part, Messieurs, de temps en temps, non aupres de LL.hh.pp.,[4] mais en répondant à mes Lettres de maniere à former une correspondance indirecte avec la Régence d'Amsterdam, telle que notre Ami la desire, dont je serai le canal de communication, et dont le commencement est indiqué dans mes deux précédentes du 2 et du 6 Octobre. Il ne s'agit présentement que d'approuver, comme une chose que vous verrez avec plaisir, que notre Ami fasse travailler à Amsterdam, par des Marchands experts, à un projet de Traité, dont celui avec la France serve de base. Notre Ami fera usage, dans sa ville, de la Lettre

3. See Sartine to the commissioners, Aug. 16.
4. The States General. See our annotation of Dumas to the commissioners, July 3.

ostensible que vous m'écrirez à ce sujet,[5] et dont je lui donnerai copie, pour engager la ville, d'abord à cette démarche, et puis à d'autres. Vous ne demanderez rien à LL.hh.PP., vous ne serez qu'auxiliaires d'un parti formé contre celui de vos ennemis, sans vous compromettre en rien, ni vous, Messieurs, ni les Etats Unis, puisque le projet ne pourra être réalisé qu'avec l'agrément des Souverains réciproques, quand ils voudront qu'on le leur propose.

L'assemblée des Etats de la Prov. d'Hollande, qui aura lieu mercredi prochain, sera précédée d'une Nouvelle Adresse, qui va être présentée à LL.hh.pp. par les Négociants d'Amst. pour réclamer tous les dommages soufferts à l'occasion des prises faites.

Est-ce bien à coup sûr que je puis me réjouir de la prise de Rhode-Island, et de celle de deux Vaisseaux de Ligne, qui faisoient partie de l'Escadre de Byron?[6]

Permettez que je salue ici bien cordialement Sir G——, et Mr. Gd. son frere.

Mr. W.L. m'a écrit deux Lettres depuis son retour à Francfort sur un bon office que je lui avois demandé précédemment. Elles sont entre les mains du g—— F——, qui me les rendra demain. Je vous en transcrirai alors 4 Lignes, qui sont tout ce qu'il me dit touchant l'affaire passée. Je suis avec respect, et toujours, Monsieur, Votre très humble et très obéissant serviteur   DUMAS

P.S. Vous avez grande raison, Monsieur, de ne pas vouloir venir ici sans l'assurance d'être reçu comme Ministre des Etats Unis de l'Amérique. Jusque-là je serai toujours l'un des premiers à le déconseiller. Mais quand j'aurai le bonheur de vous donner cette assurance, à quoi je travaille avec ardeur, soyez sûr que votre Entrée sera l'un des plus beaux [*jours*] de votre vie. Un peuple de républicains, qu'il faut bien distinguer d'avec la majorité de ceux qui le etc. . . . vous recevra, vous applaudira comme le vénérable Libérateur de sa patrie, avec

5. The letter requested by Dumas on Oct. 2.
6. Dumas' rejoicing was premature: see Emery's letter of Oct. 7.

empressement; et vous ferez couler des larmes de joie. J'en juge par celles qui m'offusquent en écrivant ceci.

Paris à S.E.M. le D. Franklin Esqr. M.P.D.E.U.

Addressed: à Son Excellence / Monsieur le Dr. Franklin, Esqr. / Ministre Plenip. des E.U. de l'Am. / à Passy..

Notation: Dumas Oct. 16. 1778

Vergennes to the American Commissioners

L (draft): Archives du Ministère des affaires étrangères; copies: Library of Congress (two), Massachusetts Historical Society,[7] National Archives

A Versailles le 17. 8bre 1778.

Par la Lettre Messieurs que vous m'avez fait l'honneur de m'e-crire le 28 aoust dernier, vous avez demandé la main levée de la saisie faite à Calais d'une partie des bagages du Sr. Smith. J'ai pris à cet egard les informations les plus exactes et il en resulte qu'il ne s'est trouvé absolument aucune trace à Calais de l'affaire dont il s'agit. Il faut donc, Messieurs qu'on se soit trompé dans l'indication qui vous a été donnée sur le nom de la ville, où la saisie contre laquelle vous reclamez, a eu lieu. Je ne puis qu'attendre les eclaircissemens ulterieurs que vous voudrez bien me donner, et aussitôt qu'ils me seront parvenus, vous pouvez compter sur mon exactitude à faire ce qui dependra de moi pour procurer au Sr. Smith la justice qui pourra lui etre due.

Les Deputés americains M. francklin

7. Misdated the 16th.

From Pierre-Joseph Buc'hoz[8]

ALS: American Philosophical Society

Monseigneur   A paris le 17e. 8bre. *1778*
  Je prend la liberté d'adresser a votre excellence deux catalogues de ma Bibliotheque. Je vous prie d'en faire passer un
dans votre Cour; Cette Bibliotheque est composée de Livres
tres rares, Surtout en histoire naturelle. Je desirerois Bien de
La vendre en gros, j'accorderais meme des Conditions for
avantageuses a L'acquereur. Ce seroit Bien dommage de la
diviser. J'ay L'honneur d'etre tres parfaitement Monseigneur
Votre tres humble et tres obeissant serviteur
                            Buc'hoz medecin de Monsieur

Endorsed: Buchoz with Catalogues Paris 17. 8bre. 1778.

From Dumas

ALS: American Philosophical Society

Monsieur   La Haie 18e. Oct. *1778*
  Mr. Huet Du Plessis, Médecin, ancien et bon ami de ma
famille, retournant en France sa Patrie, desirant de vous être
présenté, n'est point le premier qui m'ait demandé une Lettre
pour vous; mais il est le seul à qui j'aie cru jusqu'ici devoir
accorder de faire cet usage de l'amitié et correspondance dont
vous m'honorez. Son mérite, ses sentimens, et ses connoissances lui procureront auprès de vous tout ce qu'il peut sou-
haiter de plus. Je suis avec un très-grand respect, Monsieur
Votre très humble et très obéissant serviteur   Dumas

Passy à Son Excellence M. le Dr. Franklin Ministre Plenipotentiaire des Etats-Unis de l'Amérique

Addressed: à Son Excellence / Monsieur le Dr. Franklin, Esqr. /
Ministre Plénipotentiaire des / Etats-Unis de l'Amérique / etc.
etc. à *Passy.*

Notation: Dumas Oct 18. 78

---

8. This doctor turned naturalist (1731-1807) was a most prolific writer
on political economy and natural history. By 1788 he was still trying to sell
his book collection, this time to Buffon. *DBF.*

From Robert Harrison and John Lemon[9]

ALS:[1] American Philosophical Society

Honorable Sir,   Denan Prison the 18 of October 1778

This Comes With My kind adress to your Honnor hoping you will take it in Consideration to wards us Boath. I John Lemon belong to the Washington Privetere out of Plymouth in New England in Ameraca was taking By the foy [*Fowey*] frigate and was Brought into Portehmouth in England and from that sent on Bord the fox frigate that was going out to sea against my will But I Could not help my self for I Was forse to go and Was taking By a french frigate and Brought into Brest Which I thought I Could get home onc again Which I Regoice Very much at Honnor Sir I be Long to Jenerall Washington Rieffall men for month and than Enterd on Bord the Washington Priveter along with Captain martingaill By so Doing you Will oblidge your humble Sarvant

JOHN LEMON

Honorable Sir

This Comes with my kind a Dress to your honor hoping you Will not for get us Boath here Prisinors as yet hoping your Honnor Will set us at Liberty as it Lies in your Pour for I have ofen hard of your goodness Before this time Which I hope Will not feal to wards us for wee are Willing to sarve our Contry if Wee Could get home.

I Robert Harrison was bound from Newbery to nance With Captain foster and Was taking by the Wasp slope of Ware and Cared into Corke in Ireland. I Ran a Way from Corke to Dublin and ship my self on Bord a Letter of marque Bound to Jemaca and was taking by a fench frigate and Cared into Brest. Was send to Dinan Prison where wee Remain but hoping your goodness Will think of us if a Cartell should come here Wee must go to England Wee Would be sent on Bord a man

---

9. Each of the prisoners had already written independently, Harrison on Oct. 7 and Lemon, with others, on Oct. 12.
1. In Harrison's hand.

of Ware and maid fight against our Country which Would grive us Very much. By so Doing you will oblidge your humble sarvant ROBERT HARRISON

I Robert Harrison was Borne Newbery in New England north ameraca and sarved my time to Jordge swanton shipright.

I John Lemon Was Borne in Lankertser Pencevane and sarved my time to gorge Croush house Carpinter.

Sir if your Honnour Would think fit to send an answer to us or order few Liens to the Commisaries in Dinan Wee should for Ever be your most humble Sarvants Both together for Ever.

Hoping you not foget us.

Addressed in another hand:[2] To / Mr Franklin Agent for the / United States of America / Paris

Notation by John Adams: Prisoners in Dinant 18 Octr. 1778

From ——— Mané[3]   ALS: American Philosophical Society

Monsieur,   à Paris ce [18] 8bre. 1778
    J'ai eu l'honneur de présenter à l'Académie Royale des Sçiences plusieurs *Médaillons* éxécutés *au Tour*; elle en a paru satisfaite. C'est, sans doute, ce qui l'a déterminée à me demander celui d'un des plus grands Hommes de ce siécle. Par le choix du sujet, Cette célebre compagnie, qui s'honore de vous avoir pour Membre, semble avoir prévenu mes desirs; J'ai tâché de répondre aux siens; Vous jugerez mieux que personne si j'ai réüssi: Je l'ai tourné d'après un modéle en Porce-

---

2. This seems to be in the hand of George Swaller, who wrote on Oct. 21.
3. The Académie des sciences, to which he made a presentation on Sept. 2, refers to Mané as a goldsmith and "tabletier du Garde-meuble de La Couronne," *i.e.* one who manufactures chess games and other small ivory objects. He also invented pieces of heavy mechanical equipment. *Procès-verbaux*, XCVII, fols. 294 and 270.

laine de la Manufacture Royale.[4] Je prends la liberté de vous offrir, Monsieur, le pareil Médaillon que j'ai remis à l'Académie.

J'aurois pu en faire hommage à un des plus grands Philosophes de nos jours, à un de nos premiers Physiçiens, au plus profond des Politiques; J'aurois pu oser le présenter au généreux Libérateur, au sage Législateur, à l'heureux et habile Négoçiateur d'une République puissante dès son berceau: Mais j'ai cru devoir la préférence à un juste apréçiateur des Talens, à un amateur éclairé des Arts. Le Protecteur que je choisis réünit tous ces tîtres; vous ne pouriez pas en étre jaloux: ils se trouvent tous énoncés par la seule expression dont le sujet du Médaillon m'a été designé. Si la modestie vous empêche de reconnoître la ressemblance, Je me flatte que personne ne pourra méconnoître le Génie Tutelaire du Nouveau Monde. Je suis avec le plus profond respect, Monsieur, Vôtre trés humble, trés-respectueux et trés-obéissant serviteur   MANÉ

Endorsed: M. Mané with an Ivory Medaillon Paris ce 18. 8bre. 1778.

From [Joshua Steele][5]   ALS: American Philosophical Society

Dear Sir,   London 18th Octr. 1778

This comes, thro' the favour of a Foreign Minister,[6] from a Friend, that loves, esteems and honours you, as a Man, a Philosopher, and a Patriot; But who, while his Country is under the sway of Ignorance and Malevolence, dares not to put his Name to a mere philosophic letter; lest, by miscarriage and misconstruction, it should be voted into a treasonable Correspondence.

The purport of it is principally to send you a few sheets in Folio, lately published by the Society of Arts, under the Title

4. The medallion in question is discussed in Charles Sellers, *Benjamin Franklin in Portraiture* (New Haven and London, 1962), pp. 366–7.

5. For the long-time member of the Society of Arts, see XX, 312 n. BF's guess at his identity is confirmed by the handwriting.

6. He presumably sent this letter, like one on June 25, 1779 (APS), through the Spanish embassy.

of *A Register of the Premiums and Bounties bestowed by the Society* etc. which work was chiefly owing to the Assiduity of a Mr. Steele, who was the proposer, and also Chairman of the Committee intrusted with the Execution, the same, who was the Author of a philological Essay in Quarto, which I sent you about three years ago thro' the means of your old female Friend of Craven Street.[7] This Register, I must own, is not sent to you by the Society at large, but by your Friends, and Men of Honour, who know you are intitled thereto as a perpetual Member, and who do not see any particular Clause in the *Capture, Prohibitory,* or, as I may say, in the *Amputation Act*[8], that should restrain them from giving you these Philosophical Rights.

By this same opportunity, I send you a Pamphlet just come out, called the *West India Merchant*, collected from the public papers of two years past, and mostly written, as I have heard, by the Author of a Dialogue, published about twelve years ago, on the subject of the dispute with America: but, I understand, other Gentlemen also of those Colonies have been concerned in this and the like Publications.[9] Indeed, the case of the West India Planters, during this unhappy dispute, is so truly pityable, that I cannot avoid going a little out of my way to observe, that it would well become the Humanity of your Countrymen, (whose procedures shew they have not yet renounced that Virtue) notwithstanding their provocation, to

7. The register of premiums covered the years 1754–1776; it was published in London in 1778. Steele had sent BF a copy of *An Essay towards Establishing the Melody and Measure of Speech . . .* (London, 1775) by way of Mrs. Stevenson in 1775: XXII, 264.

8. The Prohibitory Act of December, 1775: *ibid.*, p. 268 n.

9. Steele, who had estates in Barbados (*DNB*), is almost certainly claiming himself as principal author of *The West-India Merchant. Being a Series of Papers Originally Printed Under that Signature in the London Evening Post . . .* (London, 1778). The dialogue was probably *An Account of a Late Conference on the Occurrences in America. In a Letter to a Friend* (London, 1766), which has been attributed to Steele: Thomas R. Adams, *The American Controversy: a Bibliographical Study of the British Pamphlets About the American Disputes, 1764–1783* (2 vols., Providence, 1980), I, 283. Of *The West-India Merchant* a reviewer wrote that "The main design of the Author is to reprobate, in every view, the American war." *Monthly Rev.*, LIX (1778), 390.

turn the force of their Naval Arms some other way; You are well enough acquainted with the narrow Conceptions of the great Vulgar in this Country, to know that the Interests of no Man, or Body of Men, are regarded by the governing Powers, whose Faces are not well known at Court, and whose Connections are not strong in Borroughs or Counties; This not being the case of the Proprietors of those poor defenceless Islands, Their Masters have not shewn the least sense of Feeling for all the Losses the Planters have suffered by the American Privateers; Therefore, tho' you might think yourselves, not only justified, but obliged in policy, to wound this Country thro' the sides of the Sugar Colonists, you have failed, so far, in that point, that the governing powers here are as insensible of those wounds, as they are of having destroyed the Grandeur and prosperity of the British Empire; a Mischief, which they will never be thoroughly sensible of, till, by a total failure in the Exchequer, they will find they are thoroughly undone.

Neither has the with-holding the Lumber and Provisions of N. America, however distressing to the Islands, wrought any Effect on the generality of this unfeeling Administration, or their Adherents; on the Contrary, it has given rise to a new and Lucrative branch of Trade, and thereby purchased a new sett of Abettors of an absurd and infamous policy; which exists by an Endeavour to furnish a scanty supply of those Commodities at an advance of above an hundred per Cent: on which Occasion, I have heard many of the planters, particularly those of Barbados and the old Islands, say, that there is nothing next to a Peace, they so ardently wish for as some species of *Flag of Truce Neutrality*, however limited, whereby they might be supplied with Lumber and provisions as heretofore, in fair Exchange for their produce; and if they could have any ground to hope, the united States would, on their part, consent to such a Cartel Treaty, they would employ all their Force to obtain a license from Parliament to negociate it. Whoever is divested of the disgracefull passions of Pride and revengefull Resentment, must see that such a friendly Communication, tho' within eversuch narrow bounds, might be the happy Means of bringing about the most natural, most profitable and firmest Connection, by the mutual Benefits of Commerce and brotherly Affection.

If there should be any West India Planters or Merchants, under Ministerial Influence, so rash and Imprudent as to do Acts that might provoke Reprisals; it will be but reasonable to make Allowance for a few deluded Fools, and not to impute their Rashness to a whole Community; And tho' our Masters, on this Side, should continue to be both unjust and unfeeling, it is to be hoped, that in all Events the rising Republic will not forget their Relation in Blood to those poor Islanders, so far, as, on any occasion, to abandon them to depredation, or to the dominion of any foreign power. I am, dear Sir, with the most perfect Respect and affection, Your very humble Servant,

A Sincere Patriot.

His Excellcy B. Franklin Esqr

Endorsed: Supposed Mr Steele 18. Oct. 1778.

Sartine to the American Commissioners[1]

Copies: National Archives, Massachusetts Historical Society, Library of Congress (two)

⟨Marly, October 19, 1778, in French: I have received your letters about Mr. Izard's complaints. The ship with its cargo has been declared a valid prize; for the government to meddle with the law would create a dangerous precedent. If Mr. Izard's request is in conformity with the treaties his claim will be favorably received and the cost of addressing a petition is not great. Had his ownership been proven earlier, it would have only been a question of verifying it. I am sorry to say, however, he will be unable to avoid the indispensable formalities His Majesty has established for allies as well as subjects.⟩

1. Published with a translation in Taylor, *Adams Papers*, VII.

From John Paul Jones

ALS: American Philosophical Society; copies: Library of Congress, United States Naval Academy Museum

Honored and Dear Sir   Brest Octr. 19th. 1778.

I hope you will find the within letters entirely free from asperity or ill Nature.[2] I have been and am, in the Eyes of Brest and of the French Fleet, considered as having incurred your Displeasure and being consequently in Disgrace. The Commissioners' refusal of my Bill, my Journey to Paris without any Visible reason, the Cabals and ungrateful misrepresentations of Mr. Simpson, and my present inactivity, are held as so many circumstantial Proofs; and my Dishonor is now so firmly beleived everywhere, that it is in Vain for me to assert the contrary. Such a Situation Destroys my Peace of Mind, and is incompatible with my Sensibility: Yet I am far more affected, beleive me, by the Indignity that has been shewn thro' me to yourself and to America, than on my own Account. I think it now beneath your Character to ask an explanation from M. De Sartine; but you are the best Judge. Had I been unconnected with him, I should this Day have Commanded more than a Frigate, without asking it, in America: And his giving me a single Frigate now after having done me so much Dishonor, and after so many Opportunities have been lost, is no recompense either to myself or to my Country. He ought now by the Laws of Hospitality, and a regard to Truth, to *Do* more than he at first proposed; instead of merely *promising*, to do less. My Heart cannot forgive him till he makes whole my injured Honor by a direct Apology and Atonement for the Past.[3]

2. The enclosures, dated Oct. 19, were to Louis XVI and the duchesse de Chartres. To the King, Jones outlined his activities and frustrations since Sartine first promised him the *Indien* through a letter from BF, June 1 (XXVI, 558–9). Ever since then, his life has been a series of humiliations; he appeals to the King because all other channels have been exhausted. To the duchess, Jones condensed the same story and begged her to present in person his letter to Louis. APS.

3. Jones had begun this campaign in a letter to Bancroft, Oct. 7 (U.S. Naval Academy): if Sartine did not apologize and prove his good inten-

My letter to the King cannot I think do Harm; and, unless you disapprove of it, I beg that it may have Course. The Duchesse De Chartres will I am persuaded undertake to deliver it into the Kings Hands: And, as you may not think fit at present to appear in the Business, either the Duc De Rochefocaulte or your Grandson will oblige me by waiting on her at the Palais Royal.⁴ The Duc De Rochefocaulte, as he understands the English so well and is acquainted with circumstances, would oblige me much if he could be present when the letter is presented to the King.

I do not wish to trouble the Duc De Chartres about this affair; as that Brave Prince has met with Vexations of his own, in my opinion, very undeservedly.⁵

Let not your Delicacy prevent my having the Honor of hearing from you: For, so far am I from blaming you as the cause of my present Unhappiness, that I am entirely convinced that you had no other Motive than my Honor and Promotion, as consistent with the Public Good. I am consequently with the Veneration of a Son who ardently wishes to render himself worthy of your Regard, Honored and Dear Sir Your very Obliged very Obedient very humble Servant

JNO P JONES

tions, Jones would have to "make his perfidy public." Bancroft's answer of Oct. 10 claimed that Sartine was ashamed of his behavior, blaming it on the cabals and intrigues of French marine officers, and was more determined than ever to secure Jones a ship. The captain would not be mollified. "If he does not make me a direct apology and attonement for the past," he apparently wrote Chaumont on Oct. 13, "painful as it will be, in Vindication of my sacred Honor I must Publish in the Gazettes of Europe the Conduct which he has held towards me." Jones sent this letter, now missing, through WTF, whom he asked to translate and forward it (Oct. 13, APS). It, as well as Bancroft's of Oct. 10, are paraphrased in Jones to JW, Oct. 20 (U.S. Naval Academy).

4. "If my letters of the 19th are delivered," Jones wrote WTF on Oct. 28, "I beg you to attend the Princess at Versailles." APS. He presumably meant the duchess.

5. The duc de Chartres had been criticized for the handling of his division of ships at the Battle of Ushant. See E. Chevalier, *Histoire de la marine française* . . . (Paris, 1877), pp. 92 ff.

His Excellency Doctor Franklin.

Endorsed: Capt Jones Brest Oct. 19. 78

From Vergennes

Copy: Library of Congress

Versailles 19. 8bre. 1778.
Le Cte. de Vergennes fait ses Complimens à Mr. Franklin et le remercie des nouvelles de l'Amerique qu'il a bien voulu lui communiquer, elles ne sont pas a beaucoup près satisfaisantes, les accidens semblent venir au secours des Anglois. Si M. Le Comte d'Estaing a du quitter Rodhes Island pour se rendre à Boston,[6] ce ne sera sûrement pas sans pouvoir justifier evidemment la Necessité du Parti qu'il aura pris. Son zele pour la Cause qu'il est chargé de deffendre et son ardeur pour la gloire ne peuvent pas être soupçonnés.

To David Hartley

ALS: Library of Congress; copies:[7] National Maritime Museum, Public Record Office; transcript: Library of Congress

Dear Sir   Passy, Oct. 20. 1778.
I received your Favour of the 9th. Instant, with a Copy of the Letter from the Admiralty Office relative to the proposed Exchange of Prisoners, in which the precise Number of those we have here is desired. I cannot at present give it you, they being dispers'd in different Ports; and indeed it will always be difficult to be precise in it, the Number continually changing by new Prisoners brought in, and some escaping. I think the List I formerly sent you was near 200*,[8] since which Sixty-odd

---

6. See John Emery's letter, Oct. 7.

7. With minor variations introduced by Hartley; see the following note.

8. Hartley added the asterisk and a marginal note: "NB In July the were about 258 and some mast men according to the list then sent wch I transmitted to the Adty in July last." See BF to Hartley, July 13. Hartley forwarded a copy of this letter to the Board of Admiralty on Nov. 5, incorpo-

have been brought into France from the North Seas by Capt. McNeil, and some by others of our Cruisers; and I just now hear that we have near an hundred more in Spain taken by one of our Privateers in two New-York Packets, one going thither, the other returning, 88 of which are Officers of your Army.[9] I wish their Lordships could have seen it well to exchange upon Account; but tho' they may not think it safe trusting to us, we shall make no Difficulty in trusting to them. And to expedite the Exchange, and save the Time that obtaining a correct List would require, we make this Proposition, that if their Lordships will send us over 250 of our People, we will deliver all we have in France. If the Number we have falls short of the 250, the Cartel Ship may take back as many of those she brings as the Deficiency amounts to, delivering no more than she receives. If our Number exceeds the 250, we will deliver them all nevertheless, their Lordships promising to send us immediately a Number equal to the Surplus. We would thus wish to commence, by this first Advance, that mutual Confidence, which it would be for the Good of Mankind that Nations should maintain honourably with each other, tho' engag'd in War. I hope this will remove all Obstructions to a speedy Completion of the Business, as the Winter approaches, and the poor Prisoners on both Sides may suffer in it extremely. I am, with great Esteem, Dear Sir, Your most obedient humble Servant   B FRANKLIN

David Hartley Esquire

Endorsed: D Fr Oct 20 1778

---

rating his addition as if it were BF's own parenthetical phrase. Philip Stephens of the Admiralty Board in turn forwarded Hartley's copy and cover letter to the Commission for the Sick and Hurt on Nov. 13, and asked its advice on how to effect the exchange while guarding against the "inconvenience" of the prisoners' overtaking the cartel. National Maritime Museum.

9. See Bondfield to the commissioners, Aug. 26 and Oct. 13.

To Vergennes   ALS:[1] Archives du Ministère des affaires étrangères

M. le Comte,   A Passy, ce 20. Octre 1778
    Mes Colleagues croyent qu'il seroit necessaire que je fusse
en Hollande, et que ma Presence pourroit y accelerer les
Choses. Ils me pressent en consequence.[2] Je crains que ce seroit plutôt les reculer que les avancer, et que ce ne soit pas le
moment de s'y presenter. Personne ne sçait mieux que votre
Excellence ce que nous convient de faire à cet egard, et je ne
puis avoir de Conseil meilleur et plus agreable que le vôtre. Si
vous voulez bien me l'accorder, je m'y conformera avec la
Confiance. J'ai l'honneur d'être, avec Respect M. le Comte,
Votre tres humble et tres obeissant Serviteur   B FRANKLIN

Notation: M. franklin / Etats unis / rep.[3]

To Wuybert, Lunt and MacKellar, Officers and the
Other Prisoners at Forton   Copy: Library of Congress

Gentlemen   Passy 20th. Octor. 1778
    I have just received yours of the 2d. Instant. I beg that you
will be assured that your long Detention, is not owing to any
Neglect of you by the Commissioners. Our first Applications
for exchanging you, were haughtily rejected. You were at that
time consider'd as Rebels, committed for High Treason, who
could only be delivered by course of Law.[4] We then did every
thing in our Power to make your situation as comfortable as
possible. When Time and Circumstances produced a Disposition to consider you in a more favourable light, we proposed
that on your being all discharg'd, we would give up all we had
here, and an Order to receive the Ballance of the number in
America;[5] this was refused, but good Mr. Hartley has finally

    1. BF must have copied (with some slips) a model prepared for him.
    2. An idea broached to Dumas on Sept. 22. BF had not yet received
Dumas' discouraging response of Oct. 16.
    3. Vergennes replied on Oct. 21.
    4. See XXIII, 360–1, 548–9, 554.
    5. In a letter of the commissioners to Hartley, June 16: XXVI, 626.

by long solicitation obtain'd an Agreement of the Lords of the Admiralty to an exchange of Man for Man, and the Pass required for a Cartel Ship to bring over as many of you as we have here to give in Return, was sent to England in September.[6] The Execution has been delay'd 'till a precise List could be sent of our Number. Of this we have only been a few days informed. By this Post I have written a Letter to Mr. Hartley, which I hope will remove that difficulty, and that those who have been longest in confinement to the number of 250. at least from the two Prisons of Forton and Plymouth will now soon be at liberty. Nothing in the Power of the Commissioners will be wanting to liberate the rest as soon as possible, for the Sufferings of so many of our brave Countrymen, affect us very sensibly. I have the honour to be Gentlemen Your most obedient and most humble Servant   B. FRANKLIN

To Messrs. Wuibert, Lunt & MacKellar, Officers and the other Prisoners at Forton

Notation: Passy 20th. Octor. 1778. Copy of a Letter from Dr. Franklin to the American Prisoners at Forton. Recd. 2d. Novem. 1778.

Abraham Livingston to the American Commissioners[7]

ALS: American Philosophical Society

⟨Charleston, October 20, 1778: I wrote you on June 10 and 22[8] that the commercial committee of Congress had ordered several vessels from here. The *Flammand*'s officers and crew refused to sail here from Massachusetts,[9] the *Mellish* was de-

---

6. On Sept. 14.

7. Published in Taylor, *Adams Papers,* VII. Livingston served as commercial and continental prize agent at Charleston.

8. Missing. The only previous communication we have found was a letter of introduction: XXVI, 455.

9. Beaumarchais' *Flammand* (or *Flamand*) had planned to pick up freight in Charleston: Morton, *Beaumarchais Correspondance,* IV, 186 (entry of July 31).

stroyed by the British at Bedford,[1] and the ship *Hayfield* and brigantine *Minerva* have been ordered to the West Indies. My hopes of sending remittances to France on the public account are frustrated; I will advise you whenever anything further occurs in the mercantile line.⟩

From Cadet de Vaux

ALS: American Philosophical Society

Monsieur le docteur   Ce Mardi 20 8bre 1778

Monsieur le lieutenant Général de Police[2] accepte le Jeudi 29 de ce mois, Jour que vous avés bien Voulu prendre pour notre rendès-vous à l'hôtel Royal des Invalides; J'aurai l'honneur d'aller vous prendre le matin, pour vous accompagner. Nous ne nous occuperons pas seulement du pain de pommes de terre, mais De tous les travaux relatifs à la Boulangerie, art qui est bien Eloignée de sa Perfection, sourtout parmi les Anglais; et que nos chers alliés les américains pourront y porter, en leurs communiquant l'ouvrage de M. Parmentier,[3] que ce chymiste aura l'honneur de vous présenter. Je suis avec le plus profond respect Monsieur le docteur Votre très humble et bien obeissant serviteur   CADET LE JEUNE[4]

1. During the British occupation of New Bedford: Silas Deane to BF, Sept. 15.

2. Jean-Charles-Pierre Lenoir (1732–1807) had been appointed Paris lieutenant of police in 1774, resigned temporarily because of a conflict of opinion with Turgot, and was reinstated in 1776. During his tenure, which lasted until 1785, he opened a bakery school, endowed the streets with better lighting, organized garbage collection, established the first pawning system (*mont-de-piété*) and fought against the use of torture. Larousse. BF always maintained excellent relations with him.

3. *Le Parfait Boulanger, ou Traité complet sur la fabrication et le commerce du pain* (Paris, 1777). Parmentier was *apothicaire major* at the Hôtel Royal des Invalides.

4. On Oct. 27 Cadet sent BF a reminder, telling him how much Lenoir was looking forward to the occasion. APS.

From Richard Penn, Jr.[5]

ALS: American Philosophical Society

Dear Sir.   London Octobr. 20th. 1778.

Nothing but Necessity cou'd have induc'd me to take the liberty of begging your Attention for a few moments, from those Various and important Affairs with which you are Entrusted and which you have Executed with so much Reputation to yourself, and Advantage to your Country. At the same time I am aware that the Name subscrib'd will not at first sight bias you much in favour of the Writer. Nevertheless I have too high an Opinion of your Character to Imagine that any Misunderstanding which might formerly have subsisted between you and any part of my Family in which I myself coud have had no Share will at all prejudice you against me or in any degree withhold you from lending me your Advice and perhaps Assistance upon the present Occasion. I flatter myself I have some slight ground to go upon in this Case, which I own I am most willing to catch at. I am Married to your late Ward the Eldest Miss Masters and have now living with me her younger Sister still under Age and of course in a manner claiming your Patronage as well as their Mother the Widow of your late Friend.[6] From this connexion it is well known to you Sir that I possess a very considerable Property in the City of Philadelphia and its Environs besides two or three Valuable Estates of my own in the Province of Pennsylvania and a whole undivided Proprietary of New Jersey, yet with all this Property I have not been able for more than two years past to procure One Shilling from that Country nor have I during that time so much as recievd a line from my Friend and Agent Mr. Tench Francis who it is probable has at this very time a

5. Penn, the former lieutenant governor of Pennsylvania, has appeared often in past volumes, most recently while delivering for Congress the Olive Branch petition (XXII, 280–1). Since then he had been living in England. He was eventually compensated by Pennsylvania for the loss of his rights as proprietor of the colony: *DAB*. See also Namier and Brooke, *House of Commons*, III, 261–2 for his future parliamentary career.

6. Mary Masters Penn (1756–1829), her sister Sarah and their widowed mother Mary Lawrence Masters: *PMHB*, XXII, 87–92. BF had been executor of William Masters' will: above, XVI, 275 n.

handsome Sum of Money belonging to me in his hands.[7] The Purse I brought with me to England is nearly Exhausted tho' it has been managed with the strictest Œconomy. I have not yet tried nor woud I willingly at present what American Security woud produce in this Country. I shoud think myself infinitely obligd to you if you coud point out to me, in what manner I coud procure either from America or in any other Way a Temporary Subsistance. I have not a doubt but that in time Matters will turn out much to the Advantage of Every body concern'd and connected with that Country, let me Entreat you Sir to favour me with an Answer to this letter under Cover to my Bankers Mesrs. Barclay Bevan & Co. No. 56 Lombard Street,[8] in doing which you will lay a lasting Obligation upon One of the many who reveres your Character and admires your Ability. Give me leave to subscribe myself Dear Sir Your very sincere Friend   RICHD. PENN

From Daniel Solander[9]   ALS: Harvard University Library

Dear Sir   London Oct. 20. 1778
    Permit me to introduce to You my Countryman Mr. John Alstroemer;[1] He is one of my best and most intimate friends, whose thirst for Knowledge intitles him to any favor You can bestow on Him. If You have a few Moments to spare, You will find [him] very intelligent. I am with great regard Dear Sir Your most obedient humble servant   DAN. SOLANDER
Dr Franklin

    7. For Tench Francis, Jr. see XIV, 160 n.
    8. The banking house in which David Barclay was a partner; for its connection with Penn see IX, 190–1 n. It helped Penn weather his wartime financial difficulties: *PMHB, loc. cit.*
    9. For the Swedish-born Fellow of the Royal Society, keeper of the natural history department of the British Museum, botanist on Cook's *Endeavor* voyages, and friend of BF, see IX, 121 n; XIV, 215 n, 285 n; XVIII, 209; XIX and XX, *passim.* This is the only extant letter between the two men.
    1. Son of the patriot and influential commercial and industrial innovator Jonas Alströmer, Johan (1742–86), like his father, was a member of the Academy of Sciences in Stockholm. From 1777 to 1780 he was traveling through western and central Europe. *Svenskt Biografiskt Lexikon.*

American Prisoners in Dinan to the American Commissioners

ALS:[2] American Philosophical Society

Gentlemen   Dennant Castle Octr: 21st: 1778

We the under Subscribed Persons having Received Your kind favour of the 15 Inst: who are the only [Santuaries?] under God we Rely on, nor do we desire our liberty from other hands than yours; being in Reallity Americans, who are farr from Imposeing upon Your Clemency (or this Goverment) and willing to Stand or fall by our Countrys Cause, as we are well assured of the Justness thereof, and Desire no Greater Happyness than to be set at liberty, and that You Gentlemen shoud Appoint us to be of Service thereto, for which we, as in Duty Bound will ever pray

> WM. KEATING from Virginia
> John Lemon—Pensylvania
> Robt: Harrison—New England
> Edward Driver—Do.
> John Nicholass—Providence
> Wm. Berry—Road Island
> Abraham Fairman Conneticutt Government
> John Williams—Do.
> Robt: Bougass } Virginia[3]
> Jams: Hamdly }

P.S. some of the above Subscribers, wrote some time ago, but are of Oppinion their letters Misscarryed, as the gave a full Acct. of themselves, & there is no Mention Made of them. We remain with due Respect your's to Comd.

2. In the hand of William Keating, who signed for all the petitioners; his own letter of Oct. 8 established his credentials more fully.

3. Lemon, Harrison and Driver were soon released, according to a subsequent petition of Nov. 15, below. Berry, Fairman and Williams attempt in that petition to answer in greater detail the commissioners' request for information about themselves. Nicholass (Nichols) may also have been released since his name does not appear on the Nov. 15 petition.

OCTOBER 21, 1778

Addressed: Messieurs Franklin, Lee, & Adams / American Ambassadors at Passey / Near Pariss / a paris

Notations in different hands: From Dinant Prisoners[4] Oct. 21. 78

John Langdon to the American Commissioners[5]

ALS: American Philosophical Society

⟨Portsmouth, N.H., October 21, 1778: Since the *Courier de l'Europe*, Captain Raffin, is ready to sail for Europe, I take the liberty of mentioning a matter advantageous to our allies and profitable to me. The British Navy was mostly furnished with masts from this port; lately I have sent to Boston all the masts for d'Estaing's squadron. Please mention to the naval minister or any appropriate person that I will furnish the French navy with masts if someone in France will contract. My commission is 5% for the cargo and disbursements and 5% on the sale of articles sent for payment.[6]⟩

James Moylan to the American Commissioners

ALS: American Philosophical Society

Honorable Gentlemen   L'Orient 21 October 1778
    Captain Thomas Bell[7] in a private Vessel belonging to Philadelphia with Tobacco, is arrived here this moment from said Town, which he left the first, and it's Bay the 10th of September last. He Brings dispatches both for you and for Government which the Commissary will forward for you with his Letters to Versailles. I therefore mention it that you may send for them on receipt. Time will not admit my saying more than

4. "Dinant Prisoners" is in JA's hand.
5. Published in Taylor, *Adams Papers*, VII. For the maritime agent for New Hampshire, see XXIV, 110; XXV, 120.
6. This is one of several unsuccessful attempts to create a French market for American masts; see Paul W. Bamford, *Forests and French Sea Power 1660–1789* (Toronto, 1956), pp. 185–8.
7. For Bell, see Deane's letter to BF of Sept. 15.

that. I remain truly Honorable Gentlemen Your assur'd humble Servant   JAMES MOYLAN

P.S. I must add that Captain McNeill is justly uneasy about his Prisoners, they are yet all on board, and as he intends to sail next week, he must be under the necessity of giving them their liberty in case your orders to receive them, do not appear before his departure, for your government.   J.M.

Addressed: The Honorable Plenepotentiary / Ministers of the United States / of America / at / Passy

Endorsed by John Adams: Mr Moylan. ansd Oct. 27.

Notation: 21. Oct 78

From Barbeu-Dubourg   ALS: American Philosophical Society

Mon cher Maitre   A Paris ce 21e. 8bre. 1778

Le Neveu d'un de mes bons Amis, jeune homme bien né, et bien elevé et qui se destine au commerce est pret à partir pour Charlestown dans la Sud Caroline. Je vous prie avec instance de vouloir lui donner quelque lettre de recommandation pour ce pays-là. Je vous en serai fort obligé. Je comptois avoir l'honneur de vous voir hier au College royal[8] et de vous en parler, mais cela ne me fut pas possible; je compte reparer cela en allant au premier jour a Passy des le matin, d'autant plus que j'ai encore a vous faire souvenir de Messieurs Gregoire et de Maubaillarcq[9] pour des Consulats. Vous reïtererai-je les assurances de mon inviolable et tendre attachement? J'espere, que vous n'en doutez point   DUBOURG

Addressed: To Dr. franklin Passy[1]

Notation: Dubourg Paris 21. 8bre 1778.

8. At the meeting of the Société royale de médecine; see Poissonnier to BF, Oct. 15.

9. The would-be consul in Brest: XXVI, 212–13, where we misread his name. Dubourg had already sent a reminder of Grégoire's candidacy in his letter above, under August.

1. For BF's jottings on this letter, see below, from ――――, of the same day.

From Silas Deane

ALS: American Philosophical Society

During the first half of September Deane was optimistic that congressional approval of his conduct as commissioner would permit his quick return to Europe.[2] Between September 19 and October 15, however, that optimism was undermined. On those two dates Henry Laurens presented to Congress letters he had received from Ralph Izard criticizing the conduct of Franklin and Deane. Meanwhile, on October 3, a similar letter from Arthur Lee was introduced into the congressional record by the committee for foreign affairs.[3] At the same time, Deane's former friend William Carmichael was testifying before Congress that the commissioner, while in Paris, had misappropriated public funds.[4] Deane, upon request, was furnished extracts from the accusatory letters,[5] but his applications to testify in person before Congress were continually frustrated. He was reduced to writing Congress in his own defense; by answering the accusations, he defended Franklin as well.[6] He also composed a highly subjective paraphrase or "translation," as he called it, of Izard's letters, which he here includes. The dispute now beginning would delay Deane's return to Europe for almost two years, provoke an angry debate in the press between him and his opponents, and greatly embitter congressional politics.[7]

2. Deane to BF, Sept. 2 and 15.

3. *JCC*, XII, 935–6, 980, 1011–12. Izard's first letter, of Feb. 16, included copies of correspondence with BF in January (above, XXV, 535–9, 550–1). That letter and the ones of April 1, 11, and June 28 are published in Wharton, *Diplomatic Correspondence*, II, 497–501, 531–3, 547–9, 629–32. The National Archives contains Izard's letter of March 1 and one written by his wife to Laurens on Nov. 24, 1777. For Arthur Lee's, dated June 1, see Wharton, *Diplomatic Correspondence*, II, 600–3. Lee had previously sent accusatory letters to his brother R.H. Lee and to Samuel Adams: above, XXV, 407.

4. Smith, *Letters*, X, 653–4 n, 707–9, 717–20; XI, 27–30. The origin of Carmichael's alienation from Deane is discussed above, XXV, 406–7, 696–7. The two men, however, were allies in the defense of Beaumarchais' right to reimbursement; see Morton, *Beaumarchais Correspondance*, IV, 224–5.

5. *JCC*, XII, 949.

6. On Oct. 12: *Deane Papers*, III, 4–41.

7. *Deane Papers*, II, 480–91; III, *passim;* IV, 1–174; Rakove, *Beginnings of National Politics*, pp. 249–74; H. James Henderson, *Party Politics in the Continental Congress* ([New York, 1974]), pp. 187–206; Edmund S. Morgan, "The Puritan Ethic and the American Revolution," *W&MQ*, 3rd ser., XXIV (1967), 3–43.

Dear Sir   Philadelphia 21st Octo: 1778
The Marquiss De La Fayette tarrying one Day longer than
I expected when I finished my Letter to Docr. Bancroft,[8] I have
spent it in looking over, and examining the Letters and dispatches of Mr. Izard, who I think on the whole, is further gone
than Lee himself, and consequently it cannot be long, before
they must both of them have their Heads Shaved, at least. I
send you inclosed a Translation of Izards Letters, which I have
obtained by the assistance of one of Our Freinds, in Congress;
like other translations it is very short of the Original, especially of those parts of them, seasoned with Epithets too abu-
sive for a modest translator to Venture upon; the sentences
underscored are nearly word for Word after the Original. I
need not add any thing to what I have said in my Letter to
Docr. Bancroft Except that the Congress have permitted these
Letters, tho' evidently wrote only to a private Freind, (or at
least the cheif of them for private information) Not only to be
introduced, and read, but to lye on their Files. Mr. and Mrs.
Bache are well, and their little ones. I dined with them a few
Days since. I have spent so much Time on this Translation,
and Copying of it, that I have no Time to add. It is now
handed about, among the Members, and will I trust have a
good Effect. The Enemy are about making an Expedition of
some Consequence, but to what part is uncertain. I fear they
will not soon evacuate this Continent intirely. Accept my constant Wishes for the continuance of Your health, and use-
fullness and be assured I count it an honor to be numbered
among your Freinds, and to suffer persecution with You for
Righteousness sake;[9] I am my Dear sir Your most sincere
Freind and Very humble Servant   S DEANE

8. Lafayette had been granted leave to return to France: see Paine's letter
of Oct. 24. We have found no record of Deane's letter to Bancroft.
9. Deane wrote as much to Congress in his "Observations on Mr. Arthur Lee's Letter of June 1, 1778," part of his extensive defense of Oct. 12:
"It gives me pleasure to reflect on the honors and respect universally paid
him by all orders of people in France,. . . . for I considered it to be an honor
to be known to be an American and his friend." Deane Papers, III, 37.

P.S. I desire the inclosed may not go out of Your hands, unless to Docr. Bancroft, or to Mr. Adams.

B Franklin Esqr

Mr. Lee has wrote, that Mr. Adams and he are agreed that they cannot live in Paris for Less than Three Thousand pounds Sterling each per Annum, and intimates as if his expences had rather exceeded that Sum.[1]

Endorsed: Mr Deane Oct. 21. 1778. Lee & Izard

A Liberal, and just Translation,[2] of the Letters of R.I. Esqre. To his Excellency H.L. Esqre. Done for the benefit of those Americans, who are ignorant of the Language, in which they were written.

Dear Sir

I write this to You, and desire you to communicate it to my Countrymen in Congress, *who I hope exert themselves in my favor.* If you and they are satisfied that my former Letters have made the impressions I wish, you will then be so good as to lay this before Congress; if on the contrary you think their Minds are not properly prepared you will withold it, as I do not wish it publicly known, 'till it is likely to produce the desired effect. *My situation here is very tormenting;* I have received Two Thousand Louis D'Orrs of the public money as I informed you in my Letter of [*blank in* MS] and have done nothing in my proper department: but my Letters will convince you I have not been idle.

Upon my coming to This place I found the Commissioners at Variance, I wished, to be on the side of Franklin and Deane but the former was too wise to be my dupe, and treated Me with reserve, the latter too haughty to be guided by me and treated

1. Lee to the committee for foreign affairs, June 1: Wharton, *Diplomatic Correspondence,* II, 602.
2. In a very loose sense. The "translation" is, in fact, a composite of individual passages taken out of context and combined in no apparent order. The underlined sections, which do reflect the spirit of Izard's arguments, are in only some cases faithful to the original language. Excerpted and then juxtaposed, Izard's phrases are here presented in a light which deliberately heightens their malevolence.

me with contempt, which you know was too mortifying for me to bear. I had therefore nothing left, but either to cross the Alps or fall in with a Man, *whom from many years acquaintance I knew was not accounted the mildest and best natured in the World.* I chose the latter, and how busily I have been engaged, the present as well as former Letters with the inclosed papers will sufficiently evince. I do not want to be troublesome to my Freinds by solliciting their Interest in my Favor, as it would be much more agreeable, they would take a hint, and without forcing me to a direct Application, procure me a post, and place most suited to my inclination and ambition. Favors unasked confer a higher gratification. I thought I had spoken plain enough before, and sufficiently explained my wishes, when *I told you I was willing to Act as Envoy or Minister Plenipo. for Italy, in which case it would be Necessary to have as many Commissions as there are Courts* that so I might Travel in State from Court to Court and reside where I pleased without being confined to Florence or Leghorn; at the same Time I informed You *that it would be still more agreeable to be appointed for Versailles untill the British Ministry* return to their Senses and by *Acknowledging Our independance give an Opportunity of sending me to the Court of London, which has ever been the heighth of my Ambition.* I could not entertain a doubt of being gratified in one or other of these points, and that my first excuse for not crossing the Alps namely that the Tuscan Minister had informed me "his Master did not wish to see me, though he entertained a good Will for America, untill France took a decided part in our favor as by the conduct of France he meant to regulate his Own." That this Excuse I say would have served my Turn, untill I should receive Your Answer. Unfortunately France has come to a Determination, has signed a Treaty with Us, acknowledged Our independance and sent a Fleet to Assist and a Minister to reside in America, and still I am here without having received a Line from you or the Commttee. for foreign Affairs, or from Congress, and with only a simple Commission for the Court of Tuscany. For this Reason I intimated my pleasure to you that you should oppose the ratification of the Treaties, and set matters again afloat, assigning the best Reasons I was then able to devise, interspersing with a Liberal hand as much

587

personal Abuse on Franklin and Deane who had in spite of my endeavors brought this matter to so speedy an issue, as I thought was sufficient at least to convince You how much they Thwarted my Views, and how much I hated them, and therefore that they ought to be removed with disgrace, and infamy, and untill I could know the Effect of this I cast about for another reason for my not leaving this place. Luckily the Broils in Germany furnished a very ostensible one. I got the Tuscan Minister to say that *his Master wished me not to appear at his Court untill he knew what part the Court of Vienna would take, as by the Conduct of that Court with which he is so intimately connected he must regulate his own.* Before that is done I hope for Your Answer, and that Congress will gratify me so far as to disgrace Deane, and remove Franklin to make room for me at Versailles, when I assure them that they have acted very foolishly in the Appointment of Mr. Deane *who is every way unqualified for the Trust reposed in him.* It may be said Congress knew him well before they trusted him, he having been for some considerable Time a Member of that Body; *but I say search the whole World through and a more unfit person could not be found,* And as I hope they will allow Me to be a better judge of Men, Manners and Abilities, I say again *he is totally unqualified for the post he has filled, and not to be trusted in future.* This I hope is sufficient. But if not I do assert nay I [can?] prove that he is a *New England Man*; and though he has sent you supplies of Arms, Ammunition, and Cloathing, fitted out Vessels &c. without deigning to consult my worthy Friend A. Lee Esqr. Nay I may say has almost without him brought about the Treaty and has procured a Fleet and Minister to be sent you without the knowledge of A. Lee Esqr. or my self, yet I affirm, nay I will swear if You require it, *that he has such a hauteur about him that no body can do business with him.* And as to Franklin he is a crafty old knave, he would not let me have a Copy of the Treaty after it was signed though he knew how Anxious I was to have it, and how much advantage I could have made of it. *In my Conscience I beleive he has neither honor nor honesty; he has Abilities it is true but so much the worse, when these are not under the restraint of Virtue and Integrity,* And *I declare before God he is under the restraint of neither.* And if Congress still doubt it I can get Doctr. [*blank*] so celebrated in*³ the *quinzaine D'Anglais* who is as honest an Irishman as ever attended a Court with a Straw in his Shoe And Monsr. [*blank*] my two intimate Freinds together with Thornton and twenty such like to confirm it by their Oaths also. But it will be said perhaps, he has during a long Life of upwards of Seventy Years supported a good Character, and that his reputation is established, and high throughout Europe. I deny the Fact, did not Mr. Wedderbourne abuse him? But if it were even so does not that even prove what Fools they are, to think well of a Man who has treated me with Contempt? who refused to consult me on the Treaties or to let me have a Copy of Them after they were finished and when I called upon him to explain his conduct and wrote to him again, again and again, and sent my Secretary John Julius Pringle to catechise him in person at last sent Me word "*have patience and I will pay thee all.*" But I have sent him a Roland for his Oliver. I have shewn him that he did not understand the Text, and desired him to read over the whole Chapter.

However if after all I have said *Congress cannot be induced to dismiss him wholly, there can be no Objection to his being sent to Vienna*, he will do well enough there notwithstanding what I have said of him, but he is not to be trusted at Versailles, which is the place I have fixed on for myself; and You may tell Congress so.

I am my Dear Sir &c. &c.

Endorsed: Mr Deane's Version of Mr Izard's Letters

3. *Footnote in* MS: "*The reader is referr'd to a peice intitled *quinzaine D'Anglais*, or the Englishman's fifteen Days at Paris, in which a certain Irish Doctor acts a Capital part. He is a known and real Character, and often seen with Mr R.I., especially about the Time the Treaty was executed." The piece, published under the pseudonym of Dr. Stearne, was Jean-Jacques Rutlidge, *La Quinzaine anglaise à Paris, ou l'Art de s'y ruiner en peu de temps* (London, 1776).

From ―――[4]   AL: American Philosophical Society

ce 21 8bre. 1778

Monsieur franklin est suplié de vouloir bien se rappeller l'Engagement pris avec Madame helvetius de diner aujour-dhuy mercredy a auteüil chez M. hebere ou il sera toujours desiré avec la meme ardeur.[5]

Addressed: A Monsieur / Monsieur franklin / a Passy

To the Abbé Martin Lefebvre de La Roche[6]

AL: Bibliothèque Nationale; copy: Duke University Library

[October 21, 1778][7]

M. Franklin n'oublie jamais aucune Partie ou Me. Helvetius doit être. Il croit même, que s'il etoit engagé d'aller à Paradis ce matin, il ferai Supplication d'être permis de rester sur terre jusqu'à une heure et demi, pour reçevoir l'Embrassade qu'elle a bien voulu lui promettre en le rencontrant chez M. Turgot.

Addressed: A Monsr. / Monsieur l'Abbé de la Roche / Auteuil

4. In an unknown hand.

5. BF started to draft an answer on the address sheet of Dubourg's letter of the same day: "M.F. ne manquera pas de se rendre aujourdhuy chez M. Hebere, ou."

6. One of the habitués of Madame Helvétius' circle, about whom JA remarked, "These Ecclesiasticks . . . have as much power to Pardon a Sin as they have to commit one, or to assist in committing one": Butterfield, *John Adams Diary*, IV, 58–9. Born in 1738, de La Roche had been chaplain and librarian to the Duc de Deux-Ponts. By 1778 he lived in a pavilion on the grounds at Auteuil, along with Cabanis and—occasionally—the abbé Morellet. They all became close friends of BF.

7. We presume this is in answer to the reminder BF had received earlier in the day about the dinner at Hébert's.

From Samuel W. Stockton

ALS: American Philosophical Society

Sir.   Frankfurt on the Maine Octr. 21st. 1778.

From your kind permission given when I had the honor of seeing you last, I take the liberty of requesting your care of a letter for me, which my worthy friend Mr. Dumas of the Hague writes me, came to his address, and which he enclosed to the Plenipotentiaries &c. at Passy, a day or two before I left Paris, supposing it would find me there.[8] I shall be much indebted for your enquiry respecting it, and when received for your trouble in forwarding it under cover to Mesrs. Frederick Gontard & Fils Banquiers a Frankfort sur le Maine.

Mr. Dumas also writes, that, by a ship arrived at Bourdeaux, it is said, Rhodes-island is taken and the B. troops there are made prisoners; I pray God you may speedily receive an authentic confirmation of this important news.

Private letters from Paris received by a banker in this city also say that The Court of Spain had resolved on taking an immediate and open part in favor of Am——a, you best know if there is any foundation for it.

In the English papers of the 6th, 8th and instant, which perhaps you have not yet seen, there are ministerial paragraphs declaring the great discontent that prevail in France on account of the late captures,[9] against Monsieur Sar——e and yourself, who, they say, are looked upon as the chief causes of the war, and they give out that you were obliged to take refuge at Ver[saille]s to avoid the resentment of the mob. Your popularity in F—— is too well known to suffer such fabrications to meet with the least credit, or to give uneasiness to any of your friends. I have the honor to be, with the higest respect and esteem Sir Your most obliged and most obedient Servant

SAML. W. STOCKTON.

8. Most probably the letter enclosed in Dumas' of Oct. 2.

9. The captures of merchant ships returning without convoy from the West Indies for which Sartine was blamed: see Bondfield's letters of Aug. 29 and Oct. 13. For a sample of the news items Stockton is recounting see *The Public Advertiser* of Oct. 6.

OCTOBER 21, 1778

Addressed: The Honorable / Benjamin Franklin Esqr. / Minister Plenipotentiary / for the United States of America / a Passy / pres Paris. / au soin du Monsr. Bethman[1]

Endorsed: Mr Stockton

Notation: Oct. 21. 1778.

From George Swaller   ALS: American Philosophical Society

Sir   Denan Octor 21st, 1778

This is to inform I am and American Born in Baltimore and served my time to the say to Mr. Isaac Vanbevres Justice of Peace living upon falspoint.[2] And I was taken in a Brig called the rizing States taken by the Terrible a Ship of 74 Guns belonging to the Englinsh and was sent to the Aspital being unwel from whench I made my Escape and was taken by the press Gang and sent on Board the fox where I remained untill I was taken By the Junon Frigate belonging to the French. And I take this opertunity of writing to you to let you know I want to serve my native Country as I have a Wife in Philadelphia living in Shippen Street she is the Daughter to Joseph Hunter and I was in Mr. Colwels employment during the time I lived in Philadelphia. I would have sent my Name along with the rest of the Men only I was in another Castle from them and did not know untill after they had sent it. So I take this opertunity of writing to your Honour in hopes it would an-

1. His employer William Lee's banker: xxvi, 264 n. For further details about the Bethmann brothers see Behrends' letter of Oct. 28.
2. Swaller himself has left no traces, but the names he mentions might have been known to BF. "Vanbevres" was probably a member of the Van Bebber family, who were among the first settlers of Germantown. Early in the 18th century Isaac and Matthias Van Bebber, gentlemen of means, moved to Maryland where the latter became a justice of the peace: *PMHB*, IV, 39–41. Joseph Hunter might have been the resident of Carlisle, Pa., whose cousin James lived in Philadelphia; BF had dealt with a James Hunter in 1757 and again in 1775, as trustee for Hunter's children: *PMHB*, xxviii, 108–9; above, VII, 99 and xx, 44–5. "Mr. Colwels" was most likely one of the many Philadelphia Caldwells.

592

swer as well. So I hope your Honour will send me home to my Country once more and no more at present from your Humble servant   GEORGE SWALLER

Addressed: Mr Franklen Agent for / the United States of America / in / Paris

Endorsed: Geo Swaller Prisoner, Dinan Octobre 27. 1778.

From Vergennes
Two copies: Library of Congress

A Versailles le 21. 8bre. 1778.

J'ai reçu, Monsieur, la lettre que vous m'avez fait l'honneur de m'écrire hier. Je connois assez les dispositions presentes de la Hollande pour croire que votre presence n'y avanceroit pas plus vos affaires que le fait l'ami secret avec lequel vous êtes en Correspondance. Vous avez sans doute beaucoup de Partisans dans cette republique qui font des voeux pour le succes des Etats unis de l'amerique, mais il faut le Concours des differentes provinces pour former une resolution, et je ne crois pas que leur reunion fut possible pour conclure le traité reciproque qu'on veut bien ébaucher, mais qu'on ne vous dissimule pas qu'on ne signera que lorsque les Etats Unis auront obtenus de l'Angleterre la Reconnoissance de leur Independance. J'ai l'honneur d'etre avec un sincere attachement, Monsieur, votre tres humble et très obeissant serviteur

(signé) DE VERGENNES

M. Franklin

From Jérémie Witel[3]   ALS: American Philosophical Society

This letter provides the only contemporary evidence of an incident which would come back to haunt Franklin in 1782 and 1783: his subscription to, and subsequent reluctance to pay for, a pirated Swiss edition of the *Encyclopédie*. On February 11, he had received a visit from Jean-Pierre Duplan, co-director of the Société Typographique de Lausanne, whose firm was embroiled in a bitter and complex publishing war with rivals in France and Switzerland.[4] What Duplan offered was a new edition of the *Encyclopédie* in octavo, 36 vols. of text and 3 of plates, less expensive than the quarto and folio editions available in Paris. Franklin, apparently delighted with the idea, agreed in conversation to a subscription, and may have even promised to help publicize the volumes. What Duplan had no doubt neglected to tell the Doctor was that importation of his unauthorized edition into France was illegal.

Whether or not Franklin ever learned of his unwitting indiscretion is unclear;[5] all we do know is that by November, 1782, the Society had sent him the first ten volumes of text but had not received a penny. The total price of the subscription was £225 payable to Ferdinand Grand, as they reminded him again on August 30, 1783.[6] There the one-sided correspondence ends, with the Society's final plea for help in marketing the remainders in America falling on unresponsive ears.

Monsieur   Paris le 21e. 8bre 1778
    Connoissant votre gout pour les Lettres et les rélations que vous avés avec la Societé Typographique de Lausanne, j'ose prendre la liberté de m'annoncer auprès de vous comme un de

3. Son-in-law and business associate of Samuel Fauche, *imprimeur du roi* in Neuchâtel, who had formerly been a partner in the Société Typographique de Neuchâtel but was now working for the rival publishing consortium of Lausanne-Berne.
4. Duplan to BF, Nov. 10, 1782. APS. Duplan's full name was kindly supplied by Prof. Robert Darnton of Princeton University. For a detailed account of the publishing wars see his *The Business of Enlightenment: a Publishing History of the Encyclopédie 1775–1800* (Cambridge, Mass. and London, 1979).
5. He did, however, pay 852 *l.t.* for what was probably a folio edition, at some point before March, 1778: see XXVI, 235 and its note referring to Deane's accounts of that date.
6. See Duplan's letters to BF, Nov. 10, 1782 and Aug. 30, 1783 (APS).

594

ses associés. Je désirerois en conséquence avoir l'honneur de vous entretenir sur quelques sujets rélatifs à ce commerce.[7] Etranger à Paris j'ignore absolument ce qu'il faut faire, pour avoir accès chez une Personne chargée d'un Ministère aussi important que le votre. Mais sur la seule réputation de votre caractére, j'ai cru qu'une lettre simple (accompagnée de l'incluse de la part de Monsieur de Haller)[8] pourroit ne vous pas déplaire, et me procurer l'honneur de savoir directement votre heure la plus commode. J'ay l'honneur d'ête avec le plus profond respect Monsieur Votre tres humble et tres obeissant serviteur   J WITEL pour S. FAUCHE[9]

Hotel de thou Rue des Poitevins, maison Pancouke.

7. Witel had been selling octavo subscriptions in the French provinces, and had gone to Paris in mid-September. Constantin Lair to the Société Typographique de Neuchâtel, Nov. 11, 1778 (STN archives, MS 1172), communicated by R. Darnton.

8. The enclosure was a letter dated Oct. 19 from Girardot, Haller & Cie. to BF recommending the bearer, "Mr. Foache, bookseller of Naifchatel." BF endorsed the letter, "Girardot & Haller recommending Witel or Foache." APS.

9. This letter evidently produced an interview. In 1784 Witel engaged BF in a correspondence, recalling their conversation in Paris, about the feasibility of his establishing a French publishing and bookselling house in America along with his two brothers-in-law. The Doctor's answer was kind but scarcely encouraging: there were not enough French readers in America to support three families in trade. Witel stayed in Switzerland, therefore; one of the Fauche sons went on to America and the other, later known as Louis Fauche-Borel, became one of the most celebrated secret agents under Louis XVIII. For Samuel Fauche see the *Dictionnaire Historique de la Suisse*. See also Witel and Fauche to BF, Oct. 24, 1784, and BF's reply of Nov. 15 (APS); and Louis Fauche-Borel, *Mémoires de Fauche-Borel* (4 vols., Paris, 1829), I, 24, 34.

The Continental Congress to Louis XVI: Letter of Credence for Franklin as Minister Plenipotentiary to France[1]

L (draft):[2] National Archives; LS:[3] American Philosophical Society, Historical Society of Pennsylvania; copies: Archives du Ministère des Affaires Etrangères, National Archives, South Carolina Historical Society

[October 21, 1778][4]

Great faithful and well[5] beloved Friend and Ally

The Principles of Equality and Reciprocity on which you have entered into Treaties with us, give you an additional security for that good Faith with which we shall observe them from Motives of Honor and of Affection to Your Majesty. The distinguished Part you have taken in the support of the[6] Liberties and Independence of these States cannot but inspire them with the most ardent Wishes for the Interest and the Glory of France. We have nominated Benjamin Franklin Esqr. to reside at your Court in Quality of our Minister Plenipoten-

---

1. Upon BF's election as minister plenipotentiary (see Deane to BF, Sept. 15) Congress appointed a committee to prepare this letter of credence and to draft instructions for him. The original committee members were Gouverneur Morris, Samuel Chase, William Henry Drayton, Samuel Adams and Richard Henry Lee; John Witherspoon was added on Oct. 13 and William Duer on Oct. 24. This document was brought before Congress on Oct. 21 and promptly adopted: *JCC*, XII, 908, 1005, 1035–6, 1061.

2. In Morris' hand. Above it is written "Your Committee to whom it was referred to prepare a Letter of Credence to his most Christian Majesty notifying the Appointt. of Benjamin Franklin Esqr. to be the Minister Plenipotentiary of these States at the Court of France and also the Draft of Instructions to the said Minister &ca. Report." Following it are drafts of BF's instructions, the plan of an attack upon Quebec and the observations on the finances of the United States, all printed below, under Oct. 26.

3. Signed by Henry Laurens as president of Congress and providing the date. It is divided into paragraphs and bears slight differences in capitalization as well as the change noted in the next two footnotes: *JCC*, XII, 1035–6.

4. Each LS bears this date, as does the National Archives copy.

5. The word "well" does not appear in the LS or in either copy.

6. Substituted after "taken" for "to support the," which has been lined out.

tiary that he may give you more particular Assurances of the grateful Sentiments which you have excited in us and in each of the united States. We beseech you to give entire Credit to[7] every Thing which he shall deliver on our Part especially when he shall assure you of the Permanency of our Friendship. And we pray God that he will keep your Majesty our Great faithful and beloved Friend and Ally in his most holy Protection. Done at Philadelphia the [*blank in MS*] Day of [*blank in MS*] 1778. By the Congress of the united States of North America your good Friends and Allies.

H.L. President

CHA THOMSON Secy

To Our Great Faithful & Beloved Friend & Ally Louis the sixteenth King of France & Navarre

The American Commissioners to Ralph Izard

AL (draft): Massachusetts Historical Society; two copies: National Archives

Sir   Passi Oct. 22. 1778

We have just now the Honour of a Lettre from M. De Sartine dated the 19, which We suppose is his Excellencys Ultimatum concerning your Effects taken in the Nile, and We therefore take the earliest opportunity to inclose you a Copy of it that you may be able to take your Measures in Consequence of it, in which We suppose there is no Time to be lost. We have the Honour to be with great Respect, Sir your most humble and obedient Servants.[8]

The Hon. Ralph Izzard Esq.

---

7. Substituted after "beseech you to" for "place [?] entire Confidence in," which has been lined out.

8. Izard on the following day thanked the commissioners for their trouble, even though it had "proved ineffectual." APS. We do not know the outcome of the episode.

The American Commissioners to Matthew Ridley

AL (draft): Massachusetts Historical Society; two copies: National Archives

Sir   Passy Octr. 22. 1778

We have received your Letter dated Paris September 29 1778, with the valuable Present to the united States of America, of a Manuscript Book of the Commissioners of the English Navy, containing a Description of the Dimensions, Guns, Men &c. of most Ships, in Commission at the Time when it was written. We thank you, Sir for this Instance of your Attention and good Will to our Country, and for the respectfull Expressions of your Wishes for her Prosperity. We shall transmit to Congress an Account of this Benefaction, and shall send the Book itself by the first safe opportunity. And We wish that you and your Posterity may enjoy the Benefit of this Repertory of naval Knowledge, in the Security of your and their Rights and Interests of every Kind. We are, Sir, with much Respect, your most obedient humble Servants.

Mr Mathew Ridley at Nantes.

To Vergennes[9]   ALS: Archives du Ministère des affaires étrangères

Sir   Passy, Oct. 22. 1778

I am perfectly of the same Sentiments with your Excellency respecting Count d'Estaign. I know his Zeal for the Cause, and have a high Opinion of his Abilities.[1] I have therefore not the least doubt but that his going to Boston was a Measure absolutely necessary, and will appear to be for the common Good. We just now learn that our Troops on Rhodeisland had made good their Retreat without the Loss of a Man.[2] I have

---

9. In answer to Vergennes' of the 19th.

1. BF appears to have known d'Estaing for more than a year; the admiral had contacted him soon after his arrival in Paris: XXIII, 67.

2. See Deane to BF, Sept. 2, for the successful retreat.

the honour to be with great Respect, Your Excellency's most obedient and most humble Servant   B FRANKLIN

His Excellency the Count de Vergennes.[3]

From Richard Bache   ALS: American Philosophical Society

Dear and Honored Sir   Philadelphia October 22. 1778

My last to you was dated in July, which I sent via Boston, and Copy via Maryland. I have not had the pleasure of a Line from you since, except the introductory Letter you honored me with, by the hands of Mr. Gerard,[4] which he sent into the Country to me, where I remain'd with my family 'till about a Month ago, when we moved bag and baggage into Town, with the pleasing hope, that we should not again be obliged to quit it. In my last I mentioned my fears, that Captain Frederick de Wernecke, whom you commissioned me to inquire after, had perished; but I have lately learned, and have the pleasure to assure you and his Relations, that not long ago he was alive and well, at Williamsburg in Virginia, in which State he holds a Commission, and has resided for some time past.[5] Mr. Lutterloh's answer to the Count de Wittgenstein's demand is, (as I mentioned in my last) that he had remitted the money to his Wife in England, with directions to her to pay it, but he thought the Count's demand had not been so much. I have not had time to inquire into the Duchess de Melforts Business in the Jerseys, I hope soon to have an opportunity of doing it. I wish I could hear from you respecting the Types I have so often wrote to you about, telling you that I had sold them to the State of Virginia, and that it is left to you to fix the price, as I knew nothing of their cost or value. The Six cases of

3. A file clerk has noted that BF enclosed extracts of American news of July 30, Aug. 13 and 20, Oct. 7 and 13. Presumably Emery's news of Oct. 7 about the Rhode Island retreat, acknowledged by Vergennes on the 19th, had been sent in another form.

4. RB's letter is above, July 14; for BF's, see XXVI, 202–3.

5. For Warnecke, Lutterloh's debt to Wittgenstein, and the duchesse de Melfort's lands, see RB's letter of July 14.

OCTOBER 22, 1778

Types made use of for the printing the continental Money Congress have taken, and I am much at a loss what to charge them for them. I should be glad therefore to hear from you on this subject, and you will be pleased when you are fixing the prices of these articles, to attend to the depreciation of our money, which I am sorry to observe is as Six to one. Where this evil will stop, unless the Enemy leave the Continent soon, I know not. I congratulate you upon your being appointed Minister Plenepotentiary to the Court of France, this must give great pleasure to your *Friends* Messrs. Izard, Lees &ca. who, I hear, are very profuse in their abuse of you, and are taking and persuing every method to injure you on this side the water; their efforts I trust will prove inefficacious. I am informed they lay some stress upon your employing as a private Secretary your Grandson, whom they hold out as unfit to be trusted because of his fathers principles;[6] this has been hinted to me; but whether this be so or not, sure I am, that this was an argument made use of by your friend Mr. Roberdeau, upon the votes being called for on your late appointment, and he had influence enough to carry the vote against you for this state, and it seems pretty remarkable that this State was the only one that voted against you on this question.[7] Mr. Roberdeau also urged the same reasons against the

6. BF must have been greatly wounded by this remark for he answered on June 2, 1779 in uncharacteristically emotional language. Praising WTF's industry, integrity, and business acumen, he took credit for fixing the young man in "honest republican Whig principles." Affording a rare glimpse into his private feelings, BF spoke of the pleasure he felt in his grandson's companionship and of the comfort he derived from the thought of having, if need be, "a child to close my eyes and take care of my remains": Smyth, *Writings*, VII, 345.

7. BF's election is discussed in Deane's letter of Sept. 15. From the present letter we learn that Robert Morris voted for him, Daniel Roberdeau against him. The swing vote must have come from the only other Pennsylvania delegate in attendance that day, William Clingan, for whom see *Biographical Directory of the American Congress, 1774–1961* ([Washington], 1961). Neither the debate nor the vote was recorded but see *JCC*, XII, 911 and Burnett, *Letters*, III, lviii–lix for the delegates in attendance. The vote is consistent with the prevailing divisions within the delegation: H. James Henderson, *Party Politics in the Continental Congress* ([New York, 1974]), p. 166.

exchange of Governor Franklin, *"he had a son living with you, and much evil might ensue to the United States."* I must acquit your friend Mr. Morris from the imputation of suffering any such weak reasons to influence his mind, but there was a majority in the State against him. Governor Franklin however is exchanged, and I expect is gone, or will shortly go for England.[8] Inclosed you have the first Bills of four sets of Exchange for 486 Dollars, being a years Interest on 8100 Dollars in the Loan office, from the 10th. Septr. 1777 to 10 Septr. 1778.[9] The Interest accruing antecedent to that date I received in Continental money, and have passed to your Credit, this mode is persued in paying off Interest to every body else.

Since writing the above I have had an opportunity of conversing with Mr. Deane, who has shewn me what he calls a *translation* of Izards and Lee's Letters, which he purposes sending to you;[1] I shall endeavor to see the originals, and if possible get copies of them to send to you by some other opportunity. Mr. Deane has convinced me that the Junto here lay *great* stress, in their operations against you, on Temple's being so near you, and that they have had some thoughts of bringing in a motion to have him removed at a distance from you; this is perhaps too delicate a point for *me* to touch upon, but I trust you know me well enough to view it in the light I mean it, and to believe that my mentioning it to you is the result of a tender and virtuous principle. Sally writes by this conveyance to you and dear Ben, she will give you an account of the situation of the family, I was pretty full on this subject the last time I wrote. This I hope will be handed you by the Marquis De Fayette, who returns to his own Country crowned with Laurels; the reputation he has established in this Country as a Soldier and a Gentleman, will I trust render him ten times

8. Governor Franklin had been exchanged for John McKinley, former president of Delaware, and was preparing to leave for New York: *JCC*, XII, 911–12; William H. Mariboe, "The Life of William Franklin . . . " (Ph.D. diss., University of Pa., 1962), p. 484.

9. The money that BF, on departing for France, had left with RB to invest: XXIII, 280–1 n. At a rate of 5:1, $486 would be equivalent to £2430, perhaps an explanation for the final notation, below.

1. He did, on Oct. 21.

dearer to his friends and connections in his own. I have not had the honor of being much acquainted with him, but this I know for certain, that his charactor stands high among us. My Love to Temple and Ben. Accept yourself my dutifull Regards, and believe me to be Dear Sir, Your ever affectionate Son

RICH. BACHE

P.S. In one of your Letters recd. some time ago, you hinted at some commercial advantages that might be thrown in my way, but have never since touched upon the subject.[2] All I can say is, that I should be very glad to embrace any offers of that kind, for my Salary as P.M. General will scarcely afford me Salt to my Porridge.

Dr. Benjn. Franklin

Notations in different hands: Rich. Bache phyladelphia 22m. 8bre. 1778. / Bache Rich. 22, 8bre. 1778. Bills of setts for 286

486
  5
2430

From Sarah Bache

ALS: American Philosophical Society

Dear and Honoured Sir   Philadelphia, October. 22d. 1778

This is the first opportunity I have had since my return home of writing to you. We found the House and Furniture in much better order than we could expect, which was owing to the care the Miss Cliftons took of all we left behind.[3] My being removed four days after my little Girl was born[4] made it impossible for me to remove half the things we did in our former flight. I have much to tell you but my little Girl has the small Pox just coming out and a good deal restless tho in a fine way, she takes up most of my time as I have none but a very young Girl to attend her. She is a fine Brown lass, but her sparkling

2. We have no record of such hints. Bache was Postmaster General.
3. Anna Maria Clifton and her sisters, old friends of the Franklins: see XVI, 262 n; XXIII, 425–6; XXVI, 488.
4. Elizabeth or Eliza Franklin Bache was born Sept. 10, 1777: I, lxiv.

black eyes make up for her skin, and when in health she has a good colour. I would give a good deal you could see her, you cant think how fond of kissing she is, and gives such old fashioned smacks. General Arnold says he would give a good deal to have her for a school Misstress to teach the young Ladies how to kiss.

M. Gerard[5] has been several times to see us, and has dined with us. We like him very much. He promises to be very friendly and come often. He brought me one of your Clay pictures, the one you sent me,[6] since I recev'd the other I gave to Mr. Hopkinson[7] who admired it very much and loves you. He is going to frame and Glaze it. I promised him when in Manheim to send to you for one. We have not long been return'd home. I chose to stay in the Country on the Childrens account till the summer was over, and if it had suited Mr. Baches business it would have been better to have stay'd there altogether. Their is hardly such a thing as living in town every thing is so high the money is old tenner to all intents and purposes. If I was to mention the prices of the Common necessaries of life it would astonish you. I have been all amaizment since my return such an odds has two years made, that I can scarcely beleive I am in Philadelphia. This time twelve month when I was in town I never went out nor bought any thing leaving it till I got up again, expecting we should stay, so that we ran away quit unprovided. I had two peices of linnen at the weavers it has been there these eighteen months, and if it had not been for my Friends must have suffered as it could not be bought were we were. I should tell you that I had seven table Cloths of my own spinning cheifly wove before we left Chester county. It was what we were spinning when you went. I find them very usefull and they look very well, but they now ask four times as much for weaving as they used to ask for the linnen, and Flax not to be got without hard money. I am going to write to Cousin Jonathan Williams to

5. The French minister, Conrad Alexandre Gérard.
6. One of the Nini medallions, acknowledged by her husband in January: xxv, 553–4.
7. Francis Hopkinson also wrote BF on this date, below.

purchaise me linnen for Common Sheets and many other articles. The Children as well as myself want linnens and common cloaths. Buying them here is out of the Question. They realy ask me six dollars for a pair of Gloves, and I have been obliged to pay fifteen pound fifteen shillings for a common Gallomanco[8] peticoat without quilting, that I once could have got for fifteen shillings. I buy nothing but what I realy want, and wore out my silk ones before I got this, I do not mention these things by way of complaint, I have much less reason to complain than most folks I know, besides I find I can go without many things I once thought absolutely necessary. I shall write to Temple by this opportunity. Mr. Bache who sincerely loves him and wishes him every kind of happiness, has been a good deal distress'd wether or know he should mention to you what he has about him, as it was a delicate Subject, but he as well as your other Friends thought it best you should know what is doing on this side the water, what wicked things pride and ambition make people do. But I hope these envious men will be disapointed in every scheme of theirs to lesen your Character, or to seperate you from those you love, your knowing their intentions in time may be a means of disapointing them in their plan. I have wrote to dear little Ben it makes me happy to hear he behaves so well. Mr. Deane gives him a very good character. Willy is a fine fellow and is just gone to a new school. Smith[9] acted such a part last winter, besides the Trustees are almost all Tories, that his Papa is not willing he should go to the Academy. He went to a German School at Manheim their being no other, and Mr. Morris bringing his

8. Calamanco, a woollen stuff originally made in Flanders and woven so that one side is plain, the other checkered.

9. William Smith (1727–1803) was provost of the College, Academy, and Charitable School of Philadelphia, as the University of Pennsylvania was then known. At the end of August, 1777, when Howe was advancing against Philadelphia, he and forty other prominent citizens suspected of toryism were arrested by order of the Continental Congress. Smith was paroled, after promising to appear on demand, but was not discharged until June 30, 1778, after the British evacuation. Thomas F. Jones, *A Pair of Lawn Sleeves: a Biography of William Smith* ... (Philadelphia, New York, London, [1972]), pp. 117–18, 124.

Family to town two months before us, left Will none but Dutch Boys to play with so that he learnt to speak their Language very fluently but I am afraid he will loss it here. As soon as my little Betsy gets well I will sit down and give you a little History of every thing about the house. The Chest of papers you left with Mr. Galloway Mr. B. went up about. Bob brought them to town.[1] The lid was broke open and some few taken off the top, Mr. B collected those about the flour [floor] had it naild up and they are all safe here. Mr. Galloway took not the least care of them, and used you as he did every body else very ill. Honest Pritchard[2] has made a little fortune and gone home to Wales. He talks of returning. He came to Manheim last Winter and paid me the whole of his account.

Their is many has desired to be remembered to you that its impossible to name them all, but Willy's duty with Bety's and mine I must beg you to accept being as ever Your Dutiful Daughter   S Bache

Dr. Franklin

Notations: Bache 22 Oct. 1778 / Bache Phyladelphie 22 8bre. 1778.

From Francis Hopkinson[3]

ALS: American Philosophical Society

My dear Friend.   Philada. 22d. Octr. 1778.

Had I consulted my own Inclinations more than your Ease, you should have frequently heard from me since you left us; but knowing your Correspondence to be extensive and your Engagements important, I have avoided offering myself to your Notice lest I should intrude on more weighty Concerns. I would not, however, carry this Delicacy so far as to run the

1. RB had promised to examine BF's papers in his letter above, July 14. Bob was the black slave whom BF, in his will, directed Bache to free "immediately" upon his death: Smyth, *Writings*, X, 495.
2. William Prichard had applied for help to BF when he first arrived in Philadelphia, in 1776. See XXII, 472–3.
3. This is his first private letter, as far as we know, since April 23, 1770.

Hazard of being entirely forgot by one who was my Father's Friend to the last,[4] and whom I am very proud to call mine. A Continuance of your Regard will be a real Gratification to me and flatter my Vanity, as I can truly say I both love and honour you. I have suffered much by the Invasion of the Goths and Vandals. I was obliged to fly from my House at Borden Town with my Family and leave all my Effects in *Statu quo*; the Savages plundered me to their Heart's Content, but I do not repine, as I do really esteem it an honour to have suffered in my Country's Cause and in Support of the Rights of human Nature, and of civil Society. I have not Abilities to assist our rightious Cause by personal Prowess and Force of Arms, but I have done it all the service I could with my Pen, throwing in my Mite at Times in Prose and Verse, serious and satirical Essays &ca.[5] The Congress have been pleased to appoint me Treasurer of Loans, for the United States with a Salary of 2000 Dollars.[6] Could our Money recover it's former Value, I should think this a handsome Appointment—as it is, it is a Subsistance.

Mrs. Bache has been so good as to lend me your portable Electrical Apparatus, which I have got in excellent Order, and shall take great Care of; it is a great Amusement to me, and I hope you will not be offended with her and me for this Liberty. I wish to borrow also your little Air Pump, which is at present much out of Order, but I will clean it and put it to Rights if she will let me have it. Whatever she lends me shall be punctually restored on Demand, in good Repair. N.B. Your Gim-cracks have suffered much by the late Usurpers of our City.[7] But I will not detain you longer with my uninteresting

4. For Thomas Hopkinson, who died in 1751, see I, 209 n.

5. At least one book had been taken from Hopkinson's library in Bordentown during the occupation by Donop's troops in December, 1776. In the raid of May, 1778, when many houses were burned to the ground, Hopkinson's was allowed to be saved. George E. Hastings, *The Life and Works of Francis Hopkinson* (Chicago, [1926]), pp. 229–33. For a discussion of Hopkinson's writings see *ibid.*, 281 ff.

6. His letter of Sept. 18 is written in that capacity.

7. "Gim-cracks": mechanical devices. On June 4, 1779, BF replied: "I am glad that the Enemy have left something of my Gimcrackery that is capable

Chat. Sincerely wishing you a long Continuance of Health and Ease, and all the solid Comforts which a *good Man* enjoys in the decline of Life, I am, dear Sir, Your ever affectionate and unfeigned Friend FRAS HOPKINSON

Dr. Franklin

Notation: fras hopkinson. Phyladelphie 22. aout[*sic*] 1778.

From Louis-Félix Guynement de Kéralio-Luxembourg[8]

ALS: American Philosophical Society

Jeudi 22. 8bre 1778

J'ay l'honneur d'assurer Monsieur franklin de Mon Respect Très humble, et de le prier de vouloir bien me faire part des Nouvelles qu'on m'a dit qu'il a Reçues d'Amerique, afin que Je les fasse passer a Madame La Comtesse Douairiere de Deux Ponts et au Chevr. de Keralio mon frere.

Monsieur franklin peut m'envoyer ces Nouvelles en Anglois ou en françois, selon qu'il lui sera plus commode.

DE KERALIO

Addressed: A Monsieur / Monsieur franklin chez M. de Chaumont / A Passy

Notation: De Keralio Paris 22e 8bre. 1778

---

of affording you Pleasure. You are therefore very welcome to the Use of my Electrical and Pneumatic Machines as long as you think proper." APS.

8. The brother of the chevalier; see Kéralio's letter, Sept. 10.

Richard Grinnell to the American Commissioners

ALS: American Philosophical Society

on Board the General Mifflen[9] Oct. the. 23d 1778
It is with Pleasure that I Can Inform your honnours that this
Day a Rived heare the Brigg Interprise Capt. Paul Peas[1] from
London Bound to the Braizels. She was Taken by Belpoole
french frigate of thirty two Guns.[2] I have the pleasure of In-
formeing your honnours that Capt. Francis Macy in the Ship
Pitt from London was Taken the Same time by the Venger
french man of war of 64 Guns[3] and one other of the whalemen
at Same time name not Known. The Ship Pitt is the Ship I
Came from Rhodisland in. I have been on Board the Prise.
The Poast is Just going. Excuse hast. Capt. Mackneile will not
Sail Soon. I am your honnours obedent. Servant

RICHD. GRINNELL

Addressed: To / The / Honourable / Beniaman Franklen / Arthur
Lee and Adams / att Passy Near Parris

Notation: Capt. Grinnell Oct. 23. 78.

---

9. Daniel McNeill had clearly acted on JA's recommendation to find a
place for Grinnell on the *General Mifflin*: see the annotation to Grinnell's
letter of Sept. 15.
1. A Nantucket whaling captain, according to Grinnell's account to JA:
Butterfield, *John Adams Diary*, II, 320. Pease appears in Griffith Williams'
undated list, "Friends to American Liberty are friends to Mankind," at the
Hist. Soc. of Pa.
2. The *Belle-Poule*, 30 guns, commanded by de La Clocheterie, out of
Brest: Amblard-Marie-Raymond-Amédée, vicomte de Noailles, *Marins et
Soldats français en Amérique* (2d ed.; Paris, 1903), p. 374.
3. Francis Macy also appears on Williams' list, *loc. cit.* The French ship
in question, The *Vengeur*, was commanded by d'Amblimont, out of Brest:
de Noailles, *op. cit.*, p. 373.

The Massachusetts General Court to the American Commissioners

ALS: American Philosophical Society; copy: Library of Congress

Council Chamber Boston

May it please your Honors,   Octr. 23d. 1778

Agreeable to the Directions of the Genl. Assembly of this State, I do myself the Honor to transmit One hundred Copies of An Act intitled "An Act to prevent the return to this State of certain persons named and described and others who have left the same and joined our inveterate and Cruel Enemies;"[4] in Order that the same may be made public for their Government. Doubtless many of those mentioned in said Act, since they have found that the low Arts and Wicked Designs of our Enemies have been frustrated, will have that *Modesty* peculiar to themselves to Attempt a return; but I hope if they should be so daring, that Just Vengeance of our Countrymen will fall upon them. Your Honors will perceive that I am directed to transmit five hundred Copies of said Act, which I shall endeavour to comply with by five different Opportunities. I am with every sentiment of Esteem Your Honors, most Obedient and very humble Servant   JOHN AVERY, Dy. secy.[5]

Addressed: (On Public Service) / Their Excellency's / Benjamin Franklin, Arthur Lee and / John Adams Esqrs. / Commissioners at the Court of France / Paris

Notations in different hands: Jn. Avery Oct 23. 78 / D. Secretary, Mass: Bay.

---

4. *State of Massachusetts-Bay. In the Year of Our Lord One Thousand Seven Hundred and Seventy-Eight. An Act to prevent the Return to this State of certain Persons* ... (Boston, 1778). The act named hundreds of persons, with Thomas Hutchinson at the head of the list, who, if they returned, would be jailed and then transported out of state; a second return would mean the death penalty. The act was passed on Oct. 16.

5. John Avery (1739–1806), although bearing only the title of deputy secretary, was actually secretary of the commonwealth: *Sibley's Harvard Graduates*, XIV, 384–9.

Pierre Rïou[6] to the American Commissioners

ALS: American Philosophical Society

Messieurs   Brest Le 23e 8bre 1778.

Le Sr. Riou ainé Neg[ocian]t a Brest et Interprette Breveté pour les affaires de Sa Majesté seulement a l'honneur de re-montrer tres humblement a Messieurs Les Plenipotentiaires des Etats unies de L'amerique, que Le Corsaire ameriquain Le Hamden de Piscatua sous le commandement de thomas Pic-keren Esqr. arivé en ce port y a fait conduire le 6. de ce Mois une Prise par Luy faitte le 2e du present sous pavillon et Commission angloise en Datte du 29e du passé. La meme Raison qui a Doné Lieu a la vante sans formalité de justice, de la prise Le Lord Chatham conduitte precedemment en ce Port par La fregatte des Etats unies Le Ranger a authorisé Le Dit Capne Pickeren a Disposer de Sa Dite prise et Carguaison en consequence m'a muny d'un Pouvoir d'en traiter. Au Dessus de quoy J'ay Recu des offres de Gré a Gré et aÿ contracté le 16. de ce Mois pour le Batiment et Carguaison avec des Neg[ocian]ts de cette ville.

Messieurs de L'amirauté de cette ville me notifierent hier ainsÿ qu'au Dit Capne Pickeren un Extrait d'une Declaration du Roy, du 27e 7bre Dernier, qui n'a eté enregistré que de hier a Leur Greffe par Laquelle il appert qu'a l'avenir Les Vantes et Livraison de Prises faitte par Les Corsaires des Etats unies se feront du consentement et en presance des Dits officiers de L'amirauté.

Permettes moÿ de vous observer que L'Enregistrement de cette Declaration etant posterieure a La Vante et Livraison faitte par Le Capne Pickeren, il semble qu'elle ne Doit pas avoir un effet Retroactif capable D'annuler une vante et Li-vraison faitte precedemment.

Si L'on Met cette Declaration a execution le Capne Pickeren va se trouver arreté. Il ne peut Donc Mieux faire Dans la Cir-constance que de Reclamer votre Justice pour qu'il vous plaise Luy procurer par le Retour du Courier une ordre du Ministre

6. For this interpreter who first came to the commissioners' attention in connection with Jones's arrival in Brest, see XXVI, 419 n.

de la Marine qui Deffende a Messieurs les officiers de L'amirauté ou tout autre pretandant de former D'obstacle a son Depart et a La Rantrée d'une partie de fonds qui Luy sont Dus
par Billets et qui Le Mettroit Dans la Dure Necessité de ne
pouvoir faire face aux Depances considerables de sa Relache
pour Victualles et Equipement. Noté Je vous prie que L'equipage a Deja Recu de Grandes avances acompte de Leur parts
de Prise et qu'il y auroit de L'impossibilité a Leur faire Retourner ce qu'ils ont Reçu si cette Declaration aneantissoit la vante
faitte le 16e ou que par quelque autre Reglements Inconnu La
proprieté entiere du Batiment Leur fut Disputée.[7] Remarqué
aussy que ce batiment La Constance de Bordeaux prise Dont
il est question avoit eté pris par un corsaire de Guernezey Le
29e 7bre sur les francois et que ce Batiment est Dans le meme
cas que L'une des Prises conduite a Lorient par le Capne Mac
Niels du General Miffling.

Vos Instructions Relativement au Retard Considerable et a
la perte Evidente et Inexprimable que souffriroit Les armateurs Le Capne et L'Equipage du Corsaire le hamden de 22.
canons et de 120. hommes d'equipage, si son expedition etoit
Retardée paroissant Meriter votre attantion, me Done Lieu
D'Esperer qu'aiant Egard a La Demande que j'ay L'honneur
de vous faire au Nom de L'armateur, Du Capne et de L'equipage en General, vous aurez pour agreable de m'honorer de
votre prompte Reponse sous le couvert de Mr. Faisolle de ville
Blanche[8] Commissaire ordonateur de la Marine. Ce qu'attan-

7. Riou is arguing, in other words, that, should the new law be applied
retroactively to the sale of the *Constance*, not only would the transaction
have to be made in the presence of admiralty officers of the city, but Pickerin's presence in Brest would permit the reclaiming of prize money distributed to himself and the crew, creating complications and expensive delays. Therefore there is a practical argument for ordering him out of the
port as well as a case to be made about the applicability of recent legislation. The case involved an extensive exchange of memoirs during the following months and well into 1779. See Sartine to the commissioners, Sept.
16, for differences in French and English legal precedent.

8. Faissolle de Villeblanche is briefly identified in Didier Neuville, ed.,
État sommaire des Archives de la Marine antérieures à la Révolution (Paris, 1898),
p. 137 n.

dant J'ay l'honneur D'etre avec Le Respect possible Messieurs Votre tres humble tres obeissant serviteur RIOU AINÉ

Addressed: A Monsieur / Monsieur Le Dr. Franklin / A Passi

Notation: Riou ainé. Brest 23. oct. 78.

From Dumas

ALS: American Philosophical Society; AL (draft): Algemeen Rijksarchief

Monsieur,   La haie 23. Oct. 1778.
Voici, comme je l'ai promis dans ma derniere, ce que m'écrit Mr. W.L. de Francfort, en date du 4 de ce mois
"I have been but a few days returned from Paris. Until I got there, I did not know how deeply you have been engaged in a very important business. It might have been well if the Gentlemen had made me acquainted with it before. However all I will add is, that I heartily wish you success."[9]
Je fis hier une démarche qui, à ce que je pense, embarrasse beaucoup certaines gens, et fournit à nos amis une arme, qui pourra devenir en son temps redoutable entre leurs mains. Mais il n'est pas temps encore de vous en parler.
J'attends la Lettre ostensible, qui donne à connoître que la proposition de nos amis, de faire travailler au projet en question, vous fait plaisir, Monsieur, et a votre encouragement. J'ai lieu de croire que vous avez eu ou aurez une Conférence là-dessus avec ————. Ainsi, après ce que j'ai dit précédemment, je crois n'en devoir dire rien de plus; à moins que le g—— F—— ne le veuille. J'ajouterai seulement, que je ne vois aucun inconvénient à ce que la Lettre seroit signée par vous seul. Ainsi faites comme vous jugerez à propos.
Les Etats de la Province sont assemblés. Il ne s'y est rien traité encore d'important. On attend demain l'adresse des Négociants d'Amst——, pour réclamer les dommages.

---

9. We have not found this letter. We assume it signifies that Lee finally realized there was an official negotiation in process for a treaty and loan.

Dans un Entretien particulier de notre Ami avec un Grand Personnage, il lui a fortement représenté le mécontentement de toute la Bourse de sa ville, à cause des délais sur délais que fait naître certain Capitaine (fort porté pour les Anglois) commandant un vaisseau de 50 Canons au Texel, destiné à convoyer une Flotte de vaisseaux Marchands, dont une partie est venue de la Baltique, relâcher exprès pour cela au Texel, chargée de bois, mâture, etc.; lui ayant laissé passer l'opportunité d'un bon vent d'Est, qui avoit soufflé plusieurs jours, etc. etc. On a été interdit et mortifié de ces plaintes. Elles ont été faites aussi à Messrs. de l'Amirauté, qui ont donné ordre au Capitaine de partir incessamment. On vient de m'assurer qu'il est enfin parti.

J'ai une Lettre de Mr. Austin, qui est toujours à Amsterdam et le plaisir d'apprendre qu'il est content des politesses que mes amis lui ont faites à Leide et à Amsterdam. Il m'a promis votre portrait en relief, qu'il a à Rotterdam.[1] Je l'attends avec empressement, parce qu'il m'a dit qu'il étoit fort ressemblant. Vous aurez, Monsieur, pour Satellites dans ma chambre, Newton, Voltaire, Rousseau, Montesquieu et l'Imperatrice de Russie, qui vous entoureront. Je suis avec le plus respectueux attachement, Monsieur Votre très humble et très obéissant serviteur   DUMAS

Paris à S.E.M. le Dr. Franklin Min Plenip. des E.U. de L'Am.

Addressed: à Son Excellence / Monsieur le Dr. Franklin Esqr. / Min. Plenip. des E.U. de l'Am. / à *Passy.*/.

Notation:[2] Dumas Oct. 23. 78

1. Doubtless the Nini medallion.
2. In addition to this notation there are several unrelated numbers and columns of figures.

From —— Dumoulin

ALS: American Philosophical Society

Monsieur,   Paris 23. 8bre 1778
   Madame la Comtesse De chateaurenault,[3] belle mere de M.
le Comte D'Estaing desirerait avoir l'honneur de vous voir,
permettés moy d'avoir celuy de vous demander, si elle vous
trouvera chés vous, demain L'aprés midy, à cinq heures. Je suis
avec respect, Monsieur, Votre trés humble et trés obeissant
serviteur   DUMOULIN[4]

Monsieur Franklin

Notation: Dumoulin Paris 23. 8bre 1778.

   3. Marie-Françoise de Bournonville married Emmanuel, comte and later
marquis de Châteaurenault (d. 1739), son of a famous admiral. Their
daughter Marie-Sophie (b. 1727) became d'Estaing's wife in 1746. *DBF*
under Châteaurenault; Jacques Michel, *La vie aventureuse et mouvementée de
Charles-Henri, comte d'Estaing* ([n.p., 1976]) p. 14.
   4. His identity eludes us. At about this time he sent an undated note
saying he was very anxious to learn what had happened to d'Estaing since
he left Sandy Hook. APS.

From Daniel Hopkins[5]

ALS: University of Pennsylvania Library

Sir,   Boston Octr. 23d 1778.
I take the Liberty to inform you that I have a Brother in
Law among the American Prisoners in England, his Name is
John Palmer; he was captured about 18 months since.[6]
I can think of no way to effect his Liberation, except thro'
your Influence. I sincerely wish your Interposition in the affair. Confiding in your Disposition to use the best means to
effect so desirable an Event, am with great Respect, Your most
obedient Servant,   DANL. HOPKINS.
                                          Member of the Council.

Honle. Benjamin Franklin Esqr

Addressed: (On Public Service) / Honble Benja. Franklin Esqr. /
France

From Samuel Nuttle[7]   ALS: American Philosophical Society

           Havre de Grace 23d. October 1778 at the house of
My Lord   D. Chauvel & fils
In Consequence of the Protection, which your Lordship
was pleased to grant to me, I have obtain'd justice from the
Court of France; Mr. Necker Director General of the finance

5. Born in Waterbury, Conn., and a 1758 graduate of Yale, this pastor
and patriot (1734–1814) spent most of his adult life as a preacher in Salem.
A member of the Governor's Council from 1776 to 1778, he served as a
delegate to the Third Provincial Congress of Massachusetts in the spring
of 1778 and to the successor body, the General Court: Franklin B. Dexter,
Biographical Sketches of the Graduates of Yale College (6 vols., New York, New
Haven, 1885–1912), II, 533–4. Hopkins wrote again to BF on the subject of
prisoner release, April 13, 1782 (APS), indicating that he had an "agreable"
response to this one; BF's answer has not been found.
6. Presumably the John Palmer who was captured on the prize of the
Warren and committed to Forton prison on June 26, 1777: Kaminkow, *Mariners.*
7. A Philadelphia ship captain who had carried letters from London between BF and his wife a decade earlier: XIV, 23 n. On Aug. 29 he had both

has judged irregular the Seizure made on the 14 Guns on Board the Two Brothers, and has order'd the Custom house Officers to deliver them up. Upon my going to receive them I was surprized to find, that they wanted me to pay the Charges, which they themselves had occationed, which I don't think myself bound to pay as the seizure has been acknoleg'd injust and against the ordinance. Nevertheless if it is your Lordships approbation, I shall be ready Not only to pay them, but also lay aside all demand for the Damages they have occationed me. M. Tommasine[8] has assured me, that it was not the Director General's Intentions, that I should pay the Charges; I mean M. Necker to whom this affair concerns and Not to M. de Sartine.

I also take the Liberty to Lay before your Lordship that 'though I receive the Guns I shall not be able to go on in arming the Vessel, for want of a possitive order from M. Necker to this Custom-house to let me put on board all Nessacary Amunition and arms. This is what I humbly request of your Lordship. I am with the Greatest Respect My Lord Your Lordships Most Obedient Humble Servant   SAMUEL NUTTLE

From Genet
AL: American Philosophical Society

V[ersai]lles oct 24 [1778]

Genet takes the respectful liberty to transmit to his Honour M. Franklin several very interesting papers from the Royal american Gazette.[9] He would be exceedingly Happy, for the affection he has to the américan Cause, if he could enrich his next number (58) of the *affaires d'angleterre*, with the just and pointed observations that will offer themselves to His honour while reading these papers, wherein are such aspersions and

---

taken an oath of allegiance before the American Commissioners and, with the ship's owner David Chauvel, signed a letter of marque for the *Dr. Franklin* in the presence of WTF and Jonathan Loring Austin. APS.

8. Conceivably Jean-François Tolozan who was an *intendant du commerce*: *Almanach Royal* . . . for 1778, pp. 191–2.

9. The well-known Loyalist paper.

Lyes as deserve the animadversion of all persons having to heart the interest of truth and the success and crédit of the alliance.[1]

His honour's observations would be made use of by M. Genet, as from some writer in London without mentioning at all His Honours name, that deserves to appear in a more ennobled field.

M. Genet is sure the Count de Vergennes, would not be displeased with it: on the contrary. Undoubtedly the next *courier de l'Europe* will report all these papers translated into French for every body here and elsewhere to read[2]—it is fit the field of battle shou'd not remain to the English and it wou'd, till the american papers in answer to the Commissioners, either by W.H. Drayton or other able pens,[3] could arrive in Europe. It is therefore necessary that something be said on that account.

Notation: Genet

Franklin and John Adams to Genet

AL:[4] Library of Congress

Passy, Oct. 23. [*i.e.*, on or after October 24, 1778][5]
Messrs. Franklin and Adams present their Compliments to Mr. Genet, with Thanks for communicating the Papers, which

---

1. Genet made a similar request of Adams and Arthur Lee on the same day: Taylor, *Adams Papers*, VII. Cahier LVIII of the *Affaires* was largely devoted to the attempts of the Carlisle commission to seduce Congress into peace; see also BF or Arthur Lee to Genet, under Oct. 26.
2. The Oct. 23 issue of the *Courier de l'Europe* (IV, 259–61) carried statements by Gov. Johnstone and his fellow members of the Carlisle commission.
3. Congressional delegate William Henry Drayton, whose letter of Sept. 4 to the Carlisle commission (Smith, *Letters*, X, 559–70) appears in translation in the *Affaires*, XII, part II, cahier LVIII, cclxii–cclxxxviii.
4. In BF's hand.
5. We presume BF dated this letter erroneously, for it is in response to Genet's of the 24th to each of the commissioners.

they will read and consider, and furnish him with such Notes upon them as may occur.[6]

From Jean-François Fournier fils[7]

ALS: American Philosophical Society

Monsieur   de Paris ce 24. d'Octobre 1778.

J'ai l'honneur de vous prévenir que vôtre fonte de Gros Romain et l'italique est finie. Elle pèse le tout ensemble assorties, de cadrats, et espaces, deux cent soixante et une livres, à vingt quatre sols la livre sera la somme de trois cent treize livres quatre sols. Marqué moi s'il vous plait comment on vous l'envera si vous jugez à propos que je la fasse emballé dans deux boëte pour l'envoyer a sa destination, comme il vous plaira. Je m'aquiterai de vos ordres ce qu'attandant j'ai l'honneur d'être avec le plus profond respect Monsieur Votre trés humble et trés obeissant serviteur   J.F. FOURNIER FILS
rüe du foin St. jacque
visavis la rüe Boutbrie à paris

Addressed: A Monsieur / Monsieur Le Docteur / Francklin, même Maison de / Mr. chaumon / *à Passy*

Endorsed: Fournier fils

From Thomas Paine

ALS: American Philosophical Society

Dear Honored Sir   Philadelphia Oct. 24th. 1778

I congratulate you on your accession to the State of Minister Plenipotentiary. Could you have lived to fill a particular point in the Circle of human Affairs, it would have been That to which you are now so honorably called.

---

6. They were as good as their promise; JA's reply is printed in Taylor, *Adams Papers*, VII, after Oct. 24, BF or Arthur Lee's below, under Oct. 26.

7. For this member of the Fournier family see XXIV, 500 n. A little over a year had elapsed since BF had ordered types from his firm: XXIV, 500–1. An entry dated Oct. 29 in BF's *Waste Book* indicates a payment of 321 *l.t.* 4 *s.* to Fournier fils for types. The notation "self" appears beside it.

We rub and drive on, all things considered beyond what could ever be expected, and instead of wondering why some things have not been done better, the greater wonder is we have done so well. As I wish to render the History of this Revolution as compleat as possible I am unwilling to begin it too soon, and should be glad to consult you first, because the real Motives of the British King and Ministry in commencing the War will form a considerable political Part.[8] I am sufficiently perswaded myself that they wished for a Quarrel and intended to annex America to the Crown of England as a Conquered Country; they had no doubt of Victory and hoped for what they might call a Rebellion, but we have not, on this Side the Water, sufficient proof of This at present. I intend to embellish it with plates of heads Plans &c which likewise cannot be perfected here.

I enjoy thank God a good Share of health and hopes and tho' my Situation is no ways advantageous, it is nevertheless agreeable. I have the pleasure of being respected and I feel a little of that satisfactory kind of pride that tells me I have some right to it. I am not much harried in the Secretary department,[9] and have sufficient leisure for any thing else.

At this Time the public expectations run high on the Enemy quitting New York, but for what or where is all uncertain, neither do I beleive they know what to do themselves.

The Marquiss de Fayette returns with the warmest Thanks from this Country.[1] His Amiable and benevolent Manners

8. For Paine's projected history see XXIV, 205.
9. As secretary of the committee for foreign affairs.
1. Lafayette had asked leave to rejoin the French army. He was queried by a congressional committee about French participation in joint military operations against Canada, but, probably on the advice of Gérard, replied noncommittally. On Oct. 21 he was granted leave by Congress and promised "an elegant sword" (to be presented by BF): Meng, *Despatches of Gérard*, pp. 339–40, 346–7; *JCC*, XII, 1034–5, 1054; Idzerda, *Lafayette Papers*, II, 16–17, 191–5. He sailed from Boston on January 11, 1779, on the American frigate *Alliance*, carrying BF's instructions as minister plenipotentiary (below, Oct. 26), but was not content to be a mere messenger. Anxious to avenge the French and American defeat at Newport, he apparently was able to convince BF to exceed his instructions by asking Vergennes to send a French expedition against Rhode Island (below, Feb. 25).

have been a living contradiction to the narrow spirited declarations of the British Commissioners. He happily returns in
safety, which, considering the exposures he has gone thro', is
rather to be wondered at.

A large Detachment is Sailed from N. york Destination
unknown[2]—probably for Boston, but as you will receive later
Information than this Letter can Convey, any thing which I
may mention will be of little use. I am, with every wish for
your happiness Your obliged and Affectionate Humble Servant   T PAINE

Please to presant my Compts. to your Grandsons.

Addressed: His Excellency / Benjamin Franklin / Paris / Favor /
Marquis de Fayette

Endorsed: Mr Paine Oct. 24. 78

Notation: Mr. Paine

From Elizabeth Hubbart Partridge

ALS: American Philosophical Society

Boston Octr 24 1778
Honored and *Ever Dear* Papah   [–January 2, 1779]
    Allow me to Address you by that Tender Appilation: which
you once Intitled me to Use;[3] and to thank you for your
Agreeable Favour of Feby: 28. Could you know the Pleasure
that Every line from you gave me, I flatter my Self I should be
Offener indulged with Hearing from you, as I know you Delight in Communicating Pleasure; even to the Undeserving.

    I waited along Time to give you an Account of some Signial
Success of Our Armes: but the Letter I wrote you, with the
Account of the Monmouth Battle and General Lee's Disgrace
was taken. I again enclose the Paper, as their is a possibility
that it may not have Reached you.[4]

2. The detachment, as noted in our annotation of Deane's letter of Sept.
15, was to reinforce Florida and to attack St. Lucia.
3. BF's letter to her, March 5, 1756, is signed "Your affectionate Papa."
4. Neither this one nor BF's letter of Feb. 28 have been found.

I Love, I almost Adore the French Ladies, for their kindness to you; but let me Intreet you my Dear Papah not to let that Influence you to stay One Day longer in France, then the Servis of your Country Requieres: beleive me their is Hundreds hear as Amiable that are Impatient to Render you every Servis. I have One very Amiable Girl[5] that with her Mamah longs to see, and Converse with you: She desiers I would Present her Respectfull Regards to you.

I had the Pleasure to hear from Aunt Mecome a few Days sence. She with your Neice and all Our other Friends their ware Well. I hear by a Gentleman from Phila. that Cousin Beach and Family were Well, and that She has another Fine Babey, on which I Congratulate you; I Wish their was a Thousand of them, and all as Good as I think their Grand Papah.

I enclose you the late Papers and their is no thing New, but what they Contain, Except that is generally beleived, that the Kings Troops are Leaving New York.

I send you all the News I can Collect: and you once Told me, their was no Trade without a Return, then Sir let me beg the Favour of you, if you have any thing New that is proper to be known; that you would Communicate it to me: my best Friend: is a Sincere freind to the Libertyes of his Country, Anxiously Concern'd for his Welfair, and Curious in his Enquieries, so that to have an Opportunity to give him satisfaction Will quite double the Pleasure I feal.

Mr. Partridge[6] presents his Respectfull Regards to you, and would think him self Happy in an Acquaintance with you: I am not yet out of hopes of your fulfiling your Promis, of Spending eight, or Ten Dayes with Us, in the little Roome on the Wall.

Brother's and Sister[7] desier their affectionate Regards may be presented to you.

That whatchfull Angles may Gard your Preacious Life, and

5. Her step-daughter Rebecca Partridge: XXII, 38 n.
6. Elizabeth's husband Samuel Partridge: XIX, 30 n.
7. Tuthill Hubbart (identified in v, 118 n) and Susannah Hubbart (VII, 95 n).

OCTOBER 24, 1778–JANUARY 2, 1779

that Health and every other Blessing may attend you is the Ardent Prayer of Dear Sir Your affectionate Daughter

ELIZA: PARTRIDGE

P.S. You have told me, that postscrip's ware generally more attended to then the Letter. I theirfore take the Liberty in a postcrip to beg the Favour of your Picture in Miniture; of a Size proper to Ware on the Neck, in as good a Frame as you can get, (I wish I could afford to Decorrate it with Diamonds) and let me know the Cost, and I will Remitt it, to you, with Greatfull thank's.   E P

Jan. 2 1779

The enclos'd Petition is from Our Worthy Friend, Mr. John Green,[8] any Servis that you can Render him in his Way, will be Serving the Publick; and very much oblige one of the Best of Men, and your Humble Servant. Though this scrawl has waited so long for a Conveyance I have nothing new but what the enclosed Papers furnish and the Compliments of the Season.

Endorsed: Mrs Patridge

Notation: Eliza. Patridge Boston 24 8bre. 1778.

From ——— Demolon   ALS: American Philosophical Society

⟨Moulins en Bourbonnois, October 25, 1778, in French: I have a brother in Nantes who makes a living by his knowledge of mathematical and geometric principles. Capt. Le Maire, who has a commission to bring artillery and men of talent to Vir-

8. Possibly John Green (1731–87), a Boston printer whose firm, Green and Russell, was active from 1755 to 1775 and published the *Massachusetts Gazette and Boston Post-Boy*. After the evacuation of Boston by the British, Green became interested in the *Independent Chronicle*. He was known as a "man of steady habits, true to his engagements and well respected." Benjamin Franklin, V, ed., *Boston Printers, Publishers and Booksellers* ... (Boston, Mass., [1980]), pp. 221–8. In his reply to this letter, Oct. 11, 1779, BF makes no reference to this man but does mention an inquiry about printers' types, which presumably was the subject of Green's petition. University of Pa. Library.

ginia, solicits him to enter the service of that state. He flatters my brother that you and Mr. Lee would provide letters of recommendation, should he decide to go, and that he would be assured of the rank of captain of artillery, even though he would only be expected to occupy himself with geometry. I think my brother is too casual about the proposition; he is virtually prepared to leave without an adequate understanding of the chance he is taking in this expatriation. Would you kindly inform me of your intentions so that I can better advise him?[9])

From Aimé (Amé)-Ambroise-Joseph Feutry[1]

AL: American Philosophical Society

Ce 25. 8bre. 1778.

M. Schedel, négociant de Nuremberg en franconie, établi à Rouen, connu à La manufacture du Clos-Le-Prestre, desire d'avoir l'honneur d'assurer Monsieur Franklin de son respect, et de Lui faire quelques propositions etc.

Feutry Lui a promis de l'informer du moment où M. Franklin pourra L'entendre.

Endorsed: Schedel Manufacturier

Franklin or Arthur Lee (?) to Genet

Printed in *Affaires de l'Angleterre et de l'Amérique* XII, part II, cahier LVIII, pp. ccxxv–ccxl

[*c.* October 26, 1778]

On October 24 Genet wrote each of the commissioners asking a response to a number of articles in a New York loyalist newspaper.[2]

9. We do not know whether BF responded to this request which he apparently misunderstood; he endorsed the letter: "Demolon Wants Employ for a young Man Moulins 25. 8bre 1778."
1. The only appearance in this volume of BF's prolix literary friend, identified in XXIII, 557 n.
2. Genet to BF, Oct. 24; Taylor, *Adams Papers,* VII. BF and JA promised a reply; see their letter to Genet published under Oct. 24.

The *Affaires* in its cahier dated October 26 (but probably published somewhat later) printed three such responses. The third of these (pp. ccxl–ccxlvii) was a translation of Adams' and is published in the *Papers of John Adams*.[3] The first (pp. ccxxvi–ccxxxv) is written in such a pedestrian style (and contains historical inaccuracies[4]) that it could scarcely have been composed by Franklin. We publish the second which might well have been written by either Franklin or Lee.

No. II.

On dit que le Diable cite quelque fois l'Ecriture Sainte pour en venir à ses fins. D'après ce principe nous voyons les Commissaires de la Grande-Bretagne citer dans leurs remontrances au Congrès du 7 Août "les moyens imaginés par les hommes pour adoucir les horreurs de la guerre, pour faciliter le rétablissement de la paix, la foi des cartels, des capitulations militaires, des conventions et traités qu'on stipule même pendant la continuation des hostilités."[5]

Si le Congrès veut bien se donner la peine de répondre à cette réquisition, il lui sera tres-aisé de faire voir que les Généraux Anglois ont follement rompu pendant toute la guerre chacun des traités et conventions qui avoient été signés. Le Général Gage a violé ouvertement une convention solemnelle en retenant un grand nombre d'Habitans de Boston après qu'ils eurent rendu leurs armes, comme une condition en vertu de laquelle il devoit leur être permis de sortir de la Ville avec leurs effets.[6]

Les Soldats Américains faits prisonniers par capitulations au fort des Cèdres dans le Canada sont un autre exemple bien

3. Taylor, *Adams Papers*, VII. In *Lee Family Papers*, reel 5, frames 617–21, there is reproduced an unsigned and, as far as we know, unpublished 14-page literary piece, dated after Oct. 24, dealing with many of the same subjects as the present three articles.

4. *E.g.* by stating on p. ccxxviii that BF and Lee delivered a congressional petition to the King on Dec. 31, 1774. Actually, the petition was delivered on Dec. 24 to Lord Dartmouth: see XXI, 398–9.

5. Stevens, *Facsimiles*, XI, no. 1125, p. 1. This petition protested the detaining of Burgoyne's troops who had laid down their arms on the agreement they would be returned to England.

6. Gage's treatment of the inhabitants of Boston had provoked earlier complaints from BF: see, for example, XXII, 92.

frappant du peu de respect qu'ont les Anglois pour les capitulations. Ils souffrirent que ces misérables prisonniers fussent écharpés et égorgés par les Sauvages aussitôt qu'ils se furent rendus.[7]

Ce fait parut d'une atrocité si révoltante, que le Congrès se crut obligé d'en faire informer, et après avoir reçu les preuves les plus évidentes, il prit les résolutions suivantes le 10 Juillet 1776.

Arrêté que les Anglois, en pillant le bagage des soldats de la garnison des Cèdres, en les dépouillant de leurs habits et en livrant ces soldats aux Sauvages, ont *violé la capitulation.*

Arrêté qu'en massacrant les prisonniers de guerre ils ont manifestement et inhumainement outragé les loix de la nature et le droit des gens, que les auteurs, fauteurs et instigateurs de cette barbarie mériteroient d'être punis séverement.

Arrêté que si l'ennemi se permettoit à l'avenir de pareils actes de violence, en mettant à mort, tourmentant ou maltraitant de toute autre maniere quelconque les prisonniers détenus chez lui, on aura recours aux représailles comme le seul moyen de prévenir l'éffusion du sang humain.[8]

Le Congrès crut qu'il étoit convenable de menacer d'agir de représailles. Mais les prisonniers Anglois bien loin d'en avoir été la victime n'ont au contraire reçu pour tous traitemens que ceux que l'humanité croit devoir aux malheureux.[9] Après ces observations sur les procédés de l'armée Angloise et sur les résolutions que le Congrès a prises en conséquence, il étoit suffisamment autorisé à ne rendre aucun compte des motifs qu'il a eu de retenir l'armée du Général Burgoyne. Mais dans cette circonstance comme dans toutes les autres, il n'a agi que d'après les principes les plus vertueux.

Sans publier, à l'instar des Commissaires Anglois, une suite de maximes rebatues et de lieux communs sur la foi due aux Traités et aux Capitulations, il connoissoit toute la force de ces Traités et il auroit rempli en tout point la convention faite avec

7. See XXII, 497 n. Six or seven American captives were killed and the remainder threatened: *JCC*, v, 534–7.

8. *Ibid.*, pp. 538–9.

9. A point on which BF prided himself: XXV, 66.

le Général Burgoyne, si celui-ci ne l'avoit déclarée rompue sous les plus frivoles prétextes. La conduite ultérieure du Général Anglois a donné les plus fortes raisons de croire que son intention étoit d'agir comme si la convention eût été réellement rompue de la part des Américains et de joindre son armée à celle du Général Howe. Le 8 du mois de Janvier dernier le Congrès a exposé de la maniere la plus ample et la plus satisfaisante les motifs de sa conduite; ils ont été rendus publics et il n'y a pas d'homme raisonnable qui ne les ait approuvés.[1] Son arrêté finit de la manière suivante:

L'accusation faite par le Lieutenant général Burgoyne dans sa lettre au Major général Gates du 14 Novembre, d'une violation de foi publique de la part de ces Etats,[2] n'est fondée sur aucune expression des articles de la Convention de Saratoga; cette accusation dévoile pleinement l'intention du Général Burgoyne, et elle donne de justes sujets de craindre qu'il ne se serve de cette prétendue infraction à la convention pour se dégager lui et l'armée à ses ordres de l'obligation où ils se trouvent à l'égard de ces Etats-unis; et la sureté que ces Etats ont eue dans l'honneur personnel du Général Burgoyne, étant détruite par-là. En conséquence, arrêté que l'embarquement du Lieutenant général Burgoyne et des troupes à ses ordres, sera suspendu jusqu'à ce qu'une ratification claire et formelle de la convention de Saratoga soit convenablement notifiée au Congrès par *la Cour de la Grande-Bretagne.*

La Cour de la Grande-Bretagne n'a point fait la notification qui est requise ici. D'après tout ce que les Commissaires du Roi ont déjà publié, il ne paroit pas même qu'ils soient autorisés à faire des ouvertures relativement à cette affaire. Une partie de l'armée du Général Burgoyne consistoit en Canadiens, qui en vertu de la convention de Saratoga ont été renvoyés dans leur pays. Il est stipulé par l'Article IX de cette convention que ces Canadiens seront tenus, ainsi que les autres troupes, de ne point servir pendant la guerre actuelle

1. *JCC*, x, 29–35. The quotation which follows is given on p. 35.
2. This letter is published in F.J. Hudleston, *Gentleman Johnny Burgoyne* ... (Indianapolis, [1927]), pp. 254–6.

dans l'Amérique Septentrionale. Personne n'ignore que le Général Carleton a traité avec mépris la susdite convention, et qu'il a forcé tous ceux qui avoient été renvoyés de faire le même service militaire auquel ils auroient été assujettis, s'il n'y avoit pas eu de capitulation. Il faut que les Commissaires Anglois soient petris d'impudence pour s'étendre comme ils le font sur la foi et le respect dûs aux traités, tandis que l'objet de leur voyage en Amérique et de leur conduite depuis qu'ils y sont arrivés, a été de persuader au Congrès de violer les Traités qu'il a solemnellement contractés avec la France. Pour parvenir à leur but, il n'y a pas de ressorts qu'ils n'ayent fait jouer. La flatterie a été la premiere arme qu'ils ont essayée. Ils ont dit aux Membres du Congrès que Rome et l'ancienne Grece ne pouvoient pas se vanter d'avoir produits de si grands hommes que ceux qui composoient le Sénat Américain.[3] Lorsqu'ils ont vu que la vertu de nos Sénateurs ne se laissoit point ébranler par des éloges aussi fades, ils ont eu recours à des moyens qui depuis long-tems passent pour infaillibles dans la Grande Bretagne. La corruption, cette grande pierre de touche de la vertu, a été mise en usage. Mais cet écueil contre lequel tant de prétendus patriotes ont échoué, n'a point été dangereux pour le Congrès; et le Corrupteur a été dénoncé publiquement à l'univers comme un objet de mépris pour tous les honnêtes gens.[4] On doit naturellement s'attendre que lorsque les Commissaires Anglois auront reconnu que le Congrès ne peut se laisser vaincre par les armes qui en Europe portent presque toujours des coups irrésistibles, ils abandonneront la partie, et qu'ils commenceront à dire des injures et se montreront dignes Représentans de leurs Constituans, les Ministres Britanniques, qui en toute occasion n'ont jamais joué que le rôle le plus bas et le plus méprisable.

3. Governor George Johnstone, one of the British commissioners, wrote to several congressional delegates but we are unable to find the passage in question.

4. For a brief account of Johnstone's attempt to bribe Joseph Reed, see John F. Roche, *Joseph Reed: a Moderate in the American Revolution* (New York, 1957), pp. 137–43.

To David Hartley

Transcript: Library of Congress

My Dear Friend   Oct. 26. 1778.

I received yours without Date,[5] containing an old Scotch Sonnet full of natural Sentiment and beautiful Simplicity, I cannot make an entire application of it to present Circumstances; but taking it in Parts, and changing Persons, some of it is extreamly *a propos*. First Jenie may be supposed old England and Jamie America. Jenie laments the Loss of Jamie, and recollects with Pain his Love for her, his Industry in Business, to promote her Wealth and Welfare, and her own Ingratitude.

> Young Jamie loved me well
> And sought me for his Bride
> But saving ane Crown
> He had nothing beside
> To make that Crown a Pound
> My Jamie *gang'd to Sea*
> And the Crown and the Pound
> Were all for me.

Her Grief for their Separation is expressed very pathetically

> The Ship was a Wrack
> Why did not Jennie dee
> O why was I spared
> To cry Wae is me.

There is no Doubt but that honest Jammie had still so much Love for her as to Pity her in his Heart, tho' he might at the same time be not a little angry with her.

Towards the Conclusion we must change the Persons, and let Jamie be Old England, Jennie America and old Robin Gray, the Kingdom of France. Then honest Jenie having made a Treaty of Marriage with Gray expresses her firm Resolution of Fidelity in a manner that does Honour to her good Sense and her Virtue.

> I may not think of Jamie
> For that would be a Sin
> But Inum [I must] do my best

---

5. Hartley's letter above which BF endorsed: "Oct 4. 1778."

A good Wife to be
For auld Robin Gray
IS VERY KIND TO ME

You ask my Sentiments of a Truce for 5 or 7 Years in which
no mention should be made of that stumbling Block to England the Independence of America. I must first tell you fairly
and frankly that there can be no Treaty of Peace with us in
which France is not included. But I think a Treaty might be
made between the three Powers in which Englands expressly
Renouncing the Dependence of America seems no more necessary than her renouncing the Title of King of France, which
has always been claimed for her Kings. Yet perhaps it would
be better for England to act nobly and generously on the Occasion by granting more than she could at present be compelled to grant, make America easy on the Score of Old
Chains [Claims] cod. [concede?] all that remains in North
America, and thus conciliate and strengthen a Young Power
which she wishes to have a future and serviceable Friend. I do
not think England would be a loser by such Cession. She may
hold her remaing Possessions there, but not without vast Expence; and they would be the Occasion of constant Jealousies,
frequent Quarrels and renew'd Wars. The United States continually growing stronger will naturally have them at last; and
by the generous Conduct above hinted at, all the intermediate
Loss of Blood and Treasure might be spared; and a solid lasting Peace promoted; This seems to me good Counsel, but I
know it can't be followed.

The Friend you mention must always be welcome to me
with or without the Cheese,[6] but I do not see how his coming
hither could be of any Use at present, unless in Quality of a
Plenipotentiary to treat of a sincere Peace between all the Parties.

Your Commissioners are acting very indiscreetly in America. They first spoke disrespectfully of our good Ally. They
have since called in question the power of Congress to treat
with them; and have endeavour'd to begin a Dispute about the
detention of Bourgoynes Troops; an Affair which I conceive

6. See annotation to the Oct. 4 letter.

629

not to be within their Commission. They are vainly trying by
Publications to excite the People against the Congress. Governor Jonston has been attempting to bribe the Members; and
without the least Regard to Truth has asserted three Propos-
tions which he says, he will undertake to prove; The two first
of them I know to be false and I believe the third to be so.[7]
The Congress have refused to treat with the Commissioners
while he continues one of them, and he has therefore resigned.
These Gentlemen do not appear well qualify'd for their Business. I think they will never heal the Breach; but they may
widen it. I am ever, my very dear Friend Yours most Affectionately   N.A.[8]

Notation: to David Hartley

Marie-Nicole Grossart de Virly Gérard[9] to the American Commissioners

Copy:[1] Harvard University Library

Messieurs   a Versailles ce 26 Oct. 1778
J'avois envoyé a mon Mari, mon portrait et celui de ma fille,
sur une Boete que M. Williams de Nantes a fait partir par un

---

7. George Johnstone of the Carlisle commission. BF is apparently referring to Johnstone's reply of Aug. 26 to the Aug. 11 resolution of Congress.
Johnstone alleged that Congress had used the attempted bribe as a rationalization for their refusal to negotiate with the commission. He accused
Congress of violating the Saratoga Convention respecting the disposition
of Burgoyne's captured troops, and finally claimed that he was unmoved
by the contempt in which Congress held him: Stevens, *Facsimiles*, XI, no.
1132. The affair dominated the American press: Weldon A. Brown, *Empire
or Independence: a Study in the Failure of Reconciliation, 1774–1783* (University,
La., 1941), pp. 277–80.

8. Signifying, perhaps, North America, in apposition to Hartley's G.B.

9. Daughter of a farmer general and since 1768 wife of Conrad-
Alexandre Gérard, with whom she had one daughter, Alexandrine (1771–
90): Meng, *Despatches of Gérard*, pp. 38–9; Jean-Pierre Samoyault, *Les bureaux du secrétariat d'état des affaires étrangères sous Louis XV* (Paris, [1971]),
pp. 288–9.

1. In the hand of Arthur Lee. A copy was sent with the commissioners'
letter to Schweighauser of Nov. 1, below.

vaisseau qui a ete pris et conduit a Grenezay. M. de Chaumont m'a dit Messieurs que vous auriez la bonté pour moi et mon mari d'employer votre Correspondant a Nantes, qui a son gendre fils du Maire de Grenezay[2] pour [racheter?] cette Boete qui ne peut intéresser le preneur que pour la valeur de quelques cercles d'or qui sont de peu de consequence. Je vous demande pardon Messieurs, de reclamer votre entremise dans un objet si peu consequent, mais l'amitié que vous avez pour mon mari me répond de l'interet que vous metterez a me procurer cette satisfaction. Je suis Messieurs Votre tres humble et tres obeissante Serviteur   DEVIRLY GERARD

a Messieurs M. Franklin Lee & Adams Deputés des Etats Unis

Sartine to the American Commissioners[3]

Copies: Massachusetts Historical Society, National Archives, Library of Congress (two)

⟨Marly, October 26, 1778, in French: The second part of your letter of October 12 deserves a response as well as the first, to which I have already replied. Although it would serve a double purpose if all American sailors remaining in British service by inertia or coercion could be returned to their native country, the matter poses difficulties. I shall take up the question of the impressed seamen with His Majesty. I have given orders to put at your disposal the four prisoners in Dinan whose release you request.[4]⟩

2. Schweighauser's son-in-law Pierre-Frédéric Dobrée was a native of Guernsey; see his letter of Aug. 11 and Chaumont's of July 5.

3. Published in Taylor, *Adams Papers*, VII.

4. Presumably the men named in the commissioners' letter of Oct. 15 to the prisoners: Harrison, Lemon, Driver and Nichols.

From Madame Brillon

ALS: American Philosophical Society

ce lundi [October 26, 1778] a la thuillerie[5]

Je reprends mes engagements avéc vous mon papa; mon coeur a promis au vostre, c'est le plus sacré de tous les contrats: je vous écrirai, vous dirai que je vous aime, que vous étiés bien désiré ici[6]—en arrivant, maman me dit avant de m'enbrassér *ou est il ce bon papa*—il ne viendra pas—*ma fille voila ou je le logeois pour qu'il fut commodément*—il auroit été trés bien—*ma fille veut tu disnér; j'avois préparé tout ce que mr. franklin aime*—maman je ne doutte pas de vos soins—*voila ou tu l'aurois conduit dormir aprés son disné; voila ou il auroit joué aux échécs avec toi; j'avois fait nétoyér mes allées; j'avois tant d'envie de le rendre heureux!*—mon papa, en venant ici vous en auriés fait, bien des heureux! Si le tems devient plus beau, si vous prévoÿés avoir un ou deux jours de libérté ne viendrés vous pas nous voir, mon coeur vous appélle, le vostre ne l'entend t'il pas? óh oui il l'entend; mon papa m'aime comment ne m'aimeroit t'il pas, mon áme réunit pour lui tous les sentiments! Mon chér papa je vous aime au plus possible rien n'est plus vrai; je vous aimerai toujours c'est encore bien vrai! Toujours je chérche tous les moyens de vous plaire, et je ne serai vraiment heureuse que lorsque je lirai dans vos yeux que vous éstes content de votre fille; adieu mon aimable papa voila ma proféssion de foi amicalle je suis bien dévotte de l'amitié; son culte est doux a mon coeur, surtout quand ce culte s'addrésse a vous. J'ai l'honneur d'éstre mon chér papa Votre trés humble et trés obéissante sérvante   D'HARDANCOURT BRILLON

Addressed: A Monsieur / Monsieur Franklin / A Passy

---

5. This is the first of a group of three letters sent by Mme. Brillon from her mother's country house in Franconville, a village located near Pontoise in the valley of Montmorency. The date is inferred from her next letter which, for once, is clearly dated: Nov. 2, 1778.

6. See her letter of Sept. 30.

From the Continental Congress: Instructions, Plan of an Attack upon Quebec and Observations on the Finances of America

(I) LS: American Philosophical Society, Historical Society of Pennsylvania; draft: National Archives;[7] (II) DS: American Philosophical Society; draft: National Archives; (III) DS: American Philosophical Society, South Carolina Historical Society; draft: National Archives; copy: Archives du Ministère des affaires étrangères

These documents, like Franklin's letter of credence,[8] were drafted by Gouverneur Morris, but unlike it proved highly controversial. Gérard, for example, in discussing the instructions with Morris, strongly objected to the idea in article VII that the common cause would be served by the British Navy's withdrawing ships from America to Europe.[9] Congress, moreover, quibbled over the wording of the first article, reversed its initial decision to remove the fifth, and rejected altogether what Morris had proposed as the final one.[1] The major source of dispute, however, was the annexed proposal for a joint Franco-American attack on Quebec. Morris discussed it with Gérard, who was cool to the idea. The American told him that the United States, although intending to retain Canada, was willing to leave Florida (and perhaps even the navigation on the Mississippi) entirely to France's prospective ally Spain, and would be pleased to see the Newfoundland fishery in French hands.[2] Although Gérard remained sceptical, Congress included plans for the proposed attack along with Franklin's instructions.[3] Soon thereafter opposition arose from a new quarter. George Washington, suspicious of a French army in North America, wrote a lengthy letter to Laurens on November 11, opposing the planned attack.[4] After a congressional

7. In the hand of Gouverneur Morris and run together continuously with the drafts of II and III.

8. Above, Oct. 21.

9. Meng, *Despatches of Gérard*, pp. 340–9; Max M. Mintz, *Gouverneur Morris and the American Revolution* (Norman, Ok., [1970]), pp. 114–16.

1. These alterations are cited in detail, below.

2. Meng, *loc. cit.*; Mintz, *loc. cit.*

3. *JCC*, XII, 1039–52, 1064. Congress also ordered that the plan for attacking Canada be communicated to Gérard and that the reasons for the attack be explained to him: *ibid.*, p. 1053. The French minister sent a translation of the plan to Versailles: Meng, *Despatches of Gérard*, p. 349.

4. Fitzpatrick, *Writings of Washington*, XIII, 223–44; see also *ibid.*, pp. 254–7 and Idzerda, *Lafayette Papers*, II, 205–7.

committee met with the general, Congress wrote Lafayette on January 3, 1779, to rescind the request for assistance in attacking Canada.[5] Lafayette had already sailed, however, and did not receive the request for several months.[6]

I.

Draught of Instructions &ca.

Sir,   [October 26, 1778][7]

We the Congress of the United States of North America, having thought it proper to appoint you their Minister plenipotentiary to the Court of his most Christian Majesty, you shall in all things according to the best of your knowlege and Abilities promote the Interest and honor of the said States at that Court with a particular Attention to the following Instructions.

1st. You are immediately to assure his most Christian Majesty, that those States entertain the highest sense of his Exertions in their favor, particularly by sending the respectable Squadron under the Count D'Estaign which would probably have terminated the war, in a speedy and honorable manner if unforeseen and unfortunate Circumstances had not intervened. You are further to assure him that they consider this speedy Aid not only as a Testimony of his Majesty's fidelity to the Engagements he hath entered into but as an earnest of that Protection[8] which they hope from his power and Magnanim-

---

5. *JCC*, XII, 1230, 1250; Idzerda, *Lafayette Papers*, II, 217. See also Jay's letter of Jan. 3, 1779 to BF, below.

6. Idzerda, *Lafayette Papers*, II, 217 n; Lovell to BF, below, Feb. 8, 1779. By the time the revised instructions arrived, BF had already exceeded his original orders: see our annotation of Paine's letter of Oct. 24.

7. So dated above Laurens' signature, although the instructions were approved by Congress on the 22nd: *JCC*, XII, 1039–42. During the interim the final article of the instructions had been inserted and the decision made to combine the instructions with the plan of attack on Quebec: *ibid.*, p. 1064 n.

8. Congress rejected an attempt to substitute the words "further assistance" for "protection" and then rejected a move to strike the entire sentence beginning "You are further to assure him." *JCC*, XII, 1036–8.

ity, and as a Bond of Gratitude to the Union founded on mutual Interest.

2dly. You shall by the earliest opportunity and on every necessary Occasion assure the King and his Ministers that neither the Congress nor any of the States they represent have at all swerved from their Determination to be Independent in July 1776. But as the Declaration was made in face of the most powerful Fleet and Army which could have been expected to operate against them and without any the slightest Assurance of foreign Aid, so altho in a defenceless situation and harrassed by the secret Machinations and Designs of intestine foes they have under the Exertion of that force during three bloody Campaigns, persevered in their Determination to be free. And that they have been inflexible in this determination, notwithstanding the Interruption of their Commerce the great sufferings they have experienced from the Want of those things which it procured and the unexampled Barbarity of their Enemies.

3dly. You are to give the most pointed and positive assurances that altho the Congress are earnestly desirous of Peace as well to arrange their Finances and recruit the exhausted state of their Country as to spare the further Effusion of blood yet they will faithfully perform their Engagements and afford every assistance in their power to prosecute the war for the Purposes[9] of the Alliance.

4thly. You shall endeavor to obtain the King's consent to expunge from the Treaty of Commerce the eleventh and twelfth Articles as inconsistent with that Equality and reciprocity which form the best surity to perpetuate the whole.[1]

5thly. You are to exert yourself to procure the consent of the Court of France, that all American Seamen who may be taken on board of British Vessels, may if they chuse, be permitted to enter on board American Vessels; in return, for

9. In the draft and other LS, "great Purposes."

1. A matter which soon would be accomplished: see Vergennes' letter of Oct. 31 arranging a date for the declarations annulling the articles to be exchanged. The declarations themselves are given above, Sept. 1. Gérard suggested the French might refuse, as a lesson to the Americans: Meng, *Despatches of Gérard*, p. 346.

which you are authorised to Stipulate that all Frenchmen who may be taken on board of British Vessels, by Vessels belonging to the United States shall be delivered up to persons appointed for that purpose by his most Christian Majesty.[2]

6thly. You are to suggest to the Ministers of his most Christian Majesty, the advantage which would result from entering on board the Ships of these States, British seamen who may be made Prisoners, thereby impairing the force of the Enemy and strengthening the Hands of his Ally.

7thly. You are also to suggest the fatal consequences which would follow to the Commerce of the Common Enemy if by confining the war to the European and Asiatic seas, the coasts of America could be so far freed from the British fleets as to furnish a safe Asylum to the Frigates and Privateers of the allied Nations and their prizes.

8thly. You shall constantly inculcate the certainty of ruining the British Fishery on the Banks of Newfoundland and consequently the british Marine by reducing Hallifax and Quebec since by that means they would be exposed to alarm and plunder, and deprived of the necessary supplies formerly drawn from America. The plans proposed to Congress for compassing these Objects are herewith transmitted for your more particular Instructions.[3]

9thly. You are to lay before the Court, the deranged state of our finances together with the causes thereof and shew the necessity of placing them on a more respectable footing in

2. This article, not in Morris' draft, was submitted in the hand of William Duer and then approved. The following article, originally numbered five, was first rejected and then restored. *JCC*, XII, 1041 n. Gérard had proposed to Morris that the Americans exchange one of the prisoners they held for each French-held prisoner wishing to serve aboard an American ship: Meng, *Despatches of Gérard*, pp. 341–2.

3. Part II of this document. Gérard explained the American reasoning behind the proposed joint attack on Quebec: the plan was posited on an impending British evacuation of New York and, although the Americans could conquer Canada without French help, this assistance could permit the conquest of both Quebec (supposedly garrisoned by only 600 men) and Halifax in a single campaign. Meng, *Despatches of Gérard*, pp. 342–3. Gérard was dubious of the plan, as well he might have been, since it was grounded in false intelligence and wishful thinking.

order to prosecute the war with Vigor on the part of America. Observations on that subject are herewith transmitted and more particular Instructions shall be sent whenever the necessary steps previous thereto shall have been taken.[4]

10thly. You are by every means in your power to promote a perfect harmony, Concord and good Understanding not only between the Allied powers but also between and among their subjects that the connection so favorably begun may be perpetuated.

11thly. You shall in all things take care not to make any Engagements or stipulations on the part of America without the consent of Congress previously obtained.[5]

We pray God to further you with his Goodness in the several Objects hereby recommended and that he will have you in his holy keeping.

Done at Philadelphia the twenty sixth day of October 1778.
In Congress   HENRY LAURENS
                                                  President

Attest CHA THOMSON Secy.

To the honorable Benjamin Franklin Esqr. Minister Plenipotentiary of the United States of North America To the Court of France.

Endorsed: Instructions from Congress 1778 / Instructions from Congress 1778 to BF.

II.

Plan of Attack

1. That a number of men be assembled at Fort pitt from Virginia and Pensilvania amounting to 1500 rank and file for

4. Part III of this document. For Gérard's comments on America's financial straits see Meng, *Despatches of Gérard,* p. 346.

5. Morris' proposed final article, which was rejected, read: "You shall endeavor to gain Intelligence of the Views, Objects and Designs of the French Court as far as they may relate to or affect the Interests of these States; and of the Characters and Abilities of the Ministers and communicate the Result of your Enquiries and Observations to Congress from Time to Time."

which purpose 3000 should be called for and if more than 1500 appear the least effective be dismissed. To these should be added 100 light cavalry one half armed with lances. The whole should be ready to march by the first day of June, and for that purpose they should be called together for the 1st. day of May, so as to be in readiness by the 15th. The real and declared Object of this Corp should be to attack *Detroit* and Destroy the Towns on the route thither of those Indians who are inimical to the United States.

2dly. That 500 men be Stationed at or near Wyoming this Winter to cover the frontiers of Pensilvania and New Jersey to be reinforced by 1,000 men from those States early in the spring, for this purpose 2,000 men must be called for to appear on the 1st. of May, so as to be in readiness by the 15th. They must march on the 1st. of June at the farthest for *Oncoquaga* to proceed from thence against *Niagara*. This is also to be declared.

3dly. That in Addition to the Garrison of Fort Schuyler or Stanwix 1500 Men be stationed this winter along the Mohawk river, and preparations of every kind made to build Vessels of Force on Lake Ontario early next Spring And to take post at or near Oswego; a reinforcement of 2,500 Men from the Militia of New york and the Western parts of Connecticut and Massachusets must be added to these early in the spring for which purpose a Demand must be made of 5,000. A Party consisting of 500 Regular Troops and 1,000 Militia must march from Schenectady so as to meet those destined to Act against *Niagara* at *Oncoquaga*. They should be joined by about 100 light Dragoons armed As aforesaid together with all the Warriors which can be Collected from the friendly Tribes. In their march to Niagara they should destroy the Seneka and other Townships of Indians who are inimical.

4thly. That 2,500 men be marched from Fort Schuyler as early as possible after the middle of May to Oswego and take a post there or in the Neighbourhood to be defended by about 500. men That they be also employed in forwarding the Vessels to be built for Securing the Navigation of Lake Ontario and in making Excursions towards Niagara so as to keep the

Indian Country in Alarm and facilitate the operations in that Quarter.

5thly. That a number of Regiments be cantoned along The upper Parts of Connecticut River to be recruited in the winter so as to form a body of 5,000 Regular Troops rank and file and every preparation made to penetrate into Canada by the way of the River St. Francis. The time Of their Departure must depend upon Circumstances And their Object be kept as secret as the nature of the thing will permit. When they arrive at the St. Lawrence they must take a good Post at the mouth of St. Francis and turn their attention immediately to the reduction Of Montreal, St. Johns and the North end of Lake Champlain. These Operations will be facilitated by the several movements to the westward drawing the attention of the enemy to that Quarter. If successful so as to secure a passage across the Lake farther reinforcements may be thrown in and an Additional retreat secured that way. The next operation will be in Concert with the Troops who are to gain the Navigation of Lake Ontario &c. This Operation however must be feeble so long as the Necessity exists of securing their rear towards *Quebec*. Such detachment however as can be spared Perhaps 2,000 with as many Canadians as will join them are to proceed up *Cadaraqui*[6] and take a post defencible by about 300 men at or near the mouth of Lake *Ontario*. They will then join themselves to those posted as Aforesaid at or near *Oswego* and leaving a Garrison at that post proceed together to the party at or near *Niagara* at which place they Ought if possible to arrive by the middle of September. The Troops who have marched against *Detroit* should Also whether Successful or not return to *Niagara* if that post is possessed or beseiged by the Americans as a Safe retreat can by that means be Accomplished for the Whole in Case of Accidents.

On the Supposition that these Operations Succeed still another campaign must be made to reduce the City of *Quebec*. The American Troops must Continue all winter in *Canada*. To supply them with Provisions Cloathing &c. will be difficult if

6. Presumably the Châteaugay.

not impracticable. The expence will be ruinous. The Enemy will have time to reinforce. Nothing can be attempted Against Halifax. Considering these circumstances it is perhaps more prudent to make Incursions with Cavalry, light Infantry and Chasseurs to harrass and Alarm the Enemy and thereby prevent them from desolating our Frontiers which seems to be their Object During the next Campaign.

But if the reduction of Halifax and Quebec Are Objects of the highest importance to the Allies they must be attempted.

The importance to France is derived from the following considerations.

1st. The fishery of Newfoundland is justly considered As the basis of a good Marine.

2dly. The possession of those two places necessarily secures to the party and their friends the Island and Fisheries.

3dly. It will strengthen her allies and guarantee more Strongly their freedom and Independence.

4thly. It will have an Influence in extending the Commerce of France and restoring her to a Share Of the Fur trade now Monopolized by Great britain.

The importance to America results from the following Considerations.

1st. The peace of their Frontiers.

2dly. The arrang'ment of their Finances.

3dly. The accession of two States to the Union.

4thly. The protection and Security of their Commerce.

5thly. That it will enable them to bend their whole Attention and resourses to the Creation of a marine which will at once Serve them and Assist their Allies.

6thly. That it will secure the Fisheries to the United States and France their Ally to the total exclusion Of Great britain.[7]

Add to these considerations

1st. That Great britain by holding those places will infest the Coasts of America with small Armed Vessels to the great Injury of the French as well as American trade.

2dly. That her possessions in the West Indies materially De-

---

7. Lined out in the draft is an alternate beginning to this paragraph, "The effect in securing of the Fisheries above stated."

pend on the possession of Ports to supply them With bread and Lumber and to refit their Ships and receive their Sick as well soldiers as Seamen.

In Order then to secure as far as human wisdom Can provide the reduction of those places aid must be Obtained from France.

Suppose a body of from 4,000 to 5000 French Troops Sail from Brest in the begining of May under Convoy Of four Ships of the Line and four Frigates.[8] Their Object to be avowed but their Cloathing Stores &c. such as designate them for the West Indies. Each Soldier must have a good blanket of a Large Size to be made into a Coat when the Weather grows cool, Thick cloathing for these Troops should be sent in August so as to arrive at such place as Circumstances by that time may indicate by the begining of October. These troops by the end of June or begining of July might Arrive at *Quebec* which for the reasons already assigned they would in all probability find quite defenceless. Possessing themselves of that City and leaving there the Line of Battleships the marines and a very small Garrison with as many of the Canadians As can readily be assembled, for which purpose spare Arms Should be provided which might be put up in boxes and marked as for the Militia of one of the French Islands. The Frigates and Transports should proceed up the river St. Lawrence and a Dis Embarkation take place at the Mouth of the river St. Francis. If the Americans are already At that place the troops will cooperate for the purposes Above mentioned. If not a post must be taken there and Expresses sent &c. In the Interim three of the Frigates with four of the smallest Transports should proceed to Montreal and if possible possess that City, when the Nobles and Clergy should be immediately called together by the General who should if possible be well Acquainted with The manners both of France and of the United States. The Troops should bring with them very ample provisions especially of

8. Writing to d'Estaing in August Lafayette had envisaged a French force of 6,000 to 10,000 men for use in North America; there are several similarities between Lafayette's plan and that of Congress. See Idzerda, *Lafayette Papers*, II, 145–6.

Salted Flesh as they will come to a Country exhausted by the British Army. By the latter end of July or about the middle of August the reduction of *Canada* might be so far compleated that the ships might proceed to the Investiture of Halifax taking On board large supplies of Flour, a part of the Troops might march and be followed by the sick as they recover. A considerable body of American Troops also might then be spared for that Service which with the Militia of the States of Massachusets and New hampshire might proceed to the attack of Halifax so as to arrive the begining of September and if that place should fall by the begining or middle of October, The Troops might either proceed against Newfoundland or remain in Garrison until the Spring at which time that Conquest might be compleated. If Halifax should not be taken then the Squadron and Troops would still be in time to Operate against the West Indies.

Sir   To the honorable Benjamin Franklin Esqr.[9];

The above plan referred to in your Instructions You shall lay substantially before the French Minister. You shall consult the Marquis De La Fayette on any Difficulties which may Arise and refer the ministry to him as he hath made it his particular study to gain Information on those important points. In Congress   HENRY LAURENS
                                                        President

Attest CHA THOMSON Secy.

Endorsed: Plan for Attacking Canada

III.

Observations on the finances of America

At the commencement of the war, it was obvious that the permanent revenues and resources of Great Britain must eventually overballance the sudden and impetuous sallies of men contending for freedom on the spur of the occasion with-

9. Morris' draft also includes this explanatory note, and the one at the end of III. Morris in a slip of the pen wrote William Franklin in this line, then crossed out "William" and substituted "Benjamin."

out regular discipline, determinate plan or permanent means of subsistence.

America having never been much taxed nor for a continued length of time, being without fixed government and contending against what once was the lawful authority, had no funds to support the war notwithstanding her riches and fertility. And the contest being upon the very question of taxation the laying of imposts unless from the last necessity would have been madness.

To borrow from individuals without any visible means of repaying them and while the loss was certain from any ill success was visionary.

A measure therefore which had been early adopted and thence become familiar to the people was pursued. This was the issuing of paper notes representing specie for the redemption of which the public faith was pledged.

As these were to circulate from hand to hand there was no great individual risque unless from holding them too long, and no man refused to receive them for one commodity while they would purchase every other.

This general credit however did not last long. It menaced so deeply the views of our enemies who had built their hopes upon the defect of our resources that they and their partizans used every effort to impeach its value. Their success in one instance of this kind always made room for another, because he who could not relieve his wants with our paper, would not part with his property to procure it.

To remedy this evil the States as soon as formed into any shape of legislation enacted laws to make the continental paper a lawful tender and indeed to determine its value fixing it by penalties at the sum of specie expressed on the face of it. These laws produced monopoly throughout.

The monopoly of commodities, the interruption of commerce rendering them more scarce, and the successes of the enemy produced a depreciation of the paper. And that once begun, became in itself a source of further depreciation. The laws devised to remedy this evil either increased, or were followed by an increase of it.

This demanded more plentiful emissions, thereby increasing the circulating medium to such a degree as not only to exclude all other, but from its superabundant quantity again to increase the depreciation.

The several States instead of laying taxes to defray their own private expences followed the example[1] of Congress, and also issued notes of different denominations and forms. Hence to counterfeit became much easier, and the enemy did not neglect to avail themselves of this great tho base[2] advantage. And hence arose a farther depreciation.

Calling the husbandman frequently to arms who had indeed lost the incitements to industry from the cheapness of the necessaries of life in the begining compared with other articles which took a more rapid rise soon reduced that abundance which preceeded the war. This added to the greater consumption together with the ravages and subsistance of the enemy at length pointed the depreciation to the means of subsistence.

The issues from this moment became enormous and consequently increased the disease from which they arose, and which must soon have become fatal, had not the successes of America and the alliance with France kept it from sinking entirely. The certainty of its redemption being now evident, we only suffer from the quantity.

This however not only impairs the value simply in itself, but as it calls for continued large emissions, so the certainty that every thing will be dearer than it is, renders every thing dearer than it otherwise would be. And vice versa could we possibly absorp a part of the inundation which overwhelms Us, every thing would be cheaper from the certainty that it would become cheaper.

The money can be absorbed but three ways.

The first is by taxation, which cannot reach the evil while the war continues. Because the emissions must continue to supply what is necessary over and above even the nominal produce of taxes. And the taxes cannot be very productive by reason of the possession of part and the ravagement of other

1. First drafted as "the easy but dangerous Example." For the issuance of continental currency see Ferguson, *Power of the Purse*, pp. 25–47.
2. First drafted as "dangerous."

parts of the country by the enemy and also from the weakness of governments yet in their infancy, and not arrived to that power, method and firmness which are the portion of elder States.

The second method is by borrowing, and is not efficient, because no interest can tempt men to lend paper now which paid together with that interest in paper a year hence will not probably be worth half as much as the principal sum is at present. And whenever the case shall alter, then in proportion to the appreciation will be the loss of the public on what they borrow, to say nothing of the enormous burthens for which they must pay interest in specie or what is equal to it if so much of what hath been emitted could be borrowed as to render the remainder equally valuable with silver.

The last method is, by very considerable loans or subsidies in Europe, and is the only mode at once equal to the effect desired and freed from the foregoing exceptions. For if such a sum is drawn for at the advanced exchange as by taking up the greater part of our paper to reduce the exchange to par, The paper then remaining will be fully appreciated, and the sum due will not nominally (and therefore in the event really) exceed its real value.

But to this mode there are objections.

1st. Subsidies by any means equal to our necessities can hardly be expected while our allies being engaged in war, will want all the money they can procure. And

2dly. Loans cannot probably be obtained without good guarantee, or other security which America may not perhaps be able to procure or give.

But until our finances can be placed in a better situation, the war cannot possibly be prosecuted with vigor and the efforts made feeble as they must be, will be attended with an oppressive weight of expence rendering still more weak the confederated States.

This will appear from the foregoing observations and also from this that the present and in all probability the future seat of the war also, that is the middle States are so exhausted that unless by the most strenuous voluntary exertions of all the inhabitants no great number of men can possibly be subsisted.

And such exertions cannot be expected without the temptation of money more valued than ours is at present.

Sir, To the honorable Benjamin Franklin Esqr.

The above observations referred to in your instructions You shall lay substantially before the French ministry and labor for their assistance to remove the difficulties there stated. In Congress

HENRY LAURENS
President

Attest CHA THOMSON Secy

Endorsed: Observations on the Finances of America

From Jean Charles de Zinnern[3]

ALS: American Philosophical Society

Monseigneur! Bude en Hongrie le 26 Octobre 1778

L'atachement que j'ai a vos affaires, est au dessus de mes expressions. Je suis né sujet d'un grand Monarchie sous un gouvernement doux, mais je ne sais pas dans quel transport de joie je deviens, en cas que j'entende, ou que je lise de vos progrès.

Monseigneur de vous dire la verité, je vous regarde, et tous les chefs de votre nouvelle Republique comme des anges destinés du ciel pour soulager le genre humain sous votre direction: je prie Dieu incessament, qu'il vous ait sous sa sainte et digne garde: ce sont la de mes voeux quotidiens. Outre cela pour temoigner mon affection au publique j'ai composé un ouvrage en latin intitulé Notitia historica de Coloniis foederatis in America.[4] J'en ai un autre de viris illustribus Americae:[5]

3. Actually Johann (or Janos) Zinner; the final "n" was added to the signature according to a now obsolete German grammatical convention.
4. There is no evidence that this was ever published.
5. Probably his *Merkwürdige Briefe und Schriften der berühmsten Generäle in Amerika* ... (Augsburg, 1782). It contains an account of BF's career, his letter to Admiral Howe of July 20, 1776, as well as writings of both Loyalists and Patriots. From information kindly provided by Katalin Halácsy, Budapest.

mais il faut que j'atende la fin de guerre presente, qui me bien fournit de la matiere pour mieux tracer le caractere de vos heros admirables. Il est vrai, j'en ai beaucoup de doutes; c'est pourquoi je suis parti les jours passés de Bude a Vienne pour y rencontrer Mons. Lee,[6] qui etoit la; mais a mon arrivée je ne l'ai pas trouvé. Secretaire d'Ambassadeur de France m'a conseillé de prendre ma confiance a vous. Monseigneur c'est vous donc, que je prie tres humblement de me faire savoir la patrie de Messieurs Wassington, Hankok, Putnam, Gates, Charles Lée, Arnold: comme aussi les anecdotes de leur vie passée. Les gazettes ne debitent rien de cette chose la: particulierment de Mons. Arnold: on le fait tantot un Allemand de Maienz,[7] tantot un Ameriquain de Connecticut, tantot un Capucin cidevant, tantot un epicier de Norvich. Quant a vous Monseigneur, je vous prens pour un Bostonien un genie superieur, et un instrument principal de tout ce qui se passe pendent la guerre. Entre autre je voudrois aussi bien savoir ce qu'il en est que la Gazette de divers endroits mande, que Mons. Charles Lee n'a pas fait son devoir près de Montmouth en Nouvelle Jersey, et que le Congres lui a oté le commendement a cause de trahison.[8] C'etoit une conduite mechante; mais je suspends ladessus mon sentiment, jusqu'a votre reponse, si vous la jugerez a propos.

Puis si vous voulez vous servir de moi dans quelque occasion, vous n'avez que commander, ce sera mon vrai plaisir. J'ai de la connoissance en Hongrie j'en ai beaucoup a Vienne. Je suis persuadé, qu'il ne vous importe pas autant a present d'avoir un commerce avec les Autrichiens, que de pouvoir passer au monde en Etat Souverain et independent de l'Angletterre. Vous en faites tres sagement; mais Mons. Lée n'est pas venu

6. William Lee, who had been in Vienna in June but was back in Frankfurt by mid-July.

7. See xxv, 359, for the letter from George Arnold to BF.

8. The Supplement to the *Gaz. de Leyde* for Sept. 4, 1778, commenting on the battle of Monmouth of June 28, related that the *New-Jersey Gazette* of July 1 had criticized Gen. Lee's conduct and that he had defended himself in two letters to the newspaper. In the issues of Sept. 11, 22, and 25 the *Gaz. de Leyde* published those letters and Washington's report to the president of Congress of July 1.

bien a propos: il auroit falu prendre un autre chemin, dont je vous ecrirai un autrefois.

Aiez donc la bonté de me resoudre mes doutes signés, et de m'accorder vos bonnes graces, et votre precieuse amitié, que je regarderai comme le plus grand bien de ma vie. Je me ferai un devoir de repondre a vos commendements, et d'etre toujours avec un tres profond respect de Votre Excellence tres humble serviteur

JEAN CHARLES DE ZINNERN
Prefet dans l'Academie Impl. Royal. a Bude.[9]

Endorsed: J. Charles Zinnern Bude 26 8bre 1778.

The American Commissioners to Daniel McNeill[1]

AL (draft): Massachusetts Historical Society; two copies: National Archives

⟨Passy, October 27, 1778: We received yours of October 12 concerning your prisoners. On the basis of the King's regulations on prizes and prisoners, published at the same time, we assumed no special ministerial order was necessary and that officers in the ports were instructed to secure prisoners as provided in articles 7 and 15.[2] Moylan's letter of October 21 describes your difficulty. We shall apply to the minister at once for the necessary orders. Meanwhile secure the prisoners carefully as we anticipate an exchange. If you must sail before orders arrive, assure the port officers that we shall defray their expences in securing the prisoners. You are right to insist on a judicial decision about your prize.⟩

9. Probably the present Eötvös Loránd Tudományegyetem, founded as a Jesuit college in the sixteenth century. It was secularized in 1773 and moved to Buda in 1777. *International Handbook of Universities* . . . (8th ed., New Berlin, N.Y. [1981]), p. 504.

1. Published in Taylor, *Adams Papers*, VII.

2. See Sartine's letter to the commissioners of Aug. 16, and Wharton, *Diplomatic Correspondence*, II, 685–7, for the regulations which went into effect on Sept. 27. On Dec. 22, Sartine promised the commissioners to issue specific orders to officers in the individual ports respecting provisions for prisoners taken by Americans (Library of Congress).

The American Commissioners to James Moylan

AL (draft): Massachusetts Historical Society; two copies: National Archives

Sir   Passy Octr. 27. 1778

We received your Favour of the 12 Instant. You will see by the enclosed to Capt. McNeill, which We leave open for your Perusal, the State of the Affair of the Prisoners. In Case of his being obliged to Sail, before he can receive the Ministers particular orders for their Reception, We desire you would take care of them, if Mr. Schweighausers Agent Mr. Puchelberg declines it.[3] We are much obliged by your early Information of the Arrival of the Vessell from Philadelphia; and shall be so for any News you may from Time to Time communicate to us. We have the Honour to be.

Mr Moylan

The American Commissioners to Schweighauser[4]

ALS: Massachusetts Historical Society; two copies: National Archives

⟨Passy, October 27, 1778: We have received yours of September 27[5] and approve your handling of the *Thérèse* and her cargo. We think you should sign the receipt to Mr. Williams, through the words United States, and omit what follows.[6] He should discharge any demands against him and notify us, who stand behind him, without the additional complication of involving you. As to the *Directeur des fermes*, give him an account of the tobacco delivered him; do not change the price which is settled by contract but inform us of the going rate for tobacco at the time this was delivered. Messrs. Bondfield and Haywood[7] have offered space for freighting; contract with

---

3. He already had: see Moylan and McNeill's letters of Oct. 12.
4. Published in Taylor, *Adams Papers*, VII.
5. Actually Sept. 26.
6. For the transfer of responsibility for the arsenal see annotation to the Schweighauser letter of Sept. 26.
7. William Haywood, currently of Bordeaux, Bondfield, and John Gale of Edenton, N.C. posted bond for a letter of marque for the *Governor Living-*

them to ship the American goods held by you and Williams if you think their proposal reasonable.⟩

Jonathan Loring Austin to the American Commissioners[8]
ALS: American Philosophical Society

⟨Amsterdam, October 27, 1778: I will sail for St. Eustatia next Wednesday or Thursday, as no direct passage for America is available. Had I been able I would have told you sooner, so you could send more dispatches. I doubt that Admiral d'Estaing is in the precarious situation reported by the English newspapers. American affairs provoke conflicting opinions in the coffee houses here. I will take good care of your letters for Congress, and will be honored by any further mention of me.[9] May all possible success attend your negotiations.[1]⟩

Dumas to the American Commissioners[2]

ALS: American Philosophical Society; AL (draft): Algemeen Rijksarchief; copy: National Archives

⟨The Hague, October 27, 1778, in French: Last Saturday [Oct. 24] I received your letter of October 10.[3] The Grand Facteur is very satisfied with it. Our friend [van Berckel] was pleased and assured me several times it would make a good impression on the burgomasters of Amsterdam. He strongly recom-

---

ston, before JA and Arthur Lee on Oct. 26. APS. Gale ultimately became her captain: Boyd, *Jefferson Papers*, III, 90–1.

8. Published in Taylor, *Adams Papers*, VII.

9. See the commissioners' letter to the president of Congress, Sept. 22.

1. Austin reached St. Eustatia in February, 1779, and in April had an eventful passage to Virginia, narrowly escaping capture by a British privateer. Compensated by Congress for his services in Europe he returned to Boston at the end of May: *Sibley's Harvard Graduates*, XVI, 305.

2. Published in Taylor, *Adams Papers*, VII.

3. See our annotation of that letter for a discussion of its dating.

mended that I assure you the mention of England was made only to clarify the position of the city.

The merchants' address was presented to their High Mightinesses. I enclose their petition to the stadholder. Lord Suffolk[4] has promised to return the captured Dutch vessels and pay for their cargoes but says his ambassador will propose changes to the Anglo-Dutch treaty. He says it is a measure of his King's moderation that he has not yet requested that the republic give Britain the assistance the treaties require. We believe Suffolk's response was actually written here.[5]

The secretary of the States General[6] feels himself insulted by the merchants' accusation that he is pro-English. I will send you a translation of their address[7] as soon as it is finished and one to Congress, but the work is time-consuming and my hand trembles.⟩

From the Marine Committee

LS:[8] Yale University Library; copies: National Archives, Library of Congress

Marine Committee of Congress Philadelphia
Honorable Sir   October 27th. 1778.

This will go by a Continental Frigate from Boston which Congress have ordered to carry their dispatches as well as to accommodate the Marquis de la Fayette and his Suit with a passage to France.[9] The Captain will on his arrival immediately inform you thereof, and we have directed that he get his

4. British secretary of state for the northern department.
5. *I.e.* by the British ambassador Sir Joseph Yorke.
6. Hendrik Fagel who, Dumas believed, deserved the accusation.
7. Against the augmentation of the Dutch army; Dumas had promised on Sept. 9 to send a copy.
8. The postscript is in Lee's hand.
9. The frigate was the *Alliance,* Capt. Pierre Landais (*DAB*). For Lafayette and his passage see Paine's letter of Oct. 24.

OCTOBER 27, 1778

Vessel in readiness to follow any Orders which you may think proper to give which Orders he is to Obey.

Should you send him back with dispatches he will take in any Stores for the use of the States that may be in readiness at the Port where he may arrive, so as not to incommode the sailing or fighting of his Vessel. We have the honor to be Honorable Sir Your most Obedient Servant

RICHARD HENRY LEE Chn.

P.S. As the Marquis de la Fayette may have occasion to write by the return of this Frigate, please to let him have timely notice. R.H. LEE

The Honorable Benjamin Franklin Esqr

Endorsed: Marine Committee of Congress Oct. 27. 1778 relative to the Frigate Alliance

From Robert Niles

ALS: American Philosophical Society

Sir Bourdeaux Octor 27th 1778

This may advise you that I have had the misfortune Of being taken. I Sailed from Nants the 28th of august. The Next morning at day light fell in with the Ship Beezly Capt. Noah Gautier of Jersey who Chased me Seven hours When the Wind blowing very fresh and The Sea high Came up With and Captured me, after Maning the vessel Sent her to Jersey. Capt. Barns is Also taken and Carried into Guernsey.[1] My mail With all the letters I Commited to the Sea. I have been Treated much better than I expected. The Capt. has Been so kind as to put me With two of my people on board Of a dutch Vessel bound here. All the other people Were put on board the Seaford Ship of War[2] and ordered To do duty. I Shall Seek for a passage to Some part America as Soon as possible. I Shall be oblidged to Make application to Mr. Bonfield for Some money to Defray my Charges here and get me out of the

1. Grinnell had already reported the capture of Niles's *Spy* and Barnes's *Dispatch* to the commissioners on Sept. 15.
2. The *Seaford* was a twenty-two gun frigate launched in 1754.

652

Country Which I hope your honour Will not disaprove of as I am Moneyless. I am Sir your most obedient humble Servant

ROBT NILES

Addressed: The Honbe. / Benjamin Franklin Esqr / Paris / á Passy / Prés Paris

Notation: Captn. Niles Capt. Oct. 27. 1778.

From Thomas Pottar[3]   ALS: American Philosophical Society

Havre de Grace prison October 27th. 1778

May it plase your Excellency

To pardon the Liberty I take in trubling your honor to aquaint you that in the year Sevnty Six I left Amerca with Capt. Sheffild in the whale fishen and was bound to Holland with Our Oil[4] but had the Misfortin to be takin in the English Chanel by the gray hound Cutter,[5] whar I was Kept til I Run a way up to London, and Could get no Opurtunity of geting home to my father and was a bleched to hide for a long time from the Press, till I got on Bord of a Brig which Belonged to the frinds of Amerca, The Owner name which I make no dout you Know, is Mr. Williams,[6] in wappin [Wapping] and Mr.

3. He wrote again April 7, 1779, from the same prison with the same request; that time his name was spelled Potter. APS. Thomas was probably the son (b. 1756) of Rhode Island Captain James Potter. His brothers were James C. (1754–90) and Joseph Wanton (1762–1846): Charles E. Potter, *Genealogies of the Potter Families* . . . (Boston, 1888), [pt. 4], 21, and James N. Arnold, *Vital Record of Rhode Island* . . . (21 vols., Providence, 1891–1912), IV, [pt. 2], 110; XIV, 193.

4. Grinnell's letter of Oct. 7 speaks of a whaling ship, the *George*, commanded by Aaron Sheffield bound for Holland, although there is a discrepancy in dates of departure. See also Butterfield, *John Adams Diary*, II, 319, for a mention of Sheffield.

5. The *Greyhound* cutter, under the command of Lt. John Bazeley, was ordered in November, 1775, to cruise between Dover and Calais: *Naval Docs.*, III, 358.

6. For whom see his letters of Oct. 2 and 30.

Powel,[7] that what Ever Monny I had to Spar I Gave to Relive my Contry men, the brig was Command by our Capt. Clark,[8] who is an Amerca, but this Voydge had the Missfortin to be takin, by a french prvter and brought in har, would for Ever be thankful to your honor to Remove me to Amerca or on bord Aney Amercan priveteer, my broth is now Captain of an Amerca privateer and my fathr is well known to the Congres his nam is Capt. Jams Potter, now in Amerca. I Rest your honors most Obedgent Humble Servant   THOS. POTTAR

would be thankful to your honr to make one of your Sarvants Send me an Ancer

Addressed: To / His Excellency Benn. Franklin / Paris

Notation: Thos Potter Whaleman 27 Octr. 1778

From the Committee for Foreign Affairs

ALS:[9] American Philosophical Society; two copies: National Archives

(In Committee for foreign Affairs), Philada. Octr.
Honorable Sir   28th. 1778.
    As the Marquis De la Fayette will deliver this, we refer you to his Conversation in addition to the Gazettes for an Account of the Movements of the Enemy. He will doubtless gain some further Knowledge of them before he leaves Boston than what we are now possessed of. We shall speedily have Opportunities of forwarding Duplicates and Triplicates of what he now

7. Thomas Powell appears in Griffith Williams' "Friends to American Liberty are friends to Mankind," an undated list at the Hist. Soc. of Pa. which also includes Aaron Sheffield.
    8. Probably Elisha Clark of the *Columbus*, captured in the Channel when returning from a whaling voyage to Brazil and taken into Havre de Grace, according to Griffith Williams, below, Oct. 30. Clark is also listed among "Friends to American Liberty."
    9. In Lovell's hand.

delivers; and upon any material Event we shall dispatch a Vessel occasionally.[1]

Inclosed with other Papers is a Resolve of Congress of the 22d which we have officially sent to all the Commissioners.[2] We must earnestly request that, as we shall have Opportunities of frequently conveying to you Gazettes and other Species of American Intelligence, you would strive to communicate, in the best and speediest Way to the Gentlemen at other Courts what they are alike interested to know that they may prosecute in the best Manner the Service of these States abroad.

An exact Copy of your Credentials is among the Papers herewith. We wish you Success in this new Commission; and are with much Regard Sir Your most humble Servants

RICHARD HENRY LEE
JAMES LOVELL

Honble. Doctr Franklin

Addressed: Honorable / Benjamin Franklin Esqr. / Minister Plenipotentiary / from the United States / of America / France / favd. by Majr. Genl. / Marqs. Dela Fayette

Endorsed: Committee for Foreign Affairs Philada Oct. 28. 1778. with New Commission News to be communicated.

1. Lafayette carried BF's letter of credence (above, Oct. 21), his instructions, the plan for attacking Canada, and the observations on finances (Oct. 26).

2. The resolution, also sent to Izard, William Lee, and JA, reads: "That the Committee for Foreign Affairs be directed to inform the minister plenipotentiary at the court of France, and the commissioners of the United States at the respective courts in Europe, that it is the desire of Congress, that harmony and good understanding should be cultivated between the ministers, commissioners and representatives of this Congress at the respective courts of Europe, and that such confidence and cordiality take place among them as is necessary for the honour and interest of the United States." Smith, *Letters,* XI, 140–3; *JCC,* XII, 1053–4. A copy of this resolution (APS) bears BF's endorsement: "Resolve of Congress Oct. 22d 1778 Good Agreement among the Ministers."

From Johann Adolf Behrends[3]

ALS: American Philosophical Society

⟨Frankfurt am Main, October 28, 1778, in Latin: I am asking my good friend Mr. Bethmann,[4] who is leaving for France, to bring you this letter. It expresses my admiration for you as founder of the fatherland, doctor of the human race on the matter of bodies' electrical energy and illustrious member of the Republic of letters; most of all it tries to convey my boundless esteem for you as a human being. I burn with desire to meet you and render any service I can. Accept my congratulations on your appointment as foreign member of the French Royal Society of Medicine. May God grant you the freedom of your country!⟩

The American Commissioners to Van Berckel[5]

AL (draft):[6] National Archives

⟨Passy, October 29, 1778: Some of your propositions[7] can only be discussed in a personal interview. We wish you or

3. He signs himself Joann. Adolph. Behrends, M.D. Reipublicae Moeno francofurtensi Phÿsicus. Behrends (1740–1811) was appointed doctor for the city orphanage in 1782 and named first administrator at the medical institute founded by Frankfurt's noted benefactor, Johann Christian Senckenberg. He was the author of *Der Einwohner in Frankfurt in Absicht auf seine Fruchtbarkeit, Moralität und Gesundheit geschildert* (Frankfurt, 1771): *Biographisches Lexikon der hervorrangenden Aerzte aller Zeiten und Völker*, August Hirsch, ed. (6 vols., Vienna and Leipzig, 1884–88), I, 372.

4. Either Johann Philipp (1715–1793), Simon Moritz (1721–1782) or Peter Heinrich Metzler (1744–1800) of the Frankfurt banking firm, Gebrüder Bethmann, which became the city's leading competitor to the House of Rothschild: Udo Heyn, *Private Banking and Industrialization: the Case of Frankfurt am Main, 1825–1875* (New York, 1981), p. 169 and *passim*. In an undated note, Bethmann indicates that he did stop by to see BF and JA one evening, without success, and would call again the following day. APS.

5. Published in Taylor, *Adams Papers*, VII.

6. In Arthur Lee's hand. The editors of the *Adams Papers* speculate that this letter was never sent; we find their reasoning persuasive.

7. Above, Sept. 23.

someone authorized by you might meet one of us at Aix-la-Chapelle or any other place you may judge more convenient. We also leave to you the selection of fictitious names to be used when meeting.⟩

The American Commissioners to Vergennes[8]

LS:[9] Archives du Ministère des affaires étrangères; AL (draft): Massachusetts Historical Society; two copies: National Archives

⟨Passy, October 29, 1778: We are ready to execute and exchange the declarations concerning the omission of the 11th and 12th articles of the treaty of commerce,[1] and ask you to appoint a day for us to wait on you.⟩

From François-César Le Tellier, Marquis de Courtanvaux[2]

AL: American Philosophical Society

Ce Jeudy. 29. 8bre. 78.

Le Mis. de Courtanvaux fait mille Complimens à Monsieur Franklin, comme il a oublié de Lui dire hier que s'il avoit quelques compatriotes avec Luy, il seroit bien Le maître de Les amener diner, parcequ'ils seront recus avec plaisir. Il Le prie de recevoir les assurances de son sincere attachement.

Addressed: A Monsieur / Monsieur Franklin / deputé des Etats Unis / de L'amérique Septentrionale / A Passy.

8. Published in Taylor, *Adams Papers*, VII.
9. In the hand of BF's secretary Nicolas-Maurice Gellée: XXVI, 287 n.
1. Above, Sept. 1. We are unable to account for the delay.
2. For this military man turned scientist see above, XV, 34 and XXIII, 84.

From Richard Gridley[3]

ALS: American Philosophical Society

Dear Sir   Boston October 29 1778

Possibly you may remember the Conversation we had at General Washingtons Quarters at Cambridge, relating to Mines;[4] which I said we had a Great plenty of in this Country; and an observation I then made to you, that Congress need not be Timerous in Emiting Paper Currency, as the Mines if properly Attended to, woud enable them to Redeem their paper Currency; and otherwise be of Infinite Service to the States. My son Joseph[5] is the bearer of this, who is in the mercantile way, by whom I have sent a number of Samples of Mines, many of them are Valuable, and in good Situations for working Shafts, and Levels, and all of them well wooded and water'd; I have directed my son to shew you the Samples,[6] that you may if you think proper, direct him where the Samples may be examin'd, and if on examination any of them shou'd be found Valuable, by the French Mineralists, I am persuaded it will be a pleasure and Satisfaction to you, because great Remittances may be made to France &c. in return for their Manufactures; and as soon as our Troublesome Times are

3. A soldier and military engineer (1710–1796) who was at this time engineer general of the eastern department. In 1770 he had purchased from Edmund Quincy one half of iron-rich Massapog Pond in Sharon, Mass. Together with Quincy, Gridley began smelting iron ore and eventually manufactured cannon for the army. *DAB*; Daniel T.V. Huntoon, "Major-General Richard Gridley," *Magazine of History*, VII (1908), 338 and VIII (1908), 29.

4. Gridley can only be referring to October, 1775, when BF visited Washington's camp as chairman of a committee to evaluate the continental army. As a result of its report Gridley, who was serving as colonel of artillery, was dismissed. See XXII, 238.

5. Joseph was Gridley's fourth child, born in Boston in 1736: Boston, Record Commissioners, *Report*, XXIV (1894), 225. He established himself as a merchant in Nantes, applied unsuccessfully for a consulship, and remained in France until 1780 when he told BF he wanted passage to America, but was in extremely poor health. There is no indication that he arrived home. Joseph Gridley to BF, Feb. 25, 1779 and March 28, 1780, APS.

6. BF evidently showed the samples to the celebrated mineralogist Balthazar Georges Sage (XXV, 678 n) since his letter to Joseph Gridley, March 17, 1779 (Library of Congress), mentions Sage's report on them.

over, may publickly and privately be carried on; I woud have sent more Samples of Mines, but had so little notice of my sons going, I had not time enough to send for them: I am desirous you shou'd have the Inspection of them, and get such Tryals made of them as may Convince you of the reality; I have no motive but the general Good, which I doubt not will be a Sufficient Apology for giving you the Trouble of this Information; and am Dear Sir with the Greatest Veneration and Sincerity Your Most Obedient Humb Servant

RICHD. GRIDLEY

His Excellency Benja. Franklin Esqr

Notation: Richard Gridley, Boston 29. 8bre. 1778. concerning the Mines of America.

The American Commissioners to Sartine[7]

AL (draft): Massachusetts Historical Society; copies: National Archives (two); incomplete copy: Archives nationales

⟨Passy, October 30, 1778: We are honored by your letter of October 26 and grateful for the prompt release of some of our countrymen imprisoned at Dinan. We have received another petition from prisoners at Brest;[8] it appears that there are ten of them, only four of whom we had heard from, letters from the other six having miscarried. We would appreciate a similar clemency extended to them and enclose their most recent communication. A letter received last night from Lorient informs us that three British whaling vessels manned by Americans have been captured by French frigates and cruisers.[9] We have collected detailed intelligence on the valuable English

---

7. Published in Taylor, *Adams Papers*, VII.

8. Actually, Dinan; see above, from American Prisoners at Dinan, Oct. 21.

9. Grinnell's letter of Oct. 23. The information which follows had also been furnished by Grinnell both orally and in writing: see his memorandum of Oct. 7 and Butterfield, *Adams Diary*, II, 319–20. See also below, the American Commissioners to the President of Congress, Nov. 7, where the same scheme is proposed.

whale fishery off the coast of Brazil. About seventeen vessels have sailed in the past two months. The officers and most of the men are Americans.[1] Last year the English newspapers falsely reported that a convoy would accompany the fleet. In fact it is defenceless and could easily be overpowered. A single frigate or privateer sent in early December when the fleet is loaded with bone and oil would suffice to capture an extremely valuable cargo and free the Americans involved. Whenever the British have captured American vessels they have given the whalemen a choice of fighting their own countrymen or entering the whale fishery. Many have chosen the latter. We hope that His Majesty's service may send a frigate from here or the West Indies to seize both a profitable branch of commerce and a nursery for seamen.⟩

Dumas to the American Commissioners[2]

AL: American Philosophical Society; AL (draft): Algemeen Rijksarchief

⟨The Hague, October 30, 1778, in French: As a result of the merchants' address the Assembly of Holland will reconvene next Wednesday, the corps of nobility of the province has withdrawn a counter-address and an important personage[3] seems to be alarmed. The British party is also concerned.

The Grand Pensionary is displeased by Suffolk's reply.[4] I

1. Here the commissioners list the following names: Aaron Sheffield from Newport, William Goldsmith and Richard Holmes from Long Island, John Chadwick, Francis May (Macy), Reuben May (Macy), John Meader, Jonathan Meader, Elisha Clark, Benjamin Clark, William Ray, Paul Pease, Bunker Fitch, Reuben Fitch, Zebbeda Coffin and another Coffin (probably Richard or Hezekiah), Andrew Swain, a second William Ray and ———— Delano, all of Nantucket, and John Locke of Cape Cod. A number of these men appear in Griffith Williams' undated list in the Hist. Soc. of Pa., entitled "Friends to American Liberty are friends to Mankind," from which we have supplied an occasional first name. Spellings vary. One of the Rays is probably William Wray, called "first friend" by Williams.
2. Published in Taylor, *Adams Papers*, VII.
3. The *stadholder*.
4. To Dutch protests about the British seizure of their ships: see Dumas to the commissioners, Oct. 27.

660

have given him a printed copy of the Franco-American treaty and told him you felt he could proceed in the manner he judged most agreeable to the republic. Seeing him amazed and at a loss for words I made him understand he owed you a reply, which I told him you expected, and gave him an extract of Mr. Franklin's letter of September 22.[5] He read it carefully and smiled at the ending. I volunteered to convey to you anything he might like and beseeched him to believe me as zealous for the welfare of this republic as I am a friend of the Americans. He answered, "I do not doubt it." I gave our friend van Berckel an account of the meeting and a copy of the excerpt. I told him I was giving his city something it could use to raise charges if your overture was repressed; he agreed and thanked me profusely. On the 28th an important person in whom we can have full confidence but who requested anonymity asked me to tell Mr. Franklin that there are serious but secret reasons which impose the need for delay on the Grand Pensionary. I have noticed that of late our friend has softened his attitude toward the Grand Pensionary. I received the papers Mr. [Arthur] Lee sent and forwarded a copy to the printer at Leyden. P.S.: I have received a violently anti-British 180-page Dutch brochure which will serve to further arouse this nation.⟩

Fairholme & Luther to the American Commissioners

ALS: American Philosophical Society

St. Martins Isle of Rhè 30th.
October 1778

Honorable Gentlemen

Inclos'd we make bold to send you a copy of what we wrote yesterday to Mr. De Saint Cristau one of the Farmers General[6] with regard to a cargo of fish taken in the Brigg the Lord

---

5. Dumas here cites the letter and notes some transitional passages which he has inserted; see Taylor, *Adams Papers*, VII.

6. Adam-François de Saint-Cristau, son of the director of the treasury of the Estates of Brittany, had been a member of the *ferme* since 1772: Yves Durand, *Les Fermiers généraux au XVIIIe siècle* (Paris, 1971), p. 106.

Grovenor by the Continental Friggat the Providence Capn. Abraham Whipple.[7] At the first arrival of the above prize, we got liberty to put the fish on Shore for to export it to Spain, but after it was landed and when we intended to export it the Farmers insisted on our paying the duty of entry which was £11 4 s. per Quintal on which our John Luther went to Paris and applied to the worthy and Honble. Messrs. Franklyn and Dean who were so kind to assist him, and got an order from Mr. Necker with permission to sell it (in this Island only) free of duty if we thought proper or else to export it for Spain without paying the duty of entry as we had declar'd it at our Custom house, but as the hostilities between France and England was then begining and still continues we think the risk too much. We wou'd willingly send it to Bordeaux, Nantes, or Rochelle to be dispos'd off, as the quantity is too great for the consumption of this Island. There were lately two prizes with fish and one with Coals and bottles brought into Nantes by American arm'd Vessels who got liberty to pay duty at the rate of 10 per Cent of the amount of the Sales which is more advantagious than the paying the one half of the duties as it is now reduced by the new ordinance.[8] We therefore most humbly request your honours will be pleas'd to intercede for us with Mr. Necker that he may obtain for us the liberty of paying the 10 per Cent on the amount of Sale only. It will be always so much duty coming into the farmers general. Other-

7. A strange confusion seems to have taken place. The enclosed letter to Saint-Cristau, of Oct. 29, refers to a cargo of cod and cod oil brought to the Ile de Ré by the *Boston*, Capt. Silas Ewers, in November, 1777. This is an episode that had already been discussed by Fairholme & Luther in a letter to Silas Deane of April 3 (APS). The present letter, however, mentions the *Lord Grosvenor*, Capt. Abraham Whipple's prize, whose cargo was primarily made up of wine, not fish, and which was the object of the firm's June 5 letter to BF. Both wine and fish were subject to regulation by the farmers general, as Fairholme & Luther explained to BF in their letter of July 3. In fact, the *Lord Grosvenor*'s cargo had been sold in Nantes as early as July 12: accounts of the sale that day, signed by Schweighauser, are among JW's accounts at the National Archives.

8. Of Aug. 27, whose provisions are further described in the enclosure.

wise by their refusal we will be oblig'd to send it to Spain at all risks as the fish is so much damag'd that it will not support the paying the duties which is £5 12 s. per Quintal. Your honours kind intercession will ever be acknowledg'd with the most sincere gratitude by Honorable Gentlemen Your most obedient humble Servants   FAIRHOLME & LUTHER

Notations: Letter from Fairholme & Luther. / Fairholme & Luther 30th. Oct. 78.

Vergennes to the American Commissioners

L (draft):⁹ Archives du Ministère des affaires étrangères; copies: Library of Congress (two), National Archives, Massachusetts Historical Society; transcript: National Archives

A Versailles le 30 8bre. 1778

J'ai reçu Messieurs, la réponse que vous m'avez fait l'honneur de m'adresser concernant les arrangements a prendre avec les regences barbaresques pour la sûreté du pavillon américain dans la méditerrannée.¹ Je pense qu'avant que le Roi puisse faire des tentatives pour seconder vos vües à cet égard, il est convenable que vous soyez munis de plein-pouvoir de la part du Congrès, et surtout que vous soyez non-seulement autorisés a proposer les donatives qu'il pourra être question de répandre, mais aussi munis des fonds nécessaires pour les réaliser.² Lorsque tous ces préliminaires seront remplis, vous pouvez être assurés, Messieurs, que le Roi se portera avec empressement à seconder autant qu'il pourra dependre de luy les desirs et les vües du Congrès.

Mrs. Franklin, Adams et Lée

9. In the hand of Gérard de Rayneval.
1. Above, Oct. 1.
2. Without bribes or tribute the states of Barbary were hardly likely to conclude a treaty or to stop molesting American ships: James A. Field, Jr., *America and the Mediterranean World 1776–1882* (Princeton, 1969), pp. 29–32.

show you their sense of his merit and I do assure you that the Sentiments of the people at Large and of the Army are the Same. These public testimonies being extremely agreable to him, I hope you will pardon the Liberty I take as his freind, of hinting to you, what a satisfaction it will be to his Noble Family that the Ministry should be acquainted by you rather than any one Else of the opinion entertained of Him here. For which reason, May it not be proper to put the resolves letters &c. into the hands of the Ministry instantly on the receipt of them and before the Marquis makes his appearance at Versailles.

I am sure all the consequence he can derive from the influence of his Family or from his own merit will be exerted for our Interest because he thinks them blended with those of his Nation, and I know that Personally he ardently desires to cultivate your freindship and to merit your Esteem. He will inform you of the Parties in our Congress and in our Army, Parties which at another time might have been fatal and are now dangerous. There are seeds of great Evils scattered abroad, and I am much afraid that there [are] some among us who would ape Cromwell, if they can disgust our fairfax so much as to make him seek retirement and to effect this no Endeavors are wanting of those, who are his yours and the Enemies of every one who are obstacles to the gratification of their Private Ambition.[6]

You will find there are Wotherburnes[7] in France as well as in England and Philippics, where if the Execution doth not answer the Intention tis not the fault of the Writers. I beg you to make the proper compliments of remembrance to Dr. Bancroft and your Grandson and that these Gentlemen would mention me to such of my Old Acquaintance as do me the honor not to forget me. I am with much truth and respect Your Excellencys Most Obliged and Most Humble Servant

WM. CARMICHAEL

6. A reference to the "Conway cabal" against Washington ("Fairfax"), Horatio Gates being the potential Cromwell.

7. Alexander Wedderburn, who had humiliated BF before the Privy Council: XXI, 37–70.

P.S. I find that it will be agreable to the Marquis that his own Cutler should be imployed to make the Sword presented Him by Congress.[8] As proper devices are directed in the execution of the Workmanship, perhaps allusions to the scenes of actions in which he most distinguished Himself might be suitable. The most remarkable were Brandewine where he was wounded Glocester where he drove Ld. Cornwallis, Barren Hill from whence he effected a retreat altho nearly surrounded by the whole British Army & the Schuyllkill in his rear, Monmouth & Rhode Island from whence he imbarked in the last boat. The Address of his Cutler is Leger Fourbissier Derriere L'Opera à Paris[9]

Endorsed: Mr Carmichael Oct. 30. 78 State of Congress

From Griffith Williams ALS: American Philosophical Society

Dear Sir,   London Octr. 30. 1778.

By the way of Havre de Grace I have taken the Liberty to Send you few lines.[1] My last[2] by Captn. Barnard he informs me you received Safe. From the Active part I have taken to Assist the Unfortunate Americans on this Side the Water I have to request a little indulgence in their behalf on your Side. Viz. Captn. Elisha Clarke Master of the Columbus belonging to Nantucket now Confin'd with his Crew in Havre de Grace being taken a few weeks Ago in the Channel on his Voyage to the Brazils. I am well aware that the Southern Whale Fishery Carried On by this Country is deem'd injurious to the United States. On the Other hand I'm Convinced that whenever the Wretched Ministers of this Country Understand the interest of the People One half as well as their Own, Peace with America

8. See Paine's letter of Oct. 24.

9. BF took the advice and Liger sent his receipted bill on Aug. 24, 1779 (APS).

1. Williams sent this by way of Elisha Clark who apparently did not forward it until he reached Bilbao, on parole: see below, Dec. 5.

2. Of Oct. 2.

will be the result, the more liberal and extensive the better. America deserves more then She Claims. At whatever Period that happy day Arrives, that Fishery from this Country will naturally dissolve and dissolve to the Mutual advantage of both Countries. In the first Place the Outfitts for those Voyages from England is enormously expensive, in the Second place the outfitts from America inconsiderable. So of Course it will be the Object of America to pursue the Fishery and the Object of Britain to receive the produce of that Fishery in exchange for her manufactures. I Speak from experience having had Some tryal in the Adventure. However not to dwell on Speculation, if there is a possibility of Accomplishing the liberation of Captn. Clarke and his Crew being Chiefly Americans Should esteem it exceeding Kind. From Principles he is highly attach'd to his Country and has Acted on various Occasions in the Most Generous Manner to his Countrymen in distress. Its on his request I make this Application to you, if it Cannot be done with Consistancy, I would not wish to be too Urgent, however unsuccessful there is a Satisfaction in the Attempt. I wish a Generous Cartel was establish'd between the diffrent powers at War, there Can be no Advantage in Keeping men in Captivity. Its likely the *Kings Ambassador* with a haugtyness becoming a *Scot*[3] may refuse to hearken to the Claims of Humanity but when in the language of his Countrymen Passively Asks mercy of the Mortal Image they Worship. Freemen revolts at Such Idea of Idolatry. To Conclude however Culpable those Americans now Concern'd in the Southern Whale Fishery may be held in America, I do Aver that when Circumstances are properly Stated they will deserve the Pity of their Countrymen instead of their Censure, from the diffrent attempts they have made to go home, from their being here at a Great expence and having but Small property. Something must be done for Subsistance. Tis true they embark'd in the fishery before mention'd, and Spar'd in the most liberal manner what they Could to Assist Others in distress. If in

3. Presumably David Murray, Lord Stormont, recalled as ambassador to France in March, 1778.

consequence of what I have Stated it is in your power to effect what is herein requested you'll Confer an Obligation on Your Humble Servant &c.   G. WILLIAMS

Addressed: To / His Excellency / Benjn. Franklin Esqr / Paris

Vergennes to the American Commissioners

Copies: Library of Congress, National Archives, Massachusetts Historical Society

Versailles 31. Oct. 1778

Vous me demandez, Messieurs, un jour pour l'Echange des Declarations concernant l'Omission des onzieme et douzieme Articles du Traité de Commerce.[4] Si lundi prochain deux novembre peut vous convenir, je serai charmé d'avoir l'honneur de vous recevoir et je me flatte que vous voudrez bien me faire Celui de diner le même jour chez moi. J'ai l'honneur d'être avec une parfaite consideration, Messieurs, Votre très humble et très obeissant serviteur   signé DE VERGENNES

Messrs. Franklin Lee & Adams

From Veuve Babut & Labouchere[5]

ALS: American Philosophical Society

Monsieur   Nantes le 31. 8bre 1778.

Nous avons l'honneur de remettre a votre Excellence deux paquets qui se sont trouvés dans le Brigantin La Lucie[6] Capitaine De Groot qui vient d'arriver dans notre Riviere etant parti de la Delaware le 20. 7bre. S'il nous en parvenoit quelqu'autre nous les acheminerions avec la meme Exactitude.

---

4. Above, Oct. 29.

5. Listed among the lesser *armateurs* of Nantes in Villiers, *Commerce colonial*, p. 406, where they ranked forty-second in wealth.

6. A brig *Lucy* had been registered in the port of Philadelphia since June 16, 1774: *PMHB*, XXVIII, 488.

Nous sommes avec le plus profond Respect Monsieur de votre Excellence les trés humbles et trés obeissants Serviteurs

Ve. Babut & Labouchere

Endorsed: Babut & Labouchere Nantes 31 8bre. 1778.

From Sausset & Masson

ALS: American Philosophical Society

Monsieur,   A Beaune, le 31 8bre. 1778

L'opinion où nous sommes que vous pouvez faire usage des vins de Bourgogne, nous fait vous offrir nos soins pour vos commissions de cette espece: en les agréant, vous nous honorerez infiniment.

Nous pouvons vous annoncer, Monsieur, que généralement les vins sont, cette année, très-fermes, d'une riche couleur, du goût le plus agréable, francs et vineux, recueillis par le plus beau temps, et ayant eu, pendant toute l'année, une chaleur extrême qui n'a pas peu contribué à leur donner le moëlleux qu'on leur trouve, et qui caractérise toujours les bons vins. Nous ne regrettons dans la récolte, que sa modicité qui a influé, ainsi que la bonne qualité, sur la nature des prix que vous trouverez au Bordereau ci-contre qui contient également les prix des vins vieux.[7]

Si aucuns d'eux vous conviennent, et que vous daigniez nous donner la préférence pour vos ordres, vous connoîtrez, Monsieur, que nous ne recherchons votre confiance, que pour vous être agréablement utiles, et par-là mériter de votre part les égards que l'on a ordinairement pour d'honnêtes Négociants. Nous sommes avec le plus profond respect, Monsieur, Vos très-humbles et très-obéissants serviteurs

Sausset et Masson

Endorsed: Saussett & Masson Vins de Bourgogne

Notation: 31. Oct. 1778.

7. A price list is enclosed.

To Anne-Catherine de Ligniville Helvétius

Reprinted from William Temple Franklin, ed., *Memoirs of the Life and Writings of Benjamin Franklin, L.L.D., F.R.S., &c* ... (3 vols., 4to, London, 1817–18), III, 332.

Arranging a party with Mme. Helvétius was not always an easy enterprise. Two undated notes, in as many hands, allow us a glimpse into the complexity of getting friends together. Taking up the pen herself, for once, the lady begged Franklin to enquire from Turgot whether the dinner proposed for the following day was really taking place. It seemed to hinge on whether or not M. de Lafreté had returned from Marly. She concluded: "Je vous embrasse de toute mon ame." Bethia Alexander, writing on behalf of her father and sister, deplored that a certain party, to be held at Auteuil on the following Saturday, was now in jeopardy because Mme. Helvétius, one of the guests, "had most unluckily forgot a prior engagement she had taken to meet Monsieur Turgot at Paris."[8]

Far from resenting the widow's forgetfulness, Franklin used it at some later date (1779?) as the theme of one of his most charming Bagatelles, the "Lettre à Mme. de Lafreté." In the following document, he muses on the reasons of her popularity as a hostess.

[October, 1778?][9]

... And now I mention your friends, let me tell you that I have in my way been trying to form some hypothesis to account for your having so many, and of such various kinds. I see that statesmen, philosophers, historians, poets, and men of learning of all sorts, are drawn around you, and seem as willing to attach themselves to you as straws about a fine piece of amber. It is not that you make pretension to any of their sciences; and if you did, similarity of studies does not always make people love one another. It is not that you take pains to engage them: artless simplicity is a striking part of your character. I would not attempt to explain it by the story of the ancient, who,

---

8. These two undated letters are in the APS.

9. The date is guesswork, based on tenuous psychological clues. By the end of the summer, BF, held somewhat at a distance by Mme. Brillon, started gravitating toward the intellectually stimulating circle of the woman she called "mon aimable rivale," and whom he dubbed "Notre-Dame d'Auteuil." His visits to her house, about a mile away from the Valentinois, became so frequent that his place at table was always set.

Anne-Catherine de Ligniville Helvétius

being asked why philosophers sought the acquaintance of kings, and kings not that of philosophers, replied, that philosophers knew what they wanted, which was not always the case with kings. Yet thus far the comparison may go, that we find in your sweet society, that charming benevolence, that amiable attention to oblige, that disposition to please and be pleased, which we do not always find in the society of one another. It springs from you; it has its influence on us all; and in your company we are not only pleased with you, but better pleased with one another, and with ourselves. I am ever, with great respect and affection, &c.   B.F.

From Edward Bancroft   ALS: American Philosophical Society

Dear Sir   Monday Evening. [October, 1778 or after][1]
I have a few Lines from Mr. Deane dated Philadelphia 6th. Septr. 1778 and refering to Packets which he had just Sealed; I suppose they must have come under Cover to you, and beg you will in that Case send them by the Bearer. I am with the utmost respect and Devotion Dear Sir Yours
                                                EDWD. BANCROFT

Addressed: A Monsieur / Monsr. Franklin / Passy

Notation: Edw. Bancroft

From ——— Cox   AL: American Philosophical Society

Saturday Morning. [before or during October, 1778][2]
Mr. Cox presents his Compliments to Doctr. Franklin. Cannot do himself the Honor of dining with him on Thursday next,

1. Lacking the letter from Deane to Bancroft we cannot know the date of this letter, but this is the earliest possibility. See Deane to BF, above, Sept. 15 for Deane's surviving correspondence.
2. So dated because John G. Frazer, in his letter to Craddock Taylor of June 7, 1779 (APS), states that he and Mr. Cox of Philadelphia had been in the south of France in October, 1778.

Mr. C. having determined to sett out, on Tuesday, for the South of France.

Addressed: His Excellency / Benj. Franklin Esqr: / Passy.

From [Jean-Baptiste Le Roy][3]

AL: American Philosophical Society

Dear Sir   [October, 1778]
    Just arrived from Paris I send to know whether you have at last received your Dispatches. They say in Paris Strange news about M. D'Estaing. I wish you my Dear friend a very good Night. If it was not too late I had been to play a game at Chess with You.

Addressed: Dr. Franklin

Notation: Le Veillard?

3. Identified by the handwriting and dated by the reference to the strange news about d'Estaing, presumably his abandonment of the siege of Newport, which was learned in Paris in October: see Vergennes' letter of Oct. 19.

Index

Compiled by Jonathan R. Dull
(Semicolons separate subentries; colons separate divisions within subentries.)

From William Carmichael

ALS: American Philosophical Society

Sir   Philadelphia, October 30th 1778

The return of the Marquis de la Fayette gives me an opportunity which I seize with pleasure of renewing my assurances of respect and Gratitude to you.[3] I have thro the course of the Summer taken the liberty of transmitting you such accounts of our internal Situation as might contribute to your information, tho' by no means to your satisfaction.[4] The Marquis will fill up the out Lines which I but faintly sketch, for it is not only the knowledge of arms which he has endeavoured to acquire here, but that of Men. Altho' he has been in a good scool, I am afraid there are many of the Capital figures, which a good Painter would not chuse to copy. I have had the misfortune of being obliged to view them too near During some months past and I cannot say my enthusiasm has increased by the circumstance. Under the hands of Mr. A. Lee There might arise many admirable Caricatures. I never conceived that it was possible, that a body of men, some of whom are certainly men of Abilities and many of them honest could have met together to so little purpose.[5]

Their Finances, their foreign affairs their Internal Police are much in the same situation I found them on my arrival at york Town, Except that a letter of Credence [*and*] some instructions are made out for you as Minister at the Court of Versailles, of which the Marquis is bearer.

No one but Himself has known how to reconcile the clashing parties of this Continent to his own views, by this you may judge not only of his amiable character but of his discretion. The resolves of Congress Letters &c. in his favor will

---

3. Carmichael had been in correspondence with Lafayette over the summer and autumn: Idzerda, *Lafayette Papers*, II, 83, 99–101, 207–9, 215–6, 488; see *ibid.*, pp. 199–202, for the present letter and details on its composition.

4. Carmichael's last extant letter is of May 14: XXVI, 450–2.

5. In November Maryland elected Carmichael to Congress: Smith, *Letters*, XI, xix. He had recently testified to Congress about Silas Deane: see Deane's letter of Oct. 21.

to, 159, 267, 467, 506; mentioned, lxv, 28 n, 442; letter from, 49–50

Chaumont, Marie-Thérèse Le Ray de (Jacques-Donatien's wife): greetings to, 467, 506; Macaulay sends books to, 474; mentioned, 442

Chauvel, David, 615, 616 n

Chesapeake Bay, many French vessels in, 492–3, 508

Chess, BF, others play, lxv, 162, 378, 431, 632, 672

Chester (Dutch sloop), 482–3

Chesy, ——— de, 17 n

Chevalier, ———: captured with La Plaigne, 540–1; letter from, *inter alia,* 539–42

Chew, Benjamin: inquires about Dick, 278–9; identified, 278 n; letter from, 278–9

Child, Capt. ———, 385

Choisenet, ———, 26

Choiseul, Etienne-François, duc de, 103

Christin, ——— (clockmaker): sends inventions, 425–6; letter from, 425–6

Cicero: quoted, 435 n

Cincinnati, Order of the, 512 n

Clairbois. *See* Vial du Clairbois, Honoré-Sébastien.

Clark, Capt. Benjamin, 660 n

Clark, Capt. Elisha: captured, 654; identified, 654 n; imprisoned, 666; mentioned, 660 n

Clear (or Cleary), abbé Patrick: asks BF's help in recovering brother's estate, 195–7; identified, 195–6 n; BF assists, 197 n; letter from, 195–7

Clear (or Cleary), Esther, Margaret, Mary, Patrick, Simon (Timothy's children), 196

Clear (or Cleary), Timothy: estate of, 195 n, 196

Clear (or Cleary), ——— Campbell (Timothy's late wife), 196

Clermont, Louis de Bourbon-Condé, comte de, 27

Clifton, Anna Maria, 602

Clingan, William (Pa. delegate): identified, 600 n; opposes BF's election as minister plenipotentiary, 600 n

Clinton, Gen. Henry: in 1778 campaign, 13, 185 n, 250, 373, 408, 451; relieves

Howe, 132 n; letter of, in London paper, 360; mentioned, 43, 191–2

Clos-Le-Prestre (manufactory), 623

Clothing: Bondfield offers, 551. *See also* Uniforms.

Clouet, Louis: asks help in contacting Fouquet, 207–8; identified, 207 n; letter from, 207–8

Club of Thirteen: members of, support D. Williams, 354–5; BF member of, 354 n

Cochran, Charles B. (Robert's son): BF thanked for attentions to, 262–3; and BFB, 262 n; identified, 262 n

Cochran, Robert: thanks BF for attentions to his son, 262–3; identified, 262 n; plans trip to France, 263; letter from, 262

Cockpit. *See* Privy Council.

Coder, Henry: and Barbeu-Dubourg suggest military operations, 326, 406 n; identified, 406 n; letter from, 406

Coderc, Gabriel-Aphrodise de (H. Coder's brother): and d'Argout incident, 406–7 n

Coffee, advice on use of, by naval crews, 80

Coffin, Capt. Richard (or Hezekia), 660 n

Coffin, Capt. Zebbeda, 660 n

Coffyn, Francis (American agent at Dunkirk): and Amiel, 60, 61, 63, 64: Poreau, 61, 63, 64, 69–70, 82 n: Grinnell, 64: Hinman, 276 n: Bancroft, 480; sends intelligence, 60–1; aids American seamen, 61, 82; sends certificates in his defense, 64, 69, 81–2; asks approval of his conduct, 69–70; reports on escaped prisoners, 480; letters from, 60–1, 64, 69–70; letter to, 81–2

Coleman, Capt. Thomas, 451

Collas, Jane Mecom, 192 n, 301

Collas, Peter: captured, released, 192, 257, 404–5, 519, 526; plans return to America, 192, 301; empowers commissioners to act in *Triton* case, 192–3; identified, 192 n; BF, Ridley assist, 192 n, 301; carries Mecom letters, 257; sails on *Dispatch,* 301, 404–5, 519; to carry JW letter, 308; receives money for prisoner relief, 519 n; wishes, receives help in recovering his goods, 519, 526, 548; mentioned, 491; letters from, 192–3, 301, 519

INDEX

Dispatch (continued)
652; mentioned, 160 n
Dobrée, Marie-Rose (Peter's wife), 49 n
Dobrée, Peter Frederick (Schweighauser's son-in-law): accusations against, 49–50, 240–1, 424 n, 429; marriage of, 49 n; reports captures, 405; and dispute over sale of *Drake*, 538; mentioned, 631 n; letter from, 240–1
Dobrée, Thomas (Peter's father): accusations against, 241 n, 429; identified, 405 n; mentioned, 405
Dohrman, Arnold Henry, 451
Dolgorouki, Prince Vasily Vladimirovich, 101 n
Dolphin (merchantman), 251
Donop, Carl Emil, count von, 606 n
Dort (Netherlands): Dumas praises pensionary of, 381
Douglass, Andrew (justice), 522
Douglass, Andrew (petitioner): recounts sufferings, asks assistance, 521–2; letter from, 521–2
Douglass, George, 522
Douglass, John (assemblyman), 522
Dove (schooner), 126 n
Dover: uncertain communications between Calais and, 23; American prisoners taken to, 480
Drake, H.M.S. (sloop of war): captured by *Ranger*, 84 n; Wilkinson pilot for, 254 n; plundered, 277 n; sale of, 277 n, 536–9
Drayton, William Henry (congressional delegate), 596 n, 617
Dresden (Saxony): Prussian troops in, 116
Dr. Franklin (letter of marque), 616 n
Drill, planting: Tull invents, 466 n
Driver, Edward (prisoner): asks assistance, 547–8, 558, 581; freed, 581 n; mentioned, 542 n; letters from, *inter alia*, 547–8, 581–2
Dropsy: tobacco ash supposed cure for, 28
Du Bouchet, Denis-Jean-Florimond de Langlois de Mautheville, chevalier (comtesse de Conway's brother), 473 n
Dubourg de la Blanchardiere, ——— (Barbeu-Dubourg's nephew), 194, 326–7, 540
Duc de Choiseul (merchantman), 95 n
Du Chaffault de Besné, Louis-Charles, comte: wounded, 212; identified, 212 n

Duchesse de Grammont (merchantman), 152, 155, 274
Du Coudray, Philippe-Charles-Jean-Baptiste Tronson, 111 n
Duer, William, 596 n
Dumas, Charles-Guillaume-Frédéric: communicates treaty of commerce, 31, 116, 129 n, 150, 168, 214 n, 511, 660–1; and Berckel, 31, 116, 168, 214, 273, 344–6, 352–3, 376, 381, 388–90, 396, 454 n, 487, 510, 529–30, 562–3, 612, 650–1, 661: La Vauguyon, 31 n, 116, 129–30, 214, 272, 316–17, 352–3, 376–7, 396, 487, 511, 563, 612, 650: Carmichael, 32: Bleiswijk, 116, 129 n, 150, 168, 381, 660–1: de la Lande, Fynje, 117, 273, 390 n: Congress, committee for foreign affairs, 128, 142, 185, 344–6, 389, 651: G. Grand, 272–3, 284, 317, 346–7, 389–90, 487, 563: W. Lee, 344–5, 347, 389–90, 563, 612: Huet du Plessis, 565; reports Dutch political news, 31, 116–17, 129–30, 186, 344, 353, 380–1, 388, 396, 563, 612, 651, 660–1: de Neufville-W. Lee meetings, 343–6, 376–7, 388–90; identified, 31 n; uses code names, 31 n; sends military, diplomatic news, 31–2, 116–17, 129–30, 150, 167–8, 185, 317, 396, 651, 660–1; commissioners pay, 117, 142: recommend Congress compensate, 128; notified of ratification of Franco-American treaty, 129; provides news to Dutch papers, 130, 186, 661; visits French embassy daily, 272, 316; praises *Gaz. de Leyde*, 316; visits Salgas, Hutton, 316–17; and proposed Va. loan, 345–7, 376, 388–90; and proposed Dutch-American commercial treaty, 352–3, 379, 388, 396, 448, 487, 510–11, 529–30, 562–3, 612, 650–1; BF asks for advice about proposed Dutch mission, 448, 563–4; and commissioners' loan, 486–7; as intermediary with Amsterdam burgomasters, 487, 562; forwards letter for Stockton, 487, 591; Austin visits, 510, 613; inquires about supposed capture of Newport, 563, 591; on BF's popularity in Netherlands, 563–4; Vergennes praises, 593; awaits BF portrait, 613; criticizes Fagel, 651 n; A. Lee sends papers to, 661; letters from, 31–2, 116–17, 129–30, 150,

688

1763), 144 n: Anet, 332, 360 n, 397, 416–17, 431, 437, 460 n, 471–2, 476–8: Moulin-Joli, composes "Ephemera," 430–5: Netherlands (1761, 1766), 448 n: Ireland (1771), 496: Washington's headquarters (1775), 658; aids impecunious authors, 148–9; has difficulties with French language, 153 n, 333, 433, 531 n, 576 n; uses letterpress, 161; as scientist, inventor, 176 n, 236, 328–9, 506–7, 606; is ignorant of Bancroft's, Deane's speculations, 229; visitors' book of, 341; and liturgical reform, 354 n; writes "moral work," 355; health of, 430–1, 480, 496–9; proposed mission of, to Netherlands, 448, 563–4, 576, 593; intends to pay grandchildren's expenses, 462; Canadian mission of (1776), 497; denies having written address to Irish, 504; throws aside title of doctor, 561 n; as possible minister to Vienna, 589; directs freeing of slave, 605 n; exceeds instructions by asking Vergennes for French expedition, 619 n, 634 n; sends poem to Hartley, signs himself "N.A.," 628–30; examined before Privy Council (1774), 665 n; For new writings see "Bagatelles"; "Ephemera."

Franklin, Deborah, 37

Franklin, Elizabeth, 97

Franklin, William: exchange of, lxvi, 90, 600–1; BF, WTF suspected because of links to, lxvi–lxvii, 600–1, 604; and Walpole Company, 86; corresponds with R. Bache, 90; imprisoned, 97

Franklin, William Temple: BF criticized for employing, lxvi–lxvii, 600–1, 604; keeps accounts, 21 n, 319 n, 365, 462, 481 n; greetings to, 42, 53, 78, 159, 308, 394, 602, 665; meets pretty girls, 48; Mme. Conway appeals to, for news of her husband, 78 n; invitations to, 79, 236, 432 n, 441, 475; letters in hand of, 135–42, 145–6, 146, 259, 446–7, 553–4; criticized by J. Smith, 292–3; and JW, 308, 539 n: Le Maire, 363, 560 n: JA, 365, 462: Lombart brothers, 524 n: Jones, 573 n; with BF, to visit Anet, 333; supposed commission for, 404, 406 n; BF to pay expenses of, 462; BF describes feelings for, 600 n; witnesses document, 616 n;

mentioned, 42 n, 386, 419 n, 473 n, 475; letters to, 42–3, 48

Franklin stove: Morand wishes engraving of, 506–7

Franquelin, —— (great-grandfather of Saint-Sauveur), 393

Fraser, William (Admiralty undersecretary), 422 n

Frazer, John G.: identified, 78 n; and Cox in south of France, 671 n; mentioned, 78

Frederick II (King of Prussia): and Bavarian succession crisis, war with Austria, 116, 128, 174, 185 n, 212, 536

Frederick August (elector of Saxony), 556

Frederick Augustus, Duke of York, 264 n

Frères Amis (Masonic Lodge), 75 n

Frigates: French, captured by Keppel, 31–2, 141: left in Chesapeake, 376: cruise in North Sea, 402 n: capture Lisbon packet, 551; Jones suggests naval operations for, 45; sought for S.C. navy, 47 n, 67, 98–9, 118–19; American, have trouble with prizes, 107; British, supposedly captured by French, 130, 404; being built in Netherlands, Kerguelen wishes to command, 410, 452; Spanish, pursue English privateer, 551

Froment, Louis (brewer), 18–19

Fusils: JW repairs, 21 n, 35, 63 n, 68, 449, 455–6, 463, 649; aboard Duchesse de Grammont, 152 n; for Va., Le Maire, others inspect, 361–3 n, 386–7, 429–30, 559

Fynje (Finye), Hendrik (associate of Dumas), 117 n, 273 n, 390 n

Fyot, François-Marie: invites BF to demonstration of his mechanical pulley, 209–11; identified, 209 n; letter from, 209–11

Gadd, Charles: wishes consulship, 385; letter from, 385

Gadsden, Christopher: recommends Gillon, 98–9; identified, 98 n; letter from, 98–9

Gage, Gen. Thomas, 221–2, 624

Gaiault de Boisbertrand. See Boisbertrand, René-Etienne-Henry Gaiault de.

Galbert, Gaspard, vicomte de: sugar belonging to, taken from Isabelle, 512; identified, 512 n; letter from, 512

Gale, John: commissioners assist, 359 n;

INDEX

Gale, John (*continued*)
identified, 649–50 n; captain of *Governor Livingston*, 650 n
Galloway, Joseph, 90, 605
Gálvez, Bernardo de (governor of Louisiana), 151
Ganot, Louis de Recicourt de: Le Roy relays parents' request for news about, 110–11; identified, 111 n
Garson, Bayard & Cie. (Paris bankers), 540
Gates, Gen. Horatio, 13, 191, 360, 524 n, 626, 647, 665 n
Gauthier, Marc-François (convict): freed from confinement to serve as American gunner, lxv, 289–90; offers services, begs help, 50–2; Jones as intermediary for, 50 n; letter from, 50–2
Gautier, Capt. Noah, 652
Gautier, —— (deceased), 532 n
Gautier, —— (Frenchman), 443
Gayton, Adm. Clark, 239, 488
Gazette de divers endroits. See *Gazette de Leyde*.
Gazette de Leyde, 186 n, 273, 316, 473 n, 661
Gazette de Yorktown. See *Pennsylvania Gazette*.
Gellée, Nicolas-Maurice (BF's secretary): letter in hand of, 657; identified, 657 n
General Arnold (packet): brings newspapers, packets, 12 n, 20, 177; arrival in France of, 177; new captain for, 260, 290, 308; orders for, readiness of, to sail, 267–8, 290, 305, 387
General Court, Mass.: asked to aid St. Pierre, Miquelon, 87, 106, 107, 177–8; prohibits return of Loyalists, 609; Hopkins serves in, 615 n; letter from, 609. *See also* Council, Mass.
General Mifflin (privateer): prizes of, 291, 304, 305, 318, 382, 405, 412, 415, 440, 467, 512, 537, 543–4, 611; cruise of, described, 291 n, 304 n, 305; arrives at Lorient, 291 n, 305; prisoners of, 304 n, 305, 323, 399 n, 543–4, 574–5, 583, 648–9; JA's proposals for, 404 n; ex-prisoners among crew of, 543; sailing plans of, 583, 608, 648
General Putnam (privateer), 442
Genet, Edme-Jacques: as editor of *Affaires de l'Angleterre et de l'Amérique*, 22, 154–5,

211, 226, 616–18, 623–4; sends BF London newspapers, 22–3, 156–7; forwards letter to Bridgen, 23; proposes journal on American affairs, 155–7; and JA, 185 n, 617 n; sends copies of *Royal American Gazette*, publishes rebuttals, 616–18, 623–4; and Lee, 617 n; letters from, 22–3, 154–7, 211, 226, 616–17; letters to, 617–18, 623–7
Geneva: code of laws for, 282
Genlis, Charles-Alexis Brulart, comte de: and Jones, Chartres, 421–2, 440; identified, 422 n
Genoa: possible American loan in, 299, 300, 473; in War of Austrian Succession, 369
Gentil & Orr (merchants), 436–7 n
Gentille (French frigate), 402 n
George, Prince of Wales, 264
George III: Americans forbidden to pray for, lxiii; BF criticizes, suspects is behind "Weissenstein" proposals, lxvii, 4–10; message to Parliament by, 141; supposedly plans to offer independence if America breaks French treaty, 174; visits Portsmouth, 371–2; mentioned, 40 n, 309, 316–17, 415, 619, 624 n
George (whaling ship), 514, 653 n
Georgia: de la Plaigne agent of, 74 n, 127, 194 n, 539–41; ships carrying supplies for, 540; mentioned, 368
Gérard, Alexandrine (Conrad-Alexandre's daughter): portrait of, 630–1; identified, 630 n
Gérard, Conrad-Alexandre: French government uses as chief contact with Americans, lxii; and Baches, 90, 599, 603: Lafayette, 619 n: G. Morris, 633, 636 n; arrives in America, 90 n, 407; appoints consul, 326 n; commissioners' letter sent to, 383 n; cool to Canadian attack, 619 n, 633; wife sends portraits to, 630–1; suggests giving lesson to Americans, 635 n; comments on American affairs, 636 n, 637 n
Gérard, Marie-Nicole Grossart de Virly (Conrad-Alexandre's wife): asks commissioners' help in recovering portraits, 630–1; identified, 630 n; letter from, 630–1

694

Holy Roman Empire: W. Lee accredited to, lxiii. *See also* Germany.

Hommets, ———— des, 218 n

Honsberg, François: and Stadel offer steel, 228; identified, 228 n

Hope, Thomas and Adrien (Dutch bankers): forward Welsh letter, 57–8; on good terms with British, 129–30

Hopkins, Daniel: asks help for J. Palmer, 615; discusses prisoner relief, 615 n; identified, 615 n; letter from, 615

Hopkinson, Francis (treasurer of loans): sends list of bills of exchange, 417–18; appointment of, 417 n, 606; identified, 417 n; BF portrait given to, 603; property of, plundered, 606; RB loans BF inventions to, 606; writings of, 606; letters from, 417–18, 605–7

Hopkinson, Thomas (Francis' father), 606

Horace: quoted, 434

Horneca, Fizeaux & Cie. (Amsterdam bankers): and Grand brothers, lxiii, 178 n, 389 n; and commissioners' proposed Dutch loan, lxiii, 310 n, 322, 367, 375, 388–90, 415–16, 484; pays Hancock, 178; Lee objects to, 322 n; letters from, 375, 415–16; letters to, 322, 484

Hornet (sloop of war, U.S.N.), 190 n, 238

Horse-hoing Husbandry (Tull), 466 n

Hortalez, Roderigue & Cie. (Beaumarchais' company): charters ships, 59 n, 358, 381–2, 395, 454, 463, 508, 577 n; accounts of, 59 n, 358–9 n, 381–2, 382–3, 584 n; subsidized by French government, 358 n, 383. *See also* Beaumarchais.

Hôtel Royal des Invalides: BF to meet Parmentier at, 578

Houdetot, Sophie de la Live de Bellegarde comtesse d': and Saint-Lambert, 495 n

Howe, Adm. Richard: at New York, 250 n; combats d'Estaing, 337 n, 338, 513–14 n, 550–1; reinforced by Byron, 408; mentioned, 527

Howe, Gen. William, 132, 191, 222, 373, 604 n, 626

Hubbart, Judith R. (C. Greene's sister), 258 n

Hubbart, Susannah, 621

Hubbart, Thomas: identified, 258 n; mentioned, 258

Hubbart, Tuthill: identified, 258 n, 621 n; sends regards, 621; mentioned, 258

Hudson Bay: Jones suggests attacking ships of, 45

Huet du Plessis, ————, 565

Hugot, ———— (locksmith), 218

Hunter, James, 592 n

Hunter, Joseph: Swaller's father-in-law, 592; identified, 592 n

Hunter (prize), 291

Hurlot, J., 531–2

Hutchinson, Gov. Thomas, 379, 609 n

Hutton, James: attends wedding, 264–5, 316; travels of, 264–6, 296, 316–17; requests pass for ship to Labrador, 265, 296; and Moravian party going to Bethlehem, Pa., 266–7, 296 n: Georges Grand, 284, 296, 309, 317: Montgomery monument, 296: Dumas, 316–17; rumors about negotiations with BF, 316; mentioned, 251 n; letters from, 264–7, 296

Hutton, Louise B. (James's wife), 296

Hydrogen: Strzecki's experiments on, 100; Ingenhousz's experiments on, 505

Hylton, Daniel L.: part owner of *Sally*, 451; identified, 451 n

Ile de Ré, 35–6, 109 n, 661–3

Independent Chronicle (Boston newspaper), 622 n

Indians, American: British use of, atrocities supposedly committed by, 625

Indien (frigate): Jones as possible captain of, 32 n, 402, 458–9, 572 n; sold to French government, 410 n; Nassau reports on construction of, 458 n

Indigents: Pelletier sends memoir on, 179–80 n

Indigo: sent from S.C., 454

Inflammable air. *See* Hydrogen.

Ingenhousz, Jan: Hutton reports in good health, 267; carries description of BF's symptoms, 497; and Pringle, 497, 504–5; postpones Paris visit to remain in London, 504–5; discusses Mesmer, hydrogen, smallpox inoculations, 505–6; as Maria Theresa's physician, 505 n; letter from, 504–6

"Inglesina, L'": as sobriquet for C. Davies, 456 n

tempts to aid, 361–2, 560–1; refuses to repay Desplaces' loan, 465–6; JW relates ill treatment suffered by, 559–60; attempts to recruit Demolon, 622–3; letters from, 386–7, 428–9, 452–3; 494; letters to, 361–4, 560–1

Lemon, John (prisoner): asks liberty, 547–8, 558, 566, 581; freed, 581 n; mentioned, 542 n; letters from, *inter alia*, 547–8, 566–7, 581–2

Le Neutre, ——— (Paris merchant), 24

Lenoir, Jean-Charles-Pierre (lieutenant general of police): and BF, to meet Parmentier, 578; identified, 578 n

Le Normand (Le Normant), Simon-Emmanuel-Julien: Bondfield introduces, 260; identified, 260 n; Holker recommends, 324; mentioned, 267

Le Roy, Agatange, 326 n

Le Roy, Basile (Jean-Baptiste's son): death of, 289 n, 441–2, 480 n; burial of, 411, 480 n

Le Roy, Jean-Baptiste: as reference for J.-F. Henry, 17 n; asks recommendation for Robinot, 56, 305–6; dinner invitations to, 79, 100–1; and Mme. de Marcenay, 79, 100–1, 289 n, 306; asks BF to meet Kossakowski, Strzecki, witness scientific experiment, 100; BF dines with, 100 n, 499 n; relays parents' request for news of Ganot, 110–11; and d'Arcy, 147 n, 499 n; and BF, Lavoisier, advise on powder magazine, 237 n; death, burial of son of, 289 n, 411, 441–2, 480 n; forwards request from Caraman, 306; discusses Forster's scientific observations, 328–30; inquires about d'Estaing, 378, 672; plays chess with BF, 378, 672; to attend von Sickingen experiment, 391; greetings to, 467; defends Mesmer, presents paper on animal magnetism, 506; mentioned, 81; letters from, 56, 100–1, 110–11, 305–6, 328–30, 378, 411, 441–2, 672

Le Roy, Pétronille (Jean-Baptiste's wife): BF has tea with, lxiv; and death of son, 441–2, 480; greetings to, 467; invitation from, 480; BF's nickname for, 480 n; mentioned, 100; letter from, 480

Lesguillon, ——— : makes inquiries on behalf of servant, 534; letter from, 534

Lestarjette, Louis: father inquires about,

95–6; carries Beaumarchais letters, reaches S.C., 95 n

Letterpress: copy of BF letter made on, 161

"Lettre à Mme. de Lafreté" (BF), 670

Levacher de La Feutrie, ——— , 314

Le Vassor de la Touche, Louis-René-Madeleine (later comte de Latouche-Tréville): identified, 78 n; mentioned, 78

Le Veillard, Louis-Guillaume: forwards accusations against Dobrée, 49; drafts French letters for BF, 81 n, 154 n, 365 n; nicknamed "le grand voisin," 162; and Mme. Brillon, 162, 333, 416–17; entertains BF, 403; country house of, 417 n

Levent, ——— : asks BF to contribute information to *Almanach des Marchands*, 114–15; letter from, 114–15

Leveux, Jacques: assists Leger, Barnes, 238: Murfey, 306–7: Rolandeau, 307; letters from, 238, 306–7

Lexington (brig, U.S.N.), 23, 58, 153

Leyden (Netherlands): siege of, 369

"Libertati, Pierre": requests commission, 105–6; letter from, 101–6

Liberty (brig), 451 n

Liberty (merchantman), 290

Licorne (French frigate), 32 n, 60–1

Liger, ——— (swordmaker): suggested to make Lafayette's sword, 666

Lightning: effects of, discussed by Forster, Le Roy, 328–30

Lightning rods: debate over proper shape of, 41; in Palatinate, demonstrated by Hemmer, 457. *See also* Powder magazine; Purfleet.

Limbourg (Austrian? regiment), 195

Limozin, Andrew, 129 n

Lindau, ——— , baronne de, 28

Lindau, ——— , de (prisoner), 28

Lippe-Bückeburg, Friedrich Wilhelm Ernst, graf von, 102

Lisbon: P. Clear at Irish College of, 197; dismasted British ship at, 243 n; packet, captured, 551

Liturgy on the Universal Principles of Religion and Morality (Williams), 354 n

Lively (captured British frigate), 402 n, 542

Lively (privateer), 540

Lively (schooner), 513

Livingston, Abraham: sends rice and indigo, 454; unable to send cargoes from

Ottoman Empire: Rulhière's research on, 38; war predicted between Russia and, 185 n

Our Lady of Mount Carmel and St. Anthony (snow), 554 n

Packet boats: captured by American privateer, 551; from Lisbon, captured by French frigate, 551

Paine, Thomas: as author of *Common Sense*, 466; proposes history of Revolution, sends war news, 618–20; as secretary of committee for foreign affairs, 619 n; letter from, 618–20

Palais Royal: BF pays courtesy call at, 37

Palatinate (German principality): von Sickingen represents at French court, 391 n; emigration to America from, 457; lightning rods in, 457. *See also* Karl Theodor.

Palatine Academy of Sciences: *Transactions* of, sent BF, 457

Pallas (French frigate), 32 n, 60–1

Palma (Canary Islands): governor of, seizes prize, 184–5

Palmer, John (prisoner): D. Hopkins asks help for, 615; identified, 615 n

Palmes, Capt. Richard: identified, 387 n; mentioned, 387

Panchaud, Isaac and Jean-François (bankers): identified, 37 n; mentioned, 37

Pancoucke, Charles-Joseph (publisher), 200 n

Panebeuf, Anne-Joseph de, 27

Paradiso, Il (Dante), quoted, 342

Paramaribo (Dutch Guayana), 317

Paraut, ——— (merchant), 436

Parfait Boulanger . . . , Le (Parmentier), 578 n

Paris: intelligence from, 212–13; musical disputes at, 431–2

Parliament: BF distrusts, 4, 6–10; responds to king's message, 141; bill in, to repeal Declaratory Act, 371; Vaughan expects dissensio in, 372; reopening of, 503 n. *See also* Commons; Lords.

Parmentier, Antoine-Augustin: BF begins association with, lxvi; and Cadet de Vaux, work on potatoes, lxvi, 520–1, 578; identified, 521 n, 578 n; Lenoir, BF to meet with, 578

Parr, William: Rieger asks BF to forward letters to, 535; identified, 535 n

Parsons, R. (William's wife): difficulties of, 215–16, 244–6, 248, 269–71, 489–90; BF plans to give guinea to, 246 n, 248; letters from, 244–6, 269–71, 489–90; letter to, 246–8

Parsons, William: asks assistance, 215–17; Hickey brings letter of, 215–16, 244, 246; offers services, 215–16, 244–8; BF gives money to, 247–8, 343; pretended illness of, 269; attempts to raise money on Irish property, 489; threatened by wife's landlord, 489–90; letter from, 215–17

Parsons, Sir William (William's cousin), 215

Partridge, Elizabeth: sends petition, war news, family news, asks for portrait, 620–2; letter from, 620–2

Partridge, Rebecca (Elizabeth's stepdaughter), 621

Partridge, Samuel (Elizabeth's husband), 621

Pascal, ——— and ——— (cousins, Marseilles merchants), 217 n

Paschke, Frederic: father wishes blessings sent to, 25; identified, 25 n

Paschke, Martin (Frederic's father), 25

Passports: for salt ships, 463–4. *See also* Prisoners, American; Prisoners, British.

Pataski. *See* Pulaski.

Patience (*Ranger*'s prize), 277 n, 293–4, 313. *See also* Ranger.

Pattullo, Henry: offers proposals for American land cultivation, 549; identified, 549 n; letter from, 549

Pauly, Jh. Dl. (Joseph Daniel?), 177 n, 251

Paulze, Jacques (farmer general): asked on behalf of Peltier to waive requirement, 259; identified, 259 n; letter to, 259

Payne, Capt. Benjamin, 223 n

Pease, Capt. Paul, 608, 660 n

Pelletier, ———: sends memoir on taxation, indigents, 179–80; letter from, 179–80

Pellizer-Garcia, Joseph-Emmanuel, de, abbé: asks patronage, 28; identified, 28 n

Peltier-Dudoyer, Jean (Beaumarchais', Montieu's agent), 259, 454, 463

Penet, Pierre: forms partnership with

293–5, 313, 319–20, 360, 459; prizes of, 32, 84, 112 n, 121, 167, 197, 213, 237–8, 277, 293, 298 n, 536–9, 610; Simpson commander of, 44, 108–9, 110, 122 n, 167, 187, 254–5, 277; Sartine suggests new captain be named for, 48; captures *Drake*, 84 n; raids Whitehaven, 84 n, 224 n, 237; Schweighauser provides money, supplies for, 108, 167, 287; to cruise with *Boston, Providence*, 109, 167, 186–7, 277; Livingston prospective captain of, 110 n, 167; Delap and, 112; jw and, 112, 153 n; Odea helps outfit, 153 n; prepares for sailing, 167; encountered at sea, 213; return voyage of, 213, 293, 325, 358; Jones wishes personal property from, 224, 237, 277 n; Jones proposes Hinman as captain for, 255; Whipple attempts to settle affairs of, 277; Bersolle refuses supplies for, 287 n; Hall acting commander of, 287 n

Ratisbon: diplomatic dispatches from, 167 n

Ray, Judith. *See* Hubbart, Judith R.

Ray, Capt. William, 660 n. *See also* Wray, Capt. William.

Ré, Ile de. *See* Ile de Ré.

Read, Capt. Thomas: arrives in France, 159, 172; identified, 159 n; Schweighauser to provide cargo for, 175; sailing orders for, 175, 395; asked to provide passage for Fowler, wife, 286–7; requests permission for Mediterranean cruise, 300–1; letter from, 300–1; letters to, 175, 286–7

Réaumur, René-Antoine Ferchault de: treatise of, 432 n

Recicourt de Ganot. *See* Ganot.

Reculès de Basmarein & Raimbaux (merchant firm), 304, 404 n

Reed, Lt. Benjamin, 73–4, 77–8, 88 n, 121

Reed, Joseph, 627 n

Reed, Capt. ———, 290

Régie des poudres, 15, 207 n, 236 n

Regiments, American: 4th Continental Artillery, 25 n; Pulaski's legion, 25 n

Regiments, French: Monsieur's *garde du corps*, 79 n; Conflans hussars, 103; Legion of Conflans, 103; Legion of Lor-

raine, 104; Mailly, 104 n; Royal grenadiers, 105 n; Cap, 190; *Chevaux légers de la garde du roi*, 438; Metz artillery, 438

Register of the Premiums and Bounties Bestowed..., A (Society of Arts), 568–9

Regnier, ———: translates constitution, 200

Reichel, John Frederick, 266

Reinhold, Lappenberg & Schmieman (merchants), 23

"Rendez-vous de la République des Lettres." *See* "Agence générale de correspondance pour les sciences et les arts."

Renommée (French frigate), 402

Reprisal (brig, U.S.N.), 418–19

"Reprise": explanation of translation of, 544 n

Reuschenberg, baron ———, 183–4

Revenge (cutter): Hodge and Ross claim ownership of, 70–1; difficulties in Spain of, 71; prizes of, 71–2, 184, 552–4; prisoner taken by, 197–8; Hodge follows Deane's orders concerning, 520; Spanish protest seizure of ship by, 552–4

Rhode Island. *See* Newport.

Rice: de Reine sends seeds for, 80–1; sent from S.C., 454; embargo on, 492

Richard, Capt. Jacques: ordered to turn over *Thérèse*'s cargo to Schweighauser, 414; identified, 414 n; letter to, 414

Richard, ———: asks news, 29; letter from, 25–9

Richelet, ———: extends invitation to visit, 123–4, 154 n; letter from, 123–4

Richmond, Charles Lennox, Duke of, 302, 374

Ricot, Capt. Pierre, 27

Ridley, Matthew: returns to America, 142 n; assists Collas, 192 n; inquires about Thornton, 232; identified, 232 n; Digges cites as reference, 421; sends book on British navy, 471, 598; mentioned, 19 n; letter from, 471; letter to, 598

Rieger, Jacob: reports on German public opinion, 535–6; identified, 535 n; letter from, 535–6

Rïou, Pierre, interpreter at Brest: advises on Pickerin's prize, 610–12; identified, 610 n; letter from, 610–12

Rising States (privateer), 491 n, 592

Toulouse, Parlement of, 285
Tournelle, ———— de (consul): forwards packet, 518; letter from, 518
Tours: advantages of, extolled, 301–2
Tourton, Fleury, banker: forwards Ingenhousz letter, 506; identified, 506 n
Trade, American: with France, 59–60, 318, 492–3, 508, 577–8, 582 n: French West Indies, 138 n, 259, 578: Italy, 313: Britain, predicted resumption of, 373: Netherlands, 376–7, 453–4, 487: Sweden, 385: Kingdom of Two Sicilies, 518–19, 525–6: Spain, 527, 551; BF's views on, 137–8
Trade, British: effects of war on, 372–3; with America, predicted resumption of, 373: France, 482, 485. See also Convoys; Jamaica; West Indies, British.
Trade, Dutch, excluded by French, 353
Trade, French: with America, 59–60, 318, 492–3, 508, 577–8, 582 n: England, 482, 485; imperiled by lack of convoys, 318, 551, 591
Traill, James (consul): identified, 436–7 n; mentioned, 436
Traité des Prairies Artificielles (Mante), 349 n
Transactions of Palatine Academy of Sciences. See Palatine Academy of Sciences.
Travallosos, ————, marqués de (commandant at Canary Islands), 184
Treasure fleet. See Spain.
Treaty of Alliance: commissioners, Vergennes exchange ratifications of, lxiii, 128, 129; ratification of, arrives in France, 34 n, 57, 70, 128, 134, 151; reception of, in America, 67, 134; Vergennes sent congressional resolution about, 115; Vergennes claims is in effect, 146; Bancroft uses knowledge of, to speculate on stock exchange, 229, 377 n; copy of, destroyed by Anderson, 450
Treaty of Amity and Commerce, Dutch-American: drafted by Lee, Neufville, lxiii, 31 n, 344 n, 416 n, 445, 454 n; Dumas' involvement in, 352–3, 379, 388, 396, 448, 487, 510–11, 529–30, 562–3, 612, 650–1; BF, commissioners discuss, 379, 396, 445, 448, 562–3; Amsterdam burgomasters wish, 453–4, 487, 510, 529–30, 562–3, 612, 650–1, 661; British recognition of American independence

prerequisite for, 453–4, 510, 530, 593, 650–1
Treaty of Amity and Commerce, Franco-American: commissioners, Vergennes exchange ratifications of, lxiii, 128, 129; articles dropped from, lxiii, 128, 137, 150 n, 173, 330–2, 635, 657, 668; communicated to Dutch political leaders, 31, 116, 129 n, 150, 168, 214 n, 381 n, 511, 660–1; ratification of, arrives in France, 70, 128, 134, 151–2, 450; Vergennes sent congressional resolution about, 115; appointment of consuls authorized by, 128–9; reception of, in America, 134; BF discusses disputed articles in, 137–8; Lees', Izard's objections to, 138 n, 587–8; British informed of, 170–1; France promises good offices with Barbary states in, 300, 313, 468, 663; Congress publicizes, 377 n, 400; article 16 of, on shipment of goods on enemy ships, 460, 513, 533; mentioned, 159, 377–8, 400
Tren, Abel, 515
Tressan, Louis-Elisabeth La Vergne, comte de, 476 n
Trevose (Galloway's estate), 90
Tristan-Brision, ———— abbé de: forwards letter, 218; letter from, 218
Triton (brig), 192–3
Trottier, ————: offers house for sale or rent, 301–2; letter from, 301–2
Truman (Trumans), John, 197
Truman, Thomas (prisoner), 197–8
Trumbull, Jonathan (governor of Conn.): and Niles, 134; corresponds with van der Capellen, 366; letter to, 134–5
Tryon, William (former colonial governor), 132
Tschiffelÿ (Tschiffeli), Johann Rudolph: volunteers to translate constitutions, 200–1; identified, 200 n; letter from, 200–1
Tuamotu Archipelago: formation of, discussed by Forster, 328
Tucker, St. George: identified, 120 n; mentioned, 120
Tucker, Capt. Samuel: and Moylan, 33, 193: Livingston, 34, 62, 87, 131, 174–5, 291–2, 323: Whipple, 87–8, 131, 186–7: McNeill, 305; returns to Lorient, 33, 34, 59; prizes of, 33, 34, 59, 62, 87–8, 121,